To Fred Bronson, for many reasons.

ACKNOWLEDGMENTS

In the 1989 edition of *The Hollywood Reporter Book of Box Office Hits,* I made a statement that I knew would someday come back to haunt me. The Acknowledgments in it began: "This book could probably not have been written if I lived in Albuquerque, or Sioux Falls, or even my former hometowns of New Haven and Palm Beach." I went on to sing the praises of Southern California's proximity to the source of my subject matter, as well as the good fortune I had in finding a fabulous research assistant, Marcia Rovins.

Cut to (as they say in movie lingo) Carefree, Arizona, 1995. Day. The author, now a confirmed desert rat, working from her home computer, running up huge telephone bills, feeding page after page into her fax machine, now finds that one can be a writer anywhere in the country. What a discovery! Hollywood, California, is *not* the center of the universe—it just seems that way when you're writing about it. Welcome to the world of high tech.

Make no mistake—I am still electronically connected to Southern California, and would still probably not have been able to write this book were it not for the help of my trusted allies there. My special thanks, as always, go to Marcia Rovins for her usual top-notch job of researching not only the "big stuff" but also the little nit-picky details that only she seems able to discover.

And, as always, I must thank Fred Bronson for his support and lifelong friendship. No wonder the word "friend" contains "Fred." He defines it.

Others who are owed a debt of gratitude for this edition: Kandy Fong, Ettore Zuccarelli, and Mitch Lewis. Also the Brothers Sherman, especially Richard, a great and charming musician.

Once again I am indebted to those wonderful folks at Eddie Brandt's Sturday Matinee in North Hollywood, California, for photo assistance.

I would also like to thank everyone at Billboard Books for their support, especially my editors, Ginny Croft and Paul Lukas.

And, once again, thanks collectively to all those who were so instrumental in the first edition. It is on your shoulders that this book stands.

THE HOLLYWOOD REPORTER BOOK OF

BOX OFFICE HITS

REVISED AND ENLARGED EDITION

❖ ❖ ❖

SUSAN SACKETT

BILLBOARD BOOKS
An imprint of Watson-Guptill/New York

Research Assistant: Marcia Rovins
Senior Editor: Paul Lukas
Book and Cover Design: Bob Fillie, Graphiti Graphics
Jacket Illustration: David Myers
Production Manager: Ellen Greene

Revised and enlarged edition first published 1996 by Billboard Books,
an imprint of Watson-Guptill Publications, a division of Billboard
Publications, Inc.,1515 Broadway, New York, NY 10036

Library of Congress Cataloging-in-Publication Data

Sackett, Susan
    The Hollywood reporter book of box office hits / Susan Sackett
       p.   cm
    Includes bibliographical references.
    ISBN 0-8230-7549-4
    1. Motion pictures—United States—History.
    2. Motion pictures—United States—Awards.
    3. Motion pictures—United States—Statistics.
    4. Film credits—United States. I. Title.
    PN1993.5.U6S18 1990
      791.45´75´0973—dc20   89-48076
                              CIP

Manufactured in the USA

1 2 3 4 5 6 7 8 9 / 04 03 02 01 00 99 98 97 96

CONTENTS

1980–1989

1990–1995

APPENDIXES

INTRODUCTION

It seemed like a dream assignment. Imagine—watching movies and getting paid for it! All I had to do was find a list of the top five films for each of the last 56 years, rent the cassettes, and settle down in my favorite chair to a marathon of celluloid and magnetic tape.

I love movies, especially those of the '30s and '40s, and had established credit at all the video shops in town. ("Name? Credit card numbers? Driver's license? First-born child we can take hostage if you lose the tape?") Many rainy weekends had been spent watching Hollywood classics and munching popcorn with one of my dogs curled up next to me. This would be fun—and easy.

Actually, it was easy watching the films, once I was able to determine which were on the list. I used to live in Hollywood (well, Los Angeles, really; nobody actually *lives* in Hollywood). So it seemed a simple thing to call upon my many friends in "the industry" and get a list of the top-grossing films of all time, by year, and wow! Crank up the microwave—here comes Orville Redenbacher! Problem was, no such list existed. Oh, there had been a few brave attempts at Top Ten lists, or lists of films that had made megabucks in the last 20 years. But to my surprise, no one had pulled together a list of the top films, year by year, and certainly not one going back to 1939.

I began combing through charts of films and discovered that the most complete figures available were not *grosses,* but *rentals.*

At first, I thought this must have something to do with videocassettes and how much money they made from people who rented them, but I soon learned that the term *rental* had nothing whatsoever to do with tapes and video. The most accurate records I was able to locate are those reported annually in that old industry bible, *Variety.* And for the most part, this is the source of the dollar figures in this book.

What is the difference between grosses and rentals? Most of us are more familiar with *gross* figures. These are the actual dollars taken in at the box office. (If a ticket costs $7.00 and Theater A sells 1,000 seats one weekend, it will gross $7,000.) These are all added together, for a total gross. The highest-*grossing* film of all time (not counting inflation) was *E. T. The Extra-Terrestrial,* which grossed $700,000,000.

Rental figures, however, are considerably lower, and represent the amount of money paid to the distributors of a film (usually a motion picture studio has its own distribution arm) by those who rent a film (generally a movie theater). Rentals are also a more accurate picture of how much a film has earned. The amount *E. T.* has made in domestic (U.S. and Canada) rentals is $228,168,939.

Once I figured out which films would be included in this book, the next step was actually *viewing* them. Surprisingly, about 99 percent of the films included in this book are available on videocassette. Most of the others appear regularly on local and cable television channels such as HBO,

Cinemax, Disney Channel, Showtime, The Movie Channel, and American Movie Classics. Thus, armed with stacks of cassettes and my trusty bag of popcorn, I began what turned out to be one of the great adventures of my life. For the next several months, I howled with laughter, cried myself silly, shook with fear, fell in love, fought several wars, traveled to outer space, and occasionally snoozed—all in front of my 60-inch big-screen TV (highly recommended for home viewing). I hired a research assistant and bombarded her with questions like "How do they train cats for the movies?" "What was the name of the mechanical shark in Jaws?" "What was the real Annie Oakley like?" and my favorite, "What ever became of _____?" It was a truly educational experience, but most of all, a great deal of fun.

It is important to bear in mind that although some of the dollar figures for films back in the '40s are well under $10,000,000, inflation must always be taken into account. You cannot, for instance, compare a 1940 film like *Boom Town*, at $4,586,415, with something like 1984's *The Karate Kid,* at $43,120,000. While the latter would appear to have earned nearly ten times the amount of the 1940 film, you could also buy a very comfortable house in 1940 for around $5,000. Of course, there is no exact formula for computing the box office inflation factor—these days, ticket prices are hitting the $7.00 range and climbing all too rapidly. Some megahits play on thousands of screens across the country simultaneously, and the population of North America has more than doubled since the '40s. All of these factors should be kept in mind when you compare rental figures.

For its annual report on rental figures, *Variety*'s cut-off point is $4,000,000; they only include films which earned at least that amount. And studios didn't keep complete records of their take from rentals in the early '40s. Generally, ranking the films by rental figures was no problem for those years, since the big hits made quite a bit of money. However, 1939, 1940, and 1941 had several gaps in the list. Joel Finler's book *The Hollywood Story* was particularly helpful in filling these positions for 1939 and 1940, but 1941 proved to be particularly elusive.

By combing through reel after reel of microfilm at the Motion Picture Academy Library, plus searching through old volumes of such '40s publications as *Motion Picture Daily, Film Daily, Film Yearly Almanac,* and *International Motion Picture Almanac,* I was able to compile a list of the top-*grossing* films of 1941, although dollar figures were not always indicated. Some of the studios were able to supply approximate figures, but most admitted that they couldn't give definite amounts. I finally settled on $1,500,000 as the best estimate for these films, a figure based on all the above sources plus some very tentative nods from the studios themselves. For 1939, 1940, and 1941, those films "tied" with the $1,500,000 amount appear in alphabetical order, as do

1947's *The Bachelor and the Bobby-Soxer* and *The Egg and I,* which each earned $5,500,000, and 1949's *Jolson Sings Again* and *The Sands of lwo Jima,* which made $5,000,000 each in rentals.

There are 45 new entries in this edition of *Box Office Hits.* Thirty-five are the lucky films that made the top five from 1989 to 1995. An additional 10 new entries have been added throughout the earlier years. Some of these films have been re-released and made additional rental dollars, enough to qualify for the top five or to have a much larger figure reported in this edition. Some have simply had their figures updated by conscientious accounting departments at the various studios and production companies. In a few cases, a film may actually have taken in less than was originally believed, and the dollar amounts have been corrected in the pages that follow. And nine movies formerly in the number-five position have dropped off the list.

One further note. In the first edition, I did not include Walt Disney's *Dumbo* with the hits of 1941, citing its running length of only 64 minutes. However, I feel that it is time for this classic to take its rightful place as the number-two film of its release year. The movie has earned $3,000,000, and that's not peanuts, especially by 1941 standards.

This book is intended as a companion to your own movie viewing, whether it's on your VCR, in a multiplex cinema, or at a 3,000-seat theater with 70-millimeter and Dolby stereo. So settle back, dim the lights, and let's go to a movie!

SUSAN SACKETT
Carefree, Arizona
March, 1996

NINETEEN THIRTY-NINE! Mention that year to any moviegoer who hasn't been living in an ice cave on Pluto and he or she is sure to blurt out "Oh, yes! *Gone With the Wind*" or even "*The Wizard of Oz.*" But to film lovers around the world, 1939 was *the* year for movies... many people claim that we've been on a downhill slide ever since.

There were 400 movies made in 1939, and the average American went to church every Sunday and to the movies three times a week. There were 15,115 movie theaters, but only 14,952 banks. That year (some use the term "watershed") saw the release of over a dozen films which now, 50 years later, we nostalgically refer to as "classics." Audiences were treated to the likes of *The Hunchback of Notre Dame*, with Charles Laughton and Maureen O'Hara; *Raffles*, starring David Niven and Olivia de Havilland; *Destry Rides Again*, with Marlene Dietrich and James Stewart; *Mr. Smith Goes to Washington*, another Jimmy Stewart winner; *Ninotchka*, starring Greta Garbo and Melvyn Douglas; *The Private Lives of Elizabeth and Essex*, with Bette Davis, Errol Flynn, and Olivia de Havilland; *Goodbye, Mr. Chips*, with Robert Donat and Greer Garson; *Only Angels Have Wings*, with Cary Grant, Jean Arthur, and Rita Hayworth; *Stanley and Livingstone*, with Spencer Tracy and Sir Cedric Hardwicke; *Dark Victory*, one of Bette Davis' finest; John Ford's classic Western, *Stagecoach;* Judy Garland and Mickey Rooney in the box office hit *Babes in Arms;* and, of course, Judy's most memorable performance of all, as Dorothy in *The Wizard of Oz.*

It would have been a memorable bumper crop if these, plus a handful of other classics, had been the full legacy of 1939. But then, two weeks before the year drew to a close, one final film was released. And it more than fulfilled the prediction of one reviewer that this picture was "likely to perform some record-breaking feats of box office magic."

GONE WITH THE WIND

METRO-GOLDWYN-MAYER
$79,375,080

O<small>N</small> D<small>ECEMBER</small> 15, 1939, *Gone With the Wind* premiered.

The long-awaited event was treated like a local holiday. In fact, the governor of Georgia declared one, and the mayor of Atlanta, where the film had its premiere, held a three-day festival. The theater, which seated only 2,500 people, sold tickets for this once-in-a-lifetime event for 10 dollars apiece, a hefty price, considering that tickets usually went for 25 cents.

With tickets costing only two bits, it's easy to see why the film's producer, David O. Selznick, was concerned about making back the $3,900,000 in production costs. That's a lot of quarters. Yet he needn't have worried. For nearly 35 years thereafter, *GWTW* held the number-one position, earning over *25 times* its initial outlay. This would be equivalent to a film costing $40,000,000 today—not an uncommon figure for a "special effects"–type film of the '80s—making over *one billion dollars* in rentals!

The critics, not surprisingly, were unanimous in their praise. *The Hollywood Reporter* reviewer said: "This is more than the greatest motion picture which ever was made. It is the ultimate realization of the dreams of what might be done in every phase of film wizardry, in production, performance, screen writing, photography, and every other of the multitude of technical operations which enter into the making of a picture." *Variety* called it "one of the truly great films, destined for record-breaking box-office business everywhere." And while *The New York Times* thought the film was "a handsome, scrupulous and unstinting version of the 1,037 page novel," the reviewer also pulled his punches by asking, "Is it the greatest motion picture ever made? Probably not . . ." Today, of course, many film historians beg to differ.

Gone With the Wind is often noted as one of the most mystery-shrouded films of the century. All kinds of myths and legends were born when Margaret Mitchell's book first appeared in 1936. After millions had read the book and she had sold the rights to Selznick for $50,000 (eventually he gave her another $50,000, the first amount seeming so inadequate to him), more rumors began. To this day, many of these still persist. For example, it is a commonly held belief that she envisioned Clark Gable in the part of Rhett Butler when she wrote the novel.

Actually, Margaret Mitchell Marsh began the novel in 1926, while bedridden from an ankle injury. Having read every book in the Atlanta public library, she decided to follow through with her husband's suggestion that she write one of her own. She began the task that would take her 10 years to complete—but wrote the last chapter first! And in 1926, Clark Gable was an obscure actor touring in stock com-

---

Screenplay by Sidney Howard

Based on the novel by Margaret Mitchell

Produced by David O. Selznick

Directed by Victor Fleming

CAST

Scarlett O'Hara	Vivien Leigh
Rhett Butler	Clark Gable
Ashley Wilkes	Leslie Howard
Melanie Hamilton	Olivia de Havilland
Mammy	Hattie McDaniel
Prissy	Butterfly McQueen

ACADEMY AWARD NOMINATIONS

13 nominations, 8 wins*

*Best Picture
 Best Actor (Clark Gable)
*Best Actress (Vivien Leigh)
*Best Supporting Actress (Hattie McDaniel)
 Best Supporting Actress (Olivia de Havilland)
*Best Director (Victor Fleming)
*Best Screenplay (Sidney Howard)
*Best Color Cinematography
*Best Interior Decoration
 Best Sound Recording
 Best Original Score
*Best Film Editing
 Best Special Effects

William Cameron Menzies was awarded a special plaque for outstanding achievement in the use of color for the enhancement of

panies. It is very doubtful she had ever heard of him.

Another rumor that crops up frequently is that she never even wrote the book; this is a kind of "Shakespeare syndrome" that frequently surrounds unknown writers who produce bestsellers. Friends who visited her never saw her working on a manuscript. This is because she was secretive about her work, writing the book on pieces of paper which she would stuff into envelopes. Whenever friends dropped by, she would hide these under the sofa cushions. Later, she moved the stacks of envelopes into closets, never seriously intending to publish the novel. When she finally did turn the manuscript over to a publisher, it consisted of a mass of paper squeezed into a suitcase, untitled and lacking a complete first chapter. And Margaret, who was now having second thoughts, cabled the publisher, "Please send manuscript back. I've changed my mind." Fortunately, he ignored her request.

Mitchell overcame her shyness at least long enough to attend *Gone With the Wind*'s premiere in Atlanta. In fact, one of the classic comments about the film has been attributed to her. *Hollywood Anecdotes* reports that after watching the high crane shot of the Atlanta station where Scarlett attends the wounded and dying Confederate troops, Mitchell turned to Clark Gable and whispered, "Mah Gawd, if we'd o' had as many soldiers as that, we'd o' won the woah!"

From the day the cameras began rolling on the film production, the rumor mills also began to turn. In an oft-recounted story, the search for the perfect Scarlett O'Hara had been conducted all over the country, and Selznick had interviewed 1,400 actresses. The most extensive screen tests in the history of motion pictures were made for this role. Sixty actresses tested, with 165,000 feet of film shot, costing $105,000 (enough to shoot a minor movie in those days). A nationwide poll of movie fans showed their first choice to be Bette Davis (43 percent), second was Katharine Hepburn (14 percent), Norma Shearer was third (12 percent), Miriam Hopkins fourth (6 percent), and miscellaneous other actresses received the remainder of the public's votes.

Ignoring the public, Selznick had selected the three screen tests he liked best—those of Joan Bennett,

Jean Arthur, and Paulette Goddard. Yet Scarlett O'Hara had still not been cast when the first scene—the burning of Atlanta—was filmed. As the old tear-down sets on the backlot (including the native fortress/gate from 1933's *King Kong*) were consumed by flames, Selznick is said to have been introduced to a charming young lady who was a visitor on the set. This little-known English actress named Vivien Leigh so bedazzled him with her face aglow in the firelight that he immediately agreed with his brother Myron, who introduced him to Vivien with those now-immortal words "I want you to meet Scarlett O'Hara!" The possibility that this story was concocted by the publicity department was never denied by Selznick, who when interviewed later would only comment, "You may be right."

And for what turned out to be the most memorable role in movie history, Vivien Leigh received the paltry sum of $15,000 for her performance.

There was never any doubt in Selznick's or the public's mind, however, about who would play the role of Rhett Butler. Once the book was published, Clark Gable was the only actor ever seriously considered. Yet Gable himself almost turned down the role. According to *Academy Award Winners,* the actor's initial reaction was "*I* don't want the part for money, chalk or marbles"—but a $2,500 weekly paycheck, plus $100,000 bonus, probably went a long way toward changing his mind. Later Gable disclosed the real reasons for his hesitation: "I was scared when I discovered that I had been cast by the public. I felt that every reader would have a different idea as to how Rhett should be played on the screen, and I didn't see how I could please everybody."

Keeping track of the film's writers and directors soon became as much a public pastime as guessing who would be Scarlett. At least 10 writers worked on the screenplay. Although Sidney Howard was credited and received the Oscar for Best Screenplay, other drafts were written by F. Scott Fitzgerald, Jo Swerling, Ben Hecht, John Balderston, John Van Druten, and Michael Foster. Selznick himself did the final rewrites. Three directors also had a hand in the production. George Cukor was on the set the first day, January 26, 1939. Three weeks later he was fired, according to some, at the behest of Clark Gable. His

replacement was Victor Fleming, who received full screen credit, although having just completed *The Wizard of Oz,* Fleming eventually succumbed to sheer exhaustion, leaving the final week's shooting to Sam Wood (*Goodbye, Mr. Chips*).

One line that presented a bit of a problem to all the scriptwriters is that immortal one delivered by Rhett Butler at the story's end, "Frankly, my dear, I don't give a damn." Audiences familiar with Mitchell's book were placing bets as to whether the line would be allowed. Although today there is probably nothing that can't and hasn't been said on screen, audiences' easily outraged ears were protected in those days by a Hollywood censorship bureau known as the Hays Office. In 1922, former Postmaster General Will Hays was appointed president of the Motion Picture Producers and Distributors of America. This self-regulatory board immediately compiled a list of 11 "don'ts" and 25 "be carefuls." This later became known as the Motion Picture Production Code, and was with us through the '60s.

Although the word "damn" was a big no-no, it had gotten by the censors at least three times in the past. In 1932, Emma Dunn exclaimed, "Well, I'll be damned" in *Blessed Event,* and Fred Stone had cursed on screen by saying "Damn you" in *Alice Adams,* a 1935 film. "Damn" was uttered by both Leslie Howard and Marie Lohr in *Pygmalion* (1938).

Somehow, these precedents didn't seem to count, and the Hays Office stubbornly refused to let the word remain in the script. In an impassioned letter, Selznick pleaded with Hays:

"The word as used in the picture is not an oath or a curse…The omission of this line spoils the punch at the very end of the picture and on our very fade-out gives an impression of unfaithfulness after three hours and forty-five minutes of extreme fidelity to Miss Mitchell's work…"

Hays finally relented, but fined Selznick $5,000 for having violated the Production Code.*

---

*However, the word "miscarriage" was strictly *verboten,* and the book's sentence "Cheer up, maybe you'll have a miscarriage" was revised in the film to "Cheer up, maybe you'll have an accident."

Clark Gable and director Victor Fleming (right) watch as a technician takes a light reading on Vivien Leigh.

On November 7, 1976, *Gone With the Wind* had another debut, this time on the small screen. Again, records were set. Aired in two parts, the first part scored a Nielsen rating of 47.6 (47.6 percent of all sets were tuned to the film) and a 65 share (65 percent of all sets turned on were tuned to *GWTW*). The second day's showing had equally impressive numbers. In 1978, CBS paid $35 million to MGM for the rights to televise *GWTW* 20 times over the next 20 years, the highest fee ever paid for TV rights to a movie.

Since then, *Gone With the Wind* has become available for viewing in our living rooms at any time on videocassette. Yet in 1989, a restored print of the film began breaking box office records all over again when it was released to the theaters.

Ted Turner, the controversial Atlanta businessman who had bought the MGM film library in 1985, spent two years and $250,000 restoring the print for its 50th anniversary re-release. The premiere screening at the 5,874-seat Radio City Music Hall in New York was a sellout, with seats going for $12.50 apiece (cheap, by the Atlanta 1939 premiere prices). On hand then, as she had been 50 years earlier, was Butterfly McQueen ("Prissy"), one of the film's few surviving cast members at the time.

Nearly all of the cast of *Gone With the Wind* are themselves gone.

Clark Gable ("Rhett Butler") died of a heart attack in 1960.

Vivien Leigh ("Scarlett O'Hara"), plagued by tuberculosis and physical exhaustion through much of her career, died in 1967.

Leslie Howard ("Ashley Wilkes") was killed in a plane crash in 1943 on a secret mission for the British government.

Hattie McDaniel ("Mammy"), the first black Oscar winner, died in 1952.

Margaret Mitchell was hit by a car and died in 1949.

David O. Selznick died in 1965.

Butterfly McQueen died in a house fire in 1995.

Sidney Howard won an Oscar posthumously for Best Screenplay. He died in August 1939 when he was crushed to death by a tractor at his Massachusetts home.

THE WIZARD OF OZ

METRO-GOLDWYN-MAYER
$4,759,890

HAD *GONE WITH THE WIND* never been made, 1939 would still have been a wonderful year to be a moviegoer. Even as *Gone With the Wind* was being completed, MGM released what has since become one of the best-loved films of all time.

Initially, *The Wizard of Oz* was a flop. Costing $2,777,000, it took over 20 years to earn back its money. Part of the problem was that its early audience consisted almost entirely of children, and children's tickets were generally half-price or less. It wasn't until NBC and later CBS bought the film for television that MGM began to show a substantial profit.

It opened in New York on August 17 to huge lines and critical acclaim. *The Hollywood Reporter* noted that people began lining up at 5:30 A.M. and that by 8:00 there were 15,000 people standing four abreast. *The Hollywood Reporter* called the film an artistic hit.

In 1900, L. Frank Baum published his book, *The Wizard of Oz,* and in 1925, Chadwick Pictures produced a silent version of it, marked by Oliver Hardy's portrayal of the Tin Woodman. In 1938, MGM purchased the rights to the children's story from Samuel Goldwyn for $75,000.

From the beginning, MGM's production was plagued with problems, not the least of which was the casting of the lead character, Dorothy. Studio chief Louis B. Mayer wanted that box office-drawing moppet, Shirley Temple, who, at nine years old, was just the right age. But she was under contract to 20th Century-Fox, and Darryl F. Zanuck refused to loan her out. MGM took stock of its own contract players and came up with a second choice—16-year-old Judy Garland (who ended up having her breasts taped flat each morning by the wardrobe department in order to appear as childlike as possible).

Other problems beset the cast. Buddy Ebsen was set as the Tin Man. Scenes with him in the role were shot for two weeks, and then he collapsed, hospitalized from an allergic reaction to the aluminum dust they had used to powder his face to give the Tin

Man his silvery appearance. He was replaced by Jack Haley in what became his most famous role.

Margaret Hamilton, who appears as the Wicked Witch of the West (total time on the screen: 12 minutes), ended up bedridden for six weeks after receiving severe burns on her hand during the broomstick-burning sequence.

There were production problems as well. After five weeks of filming at a cost of $80,000, a lavish musical number called "The Jitter Bug" was

---

Screenplay by Noel Langley, Florence Ryerson, and Edgar Allan Woolf

Adaptation by Noel Langley

From a book by L. Frank Baum

Songs written by E. Y. Harburg and Harold Arlen

Produced by Mervyn LeRoy

Directed by Victor Fleming

CAST

Dorothy	Judy Garland
Prof. Marvel (The Wizard)	Frank Morgan
Hunk (The Scarecrow)	Ray Bolger
Zeke (The Cowardly Lion)	Bert Lahr
Hickory (The Tin Woodman)	Jack Haley
Glinda (The Good Witch)	Billie Burke
Miss Gulch (The Wicked Witch)	Margaret Hamilton

ACADEMY AWARD NOMINATIONS

*6 nominations, 2 wins ***

Best Picture
Best Color Cinematography
Best Interior Decoration
*Best Song ("Over the Rainbow," music by Harold Arlen, words by E. Y. Harburg)
*Best Original Score
Best Special Effects

Judy Garland received a special award for her outstanding performance as a screen juvenile during the past year (miniature statuette).

---

dropped after the first preview. (Recently, this "lost" footage has been restored on the laser-disk and home video versions.) Louis Mayer wanted to remove the song "Over the Rainbow," but fortunately, this was one decision by the studio boss that didn't stand.

Like *Gone With the Wind, The Wizard of Oz* also had its share of writers and directors. In all, 10 writers took turns working on the script. The number of writers seems odd by today's standards, but back then, studios hired writers by the ream and sat them down in a room where they wrote more or less on an assembly-line basis. Directors were frequently replaced as well, and *Wizard* had four. Richard Thorpe started it off, working for two weeks, and then was replaced by George Cukor, who lasted three days. Victor Fleming came in and worked four months, long enough to wind up with his name on the screen. When he was hired away by David O. Selznick to direct *Gone With the Wind,* the studio brought in King Vidor, who directed the final 10 days—sort of like a chief surgeon asking a less skilled doctor to "close" following an operation.

On November 3, 1956, a milestone in the saga of *The Wizard of Oz* was reached. For the first time, the movie was shown on television. With this first appearance on CBS, a whole new generation discovered the magic of Oz. By 1989, with the 31st airing, it was calculated that the movie had been seen in more than 473,000,000 households since its first telecast.

In 1989, MGM/UA/Turner Home Video released a 50th Anniversary video of *The Wizard of Oz,* utilizing warm sepia tones for the Kansas scenes as per the 1939 original. In 1993, home theaters were treated to "The Ultimate Oz," a deluxe laser disc boxed set containing restored soundtrack, "lost" footage, outtakes, the original trailer, a continuity script, stills, and a poster. Included in both tape and laser versions are the "Jitter Bug" number, a Ray Bolger/"Scarecrow" dance sequence, and some of the Buddy Ebsen footage.

There really is "no place like home."

MR. SMITH GOES TO WASHINGTON

COLUMBIA
$3,500,000

NINETEEN THIRTY-NINE was a busy year for James Stewart—he made five films in all. But unquestionably, the best of them was *Mr. Smith Goes to Washington.* Stewart was 31 years old when he was signed to star as the wide-eyed, idealistic young senator from Wisconsin who single-handedly takes on a corrupt Congress.

The film opened to a storm of controversy. After a disastrous premiere in Washington, D.C., to a room packed with Supreme Court justices, cabinet members, senators, and other political dignitaries, the picture was lambasted by the local press. Director Frank Capra was labeled a traitor, along with Columbia Pictures president Harry Cohn. Cohn received an urgent cablegram from the United States ambassador to England, Joseph P. Kennedy, saying that *Mr. Smith* ridiculed democracy, could be construed by our European allies as pro-Axis, and thus should be withdrawn from European distribution. Members of the U.S. Senate had even harsher words, crying "It stinks!" and "I've

Screenplay by Sidney Buchman

Based on a story by Lewis R. Foster

Produced and directed by Frank Capra

CAST

Saunders	Jean Arthur
Jefferson Smith	James Stewart
Senator Joseph Paine	Claude Rains
Jim Taylor	Edward Arnold
Governor Hopper	Guy Kibbee

ACADEMY AWARD NOMINATIONS

11 nominations, 1 win*

Best Picture
Best Actor (James Stewart)
Best Supporting Actor (Harry Carey)
Best Supporting Actor (Claude Rains)
Best Director (Frank Capra)
*Best Original Story (Lewis R. Foster)
Best Screenplay
Best Interior Decoration
Best Sound Recording
Best Score
Best Film Editing

never seen a member as dumb as that boy!" The ultimate epithet was hurled by one member of Congress, who labeled the film "just something from Hollywood."

But the majority of the media loved the film. *The Hollywood Reporter* headlined: " 'MR. SMITH GOES TO TOWN; DUE FOR BOX OFFICE SUCCESS," and went on to say that "Frank Capra has another smash hit....James Stewart is the perfect choice for the role...under Frank Capra's guidance, Stewart turns in the finest performance of his career." *The New York Times'* reviewer was equally generous with his praise: "[Capra] has paced it beautifully and held it in perfect balance....James Stewart is a joy for this season, if not forever. He has too many good scenes, but we like to remember the way his voice cracked when he got up to read his bill." No Method acting here—Jimmy Stewart hired a doctor who sprayed his throat periodically with bichloride of mercury in order to hoarsen his voice in

that famous scene.

The film was so successful that it spawned a number of imitators, including a short-lived television series starring Fess Parker (September 1962 to March 1963) and a Tom Laughlin movie vehicle, *Billy Jack Goes to Washington* (1977).

But perhaps the highest tribute that could be paid to a film was one given by a former actor...who also happens to be a former President. Ronald Reagan, when asked to reflect on the film that most affected his life, cited *Mr. Smith Goes to Washington.* He said: "When Jimmy Stewart walked the halls of the Capitol building, I walked with him. When he stood in awe of that great man at the Lincoln Memorial, I bowed my head too. When he stood in the Senate chamber and refused to knuckle under to the vested interests, I began to realize, through the power of motion pictures, one man can make a difference."

1939

THE HUNCHBACK OF NOTRE DAME

RKO
$1,500,000

"Why was I not made of stone like thee?"

WITH THESE PLAINTIVE WORDS, one of the most memorable films of any decade draws to a close. Based on the classic novel by Victor Hugo, *Hunchback* had been made as a silent film in 1923 with the "Man of a Thousand Faces," Lon Chaney. Many thought this performance would never be equaled. But Charles Laughton managed to make the hunchbacked Quasimodo not only monstrous but pitiably human. What could be more moving or dramatic than when he lifts Esmeralda (Maureen O'Hara, in her American screen debut), gleefully bellowing "Sanctuary! Sanctuary!"?

Playing the role of the deformed bellringer was no easy task. Although Laughton's makeup had been lightened from the 34 pounds that Chaney wore to a mere 6, it was still a chore for Perc Westmore's assistant, makeup artist Gordon Bau, who spent five and a half hours each day applying a sponge-rubber right cheek and false eye socket that covered Laughton's own right eye. The RKO special effects department even found a way to make this false eye open and blink on cue. So realistic was the effect that

Variety warned moviegoers in its review of *The Hunchback of Notre Dame,* "Charles Laughton's grotesque makeup…is not exactly palatable for patrons sensitively inclined."

This film enjoys immense popularity even today, to the extent that it is a mainstay of many independent television stations—in one week it was listed three times on three different stations. With the advent of the controversial process of colorization, many people who would not normally watch a black-and-white film (for reasons unfathomable) will be pleased to note that this movie is not hurt one bit by the colorization process. In fact, the colorization actually enhances the exterior shots, especially the marketplace with its bright blue sky (although, as in most colorized pictures, the clothing all too often seems to run to tans and greens).

Screenplay by Sonya Levien

Adaptation by Bruno Frank

From a novel by Victor Hugo

Produced by Pandro S. Berman

Directed by William Dieterle

CAST

The Hunchback . . . . . .Charles Laughton
Frollo . . . . .Sir Cedric
                    Hardwicke
Clopin . . . . .Thomas Mitchell
Esmeralda . . . . .Maureen O'Hara
Gringoire . . . . .Edmond O'Brien

ACADEMY AWARD NOMINATIONS

2 nominations, no wins

Best Sound Recording
Best Score

JESSE JAMES

20TH CENTURY-FOX
$1,500,000

"After the tragic War Between the States, America turned to the winning of the West. The symbol of this era was the building of the transcontinental railroads. The advance of the railroads was, in some cases, predatory and unscrupulous....It was this uncertain and lawless age that gave the world, for good or ill, its most famous outlaws, the brothers Frank and Jesse James."

—PROLOGUE

IN THE LATE '30s, the "A" Western made a comeback, and each studio rushed its own box office hopeful into production. None were more successful than Fox's *Jesse James,* which boasted a top cast with Tyrone Power and Henry Fonda, as well as the prestigious director Henry King. Portraying the outlaw as a Robin Hood of the Old West, Power was the first in a long line of future Jesses, among them Lawrence Tierney, MacDonald Carey, Audie Murphy, Robert Wagner, and Dale Robertson. But the plum role here was that of brother Frank, aptly played by Fonda. So well received was his characterization that a year later a sequel was made, *The Return of Frank James,* with Fonda reprising his part.

The making of *Jesse James* was fraught with mishaps. Henry Fonda suffered powder burns on his leg when his horse reared and his gun accidentally fired its blanks. Tyrone Power stepped on broken glass while surfing on the Elk River and sliced open his foot. Lon Chaney, Jr., sprained his ankle in a fall. The next day the cinch on his saddle snapped and he took a spill that left him unconscious. But much worse was the death of a horse in the scene in which a stuntman covering for Power rides his horse over a cliff.

Horses don't take kindly to jumping off cliffs, so a slide was constructed and covered with vegetation. At the last minute, a crew member drew aside a blanket and the horse went over. But the horse slipped, injured itself on landing in the lake, and drowned. A second take with a second horse was more successful: the stuntman separated from the horse but reseated himself underwater, and both emerged from the lake unscathed.

The public outcry was so enormous that Hollywood arranged for the American Humane Association to become the official watchdog for animals used by the industry. More than half a century later, there is still an AHA rep on the set when animal actors are in use. Perhaps Jesse James did some good after all.

Screenplay by Nunnally Johnson

Based on historical data assembled by Rosalind Shaffer and Jo Frances James

Produced by Darryl F. Zanuck

Directed by Henry King

CAST

Jesse James	Tyrone Power
Frank James	Henry Fonda
Zerelda (Zee)	Nancy Kelly
Will Wright	Randolph Scott

THE FILM industry had peaked in 1939. Not that it was all downhill from there, but there would never be another year with so many memorable films. With half of Europe overrun by Hitler, the motion picture industry, dependent on foreign revenue for much of its income, began to feel the pinch well before the rest of the United States. In January, 1940, there were 17,000 movie houses in the U.S., 36,000 in Europe, and 7,000 in the Far East. As World War II cut deeply into the revenue, studio output declined drastically, in some cases by one-third.

1940

It would be nearly two years before the Yanks entered the war, but Hollywood went to war even sooner and continued producing films of that genre throughout the decade and well into the '50s. We would not recover quickly.

With so many of our men and boys overseas, it's not too surprising that the top box office draws were mostly male. A survey by Variety showed that the top stars of the early '40s were Clark Gable, Mickey Rooney, Spencer Tracy, Errol Flynn, Bette Davis, and Gary Cooper. Bing Crosby, Cary Grant, and an emerging box office star named John Wayne would dominate the second half of the decade.

1949

1

FANTASIA
WALT DISNEY PRODUCTIONS
$41,660,000

IT WAS a great year for Walt Disney. Following close on the heels of his *Pinocchio* success, the studio released *Fantasia,* which took three years and $2,280,000 to make. Walt collaborated with conductor Leopold Stokowski, and the film was originally planned as a short subject. Eventually Walt and Stokowski agreed on a full-length concert feature, and a program was selected. Works illustrated were Bach's "Toccata and Fugue in D Minor," Tchaikovsky's "The Nutcracker Suite," Stravinsky's "The Rite of Spring," Beethoven's "Pastoral Symphony," Ponchielli's "Dance of the Hours," Moussorgsky's "Night on Bald Mountain," Schubert's "Ave Maria," and the most memorable number, Dukas' "The Sorcerer's Apprentice."

Walt Disney's lovable Mickey Mouse was chosen to represent the Sorcerer in the film's set-piece. The little guy had come a long way since he appeared in the first sound cartoon, *Steamboat Willie,* in 1928. In fact, Mickey almost didn't get off the ground back then. MGM's Louis B. Mayer refused to put the young Disney under contract after seeing a preview of his first Mickey cartoon, fearing that pregnant women would be frightened by a 10-foot-high rodent on the screen.

"The Sorcerer's Apprentice" had originally been intended simply as a short, one of Disney's classic *Silly Symphony*'s. It was completed in 1938, but ran so far over budget that Disney decided the only way he could make a profit from this "featurette" was to incorporate "The Sorcerer's Apprentice" into a full-length feature.

Other segments proved equally imaginative. The Bach Fugue is particularly vivid, opening with images fading into an undulating, abstract sea of rolling, pitching colors dotted with gem-like sparkles. The Fugue builds into swirling circles of vaporous clouds rising into pillars, climaxing with a red-fire sun outlining the silhouette of the conductor. The number became an unintentional hit with latent flower children who toked up and turned on to its re-release in the late '70s.

For the Igor Stravinsky "The Rite of

Based on original soundtrack by Leopold Stokowski

Conducted by Irwin Kostal

Produced by Walt Disney

Production supervision by Ben Sharpsteen

Directed by Samuel Armstrong, James Algar, Bill Roberts, Paul Satterfield, Hamilton Luske, Jim Handley, Ford Beebe, T. Hee, Nohrm Ferguson, and Wilfred Jackson

ACADEMY AWARD NOMINATIONS

In 1941 the Academy of Motion Picture Arts and Sciences awarded Leopold Stokowski and his associates a certificate for their unique achievement in the creation of a new form of visualized music.

That same year, Walt Disney, William Garity, John N.A. Hawkins, and the RCA Manufacturing company received a certificate from the Academy for their outstanding contribution to the advancement of the use of sound in motion pictures through the production of *Fantasia.*

Walt Disney was also awarded the Irving G. Thalberg Memorial Award in 1941.

Spring" segment, Disney consulted with paleontologists from Cal Tech and assembled a herd of pet iguanas and a baby alligator so that animators could study their movements. Dinosaurs were a particular fascination for Disney; not only were they used in *Fantasia,* but they were the centerpiece of the Ford exhibit Disney designed for the 1964 World's Fair, as well as in a diorama at Disneyland and at the Exxon "Energy" exhibit at Epcot Center in Florida. Despite the lavish treatment given his work, however, Stravinsky is said to have despised the battling dinosaurs and Stokowski's conducting with equal vehemence.

The Hays Office managed to earn its keep on this animated feature when Disney animators drew bare-breasted female centaurs in Beethoven's "Pastoral Symphony" segment. They insisted that the "centaurettes" be completely redrawn with flowers hiding the offending area.

"The Dance of the Hours" was another memorable segment. Long after much of the film had been forgotten, most folks remembered the ostriches, elephants, and dancing hippos dressed in tutus, flirting with gal-

lant alligators. People familiar with the '60s Allan Sherman comedy album "My Son, the Folksinger" will recognize the melody as "Hello Mudduh, Hello Fadduh."

The film opened to mixed reviews, most critics unsure what to make of the innovative production. It didn't do very well in its initial run, which had to be limited to theaters that installed a special sound system. It wasn't until its re-release in the '70s that *Fantasia* became a box office hit. A 50th anniversary re-release became a special event in 1990. Faded prints of *Fantasia* could be discarded after the film was completely restored to its original color. Also, the original 1940 version had broken new ground as the first movie released in stereophonic sound, dubbed "Fantasound" by Disney, with three speakers used— one behind the screen and one on either side. Using the original soundtrack, an updated, Dolby one was added to the new print. Gone are the hisses and sputters heard on worn prints, replaced by a re-mastered clear, rich new soundtrack. *Fantasia* has been released on both videocassette and laser disc, perfect viewing as well as listening for the home theater.

In 1993, Walt Disney Productions began filming a long-awaited sequel— actually an expansion—to the original *Fantasia.* Called *Fantasia Continued,* the new film is planned to retain four of the original numbers— "The Sorcerer's Apprentice," "The Nutcracker Suite," "Dance of the Hours," and "Night on Bald Mountain"—while retiring others in favor of some new presentations. According to Roy Disney (nephew of Walt) in *Parade* magazine, the new opening will feature a three-and-a-half-minute version of Beethoven's "Fifth Symphony." Other classics added include Elgar's "Pomp and Circumstance," Shostakovich's "Piano Concerto No. 2," Respighi's "The Pines of Rome," and Saint-Saëns' "Carnival of the Animals." James Levine of New York's Metropolitan Opera is conducting the new score, and the film's expected release date is 1998.

2

PINOCCHIO

WALT DISNEY PRODUCTIONS
$40,442,000

WALT DISNEY premiered *Snow White and the Seven Dwarfs* in 1937 and established his reputation as one of the true geniuses of the century. This first feature-length animation created a new genre and paved the way for the many Disney classics that would follow.

The first of these was *Pinocchio*. Production began in 1937, with an unprecedented budget of $2,600,000. Taking inflation into account, it would require more than $50,000,000 to produce today.

The story of "Pinocchio" was written by Carlo Lorenzini (*nom de plume:* C. Collodi) and first published in Rome in 1881. Translations appeared in more than 200 languages and dialects. Staff members called Walt's attention to the story, originally written in installments for a weekly magazine. He liked it and felt that the characters were perfect for the medium of animation because of their fanciful qualities.

Particularly memorable among these characters is Jiminy Cricket, Pinocchio's mentor. His rendition of "When You Wish Upon a Star" has become an anthem for all things Disneyana. Years later, the Academy Award–winning song struck a chord in the heart of director Steven Spielberg, who used it to inspire awe in *Close*

From the story by C. Collodi

Produced by Walt Disney

Directed by Ben Sharpsteen and Hamilton Luske

VOICES

Pinocchio . . . . .Dick Jones
Geppetto . . . . .Christian Rub
Jiminy Cricket . . . . . .Cliff Edwards
The Blue Fairy . . . . . .Evelyn Venable

ACADEMY AWARD NOMINATIONS

2 nominations, 2 wins*

*Best Song ("When You Wish Upon a Star," music by Leigh Harline, words by Ned Washington)

*Best Original Score

Encounters of the Third Kind.

An interesting commentary on Collodi's times can be found in the characterization of the whale, Monstro, whose very name evokes his station in life. To environmentally conscious audiences of the '80s and '90s, it seems unbelievable that these gentle giants of the sea could have been given such bad press. Not since *Moby Dick* had a whale been viewed with this much fear and malevolence.

Pinocchio himself was drastically changed from the book's concept of the puppet who wants to be a real little boy. In Collodi's story, the puppet listens to a cricket who wants to be his conscience, squashes him with his foot, and goes out into the world as a juvenile delinquent. Very un-Disney.

Pinocchio's voice was supplied by child actor Dick Jones, who at the time had already appeared in almost 40 Westerns. Billed as "Little Dickie Jones," he had been discovered at age five by Hoot Gibson. After appearing in a string of "B" Westerns, Jones moved on to such major productions as *Mr. Smith Goes to Washington, Destry Rides Again,* and *Virginia City.* A radio-show veteran, he found doing the voice for Pinocchio similar to performing on radio. According to Jones, quoted in a Disney press release, "We had a script and would read right into the microphone. They had an 8-mil-limeter camera that they used to photograph my lips as I spoke, so the animators could make Pinocchio's lip movements as realistic as possible." In order to "get into the part," Jones recorded his dialogue dressed in a Pinocchio costume complete with blue short pants, suspenders, a white shirt with a fluffy collar on it, and a cap with a feather. Forty-seven years later Charles Fleischer used the same technique on another Disney film when he donned a rabbit suit to record his dialogue as the title character in *Who Framed Roger Rabbit.*

Pinocchio premiered on February 7, 1940, marred by a publicity stunt that backfired. The gimmick itself was bizarre: Disney studios hired 11 midgets dressed in Pinocchio costumes and placed them atop the theater marquee, where they were instructed to frolic about. Around lunchtime, some kind soul sent up some refreshments, including a couple of quarts of liquor. By mid-afternoon the merry Pinocchios were frolicking stark naked, belching loudly, and shooting craps on the marquee. Police were summoned and carted off the jolly lads in pillowcases.

Despite this rough beginning, audiences all over the world fell in love with the little wooden puppet, making *Pinocchio* one of the most beloved films of all time.

BOOM TOWN

METRO-GOLDWYN-MAYER
$4,586,415

ONE OF THE HOTTEST casts ever to appear in a '40s film—Clark Gable, Spencer Tracy, Claudette Colbert, and Hedy Lamarr—made *Boom Town* a powerhouse at the box office, which was exactly what MGM was banking on. These were the most popular stars at the beginning of the decade, and the studio probably would have had a hit no matter what the quartet appeared in. *Time* noted, "Like most movies that are built on the theory that four stars are better than one, *Boom Town* is not so much a picture as a series of personal appearances." Had Disney's *Pinocchio* and *Fantasia* not enjoyed such prosperity from their many re-releases over the years, *Boom Town* would certainly be considered the number-one film for 1940.

The story is a simple one—environmentally disinterested "wildcat" oil drillers find love and big bucks in the West Texas oil fields, a premise that would again be used successfully in the 1956 hit film *Giant*. State-of-the-art special effects of oil-well gushers and spectacular fires caught the attention of the Motion Picture Academy, which nominated *Boom Town* for a Special

---

Screenplay by John Lee Mahin

Based on "A Lady Comes to Burkburnett" by James Edward Grant

Produced by Sam Zimbalist

Directed by Jack Conway

CAST

Big John McMasters . . .Clark Gable
Square John Sand . . . .Spencer Tracy
Betsy Bartlett . . . . . . .Claudette Colbert
Karen Vanmeer . . . . . .Hedy Lamarr
Luther Aldrich . . . . . . .Frank Morgan

ACADEMY AWARD NOMINATIONS

2 nominations, no wins

Best Cinematography
Best Special Effects

Effects Oscar. (Watch for Mickey Rooney's father, vaudeville entertainer Joe Yule, in the minor role of "Ed Murphy.")

Female audience members were swooning by now over Clark Gable, lately of *Gone With the Wind*. Ironically, Gable himself was the son of an Ohio farmer-turned-oil-driller. In 1915, at the age of 14, he left school to work in a tire factory in nearby Akron. There he saw his first play and was hooked. Stock company bit parts followed. An MGM screen test found him turned down by that studio, as well as by Warner Bros. Producer Darryl F. Zanuck declared, "His ears are too big. He looks like an ape." He was eventually signed by MGM, and it was on a loan-out to Columbia that the highly successful *It Happened One Night* (1934) was made. Gable and co-star Claudette Colbert both won Academy Awards for their roles. *Boom Town* marked their first screen reunion, much to the delight of movie audiences.

THE GREAT DICTATOR

UNITED ARTISTS
$3,500,000

"This is a story of a period between two World Wars—an interim in which Insanity cut loose, Liberty took a nose dive, and Humanity was kicked around somewhat."
—OPENING CARD

HE WADDLED like an anthropomorphic penguin in baggy pants, twirled a cane, and could usually be found beneath a too-small bowler hat. He was "The Little Tramp," the silent clown beloved by millions of filmgoers the world over. They'd been waiting decades for their character to utter his first words. In 1940, he made up for lost time.

The Tramp was, of course, the ongoing creation of one of the 20th century's most gifted artists, Charles Chaplin. He first appeared in early Mack Sennett "Keystone Kops" films in 1914, and audiences immediately warmed to him. But even after the success of "talkies" in the late '20s and throughout most of the '30s, Chaplin refused to make anything but silent films. Some of his best work occurred during this period—classics like *City Lights* (1931) and *Modern Times* (1936). Taking a cue from the title of the latter, it was to be his final silent picture. In 1937, Charlie Chaplin began working on his first talkie.

Perhaps he got the idea for this new venture one day by looking at his own reflection in the mirror while in "Tramp" get-up. For in addition to the trousers, cane, and hat, the character had the most peculiar mustache and bore an uncanny resemblance to one Adolph Hitler. It seemed natural, then, for his character to play the European megalomaniac whose menace was becoming clearer in those final pre-World War II days. But Chaplin, creative genius that he was, played not only the evil dictator but his antithesis as well. In his masterpiece, *The Great Dictator,* Chaplin was both protagonist and antagonist, playing characters as opposite as their not-so-subtle good and evil counterparts.

In the role of a gentle Jewish Barber, Chaplin was able to enact a familiar and comfortable character, essential for audience identification. Early in the film, we see typical Tramp antics as he bumbles his way through World War I, lands in the hospital, and suffers amnesia long enough for "Adenoid Hynkel," dictator of Tomania, to come to power and begin his purge of the Jews. His buddy from the service is now a Gestapo leader and is surprised on learning of the Barber's ethnic origins. "I always thought of you as an Aryan," he says. "I'm a vegetarian," the befuddled little Barber innocently replies.

In his turn as the Tomanian dictator, Chaplin spouts a pseudo-German dialect that would serve as the blueprint for this sort of babble in routines of future comics such as Danny Kaye, Sid Caesar, and Harvey Korman. But one of his finest moments is true to his roots as a great mime, when, with impeccable timing, he does a balletic number, tossing about an air-filled globe of the world he plans to rule.

Not content to take a chance on having audiences "get it," Chaplin ended his tour-de-force by writing a daring and unprecedented finale to the film. Toward the end of the picture, the Barber and the Dictator, bearing a striking resemblance to each other, have accidentally swapped places. The Tramp/Barber is thrust forward to make a conquering speech to his "people," but it is Chaplin himself who steps out of character and speaks, his natural gray-streaked hair now untouched by the makeup department. In a stirring and poetic plea for sanity in the world, he intones, "The soul of man has been given wings…we have lost the way. Greed has poisoned men's souls, has barricaded the world into hate…Do not despair…the power [the dictators] took from the people will return to the people, and so long as men die, liberty will never perish…In the name of democracy, let us all unite…Let us fight to free the world, to do away with national barriers, to do away with greed, with hate and intolerance…In the name of democracy, let us all unite. We are coming out of the darkness into the light; we are coming into a new world."

Audiences and critics alike raved over *The Great Dictator. The New York Times* reviewer called it "perhaps the most significant film ever produced." But despite the brave end speech, the curtain dropped down too quickly on the stage of the real world. It would be five more years before Chaplin's enlightened world could emerge.

Screenplay, Produced and Directed by
  Charles Chaplin

CAST

Adenoid Hynkel/	
Jewish Barber	Charles Chaplin
Benzini Napaloni	Jack Oakie
Hannah	Paulette Goddard
Schultz	Reginald Gardiner
Garbitsch	Henry Daniell

ACADEMY AWARD NOMINATIONS

5 nominations, no wins

Best Picture
Best Actor (Charles Chaplin)
Best Supporting Actor (Jack Oakie)
Best Original Screenplay (Charles Chaplin)
Best Original Score

REBECCA

SELZNICK
$3,000,000

"Last night I dreamt I went to Manderley again."
—OPENING LINE

EVEN AS David O. Selznick was shooting his masterpiece, *Gone With the Wind,* the obsessed producer was simultaneously working on another project that he was sure would top the story of Scarlett and Rhett (as if anything ever could!). He was convinced that he had all the ingredients and, had that first picture never been made, he would surely be remembered for *Rebecca.* For it, too, is a masterpiece in its own right.

It was Alfred Hitchcock's first American film. In 1939 the successful British director, having gained a reputation for making chilling suspense films, left his native land at Selznick's behest to film Daphne du Maurier's

Screenplay by Robert E. Sherwood and Joan Harrison

Adaptation by Philip MacDonald and Michael Hogan

From the novel by Daphne du Maurier

Produced by David O. Selznick

Directed by Alfred Hitchcock

CAST

Maxim de Winter	Laurence Olivier
Mrs. de Winter	Joan Fontaine
Jack Ravell	George Sanders
Mrs. Danvers	Judith Anderson
Giles	Nigel Bruce

ACADEMY AWARD NOMINATIONS

*11 nominations, 2 wins**

* *Best Picture
  Best Actor (Laurence Olivier)
  Best Actress (Joan Fontaine)
  Best Supporting Actress
    (Judith Anderson)
  Best Director (Alfred Hitchcock)
  Best Screenplay
* *Best Cinematography, Black and White
  Best Interior Decoration, Black and White
  Best Original Score
  Best Film Editing
  Best Special Effects

atmospheric tale of the "second Mrs. de Winter" (we never learn her name, Rebecca being the name of the deceased first Mrs. de Winter). In true Hitchcock style, we are shown how the power of the dead can affect the living, a theme Hitch successfully explored in his later box office hits *Spellbound, Psycho,* and another marriage of Hitchcock with du Maurier storytelling, *The Birds.*

Casting Laurence Olivier and Joan Fontaine in the lead roles contributed to the box office success. Fontaine, in her first major role, was a big draw for fans curious to see the latest David O. Selznick "discovery," and the role established her as a major star (the following year, she won the Academy Award for Hitchcock's *Suspicion*).

Hitchcock cast Leo G. Carroll in the minor part of "Dr. Baker." Five years

later, the director again used Carroll as a doctor with a much more important role in the thriller *Spellbound.* (Television audiences may recognize Leo G. Carroll as "Mr. Waverly" from the '60s series "The Man From U.N.C.L.E.")

Critics were lavish in their praise of the British director. *Variety* hailed the film as "an artistic success" while noting that its box office draw might be limited. *The New York Times* called *Rebecca* "an altogether brilliant film, haunting, suspenseful, handsome and handsomely played."

Alfred Hitchcock continued to be one of the most successful directors of all time, with a career spanning 53 years—from the 1923 British film *Always Tell Your Wife* to the 1976 hit *Family Plot.* He died in 1980 at the age of 81.

1

SERGEANT YORK

WARNER BROS.
$6,135,707

"We are proud to present this picture and are grateful to the many heroic figures still living, who have generously consented to be portrayed in its story. To their faith and ours that a day will come when men will live in peace on earth, this picture is humbly dedicated."

—PROLOGUE

O UT OF THE Tennessee mountains came a simple, pacifistic man whose religious upbringing taught him that killing was wrong. But the Army thought differently, and the young conscientious objector Alvin C. York, already a crack shot with rifle and pistol, was denied the exemption he desperately wanted. As a corporal in the Infantry, he took part in the Argonne-Meuse offensive in France, and on October 8, 1918, he single-handedly crushed a German machine-gun nest, killing 25 soldiers and taking 132 prisoners. Having proven himself an effective killing machine, this World War I "Rambo" was made a sergeant and awarded the Croix de Guerre, France's highest honor, as well as the Congressional Medal of Honor.

In 1941, at a time when America's thoughts were turning more and more to the possibility of involvement in another deadly world war, Warner Bros. chose to make *Sergeant York,* a film about this number-one hero of the First World War. It was not really what you would call a recruitment film, but did a great deal more than any "Uncle Sam wants you" movie to sound the reveille and send home its patriotic message. *Variety* called the film, "as timely as a White House fireside chat, a moving and effective presentation in thrilling entertainment terms of what is meant by 'the American way of life'...Gary Cooper appears in the title role for which he seems singularly suited and well chosen."

It was not an accident that Gary Cooper was given this part. In 1940, Jesse Lasky bought the rights to York's life story, and the war hero agreed to let Lasky film it after being convinced that it would inspire a new generation of soldiers. But York insisted that he oversee the production, that his wife

be played by a demure young lady and not a Hollywood sex goddess (Joan Leslie got the part), and that Gary Cooper play York. Cooper later won the Academy Award for Best Actor in this role (and a second Oscar for Best Actor in 1952 in *High Noon*). The actor also received the "Distinguished Citizenship Medal" from the Veterans of Foreign Wars, a ceremony with the real Alvin York in attendance.

Director Howard Hawks had no problems with the casting of Coop as Sgt. York. In fact, he considered it a stroke of luck. "You'd watch him do a scene," Hawks later said, according to *All-Time Box-Office Hits,* "and you'd go home worrying about whether you had it. And then you'd look next day at the rushes—and there was more there than you wanted in the first place."

Again, as with many films of the '30s and '40s, a team of writers worked to turn this into a memorable screenplay. The script was based on the diary of Sergeant York himself as edited by Tom Skeyhill. The teams of Abem Finkel and Harry Chandlee, Howard Koch and John Huston were credited with the writing chores.

Especially noteworthy here is the musical score. Listen carefully and you'll hear, very subtly, the strains of "Give Me That Old Time Religion" used to underscore the scene whenever Walter Brennan appears on the screen as the pastor, or when York is torn between his religious teachings and his duty to his country.

Another familiar member of the cast is a very young June Lockhart, who plays York's sister Rosie. Television fans will remember her as Timmy's mom on "Lassie," as well as the mother on "Lost in Space."

York married in 1919 and settled on a farm donated to him by the state of Tennessee. He established the York Foundation and a Bible school, and donated his share of royalties from the movie to that school. For years, the IRS claimed they were owed several thousand dollars in income tax on the money that he earned from the film, but in 1961 a public subscription cleared his debt. York died on September 2, 1964, at the age of 76.

Screenplay by Abem Finkel, Harry Chandlee, Howard Koch, and John Huston

Based on the diary of Sgt. Alvin C. York

Produced by Jesse L. Lasky and Hal B. Wallis

Directed by Howard Hawks

CAST

Alvin C. York . . . . .Gary Cooper
Pastor Rosier Pile . . . .Walter Brennan
Gracie Williams . . . . .Joan Leslie
Major Buxton . . . . . . .Stanley Ridges
"Pusher" Ross . . . . . .George Tobias

ACADEMY AWARD NOMINATIONS

11 nominations, 2 wins*

Best Picture
*Best Actor (Gary Cooper)
Best Supporting Actor
  (Walter Brennan)
Best Supporting Actress
  (Margaret Wycherly)
Best Director (Howard Hawks)
Best Original Screenplay
Best Cinematography, Black and
  White
Best Interior Decoration
Best Sound Recording
Best Scoring of a Dramatic Picture
*Best Film Editing

2

DUMBO

WALT DISNEY PRODUCTIONS
$3,000,000

country by storm. *Time* magazine, famed for its annual "Man of the Year" issues, dubbed Dumbo "Mammal of the Year," adding, "The most appealing new character of this year of war, he is almost sure to end up in the exclusive kingdom of children's classics."

Ironically, the picture nearly didn't get made. Walt Disney himself was not a great fan of the original story, which arrived on his desk in manuscript form in 1939. At first, he tried to make it into a routine "short." Eventually, he had one of his crack writing teams rework the story. Joe Grant and Dick Huemer were assigned the task, but knowing their boss's short attention span with long treatments, they decided to write episodically, doling out the story one event at a time. According to a *Time* magazine interview at the time, the team was barely one-quarter of the way through their story when Disney stormed into their office, praising their work and demanding to know, "What the hell happens tomorrow?"

Tomorrow, of course, the film was released, and re-released over the years. Chalk up another classic for Disney.

C LOCKING IN AT a mere 64 minutes, Walt Disney's *Dumbo* barely qualified as an animated "feature." But shortly after this 1941 entry into the beloved Disney menagerie hit the screen, theater owners quickly realized that this elephant could fly, and in more ways than one. (Exhibitors added cartoons and shorts for fillers, to round out the program.)

On the surface, the story of the blue-eyed baby elephant delivered by the stork to Mrs. Jumbo seems simple enough. Christened Dumbo by the circus's tongue-wagging matronly elephants, the little guy is soon the object of ridicule because of his outsized ears. Further difficulties ensue when his mom tries to intercede and she is chained in a circus car, leaving her baby to fend for himself. In typical Disney fashion, Dumbo is soon mentored by a new-found friend, in this case a circus mouse named Timothy (think: Jiminy Cricket and Pinocchio). Naturally, Timothy's young charge gets into trouble—but with alcohol? Somehow, the little pachyderm man-

ages to ingest a serious amount of champagne (accidentally dumped into his drinking water by inebriated clowns—yes, this *is* a children's picture!), enough to get him sloshed to the point where he's seeing "Pink Elephants on Parade." It's one of the movie's cleverest musical production numbers, now hailed as a classic moment in the film. (Other songs include: "Look Out for Mr. Stork," "When I See an Elephant Fly," "All Aboard," and the Academy Award–nominated "Baby Mine.") Following this incident, Dumbo learns he can fly by spreading his enormous ears. Soon he's the hit of the Big Top, his mother is released from her confinement, and there's a happy Disney ending.

Since anyone who had ever felt different or alienated (and that included just about everyone at one time or another) identified with the critter, *Dumbo* was an instant hit. It was the perfect, uplifting film for the early war years, premiering barely two months before Pearl Harbor. By Christmas, the movie had taken the

---

Screenplay by Joe Grant and Dick Huemer

Based on a book by Helen Aberson and Harold Pearl

Produced by Walt Disney

Directed by Ben Sharpsteen and additional segment directors

CAST (VOICES)

Timothy Mouse . . . . . .Edward Brophy
Ringmaster . . . . .Herman Bing
Elephant . . . . .Verna Felton
Stork . . . . .Sterling Holloway
Jim Crow . . . . .Cliff Edwards
(Note: Dumbo never speaks)

ACADEMY AWARD NOMINATIONS

2 nominations, 1 win*

*Best Scoring of a Musical Picture
Best Song ("Baby Mine," music by Frank Churchill, words by Ned Washington)

DIVE BOMBER

WARNER BROS.
$1,500,000*

JUST FOUR MONTHS before the Japanese attack at Pearl Harbor, in August, 1941, *Dive Bomber* was released. It was another "recruitment" film, depicting the brave men who took off from carrier decks to fly bombing missions. The picture was made with the cooperation of the United States Navy and a bunch of technical advisors, duly thanked in the credits. But the real heroes of the film are naval flight surgeons, to whom the picture is dedicated "in recognition of their heroic efforts to solve the immensely difficult problems of aviation medicine."

While this film could be called the *Top Gun* of its day, it is certainly dated. Today's audience may enjoy watching this as a curiosity piece—the "modern" equipment has an ancient, historical appearance. The directing is very static, and the "wipe" technique

between scenes is overdone. It is startling, too, to see how frequently all the doctors take cigarette breaks, lighting up whenever the tension mounts. One surgeon even offers a cigarette to a dying patient so his last moment on Earth will be a pleasant one!

The film starred Errol Flynn, an Australian national who became a naturalized American citizen in 1942. He was every man's vision of the dashing young Naval officer/surgeon. Ironically, Flynn made no effort whatsoever to take part in the war, unlike many Hollywood stars of the day.

Co-starring as an old-line pilot is Fred MacMurray, a dashing leading actor of the '40s. Born in Kankakee, Illinois, in 1908, MacMurray began his career as a saxophonist, and by the '30s he had signed with Paramount, playing the lead in a variety of films. He found his forte in comedy, and today's audi-

ences probably best remember MacMurray as a staple of '60s Walt Disney comedies, as well as the star of the TV series "My Three Sons." MacMurray died on November 5, 1991.

An unintentional laugh comes for today's audience when a character named "Lucky" remarks that he's just been transferred to San Diego from Pearl Harbor. With that attack still four months away, he was aptly named.

---

*Positions 3, 4, and 5 are "guestimates" based on figures reported for high-ranking films early in the '40s. Since records weren't kept for films that were not re-released (and therefore brought in rentals of less than $4,000,000, *Variety*'s cut-off), these figures are derived from compilations of reports in the trade papers as well as raw estimates from the studios themselves. The films 3 through 5 all earned roughly the same amount and appear in alphabetical order.

Screenplay by Frank Wead and
   Robert Buckner

From a story by Frank Wead

Produced by Hal B. Wallis

Directed by Michael Curtiz

CAST

Doug Lee . . . . .Errol Flynn
Joe Blake . . . . .Fred MacMurray
Dr. Lance Rogers . . .Ralph Bellamy
Linda Fisher . . . . . . .Alexis Smith
Art Lyons . . . . .Robert Armstrong

ACADEMY AWARD NOMINATIONS

1 nomination, no wins

Best Cinematography, Color

4

HONKY TONK

METRO-GOLDWYN-MAYER
$1,500,000*

ELIZABETH COTTON (LANA TURNER) after a kiss: "*I want you to stay away from me.*"

"CANDY" JOHNSON (CLARK GABLE): "*No, you don't. Why don't you jump in and get wet all over.*"

IT WAS SCENES like this, between two of the biggest stars of the '40s, that MGM was counting on to make *Honky Tonk* a box office bonanza, and they weren't disappointed. Fans weren't disappointed, either. If the plot seemed familiar—the story of a gambling-hall hustler (Gable) and his sparring partner and eventual wife—that was because it was derivative of many an Old West yarn.

When *Honky Tonk* opened, however, most reviewers ignored the thin plot about an Old West con artist "fleecing the sheep" and moved on to the chemistry between Miss Turner and Mr. Gable. Said *The New York Times:* "Miss Turner is not only beautifully but ruggedly constructed…Mr. Gable snarls, wrinkles his eyes and occasionally becomes condescendingly tender,

but usually he keeps his chin well out in front. One could hear rapturous sighs all over the Capitol mezzanine yesterday…Miss Turner gives a competent, if limited performance and Mr. Gable again shows off his muscles." *Newsweek* also thought the virtues of the two leads were the film's strong points, terming *Honky Tonk* "a horse opera without the horses," and adding that MGM's main purpose in making the film seemed to be the "glamour merger" of Gable with Turner and "the promise of exciting and unpre-

dictable variations on the tender passion."

Honky Tonk's producer, Pandro S. Berman, was one of the most ubiquitous filmmakers of all times. His work spanned four decades, with his name appearing on dozens of important movies, including *The Gay Divorcee, Top Hat, The Hunchback of Notre Dame, National Velvet, The Three Musketeers, Father of the Bride, Ivanhoe, The Blackboard Jungle, Tea and Sympathy, The Brothers Karamazov, Butterfield 8,* and many others.

This movie was really a lark for Berman. The casting of Frank Morgan as Judge Cotton, father of Lana Turner's character, was not unusual since he was a Metro contract player. And when it came time to select his wardrobe, he was attired in almost the exact same outfit he wore in *The Wizard of Oz.* Add to that Gable's character looking like Rhett Butler, and we get something akin to *Gone With the Wind* meets *The Wizard of Oz.*

Screenplay by Marguerite Roberts and John Sanford

Produced by Pandro S. Berman

Directed by Jack Conway

CAST

"Candy" Johnson	Clark Gable
Elizabeth Cotton	Lana Turner
Judge Cotton	Frank Morgan
"Gold Dust" Nelson	Claire Trevor
Mrs. Varner	Marjorie Main

---

*Rough estimate. See footnote on page 33.

THE PHILADELPHIA STORY

METRO-GOLDWYN-MAYER
$1,500,000*

FOUR-TIME Academy Award winner Katharine Hepburn is one of the true legends of Hollywood. She arrived in California from her native Hartford, Connecticut, in 1932 and immediately began shocking the community by wearing slacks (then referred to as "men's pants"), driving a station wagon (classified at the time as a "truck" for lack of a better descriptive term), and sitting on curbstones, since studios didn't provide benches for stars whose feet hurt. She was unique and head-strong, a lot like her character "Tracy Lord" in *The Philadelphia Story.*

The story centers on a Philadelphia "Main Liner" (wealthy woman) played by Katharine Hepburn. On the eve of her wedding to hubby number two, she must fend off the advances of her ex, C. K. Dexter Haven (the ever-dashing Cary Grant). At the same time, she develops an infatuation with an amorous reporter, played by Jimmy

Screenplay by Donald Ogden Stewart

From the play by Philip Barry

Produced by Joseph L. Mankiewicz

Directed by George Cukor

CAST

C. K. Dexter Haven . . . .Cary Grant
Tracy Lord . . . . .Katharine Hepburn
Macaulay Connor . . . . .James Stewart
Elizabeth Imbrie . . . . . .Ruth Hussey
George Kittredge . . . . .John Howard

ACADEMY AWARD NOMINATIONS

6 nominations, 2 wins*

Best Picture
*Best Actor (James Stewart)
Best Actress (Katharine Hepburn)
Best Supporting Actress (Ruth Hussey)
Best Director (George Cukor)
*Best Screenplay (Donald Ogden Stewart)

Film had a pre-release of limited showing in December, 1940, which qualified it for the 1940 Academy Awards. Officially, however, the movie wasn't released until January 10, 1941, as per a Theatre Guild agreement, so as not to conflict with the road-show performances.

Stewart. This ménage à quatre delighted audiences eager to see which suitor would win the blue-blooded hand of Miss Hepburn.

A highly successful Broadway play, *The Philadelphia Story* was still playing in road companies when the film was released. Having optioned the film rights when signing for the stage play, Miss Hepburn had secured the part for herself, along with rights of approval on director and co-star.

Hepburn had performed the part hundreds of times, a distinct advantage when it came to putting the play on film. Still, director George Cukor found working with her difficult. "I have no pedestal for Miss Hepburn," he wrote in *The Hollywood Reporter* shortly after the film's completion. "She can be wrong. She can be difficult. We have had our arguments. But Miss Hepburn can most sincerely be judged by the almost tearful affection with which the crew regarded her at the completion of *The Philadelphia Story.*"

The film was even more successful than the play, and it didn't hurt that her two co-stars were Cary Grant and Jimmy Stewart. For his performance

as the love-struck reporter, Stewart received an Oscar. At his father's request, the young actor shipped the award back to his hardware store in Pennsylvania, where it was displayed in the front window for 20 years.

Years later, Stewart, who has often been called one of the greatest American actors of all time, commented on his seemingly effortless acting technique in an interview on the television magazine show "Entertainment Tonight": "You try to go through and do this part and not have the acting show."

Jimmy Stewart's performance certainly captured the attention of the critics. *The Hollywood Reporter* remarked: "How that boy does troupe. Nobody in pictures...that we have ever seen could have given Macaulay Connor what that role required, and his performance meant so much to that of Miss Hepburn."

In 1956, *High Society,* a Cole Porter musical version, was produced. It starred Grace Kelly, Frank Sinatra, and Bing Crosby, and, while popular, it didn't match the success of the original.

---

*Rough estimate. See footnote on page 33.

1

BAMBI

WALT DISNEY PRODUCTIONS
$47,265,000

WALT DISNEY had begun work on *Bambi* in 1937, right after *Snow White and the Seven Dwarfs*. But the project had several setbacks, including the high cost of making the film of Felix Salten's successful book.

From its inception, Walt wanted *Bambi* to be different from the cartoon style of its predecessors. "I respect nature very much, and by watching and observing the habits of creatures of nature, man can learn a lot," Walt stated in a press release. To ensure authenticity, Walt (he preferred to be addressed by his first name) hired top artists and instructors and brought them to the studio to lecture his animators on animal drawing and anatomy. An actual deer carcass was brought in so the animators could dissect it and study the ligaments and musculature. Two live fawns were sent to the studio courtesy of the Maine Development Commission. Appropriately dubbed "Bambi" and "Faline," they were kept in a pen outside the animation building. Later, a menagerie of two skunks, birds, squirrels, chipmunks, and rabbits were added to the Disney on-lot zoo.

One of the studio's biggest concerns from the start was how to superimpose personalities on realistically drawn animal characters and still maintain their believability. Whereas the animal characters in *Snow White* and *Pinocchio* had been cartoonlike, Bambi and his friends were anthropomorphic, intended to be taken seriously by the audience.

The animators solved this problem by paring dialogue down to a compact 900-word script. Great care was taken in animating the mouths of the creatures so that they moved in a manner suggesting delivery of dialogue while mimicking true animal movement.

To further add to the realism, Disney animators studied up on child behavior and development, learning to adapt the expressions of human toddlers to the various animals. This also proved helpful in establishing the personalities of the young animals.

Additional research was required for the forest backgrounds that would be the setting for *Bambi,* and the studio sent artist Jake Day on a photographic safari to the Maine woods. Day spent five months sketching and photographing the Katahdin wilderness in the Baxter Game Preserve. His volumes of meticulously detailed sketches and photos not only were used for *Bambi,* but later became the basis for Disney's award-winning series of True-Life Adventures, documentary movie shorts depicting various nature themes.

It is the animated characters themselves who take center stage: Bambi, the little fawn who grows to be a great forest prince; Thumper, his rabbit pal who manages to say all the wrong things; Flower, the shy skunk; and a score of quintessential big-Disney-eyed forest critters.

Although no voice credits were given to the youngsters who portrayed Bambi and his playmates, Walt Disney Studios later released the name of the child who read the part of Thumper. Peter Behn was only four years old when he came in to audition for the part. The son of a veteran Hollywood screenwriter, Peter was first brought in to vocalize the bunny family for the scene in which Bambi learns to walk. According to a Disney press release, when Peter said, "Did the young prince fall down?" someone whispered, "Get the kid out of here; he can't act." The production staff listened to the tapes later and discovered Peter had the perfect voice for Thumper. It took some scrambling to locate him after his dismissal the previous day.

Bambi is essentially a children's story, and even today eager parents will rush off to the latest re-release, or sit restless youngsters down in front of the TV set, plop a cassette in the VCR, and catch a few moments' peace. Yet there is something very adult about the underlying themes in the film. Early on, young Bambi is warned by his mother to take care when "Man [is] in the forest." Later Bambi is orphaned when hunters (Man) shoot and kill her. Was there ever a sadder murder on screen? Mercifully, Disney didn't dwell on this scene, and quickly followed it with a song and the promise of Spring. Still later, in some of the most exciting animation ever created, a fire roars through the forest. The cause: Man. The point could not have been better made if the film had been produced by the Sierra Club.

Most audiences, including the critics, saw it as just plain exciting entertainment, which it definitely is. *The Hollywood Reporter* said: "The feature is by far the most realistic achievement of the Disney merchants of magic. It likewise boasts the most beautiful effects…it is more like a free painting artfully lit and hung, actually a work of love by craftsmen who have remained young in heart. It will make millions happy and bring millions to the box office."

Actually, the film didn't do well in its initial release, and it took many years for it to turn a profit. Bob Thomas' *Walt Disney* quotes Disney as saying: "I think back to 1942 when we released that picture and there was a war on, and nobody cared much about the love life of a deer, and the bankers were on my back. It's pretty gratifying to know that *Bambi* finally made it."

In 1942, Walt Disney halted his feature filmmaking. He chose to use the studio for working on government films to help with the war effort. *Bambi* would be his last commercial effort for the duration of the war.

From the novel by Felix Salten

Story adaptation by Larry Morey

Produced by Walt Disney

Directed by David D. Hand

VOICE

Thumper . . . . .Peter Behn*

ACADEMY AWARD NOMINATIONS

3 nominations, no wins

Best Sound Recording
Best Song ("Love Is a Song That Never Ends," music and words by Frank Churchill and Edward Plumb)
Best Scoring of a Dramatic or Comedy Picture

---

*While no voice credits are given in the film, "it is known," according to *The Disney Films,* "that Peter Behn did the voice of Thumper."

2

MRS. MINIVER

METRO-GOLDWYN-MAYER
$5,390,009

many Americans as a graduation song.

In case you missed the message, the end slide announces: "America needs your money. Buy defense bonds and stamps every pay day."

Mrs. Miniver turned out to be the most financially successful film of 1942, and it was only because of re-releases of *Bambi* that it did not achieve number-one status in the long run. In 1950, a sequel, *The Miniver Story,* was produced. It bombed (no pun intended), unable to capture the mood, or the need, of the original.

Screenplay by Arthur Wimperis, George Froeschel, James Hilton, and Claudine West

From the novel by Jan Struther

Produced by Sidney Franklin

Directed by William Wyler

CAST

Mrs. Miniver . . . . .Greer Garson
Clem Miniver . . . . . . .Walter Pidgeon
Carol Beldon . . . . .Teresa Wright
Lady Beldon . . . . .Dame May Whitty
Foley . . . . .Reginald Owen

ACADEMY AWARD NOMINATIONS

12 nominations, 6 wins*

*Best Picture
 Best Actor (Walter Pidgeon)
*Best Actress (Greer Garson)
 Best Supporting Actor (Henry Travers)
*Best Supporting Actress (Teresa Wright)
 Best Supporting Actress (Dame May Whitty)
*Best Director (William Wyler)
*Best Screenplay (Arthur Wimperis, George Froeschel, James Hilton, and Claudine West)
*Best Cinematography, Black and White
 Best Sound Recording
 Best Film Editing
 Best Special Effects

Greer Garson gave the longest acceptance speech ever made at an Oscar ceremony—it lasted over an hour.

"This story of an average English middle-class family begins with the summer of 1939: when the sun shone down on a happy, careless people, who worked and played, reared their children and tended their gardens in that happy, easygoing England that was so soon to be fighting desperately for her way of life and for life itself."
—OPENING CRAWL

OF ALL THE FILMS made about and during World War II, *Mrs. Miniver* had the most impact. Winston Churchill wrote to Louis B. Mayer, saying its propaganda was worth a hundred battleships. The American public ate it up; the film did much to increase the empathy of Americans for their English allies besieged by Hitler's "blitz." And in its portrayal of the brave Englishwoman and her family adjusting to the day-to-day problems of coping with the war, *Mrs. Miniver* served as an inspiration to Americans fearful that their lives might

one day similarly be disrupted.

The film had an impact on the Germans, too. Hitler's henchman Goebbels cited the film as "an exemplary propaganda film for the German industry to copy." Churchill ordered leaflets of the film's inspirational closing speech dropped behind enemy lines. The message, delivered by Henry Wilcoxon as the Vicar, is nearly as rousing as Lincoln's Gettysburg Address:

"This is not only a war of soldiers in uniform. It is a war of the people, of all the people, and it must be fought not only on the battlefield, but in the cities and in the villages; in the factories and on the farms; in the homes and in the heart of every man, woman and child who loves freedom… this is the people's war…fight it with all that is in us, and may God defend the right."
Thus stirred, the people sing "Onward Christian Soldiers" in the bombed-out cathedral, followed by a chorus of "Pomp and Circumstance"—familiar to

CASABLANCA

WARNER BROS.
$4,750,000

"Play it, Sam. Play 'As Time Goes By.'" —INGRID BERGMAN
"You've played it for her, you can play it for me. Play it!" —HUMPHREY BOGART

EVERYBODY COMES TO RICK'S. That was the unproduced play that became the immensely successful movie *Casablanca.* The title change by producer Hal Wallis was fortuitous: just as the film was being released in November of 1942, the Allies serendipitously landed in Axis-occupied Casablanca, and the North African city's name was suddenly ubiquitous.

Other changes occurred which no doubt helped *Casablanca* become one of the favorite films of all time. As in *Gone With the Wind,* this picture owes a lot to the chemistry between the two leads, Humphrey Bogart and Ingrid Bergman. But these two great stars were not always everyone's first choice. Some of the names kicked around by Wallis and director Mike Curtiz were Ann Sheridan, Hedy Lamarr, and Michele Morgan for Ilsa, and George Raft and Ronald Reagan for Rick.

The Germans considered this a propaganda film, and it wasn't until after World War II that it was allowed to play in Germany. Even then, the censors took scissors to it and deleted 20 minutes of footage. All references to Nazis were axed, including all of Conrad Veidt's scenes as a Nazi high commander.

In 1987, for a private showing at the Rio Film Festival, Joao Luiz Albuquerque re-edited a print and changed the ending to show Ingrid Bergman not getting on the plane, but coming back into the arms of Bogey. ("We'll always have Paris…and Casablanca"?)

Many remakes have been attempted, but none have ever been successful. Back in 1943, a sequel was planned and a writer put under contract, but it was nixed almost immediately. A 1955 television series made a brief appearance on ABC, with Charles McGraw re-creating the role of Rick, but it didn't last more than seven months.

In 1983, the British Film Institute polled its members on the 30 best movies of all time. Out of a total of 2,000 films nominated, *Casablanca* was overwhelmingly the number-one choice.

Today *Casablanca* has the honor of being the most often-repeated movie on U.S. television, according to a recent survey conducted by *TV Guide.*

And you'd think that with a film this popular, people would know that no one in the movie ever says, "Play it again, Sam."

Screenplay by Julius J. Epstein, Philip G. Epstein, and Howard Koch

From a play by Murray Burnett and Jean Alison

Produced by Hal B. Wallis

Directed by Michael Curtiz

CAST

Rick . . . . .Humphrey Bogart
Ilsa Lund . . . . .Ingrid Bergman
Victor Laszlo . . . . .Paul Henreid
Capt. Louis Renault . . .Claude Rains
Major Strasser . . . . . .Conrad Veidt
Señor Ferrari . . . . . . .Sydney Greenstreet
Ugarte . . . . .Peter Lorre

ACADEMY AWARD NOMINATIONS

*8 nominations, 3 wins **

*Best Picture
 Best Actor (Humphrey Bogart)
 Best Supporting Actor (Claude Rains)
*Best Director (Michael Curtiz)
*Best Screenplay (Julius J. Epstein, Philip
 G. Epstein, and Howard Koch)
 Best Cinematography, Black and White
 Best Scoring of a Dramatic or Comedy
 Picture
 Best Film Editing

Hal B. Wallis was honored with the Irving G. Thalberg Memorial Award.

Award nominations were for the year 1943, although the film was released in a limited run in November, 1942.

YANKEE DOODLE DANDY

WARNER BROS.
$4,719,681

"Ladies and gentlemen, my mother thanks you, my father thanks you, my sister thanks you, and I thank you." —GEORGE M. COHAN

IN A YEAR laden with war movies, *Yankee Doodle Dandy,* the musical biography of George M. Cohan, gave film audiences a chance to catch their breath. Yet even this movie had an inspirational "let's go get 'em" message with rousing patriotic renditions of "You're a Grand Old Flag" and "Over There" ("…and we won't come back till it's over, over there!"). *Time* noted that the song "is enough to send movie audiences straight off to battle."

Maybe so, but mainly it sent them straight to the box office. And reason number one was the new singing and dancing sensation James Cagney. His performance as Cohan made him the first actor to receive an Academy Award for a musical performance.

It was almost inevitable that George M. Cohan would become the subject of an autobiographical film. The celebrated actor, singer, dancer, songwriter, playwright, and screenwriter was one of the most gifted talents of the early 20th century. He was born on the 3rd (not the 4th) of July in 1878 to an Irish family originally named Keohane. By the time of his death in 1942, he had written over 500 songs, created 41 musicals and plays, and produced 130 others.

It was Cohan himself who insisted Cagney play him. Audiences remembered Jimmy Cagney as the tough who smashes Mae Clarke in the face with a grapefruit in *The Public Enemy* (Warner Bros., 1931). But Cohan was familiar with Cagney as an ex-Broadway hoofer, and Cagney spent four months in rehearsals, perfecting the "hitch" and other mannerisms that would become the mainstay of future impressionists. And it didn't come easy—he sprained his ankle twice while perfecting a Cohan-esque stiff-legged dancing style.

Like George M. Cohan, whose family formed the act "The Four Cohans," Cagney managed to bring his own family members into the act. His brother, William, associate-produced many of his films, including this one, and his sister Jeanne acted and also appeared in *Yankee Doodle Dandy.*

On April 10, 1968, the highly successful play *George M!,* the musical account of the life of Cohan, premiered on Broadway and ran for many years. Joel Grey and Bernadette Peters starred in this tribute to Cohan, replete with all his famous tunes.

On July 4, 1985, *Yankee Doodle Dandy* had the dubious honor of being the first computer-colorized film released when entrepreneur Ted Turner, who owns 3,500 films of the MGM library,* premiered the movie on his Turner Broadcasting System. It opened a floodgate that eventually saw the issue of colorization being debated before a congressional committee, with many directors and stars opposed to the practice on the grounds that it diminishes the visual quality of films that were intended to be seen only in black and white. The controversy continues today, with the only resolution in the hands of the television viewer, who has the option of turning off all color on the TV set and viewing the film in its original monochrome hues.

*MGM bought the rights to many early Warner Bros. and RKO films, which Turner acquired with his purchase of the MGM library.

Screenplay by Robert Buckner and Edmund Joseph

From original story by Robert Buckner

Produced by Hal B. Wallis

Directed by Michael Curtiz

CAST

George M. Cohan . . . . .James Cagney
Mary Cohan . . . . .Joan Leslie
Jerry Cohan . . . . .Walter Huston
Sam Harris . . . . .Richard Whorf
Fay Templeton . . . . . .Irene Manning

ACADEMY AWARD NOMINATIONS

8 nominations, 3 wins*

Best Picture
*Best Actor (James Cagney)
Best Supporting Actor (Walter Huston)
Best Director (Michael Curtiz)
Best Original Story
*Best Sound Recording
*Best Scoring of a Musical Picture
Best Film Editing

RANDOM HARVEST

METRO-GOLDWYN-MAYER
$4,665,501

I T WAS THE YEAR of Greer. Following her success as Mrs. Miniver, Greer Garson starred in the melodramatic hit *Random Harvest,* which had critics rushing to their thesauruses, making lists of superlatives. Gushed *The Hollywood Reporter:* "One of the truly fine motion pictures of this or any year…an emotional experience of rare quality. Rave press notices cannot fail to greet the excellence of its production, direction, performances and craftsmanship, for there can be no fault to find with any phase of the great, enduring love story it stirringly brings to life." Not only the critics, but audiences too, were enthralled by this romantic story of a man who marries while suffering from amnesia, only to get his memory back, return to his former life, and become amnesic about his wife. This soap-operatic premise was actually the basis of a major novel by James Hilton (author of *Lost Horizon,*

Screenplay by Claudine West, George Froeschel, and Arthur Wimperis

Based on the novel by James Hilton

Produced by Sidney Franklin

Directed by Mervyn LeRoy

CAST

Charles Rainier . . . . . .Ronald Colman
Paula . . . . .Greer Garson
Dr. Jonathan Benet . . .Philip Dorn
Kitty . . . . .Susan Peters
Dr. Sims . . . . .Henry Travers

ACADEMY AWARD NOMINATIONS

7 nominations, no wins

Best Picture
Best Actor (Ronald Colman)
Best Supporting Actress (Susan Peters)
Best Director (Mervyn LeRoy)
Best Writing, Screenplay
Best Interior Decoration, Black and White
Best Scoring of a Dramatic or Comedy Picture

Sidney Franklin, who produced the two Garson movies of 1942 (*Mrs. Miniver* and *Random Harvest*), received the Academy's Irving G. Thalberg Memorial Award.

among other classics), and film audiences, eager for a respite from war films, made *The Hollywood Reporter*'s box office prediction a reality.

Kudos went to Greer Garson, with much of the attention centering on her legs, which made their first (and tasteful) appearance in this film. *Time* went so far as to say, "Random Harvest…is distinguished by (1) a moving love story, (2) the unveiling of Miss Garson's interesting legs." And *The New York Times* noted that "[Miss Garson] is modestly permitted to show off her dimpled knees." With all this attention showered upon Garson's gams, it's a wonder these critics were even aware of Ronald Colman's fine co-starring performance. His role as

the World War I shell-shocked amnesia victim was certainly one of his most memorable, and once the reviewers recovered from the sight of his leggy co-star, they had equal praise for Colman. The Academy confirmed this by honoring him with a nomination for Best Actor.

One of the most dashing heroes of the '30s and '40s, Ronald Colman first began his career in silent films. With his mellow, British-accented voice, he moved easily to "talkies," starring in a number of memorable films such as *Arrowsmith* (1931), *A Tale of Two Cities* (1935)—in which he utters those unforgettable lines, "Tis a far, far better thing I do than I have ever done"—and *Lost Horizon* (1937).

1

THIS IS THE ARMY

WARNER BROS.
$8,500,000

THOUSANDS OF Americans had already seen *This Is the Army* as a touring road show conceived to make money for the Army Relief Fund. In fact, the combined efforts of film and play netted that fund $10,000,000.

Basically an all-soldier revue, the stage show's 350 soldiers appear in the film along with an all-star Warner Bros. cast. The movie is comprised of a string of production numbers featuring singing and dancing soldiers. Many of the numbers are memorable, including songstress Kate Smith greeting the audience with "Hello, everybody. It is my privilege to introduce a new song—'God Bless America.' "

It's a beautiful number, guaranteed to send a tear down the cheek of nearly any American seeing it today. In fact, it has often been suggested that should "The Star Spangled Banner" ever be replaced as a national anthem, Irving Berlin's tune would be a suitable substitute.

But the best number in the whole movie comes when the audience is treated to none other than composer Irving Berlin himself, decked out in his old World War I doughboy uniform, gently singing a version of his own song "Oh, How I Hate to Get Up in the Morning." An amusing anecdote has it that as this bit was being filmed, someone on the set remarked, "If the fellow who wrote this song could hear this guy sing it, he'd roll over in his grave."

When Kate Smith sings her "God Bless America" number, there is a montage showing Americans in their homes, thinking about their sons at war, going about their daily lives. And in one home sits Ronald Reagan, reading *Variety*. Future President Reagan (billed in the credits as Lieutenant Ronald Reagan) had a fairly large part in this film as the son of a theatrical producer (played by George Murphy).

Mostly, though, *This Is the Army* is a vaudeville show with the emphasis on song and dance, featuring a few dreadfully boring comedy routines. One spectacular number is a minstrel show featuring the tune "Mandy." With a giant banjo in the background, tap dancers in blackface are partnered with black women—who turn out to

be guys in drag. Seen today, the whole number is really a sad commentary on the racism that was so acceptable in those days. There were racial clichés aplenty, right down to a tap-dancing black unit of soldiers.

The Navy wasn't left out either. There is a big production number with a Navy battleship on stage. Not to be outdone, the Army Air Corps bit has a plane on stage with turning propellers.

Critics couldn't praise it enough. *Variety* wrote: "After the history of World War II is written, the Warner Bros. filmization will stand out like the Empire State Bldg. amidst the many other highlights in the motion picture industry's contributions to the home front and war front. It's that kind of all-embracing job." They summed up with the trademark showbiz term "It's socko!" *The New York Times'* reviewer agreed, calling *This Is the Army* "buoyant, captivating, as American as hot dogs or the Bill of Rights…it is, from beginning to end, a great show…A bouquet to Warner Brothers who have waived all profits in the venture."

Following the film's release, the touring company continued to perform for live audiences, heading overseas to Great Britain, and then to combat areas of Europe, the Near East, and the Pacific. Having been seen by 2,500,000 American soldiers, the show closed in Honolulu on October 22, 1945. For his contribution, Irving Berlin was decorated with the Medal of Merit by General George C. Marshall.

Born Israel Isidore Baline in Russia on May 11, 1888, Berlin and his Jewish parents fled the *pogroms* when he was five, settling in New York's Lower East Side. By the time he was a teenager, he was a singing waiter selling songs on the side. His first big hit was "Alexander's Ragtime Band" (1911), and in the course of his career, he composed more than 1,000 tunes. His songs had such a familiarity about them that many thought they were old American folk songs. Among his best-known ones are "White Christmas," "Blue Skies," "Easter Parade," and "There's No Business Like Show Business." When he passed away in 1989 at the age of 101, he was mourned as a national hero.

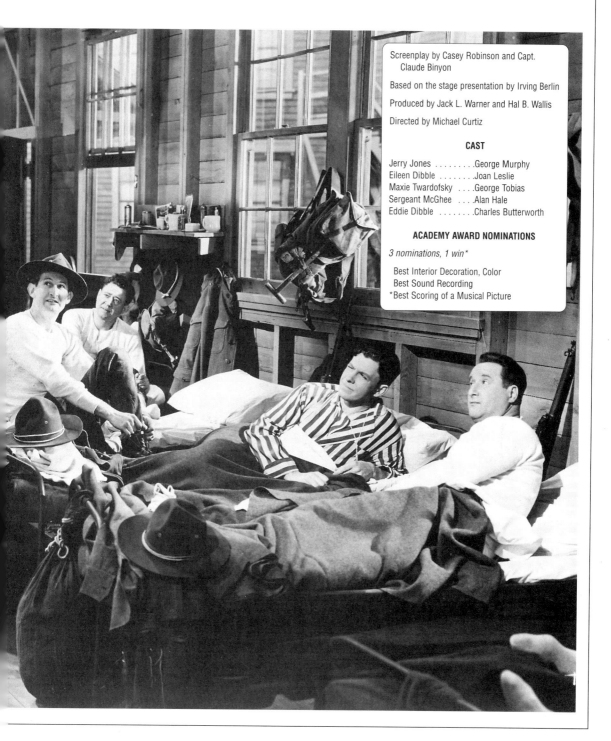

Screenplay by Casey Robinson and Capt. Claude Binyon

Based on the stage presentation by Irving Berlin

Produced by Jack L. Warner and Hal B. Wallis

Directed by Michael Curtiz

CAST

Jerry Jones . . . . .George Murphy
Eileen Dibble . . . . .Joan Leslie
Maxie Twardofsky . . . .George Tobias
Sergeant McGhee . . . .Alan Hale
Eddie Dibble . . . . .Charles Butterworth

ACADEMY AWARD NOMINATIONS

3 nominations, 1 win*

Best Interior Decoration, Color
Best Sound Recording
*Best Scoring of a Musical Picture

2

FOR WHOM THE BELL TOLLS

PARAMOUNT
$7,100,000

"Any man's death diminishes me because I am involved in Mankind: and therefore never send to know for whom the bell tolls. It tolls for thee."
—OPENING CARD (FROM A POEM BY JOHN DONNE)

PRODUCED at the height of the American involvement in World War II, the screen version of Ernest Hemingway's novel about an American fighting with Spanish Civil War soldiers is a faithful adaptation, retaining much of the original dialogue of the novel. Still, *For Whom the Bell Tolls* did not meet with unanimous critical acclaim when it was translated into a nearly three-hour-long film. While *The Hollywood Reporter* called the production "breath-taking" and *Variety* termed it "one of the important pictures of all time," *Newsweek* noted that "the film leaves a good deal to be desired," and the *New York Telegram* told its readers that "the dialogue runs on and on and drags the story to temporary halts… People simply talk too much."

Concerned about potential box

Screenplay by Dudley Nichols

From the novel by Ernest Hemingway

Produced and directed by Sam Wood

CAST

Robert Jordan	Gary Cooper
Maria	Ingrid Bergman
Pablo	Akim Tamiroff
Pilar	Katina Paxinou
Anselmo	Vladimir Sokolof

ACADEMY AWARD NOMINATIONS

9 nominations, 1 win*

Best Picture
Best Actor (Gary Cooper)
Best Actress (Ingrid Bergman)
Best Supporting Actor (Akim Tamiroff)
*Best Supporting Actress (Katina Paxinou)
Best Cinematography, Color
Best Interior Decoration, Color
Best Scoring of a Dramatic or Comedy
   Picture (Victor Young)
Best Film Editing

office mishaps, Paramount began heavily playing up the now-famous sleeping bag scene. At a time when the Hays Office insisted that even married couples have twin beds and that one foot must rest on the floor at all times, the idea of having Gary Cooper's and Ingrid Bergman's unmarried characters share a sleeping bag was downright scandalous. Compared to today's see-all bedroom scenes, this is pretty much G-rated, but in those days, what you *didn't* see was sometimes even better, and the audience filled in the rest with their libidinous imaginations.

Paramount had invested $2,000,000 in faithfully re-creating Hemingway's novel, so it is no wonder they were

concerned. The studio strove for authenticity. When costume designer Edith Head needed a tough, well-weathered outfit for Ingrid Bergman, she selected an old pair of men's trousers and a shirt from the extras' wardrobe. Producer/director Sam Wood was incensed and ordered Miss Head to custom-design a new costume. She did—copying the clothes exactly, then bleaching and re-dyeing them to look worn. When the California mountains in the background looked too lush and green to double for the rugged hills of Spain, the set designers sprayed gray paint over the landscape, even uprooting wildflowers to keep the scenery from being too pretty for the Technicolor camera.

THE OUTLAW

RKO
$5,075,000

NOT TOO MANY people remember this as a film about the life of William Bonney—a.k.a. Billy the Kid. It could hardly be termed "biographical," even though the story did have some elements of historical accuracy, such as lawman Pat Garrett's pursuit of the murderous Billy, and the young criminal's teaming up with "Doc" Holliday, an old-time gunman and former friend of Garrett. But with most of the historical facts rather clouded, this is far from a film biography. Alas, *The Outlaw* will always be remembered for Jane Russell's bustline.

When the film was released in 1943, it didn't have time to generate much business before it was pulled from release. A subsequent release in 1946 of the Howard Hughes film saw it being pulled after a week, thanks to its

being banned by the censors of the Hays Office. It was finally allowed to be seen in 1947, by which time Hughes had launched a massive advertising campaign with the much-publicized photo of Jane Russell lolling in a haystack.

Actually, she never really does much lolling in the hay. The scene goes like this:

> RIO
>
> Let me go!
>
> BILLY
>
> Hold still lady or you won't have much dress left. (ripping sounds)
>
> RIO
>
> Let me go!

All this takes place in shadow, but you get the idea.

Then there's the famous sequence where Rio (Russell) is nursing the wounded Billy back to health. When he suffers a chill, the resourceful Rio uses her body heat to warm him up ("You can bring a minister here in the morning if it'll make you feel better about it.").

Most of the attention was centered on the aforementioned chest of Jane Russell. Joseph Breen of the Hays Office wrote: "I have never seen anything quite so unacceptable as the shots of the breasts of the character of Rio...Throughout almost half the picture the girl's breasts, which are quite large and prominent, are shockingly uncovered."

Perhaps audiences agreed. They returned again and again to be shocked by Miss Russell's assets, making a pile of money for Hughes and Company.

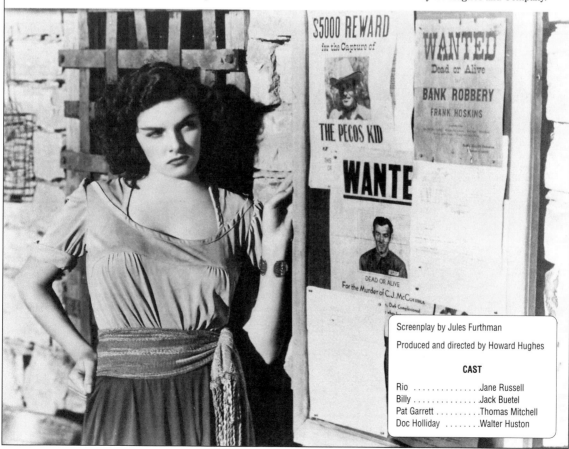

Screenplay by Jules Furthman

Produced and directed by Howard Hughes

CAST

Rio . . . . .Jane Russell
Billy . . . . .Jack Buetel
Pat Garrett . . . . .Thomas Mitchell
Doc Holliday . . . . . . .Walter Huston

THE SONG OF BERNADETTE

20TH CENTURY-FOX
$4,701,000

"For those who believe in God, no explanation is necessary. For those who do not believe in God, no explanation is possible."
— OPENING CARD

ALTHOUGH THERE WERE undoubtedly many in the audience who did not agree with the film's opening card, most people were able to dismiss this presumptuous introductory statement and enjoy the film on a dramatic level.

The tale of the young peasant French girl, Bernadette Soubirous, who has a vision of "The Lady" and later becomes a nun, is by now a familiar one, since the spring water of Lourdes has become revered by Catholics and other believers as the site of miracle cures.

Based on the best-selling novel by Franz Werfel, the film introduced 23-year-old Jennifer Jones in the title role "by arrangement with David O. Selznick." (Selznick later came to a different sort of arrangement with the lovely Miss Jones—following their divorces, the two were married in 1949.) It proved to be a fortuitous choice when the ingenue grabbed an Oscar for her performance.

The reviews were mixed. *The Hollywood Reporter* called it a "great

Screenplay by George Seaton

From the novel by Franz Werfel

Produced by William Perlberg

Directed by Henry King

CAST

Bernadette Soubirous . . .Jennifer Jones
Dean Peyramale . . . . . . .Charles Bickford
Antoine Nicolau . . . . . . .William Eythe
Prosecutor Dutour . . . . .Vincent Price
Dr. Dozous . . . . .Lee J. Cobb

ACADEMY AWARD NOMINATIONS

12 nominations, 4 wins*

 Best Picture
*Best Actress (Jennifer Jones)
 Best Supporting Actor (Charles Bickford)
 Best Supporting Actress (Gladys Cooper)
 Best Supporting Actress (Anne Revere)
 Best Director (Henry King)
 Best Screenplay
*Best Cinematography, Black and White
*Best Interior Decoration, Black and White
 Best Sound Recording
*Best Scoring of a Dramatic or Comedy
 Picture
 Best Film Editing

spiritual masterpiece…Jennifer Jones proves to be the perfect choice for Bernadette, and she gives a beautiful, moving performance of rare sincerity…It is doubly a remarkable work being her first important screen role." But *The New York Times* thought it was "tedious and repetitious; it lingers too fondly over images that lack visual mobility, and it goes in for dialectic discourse that will clutter and fatigue the average mind."

Jennifer Jones was an unknown at the time, and little publicity preceded her debut. The idea was to have her appear as pure as her character. She wore a minimum of makeup and simple peasant dress to further enhance her virginal appearance. In actuality, however, she had been married to Robert Walker since 1939, and the couple had a son, Robert Walker, Jr.

In another odd bit of casting, sexy actress Linda Darnell appears (unbilled) as the Virgin Mary. Hollywood being short on virgins, they had to make do with whoever was available.

Vincent Price does an admirable job as the adversarial Imperial Prosecutor bent on thwarting all claims of Bernadette's vision. Price died on October 25, 1993.

STAGE DOOR CANTEEN

UNITED ARTISTS
$4,339,532

DURING World War II, there was a real Stage Door Canteen in New York City (and a Hollywood Canteen on the West Coast). In time, each of these entertainment centers had a film based on it. The movies were basically an excuse to gather up famous Hollywood stars who each night dished up hot meals and entertainment to our boys before they shipped off to war. Appearing at various times throughout the film (don't blink, you'll miss them) were:

Judith Anderson	Gypsy Rose Lee
Kenny Baker	Alfred Lunt
Tallulah Bankhead	Harpo Marx
Ralph Bellamy	Elsa Maxwell
Edger Bergan & Co.	Yehudi Menuhin
Ray Bolger	Ethel Merman
Ina Clair	Paul Muni
Katharine Cornell	Merle Oberon
Gracie Fields	George Raft
Lynn Fontanne	Lanny Ross
Helen Hayes	Martha Scott
Katharine Hepburn	Ethel Waters
Hugh Herbert	Johnny
Jean Hersholt	Weissmuller
George Jessel	Ed Wynn

Screenplay by Delmer Daves

Produced by Sol Lesser

Directed by Frank Borzage

CAST

Eileen	Cheryl Walker
"Dakota" Ed Smith	William W. Terry
Jean	Marjorie Riordan
"California"	Lon McCallister
Ella Sue	Margaret Early

ACADEMY AWARD NOMINATIONS

2 nominations, no wins

Best Song ("We Mustn't Say Good Bye," music by James Monaco, words by Al Dubin)
Best Scoring of a Musical Picture

and 38 "other celebrated artists from Stage, Screen and Radio." As if that weren't enough, there were bands, big bands…as in Count Basie, Xavier Cougat, Benny Goodman, Kay Kyser, Guy Lombardo, and Freddie Martin.

This movie was filmed at a time when the words "We're in a war and we've got to win" were able to rouse the emotions of the audience. They may sound simplistic, but those were simpler times, and simple words sufficed. The soldiers and their girls were facing the very real and frightening prospect that they might never return.

In addition to featuring a heavy dose of production numbers with song and dance, this musical revue had a wisp of a plot about romance between the non-movie-star canteen workers and the servicemen visiting the famous New York rendezvous. The use of unknowns as the GIs and their gals was intended to give audiences people to whom they could relate. Besides, nearly every available professional talent was already doing a solo performance in one of the movie's big numbers. Although this could have been the "big break" many actors dream of, not one future "star" emerged from the pack of unknowns.

The film is enjoying new popularity and is frequently seen on cable television stations. It's well worth a look.

GOING MY WAY

PARAMOUNT
$6,500,000

HIS FULL NAME was Charles Francis Patrick O'Malley. He was the kindest, singingest priest ever to grace the screen. And sing he did. One of the decade's best songs (and a number-one hit at that) came from *Going My Way,* a catchy tune called "Swinging on a Star." It won a well-deserved Oscar.

Not so memorable was the title song, also sung by the old crooner himself. Can anyone hum a few bars of "Going My Way"? Thought not. It's no wonder Father O'Malley has to struggle with music publishers to get it noticed (watch for William Frawley, Fred Mertz of TV's "I Love Lucy," in the role of his publisher).

Bing Crosby, Father O'Malley's alter ego, couldn't read a note of music. But that didn't stop him from becoming

one of the most beloved singers of this century. He was born Harry Crosby on May 2, 1904, in Tacoma, Washington, and changed his name to Bing (after "The Bingville Bugle," a Sunday comic section in his hometown newspaper). In 1929, he earned $100 for appearing in a film with Douglas Fairbanks, for which he received no billing. Known mostly as a radio star, he received his big break in 1932, appearing in *The Big Broadcast.*

But he came into his own as an actor with *Going My Way.* Although both Spencer Tracy and James

Cagney were approached to play the part, neither was available. It was then that director Leo McCarey decided to offer Bing his first dramatic role. He seemed to be born to the part. According to his brother Bob, interviewed for a 1989 PBS television special, "He played Bing Crosby, 'cause he went to Jesuit school all his life." It was a role that Bing embraced with his whole life, embodying the values he had grown up with, his deep religious conviction, his innate Irish charm—all combining to make his Academy Award performance an American classic.

During the war, metal was in short supply, and Oscar statuettes were

made of plaster (they were later replaced with the real thing). Bing reportedly decapitated his plaster award one day while practicing his golf swing in the living room.

Co-star Barry Fitzgerald also turned in an Oscar-winning performance. *Life* magazine told readers to catch "a wonderful Irishman named Barry Fitzgerald. His performance is one of the half-dozen finer things seen in motion pictures." *The Hollywood Reporter* also sang his praises, declaring, "Barry Fitzgerald gives a truly brilliant performance every foot of the way…he is a joy." He received an unprecedented two nominations for the same picture—Best Actor and Best Supporting Actor (the Academy subsequently changed the rules to prevent this sort of double indemnity).

Barry Fitzgerald's portrayal of a gruff, stubbornly aging old priest was a perfect contrast for Crosby's easygoing characterization. Fitzgerald was born William Joseph Shields on May 10, 1888, in Dublin, Ireland. His early years saw him as a stage performer in

Dublin, where he changed his name to a more Irish-sounding one; this also prevented confusion with his brother Arthur Shields, also an actor. He made his film debut in Hitchcock's British film *Juno and the Paycock* (1930), and landed in Hollywood in the late '30s, where he honed his portrayals of whimsical Irishmen to the brink of near-caricatures. Among his most notable films were *Bringing Up Baby* (1938), *How Green Was My Valley* (1941), *None But the Lonely Heart* (1944), *Duffy's Tavern* (1945), *Welcome Stranger* (1947), and *The Quiet Man* (1952). He died in 1961 at the age of 73.

Fitzgerald's competition in the Best Actor category included his own costar, Bing Crosby, as well as Charles Boyer, Cary Grant, and Alexander Knox. In the Supporting Actor contest, however, he took home the prized Oscar after overcoming a field of talented actors that included Hume Cronyn, Claude Rains, Clifton Webb, and Monty Woolley.

Risé Stevens is the only cast member whose appearance in this film seems a bit contrived; her true bailiwick was as a star of the Metropolitan Opera. That's exactly how she's introduced in the picture, and her voice is obligingly showcased with her renditions of "Ave Maria," an aria from *Carmen,* and the title song.

Despite tough competition at the Academy Award ceremony for 1944 (nominated films were *Double Indemnity, Gaslight, Since You Went Away,* and *Wilson*), *Going My Way* had no trouble finding the Best Picture Oscar going its way, along with many others, for a total of seven for this audience-pleasing film. Leo McCarey proved that, like Fitzgerald, he had the luck of the Irish, and received an award for Best Director. A former silent-film director, he was never comfortable with the written word. Often while rehearsing a scene, he would tell his actors, "Forget the script and just talk it through." He usually preferred to have the cast ad-lib scenes during filming, giving scriptwriters nightmares.

On October 3, 1962, ABC premiered a television series of "Going My Way." It starred Gene Kelly as Father Chuck O'Malley and Leo G. Carroll as a crusty old pastor named Father Fitzgibbon. Kelly neither sang nor danced, but the show survived on the airwaves for a year. The 1944 film will survive, with the luck of the Irish, forever.

Screenplay by Frank Butler and Frank Cavett

From a story by Leo McCarey

Produced and directed by Leo McCarey

CAST

Father Chuck O'Malley . . .Bing Crosby
Jenny Linden . . . . .Risé Stevens
Father Fitzgibbon . . . . . . .Barry Fitzgerald
Ted Haines, Jr. . . . . .James Brown
Carol James . . . . .Jean Heather

ACADEMY AWARD NOMINATIONS

10 nominations, 7 wins *

*Best Picture
*Best Actor (Bing Crosby)
 Best Actor (Barry Fitzgerald)
*Best Supporting Actor (Barry Fitzgerald)
*Best Director (Leo McCarey)
*Best Writing, Original Story
  (Leo McCarey)
*Best Screenplay (Frank Butler and Frank Cavett)
 Best Cinematography, Black and White
*Best Song ("Swinging on a Star," music by Jimmy Van Heusen, words by Johnny Burke)
 Best Film Editing

This was the last comedy to win the award for Best Picture until Billy Wilder's *The Apartment* in 1960.

MEET ME IN ST. LOUIS

METRO-GOLDWYN-MAYER
$5,132,202

BASED ON a series of stories by Sally Benson that appeared in the *New Yorker* and were later published as a book, *Meet Me in St. Louis,* has the feeling of a stage musical. The original book, a collection of reminiscences, had warmth, charm, period costumes, a loving family—and the 1903 Louisiana Purchase Exposition (World's Fair). Producer Arthur Freed (*The Wizard of Oz*) called the book to director Vincent Minnelli's attention, and Minnelli jumped at the chance to direct. Twenty-one-year-old Judy Garland was set to star. Her last picture, *Presenting Lily Mars,* hadn't clicked with the public, and she wanted to move into more adult roles. A year after completing the film, she divorced husband David Rose and married Minnelli, with whom she had fallen in love while working on the movie.

If the film has the look of a musical,* it is because Minnelli spent his early years as a designer and art director for stage. With its series of family incidents centering around the Smith home, *Meet Me in St. Louis* was the perfect film for his talents.

Fans of Judy Garland will no doubt

Screenplay by Irving Brecher and Fred F. Finklehoffe

From the book by Sally Benson

Produced by Arthur Freed

Directed by Vincente Minnelli

CAST

Esther Smith . . . . .Judy Garland
"Tootie" Smith . . . . . . .Margaret O'Brien
Mrs. Anna Smith . . . . .Mary Astor
Rose Smith . . . . .Lucille Bremer
John Truett . . . . .Tom Drake

ACADEMY AWARD NOMINATIONS

4 nominations, no wins

Best Screenplay
Best Cinematography, Color
Best Song ("The Trolley Song," music and words by Hugh Martin and Ralph Blane)
Best Scoring of a Musical Picture

Margaret O'Brien received a miniature statuette as Outstanding Child Actress of 1944.

think of this as her picture. She sings nearly as much as she did in *The Wizard of Oz,* including such tunes as the title song, "The Boy Next Door," "Have Yourself a Merry Little Christmas" (which became a number-one record), and "The Trolley Song" ("Clang, clang, clang," and so forth). It's always a treat to audiences, even today.

If ever there was a scene-stealer, though, it was Margaret O'Brien, who was seven years old when this movie was made. The juvenile actress received second billing, and it was well deserved. Her character, "Tootie," is a somewhat morbid little creature who lops off the heads of her "snowpeople" and buries her "dead" dolls in their own cemetery. One scene called for Margaret to cry her heart out, something she usually could do on cue. For some reason, however, she was being stubborn and not a tear would flow. Vincent Minnelli solved the problem. He told her that there was a little dog that was going to be shot, and it was going to suffer terribly. "And then," Minnelli said, "THE DOG IS GOING TO DIE!" Tears began flooding down Margaret's face, Minnelli told the assistant director to roll the cameras, and they got the scene in one take. "I went home feeling like a monster," Minnelli later recalled in his book, *I Remember It Well.* "I marvel that Margaret didn't turn out to be one, too. That sort of preparation struck me as most unhealthy."

It's curious that this movie ends with almost the exact same words as does *The Wizard of Oz,* with Judy Garland delivering the closing lines. When the family finds out that they won't have to move to New York, Judy remarks about how wonderful it will be to stay, "Right here where we live. Right here in St. Louis." There's still no place like home.

---

*A musical version of *Meet Me in St. Louis* was eventually written; it played 253 Broadway performances, from November 1989 to June 1990, followed by a national tour.

SINCE YOU WENT AWAY

UNITED ARTISTS
$4,924,756

I F JUDY GARLAND was growing up over at MGM, David O. Selznick decided that Shirley Temple could have a whole new career as an adult actress, too. He cast her in a somewhat shallow part as the younger sister of Jennifer Jones in *Since You Went Away* (based on the book by Margaret Wilder)—his $2,400,000, nearly three-hour-long tribute to American families coping at home with the realities of World War II. It was a noble try, but Shirley's days as a box office draw were over.

Selznick was still obsessed with trying to top *Gone With the Wind,* and he billed *Since You Went Away* as "an epic of the homefront." He spent 127 days filming the production—only 10 days less than the record set by *Gone With the Wind.* He added popular stars to the cast, like Claudette Colbert, Joseph Cotten, Jennifer Jones, and her soon-to-be ex-husband, Robert Walker. Critics and audiences agreed he had a

success. But another *GWTW*? Never!

Part of the reason this film is so dated is its view of the world at that time. In one scene, a police officer stops Claudette Colbert and Joseph Cotten, and on learning that Cotten is shipping out, says, "Get one of them Japs for me," as he tugs upward on the corners of his eyelids while all enjoy a hearty laugh. This sort of racism, so acceptable at the time, can only make today's audiences squirm uncomfortably. To drive the message home, strains of "America the Beautiful," "Home Sweet Home," and even the words on the Statue of Liberty ("Give me your tired, your poor . . .") constantly remind us what we were fighting for. In this war story about the peo-

ple back home and how their lives are disrupted, virtually every moviegoer at the time could identify with the situations portrayed—the husband or boyfriend going away, ration coupons, the dreaded telegram from the U.S. War Department. But it doesn't evoke these emotions when viewed today. We can only watch it as a sentimental curiosity piece and shake our heads.

Still, Selznick had given the film his all. True to his legendary pursuit of perfection, Selznick requested detailed sketches from the art department, and over 1,500 scenes were drawn. In his quest for a certain scene with a particular background, Selznick sent a memo to the art department. It stated simply: "Please get me 500 sunsets."

Screenplay by David O. Selznick

From the book by Margaret Buell Wilder

Produced by David O. Selznick

Directed by John Cromwell

CAST

Anne Hilton . . . . .Claudette Colbert
Jane Hilton . . . . Jennifer Jones
Lt. Tony Willett . . . . . .Joseph Cotten
Bridget "Brig" Hilton . . .Shirley Temple
Col. Smollett . . . . .Monty Woolley
The Clergyman . . . . . .Lionel Barrymore
William G. Smollett II . . .Robert Walker
Emily Hawkins . . . . . . .Agnes Moorehead
Fidelia . . . . .Hattie McDaniel

ACADEMY AWARD NOMINATIONS

9 nominations, 1 win*

Best Picture
Best Actress (Claudette Colbert)
Best Supporting Actor (Monty Woolley)
Best Supporting Actress (Jennifer Jones)
Best Cinematography, Black and White
Best Interior Decoration, Black and White
*Best Scoring of a Dramatic or Comedy
 Picture (Max Steiner)
Best Film Editing
Best Special Effects

30 SECONDS OVER TOKYO

METRO-GOLDWYN-MAYER
$4,471,080

I N 1942, men under the command of then-Colonel James H. Doolittle flew a dramatic air raid on Japan. Two years later, this event was brought to the screen, with Spencer Tracy as Doolittle (he did little, too; it was basically a guest appearance) and Van Johnson, Robert Walker, and Robert Mitchum as some of the young fliers. The story follows the lives of a group of volunteer Air Force fliers through their training in B-52 bombers, followed by their transfer to a Naval aircraft carrier and their startling discovery that they are on a secret mission to bomb Japan. From there we pursue the saga of Captain Ted Lawson, played by Van Johnson, as he and his crew crash-land their fighter on the coast of China.

The picture is noted for its outstanding special effects, state-of-the-art work that won *30 Seconds* an Academy Award. One of the most noteworthy achievements was the model of the aircraft carrier *Hornet,* which had a flight deck 54 feet long, too big to maneuver in a 300-square-foot studio tank. To solve this problem, A. Arnold Gillespie, the model's designer, built it on hydraulic ramps that he could use to simulate the rolling and pitching

Screenplay by Dalton Trumbo

Based on the book by Capt. Ted W. Lawson and Robert Considine

Produced by Sam Zimbalist

Directed by Mervyn LeRoy

CAST

Lieut. Col. James
  H. Doolittle . . . . . . .Spencer Tracy
Ted Lawson . . . . .Van Johnson
David Thatcher . . . . . .Robert Walker
Ellen Lawson . . . . .Phyllis Thaxter
Bob Gray . . . . .Robert Mitchum

ACADEMY AWARD NOMINATIONS

2 nominations, 1 win*

  Best Cinematography, Black and White
*Best Special Effects

effect of ocean waves on a carrier.

Although no one would ever accuse this of being an antiwar or isolationist film, the screenwriter, Dalton Trumbo, did manage to work in some bits of dialogue that were about as liberal as one dared get. "I don't like killing people," remarks one sailor, "but it's a case of drop a bomb on them, or pretty soon they'll drop one on [my wife] Ellen."

Both audience and critics gave *30 Seconds* their nod of approval. *The New York Times* said: "The true and tremendous story…is told with magnificent integrity and dramatic eloquence…as a drama of personal heroism, it is nigh the best yet made in Hollywood…the film has the tough and literal quality of an Air Force documentary." Pictures like this did much to bolster the morale of those on the home front. *30 Seconds Over Tokyo* had a documentary quality to it, to the extent that *The Hollywood Reporter* called the movie "more than one of the greatest war pictures ever made…it is an all-time winner."

ONE YEAR AFTER the popular film *Stage Door Canteen* (see page 47), Warner Bros. repeated the box office success with a sister film, *Hollywood Canteen*. With practically the same story, cast, and screenwriter (Delmar Daves, now taking over as director as well), how could it miss? This time, the lonely soldier wanders into the West Coast version of the Canteen, still chock-a-block with movie stars dishing up chow and then washing the dishes. It's the standard non-plot of boy-meets-girl-and-movie-stars, right up through the picture's obligatory happy ending.

Strange as it may seem today, the glitterati in those wartime years actually did get down and mingle with the boys in uniform. In fact, the real Hollywood Canteen was founded by Bette Davis and John Garfield, who perform the welcoming chores in the movie. They are aptly assisted, to borrow another studio's slogan, by more stars than there are in the heavens. At 124 minutes, there was barely time to display the talents of Joan Leslie, Jack Benny, Jane Wyman, Jack Carson, The Andrews Sisters (singing "Don't Fence Me In" with Roy Rogers and Trigger), Peter Lorre, Ida Lupino, Alan Hale (later the Skipper on "Gilligan's Island"), Barbara Stanwyck, Craig Stevens, Joe E. Brown, Eddie Cantor, and zillions more.

Songs figured prominently. Kitty Carlisle sang "Sweet Dreams, Sweetheart." Writer M. K. Jerome and lyricist Ted Koehler were soon having sweet dreams of their own, when the tune was nominated for a Best Song Oscar (it lost to "Swinging on a Star"). Other musical numbers in the movie included: "You Can Always Tell a Yank," "Voodoo Moon," "I'm Gettin' Corns for My Country," "The General Jumped at Dawn," and "What Are You Doing the Rest of Your Life?" (not to be confused with the more recent Michel Legrand–Marilyn Bergman song of the same title). Among the many songsters and big bands appearing in the film were Jimmy Dorsey and His Band, Carmen Cavallaro and His Orchestra, the Golden Gate Quartet, and the Sons of the Pioneers (backing Roy Rogers).

Bette Davis, who was not only the co-founder, but also served as president of the real Hollywood Canteen, couldn't have been more pleased with the film's success. Most of the talent donated their time, and 40 percent of the picture's profits went to the Canteen, to help the organization continue in its good works on behalf of our fighting men.

Produced by Alex Gottlieb

Directed by Delmar Daves

CAST

Slim	Robert Hutton
Sergeant	Dane Clark
Angela	Janis Paige
Mr. Brodel	Jonathan Hale
Mrs. Brodel	Barbara Brown

ACADEMY AWARD NOMINATIONS

3 nominations, no wins

Best Scoring of a Musical Picture
Best Song ("Sweet Dreams, Sweetheart," music by M. K. Jerome, words by Ted Koehler)
Best Sound Recording

THE BELLS OF ST. MARY'S

RKO
$8,000,000

WOULDN'T IT BE GREAT if we could all "Just dial 'O' for O'Malley"? Bing Crosby's revival of the kindly priest we first grew to love in *Going My Way* outshone his performance in that first film. All the ingredients are there—the struggling young student who may miss graduation, the ailing nun (sweetly portrayed by Ingrid Bergman), and, of course, the priest with a heart of gold. Makes you wish you had a clergyman like Bing for your very own.

When Ingrid sings a little Swedish ditty, then is joined by Bing to sing the title song, it's the highlight of the film. And during the final scene between the two, when Ingrid's heart is breaking, there was not a dry hanky left in the house.

The take at the box office was phenomenal. This sequel had the unique privilege of being the first film to actually outgross its predecessor. It was RKO's most profitable hit so far.

Relying more on characterization than plot, the narrative is reinforced through a number of unrelated episodes, with Bing and Ingrid the unifying forces throughout. There is the story of a schoolgirl who may not be able to graduate; there's the crusty old industrialist who is finally persuaded to turn benefactor; there are songfests (naturally) with the Sisters gathered around the piano, and one of the best scenes in the picture—a group of uninhibited, unrehearsed five-year-olds who re-enact the Story of Christmas. Since *The Bells of St. Mary's* appeared just in time for the holiday season, the sketch was a natural. Bobby Dolan, son of the picture's musical director, doubles as the Narrator and Joseph. His wheezing, ad-libbed lines are classic: "Oh, this is Mary and I'm Joseph and we came to Bethlehem to see if we can have some place…find some place to stay. And that's all you have to know really." In the stable, an angel perches atop a ladder, surrounded by wise men and shepherds, while an 18-month-old, playing the Christ Child, waves to the audience from a clothes basket. This was all improvised by a group of kindergartners based on a rough idea given them by director Leo McCarey, who told *Time* magazine

that "it was one of the most difficult sequences I ever directed."

Many critics were enthusiastic, but others found fault with the absence of Barry Fitzgerald. Comparisons with *Going My Way* were inevitable. *The New York Times* said that "Sister Benedict has not the veracity of her counterpart character which was played by Barry Fitzgerald. She is much too precisely sugar-coated, too eagerly contrived…Although a plenteous and sometimes winning show [*Bells*] lacks the charm of its predecessor—and that comparison cannot be escaped." But *The Hollywood Reporter*'s reviewer disagreed: "The first question that will be instantly asked is how does 'Bells of St. Mary's' compare with 'Going My Way.' Both reflect the same simple sincerity of inspired entertainment. Both are tremendous credits to everyone who had a hand in the filming—actually proud credits to the entire motion picture industry…Bing Crosby's Father O'Malley is a casual joy and Ingrid Bergman's Sister Superior a portrait of quiet depth, highlighted by a sparkling sense of humor."

A true multiple talent (rare for those days), producer-director Leo McCarey is said to have based the original story of *The Bells of St. Mary's* on the real-life character of his aunt, Sister Mary Benedict of the Immaculate Heart Convent in Hollywood.* He also co-authored (with Dudley Nichols) the screenplay from his original story.

The Bells of St. Mary's is a staple of independent television stations, especially around Christmas time. A word of caution: the colorized version of this film leaves much to be desired. In the graduation sequence, for instance, the person in charge of the computer adding the color seems to have gone wild, giving the girls dresses of chartreuse, hot peach, bright yellow, and other Day-Glo colors. Best to turn your color control down all the way and spare yourself this travesty.

---

*There was also a real-life counterpart to Father O'Malley. Father Eugene O'Malley, a Chicago priest, directed the Old St. Mary's Church choir for more than 40 years until his death in 1989.

Screenplay by Dudley Nichols

Produced and directed by Leo McCarey

CAST

Father O'Malley . . . . . .Bing Crosby
Sister Benedict . . . . . .Ingrid Bergman
Mr. Bogardus . . . . . . .Henry Travers
Patsy . . . . .Joan Carroll
Patsy's Mother . . . . . .Martha Sleeper

ACADEMY AWARD NOMINATIONS

8 nominations, 1 win*

Best Picture
Best Actor (Bing Crosby)
Best Actress (Ingrid Bergman)
Best Director (Leo McCarey)
*Best Sound Recording
Best Song ("Aren't You Glad You're
    You," music by Jimmy Van Heusen,
    words by Johnny Burke)
Best Scoring of a Dramatic or Comedy
    Picture
Best Film Editing

2

LEAVE HER TO HEAVEN

20TH CENTURY-FOX
$5,505,000

THE OPENING SEQUENCE of *Leave Her to Heaven* consists of the pages of a book being turned as credits appear. This is appropriate for two reasons: one of the central characters is a writer, and the film was based upon a book that chalked up sales of over a million copies while staying on the best-seller list for 12 months. Audiences were familiar with the tale of the obsessively jealous woman who does her best (including murder) to try to spend some quality time with her gregarious husband.

Leave Her to Heaven's story is set against a background of several architectural achievements—the Santa Fe ranch house, whose look is so sought after today, is likely to send modern homebuilders to their drafting tables. There's also a beautiful Bar Harbor, Maine, mansion and some stunning scenic vistas.

Many of the critics seemed to confuse actress Gene Tierney—who faithfully portrayed the book's misguided anti-heroine and won an Oscar nomination—with "Ellen Berent," a deliberately shallow character who was jealousy personified. *Time* stated: "No amount of strenuous plot trouble—or even a long fall down a flight of steps—seems to jar Gene Tierney's smooth deadpan. Walking or sleeping,

Screenplay by Jo Swerling

Based on the novel by Ben Ames Williams

Produced by William A. Bacher

Directed by John M. Stahl

CAST

Ellen	Gene Tierney
Richard	Cornel Wilde
Ruth	Jeanne Crain
Russell Quinton	Vincent Price
Mrs. Berent	Mary Philips

ACADEMY AWARD NOMINATIONS

4 nominations, 1 win*

Best Actress (Gene Tierney)
*Best Cinematography, Color
Best Interior Decoration, Color
Best Sound Recording

in ecstasy or anger, joy or sorrow, her pretty, composed features seem to be asking the single, gamin-and-spinach question: 'Huh?'" And *The New York Times* seemed to be saying "shoot the messenger," claiming that, "Miss Tierney's petulant performance of this vixenish character is about as analytical as a piece of pin-up poster art. It is strictly one-dimensional, in the manner of a dot on an i."

The *Times* reporter didn't have any kind words for the other members of the cast, either. He saw Cornel Wilde as "equally restricted as her curiously over-powered spouse." Jeanne Crain was "colorless and wooden," and Vincent Price, Mary Philips, and Darryl Hickman were said to "mechanically play [their] roles." The reviewer did, however, enjoy the sets.

The fault may have been in the script. As the prosecuting attorney, Vincent Price's character is emotional and badgering—more a persecuting attorney. And the defense attorney should have been disbarred for putting up with this without so much as an "Objection!"

SPELLBOUND

UNITED ARTISTS
$4,970,583

THERE ARE MANY reasons why *Spellbound* became Alfred Hitchcock's most profitable film of the decade. Among them were Ingrid Bergman—who at first turned Hitch down because she thought the script was implausible—and handsome newcomer Gregory Peck as her patient/lover, a twosome that audiences found irresistible.

Peck, suffering from amnesia, believes he has committed a murder, but cannot remember the circumstances. Ingrid Bergman, as his psychiatrist, falls in love with him while trying to unlock the secrets of his tortured mind, certain he could not have committed such a crime. The solution to the film's mysteries stems from the analysis of one of Peck's recurring dreams—one of the most memorable dream sequences in cinematic history.

In an attempt to capture the "vividness of dreams," Hitchcock hired artist Salvador Dali to design the sequence. Dali proffered more than a hundred sketches and five paintings. The surrealistic number opens with 400 human eyes glaring down from

Screenplay by Ben Hecht

Based on the novel *The House of Dr. Edwardes* by Francis Beeding

Produced by David O. Selznick

Directed by Alfred Hitchcock

CAST

Dr. Constance
  Peterson . . . . .Ingrid Bergman
J. B. . . . . .Gregory Peck
Matron . . . . .Jean Acker
Harry . . . . .Donald Curtis
Miss Carmichael . . . . .Rhonda Fleming

ACADEMY AWARD NOMINATIONS

6 nominations, 1 win*

  Best Picture
  Best Supporting Actor (Michael Chekhov)
  Best Director (Alfred Hitchcock)
  Best Cinematography, Black and White
*Best Scoring of a Dramatic or Comedy
  Picture
  Best Special Effects

black velvet drapes, which are sliced by a woman with a pair of huge scissors. There is a giant pair of pliers chasing Gregory Peck up the side of a pyramid. Ingrid Bergman is draped in a Grecian gown with a crown on her head and an arrow through her neck. The statue breaks open and ants stream forth from her face. Selznick despised the sequence, and the 20-minute segment was trimmed down to a few moments.

The other treat for audiences in this suspense drama came near the movie's end. With true Hitchcock flair, the director photographs from the POV (point of view) of the gunman. We follow the gun as it points at Bergman, but then the gun is turned and aimed directly at the camera—and the audience. In a surprise that had people gasping in their seats, the gun fires at us in a sudden burst of red color (a moment easily captured by freezing frame on a VCR). This startling use of two frames of color ("Did I really see that?") in the original black-and-white print had audiences returning for a second look.

ANCHORS AWEIGH

METRO-GOLDWYN-MAYER
$4,778,679

1
9
4
5

THIS FILM marked the first major appearance of Frank Sinatra, who was then riding the crest of a teen heart-throb wave. Frankie really got to demonstrate his talent, singing and dancing with Gene Kelly, and keeping pace with the professional hoofer quite well.

In this classic screen musical, Sinatra and Kelly are sailors on liberty in Hollywood. Sinatra is a shy Brooklyn boy who's coached on picking up girls by self-assured Kelly. Both end up falling for the same gal—the aunt of a youngster (Dean Stockwell) who is ga-ga over the Navy. There's a subplot about getting the object of their affections (Kathryn Grayson) an audition with conductor Jose Iturbi, which gives the film one of its biggest musical moments. Anyone familiar today with Los Angeles' Hollywood Bowl will enjoy a look at that famous site before acoustical superstructures were added, and the production number in the film is a spectacular one, featuring row after row of precocious children whose piano lessons paid off. It's gimmicky but clever.

The highlight of *Anchors Aweigh,* though, is the musical fairy-tale num-

Screenplay by Isobel Lennart

Suggested by a story by Natalie Marcin

Produced by Joe Pasternak

Directed by George Sidney

CAST

Joseph Brady . . . . . . .Gene Kelly
Susan Abbott . . . . .Kathryn Grayson
Clarence Doolittle . . . .Frank Sinatra
Donald Martin · · · · · · .Dean Stockwell
Girl from Brooklyn . . . .Pamela Britton

ACADEMY AWARD NOMINATIONS

4 nominations, 1 win*

Best Picture
Best Cinematography, Color
Best Song ("I Fall in Love Too Easily,"
  music by Jule Styne, words by Sammy
  Cahn)
*Best Scoring of a Musical Picture

ber called "The King Who Couldn't Dance," with Gene and his animated-mouse partner Jerry (of the "Tom and Jerry" cartoons) interacting on screen. Although it broke new ground as the first Technicolor live-animated interaction, this technique, so highly touted in 1988 with *Who Framed Roger Rabbit,* was actually not an innovation at all. As early as 1909, French artist Emil Cohl pioneered the first use of matte photography to combine live action and animation in *Clair de Lune Español/Man in the Moon.* Later, the famous cartoonist Max Fleischer (creator of Betty Boop) animated a black-and-white series called "Out of the Inkwell," in which he appeared with

the characters as he drew them. But this beautiful Technicolor sequence in *Anchors Aweigh* served as a launching pad for such treats to follow as *Song of the South, Mary Poppins,* and, of course, *Roger Rabbit.*

Also a treat is the appearance of eight-year-old Dean Stockwell as a scene-stealing lad hung up on joining the Navy. Stockwell went on to a successful film career. In 1988, he played the part of Howard Hughes in the Paramount film *Tucker* and received an Academy Award nomination for Best Supporting Actor for his role in *Married to the Mob.* He also co-starred in the television series "Quantum Leap."

5

THE VALLEY OF DECISION

METRO-GOLDWYN-MAYER
$4,566,755

ANOTHER FILM based on a best-selling novel (written by Marcia Davenport), this is a Cinderella love story of an Irish girl of the 1870s (Greer Garson) who works as a servant in the home of a Pittsburgh steel-mill boss (Donald Crisp) and subsequently falls in love with his son, played by Gregory Peck. Paul Scott (Peck) must not marry beneath his station, of course, and she is forced to watch him endure a loveless marriage. The film ends with the promise that at least she and Paul can share an unconsummated love.

Just to complicate things, there is a Romeo and Juliet subplot—Pat Rafferty (Lionel Barrymore), father of Mary (Greer Garson), lost both his legs in an accident at the Scott Mill and is psychopathic in his hatred of the senior Scott (father of the man Mary loves). There was irony in Barrymore's playing this role; in 1938, at the age of 60, the actor was partially paralyzed by a combination of arthritis and a leg injury, but managed to continue his acting career even though confined to a wheel chair.

Newcomer Gregory Peck captured the immediate attention of the critics, appearing here in an early screen performance. *Variety* wrote: "Gregory

Peck, playing opposite as Paul Scott, is a standout. He has the personality and ability to command and hold attention in any scene." *Newsweek* chimed in: "Gregory Peck impersonates the intense young steel man with both the authority and the romantic appeal the role requires…the onetime guide at Radio City in New York is established as one of Hollywood's outstanding leading men."

The Valley of Decision was only Peck's third screen appearance; *Spellbound*'s release later in 1945 would see this now-legendary actor on the road to one of Hollywood's most successful acting careers of all time. Peck is one of those rarities among old-time Hollywood actors—a California native who didn't change his name. Born Eldred Gregory Peck on April 5, 1916, in La Jolla, California,

Peck graduated from San Diego State and studied pre-med at the University of California, but soon discovered he had more interest in acting. He enrolled in New York's Neighborhood Playhouse, making his Broadway debut in 1942 in *The Morning Star.* Barred from military service due to an old spinal injury from a college rowing match, he soon discovered that Hollywood was his for the taking, with many leading men away overseas serving in the armed forces. His handsome looks, warm voice, and natural acting ability have seen Peck through a career now entering its sixth decade. Among his most memorable films are *The Yearling* (1946) and *Gentleman's Agreement* (1947)—both Oscar-nominated performances—and *To Kill a Mockingbird* (1962), for which he won an Academy Award.

Screenplay by John Meehan and
  Sonya Levien

Based on the novel by Marcia Davenport

Produced by Edwin H. Knopf

Directed by Tay Garnett

CAST

Mary Rafferty . . . . . . .Greer Garson
Paul Scott . . . . .Gregory Peck
William Scott . . . . .Donald Crisp
Pat Rafferty . . . . .Lionel Barrymore
Jim Brennan . . . . .Preston Foster

ACADEMY AWARD NOMINATIONS

2 nominations, no wins

Best Actress (Greer Garson)
Best Scoring of a Dramatic or Comedy
  Picture

SONG OF THE SOUTH

WALT DISNEY PRODUCTIONS
$29,228,717

"Out of the humble cabin, out of the singing heart of the Old South, have come the tales of Uncle Remus, rich in simple truths, forever fresh and new."

—PROLOGUE

ZIP-A-DEE-DOO-DAH! What a treat this movie was for kids and adults alike. The war was over and Walt Disney was back doing what he did best—making movies with family appeal. And *Song of the South* had all the right ingredients: child actors, a kindly old storyteller, lots of animated critters, and songs—really fun songs, like the Academy Award–winning "Zip-A-Dee -Doo-Dah" and nine other tunes. (Of the film's 95 minutes, 90 of them are enhanced by music.)

The movie was based on the tales of Uncle Remus by Joel Chandler Harris, written in the late 1800s. Walt Disney had enjoyed these stories as a boy and had frequently thought about the possibility of turning them into a motion picture. He chose James Baskett, a black actor with years of stage and radio experience, to play the part of

Uncle Remus. Baskett was only 41, but his portrayal of the elderly, white-haired Uncle Remus was so convincing and endearing that the Motion Picture Academy awarded him an honorary Oscar, "for his able and heartwarming characterization of Uncle Remus, friend and storyteller to the children of the world." In addition to his role as the kindly yarn spinner, Baskett performed the voices of Brer Fox and a butterfly in the animated sequences.

Brer Rabbit, Brer Fox, and Brer Bear ("Brer" is a contraction for "brother") were some of Disney's most memorable animated characters, and their stories account for 30 percent of the film's 95 minutes. Disney animators worked for almost two years on the cartoon sequences, which are cleverly combined with live action for the most sustained interaction between the two to that time.

In years to come, Walt Disney would become noted for his ability to single out acting talent in children (remember Hayley Mills and Annette?), and *Song of the South* saw

him signing his studio's first young contract players. Seven-year-old Luana Patten was a child model who performed for the cameras for the first time in this picture, while nine-year-old Bobby Driscoll was a veteran of four previous films. Both became Disney stars. They were re-teamed in *So Dear to My Heart, Melody Time,* and *Fun and Fancy Free.* Bobby went on to do *Treasure Island,* * while Luana starred in *Johnny Tremain* and *Follow Me, Boys,* all for Disney.

Reviews were mixed. Most critics much preferred the animation to the humans. *The New York Times* noted that "the ratio of 'live' to cartoon action is approximately two to one—and that is approximately the ratio of its mediocrity to charm." *Time* wrote: "Artistically, *Song of the South* could have used a much heavier helping of cartooning. Technically, the blending

---

*Bobby Driscoll never managed to make it as an adult actor. In 1961, he had drug problems and was jailed for various offenses. He suffered a heart attack in 1968 and was found dead in an abandoned tenement. He was 31.

of two movie mediums is pure Disney wizardry. Ideologically, the picture is certain to land its maker in hot water. Tattered ol' Uncle Remus, who cheerfully 'knew his place' in the easygoing world of late 19th-century Georgia…is a character bound to enrage all educated Negroes, and a number of dam-yankees."

And therein lay the rub. The National Urban League, quoted in *Time,* called the movie "another repetition of the perpetuation of the stereotype casting of the Negro in the servant role, depicting him as indolent, one who handles the truth lightly." And the National Association for the Advancement of Colored People (NAACP), though finding "remarkable artistic merit" in the film, deplored the "impression it gives of an idyllic master-slave relationship which is a distortion of the facts."

It is important to acknowledge these comments, but a few corrections are in order. The story does not depict slavery in the South, but rather takes place after the Civil War. The film was far less degrading to blacks than was, say, *Gone With the Wind.* According to Leonard Maltin's *The Disney Films,* a Disney representative noted at the time that Walt "was not trying to put across any message but was making a sincere effort to depict American folklore, to put the Uncle Remus stories into pictures." It should also be pointed out that Uncle Remus is the only sympathetic adult character in the film. The children's white mother comes off as a short-tempered, closed-minded bitch; Uncle Remus emerges as the film's true hero.

But the bottom line on this film can be measured at the box office. The fourth successful re-release of *Song of the South* came in 1986, and millions more dollars were earned for the studio, making this the number-one film released in 1946, a half century ago. Disney must have done *something* right.

Screenplay by Dalton Reymond, Morton Grant, and Maurice Rapf

From an original story by Dalton Reymond

Animated episodes based on "Uncle Remus" stories by Joel Chandler Harris

Produced by Walt Disney

Directed by Wilfred Jackson (Animation) and Harve Foster (Live Action)

CAST

Uncle Remus . . . . .James Baskett
Johnny . . . . .Bobby Driscoll
Sally . . . . .Ruth Warwick
Ginny . . . . .Luana Patten
Aunt Tempy . . . . .Hattie McDaniel

ACADEMY AWARD NOMINATIONS

2 nominations, 1 win*

*Best Song ("Zip-A-Dee-Doo-Dah," music by Allie Wrubel, words by Ray Gilbert) Best Scoring of a Musical Picture

James Baskett received a special award (statuette) for portraying Uncle Remus, "storyteller to the children of the world."

Although officially released in November, 1946, *Song of the South* was submitted to the Academy for consideration as a 1947 release.

2
THE BEST YEARS OF OUR LIVES

RKO
$11,300,000

"The Best Years of Our Lives' is one of the best pictures of our lives." —VARIETY

I T WAS A PICTURE perfectly suited to its time. The "our" referred to in the title will not have the same meaning and effect on today's generation, but in 1946, this was the film of that generation. Based on the novel *Glory for Me* by MacKinlay Kantor (most famous for his later novel *Andersonville*), this remarkable film addresses the question of what happens to three typical veterans returning to their middle-America hometown after the war.

What is so amazing about this film, viewing it from the perspective of our present insecurity about nuclear war, is the maturity for that time. Observe this dialogue between son and father, one of the soldiers becoming reacquainted with his teenager:

SON
Say, you were at Hiroshima,

weren't you, Dad? Did you happen to notice any effect of radioactivity on the people who survived the blast?

FATHER
No, I didn't. Should I have?

SON
Well, we've been having lectures in atomic energy at school, and Mr. McLaughlin, he's our physics teacher, he says that we've reached a point where the whole human race has either got to find a way to live together or else . . .

FATHER
Or else…?

SON
That's right. Or else. Because when you combine atomic energy with the jet propulsion and radar and guided missiles, just think…

This, from a film made less that a year after we nuked Hiroshima and

Nagasaki. It seems curious that this concept was so long overlooked and that it took nearly 50 years for us to begin to move toward the goals set forth here.

Most people remember *The Best Years of Our Lives* for the performance of double amputee Harold Russell. Russell was a Canadian paratrooper who lost both hands in a grenade explosion. The performance (his first) won him an Academy Award as Best Supporting Actor, as well as a special Academy Award "for bringing hope and courage to his fellow veterans." He is the only actor ever to win two Oscars for the same role. In 1949, he published his autobiography, *Victory in My Hands.* Later he became a business executive, and in 1964 he was appointed by President Johnson as chairman of the President's Committee on Hiring the Handicapped. His only other film was a brief appearance in *Inside Moves* (1981).

Screenplay by Robert E. Sherwood

From the novel *Glory for Me* by
MacKinlay Kantor

Produced by Samuel Goldwyn

Directed by William Wyler

CAST

Milly Stephenson . . . . .Myrna Loy
Al Stephenson . . . . . . .Fredric March
Fred Derry . . . . .Dana Andrews
Peggy Stephenson . . . .Teresa Wright
Marie Derry . . . . .Virginia Mayo
Homer Parrish . . . . . .Harold Russell

ACADEMY AWARD NOMINATIONS

8 nominations, 7 wins*

**Best Picture
*Best Actor (Fredric March)
*Best Supporting Actor (Harold Russell)
*Best Director (William Wyler)
*Best Screenplay (Robert E. Sherwood)
  Best Sound Recording
*Best Scoring of a Dramatic or Comedy
  Picture
*Best Film Editing

Harold Russell was awarded a special statuette in addition to his regular Oscar.

DUEL IN THE SUN

SELZNICK
$11,300,000

D AVID O. SELZNICK continued trying to top himself. Each time he produced a picture, he was convinced that this was the masterpiece that would go beyond *Gone With the Wind*. He wrote the screenplay for *Duel in the Sun* from an adaptation of the novel by Niven Busch and cast his paramour, Jennifer Jones, opposite hunky Gregory Peck in the leading roles. He spent over $8,000,000 filming and promoting the movie, making it the costliest to that date. It had magnificent cinematography of gorgeous Western landscapes. It had a majestic score by Dimitri Tiomkin, the John Williams of his day (or perhaps John Williams is the Dimitri Tiomkin of today).

Duel made money, but it was no *GWTW*. For all its excellent production values, it was, in fact, a "horse opera," a big-budgeted, glorified Western. Never mind—the audiences loved it.

Screenplay by David O. Selznick

Adaptation by Oliver H. P. Garrett

From the novel by Niven Busch

Produced by David O. Selznick

Directed by King Vidor

CAST

Pearl Chavez . . . . Jennifer Jones
Lewt McCanles . . . . . Gregory Peck
Jesse McCanles . . . . . Joseph Cotton
Senator McCanles . . . Lionel Barrymore
Mrs. McCanles . . . . . Lillian Gish

ACADEMY AWARD NOMINATIONS

2 nominations, no wins

Best Actress (Jennifer Jones)
Best Supporting Actress (Lillian Gish)

They came to see he-man Peck in the role of antihero, and St. Bernadette (see page 46) as a half-breed tramp, clawing their way through the dirt toward each other at picture's end, each having fatally shot the other. For this scene, the picture earned the nickname *Lust in the Dust*.

Critics had a field day. *Variety* called *Duel* "raw, sex-laden, western pulp fiction...rarely has a film made such frank use of lust and still been cleared for showings." The sex was fairly tame by today's standards, but audiences then weren't used to seeing such things at the corner Bijoux. *Time* magazine quipped that "with all their frenzied galloping, *Duel*'s horses run a poor second to Sex (Jennifer Jones)... The audience eventually learns...that illicit Love doesn't really pay in the long run, but for about 134 minutes it has appeared to be loads of fun."

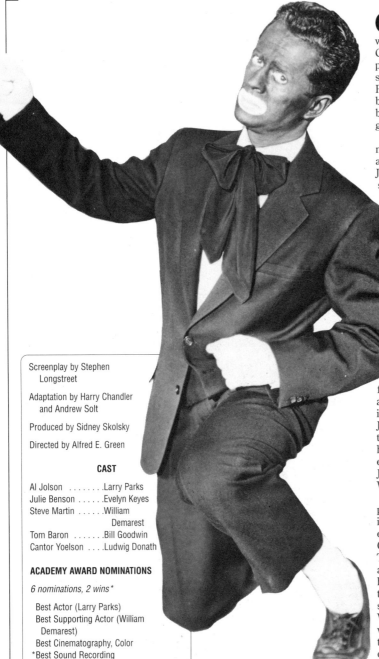

THE JOLSON STORY
COLUMBIA
$7,600,000

1946

O NCE A TOP STAR, Al Jolson was 60 when his film biography, *The Jolson Story,* was released by Columbia. He begged Columbia boss Harry Cohn for a chance to play himself, but Cohn refused and instead signed small-time Hollywood actor Larry Parks. On the basis of this successful film, both men's popularity soared, with Jolson being rediscovered by a whole new generation.

The film was peppered with Jolson's memorable songs—25 in all were used, and Larry Parks lip-synched to the original Jolson recordings. Only in the "Swanee" sequence did Jolson actually appear (he can be seen in a long shot).

The real Al Jolson was born Asa Yoelson, a talented cantor's son determined to make it big. The film portrays him as a youngster befriended by a fiddling, tumbling vaudevillian named Steve Martin (no relation to the modern actor/ comedian of that name), who becomes his mentor, and from the first moment he performs, he's hooked. Actually, "hooked" is a good word to describe his obsession with his work as portrayed here—singing is an addiction, and Jolson is an addict.

Jolson himself is best remembered for his appearance in what is often touted as "the first talkie"—*The Jazz Singer.* Originally, *The Jazz Singer* was to star George Jessel, but he demanded $10,000 more than the $30,000 Warner Bros. offered him. Eddie Cantor, the next choice, insisted the role should be played only by Jessel. Jolson received $75,000 when Jack Warner capitulated to his salary demands.

In actuality, there were several talking pictures that preceded *The Jazz Singer.* The idea of talking pictures was investigated as early as 1896, with a presentation in Germany of film with synchronized discs. The first sound-on-film was actually achieved in 1910 by Eugene Lauste, who held the first patent. By the early '20s, there were several demonstrations of sound-on-film in limited presentations. When *The Jazz Singer* arrived in 1927, it was the first talking feature film, although the process was sound-on-disc, rather than on film. Most of the movie was actually silent, with exactly 354 words being spoken, including the immortal: "Wait a minute. You ain't heard nothin' yet!"

Screenplay by Stephen Longstreet

Adaptation by Harry Chandler and Andrew Solt

Produced by Sidney Skolsky

Directed by Alfred E. Green

CAST

Al Jolson . . . . . . .Larry Parks
Julie Benson . . . . . .Evelyn Keyes
Steve Martin . . . . .William Demarest
Tom Baron . . . . . . .Bill Goodwin
Cantor Yoelson . . . .Ludwig Donath

ACADEMY AWARD NOMINATIONS

6 nominations, 2 wins*

Best Actor (Larry Parks)
Best Supporting Actor (William Demarest)
Best Cinematography, Color
*Best Sound Recording
*Best Scoring of a Musical Picture
Best Film Editing

BLUE SKIES

PARAMOUNT
$5,700,000

HEY KIDS! Let's put on a show! We'll put on some great production numbers with a lot of recycled Irving Berlin tunes like "A Pretty Girl Is Like a Melody" (previous films: *The Great Ziegfeld, Alexander's Ragtime Band*) and "Heat Wave" (*As Thousands Cheer, Alexander's…*). Then, we'll get Fred Astaire and Bing Crosby (wow!), together in the same movie. We'll get Fred to dance to "Puttin' on the Ritz," maybe get Bing to do "White Christmas." Lots of pretty chorines, of course. A plot? Naa, who needs one? This picture can't miss.

Of course, no one actually said those words…not exactly. But you could almost hear the wheels turning in the corporate heads at Paramount, and this picture, they were pleased to announce, helped pull them out of the financial doldrums—along with *The Paleface,* it became the biggest color hit of the decade. It helped put a few pennies in Bing's pocket, too. He was already on a winning streak at the box office with *Going My Way* (page 48) and *The Bells of St. Mary's* (page 54). According to *Time* magazine that year, he grossed $1,500,000 in income.

There is certainly nothing lacking in the musical department. The movie featured 22 Irving Berlin songs, including "Always," "Say It Isn't So,"

Screenplay by Arthur Sheekman

Adaptation by Allan Scott

From an original idea by Irving Berlin

Produced by Sol C. Siegel

Directed by Stuart Heisler

CAST

Johnny Adams	Bing Crosby
Jed Potter	Fred Astaire
Mary O'Hara	Joan Caulfield
Tony	Billy DeWolfe

ACADEMY AWARD NOMINATIONS

2 nominations, no wins

Best Song ("You Keep Coming Back Like a Song," words and music by Irving Berlin)
Best Scoring of a Musical Picture

"All By Myself," "Everybody Step," "How Deep Is the Ocean," "You'd Be Surprised," "See You in C-u-b-a," and "A Couple of Song and Dance Men." This last number pulls a real switch, with Astaire singing and Bing dancing. In a comment to *Time* magazine, Astaire noted: "Bing is a wonderful performer. His dancing tickles me to death. But if I said he was a good dancer, it would be the same as Bing calling me a good singer."

Blue Skies received mixed reviews. *Newsweek* dubbed it "Blue Hokum" and said that "the only fly in this ointment is a ho-hum story—and add a 'k' if you play anagrams." *The Hollywood Reporter* tempered its enthusiasm for the film with caution: "No one writes better hit tunes than Berlin, and no one better can be found to sing them than Crosby or dance to them than Astaire. It is a combination that nobody can beat. Yet strangely enough the picture leaves something to be desired…a lack of spark, vivacity or spirit."

The thread of a plot has Crosby and Astaire competing for the same girl while Bing strives to improve his career as a nightclub owner, eventually losing, then regaining, the lady in question. But most people will look past this soap-opera story and just enjoy the Crooner and Hoofer doing what they're best noted for; on that level, this is a sure-fire piece of entertainment.

1
WELCOME STRANGER
PARAMOUNT
$6,100,000

"If it ain't broke, don't fix it."

PARAMOUNT SEEMED to be ignoring the old adage when they decided to re-team *Going My Way* stars Bing Crosby and Barry Fitzgerald. The producers had them trade in their clerical collars for doctors' stethoscopes, took them out of the parish, and sent them off to a small town in Maine. Now free of his vows of chastity, Bing was even given a girl (Joan Caulfield) to woo.

Luckily for Paramount, the ploy worked, and the movie became the top grosser for the year. There were many really fine moments, like Bing and Barry fishing together—classic stuff. Along the way there were hay rides and square dances, and an appendectomy for Fitzgerald's character, who demanded a local anesthetic and a bank of mirrors so he could back-seat-drive Crosby's performance.

What there was of a plot had Jim Pearson (Bing Crosby) making an obvious play for the pretty school teacher Trudy (Joan Caulfield) at a barn dance/going away party for Doc McRory (Fitzgerald). Later, Bing helps Fitzgerald outwit the Chamber of Commerce president, who is trying to block his bid for superintendent of the town's new hospital. The more casual Crosby gets, the more crotchety and quarrelsome Fitzgerald becomes—indeed, they are almost self-parodies throughout the good-natured bantering. Typical patter: "One hundred and eighty thousand doctors in the United States and I have to get you!" bemoans Fitzgerald with the arrival of "Der Bingle."

Bing's musical performance needed no supervision. Four songs by Johnny Burke and James Van Heusen were added for spice (although this movie is really no more of a "musical" than *Going My Way*). Most memorable are "Make Mine Country Style" and Bing's crooning of "My Heart Is a Hobo." (For the record, the other two

songs were "Smile Right Back at the Sun" and "As Long as I'm Dreaming.")

It was really Bing Crosby's year—for the 12th year in a row, he was ranked among the top 10 box office draws (number 3 for 1947), not bad for a man of 43. And since Bing's "Father O'Malley" image seemed to carry over into whatever he did, even into his personal life, the critics gave a gentle nod of approval to this film. *Time* deemed *Welcome Stranger* "as pleasantly relaxed as Crosby's singing"; *The Hollywood Reporter* described it as "sparkling fun"; and *The New York Times* called the film "as genial as the day is long—just the kind of picture that is nice to have around."

Co-starring with Bing and Barry was an actress who was becoming well known to audiences of the day, although her name is little remembered today. Joan Caulfield was a former model who had been playing ingenues on Broadway before entering motion pictures in the mid-'40s. Paramount signed her to a "we'll make you a star" contract, and for a while it seemed this promise was to be fulfilled. Early films included *Duffy's Tavern* (1945), *Blue Skies* (1946), *Monsieur Beaucaire* (1946), *Dear Wife* (1950), and *The Rams of Ranchipur* (1955). In 1950, she married producer Frank Ross and announced her retirement from film (they divorced in 1960). She did, however, make appearances in several more movies, especially Westerns like *Cattle King* (1963), *Red Tomahawk* (1967), *Buckskin* (1968), and *Pony Express Rider* (1976). She also starred in two television series, "My Favorite Husband" (1953–55) and "Sally" (1957–58). Caulfield died on June 18, 1991.

Watch for an appearance by Robert Shayne as the town's petulant pharmacist. Fans of early television will recognize him as "Inspector Henderson" of "Superman" fame.

Screenplay by Arthur Sheekman

Adaptation by Arthur Sheekman and
N. Richard Nash

From a story by Frank Butler

Produced by Sol C. Siegel

Directed by Elliott Nugent

CAST

Jim Pearson . . . . .Bing Crosby
Trudy . . . . .Joan Caulfield
Dr. Joseph McRory . . .Barry Fitzgerald
Emily . . . . .Wanda Hendrix
Bill Waiters . . . . .Frank Faylen

THE BACHELOR AND THE BOBBY-SOXER

RKO
$5,500,000

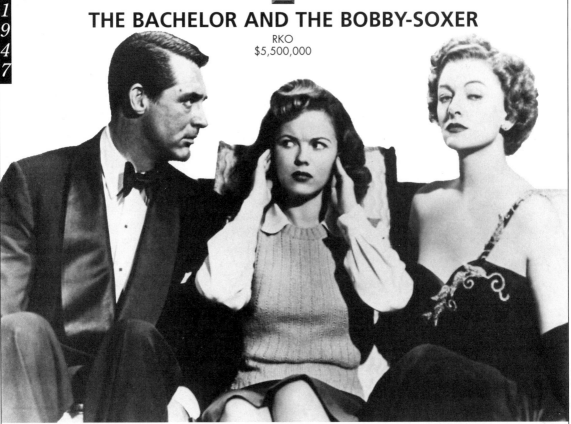

SHIRLEY TEMPLE had been flashing her dimples to the delight of audiences since her first appearance in film at the ripe old age of three, back in 1932's *The Red Haired Alibi.* Throughout the Depression-bound '30s, she kept audiences' spirits up with her endearing singing, acting, and dancing, as well as curly-head shaking and camera mugging, which she did with an equal dose of exuberance and panache. Then the unthinkable happened. She grew up.

By the 1940s, the adorable little Miss Temple, child star extraordinaire, was a blossoming adolescent. In her heyday of the mid-'30s, she was making up to five pictures a year; by the '40s, her popularity had begun to wane, and she starred in only a handful of films in the early part of the decade as she made the awkward transition from child to teenager. In 1947, David O. Selznick eagerly loaned out his former money machine to RKO (for which he received a huge, above-the-title credit stating, "Miss Temple's services by arrangement with David O. Selznick"). The result was a happy

bit of summertime fluff called *The Bachelor and the Bobby-Soxer.* Two years later, Temple's film career would be at an end.

The Bachelor of the title was heart-throb Cary Grant. Shirley's character develops a teenage crush on him and pursues him relentlessly. Her older sister, played with restraint by Myrna Loy in a choice role as a pre-woman's lib judge, tries to break up the "romance"

Screenplay by Sidney Sheldon

Produced by Dore Schary

Directed by Irving Reis

CAST

Dick . . . . .Cary Grant
Margaret . . . . .Myrna Loy
Susan . . . . .Shirley Temple
Tommy . . . . .Rudy Vallee

ACADEMY AWARD NOMINATIONS

1 nomination, 1 win*

*Best Original Screenplay (Sidney Sheldon)

---

and eventually ends up falling for Grant—no surprise here. Along the way, there's some rather stilted acting by Temple. Mugging and pouting her way through pictures was fine for a six-year-old; in an 18-year-old, it's out of place. And for today's video audiences, there are also some really dated scenes at the clean-cut, lily-white high school, populated by polite, attentive students who jitterbug and wear bobby-sox (the turned-down white socks that gave rise to a trendy '40s style and nickname for teenaged girls of the era, hence one-half of the film's title).

One of the brightest moments is an obstacle race that pits the high-school boys against Grant, pretending to try to impress Temple with his youthfulness. The scenes of the three-legged race, hurdling, and so on required a dose of agility, and the 43-year-old actor was up to the task, having worked early on as an acrobat and stiltwalker.

Screenwriter Sidney Sheldon won an Oscar for his script. Sheldon's later career included the creation of the TV series "I Dream of Jeannie" and numerous best-selling novels.

3

THE EGG AND I
UNIVERSAL-INTERNATIONAL
$5,500,000

"I'll bet you think an egg is something you casually order for breakfast. Well, I did once. But that was before the egg and I."
—CLAUDETTE COLBERT'S
OPENING SPEECH

IN ONE OF THE MORE clever openings of a '40s film, we hear the sound of a rooster crowing, but it quickly becomes apparent that this sound is actually the steam whistle on a locomotive. Claudette Colbert's character, "Betty," delivered the above narration, and audiences knew immediately that they were in for two hours of fun.

The Egg and I is certainly that…and more. The film has a lot to say about the friendship and support of neighbors, about the struggles and hardship found among farming people. The film, based on the autobiographical best-seller by Betty MacDonald, has Bob (Fred MacMurray) taking his wife Betty (Colbert) away from her familiar city life, and setting up a country chicken ranch. (Apparently,

Screenplay by Chester Erskine and Fred F. Finklehoffe

From the novel by Betty MacDonald

Produced by Chester Erskine and Fred F. Finklehoffe

Directed by Chester Erskine

CAST

Betty . . . . .Claudette Colbert
Bob . . . . .Fred MacMurray
Ma Kettle . . . . .Marjorie Main
Harriet Putnam . . . . . .Louise Allbritton
Pa Kettle . . . . .Percy Kilbride

ACADEMY AWARD NOMINATIONS

1 nomination, no wins

Best Supporting Actress (Marjorie Main)

women had no say in those days, doing whatever their husbands demanded of them.) Brave soul, she does her darndest to adjust. Help comes in the form of "Ma and Pa

Kettle," characters played by Marjorie Main and Percy Kilbride, who were introduced in this picture and subsequently went on to make one "Kettle" film a year until 1957.

These characters are really caricatures of rural people—sincere, honest, uneducated, but full of nurturing warmth. When Ma Kettle sets the table for dinner for 12 young-'uns, she merely sweeps her arm across the clutter on the table to make room for the clean dishes. Disgusting? Yes. But she's so full of love for her brood that it's hard to criticize her. And when she makes room for one more mouth to feed (Betty), your heart goes out to her. But then, she's already got such a big one.

The old "fixer-upper" theme set forth in this film has since become a frequent one in comedy films. A year later, *Mr. Blandings Builds His Dream House* found Cary Grant hard at work with hammer and nails, and the '80s saw a revival of the theme with *The Money Pit* and *Baby Boom*.

UNCONQUERED
PARAMOUNT
$5,250,000

1947

there's Boris Karloff in the role of Guyasuta, chief of the Senecas, and DeMille's own daughter, Katherine, as the chief's crafty daughter. Then there's the dialogue. Gary Cooper was forced to deliver lines like "This is greater than you or me or both of us" and "White Man's medicine is strong. Nothing can stop them." The oft-cited reason for our pushing aside the aborigines, our "manifest destiny," is expressed when Cooper notes:

> "People like the Salters [home-steaders] can never be stopped... Indians can kill them and run them off, but more will keep coming. The Salters are the New World, unconquered, unconquerable because they're strong and free—because they have faith in themselves and in God."

Fortunately, attitudes have changed in Hollywood, and there are now organizations of Native American actors which are more effective than Iron Eyes was allowed to be. But in the '40s, this view of Indians was more than acceptable; it was the norm.

Despite its problems, *Unconquered* is still good entertainment, a colorful drama in the DeMille tradition. For this reason, it is worth a watch whenever it appears on TBS and other cable stations.

"At the forks of the Ohio stands an American city, a colossus of steel, whose mills and furnaces bring forth bone and sinew for a nation. Not so long ago, a lonely outpost guarded this very spot. It was called Fort Pitt...men kept coming West, some to build their own fortunes, even at the price of Indian wars—others to build a nation—even at the price of their own lives. These are the unconquered, who push ever forward the frontiers of man's freedom."
—PROLOGUE

ALTHOUGH he touted it as a historical film, *Unconquered*'s director, Cecil B. DeMille, was more interested in doing what he did best—making a

sweeping piece of screen entertainment. He only halfway succeeded.

Listed in the film's opening credits is Chief Iron Eyes Cody, as "Indian language advisor." A full-blooded Cherokee, Iron Eyes himself makes a brief appearance in *Unconquered* as "Red Corn." Born in Oklahoma in 1907, he entered show business at the age of 12, touring with circuses and Wild West shows. He appeared in numerous films and TV episodes and acted as technical advisor on many others. His acting career was still going strong in 1991, when he died at the age of 84.

Too bad Iron Eyes wasn't consulted on more than language, since this movie is one long racial cliché. First,

Screenplay by Charles Bennett, Fredric M. Frank, and Jesse Lasky, Jr.

Based on the novel by Neil H. Swanson

Produced and directed by Cecil B. DeMille

CAST

Capt. Christopher
Holden . . . . .Gary Cooper
Abby Hale . . . . .Paulette Goddard
Martin Garth . . . . .Howard Da Silva
Guyasuta, Chief
of the Senecas . . . . .Boris Karloff
Jeremy Love . . . . .Cecil Kellaway

ACADEMY AWARD NOMINATIONS

1 nomination, no wins

Best Special Effects

LIFE WITH FATHER

WARNER BROS.
$5,057,000

ONE OF THOSE rare stories suitable for nearly every conceivable medium, *Life with Father* began as a best-selling book of sketches, reminiscences by Clarence Day, Jr., of his 1880s adolescence. In 1939, Howard Lindsay and Russell Crouse adapted the material into a play that ran on Broadway for a record eight years. Hot on the heels of that success was this film version, released in 1947, starring William Powell as Clarence Sr., the blustering paterfamilias with a heart of custard creme, and Irene Dunne as his patient yet unobtrusively independent wife, Vinnie.

That the book/play/movie was created from a string of "day in the life" events is evident in the loosely connected incidents that comprise this film. We see Clarence Jr. buying a new suit (against Father's approval); the family trying to hire a new maid; Clarence Jr. falling in love with a beautiful young lady played by Elizabeth Taylor; Vinnie struggling through a near-fatal illness; and, of course,

Screenplay by Donald Ogden Stewart

From the play by Howard Lindsay and Russell Crouse

Based on the writings of Clarence Day, Jr.

Produced by Robert Buckner

Directed by Michael Curtiz

CAST

Father . . . . .William Powell
Vinnie . . . . .Irene Dunne
Mary . . . . .Elizabeth Taylor
Rev. Dr. Lloyd . . . . . . .Edmund Gwenn
Cora . . . . .ZaSu Pitts

ACADEMY AWARD NOMINATIONS

4 nominations, no wins

Best Actor (William Powell)
Best Cinematography, Color
Best Art Direction–Set Decoration, Color
Best Scoring of a Dramatic or Comedy Picture

Vinnie persisting in getting the ever-stubborn Clarence Sr. to be baptized.

One of the Day boys, John, is played by Martin Milner, who later went on to star in the '60s TV series "Route 66" and "Adam 12."

Also credited is Mrs. Clarence Day, who served as Technical Advisor.

ZaSu Pitts, who plays Cora, had co-starring roles in the late '50s and early '60s with Gale Storm on "Oh! Susanna" and "The Gale Storm Show." Her last film appearance was in 1963, in *It's a Mad Mad Mad Mad World.* She died of cancer the year that film was released, at the age of 65.

Life with Father found new life on prime-time television a few years later. The 30-minute sitcom premiered on CBS on November 22, 1953, and lasted until July 5, 1955, with Leon Ames portraying Clarence Day, Sr., Lurene Tuttle as Vinnie, and a variety of different actors as the children. The TV version had the honor of being the first live color series on network television originating in Hollywood.

1

THE RED SHOES

RANK-ARCHERS/EAGLE-LION
$5,000,000

"The growing popularity of the ballet in Britain has been a post-war phenomenon and undoubtedly influenced [Michael] Powell and [Emeric] Pressburger to produce this, their last for Rank. Although good ballet is assured box office in London and possibly other big cities, its popularity in small towns and country districts is dubious. And in America, too, it will probably only attract a limited audience."
—VARIETY

HAPPILY, *Variety* was wrong. *The Red Shoes* has to be considered a high point in cinema, not only because it has made so much money and is a perennial favorite, but because it got off the ground (so to speak) at all. Movies were supposed to be funny, or scary, or shoot-'em-ups, or tense thrillers. But ballet? That was considered (and by many still is) highbrow "culture," certainly not mainstream fare for exhibitors.

But this film had a lot going for it, starting off with the beautiful female ballet-star-turned-actress Moira Shearer. The daughter of a Scottish civil engineer, Moira had her first dancing lessons at six and made her professional debut with the International Ballet at 15. At 16, she joined Sadler's Wells Ballet. Six years later, at the age of 22, she was signed for *The Red Shoes*, a role that demanded not only perfect dance skills but a considerable amount of acting. *The Red Shoes* is a play-within-a-play; it's the story of a dancer torn between two possessive men, as well as her career. The highlight, of course, is the performance (20 minutes long, complete with special effects) of Hans Christian Andersen's fairy tale, also titled *The Red Shoes*.

Most critics chose to ignore the rather melodramatic story, instead showering praise on Miss Shearer. *The New York Times* noted: "As the leading ballerina and the romantic heroine of the film, Moira Shearer is amazingly accomplished and full of a warm and radiant charm." *Newsweek* also commented on the young ballerina: "Perhaps Miss Shearer, an attractive 22-year-old redhead, is a little too sweet and starry-eyed to make the tragic Vicky's fate completely credible.

Nevertheless, the Covent Garden ballet star proves that she is a promising actress as well as a graceful and appealing dancer."

So much attention was heaped upon Moira Shearer that she resisted suggestions that she dance in other screen presentations. The 1950 edition of *Current Biography* quoted her as saying: "I am not ready to find satisfaction in the cinema because there I would not know how to strive for perfection. Perfection is what we strive for constantly in the ballet." She returned to Sadler's Wells for a few years, but again danced on the screen in *Tales of Hoffman* (1951). She later made a few non-ballet films, but retired in the early '60s after marrying broadcaster and novelist Ludovic Kennedy.

The picture also garnered critical praise for its fine production values, including the excellent music and Technicolor cinematography. One outstanding sequence has a point-of-view shot from the angle of the dancer's head, spinning as she "spots" (focuses on a distant point so as not to become dizzy) in the *Swan Lake* number.

J. Arthur Rank (the "Rank" in Rank-Archers/Eagle-Lion) was born in 1888, the heir to a flour and milling fortune. His first venture into the world of films was producing promotional religious films for the Methodist Church during the '30s. The British film magnate (later given the honorary title of "Lord") parlayed this modest start in films into a virtual monopoly on the British motion picture industry; by the mid-'40s, his Rank Organisation was involved in all aspects of filmmaking, including production, processing, distribution, and exhibition. At one time, his company owned more than half of all British studios and over 1,000 theaters. He died in 1972 at the age of 84.

The Archers was the name of the production company directly involved with this British production; the opening of *The Red Shoes* features the Rank logo (a man striking a gong), followed by an archery target pierced by numerous arrows, all to the accompaniment of trumpet fanfare. Eagle-Lion was the company that released this film in the United States.

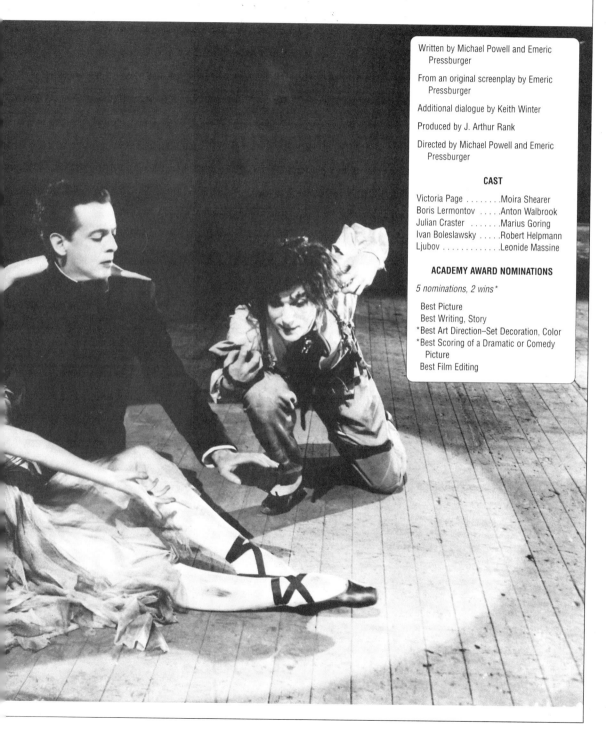

Written by Michael Powell and Emeric Pressburger

From an original screenplay by Emeric Pressburger

Additional dialogue by Keith Winter

Produced by J. Arthur Rank

Directed by Michael Powell and Emeric Pressburger

CAST

Victoria Page . . . . .Moira Shearer
Boris Lermontov . . . . .Anton Walbrook
Julian Craster . . . . . . .Marius Goring
Ivan Boleslawsky . . . . .Robert Helpmann
Ljubov . . . . .Leonide Massine

ACADEMY AWARD NOMINATIONS

5 nominations, 2 wins*

Best Picture
Best Writing, Story
*Best Art Direction–Set Decoration, Color
*Best Scoring of a Dramatic or Comedy Picture
Best Film Editing

RED RIVER

UNITED ARTISTS
$4,506,825

RED WAS CERTAINLY the color for 1948. Following in *The Red Shoes'* footsteps, *Red River* generated big business at the box office. Much of its strength lay in its production values—there was beautiful photography of sprawling Western vistas; a full and rich musical score by Dimitri Tiomkin, who by now was famous for his Westerns; plus a top-notch cast, including "The Duke," John Wayne, and a promising young newcomer, Montgomery Clift.

Critics praised just about everything and everybody. John Wayne, of course, had long been identified with Westerns—starting with *The Big Trail* in 1930—but many reviewers took special notice of Clift (it was his second film). *The Hollywood Reporter* called his performance, "a decisive bid for important screen stardom…with his charm, unaffected style and winning personality, [Clift] is a bet if ever one

has shown up in Hollywood." *Variety* called the young actor "a sympathetic personality that invites audience response. He reads the Garth character with an instinctive, nonchalant underplaying that is sock."

Clift's role was a pivotal one as the adopted son of Wayne's character; eventually there is a showdown between father and son in the film's dramatic climax, with both Wayne and Clift exhibiting their acting talent in this emotionally charged scene.

Ironically, Wayne was not Howard Hawks' first choice for the lead in *Red River.* Gary Cooper was the man Hawks had in mind, but Coop turned down the part because he didn't like the ruthless nature of the character of Tom Dunson. Montgomery Clift, however, was always Hawks' first choice for the part of Matt Garth. Eventually, Hawks signed Clift to a five-picture

deal, but *Red River* was the only picture they ever did together.

The sequence most frequently recalled is the cattle drive over the newly opened Chisholm Trail, and the resulting stampede. To make the cattle appear to be stampeding and trampling the carefully placed stuntmen, cameras were undercranked* to emphasize the speed of the running animals, which were being frightened by off-camera wranglers. It took 10 days to film, using 15 cameras, 35 wranglers, and thousands of head of cattle. Seven men were injured during the filming.

---

*Undercranking is a process of shooting at less than the normal 24 frames per second. When the film is shown, the action appears speeded up. Silent films were shot at 18 frames per second, which is why when they're shown with modern projection equipment, the people always seem to be running.

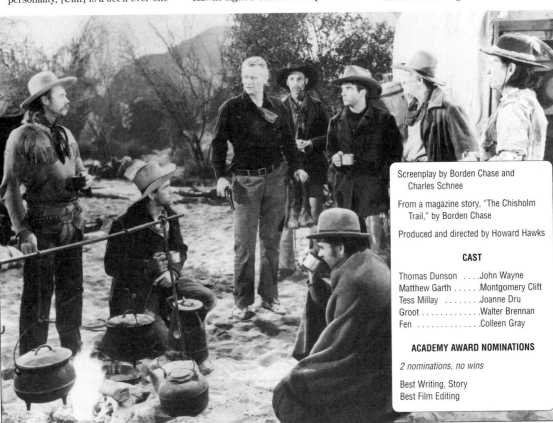

Screenplay by Borden Chase and Charles Schnee

From a magazine story, "The Chisholm Trail," by Borden Chase

Produced and directed by Howard Hawks

CAST

Thomas Dunson . . . .John Wayne
Matthew Garth . . . . . .Montgomery Clift
Tess Millay . . . . .Joanne Dru
Groot . . . . .Walter Brennan
Fen . . . . .Colleen Gray

ACADEMY AWARD NOMINATIONS

2 nominations, no wins

Best Writing, Story
Best Film Editing

THE PALEFACE

PARAMOUNT
$4,500,000

BOB HOPE'S first color picture was *The Paleface,* and it became his biggest box office success. In addition to Hope, the film had cowboys, Indians, and Howard Hughes' discovery from *The Outlaw,* Jane Russell, as Calamity Jane. All the ingredients were there, and the burlesque, a send-up of classic "shoot-out on Main Street" films like *The Virginian,* opened in time for Christmas and continued to pull in big bucks long after the holiday season.

The most notable thing about this picture, aside from the snappy dialogue bantered between Russell and Hope, is the hit song the film introduced. "Buttons and Bows" won an Oscar for its composers, Jay Livingston and Ray Evans. In the movie, Bob Hope sings it, lip-synching and faking accompaniment on a concertina. The song went to the top of the charts and became a number-one record, but not as sung by Hope. Leaving nothing to chance, the composers insisted that Dinah Shore be signed as the singer, and her recording became a smash hit. Livingston and Evans had many famous tunes in the decades that followed, including "Tammy," "Que Sera Sera," and the familiar themes to television's "Bonanza" and "Mr. Ed."

Bob Hope had been making films for many years and was a perennial

Screenplay by Edmund Hartmann and
Frank Tashlin

Produced by Robed L. Welch

Directed by Norman Z. McLeod

CAST

"Painless"
Peter Potter . . . . . . .Bob Hope
Calamity Jane . . . . . . .Jane Russell
Terris . . . . .Robert Armstrong
Pepper . . . . .Iris Adrian
Toby Preston . . . . . . .Robert Watson

ACADEMY AWARD NOMINATIONS

1 nomination, 1 win*

*Best Song ("Buttons and Bows," music
by Jay Livingston, words by Ray Evans)

favorite even back then. A successful radio career in New York brought him to Hollywood for the movie *The Big Broadcast of 1938,* in which he first sang his theme song, "Thanks for the Memory." *The Cat and the Canary* followed in 1939, and soon he was on the road to success in his series of Road pictures, beginning in 1940 with *The Road to Singapore.* He eventually made seven of these films with Bing Crosby and Dorothy Lamour. During times of military involvement, Hope pulled together teams of celebrities and took his troupe of performers overseas to entertain the troops. One of the earliest entertainers to appear on television, he has continued in that medium even today, and his frequent specials and variety programs are always certain to pull in high ratings.

Although *The Paleface* was a comedy and did not strive for authenticity, it is interesting to note that Iron Eyes Cody (see *Unconquered,* page 70) played the part of "Chief Iron Eyes" and a Native American by the name of Chief Yowlachie appears as "Chief

Yellow Feather."

If you have a VCR and rent the videocassette of *The Paleface,* you can witness for yourself how stunt doubles are effectively used in movie making. Watch the scene where the dental patient slugs "Painless Potter" (Hope), and you'll see why doubles are filmed in long shots. The man doing the flip over the counter is a terrible likeness of Bob Hope—freeze-frame just as he begins his stunt. Notice how, when he completes the back flip, the pile of towels hides him. A few seconds pass, and up pops Hope, who had been waiting behind the towels. Of course, this scene, and thousands of others like it, were never meant to be seen this way by anybody except the film editor, and in the theatrical runs there was never any chance of these things being caught.

A sequel, *Son of Paleface,* followed in 1951, with much of the same cast—plus singing cowboy Roy Rogers—but its success couldn't match the original. In 1962, Don Knotts starred in a remake, *The Shakiest Gun in the West.*

THE THREE MUSKETEERS

METRO-GOLDWYN-MAYER
$4,306,876

ACTUALLY THERE ARE *four*, not three, musketeers in Alexandre Dumas' classic novel, but poor D'Artagnan always seems to be left out of the total. And if you take into account the number of times this book has been made into film and television versions, well, there have been hundreds of musketeers. Edison made a version way back in 1911, so everything else has to be considered a remake. These came in 1913, 1914, 1921 (the famous Douglas Fairbanks version), 1935 (Paul Lukas), 1939 (Don Ameche and the Ritz Brothers!), this 1948 edition, as well as two back-to-back Richard Lester productions starring Michael York—*The Three Musketeers* and *The Four* (yes, count 'em, four) *Musketeers*.

Several elements distinguish the 1948 production, such as the lavish sets and use of color; Lana Turner as "Lady de Winter"; a fine performance by a young Angela Lansbury (of TV's "Murder, She Wrote" fame); plus June Allyson, Van Heflin, Frank Morgan, Gig Young, Reginald Owen, Vincent Price—the list goes on and on. But the best thing about this film is the actor playing D'Artagnan—the great hoofer, Gene Kelly. Gene really knew how to buckle a swash (or is it swash a buckle?).

Although critics were not in accord about the film's total merits (most found it uneven or too long), they were unanimous in their praise for Kelly. Said *The New York Times:* "Not since Douglas Fairbanks swung through the air with magic ease and landed on balconies and beefsteaks

has a fellow come along who compares with that robustious actor in vitality and grace…what's more, he looks good in plush costumes." And *Variety* agreed: "There are acrobatics by Gene Kelly that would give the late great Douglas Fairbanks pause. His first duel with Richelieu's cohorts is almost ballet, yet never loses the feeling of swaggering swordplay. It is a masterful mixture of dancing grace, acro-agility and sly horseplay."

Many of the exteriors were shot on the back lot of MGM. There is a small bridge noticeable in the European village set which was used in dozens of MGM movies. You'll see this same bridge frequently in MGM television series of the '60s and '70s, notably "Combat" and "The Man From U.N.C.L.E."

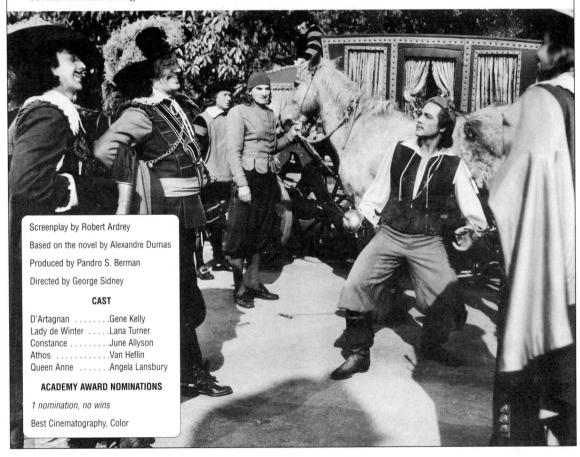

Screenplay by Robert Ardrey

Based on the novel by Alexandre Dumas

Produced by Pandro S. Berman

Directed by George Sidney

CAST

D'Artagnan . . . . .Gene Kelly
Lady de Winter . . . . .Lana Turner
Constance . . . . .June Allyson
Athos . . . . .Van Heflin
Queen Anne . . . . . .Angela Lansbury

ACADEMY AWARD NOMINATIONS

1 nomination, no wins

Best Cinematography, Color

EASTER PARADE

MGM
$4,189,997

"SMILE AND SHOW YOUR DIMPLE." That was the original title and opening lyric of a song Irving Berlin wrote back in 1917. It went nowhere, and Berlin relegated it to his "trunk," a temporary resting place for unsuccessful tunes from the persistent songster who hoped one day to resurrect it. Then, in 1933, he created a different lyric for the original melody; the new song was christened "Easter Parade." It had its chance in a revue called *As Thousands Cheer,* and proved to be a popular number.

A decade later, 20th Century-Fox, which had produced the successful Berlin songfest called *Alexander's Ragtime Band* (1938), decided to make the song a centerpiece of a new film. Eventually, *Easter Parade* wound up on the MGM lot, with Gene Kelly signed to star opposite Judy Garland.

The film seemed plagued with problems. Judy's husband, Vincente Minnelli, was set to direct. He had just directed a Kelly-Garland picture, *The Pirate,* so it seemed a natural for Minnelli to direct his wife's next film. But Judy's emotional state was precarious, as she had just returned from a period of recuperation in a mental health facility (called a "sanitarium" in those days) after finding it difficult to

work under her husband's direction. So Minnelli willingly agreed to let another man, Charles Walters, direct.

Then Gene Kelly's ankle snapped during a touch football game, and it seemed he had taken the old show business chestnut "break a leg" too literally. Fred Astaire was brought out of semi-retirement to play opposite Judy. He was nearly 50; she was a mere 25, half his age. Would the combination work?

Fortunately, the film proved to be a smash. Judy appeared radiant on the

---

Screenplay by Sidney Sheldon, Frances Goodrich and Albert Hackett

Produced by Arthur Freed

Directed by Charles Walters

CAST

Hannah Brown . . . . . . .Judy Garland
Don Hewes . . . . .Fred Astaire
Jonathan Harrow III . . .Peter Lawford
Nadine Hale . . . . .Ann Miller

ACADEMY AWARD NOMINATIONS

1 nomination, 1 win*

**Best Scoring of a Musical Picture

---

screen, despite a constant battle with her weight and a growing addiction to amphetamines. Her vocal performances and dancing opposite Astaire showed her to be in top form. Ann Miller and Peter Lawford co-starred, with Miller kicking up her heels in her typical fashion. Seventeen songs—10 vintage and seven new Berlin tunes—kept this musical in the grand MGM tradition, moving along at a steady clip. Songs included "Happy Easter," "Drum Crazy," "When That Midnight Choo-Choo Leaves for Alabam," "A Feller with an Umbrella," "When I Dance with You," "I Love a Piano," and what most considered to be the musical highlight, "A Couple of Swells." In that number, Judy and Fred appear dressed as tramps who must "walk up the avenue" to a high society ball because they're down on their luck.

The all-stops-out finale centers on the title song, "Easter Parade," as everyone does indeed walk up the avenue on Easter Sunday, decked out in their best 1912 finery. Hundreds of extras and an elaborate re-creation of New York City's St. Patrick's Cathedral sent audiences home on a seasonal high note. Today the picture is a holiday favorite on TV and at the rental counter.

SAMSON AND DELILAH

PARAMOUNT
$11,500,000

"Before the dawn of history, ever since the first man discovered his soul, he has struggled against the forces that sought to enslave him..."
—PROLOGUE, NARRATED
BY CECIL B. DEMILLE

S EX, BIBLICAL PAGEANTRY, spectacle— stir rapidly, add Cecil B. DeMille, and voilà—instant box office block- buster.

With those ingredients and more, *Samson and Delilah* became the num- ber-one film of 1949, netting Paramount its biggest take of the '40s. Part of the reason was the cast. Brawny, beefy Victor Mature was the

"and more" for the ladies in the audi- ence. He was the hunk of the year and can easily be seen as a "Rambo" proto- type by today's audiences, right down to the sweatband. As he swings the ass's jawbone, crushing all foes, it seems likely that Sylvester Stallone had to have had this image in mind when he created his "Rambo" charac- ter, who bears more than a passing resemblance to Victor Mature. Overwhelmed by the attention afford- ed him by the femmes, Mature relin- quished his title as "America's Number One Sweater Boy." *Hollywood Legends* quoted him as stating at the

time that "I can't help it if I've got something more. I'm tired of being nothing but a male strip-teaser."

As one-half of the title role, Mature's Samson was up to his ass's jawbone in women. Hedy Lamarr, at age 36, seemed a bit old for the part of Delilah, but even more bizarre was the casting of Angela Lansbury as her older sister, Semadar, since she was only 24.

Notable among others in the cast was George Reeves in the minor part of the "Wounded Messenger." Reeves, television fans will recall, later became a muscle man in his own right when he landed the part of "Superman." The one-time wrestler seemed to have a promising acting career in the late '30s, but his film roles were basically supporting ones, including a brief but memorable cameo as one of the

Screenplay by Jesse L Lasky, Jr., and Frederic M. Franc

From original treatments by Harold Lamb and Vladimir Jabotinsky

Produced and directed by Cecil B. DeMille

CAST

Delilah . . . . .Hedy Lamarr
Samson . . . . .Victor Mature
The Saran of Gaza . . . .George Sanders
Semadar . . . . .Angela Lansbury
Ahtur . . . . .Henry Wilcoxon

ACADEMY AWARD NOMINATIONS

5 nominations, 2 wins*

Best Cinematography, Color
*Best Art Direction–Set Decoration, Color
Best Scoring of a Dramatic or Comedy Picture (Victor Young)
*Best Costume Design, Color
Best Special Effects

Samson and Delilah was released at Christmas time in 1949, but was submitted to the Academy for consideration as a 1950 release.

Cecil B. DeMille picked up an honorary Academy Award statuette as a "distinguished motion picture pioneer, for thirty-seven years of brilliant showmanship."

Tarleton twins in *Gone With the Wind.* Reeves also appeared in *From Here to Eternity* (page 107). He starred as the "Man of Steel" in the weekly "Superman" television series from 1951 to 1957, and the handsome actor eventually found himself typecast after this long TV stint as "Superman." It eventually became too much for him to cope with, and Reeves took his own life in 1959.

DeMille, of course, was the acknowledged master of Biblical epic, having already made one version of *The Ten Commandments* in 1923 (another would follow in the '50s), as well as other religious spectacles such as *The King of Kings, The Sign of the Cross,* and *The Crusades.* Of his 18 sound films, 12 are built around historical situations. *Samson and Delilah*

helped kick off the '50s trend of Biblical spectaculars.

While DeMille excelled at managing crowd scenes, he was lax in other areas, for example, the unconvincing scene where Samson has to wrestle with and kill the lion. The poor beast was noticeably tranquilized into la-la-land while Samson appeared to vanquish the animal, complete with dubbed roars. Like "Superman," he bends rather fake-looking steel (or iron) in his bare hands. And the effect of his pulling down the temple would have been more believable if it had not been supported by two tiny pillars.

Critics were mixed in their appraisal of *Samson and Delilah. Time* noted that "even lovers of cinematic art who recognize *Samson and Delilah* as a run-of-DeMille epic should enjoy it as

a simple-minded spree. In its way, it is as much fun as a robust, well-organized circus." Puns on DeMille's name abounded, as in *The New York Times* review: "If ever there was a movie for DeMillions, here it is…Victor Mature as Samson is a dashing and dauntless hunk of man…Hedy Lamarr as Delilah is a sleek and bejeweled siren whose charms have a strictly occidental and twentieth-century grace and clarity."

In 1984, *Samson and Delilah* was remade as a movie for television, with Antony Hamilton as the strongman and Belinda Bauer as the Philistine temptress. Shown occasionally for late-night viewing, it is worth catching for a special reason—the part of Samson's father was played by Victor Mature, still going strong after all those years.

2

BATTLEGROUND

METRO-GOLDWYN-MAYER
$5,051,143

WHEN SOMEONE first proposed *Battleground* to MGM's Louis B. Mayer, he turned it down, convinced that the public wanted no more war movies. But in 1948, a deal was made which saw Dore Schary arriving as

Screenplay by Robert Pirosh

Produced by Dore Schary

Directed by William A. Wellman

CAST

Holley . . . . .Van Johnson
Rodrigues . . . . .Ricardo Montalban
Jarvess . . . . .John Hodiak
"Pop" Stazak . . . . . .George Murphy
Jim Layton . . . . . . .Marshall Thompson

ACADEMY AWARD NOMINATIONS

6 nominations, 2 wins *

Best Picture
Best Supporting Actor (James Whitmore)
Best Director (William A. Wellman)
*Best Story and Screenplay (Robert Pirosh)
*Best Cinematography, Black and White
Best Film Editing

boss of the studio. The first thing he did was dust off the *Battleground* script, purchased from Howard Hughes when Schary was at RKO. (Hughes also believed people were tired of war films and had refused to make the movie.) With the public having recovered sufficiently from its World War II shell shock, the picture proved a box office sensation.

Much of its success must be attributed to director William Wellman, coupled with a strong Oscar-winning script by Robert Pirosh. The message of the film about men fighting the Battle of the Bulge is delivered by Leon Ames, in the role of the Chaplain. It sums up America's feelings about the war and why we fought, but also sounds the alarm about the perceived menace of Red Communism, of grave concern at the time.

"Was this trip necessary?... Nobody wanted this war but the Nazis. A great many people tried to deal with them. Millions have died for no other reason except that the Nazis wanted them dead. In the final showdown there was

nothing left to do except to fight. There's a great lesson in this. And those of us who learned it the hard way aren't going to forget it. We must never again let any force dedicated to a super race or super idea or super anything become strong enough to impose itself upon a free world. We must be smart enough and tough enough in the beginning to put out the fire before it starts spreading... yes, this trip was necessary."

The all-star cast included Van Johnson, John Hodiak, Ricardo Montalban, George Murphy, James Whitmore, and Jim Arness (later "James" Arness of TV's "Gunsmoke").

Battleground won unanimous critical acclaim. *Variety* called it "the first great picture to come out of Hollywood treating with World War II...a fine, mature war picture of smash proportions for audience and boxoffice impact." *The Hollywood Reporter* termed the film "eloquent and compelling...the war picture for which the industry and the public have been waiting. It is a strong, realistic and gripping drama."

JOLSON SINGS AGAIN

COLUMBIA
$5,000,000

WHEN JOLSON sang again, so too did Columbia Pictures. Betting that the public would return to the theaters for a sequel to the first successful film, Columbia re-teamed Larry Parks as Al Jolson and William Demarest as his pal Steve Martin.

It is surprising that this picture did so well. There was very little original new material, with much of the film devoted to recapping *The Jolson Story* through the overdone technique of newspaper clippings.

The film begins where the first picture ended, establishing Jolson as a successful entertainer, obsessed with adulation from his audiences. Everything else in his life, from his marriage and family life to his health, is subjugated to his love of the applause ringing in his ears. In a way, the movie becomes a documentary of *The Jolson Story,* showing Al Jolson (Larry Parks) standing with the production crew and watching as his life story is being made. There is a particularly interesting sequence in which Larry Parks, playing Jolson, meets Larry Parks (played by Larry Parks). It's not nearly as confusing on the screen as it sounds, and must be seen to be appreciated for the clever bit of writing that it is.

Then are so many clips from the first film that they seem almost like filler. As the sequel recounts the details from that movie, it nearly catches up with itself…a situation that is narrowly avoided.

Despite the inevitable comparisons to the original film, *Jolson Sings Again* has some enjoyable moments, most of them coming from the original recordings of Jolson tunes, lip-synched by Parks. Since the first picture, Jolson had staged a comeback and audiences delighted to the soundtrack of favorites like "California, Here I Come," "Red, Red Robin," "Sonny Boy," and, of course, "Mammy."

Although he had found a new generation of fans following the success of the biographical films *The Jolson Story* and *Jolson Sings Again,* Al Jolson's comeback was short-lived. In 1950, a year after the latter picture was released, Jolson set off on a trip to Korea to entertain the U.S. troops stationed there during the Korean War. Shortly after returning home, he died of a heart attack.

Screenplay by Sidney Buchman

Produced by Sidney Buchman

Directed by Henry Levin

CAST

Al Jolson . . . . .Larry Parks
Ellen Clark . . . . .Barbara Hale
Steve Martin . . . . .William Demarest
Cantor Yoelson . . . . . .Ludwig Donath

ACADEMY AWARD NOMINATIONS

3 nominations, no wins

Best Story and Screenplay
Best Cinematography, Color
Best Scoring of a Musical Picture

THE SANDS OF IWO JIMA

REPUBLIC
$5,000,000

"To the United States Marine Corps, whose exploits and valor have left a lasting impression on the world and in the hearts of their countrymen. Appreciation is gratefully acknowledged for their assistance and participation which made this picture possible."
—DEDICATION

ONE OF THE MOST profound bits of philosophy ever to be expressed in any motion picture came, surprisingly, from this war film which dramatizes the raising of the flag over Iwo Jima during World War II.

Two soldiers are discussing their plight. One asks, "What's war?" The other replies, "Trading real estate for men."

Oversimplification? Yes. True? You bet. If the film said nothing else for its 110 minutes, it would be worthy of a place in movie history for having the fortitude to sum up the senselessness of war. But the line is buried in the midst of all the action and blood-and-guts that brings in audience dollars; moviegoers are not likely to line up for a "preachy" war movie, although most fans don't have any objection to some serious statements being made on the subject of war, as long as there's plenty of action. *The Hollywood Reporter* reviewer was quick to point out that there was something more happening here for those who cared (and many certainly did): "It is obvious that the picture industry is not shirking its responsibilities. To meet the public half way it is necessary to camouflage documentation and social content as entertainment. 'Sands of Iwo Jima' accomplishes this to near perfection."

The Sands of Iwo Jima has long been acknowledged as one of the best war movies ever made. *Variety* noted: "'Sands of Iwo Jima' is a real war story. There is no half way about it. The picture uses footage actually shot during combat and weaves it, with tremendous effect, into a gripping, dramatic and tragic story." And *TV Guide* calls the picture, "the granddaddy of all those basic-training-to-battlefield war stories." Director Allan Dwan superbly blended his staged battle scenes with actual war footage, and the picture benefited enormously from the acting of John Wayne, who at 42 was voted America's number-one box office star for the year, the fourth year in a row he had made the top 10. The star's popularity contributed to the box office success, making Republic's costliest production ever also its most profitable.

Others in the cast in minor roles were Martin Milner as Pvt. Mike McHugh and Richard Webb as Pfc. Shipley. Milner, whose part in *Sands* consisted of only two lines, later co-starred in TV's "Route 66" and "Adam 12." Webb went on to TV fame as the star of "Captain Midnight."

The highlight of the movie is the flag-raising over Iwo Jima. Most of the audience was familiar with the famous photo of six Marines placing the American flag atop the newly secured Mount Suribachi. Actually, this famous picture was done as a "photo opportunity" re-staged for the camera, since a first, smaller flag had been raised in the same spot earlier in the day on February 23, 1945. Joe Rosenthal captured the second, more dramatic moment on film and received a Pulitzer Prize for the picture. Of the six Marines who participated in the second flag-raising, only three survived to leave the island after further skirmishes with the Japanese.

Screenplay by Harry Brown and James Edward Grant

Based on a story by Harry Brown

Produced by Edmund Grainger

Directed by Allan Dwan

CAST

Sergeant Stryker . . . . .John Wayne
Pfc. Conway . . . . .John Agar
Allison Bromley . . . . . .Adele Mara
Corporal Thomas . . . . .Forrest Tucker
Pfc. Ragazzi . . . . .Wally Cassell

ACADEMY AWARD NOMINATIONS

4 nominations, no wins

Best Actor (John Wayne)
Best Writing, Story
Best Sound Recording
Best Film Editing

I WAS A MALE WAR BRIDE

20TH CENTURY-FOX
$4,100,000

THE TITLE says it all. The 'I' in this case was a Frenchman named Henri Rochard, who wrote the original first-person story. However, most moviegoers tend to forget the name of the character and instead remember the film's final (and best) moments when Cary Grant, as the hapless Rochard, dons his gay apparel in order to slip aboard a ship full of war brides. It seems the sexist War Department forgot to provide for male spouses of female military personnel married overseas, and in this case, a picture is worth a thousand words (see photo illustration).

Grant plays French Captain Rochard, who is assigned to track down a famous German lens grinder and persuade him to work for the French, rather than the German black-marketeers. His assistant is an American WAC lieutenant, played by Ann Sheridan, who has worked with him before and calls him a "human octopus with hands." Naturally, they fall in love and marry, making for the "war bride" problem.

Cary Grant and Ann Sheridan romped their way through a lot of interesting German locations (Bad Nauheim and Frankfurt) that showed the effects of Allied bombing. Grant, a former acrobat, did all his own stunts, one notably dangerous one involving climbing onto a guard rail that swings up in the air. By the time of this film, however, Grant was noted for his light, comedic roles, and although some found it difficult to accept an Englishman playing the part of the French captain, his action was praised by nearly all the critics. It is impossible to imagine anyone else playing the role.

The comedy film is frequently seen on various cable channels.

Screenplay by Charles Lederer, Leonard Spigelgass, and Hagar Wilde

From a story by Henri Rochard

Produced by Sol C. Siegel

Directed by Howard Hawks

CAST

Henri Rochard . . . . Cary Grant
Lt. Catherine Gates . . . Ann Sheridan
WACs . . . . Marion Marshall, Rudy Stuart
Capt. Jack Rumsey . . . William Neff

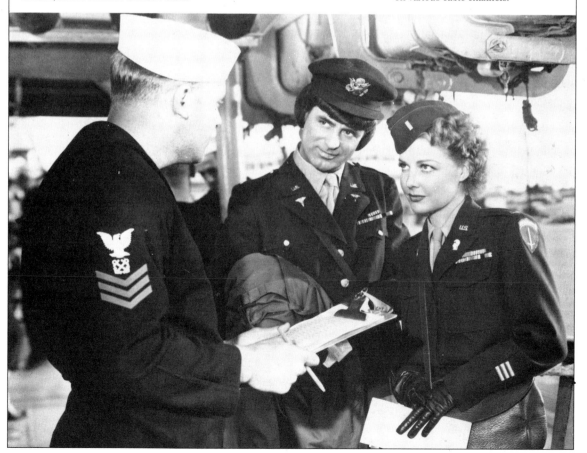

WITH THE advent of the Fifties came the demise of the motion picture theater as the sole bastion of on-screen entertainment. The reason could be summed up in one word: television. The medium was first publicly demonstrated at the New York World's Fair in 1939; by the end of World War II, there were still only 6,500 sets in existence, most of these in bars. By 1950, the number had climbed to 11,000,000.

All of a sudden, millions of moviegoers—*ticket buyers*—were staying home to watch Uncle Miltie in a dress. Attendance fell from 80,000,000 a week in

1950

1946 to only 60,000,000 in 1950, and kept dropping. Something had to be done.

Television was here to stay, and there was nothing the movie industry could do to change that. But the challenge had been presented, and the studios responded. In an attempt to woo audiences away from the hypnotic eye of the cathode-ray tube, studios produced more and more epics— biblical films, historical themes, musicals with lavish casts, and, in the words of *Silk Stockings* (1957), "glorious Technicolor, breathtaking CinemaScope and stereophonic sound."

It worked, and people began returning to theaters as box office figures surged ever higher.

1959

1

CINDERELLA

WALT DISNEY PRODUCTIONS
$41,087,000

ACCORDING TO *The Guinness Book of Movie Facts and Feats,* there have been 84 productions of *Cinderella,* ranging from an 1898 film from England called *Cinderella and the Fairy Godmother,* to everything from cartoons, live-action, ballets, operas, parodies, and even porn films. *Cinderella,* in fact, has been remade more times than any other story. There were two "Cinderella" films released the year Walt Disney brought his creation to the screen—the "also-ran" was a live-acted version from Estela Film in Spain. Walt had nothing to worry about. Thanks to numerous re-releases, the Disney classic went on to become the second-highest-grossing all-animated film ever made (*Bambi* being the first).

Cinderella was Disney's first attempt at traditional feature-length animation since *Bambi,* eight years earlier. A team of 750 animators and writers spent nearly six years adapting the story of the scullery maid who becomes the belle of the ball and marries Prince Charming. Disney chose to adapt Charles Perrault's 17th-century French fable, although variations of the Cinderella story have in fact been found in the folklore of the ancient Egyptians, Romans, and even American Indians.

The final days of World War II found Walt Disney Studios in a financial crunch. During the war, the Disney animators had devoted much of their energy to government training films, patriotic short subjects, and episodic animated packages like *Make Mine Music* and *Fun and Fancy Free.* Now Walt was anxious to make another full-length animated fairy tale. The task of creating a believable and sympathetic heroine was essential to the success of *Cinderella.* According to a studio press release, Walt told his animators, "I want to be hit right here in the heart. You have to pull for her and feel for her." Although publicly Walt Disney professed that *Bambi* was his all-time favorite, it was well known that he had a soft spot for *Cinderella,* occasionally referring to it as another favorite. The scene that he liked best was supposedly the one in which Cinderella gets her gown. In an interview with a Disney publicist, Marc Davis, one of Disney's trusty "nine old men," reported that Walt identified with Cinderella because he, too, came from very humble beginnings.

In traditional Disney fashion, the team made a number of changes, adding to and improving on the original story. Among these changes was the transformation of the Fairy Godmother from an old hag (as depicted in Perrault's original) to the grandmotherly character we see in the film. And the original's fur slipper had by now evolved into a glass model, so Disney chose to go along with this version.

But perhaps the best of these additions was a memorable musical score written by Mack David, Jerry Livingston, and Al Hoffman. The six songs composed by the trio were "So

Story by William Peet, Ted Sears, Erdman Penner, Winston Hibler, and Harry Reeves

Based on a fairy tale by Charles Perrault

Produced by Walt Disney

Directed by Wilfred Jackson, Hamilton Luske, and Clyde Geronimi

VOICES

Cinderella . . . . .Ilene Woods
Prince Charming . . . . .William Phipps
Stepmother . . . . .Eleanor Audley
Fairy Godmother . . . . .Verna Felton

ACADEMY AWARD NOMINATIONS

3 nominations, no wins

Best Sound Recording
Best Song ("Bibbidi-Bobbidi-Boo," music and words by Mack David, Al Hoffman, and Jerry Livingston)
Best Scoring of a Musical Picture

This Is Love," "A Dream Is a Wish Your Heart Makes," "Cinderella," "The Work Song," "Sing, Sweet Nightingale," and the one that earned them the Oscar nomination for Best Song—"Bibbidi-Bobbidi-Boo." The *Cinderella* record album released that year became the number-three top-selling soundtrack for 1950.

Many memorable Disney characters made their debut in this 1-hour 14-minute animated feature. The title character, with her blond hair and graceful movements, embodied the universal ideal of the "Cinderella" character created 300 years earlier by Perrault. Her "wicked" stepmother and jealously abusive stepsisters, Anastasia and Drizella, also evoked most people's childhood concepts from the original fable. The King is depicted as a well-meaning but anxious parent, while Prince Charming is

the incarnation of his name. Rounding out the human cast is an additional Disney creation, the Prince's faithful "foot-servant," the Grand Duke.

Among the featured animated animals are a crafty cat called Lucifer, a helpful dog named Bruno, and a group of resident mice with names like Jaq, Gus-Gus, Luke, Mert, Bert, Suzy, Perla, and Blossom. Their voices, part of the Academy Award–nominated sound recording, are played at high speed, so that they sound a lot like (but actually pre-date) "Alvin and the Chipmunks."

Radio star Ilene Woods provided the voice of Cinderella, while actress Eleanor Audley (who later did the voice of Maleficent in Disney's *Sleeping Beauty*) spoke the part of the Wicked Stepmother. Most notable, however, was the singing voice of Prince Charming—that of talk-show

host Mike Douglas (another actor did the speaking part).

To bring Cinderella to life, the animators were provided with a source of inspiration—a live model, 18-year-old actress Helen Stanley, who was photographed in various graceful poses. The animators studied blow-ups of her photos to achieve the right feeling in their drawings. This technique was so successful that Disney used it in *Sleeping Beauty* (again with Miss Stanley) and other animated features.

Cinderella had frequent theatrical re-releases, the last one taking place in 1987. In 1988, the Walt Disney Company finally brought *Cinderella* out on videocassette, where it soared to the top of the charts, remaining there for many weeks. Another release of the video in 1995 proved even more lucrative. At the Disney Company, at least, they all lived happily ever after.

2

KING SOLOMON'S MINES

METRO-GOLDWYN-MAYER
$5,586,000

HOLLYWOOD CONTINUED in its tradition of turning to other media for film inspiration, and in 1950, every one of the top five films was derived from another source.

H. Rider Haggard's *King Solomon's Mines* had been a very popular book ever since it was published in 1885. The first film version came in 1937, starring (Sir) Cedric Hardwicke. But Hollywood likes to top itself, and the 1950 spectacular produced by MGM had Technicolor cameras and crew, plus Deborah Kerr, Stewart Granger, and Richard Carlson, trekking 25,000 miles to Tanganyika (Tanzania), Uganda, Kenya, and Belgian Congo (Zaire) to get it all on film. The magnificent shots of Africa's wildlife—lions, giraffes, crocodiles, antelope—served as stock footage for many an MGM film to follow. Tragically, an elephant hunt was part of the script, and although this caused nary an eyebrow to be raised in those pre-conservation-conscious days, it is the one painful moment for today's viewers, aware of the plight of a species being poached to the brink of extinction.

Screenplay by Helen Deutsch

Based on the novel by H. Rider Haggard

Produced by Sam Zimbalist

Directed by Compton Bennett and Andrew Marton

CAST

Elizabeth Curtis . . . . . . Deborah Kerr
Allan Quatermain . . . . . Stewart Granger
John Goode . . . . Richard Carlson
Smith . . . . Hugo Haas
Eric Masters . . . . Lowell Gilmore

ACADEMY AWARD NOMINATIONS

3 nominations, 2 wins*

 Best Picture
*Best Cinematography, Color
*Best Film Editing

The film made good use of the local tribes, and the credits listed several Watusi natives. Then-president of Uganda Godfrey Binaisa was also given a bit part, and he would later appear in *The African Queen.*

Stewart Granger starred as the legendary Allan Quatermain. Like so many screen personalities, British-born Granger originally had a different name—James Stewart—which he changed to avoid confusion with the American actor by that name. In the '30s and '40s, Granger became a matinee idol in England. His early films included British pictures such as *So This is London* (1939), *Waterloo Road* (1945), and *Captain Boycott* (1947). In 1950, MGM signed him to a seven-year contract. *King Solomon's Mines* was the first of many adventure movies he made for the studio.

As in *Red River,* there is a stampede scene, shot with undercranked cameras to make the animals seem to run faster. To the *Variety* reviewer, it was the highlight: "The standout sequence is the animal stampede, minutes long, that roars across the screen to the terrifying noise of panic-driven hoofbeats."

In 1985 there was yet another remake, starring Richard Chamberlain and John Rhys-Davies, in an attempt to capture the *Indiana Jones* crowd. It wasn't nearly as successful.

ANNIE GET YOUR GUN

METRO-GOLDWYN-MAYER

$4,919,394

METRO'S FIRST ATTEMPT at bringing a popular stage musical to the screen proved highly successful— *Annie Get Your Gun* was the studio's first big musical hit since 1945's *Anchors Aweigh.* Although it was Ethel Merman who first belted out Irving Berlin's hit theme from this play— "There's No Business Like Show Business"—her screen replacement, Betty Hutton, did a credible job and won the approving nod of the critics. *The Hollywood Reporter* lauded her performance: "For Betty Hutton, charged with the difficult and challenging job of playing one of the greatest parts ever handed a popular singer and chanting a score without peer, the role of 'Annie' is the opportunity of a lifetime. How she is ever going to top it is a problem she will have to take up with her agent and advisors. For us and for the public, her performance ranks as an all-time great in motion picture annals."

The songs were the real stars of the show—great Irving Berlin showstoppers all. In addition to "There's No Business Like Show Business" (sung by Betty three times, in three different costumes), there was "The Girl That I Marry," "You Can't Get a Man with a Gun," and "They Say It's Wonderful."

The screenplay was written by Sidney Sheldon, later better known as a popular novelist. Sheldon's career dates back to the early '40s, when he began as a $24-a-week reader for Universal Studios. In 1947 he won an Oscar for his original screenplay of *The Bachelor and the Bobby Soxer* (see page 68). His best-selling novels of the '70s included *The Other Side of Midnight* and *Bloodline,* both of which were made into films.

Although portrayed as a tomboy in the movie, the real Annie Oakley was a quiet homebody who enjoyed doing needlepoint. Born in Darke County, Ohio, she learned to shoot at age eight in order to provide for her family. As in the movie, at 15 she defeated Frank Butler in a sharpshooting contest, and by age 16 she had married him. She joined Buffalo Bill's Wild West Show and, with her husband as her manager, toured with that company for 16 years. Standing only five feet tall, she was dubbed "Little Sure Shot" by Chief Sitting Bull, also in Buffalo Bill's show, and she proved her talent by shooting a dime out of Butler's hand and a cigarette out of the mouth of German Crown Prince Wilhelm. During World War I, she gave shooting exhibitions and instruction to American soldiers.

Her life was much happier than that of the woman who played her on screen. *The Hollywood Reporter* was right—the part was a tough act for Betty Hutton to follow. Hutton had one other success, starring in *The Greatest Show on Earth* (see page 100), but she walked out of a Paramount contract in 1952 over a dispute in which she demanded that her husband be assigned to direct her films. Only one minor film offer followed, and in 1967, having made and lost $10,000,000, she filed for bankruptcy. She married and divorced five times, and eventually ended up as a cook in a Rhode Island Catholic rectory.

Screenplay by Sidney Sheldon

From the play by Herbert Fields and Dorothy Fields

Music and lyrics by Irving Berlin

Produced by Arthur Freed

Directed by George Sidney

CAST

Annie Oakley	Betty Hutton
Frank Butler	Howard Keel
Buffalo Bill	Louis Calhern
Sitting Bull	J. Carrol Naish
Pawnee Bill	Edward Arnold

ACADEMY AWARD NOMINATIONS

4 nominations, 1 win*

Best Cinematography, Color
Best Art Direction–Set Decoration, Color
*Best Scoring of a Musical Picture
Best Film Editing

4

CHEAPER BY THE DOZEN

20TH CENTURY-FOX
$4,425,000

BASED ON THE best-selling novel by Frank B. Gilbreth, Jr., and his sister Ernestine Gilbreth Carey, *Cheaper by the Dozen* is the story of their father, Frank Sr., a motion-study expert trying to run his household brood of 12 children as efficiently as one would run a factory. Set in the 1920s, it is plotless and episodic, in some ways reminiscent of *Life with Father,* and the hilarious results were just what was needed to convince families that "Movies are better than ever" (quoth 20th Century-Fox). They turned their television sets off and made this charming film a box office hit.

The movie stars Clifton Webb as the proud and persistent Frank Gilbreth, and audiences of the time were familiar with him for his creation of the character of "Mr. Belvedere," which had already made him immensely popular. His first appearance as the pompous babysitter had been only two years earlier, and he became subsequently typecast, appearing in several more "Belvedere" films. (Years later, "Mr. Belvedere" became a popular TV

series starring Christopher Hewett.)

Jeanne Crain stars as the oldest sister, and she is given much more to do than in *Leave Her to Heaven,* where she served basically as "set dressing."

Reviews were mixed, with most critics picking up on the lack of real plot while generally praising the film's cast. *The Hollywood Reporter* described the picture as "glib, provocative entertainment." Of Clifton Webb, the trade paper remarked: " 'Cheaper by the

---

Screenplay by Lamar Trotti

Based on the novel by Frank B. Gilbreth, Jr., and Ernestine Gilbreth Carey

Produced by Lamar Trotti

Directed by Walter Lang

CAST

Frank Bunker Gilbreth	. . .Clifton Webb
Ann Gilbreth	. . . . .Jeanne Crain
Mrs. Lillian Gilbreth	. . . .Myrna Loy
Libby Lancaster	. . . . . . .Betty Lynn
Dr. Burto	. . . . .Edgar Buchanan

Dozen' will go a long way toward implementing the strong hold he already maintains on the affection of the public." But *Time* magazine disagreed, calling the film a "string of mild, rambling anecdotes" and claiming that Clifton Webb was miscast as head of the Gilbreth household: "It is not much more fun than leafing through somebody else's family album…the result is seldom comic and never moving."

The main reason for this negativity seems to be that critics were too familiar with "Mr. Belvedere," unable to separate the performance of Webb as Gilbreth from his more familiar characterization of Belvedere. Today's audiences, however, free from that stereotyping, can enjoy this film and Webb's portrayal in the spirit it was intended.

A 1952 sequel, *Belles on Their Toes,* had Myrna Loy returning as Mrs. Gilbreth, along with Jeanne Crain as her now mature daughter. As usual, the sequel couldn't match the success of the original.

COLUMBIA
$4,115,000

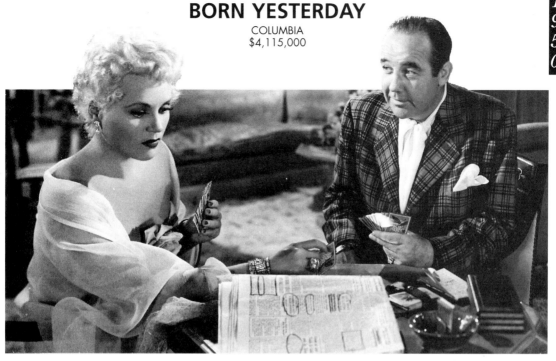

S HE HAD an IQ of 172, yet her most famous movie role would forever lock Judy Holliday in the public's mind as the quintessential dumb blonde. Yet even though *Born Yesterday* was her breakthrough role, Holliday nearly didn't get to play the part of the character she had played on Broadway for 1,642 performances.

Columbia Pictures head Harry Cohn thought Holliday was too unknown and too fat for the motion picture to be a success. But Garson Kanin, author of the Broadway version, had a plan to see his protégée ensconced as the film's star. While he was co-scripting the movie *Adam's Rib* (with his wife, Ruth Gordon, as collaborator), he created a blonde floozy character just for Judy Holliday in that film. She received rave reviews, and Cohn relented. The rest is history.

In *Born Yesterday,* Holliday plays the airhead mistress of a hot-shot junk dealer, one of the most abusive male roles ever to grace the screen, played to the hilt by tough guy Broderick Crawford. He hires William Holden to teach her some cultural refinement in the best Shavian tradition. Holden, of course, soon discovers a diamond in the hands of this roughneck, and he takes his mentoring seriously, chiding her for her lack of self-confidence

while stating the movie's theme:

"Nobody's born smart, Billie. You know what the stupidest thing on earth is? An infant!…I've got nothing against a brain that's three weeks old and empty. But after it hangs around for 30 years and hasn't absorbed anything, I begin to wonder about it. I want everyone to be as smart as they can be—a world full of ignorant people is too dangerous to live in."

In the end, she's grown considerably, all the while fulfilling boss Cohn's expectations—and more. For her convincing portrayal of Billie Dawn, Ms. Holliday was presented with the Best Actress Oscar by her peers at the Academy. Her career was tragically short-lived, however. She made a only a handful of films, including *The Solid Gold Cadillac* (1956), and one more memorable Broadway appearance, in the successful musical *Bells Are Ringing,* for which she received the Tony Award. Her final film was the screen version of that musical, released in 1960. Her health declined after that, and in 1965, she died of cancer at the age of only 42.

In 1993, a remake of *Born Yesterday* attempted to recapture some of the original's magic, but it wasn't there, as

evidenced by paltry box office receipts. The updated version starred Melanie Griffith as the dumb blonde, a role she'd made a virtual career out of, with John Goodman as the lout and Griffith's husband, Don Johnson, as the mentor. Oddly, there was little chemistry between then-real-life husband and wife Griffith and Johnson (often bafflingly true of married teams on-screen).

Screenplay by Albert Mannheimer

Based on the play by Garson Kanin

Produced by S. Sylvan Simon

Directed by George Cukor

CAST

Billie Dawn . . . . .Judy Holliday
Harry Brock . . . . .Broderick Crawford
Paul Verrall . . . . .William Holden
Jim Devery . . . . .Howard St. John
Eddie . . . . .Frank Otto

ACADEMY AWARD NOMINATIONS

5 nominations, 1 win*

Best Picture
*Best Actress (Judy Holliday)
Best Director (George Cukor)
Best Screenplay (Albert Mannheimer)
Best Costume Design, Black and White

QUO VADIS?

METRO-GOLDWYN-MAYER

$11,901,662

"Quo Vadis...whither goest thou?" Or, as modern English would have it, "Where are you going?" The answer for MGM was simple—straight to the bank. Even at a reported cost of $7,000,000, making it the most expensive film to date, the studio still came away with a huge profit. Metro had managed to place three of its releases in the top five in 1950, and they equaled that record in 1951—a feat they have not duplicated since.

Quo Vadis? was a Biblical epic set in Rome during Nero's reign. Everything about it was lavish—the sets, the costumes, the score—and it lured people out of their living rooms and away from their TVs in droves, the crowd scenes at the box office rivaling those on the screen. They came to see Peter Ustinov as Nero fiddle while Rome burned. They came to see 30,000 extras on 55 sets wearing a record 32,000 costumes. They came to watch starving lions chow down on hapless Christians. They came to be dazzled, and they were.

Peter Ustinov was perfectly cast as the sybaritic, egomaniacal Nero, a villainous, somewhat Hitleresque caricature whom audiences, with the horrors of the Second World War still vivid in their minds, could boo and hiss with unrestrained glee. *Variety* accused the actor of "scenery-chewing" and *The New York Times* claimed that "Peter Ustinov plays [Nero] in a manner to elevate Charles Laughton as a master of restraint in the role...[his] mouthing and screaming...become the most monotonous and vexing things in the film." Yet in retrospect, Ustinov's performance in *Quo Vadis?* is now seen as the quintessential Nero.

The London-born actor has made a living at unusual characterizations. Born in 1921 to a journalist-father of Russian descent and an artist-mother of French descent, Ustinov trained for the London stage. He made his acting debut at the age of 17, and later perfected his craft on stage and on the British and American screens. He won Academy Awards for *Spartacus* (1960) and *Topkapi* (1964). In 1961, the multitalented Ustinov wrote, produced, directed, and starred in *Romanoff and Juliet,* and in 1962 he produced, direct-

ed, co-scripted, and starred as Captain Edward Fairfax Vere in *Billy Budd.* His other films include *Blackbeard's Ghost* (as Captain Blackbeard, 1968), *Hammersmith Is Out* (also directed; 1972), *Logan's Run* (1976), and *The Thief of Baghdad* (1979). Ustinov continued working in film and television, appearing in *Lorenzo's Oil* in 1992, and recently writing and narrating a documentary entitled *Peter Ustinov's Russia.*

One of the minor parts in *Quo Vadis?,* that of Ursus the Slave, was played by an ex-pugilist named Buddy Baer. (Not unintentionally, his character's name, "Ursus," means "bear" in Latin.) He was the brother of famed prizefighter Max Baer, the former heavyweight champion of the world (1934), who also appeared in films. His nephew, Max Baer, Jr., appeared in the television series "The Beverly Hillbillies." Buddy also played a giant in *Jack and the Beanstalk* (1952).

In making this epic, MGM turned again to the classics, this time the novel by Henryk Sienkiewicz, which had served as the basis for two earlier

---

Screenplay by John Lee Mahin, S. N. Behrman, and Sonya Levien

Based on the novel by Henryk Sienkiewicz

Produced by Sam Zimbalist

Directed by Mervyn LeRoy

CAST

Marcus Vinicius	Robert Taylor
Lygia	Deborah Kerr
Petronius	Leo Genn
Nero	Peter Ustinov
Poppaea	Patricia Laffan

ACADEMY AWARD NOMINATIONS

8 nominations, no wins

Best Picture
Best Supporting Actor (Leo Genn)
Best Supporting Actor (Peter Ustinov)
Best Cinematography, Color
Best Art Direction–Set Decoration, Color
Best Scoring of a Dramatic or Comedy Picture
Best Film Editing
Best Costume Design, Color

---

productions of *Quo Vadis?,* one in 1912 and again in 1924.

Filming the spectacular took six months, although it was in the pre-production stages for nearly three years. The entire facilities of Rome's Cinecitta studios were given over to the production. In addition to hiring the thousands of extras (one of whom was an unknown 15-year-old named Sophia Loren), director Mervyn LeRoy scouted all over Europe for the lions required, finally securing the necessary 63 cats from circuses. To simulate realism, LeRoy resorted to stuffing empty clothing with meat, making it appear that the lions were eating actual people. Closeups were handled with fake lions attacking the extras.

For the burning of Rome sequence (yes, Nero fiddled), a miniature city was constructed, although it could hardly be called that. It consisted of several hundred scaled-down buildings on two acres of ground.

Critics roared with approval. *The Hollywood Reporter* used a banner headline to announce:

MGM's Quo Vadis Colossal industry's greatest spectacle superb drama and excellent entertainment—should run biggest grosses everywhere

The paper's reviewer noted that the press screening "left most of those in attendance limp in their astonished enthusiasm," and described the film as "the real gigantic king of all pictures, the most expensive, the largest cast, the most tremendous display of scenic, wardrobe and color investiture ever known in our business."

Not even *Gone With the Wind* had left people gasping that hard. In fact, MGM tried very hard to promote *QV* as the greatest thing since *GWTW,* taking out a three-page trade ad telling exhibitors, "The quickest way to understand *Quo Vadis'* business is to compare it with *Gone With the Wind."* *The Hollywood Reporter* continued the comparison, stating, "If *Quo Vadis* wins the best picture Oscar, it'll be the second Technicolor item to do so, first being *GWTW."*

Strangely, it won nary a one.

ALICE IN WONDERLAND

WALT DISNEY PRODUCTIONS
$7,196,000

LEWIS CARROLL'S book *Alice in Wonderland* was a project that had interested Walt Disney since 1933, when he considered a possible live-action film with Mary Pickford. Walt had always been fond of the Carroll story; back in the '20s, when he was beginning to experiment with animation, he had created a marriage of cartoon and live action in his *Alice in Cartoonland* series of shorts, with a live little girl playing in a cartoon world. In 1937, he produced a Carroll-inspired short called *Thru the Mirror,* with Mickey Mouse. Walt also thought about starring Ginger Rogers as a live Alice in a cartoon Wonderland, but he eventually dropped the idea of a live-action character, feeling the results would be disappointing.

Production finally began on an all-animated feature in 1946, and it took nearly five years and $3,000,000 to bring it to the screen. The results were disappointing both financially (it initially lost $1,000,000) and critically, and Walt found himself making apologies for it.

Much of the criticism was directed at the lack of respect for the "classics," since the Disney team had taken the liberty of reshuffling the story, adding bits and pieces from *Through the Looking Glass,* as Alice strolled "through her dream world to the accompaniment of ballads and musical nonsense" (*Variety*).

Musical nonsense? Among the songs that went unheralded at the time were tunes that have become classics today. Most notable is the White Rabbit intoning "I'm Late" and the wonderful Mad Tea Party number, "The Unbirthday Song." Even *Variety*

couldn't deny the loveliness of "All in the Golden Afternoon," with its singing flowers, terming the number a "standout." Other songs included "Very Good Advice," "In a World of My Own," "The Walrus and the Carpenter," "The Caucus Race," "March of the Cards," and "Painting the Roses Red," all by Bob Hilliard and Sammy Fain. Still others were contributed by the teams of Mack David, Al Hoffman, and Jerry Livingston, and Oliver Wallace and Ted Sears.

In this hybrid of *Through the Looking Glass* and *Alice in Wonderland,* Alice follows the white rabbit and falls down the rabbit hole, where she has adventures in a surrealistic setting, encountering Tweedledee and Tweedledum; the dope-smoking caterpillar whose words form letters in the air; the smile, tail, and occasionally all of the Cheshire Cat; the Mad Hatter and March Hare; and, of course, the King and Queen of Hearts ("Off with her head!").

The voices of the characters were a clever piece of casting; most memorable were Sterling Holloway as the "Cheshire Cat," Ed Wynn as "The Mad Hatter," and Jerry Colonna as "The March Hare."

Though not nearly as successful as other Disney animated features, *Alice* eventually made back its money, and more. Certainly nothing for Walt Disney to apologize for.

From a story by Lewis Carroll

Produced by Walt Disney

Directed by Clyde Geronimi, Hamilton Luske, and Wilfred Jackson

VOICES

Alice . . . . .Kathryn Beaumont
Mad Hatter . . . . .Ed Wynn
Caterpillar . . . . .Richard Haydn
Cheshire Cat . . . . . . .Sterling Holloway
March Hare . . . . .Jerry Colonna

ACADEMY AWARD NOMINATIONS

1 nomination, no wins

Best Scoring of a Musical Picture

SHOW BOAT

METRO-GOLDWYN-MAYER
$5,533,000

"Ol' Man River he just keeps rollin' along."

WHEN JEROME KERN first approached novelist Edna Ferber back in 1926 with the idea of adapting her novel *Show Boat* into a musical, she thought he was insane. She could hardly envision her story of a Mississippi River showboat of the late 19th century as a stage show, yet it proved to be one of the most successful ones ever. Produced by impresario Florenz Ziegfeld, *Show Boat* ran two years on Broadway, then toured the world for several more.

What convinced Miss Ferber? Jerome Kern played "Ol' Man River" for her (lyrics by Oscar Hammerstein II). She is quoted in *The New Complete Book of the American Musical Theatre* as saying: "My hair stood on end, the tears came to my eyes, and I breathed like a heroine in a melodrama. This was great music. This was music that would

Screenplay by John Lee Mahin

Based on the musical play by Jerome Kern and Oscar Hammerstein II

From the novel by Edna Ferber

Produced by Arthur Freed

Directed by George Sidney

CAST

Magnolia Hawks	Kathryn Grayson
Julie Laverne	Ava Gardner
Gaylord Ravenal	Howard Keel
Capt. Andy Hawks	Joe E. Brown
Ellie May Shipley	Marge Champion

ACADEMY AWARD NOMINATIONS

2 nominations, no wins

Best Cinematography, Color
Best Scoring of a Musical Picture

outlast Jerome Kern's day and mine." She was correct. Kern's immortal hymn to the Mississippi is so remarkably close to a true Negro spiritual that many feel it must be an American folk song.

The tune must be considered the highlight of the MGM movie version, too—in fact, all the Kern/Hammerstein songs made the soundtrack album the number-one seller for 1951. Also contributing to the film's success was Howard Keel (of *Annie Get Your Gun* fame), Kathryn Grayson, and Ava Gardner, who did her own singing for "Bill," although her voice was dubbed for the torch-song "Can't Help Lovin' Dat Man." Dancing by Marge and Gower Champion added to the appeal.

The show's popularity is still evident today, with frequent revivals by touring companies, dinner theaters, and a recent successful return to Broadway. If you can't catch a live performance of this "classic," the film is just the ticket.

A STREETCAR NAMED DESIRE

WARNER BROS.
$4,800,000

"I've always depended upon the kindness of strangers."
—BLANCHE DU BOIS

WHEN THE STAGE version of *A Streetcar Named Desire* held its pre-Broadway tryouts in New Haven and Philadelphia, the reviews were lukewarm. No one was quite sure what to make of this Tennessee Williams drama, rife with domestic violence, steamy sex, rape, and references to homosexuality. Women were embarrassed to admit they were turned on by the young lead, a relative newcomer named Marlon Brando, whose glistening biceps and torn shirts brought them to theaters in droves, despite the critics' less than enthusiastic welcome. With Jessica Tandy, Karl Malden, and Kim Hunter rounding out the cast, this play was soon a hit. *Streetcar,* as it was quickly nicknamed, rode off with a Pulitzer Prize and the New York Drama Critics Award.

The screen version seemed a natural. Elia Kazan was set to direct, but like all good Hollywood directors, he wanted to recast the film with different actors. John Garfield was his ideal Stanley Kowalski, the part Brando had created on the stage. When Garfield wasn't available, Burt Lancaster's name was submitted by well-meaning casting directors, but he was bound by contract to another studio, which refused to release him. Eventually, Brando, in his T-shirt and jeans, actually had to audition for the part he had originated and played for two years. Reluctantly, Kazan awarded him the role. His performance on the screen became the stuff of legends. Many thought he ought to have won the Oscar for his portrayal of the self-centered, brooding Kowalski. (He lost to Humphrey Bogart in *The African Queen.*)

The transition to the motion picture screen saw the rest of the cast remaining intact, with one exception. Jessica Tandy was thought to have little movie recognition, being familiar only to theater audiences, so her character of Blanche du Bois had to be recast. Vivien Leigh had created quite a sensation in the role of Blanche in London's West End, and she was signed to play the part in the film. Once again, her natural English accent was subjugated, and she acquired a southern drawl, as she had for her Oscar-winning performance as Scarlett O'Hara in *Gone With the Wind.* This time, she took on the role of an emotionally disturbed southern schoolteacher who comes to New Orleans to live with her sister, Stella (Hunter), and her low-life husband (Brando). Her performance caught the attention of the Motion Picture Academy, who rewarded her with her second Oscar. The film itself was nominated for an astounding 12 Academy Awards.

Leigh was suffering at the time with a chronic tuberculosis condition, which plagued her much of her life. It made shooting the picture tough on cast and crew alike, but Leigh insisted on continuing, falling exhausted into bed each night at 9:00. She would make only three more pictures in her career—*The Deep Blue Sea* (1955), *The Roman Spring of Mrs. Stone* (1961), and *Ship of Fools* (1965). She died two years later, in 1967, at the age of 53.

Screenplay by Tennessee Williams

Produced by Charles K. Feldman

Directed by Elia Kazan

CAST

Blanche du Bois . . . . . .Vivien Leigh
Stanley Kowalski . . . . .Marlon Brando
Stella Kowalski . . . . . .Kim Hunter
Mitch . . . . .Karl Malden

ACADEMY AWARD NOMINATIONS

12 nominations, 4 wins*

Best Picture
Best Actor (Marlon Brando)
*Best Actress (Vivien Leigh)
*Best Supporting Actor (Karl Malden)
*Best Supporting Actress (Kim Hunter)
Best Director (Elia Kazan)
Best Screenplay (Tennessee Williams)
Best Cinematography, Black and White
*Best Art Direction–Set Decoration, Black and White
Best Sound Recording
Best Scoring of a Dramatic or Comedy Picture
Best Costume Design, Black and White

DAVID AND BATHSHEBA

20TH CENTURY-FOX
$4,720,000

"Three thousand years ago, David and Bathsheba ruled over the united tribes of Israel. This story of King David's reign is based on one of the world's oldest historical narratives written by an anonymous chronicler in the Second Book of Samuel of the Old Testament." —PROLOGUE

INSPIRED BY the phenomenal success of Paramount's *Samson and Delilah,* Fox decided to jump on the Biblical bandwagon that would become so crowded during the '50s. The studio entered the race with Gregory Peck and Susan Hayward as *David and Bathsheba.* Since Biblical works were usually free of harsh censorship (you can't rewrite the word of God, after all), the film was full of lust, adultery, murder—all the good stuff. Moviegoers didn't object, and since *Quo Vadis?* would not be released for nearly three more months, there was little competition in that genre for the box office dollars.

The story of David and Bathsheba is drawn from the pages of the Old Testament, Second Book of Samuel, with

Peck as the shepherd/song composer/King of Israel, and Hayward as the notoriously beautiful and sexy Bathsheba. Problem: she's already married. Solution: send her hubby off to war, where, hopefully, he'll be killed (he is). The Hollywood ending is a bit more

---

Produced by Darryl F. Zanuck

Directed by Henry King

CAST

David . . . . .Gregory Peck
Bathsheba . . . . .Susan Hayward
The Prophet Nathan . . .Raymond Massey
Uriah the Hittite . . . . . .Kieron Moore
Michal . . . . .Jayne Meadows

ACADEMY AWARD NOMINATIONS

5 nominations, no wins

Best Story and Screenplay
Best Cinematography, Color
Best Art Direction–Set Decoration, Color
Best Scoring of a Dramatic or Comedy
  Picture
Best Costume Design, Color

---

upbeat than the original story; producers seemed more concerned about box office than total Biblical accuracy.

By the end of the year, Susan Hayward was voted the number-one female box office star, with Gregory Peck in the number-two spot (his fourth year in the top 10). Rounding out the excellent cast were Raymond Massey as the prophet Nathan, Francis X. Bushman as King Saul, and Jayne Meadows as Michal.

The critics adored *David and Bathsheba. The New York Times* called it "a reverential and sometimes majestic treatment of chronicles that have lived three millennia…in concerning itself with an ageless romance, 'David and Bathsheba' admirably achieves its goal." And *The Hollywood Reporter* predicted a "sure box office hit…a big, luxurious, spectacular production that should promote big ticket sales."

One point of interest is the depiction of the Ark of the Covenant. The design is virtually the same as in the 1981 hit film, *Raiders of the Lost Ark,* both having been drawn from the illustrations of medieval scholars.

THIS IS CINERAMA

CINERAMA RELEASING CORPORATION (CRC)
$15,400,000

"Ladies and gentlemen, this is CINERAMA!"

—LOWELL THOMAS

IT STARTS WITH a basic 35-millimeter screen. Lowell Thomas, famed world traveler, narrates a very long black-and-white documentary on the history of art, from early cave paintings through 19th-century attempts at motion pictures. We are given the impression that all that has gone before had but one goal to attain—the miraculous achievement Thomas has been leading up to for ten tedious minutes—Cinerama! With a smash cut to full color, the screen suddenly widens to three times its previous size as we enter a roller coaster, go up the ramp, then find ourselves hurtling at break-neck speed back down to a chorus of screams from the unseen patrons (we're in the front car) in the most memorable and famous point-of-view shot of all time.

Ask anyone what they know or remember about Cinerama and they will inevitably tell you, "The roller coaster ride." This sequence would be considered tame today by a generation raised on the great special effects of films like *Star Wars*, but seen as a museum piece, it is easy to understand why people were so enthralled.

To begin with, it was a big screen, a very big screen—certainly bigger than the tiny TVs in people's living rooms. It was not the first time wide-screen had been attempted, however. Back in 1896, an Englishman named Birt Acres shot a local regatta in 70-millimeter, but he soon abandoned the use of wide-gauge film as too costly. In 1929, *Fox Movietone Follies* became the first wide-screen 70-millimeter feature film shown in New York, but it was a curiosity, not ready for mass distribution.

Cinerama was developed by Frederick Waller of Huntington, New York. His original idea was to use 11 16-millimeter projectors to cover a vast area of screen. There were numerous technical problems at first, but eventually he was successful.

Through three separate 27-millimeter lenses—each of which roughly resembled the lens of a human eye—the Cinerama cameras took three pictures simultaneously on three separate rolls of film. Set at 48-degree angles to each other, each lens covered precisely one-third of the entire picture—the one on the right photographing the left third, the one on the left photographing the right third, and the one in the center shooting straight ahead. A single rotating shutter assured simultaneous exposures on each of the films, while single focus and diaphragm controls adjusted the settings on all three lenses at the same time. The footage was then shown in the theater by three projectors,

> Developed by Fred Waller
>
> Stereophonic sound concept by Hazard Reeves
>
> Produced by Merian C. Cooper and Robert L. Bendick
>
> Narrated by Lowell Thomas
>
> **ACADEMY AWARD NOMINATIONS**
>
> *1 nomination, no wins*
>
> Best Scoring of a Dramatic or Comedy Picture
>
> Producer Merian C. Cooper received an honorary statuette "for his many innovations and contributions to the art of motion pictures."
>
> Fred Waller was presented with a special Oscar "for designing and developing the multiple photographic and projection systems which culminated in Cinerama."

producing a wider-than-average image. These projectors, grounded in concrete, were locked together by motors that automatically kept the three images in perfect synchronization on the screen. Tiny comb-like bits of steel were fitted into each projector at the side of the film gate. Jiggling up and down along the edges of the film at high speed, they fuzzed the edges of the pictures to minimize the lines between them. Oversized reels that fed film to the Cinerama projectors held 7,500 feet (50 minutes' worth) of film. It was a cumbersome process at best, by today's standards, but the novelty was just what was needed to compete with television.

Audiences ate it up. Tickets were on a reservations-only basis, often sold out weeks in advance. *This Is Cinerama* ran more than two years in New York alone, and played in limited engagements around the country. Only 47 theaters in the world were able to show Cinerama, with its 97-foot-wide screen and special equipment. Had even more theaters been able to make the equipment conversion, the film undoubtedly would have made even more millions.

The medium was definitely the message. There was absolutely no story in *This Is Cinerama*. In addition to the roller coaster, the audience watched a ballet, a helicopter ride over Niagara Falls, and a church organ service (with a locked-off camera, making for one of the dullest segments ever put on film—audiences, however, were enchanted). A gondola ride in Venice, bagpipes in Scotland, the Vienna Boys Choir, and a bullfight in Spain, plus a ho-hum segment at Florida's Cypress Gardens, were all on the program. There were two excellent numbers. The first was a visit to La Scala Opera House in Italy, where a spectacular performance of *Aida* employed what seemed like half of Italy in the chorus. The second was the film's final segment, which featured a stirring flyover of the United States, including forests, wheat fields, the Golden Gate, and the Grand Canyon, all set to the music of the Mormon Tabernacle Choir.

This is the sort of film that will never be seen again by most people, since it is not suitable for release on videocassette. In 1988, there was a reissue of *This Is Cinerama* at Los Angeles' Cinerama Dome—a theater that claims to have never actually shown a film in Cinerama, and normally runs only modern blockbuster hits like *E. T.* and *Who Framed Roger Rabbit*. Most of the people in the audience were either film students or older couples, there to recapture some of the thrill they felt when Lowell Thomas first said those magic words.

Illustration from the *This Is Cinerama* program booklet shows how Fred Waller's three-camera, three-projector process works.

FIVE SPEAKERS BEHIND SCREEN

ROCKET

SOUND-CONTROL

PICTURE-CONTROL ENGINEER

AS BOATS LEAVE SCREEN, SOUND FADES AWAY THROUGH THIS SPEAKER

PROJECTOR

EXTRA SPEAKERS FOR OFF-SCREEN NOISES

PROJECTOR

PROJECTOR

MAGNETIC SOUND RECORDER

THREE SEPARATE FILMS

SOUND FROM SIX MICROPHONES RECORDED ON ONE TAPE

THREE LENSES

SIX MICROPHONES PICK UP SOUND AS BOATS MOVE

146-DEGREE ANGLE OF VIEW

THREE MAGAZINES

SHUTTER

CAMERA TAKES THREE PICTURES SIMULTANEOUSLY

THREE FILMS

PARAMOUNT
$14,000,000

1952

"This is the story of the biggest of the big tops and the men and women who fight to make it to The Greatest Show on Earth."
—OPENING NARRATION

CECIL B. DEMILLE was 70 when he directed his 69th film. He proved he was still the master of the spectacle when he took his camera crew on the road to follow the Ringling Bros. and Barnum & Bailey circus to its winter headquarters in Sarasota, Florida. The movie was the perfect vehicle for the untiring showman—as *Time* put it, "a mammoth merger of two masters of malarkey for the masses: P. T. Barnum and Cecil B. DeMille."

In some ways, *The Greatest Show on Earth* seemed almost like a documentary, with DeMille's own narration telling us of the 58,000 pounds of fireproof canvas used to make up the Big Top. Over 60 circus acts paraded through the scenario—elephants, aerialists, sword swallowers, clowns, dogs, seals, lions and tigers and bears, oh, my! The man didn't miss a trick.

Screenplay by Fredric M. Frank, Barre Lyndon, and Theodore St. John

From a story by Frank Cavett, Fredric M. Frank, and Theodore St. John

Produced and directed by Cecil B. DeMille

CAST

Holly	Betty Hutton
Sebastian	Cornel Wilde
Brad	Charlton Heston
Phyllis	Dorothy Lamour
"Buttons," a Clown	James Stewart

ACADEMY AWARD NOMINATIONS

5 nominations, 2 wins*

*Best Picture
Best Director (Cecil B. DeMille)
*Best Writing, Motion Picture Story
(Frank Cavett, Fredric M. Frank, and Theodore St. John)
Best Film Editing
Best Costume Design, Color

Cecil B. DeMille was honored with the Irving G. Thalberg Memorial Award.

Of course, there was an excellent cast, too, including Charlton Heston (here in only his second film) and Betty Hutton, doing an outstanding follow-up to her *Annie Get Your Gun* performance. The expert intercutting of her own closeups and her stunt double's performances on the trapeze are totally convincing.

And then there was Jimmy Stewart as Buttons, the doctor-turned-fugitive-clown whom we never see out of makeup. It was a dream come true for Stewart, who had always wanted to play such a part. In a recent television interview, he recalled a telegram he had sent DeMille. "I had never met Cecil B. DeMille…and I just said, 'Mr. DeMille, could you possibly find a place for me as a clown in your picture?' and two days later he wrote me back, and he said, 'You're in!' "

One of the most memorable sequences is the train wreck. To achieve the special effect, a derailment of miniature trains was filmed, then skillfully interwoven with footage of full-scale models of upended individual cars. The rest is pure DeMille.

Uncredited were cameo appearances by Bob Hope and Bing Crosby, who appear as spectators in the audience, contentedly munching popcorn.

An ABC television series of "The Greatest Show on Earth" appeared in September, 1963, and lasted for one year. It starred Jack Palance and Stu Erwin, and featured regular performers from Ringling Bros. circus.

THE SNOWS OF KILIMANJARO

20TH CENTURY-FOX
$6,500,000

"Kilimanjaro is a snow-covered mountain 19,710 feet high and is said to be the highest mountain in Africa. Close to the western summit there is a dry and frozen carcass of a leopard. No one has explained what the leopard was seeking at that altitude."
—OPENING NARRATION

THE ABOVE OPENING to the film version of Ernest Hemingway's short story "The Snows of Kilimanjaro" is also the riddle that the central character, Harry Street, must solve. The leopard comes to represent Harry's own drive as a writer, a quest that impels him to struggle toward seemingly unattainable heights. Never mind if you miss the symbolism. It's still an epic film (did Hollywood make anything else in the '50s?), reuniting Gregory Peck with Susan Hayward—*David and Bathsheba* together again. Also adding spice to the cast was Ava Gardner as Peck's first love.

Screenplay by Casey Robinson

Based on short story by Ernest Hemingway

Produced by Darryl F. Zanuck

Directed by Henry King

CAST

Harry . . . . .Gregory Peck
Helen . . . . .Susan Hayward
Cynthia . . . . .Ava Gardner
Countess Liz . . . . . . .Hildegarde Neff
Uncle Bill . . . . .Leo G. Carroll

ACADEMY AWARD NOMINATIONS

2 nominations, no wins

Best Cinematography, Color
Best Art Direction–Set Decoration, Color

Screenwriter Casey Robinson described the script to *Time* as "one-third Hemingway, one-third [Darryl F.] Zanuck, and one-third myself." And he didn't seem concerned that critics might attack him for changing the traditional Hollywood "happy ending" in which Peck's character gets to live rather than meet the death Hemingway chose for him. Most critics allowed him to get away with it, and audiences didn't protest either.

The African footage—which led *The New York Times* to dub *Snows* "an eye-filling film"—was shot by a second unit dispatched to the continent to film wildlife and panoramic scenery, while the live action was done in Hollywood and on location nearby. A technique called "rear projection" was used for the scene where Gregory Peck shoots a rhinoceros. The African unit filmed the charging rhino on location, with someone shooting the poor beast dead for the benefit of the camera. Back on the Fox soundstage, that footage was then projected on the screen behind Peck, who at the proper moment aimed his blank-loaded rifle at the screen and fired.

IVANHOE

METRO-GOLDWYN-MAYER
$6,258,000

"In the 12th Century, at the close of the Third Crusade to free the Holy Land, a Saxon knight called Wilfred of Ivanhoe undertook a private crusade of his own… [Richard the Lionhearted's] disappearance had dealt a cruel blow to his unhappy country already in turmoil from the bitter conflict between Saxon and Norman."
—OPENING NARRATION

ENTER IVANHOE, in the person of Robert Taylor, a handsome young actor whom audiences proclaimed the number-three box office star of the year (his fifth year on the list). And at his side was another (though unrelated) Taylor, Elizabeth, in her first big box office hit since *Father of the Bride.*

While this wasn't a Biblical epic, it felt like it. There were battles, great tournaments on colorfully draped horses; there were lavish costumes, great scenery, and lots of extras, this time played by Britons in their native land. Producer Pandro S. Berman was proud of the fact he had saved MGM $650,000 by shooting on location in England's MGM facility there, and

Screenplay by Noel Langley

Adaptation by Aeneas MacKenzie

Produced by Pandro S. Berman

Directed by Richard Thorpe

CAST

Ivanhoe . . . . .Robert Taylor
Rebecca . . . . .Elizabeth Taylor
Rowena . . . . .Joan Fontaine
De Bois-Guilbert . . . .George Sanders
Wamba . . . . .Emlyn Williams

ACADEMY AWARD NOMINATIONS

3 nominations, no wins

Best Picture
Best Cinematography, Color
Best Scoring of a Dramatic or Comedy
  Picture

since three of the stars were British born (Ms. Taylor, Joan Fontaine, and George Sanders all had British parentage), there was little problem with work permits for the cast.*

Second-unit direction was done by Yakima Canutt, who was noted for his work not only as a director but also as

an actor and stuntman. In *Gone With the Wind,* for example, he was the Yankee deserter shot in the face by Scarlett O'Hara. During his career as second-unit director, he filmed backgrounds and long shots for such other box office hits as *Ben-Hur* (1959), *Spartacus* (1960), *El Cid* (1961), and *How the West Was Won* (1962).

It is interesting to note that Elizabeth Taylor played a Jewish girl in this film, although she was not raised in that faith. Seven years after *Ivanhoe*'s release, she converted to Judaism. According to Ms. Taylor, in her book *Elizabeth Takes Off,* "It had absolutely nothing to do with my past marriage to Mike [Todd] or my upcoming marriage to Eddie Fisher, both of whom were Jewish. It was something I had wanted to do for a very long time."

In 1957, *Ivanhoe* became a British-produced television series starring Roger Moore, who later made "The Saint"-hood before being drafted into James Bond-age. The 30-minute program ran for a year in syndication.

---

*British labor laws insist that casting be done with British actors unless just cause can be shown for importing foreign talent.

HANS CHRISTIAN ANDERSEN

RKO
$6,000,000

"Kaye is Andersen."
—*THE HOLLYWOOD REPORTER*

AND LUCKY for RKO that he was, too. In taking Danny Kaye out of his customary comedian-entertainer roles and putting him into the part of the beloved Danish storyteller, producer Samuel Goldwyn and director Charles Vidor gave children around the world the best Christmas present ever. For it is Danny's interaction with the youngsters in this movie that gives the film its magic, as every child who has ever seen it can attest. Many years later, when Danny Kaye was working with UNICEF and needy children worldwide, it became apparent that he was truly gifted when it came to dealing with kids.

Kaye's rare talent permeates every inch of this picture. Whether he's singing one of the movie's many memorable songs to a group of children, or telling a Hans Christian Andersen story to them, it is Danny's movie all the way.

There are many charming songs. Among the most memorable are "No

Screenplay by Moss Hart

From a story by Myles Connolly

Words and music by Frank Loesser

Produced by Samuel Goldwyn

Directed by Charles Vidor

CAST

Hans Christian
   Andersen . . . . .Danny Kaye
Niels . . . . .Farley Granger
Doro . . . . .Renee Jeanmaire
Peter . . . . .Joey Walsh
Otto . . . . .Phillip Tonge

ACADEMY AWARD NOMINATIONS

6 nominations, no wins

Best Cinematography, Color
Best Art Direction–Set Decoration, Color
Best Sound Recording
Best Song ("Thumbelina," music and
   words by Frank Loesser)
Best Scoring of a Musical Picture
Best Costume Design, Color

Two People," "Anywhere I Wander," "Inch Worm," "Ugly Duckling," "Copenhagen," "Thumbelina," and, of course, the title song. The album became the number-two selling soundtrack of the year.

As popular as the film was in the United States, it was without honor in Andersen's homeland. The Danes condemned it even before it had opened there on the basis that most of the film about their beloved storyteller was also a fairy tale. But when it finally opened in Denmark eight months after its American debut, the critics lauded Danny Kaye, and Denmark's biggest newspaper avowed that "it contains both poetry and art." Danish Queen Ingrid herself attended opening night, and that ended any doubt—*Hans Christian Andersen* was at last welcomed home.

This movie should be mandatory viewing for every child, or anyone who's ever been a child. Be sure to watch for it around holiday time, when many television stations offer it as a special treat.

PETER PAN
WALT DISNEY PRODUCTIONS
$37,584,000

"You can fly, you can fly, you can fly!"

H E FLEW, he wore a feathered cap, and he refused to grow up. He touched the child in all of us, brought to us by none other than that perennial child himself, Walt Disney.

When *Peter Pan* first flew across movie screens in 1953 straight into the hearts of the audience, the Disney factory had again found gold. The plot centers on Peter Pan, The Boy Who Never Grew Up, who travels to Never Never Land with the Darling children and does battle with Captain Hook and his pirates. Many re-releases of the animated feature have since followed, including the most recent one in the summer of 1989, which found Peter Pan, Wendy, John, Michael, et al. earning their keep once again for Uncle Walt's company.

Yet Walt Disney himself was not particularly pleased with the film. He found Peter a rather cold character, one with whom he did not feel comfortable. Fortunately, several generations of children disagreed.

Back in 1939, Walt had optioned *Peter Pan* from the Hospital for Sick Children, in London, to whom Sir James M. Barrie had bequeathed ownership rights. (Until June, 1989, all for-profit productions of *Peter Pan* had to be cleared through this licensee.) When Disney took on the task of bringing the play to the screen, he tried to approximate what he felt Barrie himself might have done if animation had been at the playwright's command when his version opened in 1904. The original play directions and annotated scripts gave Disney many ideas during the three years it took to complete the $4,000,000 production.

During preparation, Walt had every one of his top animators, background painters, and character developers—over 100 artists—working on the project. More than 500,000 separate drawings were made, with more than 900 painted backgrounds, an all-time feature cartoon record to that date.

Traditionally, Peter Pan has always been played by a female. However, Walt chose Bobby Driscoll, veteran of a number of Disney films (*Song of the*

Margaret Kerry as a live model for Tinker Bell for the Disney animators.

South, So Dear to My Heart, and *Treasure Island*), to do the voice of Peter, breaking with that tradition, although the animated figure of the boy is basically androgynous.

The most drastic changes were in the character of Tinker Bell. On stage, Tink had always been portrayed as a beam of light. For his version, Disney chose to depict the pixie as a tiny humanoid with wings. If there is a scene-stealer in the movie, Tinker Bell is it. She flirts, she pouts, she even preens in front of a mirror, showing concern that she's gaining weight in the hips. When Wendy says she wants to give Peter a kiss, the little charmer literally flies into a tizzy. And at one point, Tinker Bell tries to find a way to seal Wendy's doom. Yet audiences loved this tiny vixen. Animator Marc Davis, one of the original "nine old men" who created many of the Disney animated classics, recalled to *Premiere* magazine: "I hear from a lot of people how crazy they were about that little character. She was kind of sexy, and I think there was an appeal in that." Quite possibly true, since the artist used a live 18-year-old model named Margaret Kerry to pose for sketches of Tinker Bell. Kerry had been a child actress as well, appearing under her given name of Peggy Lynch in four *Little Rascal* featurettes.

Although no voice was necessary for Tink, who never speaks, actors were required for the other parts. Noteworthy are Kathryn Beaumont as the voice of Wendy (she spoke for Alice in 1951's *Alice in Wonderland*),

From a play by J. M. Barrie

Produced by Walt Disney

Directed by Hamilton Luske, Clyde Geronimi, and Wilfred Jackson

VOICES

Peter Pan	Bobby Driscoll
Wendy	Kathryn Beaumont
Captain Hook and George Darling	Hans Conried
Mary Darling	Heather Angel
Smee	Bill Thompson

and actor Hans Conried, who read for Mr. Darling and Captain Hook.

Several teams of songwriters helped to create the music. Most famous were Sammy Cahn and Sammy Fain, who wrote "The Elegant Captain Hook," "What Makes the Red Man Red," "You Can Fly," and "Your Mother and Mine." Songs by other writers include "A Pirate's Life," "Tee Dum, Tee Dee," and the memorable "Never Smile at a Crocodile."

When Walt Disney opened his first theme park, Disneyland, in 1955, one of the rides in "Fantasyland" was a "Peter Pan" adventure. Originally it was conceived as an experience for the younger set, but today it is not unusual to find more adults than kids lined up for as long as 30 minutes to board a Pirate Ship and set sail over London with the words, "Come on everybody. Here we go-o-o-o!"

Roland Dupree and Kathy Beaumont model for Disney artists.

2

THE ROBE

20TH CENTURY-FOX
$17,500,000

"Rome. Master of the Earth, in the eighteenth year of the Emperor Tiberius, our legions stand guard on the boundaries of civilization …we have reached the point where there are more slaves in Rome than citizens…"
—OPENING NARRATION

L ONG AFTER the silly plot about a curse on Christ's crucifixion garment had been forgotten, *The Robe* took its place in cinematic history as the first movie in CinemaScope. With the gauntlet having been thrown down by the novelty of Cinerama, every studio in town rushed to achieve its own big-screen miracle in order to lure in the couch potatoes. Like Cinerama,

Screenplay by Philip Dunne

Adaptation by Gina Kaus

From the novel by Lloyd C. Douglas

Produced by Frank Ross

Directed by Henry Koster

CAST

Marcellus Gallio	Richard Burton
Diana	Jean Simmons
Demetrius	Victor Mature
Peter	Michael Rennie
Caligula	Jay Robinson

ACADEMY AWARD NOMINATIONS

5 nominations, 2 wins*

Best Picture
Best Actor (Richard Burton)
Best Cinematography, Color
*Best Art Direction–Set Decoration, Color
*Best Costume Design, Color

An Honorary Award (statuette) went to 20th Century-Fox "in recognition of their imagination, showmanship and foresight in introducing the revolutionary process known as CinemaScope."

A statuette also went to Professor Henri Chretien, Earl Sponable, Sol Halprin, Lorin Grignon, Herbert Bragg, and Carl Faulkner of 20th Century-Fox Studios "for creating, developing and engineering the equipment, processes and techniques known as CinemaScope."

CinemaScope offered a wider screen, 68 feet wide and 24 feet high, but simplified the process by requiring only a single camera and single projector. Virtually any exhibitor could utilize the system, which promised more dollars in their coffers.

With *The Robe,* 20th Century-Fox made good that promise. In the true tradition of the Biblical epic genre, the $5,000,000 production (the most expensive one of the year) had it all. Based on Lloyd Douglas's best-selling novel, there were lavish Technicolor sets and costumes, pomp and pageantry, gladiatorial contests, and a soaring musical score. The fact that handsome young actor Richard Burton played opposite beautiful young actress Jean Simmons didn't hurt, either. The film set a New York box office record, grossing close to $3,500,000 in the first 12 days.

The film's title refers to the crucifixion garment worn by Jesus. Richard Burton, as a Roman tribune assigned to carry out the crucifixion, wins Christ's robe in a game of dice. But for his "sin," he suffers from the delusion that he is cursed by the robe, deteriorating into mental agony, eventually

vindicating himself by conversion and defense of his new-found faith. Although most critics found the acting and storyline only mediocre, they were unanimous in their praise of Fox's new wide-screen process. *The Hollywood Reporter* went to a banner headline:

CINEMASCOPE, 'ROBE' TRIUMPH
PREMIERE CROWDS THRILLED
IN N.Y. BY FIRST FILM MADE
IN REVOLUTIONARY PROCESS

Publisher W. R. Wilkerson continued by saying that "CinemaScope arrived at the Roxy Theatre here last night with a bang that must certainly have been heard all over the amusement world. All the hopes and promises of 20th-Fox have been fulfilled with the presentation of 'The Robe' in a medium that holds promise of revolutionizing the making of films and their presentation throughout the world."

With success like this, Fox couldn't wait to try for more, and a year later released a sequel, *Demetrius and the Gladiators,* with Victor Mature recreating his role from *The Robe.* The sequel fell short of the mark, and the film only did about a third of the business of its predecessor.

"I never knew it could be like this."
—DEBORAH KERR TO
BURT LANCASTER

THE LINE WAS pure corn, but it was dialogue like this, along with the famous beach scene (SHE: "I've got a bathing suit under my dress." HE: "Me too.") that drew the fans to the theaters and gave Columbia a bona fide entry into the 1953 box office sweepstakes. The excellent production values made this film the most honored one in over a decade, taking top honors at the Oscars against contenders that included *The Robe, Shane, Julius Caesar,* and *Roman Holiday.* And in a year of wide-screen epics, *From Here to Eternity* was shown in basic 35-millimeter, and in black and white at that.

Adapted from the novel by James Jones, the story concerns the lives of several soldiers stationed in Honolulu just prior to the bombing of Pearl Harbor. Montgomery Clift plays a former boxer who once blinded a sparring partner and refuses to fight again, even if it means humiliation. There are several levels of storytelling here, with Clift's sergeant (Burt Lancaster) involved with the neglected wife (Deborah Kerr) of the base's captain (Philip Ober).

Aside from the good filmmaking, the picture is also remembered for the controversy surrounding its casting.

Screenplay by Daniel Taradash

Based on the novel by James Jones

Produced by Buddy Adler

Directed by Fred Zinnemann

CAST

Sgt. Milton Warden . . .Burt Lancaster
Robert E. Lee Prewitt . .Montgomery Clift
Karen Holmes . . . . . . .Deborah Kerr
Angelo Maggio . . . . . .Frank Sinatra
Alma (Lorene) . . . . . . .Donna Reed

ACADEMY AWARD NOMINATIONS

13 nominations, 8 wins*

*Best Picture
 Best Actor (Burt Lancaster)
 Best Actor (Montgomery Clift)
 Best Actress (Deborah Kerr)
*Best Supporting Actor (Frank Sinatra)
*Best Supporting Actress (Donna Reed)
*Best Director (Fred Zinnemann)
*Best Screenplay (Daniel Taradash)
*Best Cinematography, Black and White
*Best Sound Recording
 Best Scoring of a Dramatic or Comedy
 Picture
*Best Film Editing
 Best Costume Design, Black and White

This film won the most Academy Awards for any picture to date since *Gone With the Wind.*

Deborah Kerr won her role as the Captain's wife after Joan Crawford fought with the studio over her wardrobe. Columbia boss Harry Cohn wanted Robert Mitchum in the part eventually played by Lancaster. He had Aldo Ray in mind for "Robert E. Lee Prewitt," a part that went to Montgomery Clift. Eli Wallach was signed for the role of "Maggio" but subsequently withdrew in favor of Frank Sinatra, who had pressured Harry Cohn until the mogul relented.

Rumors abounded that it was Sinatra's ties to the Mafia that clinched the part for him, a point that became a scenario in another book and film, *The Godfather.* Sinatra, however, denied any outside pressure, and indeed had applied enough of his own. His singing career had been on hold due to some throat problems, and he was anxious to get back into the public eye. Leaving wife Ava Gardner on location in Africa, he flew to Hollywood and screen-tested for the part. When Wallach bowed out, Frank got the role. Although he received a reported salary of only $8,000, he was ecstatic.

In 1979, a six-hour "From Here to Eternity" television miniseries ran on NBC. A ratings success, it was tried as a weekly series on the network the following August but survived only a month.

HOUSE OF WAX

WARNER BROS.
$9,500,000

H**E WAS BORN** with the unlikely name of Sasvrai Farkasfawi Tothfalusi Toth Endre Antai Mihaly. Fortunately, by the time the Hungarian-born director arrived in the U.S. in 1942, he had shortened his name to André de Toth. He made a string of mostly crime dramas and Westerns, including *None Shall Escape* (1944), *Dark Waters* (1944), and *The Stranger Wore a Gun* (1953). That same year, Warner Bros. tapped him to direct what the studio hoped would be a monumental event in the history of motion pictures, akin to Jolson's *The Jazz Singer,* the first major talkie. De Toth was assigned to film the first commercially exploited 3-D picture, *House of Wax,* a remake of a 1933 Warner's film, *Mystery of the Wax Museum.*

There was one slight problem. The stereoscopic qualities of 3-D would be lost on the director. He had only one eye. But a man with seven unpronounceable names couldn't let a little thing like that stop him. As de Toth himself stated (as quoted in *A Pictorial History of Horror Movies*): "Beethoven couldn't hear music either, could he?"

Warner Bros. decided to throw everything but the proverbial kitchen sink at the bespectacled audience. Ladies cancanned their little can-cans at theater patrons; furniture and bric-a-

---

Screenplay by Crane Wilbur

From a story by Charles Belden

Produced by Bryan Foy

Directed by André de Toth

CAST

Prof. Henry Jarrod . . . . . Vincent Price
Lt. Tom Brennan . . . . Frank Lovejoy
Sue Allen . . . . Phyllis Kirk
Cathy Gray . . . . Carolyn Jones
Igor . . . . Charles
                    Buchinsky*

---

*A young actor who shortly thereafter changed his name to Charles Bronson.

---

brac flew at them, while wax figures in historical settings gave theater-goers the impression of actually being at Mme. Tussaud's real Wax Museum in London, the prototype for the film's museum. But the biggest three-dimensional crowd-pleasers were the paddle balls—rubber balls attached to wooden paddles (a big '50s craze)—which a barker hit toward the cringing audience. Unfortunately, all this 3-D is lost on today's home viewers renting the video, since the film was transferred "flat" to tape.

The picture was a huge success,

thanks not only to the 3-D gimmick and use of stereophonic sound (one of the first major pictures to use this relatively new technique), but to the other fine production values as well. The sets were colorful, the wax figures well made, and the acting by Vincent Price and the others as good as could be expected, given the film's corny plot about a disfigured sculptor (from a spectacular fire sequence early in the film) who murderously creates the dead bodies he needs to add realism to his wax figures.

Warner Bros. launched an all-stops-out campaign to promote the movie. A huge world premiere was held in New York City, with all of the cast plus other horror film stars in attendance. One luminary there was 70-year-old Bela Lugosi, whose "guest" was a live gorilla on a leash! To promote the film in the Los Angeles area, Vincent Price agreed to appear at a local wax museum in nearby Buena Park. He decided to play a joke, and posed as his own wax figure in a scene from the movie. "I was standing in a menacing pose with a hypodermic needle," he said (as quoted in the book *Vincent Price Unmasked*). "As the people came closer to look, I squirted water from the needle at them. It was great fun!"

"Shane! Come back!"

BRANDON DE WILDE'S plaintive call at the end of *Shane* goes unacknowledged, as our hero rides off into the sunset. But the audience heard the call, and returned to the box office again and again, giving Paramount not only a big hit but a film that has become a classic in the Western genre. It was a truly "adult" Western, a trend that was quickly copied by television when "Gunsmoke" hit the airwaves two years later.

Based on the novel by Jack Schaefer, this film had a lot going for it, not the least of which was the beautiful scenery of Wyoming's Grand Tetons National Park.

Blatantly obvious in its symbolism, *Shane* brings together the forces of good (blond-headed Alan Ladd) and evil (dark-complected, black-outfitted Jack Palance—billed as *Walter* Jack Palance) for the eternal showdown.

There's never a doubt that we are watching a morality play, with its lessons to be taught, among them: "A gun is a tool...no better, no worse than any other tool—an ax, a shovel, or anything. A gun is as good or as bad as the man using it."

Screenplay by A. B. Guthrie, Jr.

Based on the novel by Jack Schaefer

Additional dialogue by Jack Sher

Produced and directed by George Stevens

CAST

Shane	Alan Ladd
Mrs. Starrett	Jean Arthur
Mr. Starrett	Van Heflin
Joey Starrett	Brandon de Wilde
Wilson	Jack Palance

ACADEMY AWARD NOMINATIONS

6 nominations, 1 win*

Best Picture
Best Supporting Actor (Brandon de Wilde)
Best Supporting Actor (Jack Palance)
Best Director (George Stevens)
Best Writing, Screenplay
*Best Cinematography, Color

But don't get the impression that the movie is bogged down in preaching; it isn't. There's action, for instance, in what has to be the quintessential barroom brawl, a sequence that lasts a full eight minutes on screen. Fine performances were turned in by Ladd, Palance, Van Heflin as the boy's father, and Jean Arthur as Heflin's wife, who has an eye for the drifter Shane. But the old Hollywood adage about never working with children or dogs applies here (there's one of each), with Brandon de Wilde stealing many a scene. As *The New York Times* pointed out: "It is Master de Wilde with his bright face, his clear voice and his resolute boyish ways who steals the affections of the audience and clinches 'Shane' as a most unusual film."

De Wilde was born into a theatrical family and came to the Broadway stage at the age of nine in *The Member of the Wedding.* Following *Shane* and an Oscar nomination, he starred in his own TV series in the 1953–54 season ("Jamie"). He later appeared in films like *Blue Denim* and *Hud,* but met with a tragic end in 1972 in a car accident at the age of 29.

In 1966, ABC attempted a television series of *Shane.* It had a fine cast, including David Carradine and Jill Ireland, but lasted only three months.

WHITE CHRISTMAS

PARAMOUNT
$12,000,000

CHRISTMAS IN OCTOBER? It must have felt like it at Paramount Pictures when they released the movie *White Christmas* and the box office dollars began to chime like Yuletide bells.

How could they miss? Not only did the movie have stars Bing Crosby, Danny Kaye, Rosemary Clooney, and Vera-Ellen, but it had something even more wonderful.

VistaVision. Paramount's answer to Fox's CinemaScope, virtually indistinguishable from the other wide-screen format. And what better way to introduce this modern miracle of the movie house than to use proven material?

By now, Bing Crosby and the song "White Christmas" were synonymous —the holiday and the crooner were Siamese twins, joined at the warbling throat. The song harkens back to a 1942 musical, *Holiday Inn,* when Bing first sang "White Christmas." It won an Oscar for its composer, Irving Berlin, who presented it to himself onstage—the only person ever to do

Screenplay by Norman Krasna, Norman Panama, and Melvin Frank

Music and lyrics by Irving Berlin

Produced by Robert E. Dolan

Directed by Michael Curtiz

CAST

Bob Wallace . . . . .Bing Crosby
Phil Davis . . . . .Danny Kaye
Betty . . . . .Rosemary Clooney
Judy . . . . .Vera-Ellen
General Waverly . . . . .Dean Jagger

ACADEMY AWARD NOMINATIONS

1 nomination, no wins

Best Song ("Count Your Blessings Instead of Sheep," words and music by Irving Berlin)

Danny Kaye received an Honorary Award (statuette) "for his unique talents, his service to the Academy, the motion picture industry, and the American people."

that. Berlin was entitled: "White Christmas" went on to become the best-selling record of all time, with over 30,000,000 copies sold to date. Even so, the story is told of how Berlin paced the halls during the filming of *White Christmas,* nervous about how Bing would perform it this time, until Crosby told him to go back to his office and relax.

A couple of other memorable tunes rounded out the musical program. "Sisters" has become a classic since it was introduced in this picture. Best of all is the send-up treatment given to it by Crosby and Kaye in drag. Other musical numbers include "The Best Things Happen While You're Dancing," "Count Your Blessings," and reprises from earlier Berlin hits— "The Old Man" and "Mandy."

For the record, there was a plot, but it seemed incidental to the songs. Bing, Danny, Rosie, and Vera-Ellen depart warm, balmy Florida for a New England ski lodge at Christmas time, dreaming of all the snow they'll soon find. Unfortunately, there isn't any when they arrive at the inn—the ski tow is being used to dry the wash in the warm air. And wouldn't you know it, Bing and Danny's old army general is the unfortunate new owner of the inn, and because there's no snow, business is terrible. No problem for these song-and-dance men and women. Let's put on a show, round up the general's old division, and fill this puppy up to the rafters—surprise the old coot, watch him fight back the tears. Of course, it works, and of course, it snows flakes the size of tennis balls, just in time for the holidays.

Critics were definitely snowed by the production's music, Technicolor, and lavish choreographed routines coming at them in VistaVision. *The New York Times* wrote: "The colors on the big screen are rich and luminous, the images are clear and sharp...direc-tor Michael Curtiz has made his picture look good." *The Hollywood Reporter* immediately sized up the box office potential, offering these words of advice: "The exceptional theatre operator...will spare no effort to let all veterans of World War II know that this is their picture."

The film went over well with nearly everyone, not just veterans, and for the 12th year in a row, Bing Crosby was voted among the top 10 box office stars, this time perched squarely at the top. Not far behind was his co-star, Danny Kaye, at number three.

Kaye had a prolific film career both prior to and following his performance in *White Christmas.* Born David Daniel Kaminski in 1913 in Brooklyn, he was a garment center tailor's son who quit school at 13 to learn comedy as a busboy in upstate New York's "Borscht Belt." Vaudeville and nightclub work followed, and by 1939 he had landed a part in a Broadway review. In 1943, after Kaye had made a few two-reelers, Samuel Goldwyn signed him to appear in his comedies; soon a succession of films followed, including *Up in Arms* (1944), *Wonder Man* (1945), *The Secret Life of Walter Mitty* (1947), *The Inspector General* (1949), *Hans Christian Andersen* (1952; see page 103), and *Knock on Wood* (1953). Following *White Christmas,* Kaye made the popular films *The Court Jester* (1956) and *The Five Pennies* (1959). In the '60s, he had his own successful TV variety program, which won him both an Emmy and a Peabody Award. Work with UNICEF, more Broadway musical performances, and some hands-on experiences conducing the New York Philharmonic and other symphony orchestras rounded out his prolific career. He died in 1987 at the age of 74.

20,000 LEAGUES UNDER THE SEA

WALT DISNEY PRODUCTIONS
$11,267,000

"Got a whale of a tale to tell you…"

IT WAS ONLY fitting that Walt Disney be the one to bring Jules Verne's classic undersea tale, *20,000 Leagues Under the Sea,* to the screen. The two men had much in common, both being among the greatest visionaries of their times. Writing this adventure in 1869, Verne described the forerunner of the modern *nuclear* submarine, as well as predicting the aqualung. It wasn't until decades later that these things came to pass.

Verne's visions were never in better hands. For years, MGM had been toying with the idea of bringing this story to the screen, but it never got off the drawing boards. When Walt's idea

men suggested they produce an underwater adventure, he decided to purchase the property from Metro. The film was given the big-budget treatment, with $5,000,000 being spent in bringing Captain Nemo and the *Nautilus* to life. Much of the money went to secure a top cast, including James Mason as the farsighted but demented captain, along with Kirk Douglas, Peter Lorre, and Paul Lukas.

But most of the budgetary demands were for the sets and special effects. A 200-foot-long model of the submarine was built, and although much of the underwater footage was shot on location in the clear, fish-laden waters of Nassau, a great deal of photography had to be done under studio-controlled

conditions. To facilitate this, Disney built an entirely new soundstage at the Burbank studios, housing a 90-by-165-foot tank 12 feet deep.

Still more money was spent in filming the attack by a giant squid in the newly built tank. It cost $200,000 and took eight days to film the sequence, the costliest scene in the movie.

The investment paid off. *20,000 Leagues Under the Sea* did well at the box office, especially with the younger set, and the critics acclaimed it as well. *Variety* called the film "a very special kind of picture making, combining photographic ingenuity, imaginative story telling and fiscal daring…ultra high box-office around the world."

A prediction worthy of Verne himself.

Sketch for the original poster of Walt Disney's *20,000 Leagues Under the Sea.*

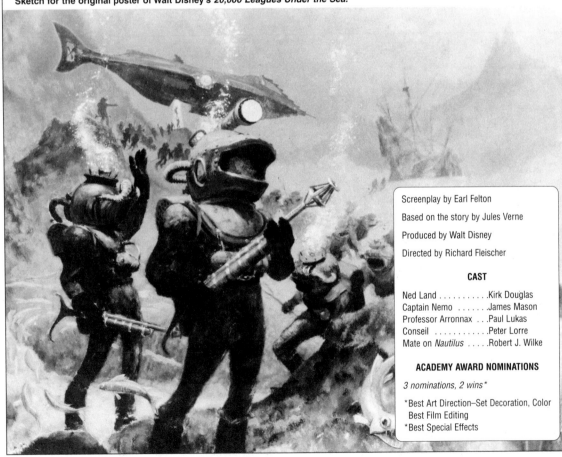

Screenplay by Earl Felton

Based on the story by Jules Verne

Produced by Walt Disney

Directed by Richard Fleischer

CAST

Ned Land . . . . .Kirk Douglas
Captain Nemo . . . . . .James Mason
Professor Arronnax . . .Paul Lukas
Conseil . . . . .Peter Lorre
Mate on *Nautilus* . . . .Robert J. Wilke

ACADEMY AWARD NOMINATIONS

3 nominations, 2 wins*

*Best Art Direction–Set Decoration, Color
 Best Film Editing
*Best Special Effects

REAR WINDOW

PARAMOUNT
$9,812,271

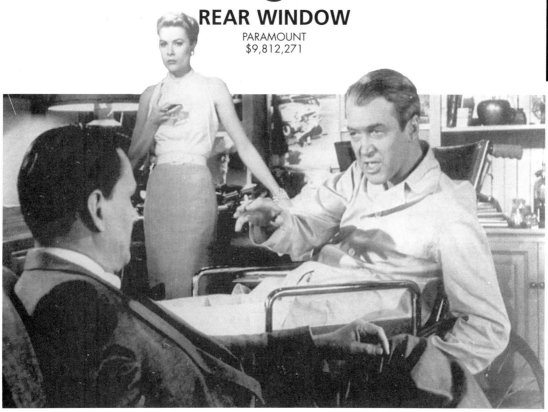

ALFRED HITCHCOCK'S *Rear Window* has become one of the most written about, studied, dissected, and analyzed films in cinematic history. It purports to be a simple story: a man (James Stewart) is confined to a wheelchair and uses the time to witness the everyday life in his Greenwich Village apartment courtyard. Chief among his observations: the murder of one of his neighbors.

The film can be viewed from almost as many angles as Stewart's courtyard. It is at once a comedy, a mystery, a psychological drama, a love story, social commentary—the list is long enough to have led to several in-depth studies of the classic film. But most of all, it is what it is supposed to be: *entertainment,* the kind only the "master of the macabre" could give us.

Hitchcock had a habit of reusing the same actors in his films. In addition to *Rear Window,* Jimmy Stewart appeared in Hitch's *The Rope* (1948), *The Man Who Knew Too Much* (1956), and *Vertigo* (1958); Stewart's co-star, Grace Kelly, was cast in two additional Hitchcock thrillers—*Dial M for Murder* (1954) and *To Catch a Thief* (1955).

Most critics never thought of Grace Kelly as an acting powerhouse, although she won the 1954 Oscar for *The Country Girl.* But Hitchcock was said to have used her for her "sexual elegance," along with her humor, warmth, and serenity. (A few years later, Prince Rainier of Monaco

Screenplay by John Michael Hayes

From a short story by Cornell Woolrich

Produced and directed by Alfred Hitchcock

CAST

Jeff . . . . .James Stewart
Lisa Fremont . . . . . . .Grace Kelly
Thomas J. Doyle . . . . .Wendell Corey
Stella . . . . .Thelma Ritter
Lars Thorwald . . . . . . .Raymond Burr

ACADEMY AWARD NOMINATIONS

4 nominations, no wins

Best Director (Alfred Hitchcock)
Best Screenplay
Best Cinematography, Color
Best Sound Recording

agreed—he married her and made her his Princess Grace in the oft-told Hollywood fairy-tale-come-true.)

Also noteworthy in the cast is Raymond Burr as the man who chops his wife up into cutlets. (Fortunately, this is never actually seen on screen.) Burr is familiar to television audiences for his portrayals of "Perry Mason" and "Ironside," but in 1954, he was virtually unknown to the public. He had appeared in a few films as the "heavy," but his name was not a household word. Only 37 years old when he was cast as the murderer in *Rear Window,* he was too young-appearing for the part as it was written, so Hitchcock had his hair died gray.

Rear Window sat on the shelf for 30 years after its initial release, finally reappearing on the big screen in 1984 and eventually on videocassette. When it was re-released, it opened a legal can of worms. In 1990, the U.S. Supreme Court ruled 6-3 that the re-release infringed on the copyright of the Woolrich short story, then owned by literary agent Sheldon Abend, who had bought the rights from the estate for a mere $650 in 1971.

THE CAINE MUTINY

COLUMBIA
$8,700,000

1954

> *"There has never been a mutiny on a ship of the United States Navy. The truths of this film lie not in its incidents but in the way a few men meet the crisis of their lives ..."*
> —PROLOGUE

IT IS FORTUNATE that this film opens with that disclaimer. So convincing is the movie, based upon Herman Wouk's Pulitzer Prize–winning novel, that audiences unfamiliar with the book thought they were seeing a re-enactment of fact.

Producer Stanley Kramer insisted on the disclaimer, stating this was his own idea and not a requirement dictated by the United States Navy. From the time the film was announced as a project by Columbia, rumors abounded that the Navy was at odds with the studio, first saying they might permit filming but only if the story was not labeled a "mutiny," later insisting the producers eliminate the character of Captain Queeg, the neurotic skipper. Columbia and Kramer got frequent coverage in the press by squelching these rumors, giving the film some good advance publicity.

When the picture was finally released, the rumors still abounded, but they only added to the attraction at

Screenplay by Stanley Roberts

From the novel by Herman Wouk

Produced by Stanley Kramer

Directed by Edward Dmytryk

CAST

Captain Queeg . . . . Humphrey Bogart
Lt. Barney Greenwald . . Jose Ferrer
Lt. Steve Maryk . . . . . . Van Johnson
Lt. Tom Keefer . . . . Fred MacMurray
Ensign Willie Keith . . . . Robert Francis

ACADEMY AWARD NOMINATIONS

7 nominations, no wins

Best Picture
Best Actor (Humphrey Bogart)
Best Supporting Actor (Tom Tully)
Best Screenplay
Best Sound Recording
Best Scoring of a Dramatic or Comedy Picture
Best Film Editing

the box office. Even *Newsweek* commented: "There must be something basically healthy about a nation whose armed services not only permit but abet the production of such clinically observant films as 'From Here to Eternity' and 'The Caine Mutiny.'" The reviewer then praised all involved, summing up by calling *The Caine Mutiny* "one of the year's best films, with a half dozen of the year's best performances."

Most outstanding was the work of Humphrey Bogart. It was a dramatic triumph for the actor most noted for playing gangsters and scoundrels. It was his last great role—less than three years later, Bogey died of cancer.

Other memorable performances were turned in by Jose Ferrer, Van Johnson, Fred MacMurray, and E. G. Marshall as the judge advocate. Marshall seemed to be born to the bar—he later went on to star as an attorney on the TV show "The Defenders" (CBS, 1961–65).

In 1988, *The Caine Mutiny* was remade as a movie for television, so be sure to check listings carefully before watching or taping to determine which version is being broadcast.

THE GLENN MILLER STORY

UNIVERSAL-INTERNATIONAL
$7,590,994

GLENN MILLER and His Orchestra rode the crest of a wave of big bands in the '30s and '40s whose popularity set millions of young people dancing to the "swing" beat. When Miller died in 1944 while serving in Europe as the Army Air Force's bandmaster, a generation mourned him. That a biographical film of his life would be made was only a question of time.

In Jimmy Stewart, Universal found the perfect actor to play the mild-mannered, spectacled bandleader. To prepare for the role, Stewart signed on with a trombone tutor named Joe Yukl, but was soon fired as a pupil when it was discovered he really had no aptitude for the "bone." Stewart said that the sounds emanating from the instrument had so upset Yukl that he took to kicking his dog. A solution was found when Stewart plugged up the mouthpiece and maneuvered the slide to approximate the correct positions. It worked, even fooling some professional musicians.

Stewart's portrayal of the bandleader was so effective, in fact, that Miller's mother sent her compliments to the actor, although, as Stewart told *KCET* magazine, "she was sorry that I wasn't better looking."

Music was the focal point, of course, with guest appearances by many popular stars of the era, including Louis Armstrong, Gene Krupa, and the Modernaires. Credited with "Musical Adaptation" was Henry Mancini, with one of his earliest screen credits.

The "Tuxedo Junction" number in which Stewart as Miller conducts his orchestra at a motion picture "scoring" session is quite accurate, giving viewers a good behind-the-scenes look at how a real session takes place. Only in the last few years has the method of scoring changed—instead of a large screen running a black-and-white print with cues for the conductor, many modern studios now use TV monitors to roll film-on tape, a much more inexpensive procedure. And, of course, there is *instant* tape playback today rather than the "wax" they promised Glenn Miller "after lunch."

Nino Tempo, who had the number-one record "Deep Purple" with sister April Stevens in 1963, appears in a bit part. Glenn Miller's friend Chummy MacGregor served as technical advisor on the film, here played by Harry Morgan (credited as "Henry" Morgan). Television fans of "M*A*S*H" may recognize him as Colonel Potter, although he is quite a bit younger here. There's no mistaking that voice, though.

Screenplay by Valentine Davies and Oscar Brodney

Produced by Aaron Rosenberg

Directed by Anthony Mann

CAST

Glenn Miller	James Stewart
Helen Miller	June Allyson
Don Haynes	Charles Drake
Si Schribman	George Tobias
Chummy MacGregor	Henry Morgan

ACADEMY AWARD NOMINATIONS

3 nominations, 1 win*

Best Story and Screenplay
*Best Sound Recording
Best Scoring of a Musical Picture

LADY AND THE TRAMP

WALT DISNEY PRODUCTIONS
$40,249,000

"In the whole history of the world, there is but one thing that money cannot buy, to wit—the wag of a dog's tail." —JOSH BILLINGS

ONE EVENING after a long day at his drawing board back in 1925, Walt Disney had forgotten a dinner engagement, so he brought home a peace offering to his bride—a puppy in a hat box. The image stayed in his mind, and in 1937 he began plans for an animated adventure about a sedate cocker spaniel. About the same time, he read a short story by Ward Greene called "Happy Dan, the Whistling Dog." When Walt joked about how the two dogs should get together, Greene wrote a story called "Happy Dan, the Whistling Dog, and Miss Patsy, the Beautiful Spaniel." Several interruptions later, the tale evolved into the now-famous *Lady and the Tramp,* one of the most beloved and enduring of the Disney classics.

One of the qualities that is so impressive about this movie is how the story is told from a dog's point of view. Anyone who has ever been owned by a dog will understand. For instance, Lady refers to her humans as "Jim Dear" and "Darling"—after all, that's what they call each other. And the cartoon is packed with commentary on human life. "Remember," cautions Jock in his Scottie's burr, "they're only humans after all." Tramp, who

describes himself as "footloose and collar-free," dismisses apes as "too closely related to humans." And then there's the wonderful dialogue about babies:

LADY
What's a baby?

JOCK
Well, they resemble humans.

BLOODHOUND
But I'd say a mite smaller.

JOCK
Aye, and they walk on all fours.

BLOODHOUND
And if I remember correctly, they beller a lot.

JOCK
Aye, and they're expensive. You'll no' be permitted to play with it.

BLOODHOUND
But they're mighty sweet.

JOCK
And verra, verra soft, Tramp. Just a cute little bundle…of trouble. They scratch, pinch, pull ears.

Aside from the love story between the two title dogs, all sorts of canine characters cavort in this animated feature (the first ever made in CinemaScope). There's a Russian wolfhound who quotes Gorky, the German-accented Dachsie, and the sultry ex-show-dog named Peg, whose voice was provided by songstress Peggy Lee.* Miss Lee also co-wrote five of the film's songs, including the jazzy number "He's a Tramp." Additionally, she provided the voices for three other characters.

As with the live-animal studies for *Bambi,* plenty of pooches were paraded through Disney's Burbank studio for the animators to study and sketch. Their thorough understanding of how dogs react and move is clearly evident to any dog owner.

Story by Erdman Penner, Joe Rinaldi, Ralph Wright, and Don DaGradi

Based on an original story by Ward Greene

Songs written by Peggy Lee, Sonny Burke, and Walt Disney

Produced by Walt Disney

Directed by Hamilton Luske, Clyde Geronimi, and Wilfred Jackson

VOICES

Darling, Peg, Si, and Am . . .Peggy Lee
Lady . . . . .Barbara Luddy
Tramp . . . . .Larry Roberts
Jock, Bull, and Dachsie . . . .Bill Thompson
Trusty . . . . .Bill Baucon

*In 1988, Peggy Lee filed a $25,000,000 suit against Walt Disney Productions, saying that in violation of her contract, the company had not secured her approval prior to releasing the videocassette version of *Lady and the Tramp.* According to *People* magazine, April 8, 1991, Lee was awarded a settlement of $3.8 million.

2

CINERAMA HOLIDAY
CINERAMA RELEASING CORPORATION (CRC)
$12,000,000

CINERAMA WAS still big cinema in 1955. When the process was first mass-shown in 1952 (see page 98), it made box office history with its "Hey, look what we can do" production. So it isn't surprising that the producers wanted to show more of their stuff before the novelty wore off.

Producer Louis de Rochemont found a unifying thread this time for the basic travelogue format, choosing a honeymooning couple from Kansas City and a young couple from Zurich, Switzerland, and putting them on the road for a *Cinerama Holiday.* The results? Your basic travelogue.

The "exchange student"–type film saw the Swiss couple, Fred and Beatrice Troller of Zurich, touring the U.S. on a Vespa motorbike, exploring the likes of such Far West sights as Las Vegas, an Apache Indian reservation, and a cocktail lounge atop San Francisco's Mark Hopkins Hotel. From the Top o' the Mark to the top of the Alps, we find the Americans, John and Betty Marsh, skiing and bobsledding, making full use of the Cinerama process à la the roller-coaster sequence from the first film. They then proceed to Paris to see High Mass at Notre Dame, the boulevards, the Louvre, and the ballet. The picture ends with the four travelers back in New York at a performance of *Cinerama.* For the finale, there is a fireworks display with the American flag, the Statue of Liberty, and the Eiffel Tower.

The couples were nonprofessionals, carefully selected from screen tests. When not skipping about the globe sightseeing, the foursome compare

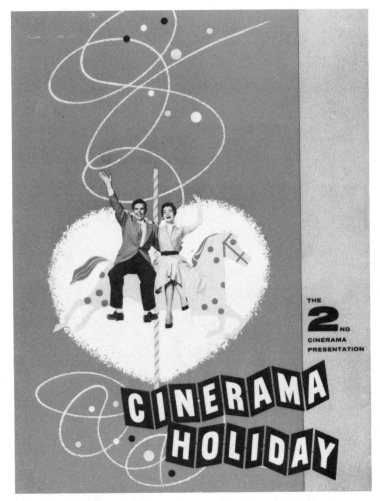

THE
2ND
CINERAMA
PRESENTATION

cultures. "Does John really do the dishes?" asks the Swiss Mrs. "Well, under pressure and without enthusiasm, he'll do some of them sometimes. Doesn't Fred?" The Alpine hausfrau is aghast. "I should say not! That's my domain!" So much for the status of women in the '50s.

Cinerama was no longer the darling of the critics, although there was general praise for the content as "a good travelogue/documentary." But on closer inspection, the process wasn't as perfect as had once been thought. *The Hollywood Reporter,* for instance, noted that "there seem to have been

some improvements in Cinerama since it was first introduced, but the lines dividing the three pictures still are there, though less visible; and in some scenes the jiggling of the two side pictures in opposite directions to the center picture is distracting and annoying. Also, the center panel often is a different color shade than the two side panels."

But for the uncritical eye of movie audiences, *Cinerama Holiday* was still a good ride even without a roller coaster, and they made it the top film of the year (surpassed in re-releases by *Lady and the Tramp*).

Based on "America Through a French Looking Glass" by Renee & Pierre Gosset

Narration written by John Stuart Martin

Adaptation by Otis Carney and Louis de Rochemont III

Produced by Louis de Rochemont III

Directed by Robert Bendick and Philippe de Lacy

Narrated by Martin Weldon

MISTER ROBERTS

WARNER BROS.
$8,500,000

THE STORY OF *Mister Roberts* successfully navigated the waters from best-seller to stage hit to screen success, but there were some land mines along the way. John Ford was signed to direct the film based on Thomas Heggen's novel and Joshua Logan's play. Ford refused to direct unless Henry Fonda, who had already played the part on stage over a thousand times, was signed to reprise the role of Lieutenant (j.g.) Roberts (Warner Bros. wanted either William Holden or Marlon Brando). But all was not roses even after the studio capitulated, and Ford feuded with Fonda, the director eventually leaving after the first week's filming. Mervyn LeRoy was quickly drafted to fill his shoes, and the two received a Hollywood rarity—a shared directing credit.

The play was transplanted to the screen virtually intact from its familiar play form, and audiences were well acquainted with the voyages of the USS *Reluctant,* affectionately called "The Bucket," as she slogged through the backwaters of the Pacific with her vital cargo of toothpaste and toilet paper. It was practically a foregone conclusion that this would be a big hit, if not the biggest hit that year. Aside from Fonda, there was an equally fine cast including James Cagney as the crusty ship's captain; William Powell as the doctor (famous for his grain alcohol/Coke/iodine/hair tonic cocktails); and young Jack Lemmon as Ensign Pulver, "easily the most engaging of Hollywood's new comedians" (*Time* magazine). The Academy thought so, too, and awarded him the Oscar.

Life magazine awarded the coveted cover spot to Henry Fonda, proclaiming "*Mister Roberts* is finally a movie."

The great publicity meant more dollars in Warner Bros.' coffers as rave reviews continued. *The New York Times* announced: "Now hear this! Another 21-gun salute is hereby accorded 'Mister Roberts'. . . to 'Mister Roberts' and all hands involved in one of the season's greatest pleasures: 'Well done!' "

In 1964, an inevitable sequel was attempted. *Ensign Pulver* starred Robert Walker, Jr. (son of Jennifer Jones and Robert Walker), and featured Walter Matthau, Burl Ives, and Tommy Sands. The film also had a pack of future big stars like Jack Nicholson, James Farentino, Larry Hagman, and James Coco. But *Ensign Pulver* lacked the warm appeal of the original. So, too, did a "Mister Roberts" television series starting Roger Smith. It survived a year on NBC (1965–66).

Screenplay by Frank Nugent and
  Joshua Logan

Based on the play by Thomas Heggen
  and Joshua Logan

From the novel by Thomas Heggen

Produced by Leland Hayward

Directed by John Ford and Mervyn LeRoy

CAST

Lieutenant Roberts . . . . .Henry Fonda
The Captain . . . . .James Cagney
Doc . . . . .William Powell
Ensign Pulver . . . . .Jack Lemmon
Lt. Ann Girard . . . . .Betsy Palmer

ACADEMY AWARD NOMINATIONS

3 nominations, 1 win*

 Best Picture
*Best Supporting Actor (Jack Lemmon)
 Best Sound Recording

4

BATTLE CRY

WARNER BROS.
$8,100,000

"They call me Mac. The name's not important. It's January, 1942. Marine outposts all over the world have fallen to the Japanese. Our ranks are empty and ill equipped. We need help. And from every part of the country, kids are answering the call."
　　　　　—OPENING NARRATION

EVEN THOUGH the war had been over for ten years, *Battle Cry* was Warner Bros.' first successful war picture. Taking a gamble on Leon Uris' best-selling 1953 novel, the studio found that the war still meant big business at the box office.

Basically a boot-camp-to-battlefield "recruitment" film, *Battle Cry* follows a platoon of baby-faced Marine recruits through basic training to their assignments in World War II in the Pacific. Along the way, the boys become men, drinking and barroom brawling, as well as falling for women in their base

of operations—in this case, New Zealand. The film climaxes with the bloody invasion of the beaches of Saipan.

As with any good drama, it was the

Screenplay by Leon M. Uris

Based on the novel by Leon M. Uris

Directed by Raoul Walsh

CAST

Major Huxley . . . . .Van Heflin
Andy . . . . .Aldo Ray
Kathy . . . . .Mona Freeman
Pat . . . . .Nancy Olson
Sergeant Mac . . . . . .James Whitmore

ACADEMY AWARD NOMINATIONS

1 nomination, no wins

Best Scoring of a Dramatic or Musical Picture

---

characters that appealed to the audience. The well-stratified cast included James Whitmore as the inevitable Old Sarge, Van Heflin as the colonel with the soft heart beneath a skin of steel, and Tab Hunter as a young collegian-turned-leatherneck. Nancy Olson provided the love interest for another young recruit played by Aldo Ray. Also in the cast were Fess Parker (of "Davy Crockett" fame), William Campbell (who would later became popular with "Star Trek" fans for having guest-starred in two episodes), and Anne Francis (another science-fiction favorite, from *Forbidden Planet*).

Excellent reviews brought encouraging news to exhibitors, who were advised to count on huge takes. They weren't disappointed. *The Hollywood Reporter* headlined " 'BATTLE CRY' REAL BIG ONE HEADED FOR B. O. BONANZA," while *Variety* predicted "good box office expectations."

War was indeed big business.

OKLAHOMA!

MAGNA THEATRE CORPORATION
$7,100,000

"Oh, what a beautiful morning!"

AND OH, WHAT a beautiful matinee and evening performance as well. An estimated 30,000,000 theatergoers had already seen the Rodgers and Hammerstein musical, which had been appearing on stages for over five years. The eagerly awaited film version delivered all that had been promised, and more.

It couldn't miss. Joseph M. Schenck, an independent producer who had recently resigned from Fox, formed Magna Theatre Corporation and promptly became one of the few independent producer/distributors ever to have a top-five film. His firm spent $5,000,000 to bring *Oklahoma!* to the big screen—and big it was. Much of the hoopla centered around Magna's new process, Todd-AO (named for developer Mike Todd and the American Optical Company). The wider- and deeper-than-normal screen went Cinerama one better—it didn't have seams. Magna Theatre Corporation's process would be successfully used in

Screenplay by Sonya Levien and William Ludwig

From the Theatre Guild Production

Book and lyrics by Oscar Hammerstein II

Music by Richard Rodgers

Based on a play by Lynn Riggs

Produced by Arthur Hornblow, Jr.

Directed by Fred Zinnemann

CAST

Curly . . . . .Gordon MacRae
Laurey . . . . .Shirley Jones
Aunt Ellen . . . . .Charlotte
 Greenwood
Will Parket . . . . .Gene Nelson
Ado Annie . . . . .Gloria Grahame

ACADEMY AWARD NOMINATIONS

4 nominations, 2 wins*

 Best Cinematography, Color
*Best Sound Recording
*Best Scoring of a Musical
 Best Film Editing

1956 for Mike Todd's *Around the World in 80 Days.*

In many ways, *Oklahoma's* arrival was reminiscent of the excitement surrounding *Gone With the Wind.* For the New York City premiere, the city held a parade for visiting Oklahoma officials and dignitaries, with Oklahoma governor Raymond Gary in the lead atop his white horse. Right behind him was a cavalcade of surreys "with the fringe on top," riding up Broadway, eventually arriving at the Rivoli Theatre, where the contingency was welcomed by composers Richard Rodgers and Oscar Hammerstein II.

But the movie's the thing, and fans of the play were not disappointed in the screen version. *Oklahoma!* has often been termed an American

opera/ballet. The memorable music sung so richly by Gordon MacRae and Shirley Jones, coupled with the staginess of the production, is operatic in style, while the surrealistic dream sequence can only be termed balletic. This gives an unevenness to the film, which alternates between a location picture with beautiful exteriors to one that is very much bound to the soundstage, with an obvious painted backdrop. Never mind, it's not meant to be reality (after all, how many people go around bursting into song?). Audiences loved it, coming back for more "corn as high as an elephant's eye." With its success at the box office, the movie *Oklahoma!* took its rightful place next to the stage play *Oklahoma!* as an American classic.

1

THE TEN COMMANDMENTS

PARAMOUNT
$43,000,000

"Those who see this motion picture produced and directed by CECIL B. DEMILLE will make a pilgrimage over the very ground that Moses trod more than 3,000 years ago."
—OPENING CREDIT

AND IT CAME TO PASS, that the legend named DeMille brought forth the most ambitious, most successful picture of his career. For DeMille, now age 75, it would also be his last. But what a finale! The legacy of *The Ten Commandments* may not last 3,000 years, but the film will certainly be around for decades to come.

This was actually a remake of the 1923 version of the film, also by DeMille. But now, with $13,500,000 at his command, DeMille showed the world how to make an epic. In the '50s era of Biblical extravaganzas, *The Ten Commandments* became the touch-

stone, surpassing those that preceded it as well as those to follow.

Ten years in the planning, three years in research and preliminary exploration, three in the writing—the film required the longest shooting schedule up to that time. Much of the footage was shot on location in the Middle East and on the Sinai Peninsula, DeMille having insisted that as many actual locales as possible be used. Over 25,000 extras took direction from the master as he perched atop his platform, happy to be in his element once again.

Much of the budget went for special effects. Most memorable of these was the parting of the Red Sea. To get the effect, shots of the actual Red Sea were matched with shots of dump tanks pouring huge amounts of water into a Paramount tank set. When the footage was reversed, the waters seemed to

part. The careful blending of these two shots produced the desired effect. The combined footage took 18 months to film, at a cost of $1,000,000.

An important part of the special effects was the use of animation. Animated "fire" was drawn to represent the finger of God burning the Commandments onto the tablets. Compare this technique with the use of similar animation in recent special effects films like *Raiders of the Lost Ark* and *Star Trek V,* and you'll appreciate how ahead of its time *Commandments* was.

Critics marveled at the film, predicting success. *Variety* speculated that "the box office returns will be mountainous...Biblical entries of the past have won marked public endorsement and this one tops them all. Its theme, its photographic magnificence and the truly powerful publicity campaign must mean that 'Ten Commandments' will run on and on."

A year later, the film had been seen by 21,900,000 people in 800 U.S. cities, and had *grossed* $26,500,000. Since the ratio of grosses to rentals generally runs 2:1, this was approximately the break-even point for Paramount. From then on, it was all gravy.

A good deal of credit for the film's success must also be given to Charlton Heston, with his portrayal of Moses one of the most outstanding characterizations in cinematic history. Heston was, and to many is, Moses— he is still sometimes jokingly referred to by the prophet's name. Garnering much of the attention was co-star Yul Brynner, whose shaved head and exotic looks had made him Hollywood's newest sex symbol. *Redbook* called him "the most exciting male on the screen since Rudolph Valentino." Brynner, whose newly released film version of his successful musical, *The King and I* (for which he would receive the year's Best Actor award), had made him a familiar face to audiences, received critical acclaim as Egyptian pharaoh Ramses II.

The last shot of the last picture of DeMille's career was taken on the director's birthday. According to an interview in Paul Boller's *Hollywood Anecdotes* with the late Yul Brynner, DeMille seemed reluctant to call it a wrap. "I could see he just didn't want to get off that boom. His one regret, I think, was that he didn't die as he finished the film. He was so sad. He kept trying to think of another shot when it was really over."

With that in mind, the picture's final card seems doubly meaningful. DeMille opted to omit the traditional "The End" for this:

"So it was written, so it shall be done."

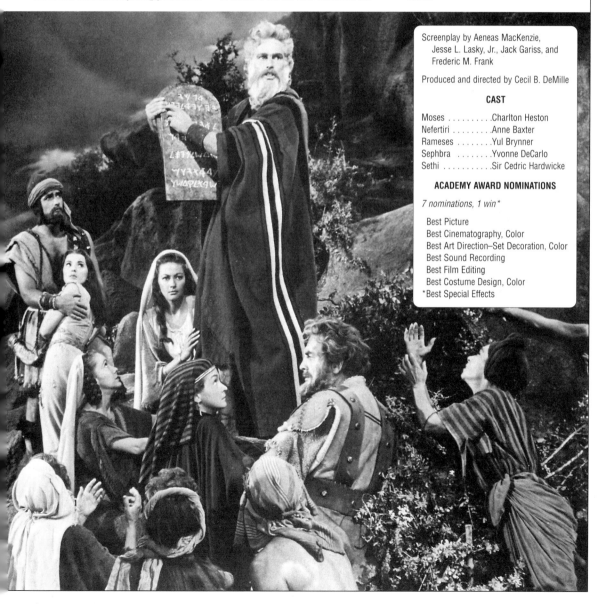

Screenplay by Aeneas MacKenzie, Jesse L. Lasky, Jr., Jack Gariss, and Frederic M. Frank

Produced and directed by Cecil B. DeMille

CAST

Moses . . . . .Charlton Heston
Nefertiri . . . . .Anne Baxter
Rameses . . . . . . .Yul Brynner
Sephbra . . . . .Yvonne DeCarlo
Sethi . . . . .Sir Cedric Hardwicke

ACADEMY AWARD NOMINATIONS

7 nominations, 1 win*

Best Picture
Best Cinematography, Color
Best Art Direction–Set Decoration, Color
Best Sound Recording
Best Film Editing
Best Costume Design, Color
*Best Special Effects

2
AROUND THE WORLD IN 80 DAYS

UNITED ARTISTS
$23,120,000

In keeping with presenting his film in the tradition of a Broadway show, ticket holders received programs; popcorn and other munchies were verboten.

On the first anniversary of *Around the World in 80 Days,* Mike Todd hosted a party for 20,000 of his most intimate friends, at which he announced his next project. It was to be a lavish picturization of Cervantes' *Don Quixote,* for which the showman had already begun construction of an exact replica of a 17th-century Spanish town. The centerpiece was to be Mrs. Todd, Elizabeth Taylor. Todd never got the chance to fulfill this fantasy. In 1958, on his way to receive an award as "Showman of the Year," his private plane crashed in the New Mexico desert, killing all aboard. The plane's name was the "Lucky Liz."

In 1989, a six-part TV mini-series of "Around the World in 80 Days" was broadcast on NBC. It starred Pierce Brosnan, Peter Ustinov, and Eric Idle, but pulled in only mediocre ratings. Mike Todd's legacy was in no jeopardy.

IN BRINGING Jules Verne's classic novel to the screen, Mike Todd, the irrepressible showman, produced his first—and only—motion picture. All producers should be so lucky.

The movie to end all movies was a celluloid three-ring circus. His oversized Todd-AO screen was front and center, of course. And with a subject like The World, the possibilities were endless. But what brought this picture to life was the balance that he struck between his forte—showmanship—and engrossing cinematic entertainment. Todd is credited with creating the "cameo" appearance, and practically everyone who had a Screen Actors Guild card appeared in this movie. His cast read like a who-was-who of Hollywood. Anchored by David Niven, Cantinflas, and Shirley MacLaine (as an Indian Princess, yet!), the parade included Charles Boyer, Joe E. Brown, John Carradine, Charles Coburn, Ronald Colman, Noel Coward, Marlene Dietrich, Sir John Gielgud, Hermione Gingold, Trevor Howard, Buster Keaton, Peter Lorre, Robert Morley, Edward R. Murrow, George Raft, Cesar Romero, Frank Sinatra, and Red Skelton. Theater patrons had

to return several times just to play "How many stars can you spot?"

Extras? Todd gave new meaning to the word, using 68,894 of them, if you can believe the press releases, plus more animals than in any other picture ever made—7,959 of them, including 800 horses, 950 burros, 2,448 American bison, and 3,800 Rocky Mountain sheep.

The film took 34 directors 160 days to make on 112 locations and 140 sets in 13 countries. The wardrobe department spent $410,000 on 74,685 costumes. Still, the total budget came in at a mere $6,000,000, prompting Todd to quip to *Time,* "I'm ashamed to admit it, it cost so little. Take *The Ten Commandments.* That cost $1,000,000 a commandment."

To ensure box office success, Mike Todd guided the film's exhibition with diligence. He sent a manual to each theater, outlining procedures for organizing the reserved seating, ticket pricing, and scheduling of two performances per day. With a running time of nearly three hours, Todd didn't want any anxious patrons watching the clock, and had theater owners remove any illuminated ones near the screen.

Screenplay by S. J. Perelman

Based on the novel by Jules Verne

Produced by Michael Todd

Directed by Michael Anderson

CAST

Phileas Fogg . . . . .David Niven
Passepartout . . . . .Cantinflas
Princess Aouda . . . . . .Shirley MacLaine

ACADEMY AWARD NOMINATIONS

8 nominations, 5 wins*

*Best Picture
  Best Director (Michael Anderson)
*Best Screenplay–Adapted (James Poe,
  John Farrow, and S. J. Perelman)
*Best Cinematography, Color
  Best Art Direction–Set Decoration, Color
*Best Scoring of a Dramatic or Comedy
  Picture (Victor Young)
*Best Film Editing
  Best Costume Design, Color

After a career with 22 nominations, composer Victor Young finally won an Oscar, posthumously—for Best Scoring.

GIANT
WARNER BROS.
$14,000,000

WHEN EDNA Ferber wrote her novel *Giant* in 1952, she couldn't have chosen a more fitting title. In the decade of the mastodon movie, this sprawling Texas saga of greed, lust, family strife, and social conflict lasting 197 minutes did everything to live up to its name.

It had a giant cast. Elizabeth Taylor proved her mettle to critics, whose attention she caught by handling the mature role with confidence and intelligence. Rock Hudson's role as cattle baron Bick Benedict was his first important one, and some later called it his best performance (it won him an Oscar nomination). *Newsweek* noted that "Rock Hudson as her rancher-husband is gigantic, relaxed, rocklike indeed, and right for the part."

The scope of the film is giant in itself. The saga of the Benedict family begins with Rock Hudson as a rugged Texan rancher married to an elegant society girl (Elizabeth Taylor). Together they raise their brood (watch for young actor Dennis Hopper as Jordan Benedict III; Hopper later became the director/star of *Easy Rider* [see page 206]). Both Hudson and Taylor do admirable jobs with their characters' evolution and progressive aging over

Screenplay by Fred Guiol and Ivan Moffat

Based on the novel by Edna Ferber

Produced by George Stevens and Henry Ginsberg

Directed by George Stevens

CAST

Leslie Benedict ......Elizabeth Taylor
Bick Benedict ....Rock Hudson
Jett Rink ....James Dean
Luz Benedict ....Carroll Baker
Vashti Snythe ......Jane Withers

ACADEMY AWARD NOMINATIONS

10 nominations, 1 win*

Best Picture
Best Actor (Rock Hudson)
Best Actor (James Dean)
Best Supporting Actress (Mercedes McCambridge)
*Best Director (George Stevens)
Best Screenplay–Adapted
Best Art Direction–Set Decoration, Color
Best Scoring of a Dramatic or Comedy Picture
Best Film Editing
Best Costume Design, Color

the 25-year span of the film. There is also a controversial (especially for its time) subplot dealing with racism against Mexicans, a theme that had been traditionally taboo in filmmaking.

Most film buffs, however, recall *Giant* as the last performance of James Dean. He had honed his "lonely rebel" character to perfection, and in the role of Jett Rink, he created one of the screen's most unforgettable personifications. *Time* called his acting "a streak of genius," adding: "He has caught the Texas accent to nasal perfection, and has mastered the lock-hipped, high-heeled stagger of the wrangler…the actor is able to press an amazing variety of subtleties into the mood of the moment, to achieve what is certainly the finest piece of atmospheric acting seen on screen since Marlon Brando and Rod Steiger did their 'brother scene' in *On the Waterfront*."

James Dean never lived to learn about the Oscar nomination he so deservingly received for his performance. Two weeks after his last scene in *Giant* was filmed, he was killed in a highway crash while driving his Porsche to a racing competition. He was only 24 years old.

4

SEVEN WONDERS OF THE WORLD

CINERAMA RELEASING CORPORATION (CRC)
$12,500,000

NINETEEN FIFTY-SIX was the year of numbers. Of the top five films, three had numerals in their titles. There were 10 commandments, 80 days in which to go around the world, and a lucky 7 (for CRC, at least) Wonders of the World.

Actually, Lowell Thomas' camera crews found themselves unable to stop at seven, and in preparing this latest entry in the Cinerama saga, his crews trekked hundreds of thousands of miles, shooting as many feet of film as they globetrotted through 32 countries

for the two-hour movie. Alas, the Cinerama crews were several thousand years too late to capture all Seven Wonders of the Ancient World. (These comprised the Hanging Gardens of Babylon, the Colossus of Rhodes, the Statue of Olympian Zeus, the Pharos Lighthouse of Alexandria, the Tomb of King Mausolus, the Temple of Diana at Ephesus, and the Sphinx and Pyramid of Cheops—the oldest manmade object in the world.)

Since the only remaining Wonder of the ancient world's famous collection is

Egypt's Sphinx and Pyramid of Cheops, Thomas decided to go in search of some modern wonders. The triple bank of Cinerama cameras recorded an impressive collage of footage of such far-flung places as New York City, Rio de Janeiro, the Sahara Desert, East Africa, the Taj Mahal in India, Mt. Fuji in Japan, Italy's Leaning Tower of Pisa, the Parthenon, and Mt. Sinai (a popular site for films this year, it would seem). And, of course, there were the obligatory crowd-pleasing scenes of spectacular American scenery, the Cinerama finale this time showcasing flyovers of the Grand Canyon, Niagara Falls, and the redwoods of Yosemite.

Set amidst this vast array of scenery was one unusual segment done in Rome. Pope Pius XII had expressed interest in the Cinerama process when the films were screened at La Scala in Milan, and the production team was only too happy to oblige when His Holiness requested a part in this latest venture. The platform housing the cameras was placed a mere two feet from the balcony the Pope would use to bless the audience gathered in St. Peter's Square. Right on cue, the Pope hit his mark and delivered his blessing. The nervous Cinerama crew was delighted, and was about to wrap when the Pope's advisors suggested another take. They felt the bright lights and cameras had made the Pontiff a bit nervous, so to the surprise of the throng below, the Pope did "take two." Later, the Pope joked with the crew, "Ah, you Americans, you always want two to make sure."

Seven Wonders of the World was the last of the Cinerama travelogues, and it wasn't until 1962 that moviegoers would see a new film using that three-camera process, this time with a plot (see *How the West Was Won,* page 160).

CINERAMA, INCORPORATED
presents the
LOWELL THOMAS
production
SEVEN WONDERS OF THE WORLD
...as seen through the greatest wonder
CINERAMA

Scenario by Prosper Buranelli and William Lipscomb

Produced by Lowell Thomas

Directed by Ted Tetzlaff, Andrew Marton, Tay Garnett, Paul Mantz, and Walter Thompson

Narrated by Lowell Thomas

THE KING AND I

20TH CENTURY-FOX
$8,500,000

Rodgers and Hammerstein's delightful score prompted people to return to box offices again and again, eager to sing along with such tunes as "Shall We Dance?," "Getting to Know You," "Whistle a Happy Tune," "We Kiss in a Shadow," and "Hello, Young Lovers." Fans also made the album the number-one seller of the year. Point of trivia: Yul Brynner's looks and charm must have distracted the person in charge of on-set wardrobe, because when Yul Brynner sings "A Puzzlement," some shots show him with an earring, some without.

Fox hoped it had at last found the elusive key to making television spin-offs from movies when they signed Yul Brynner to reprise his "King of Siam" role (sans singing) for a TV series on CBS. It debuted in September, 1972, and made it all the way to December, three months later. The movie version, and Yul, will always remain King.

Screenplay by Ernest Lehman

Music by Richard Rodgers

Book and lyrics by Oscar Hammerstein II

From the musical play based on the book
Anna and the King of Siam by Margaret Landon

Produced by Charles Brackett

Directed by Walter Lang

CAST

Anna . . . . .Deborah Kerr
The King . . . . .Yul Brynner
Tuptim . . . . .Rita Moreno
Kralahome . . . . .Martin Benson
Lady Thiang . . . . .Terry Saunders

ACADEMY AWARD NOMINATIONS

9 nominations, 5 wins*

  Best Picture
*Best Actor (Yul Brynner)
  Best Actress (Deborah Kerr)
  Best Director (Walter Lang)
  Best Cinematography, Color
*Best Art Direction–Set Decoration, Color
*Best Sound Recording
*Best Scoring of a Musical Picture
*Best Costume Design, Color

YUL BRYNNER. The Asian-born actor of Gypsy extraction made 1956 *his* year. He appeared in three films, two of them in the top five (*The Ten Commandments* and *The King and I*), and fans voted him King of the Box Office as well.

Brynner was not the first one to play the Siamese King. In 1946, Fox had produced *Anna and the King of Siam,* a straight drama taken from Margaret Landon's fictionalized biography (which was in turn based on Anna Leonowens' autobiography). In that film, Rex Harrison played King to Irene Dunne's Anna. Gertrude Lawrence was enchanted with the picture and secured the rights so that she could play Anna in a musical version. Rodgers and Hammerstein set to work writing the now-memorable music, and an unknown Brynner was cast as the

King for the stage version. When Fox decided to bring the well-known musical to the screen 10 years later, there was never any doubt about the man who would be King. Critics sang his praises; *Variety* noted that "the larger exposure via the film medium should make Brynner an international personality." Deborah Kerr, as the properly English schoolteacher, was the perfect foil for Brynner. Her singing voice had to be dubbed by Marni Nixon, a chanteuse who would later make a career of dubbing on-screen singing for less gifted actresses. *Variety* commented that Kerr's voice was "ghosted so well that it is hard to believe that it is not Miss Kerr," and credited Kerr with portraying Anna with "charm and understanding and, when necessary, the right sense of comedy."

Along with the two top stars,

1

THE BRIDGE ON THE RIVER KWAI

COLUMBIA
$17,195,000

COLUMBIA PICTURES, distributors of British-made *The Bridge on the River Kwai,* went firmly to the top of the 1957 box office with the film. Even though the profits had to be split with British producer Sam Spiegel, there was plenty to spare, since the cost of the movie was only $3,000,000.

The producers' money was well spent. Not only did they get a wide-screen, sweeping drama about British prisoners in a Japanese POW camp in the jungles of Burma, but along the way they managed to secure seven Oscars.

The scope of this film is the stuff of love affairs between Academy members and the motion picture screen. It had excellent production values—cast, crew, special effects, sound, cinematography, location sets, and score.

Because the film was made entirely on location in the jungles of what is now Sri Lanka, much of its low cost was due to the use of Ceylonese labor, elephants, and materials during the year the crew spent there. In fact, director David Lean's wife thought he spent too much time on the picture and sued him for divorce on the grounds of desertion.

Among the Academy Awards was one for writing—Best Screenplay Based on Material from Another Medium. Novelist Pierre Boulle was named as the winner, and indeed it is his name that appears in the credits. But in fact the screenplay had been co-scripted by Carl Foreman and Michael Wilson. Why were their names omitted? The late '40s and early '50s was the time of Senator Joseph McCarthy's

hearings to rout the "Red Menace" in our midst (with that infamous question "Are you now or have you ever been a member of the Communist Party?"). These witch hunts extended to the literati and film community, and several Hollywood actors, producers, directors, and writers were either jailed or blacklisted. Two such blacklisted scribes were Foreman and Wilson, whose names were deliberately omitted from the credits. Only later, when this absurd paranoia subsided, were they able to come forward and publicly take credit for their superb screenplay.

Topping the cast was a British actor known mostly to patrons of "art houses." Alec Guinness, portraying the tough, disciplinarian English colonel who defies his captors, garnered a

Director David Lean (left) and Alec Guinness relax a moment during the location filming of *The Bridge on the River Kwai.*

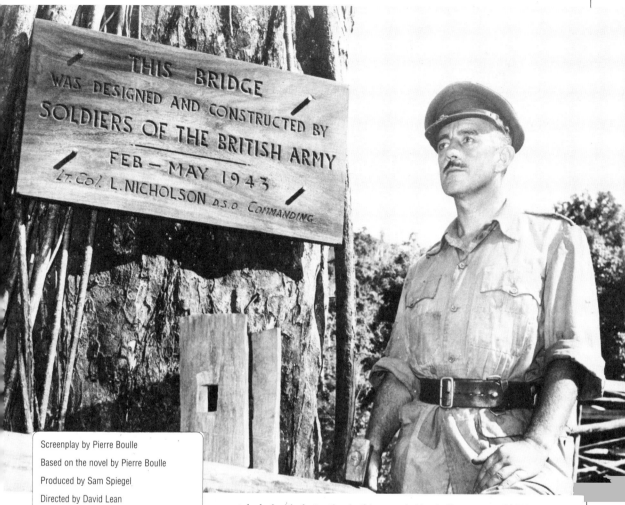

THIS BRIDGE
WAS DESIGNED AND CONSTRUCTED BY
SOLDIERS OF THE BRITISH ARMY
FEB — MAY 1943
Lt. Col. L. NICHOLSON D.S.O. COMMANDING

Screenplay by Pierre Boulle

Based on the novel by Pierre Boulle

Produced by Sam Spiegel

Directed by David Lean

CAST

Shears . . . . .William Holden
Colonel Nicholson . . . .Alec Guinness
Major Warden . . . . . .Jack Hawkins
Colonel Saito . . . . . . .Sessue Hayakawa
Major Clipton . . . . . . .James Donald

ACADEMY AWARD NOMINATIONS

8 nominations, 7 wins*

*Best Picture
*Best Actor (Alec Guinness)
 Best Supporting Actor (Sessue
   Hayakawa)
*Best Director (David Lean)
*Best Screenplay Based on Material from
   Another Medium (Pierre Boulle)
*Best Cinematography
*Best Score
*Best Film Editing

great deal of critical attention in this picture, the turning point in his career. Said *The New York Times:* "Alec Guinness does a memorable—indeed a classic—job in making the ramrod British colonel a profoundly ambitious type…He gives one of the most devastating portraits of a militarist that we have ever seen." Kudos also went to his Japanese adversary, Sessue Hayakawa, a former silent screen star, whom *The Times* labeled "superb."

But *The Bridge on the River Kwai* is David Lean's picture all the way, and all critics were quick to point out that although the film runs about two and three-quarter hours, the director achieved such intensity that it seems like only an hour or so.

In striving for authenticity, Lean chose not to use miniatures for his special effects. Instead, he had a real

bridge built, at a cost of $250,000. From the Ceylon Government Railway he purchased six old coaches and an ancient locomotive once belonging to a maharajah; these were also destroyed as the train crossed the bridge.

The "Colonel Bogie March," the film's famous theme song whistled by the stalwart soldiers, became a hit record, and soon other movies began writing marketable theme songs into their scripts.

In 1989, a nonsequel film entitled *Return from the River Kwai,* co-starring George Takei ("Sulu" of "Star Trek" fame) was released overseas. However, six years after it was made, it still had not been cleared for release in the U.S., as the courts decided whether or not the film's title was an infringement on the original property. (The film's producers argued that no one can own the name of a river.)

2
PEYTON PLACE
20TH CENTURY-FOX
$11,500,000

THE TEMPERATURE wasn't the only thing that was hot in the summer of '57 as 3,000,000 people toted copies of Grace Metalious' steamy novel, *Peyton Place,* to their favorite beach spots. And when Fox bought the film rights to the best-seller, no one thought that her novel could be filmed without cutting most of the sex out of it. They were wrong.

When *Peyton Place* hit the screens at Christmas, the majority of the scenes of suicide, abortion, adultery, rape, and murder were still intact. The film flew in the face of the by-now-impotent censors, and that was just fine with the paying public, who couldn't wait to see it all discussed up on the bigger-than-life CinemaScope screen.

It wasn't all no-holds-barred, however. Compared to today's Peeping-Tom camera with its almost clinical shots of sex acts, this was quite tame; not exactly *Bambi,* but tame. Set in 1941 in a small New Hampshire town (beautifully doubled here by Camden, Maine), the film left some taboos to be broken in screen dialogue. Four-letter words beginning with "f" were certainly not a part of its vocabulary. Nor, oddly, was the word "abortion." When the town doctor performs a then-illegal operation, he tells someone, "I

assisted her in a miscarriage." You may recall that Clark Gable wasn't even allowed to say that no-no back in '39. We'd come a long way, baby.

Casting had much to do with the film's success. Lana Turner finally played an adult role, as the mother of a teenager. Lloyd Nolan, Arthur Kennedy, Leon Ames, and a pre-"Bonanza" Lorne Greene completed the adult roster, while a crop of newcomers—Hope Lange, Russ Tamblyn, Diane Varsi, and David Nelson (yes, Ozzie and Harriet's boy)—proved their professionalism.

In true Hollywood style, Fox came up with a sequel in a 1961 movie called *Return to Peyton Place.* Most people didn't want to.

But most surprising of all was what happened seven years after the film was released. Finally, 20th Century-Fox had found the perfect vehicle for a television spin-off. "Peyton Place" went on ABC in September, 1964, and continued to run for five seasons. It was the original nighttime soap. The show made stars out of two of its cast, Mia Farrow and Ryan O'Neal, and had a stock of other prestigious actors like Leslie Nielsen, Barbara Parkins, Lee Grant, John Kerr, Wilfred Hyde-White, Lana Wood, Leigh Taylor-Young, Gena Rowlands, Barbara Rush, and Dan Duryea. It was not until June 2, 1969, that "Peyton Place" ran its full course.

Screenplay by John Michael Hayes

From the novel by Grace Metalious

Produced by Jerry Wald

Directed by Mark Robson

CAST

Constance . . . . .Lana Turner
Selena Cross . . . . . . .Hope Lange
Michael Rossi . . . . . .Lee Philips
Dr. Swain . . . . .Lloyd Nolan
Lucas Cross . . . . . . .Arthur Kennedy
Norman Page . . . . . .Russ Tamblyn

ACADEMY AWARD NOMINATIONS

9 nominations, no wins

Best Picture
Best Actress (Lana Turner)
Best Supporting Actor (Arthur Kennedy)
Best Supporting Actor (Russ Tamblyn)
Best Supporting Actress (Hope Lange)
Best Supporting Actress (Diane Varsi)
Best Director (Mark Robson)
Best Screenplay Based on Material from
  Another Medium
Best Cinematography

SAYONARA

WARNER BROS.
$10,500,000

"The pleasure does not lie in the end itself. It's the pleasurable steps to that end." —ORIENTAL WISDOM AS QUOTED IN *SAYONARA*

BASED ON James Michener's 1954 novel about American servicemen on leave in Japan during the Korean War, *Sayonara* is very much a modern *Madame Butterfly.* The tragedy centers on the theme of interracial love and marriage, something with which Michener had first-hand experience. In 1955, shortly after the novel's publication, Michener married his third wife, Mari Yoriko Sabusawa, an American of Japanese extraction.

In the film—which opens with a less-than-memorable title song by Irving Berlin—Major Gruver, played by Marlon Brando, comes face to face with his own prejudices, gradually understanding that love is more than skin deep. What we see is something akin to a religious conversion as he rushes to Red Buttons' character's defense. His conversion is complete when he meets and falls in love with a beautiful dancer. From a writing perspective, this is a model script: we have a central character who learns, grows, and eventually changes by story's end. Paul Osborn did an admirable job of translating Michener's novel to the screen and was rewarded with an Oscar.

Both Brando and Buttons were lauded by the press for their fine performances. *The Hollywood Reporter* commented: "Brando has done something in this picture that is seen so rarely that it is especially notable. He has undertaken to portray a drastic change in character and he brings it off with conviction and resolution." Until this film, Red Buttons was known primarily as a comedian. With this dramatic debut, *Variety* noted: "The performance [director Joshua Logan] gets out of Buttons, deeply moving in its sincerity, should raise the erstwhile air comic to entirely new stature. In this 'straight' part, he's excellent and his devotion and final desperation ring completely true."

Buttons' ill-fated Japanese wife was played by newcomer Miyoshi Umeki (familiar to later TV audiences as "Mrs. Livingston" on "The Courtship of Eddie's Father"), who was discovered singing in a San Fernando Valley nightclub. Her film debut was honored by the Academy with an Oscar—rare for a first performance.

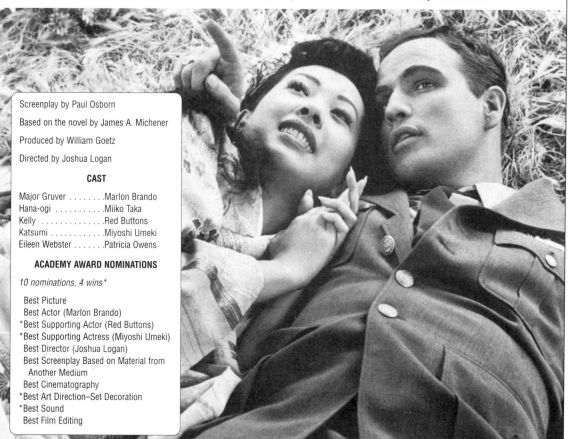

Screenplay by Paul Osborn

Based on the novel by James A. Michener

Produced by William Goetz

Directed by Joshua Logan

CAST

Major Gruver . . . . .Marlon Brando
Hana-ogi . . . . .Miiko Taka
Kelly . . . . .Red Buttons
Katsumi . . . . .Miyoshi Umeki
Eileen Webster . . . . . . .Patricia Owens

ACADEMY AWARD NOMINATIONS

10 nominations, 4 wins*

Best Picture
Best Actor (Marlon Brando)
*Best Supporting Actor (Red Buttons)
*Best Supporting Actress (Miyoshi Umeki)
Best Director (Joshua Logan)
Best Screenplay Based on Material from Another Medium
Best Cinematography
*Best Art Direction–Set Decoration
*Best Sound
Best Film Editing

4

OLD YELLER

WALT DISNEY PRODUCTIONS
$10,050,000

WALT DISNEY proved that he knew how to make a tear-jerker with *Old Yeller*. It's a charming story about a boy and his dog, but the master story-teller also gave us a basic human tale blending fun, laughter, love, adventure —and tragedy. Most people will think of this as a children's tale, but many a kid learned about real life and grew up a tad or two after watching this film.

For his story, Walt turned to an acclaimed novel by Fred Gipson, who collaborated on the screenplay with William Tunberg. Gipson described *Old Yeller* as fiction based on fact. "My grandfather owned a big yellow stray dog who could throw wild range cattle and who once rescued him from a meat-eating hog," he recounted.

The film introduced Tommy Kirk and Kevin Corcoran, two young players who were put under Disney contract and appeared in numerous films to follow. Jeff York, Chuck Connors (former baseball star and "The Rifleman" of TV fame), and Beverly Washburn rounded out the cast.

But this was really a picture about animals and *their* relationships. The

---

Screenplay by Fred Gipson and William Tunberg

Based on the book by Fred Gipson

Produced by Walt Disney

Directed by Robert Stevenson

CAST

Mrs. Coates	Dorothy McGuire
Mr. Coates	Fess Parker
Travis Coates	Tommy Kirk
Arliss Coates	Kevin Corcoran
Mr. Searcy	Jeff York
Mr. Sanderson	Chuck Connors
Lisbeth Searcy	Beverly Washburn

---

title dog was played by "Spike," who was rescued by trainer Frank Weatherwax from a Van Nuys, California, animal shelter. He paid $3.00 for his future star. Weatherwax invested $20,000 and four years in training time before Disney cast Spike as "Old Yeller." Other animals in the cast weren't that easy to come by. Where do you find a red-eyed wild boar? Disney wranglers located a herd with four-inch tusks in the back

country of central California. Buzzards had to be shipped from Florida, reptiles from Texas and Arizona, squirrels from Kentucky. A pregnant cow was located, and obliged the Disney crew by giving birth to her calf on cue.

The script called for Spike/Yeller to fight with a 500-pound bear, and the battle took place without any harm to either animal. For months, Spike was introduced to his wrestling partner Doug, a nine-year-old movie bear. They learned to play-fight, later re-creating such a scene for the cameras. Appropriate growls and yelps were all added by the sound department for effectiveness, and the animals, closely supervised by an American Humane Association representative, emerged without a single scratch.

But it is the film's sad ending that is remembered by most. Walt argued for realism. "This is a Texas farm in 1869 and the dog has rabies; there's no way he can be saved. You gotta shoot him…The kids'll cry, but it's important for them to know that life isn't all happy endings." Who said only kids would cry?

POOR WHITE TRASH (a.k.a. BAYOU)

UNITED ARTISTS
$6,000,000

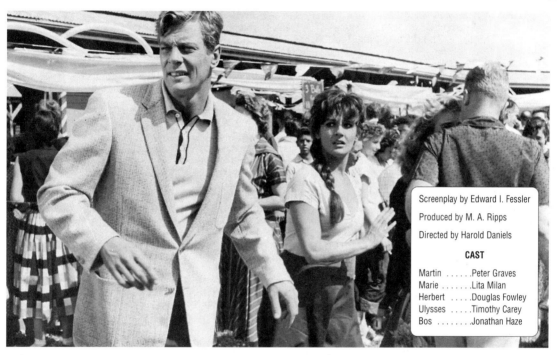

Screenplay by Edward I. Fessler

Produced by M. A. Ripps

Directed by Harold Daniels

CAST

Martin . . . . . . .Peter Graves
Marie . . . . . . .Lita Milan
Herbert . . . . .Douglas Fowley
Ulysses . . . . .Timothy Carey
Bos . . . . .Jonathan Haze

"Due to the abnormal subject matter of this motion picture, absolutely no children will be allowed with or without their parents…special uniformed police will supervise admissions. M. A. Ripps, Producer, Poor White Trash"

—ADVERTISING COPY
PROMOTING *POOR WHITE TRASH*

HISTORY DOESN'T record whether or not anyone was actually bodily removed from a theater by the "special uniformed police," but when M. A. Ripps decided his 1957 dud of a film called *Bayou* needed a boost for its 1962 re-release, he brought in the big guns to goose up his product. First, the title had to go. *Bayou* sounded like a National Geographic documentary about swamps. Something catchier, more illustrative of the film's sultry southern atmosphere was needed. *Poor White Trash* had a lot more to say about the backwater Cajuns who "fish to live, live to love and love to fight," as producer Ripps put it.

Partly because of the hype, urging patrons to "See for yourself what goes on behind those Spanish moss-covered trees," audiences were lured by these lurid suggestions, pushing this rather unworthy film into box office hit status. There were no big stars, with the exception of Peter Graves as a citified Yankee architect on a business trip to the South. Graves, fresh from his TV success in "Fury" (and pre–"Mission: Impossible") meets a fury of another sort here—a swamp fox, played by Lita Milan. Early in the film, her papa warns her, "Marie, you is near 18; most girls is married by the time they are 17, and they have family." This Cajun queen, however, is the object of another's desires—and rape. Graves to the rescue, of course, but first, the couple (and the audience) must endure endless stock footage of a hurricane as they struggle to survive. At one point, with the storm raging outside their shack, the couple begin to make love. This is toned down by more stock footage of crashing surf, except that the waves are superimposed over the couple's love-

making, giving the appearance that they are in the ocean!

Dialogue wasn't the film's strong suit, either. To wit:

MARIE
What you want from poor Cajun girl?

GRAVES
I love you, Marie. I want to marry you. Will you marry me?

MARIE
I love you too.

This, at the height of the howling hurricane. One can only imagine the howling of the audience as well.

Nevertheless, Ripps was undeterred. The ad campaign worked. His film began to take on cult status. Encouraged (he seemed to need little encouragement), Ripps tried to top himself in 1976, when he produced *Poor White Trash II* (a.k.a. *Scum of the Earth*). But not even two racy titles and the repeated threat of "abnormal subject matter" and "special uniformed police" could make this dog hunt.

SOUTH PACIFIC

20TH CENTURY-FOX
$17,500,000

"You've got to be carefully taught."
—LYRIC FROM "YOU'VE
GOT TO BE TAUGHT"

FOR THE YEAR 1958, Hollywood turned to Broadway. Every one of the top five films that year was adapted from a successful Broadway play or musical. The feeling seemed to be that if it made money on the stage, go with the film. The public confirmed that attitude, spending their box office dollars on two musicals, two comedies, and one drama.

The most successful of these was *South Pacific,* the James Michener musical adapted from his book *Tales of the South Pacific.* Again, as in *Sayonara* the previous year, the talents of director Joshua Logan were brought to a Michener property, and again the book dealt with interracial relationships. While *South Pacific* was not actually a "message" movie, the statement made by the above lyrics was the play/movie's theme in a nutshell—you have to be taught to hate all the people your relatives hate.

Although *South Pacific* was a morality play, its main emphasis was on the wonderful music of Rodgers and Hammerstein—songs like "I'm Gonna Wash That Man Right Out of My Hair," "Some Enchanted Evening," "Younger Than Springtime," "Happy Talk," "Bloody Mary," and "Bali Ha'i." Joshua Logan had brought the first version of the show to the stage in 1949, when World War II was not yet a distant memory, and the story may have had more immediacy then. Still, audiences had been humming the popular tunes for nine years when the movie hit the screens in Todd-AO and stereophonic sound, and Fox's $6,000,000 investment paid off handsomely.

Presentation in movie theaters was, as with many spectacular '50s films, "an event." People booked in advance for the privilege of seeing this film lasting 2 hours 51 minutes, with a 15-minute intermission. No one seemed to mind the length. In fact, the film proved such a success in London that it played at the same movie house there for four years.

Success came for many reasons. In addition to the love stories, there was much comic relief, as well as beautiful settings. When Mitzi Gaynor washes that man right out of her hair, she does so on one of Kauai's (Hawaii) most beautiful beaches.

While the public took *South Pacific's* screen version to their hearts, many of the critics didn't, finding fault with the cast (they missed Mary Martin and Ezio Pinza from the Broadway version), the length, the colors, and so on. *Time* found the film "about as tastelessly impressive as a ten-ton marshmallow" but then went on to predict that "nevertheless, it will probably run almost as long as it did on Broadway…and it seems sure to make yet another bale of kale."

Cast in the leads were Mitzi Gaynor as Nurse Nellie Forbush and Rossano Brazzi as her French suitor. Brazzi was a particularly puzzling choice, since although the Italian film star had caught the attention of the American public in *The Barefoot Contessa* (1954), his vocals for South Pacific all had to be dubbed by Giorgio Tozzi. Others in the cast included Ray Walston, who later starred as TV's "My Favorite Martian" and, in bit parts, Doug McClure (later star of TV's "The Virginian") and Ron Ely (later TV's "Tarzan").

Much of the film's controversy centered on director of photography Leon Shamroy's unorthodox use of color gels to establish "mood" with each use of song. Many found this technique distracting or annoying. When the film was released, Shamroy defended the process, telling *Newsweek:* "My interpretation of the South Pacific was like Gauguin painted it. I also wanted to create a change of pace. You have to think of the audience's restlessness watching the same thing for three hours. You have to change the atmosphere. So I shot the musical parts as a fantasy by sliding colored gelatin filters across the lens." The D.P.'s peers at the Academy obviously enjoyed these innovations—they gave Shamroy an Oscar nomination.

This technique may have given audiences a break then, but the color variations are jarring today when this movie is viewed on a television set via VCR—one has the urge to continually fiddle with the color adjustments.

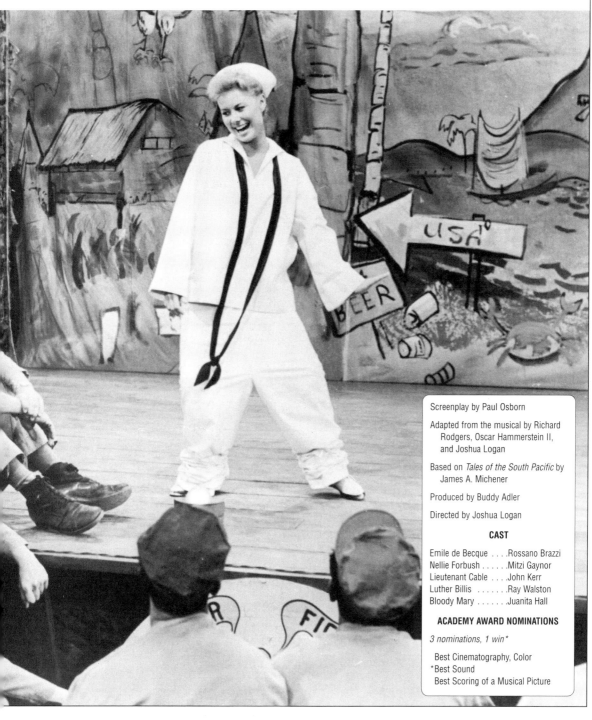

Screenplay by Paul Osborn

Adapted from the musical by Richard
 Rodgers, Oscar Hammerstein II,
 and Joshua Logan

Based on *Tales of the South Pacific* by
 James A. Michener

Produced by Buddy Adler

Directed by Joshua Logan

CAST

Emile de Becque . . . .Rossano Brazzi
Nellie Forbush . . . . . .Mitzi Gaynor
Lieutenant Cable . . . .John Kerr
Luther Billis . . . . . . .Ray Walston
Bloody Mary . . . . . . .Juanita Hall

ACADEMY AWARD NOMINATIONS

3 nominations, 1 win*

 Best Cinematography, Color
*Best Sound
 Best Scoring of a Musical Picture

AUNTIE MAME

WARNER BROS.
$9,300,000

"Life is a banquet, and most poor suckers are starving to death."
—ROSALIND RUSSELL

PATRICK DENNIS' semi-autobiographical book about his eccentric (to say the least) Auntie Mame remained on the best-seller list for 112 weeks, so it was only natural that it be converted into a play. And, as we've seen, successful plays beget successful motion pictures. With an audience pre-sold on the farce, how could it miss?

It was the role of a lifetime, and Rosalind Russell will always be remembered as Auntie Mame. She had already perfected her portrayal of the kindhearted kook on the Broadway stage as she romped through 639 performances. And since the play/film is basically a one-woman tour de force, most of the glory went to Miss Russell as well. One reason Miss Russell was able to pull it off so brilliantly was the warmth and humanism she brought to her character, who would otherwise have come off as an egocentric airhead.

Roger Smith, who played the part of her grown nephew Patrick, is best remembered as having co-starred in the television series "77 Sunset Strip," which went on the air three months before the release of *Auntie Mame*. (Those readers too young to remember that show will probably know him as the husband of performer Ann-Margret.)

Another television regular, Fred Clark, appeared in *Auntie Mame* as Mame's no-nonsense banker. Clark was also familiar to TV audiences of the '50s as "Harry Morton" on "The Burns and Allen Show." Coincidentally, he played an accountant on that program.

Contributing to the popularity of this movie were the clever sets. Mame's apartment is almost a character itself. One of the most unforgettable moments comes when she is trying to destroy her nephew's relationship, and the fun she has with the barber-chair-like sofas, which rise ceilingward. It's totally unbelievable, and yet the total absurdity of the scene works beautifully.

In 1966, Broadway was again treated to the outrageous aunt, this time in the musical *Mame*. It starred Angela Lansbury (who won a Tony Award) and ran for 1,508 performances, an even more impressive record than its predecessor.

Less impressive was the 1974 movie version of *Mame* starring Lucille Ball. Audiences loved Lucy, but not this musical fiasco.

Screenplay by Betty Comden and Adolph Green

Based on the novel by Patrick Dennis

Stage adaptation by Jerome Lawrence and Robert E. Lee

Directed by Morton DaCosta

CAST

Mame	Rosalind Russell
Beauregard Burnside	Forrest Tucker
Vera Charles	Coral Browne
Mr. Babcock	Fred Clark
Patrick Dennis	Roger Smith
Agnes Gooch	Peggy Cass

ACADEMY AWARD NOMINATIONS

6 nominations, no wins

Best Picture
Best Actress (Rosalind Russell)
Best Supporting Actress (Peggy Cass)
Best Cinematography, Color
Best Art Direction–Set Decoration
Best Film Editing

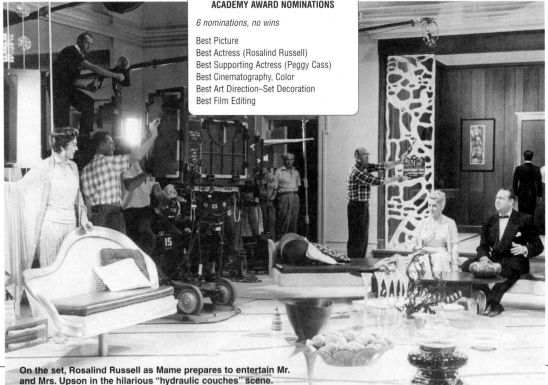

On the set, Rosalind Russell as Mame prepares to entertain Mr. and Mrs. Upson in the hilarious "hydraulic couches" scene.

CAT ON A HOT TIN ROOF

METRO-GOLDWYN-MAYER
$8,785,162

WHEN TENNESSEE Williams' stage play was brought to the screen, audiences eagerly rushed to see whether it would remain intact, since the drama unabashedly dealt with what were considered very "adult" topics—greed, lust, latent homosexuality—set to the tune of four-letter words so much a part of the Southern dramatist's realistic vocabulary. Much of this was indeed toned down for the screen, but the dramatic impact was still very much in evidence. Even more enticing to paying audiences were the fine performances of its lead actors—Elizabeth Taylor, Paul Newman, and Burl Ives.

Ms. Taylor almost didn't get the part. When MGM bought the film rights to the play, they had Grace Kelly in mind. But by the time cameras were ready to roll, Grace had landed another part, that of Princess of Monaco.

Just as Elizabeth Taylor was finishing the opening sequences of *Cat,* her husband, Mike Todd, was killed in a plane crash (see page 124). In the "show must go on" tradition, she worked throughout her grief, turning in an intense performance that drew raves from the critics. *Newsweek* wrote: "Elizabeth Taylor, who never has been known as a dramatic star of particularly commanding stature, is more than satisfactory as Maggie the Cat, the first role she has been given which is not bigger-than-life. Her ably

---

Screenplay by Richard Brooks and James Poe

Based on the play by Tennessee Williams

Produced by Lawrence Weingarten

Directed by Richard Brooks

CAST

Maggie	Elizabeth Taylor
Brick	Paul Newman
Big Daddy	Burl Ives
Gooper	Jack Carson
Big Mama	Judith Anderson

ACADEMY AWARD NOMINATIONS

6 nominations, no wins

Best Picture
Best Actor (Paul Newman)
Best Actress (Elizabeth Taylor)
Best Director (Richard Brooks)
Best Screenplay Based on Material from Another Medium
Best Cinematography, Color

---

modulated performance suggests a promising future that could extend long after the bloom is off the rose."

Ever since the death of Todd, Ms. Taylor had been comforted by his best friend, Eddie Fisher. Although married to Debbie Reynolds at the time (the "perfect Hollywood couple," proclaimed the press), Fisher suddenly dumped Debbie for Liz. A few months later, Eddie Fisher became the fourth husband of Elizabeth Taylor.

The press also took notice of Paul Newman as Maggie's latent homosexual husband, Brick. *Variety* noted: "Newman again proves to be one of the finest actors in films, playing cynical underacting against highly developed action. His command of the articulate, sensitive sequences is unmistakable, and the way he mirrors his feelings is basic to every scene."

Burl Ives was the only actor who had appeared in the original Broadway version of this film; forevermore he would be the embodiment of "Big Daddy." The one-time banjo-pickin' balladeer received kudos from the critics. Also released in 1958 was *The Big Country;* Ives won an Academy Award for Best Supporting Actor in that picture. Burl Ives died in 1995, at the age of 85.

NO TIME FOR SERGEANTS

WARNER BROS.
$7,500,000

Y ET ANOTHER Broadway hit made it to the screen in this comedy about a farmboy turned flyboy. The movie is based on Ira Levin's (later of Rosemary's Baby fame) popular play, which in turn was based on Mac Hyman's best-seller. Andy Griffith created the stage role and re-created it quite successfully in the movie.

The North Carolina native was born to play the wide-eyed draftee, whose character is not so much dumb as literal-minded in a Gracie Allenesque way. Two years later, some clever people saw the potential in Andy, and the actor took his rightful place in Mayberry on the weekly television program "The Andy Griffith Show." And since Andy had become the respectable sheriff, his hayseed character from *No Time for Sergeants* was subdivided. The "gaaaaaah-ly" that we heard so frequently from Gomer Pyle in the weekly TV series was lifted straight out of the mouth of Private Will Stockdale in *No Time for*

Sergeants. Andy also recruited actor Don Knotts from this movie's cast (listed in the film's credits as "Manual Dexterity Corporal").

Three other cast members also went on to star or co-star in television shows. Nick Adams became "The Rebel" in 1959; Will Hutchins landed the lead in "Sugarfoot" back in 1957

Screenplay by John Lee Mahin

From the play by Ira Levin

Based on the novel by Mac Hyman

Produced and directed by Mervyn LeRoy

CAST

Will Stockdale	Andy Griffith
Sergeant King	Myron McCormick
Ben	Nick Adams
Irvin	Murray Hamilton
General Bush	Howard Smith
Manual Dexterity Corporal	Don Knotts

and had just completed that show's first season when he filmed *Sergeants;* and Jamie Farr, who plays an uncredited co-pilot in this film, later became Corporal Maxwell Klinger on TV's "M*A*S*H."

Although it was popular at the time of release, this film seems slow and a bit of the humor dated when viewed on videocassette. Particularly ludicrous is the sequence in which Andy and his buddy jump from an airplane over Yucca Flats immediately after a brush with an A-Bomb test, and calmly converse while descending through a fallout cloud! No one thought this odd in those days, particularly the unsuspecting military, whose tests were carried on with virtually no protection for nearby spectators.

As you have probably guessed, a television series of "No Time for Sergeants" appeared in September, 1964. It ran for a year on ABC with Sammy Jackson playing the Griffith-created role of Private Stockdale.

5

GIGI

METRO-GOLDWYN-MAYER
$7,321,423

1958

SOMEHOW IT SEEMS unfitting that *Gigi* was number five for 1958 and not number one, since this musical film has stood the test of time much better than *South Pacific*. It proved to be the favorite film of the Motion Picture Academy for that year, when it received an all-time high number of Oscars—nine all told. And the *My Fair Lady*–like story of the tomboyish French girl blooming into lovely young womanhood continues to charm audiences as much today as it did over 30 years ago.

Gigi began with the pen of French novelist Colette, who wrote it when she was 70. In 1950, a French movie ver-

---

Screenplay by Alan Jay Lerner

Based on the novel by Colette

Lyrics by Alan Jay Lerner

Music by Frederick Loewe

Produced by Arthur Freed

Directed by Vincente Minnelli

CAST

Gigi . . . . .Leslie Caron
Honore Lachaille . . . . .Maurice Chevalier
Gaston Lachaille . . . . .Louis Jourdan
Mme. Alvarez . . . . . . .Hermione Gingold
Liane D'Exelmans . . . .Eva Gabor

ACADEMY AWARD NOMINATIONS

9 nominations, 9 wins*

*Best Picture

*Best Director (Vincente Minnelli)

*Best Screenplay Based on Material from Another Medium (Alan Jay Lerner)

*Best Cinematography, Color

*Best Art Direction–Set Decoration

*Best Song ("Gigi," music by Frederick Loewe, words by Alan Jay Lerner)

*Best Scoring of a Musical Picture

*Best Film Editing

*Best Costume Design

Maurice Chevalier won an Honorary Award (statuette) "for his contributions to the world of entertainment for more than half a century."

Gigi swept the Oscars, setting a new record for most Awards won.

---

sion was made, and was soon followed by a nonmusical Broadway play with a young unknown by the name of Audrey Hepburn. Then, in 1957, producer Arthur Freed (*The Wizard of Oz*) and director Vincente Minnelli (*Meet Me in St. Louis*) hit upon the idea of a musical. They immediately turned to Alan Jay Lerner and Frederick Loewe, the musical pair behind *My Fair Lady,* still in its unprecedented Broadway run.

Some called the result a *My Fair Gigi,* with many of the songs nearly paraphrases of those from the first musical. Compare, for example, *My Fair Lady*'s "The Rain in Spain" with *Gigi*'s "The Night They Invented Champagne," or Henry Higgins' musings in "I've Grown Accustomed to Her Face" with Louis Jordan's longing for "Gigi." Even the critics noticed the similarities. As *The New York Times* wrote, "There won't be much point in anybody trying to produce a film of 'My Fair Lady' for a while, because Arthur Freed has virtually done it with

'Gigi.' " (The producers of *My Fair Lady* must have been reading *The Times,* because it took six more years for that play to become a film.)

Chemistry was a key element in the success of *Gigi*. The cast worked well in pairs—Maurice Chevalier opposite Hermione Gingold; Leslie Caron with Louis Jordan—and occasional mixes of the above created whole new recipes for fun and song. Yet it is ironic that with all the Oscars this great musical won, not one of the film's fine cast walked away with an Award (although Maurice Chevalier received an honorary Oscar).

Leslie Caron was born near Paris to a French father and an American-born mother, a former dancer. She studied ballet, and at age 16 was discovered in a local company by Gene Kelly; he later selected her to co-star in *An American in Paris* (1951), thus launching her film career. As of 1996, she was still working in film as well as making occasional TV appearances.

BEN-HUR

METRO-GOLDWYN-MAYER

$36,992,088

"EXTRAORDINARY, OF GREATER
DIMENSIONS THAN ANY FILM OF
OUR TIME."

—*THE HOLLYWOOD REPORTER*

METRO MADE a go-for-broke move in 1959. The financially ailing studio sank $15,000,000 into a remake of an old film based on an even older novel. The film was *Ben-Hur*, considered a "spectacular" back in 1921 when the Cinematograph Corporation spent $600,000 to acquire the rights to General Lew Wallace's 1880 novel. Produced in 1926 by MGM, the silent film cost $4,000,000, starred Ramon Novarro and Francis X. Bushman, and by 1936 had grossed $10,000,000 for the studio. This proven property sitting in their Culver City vaults seemed the perfect vehicle for a remake, especially in the wide-screen, religious-epic epoch of the 1950s. Leo tossed back his mane and gave one last roar. It was the roar heard 'round the world.

Ben-Hur was the most expensive film ever made at the time of its release. It took five years of preparation, six and one-half months of shooting in Italy at the Cinecitta studios, and nine months of editing in Hollywood to produce the 3-hour 37-minute movie.

Screenplay by Karl Tunberg

From the novel by Gen. Lew Wallace

Produced by Sam Zimbalist

Directed by William Wyler

CAST

Judah Ben-Hur . . . . . .Charlton Heston
Quintus Arrius . . . . . . .Jack Hawkins
Messala . . . . .Stephen Boyd
Esther . . . . .Haya Harareet
Sheik Ilderim . . . . . . .Hugh Griffith

ACADEMY AWARD NOMINATIONS

12 nominations, 11 wins*

*Best Picture
*Best Actor (Charlton Heston)
*Best Supporting Actor (Hugh Griffith)
*Best Director (William Wyler)
 Best Screenplay Based on Material from
  Another Medium
*Best Cinematography, Color
*Best Art Direction–Set Decoration, Color
*Best Sound
*Best Scoring of a Dramatic or Comedy
  Picture
*Best Film Editing
*Best Costume Design, Color
*Best Special Effects

Vital statistics: 50,000 extras, 100,000 costumes, 300 sets. The chariot race, the film's most famous sequence, required six months of planning and two months to shoot, at a cost of $1,000,000, making it the most expensive 11 minutes moviegoers had ever seen. The film won enough Academy Awards to sink a Roman galley: 11—count 'em—11, more than any film as of 1996.

Producer Sam Zimbalist (who died of a heart attack before the film was completed) assembled some of the greatest talents in Hollywood. For his director, he chose William Wyler, whose credits included *Mrs. Miniver* and *The Best Years of Our Lives* (and in 1966, *Funny Girl*); the script was written by Karl Tunberg, with assistance from S. N. Behrman, Gore Vidal, and Christopher Fry. According to *Time,* the lines "sometimes sing with good rhetoric and quiet poetry." And for the title role, who else but Charlton Heston, late of Mt. Sinai, whom someone once called "Hollywood's resident epic hero"? Other fine cast members included Stephen Boyd as Ben-Hur's nemesis Messala, plus Jack Hawkins, Haya Harareet, Martha Scott, Sam Jaffe, and an odd assortment of several dozen credited speaking parts, such

"Rower No. 42," "Rower No. 28," and "Leper."

Stephen Boyd's biggest film was *Ben-Hur*. Born William Millar in Belfast on July 4, 1928, the actor began his stage career in childhood, and arrived in Canada when he was 18, performing on radio and in summer stock. He toured the States with a stock company in 1950, and set his sights on an acting career there. His first film break came in England, with *An Alligator Named Daisy* (1955). He also appeared in *The Man Who Never Was* (1956) and a few others before his co-starring role as Messala in *Ben-Hur*. He was featured in *Fantastic Voyage* (1966) and *The Bible* (as Nimrod; 1966), but never really had another role with the importance of Messala. In the early '70s, Boyd appeared mainly in low-budget Spanish films. He died in 1977, at the age of 49.

For this most spectacular of films there was without a doubt *the* most spectacular of scenes—the chariot race. Producer Sam Zimbalist selected Andrew Marton to direct this sequence, since Marton had successfully worked with William Wyler on the Dunkirk segment in *Mrs. Miniver*. Marton began by securing the necessary horses. The race was to be run by nine chariots drawn by four horses each, but he actually used doubles and "understudy" teams, for a total of 82 horses, all obtained in Yugoslavia. Months were spent rehearsing the teams on a duplicate race track. Chuck Heston already was a skilled rider from experience in Westerns, and his strong hands and shoulder muscles gave him an advantage. Stephen Boyd had a much rougher time of it, with his hands constantly blistered and bloody. In the filming, Heston and Boyd did all their own chariot driving except for two stunts. One stunt which Boyd did, for a close-up of him being dragged under his chariot, left him battered and bruised.

There were some accidents, although despite rumors to the contrary, there were no fatalities. Once a couple of chariots smashed into two cameras as they came out of a turn. The other serious accident occurred when stuntman Yakima Canutt's 22-year-old son Joe bounced his chariot, sailing into the air. As he landed, his chariot flipped him into a head-stand and he was thrown out between the horses. He instinctively grabbed the cross-bar, dragging behind it. Amazingly, he required only four stitches on his chin, and returned to work the same day.

It is scenes like the above, with their attention to perfection, that made *Ben-Hur* the darling of the critics and public alike. It marked the end of an era, the last of the epic blockbusters—and MGM's last number-one film to the present time.

SLEEPING BEAUTY

WALT DISNEY PRODUCTIONS
$21,998,000

THERE MUST BE a plaque somewhere on the Walt Disney lot memorializing 1959. With three of the top films of that year bearing the familiar flourish of the "Walt Disney" signature, 1959 can only be called "The Year of Disney." Together, *Sleeping Beauty, The Shaggy Dog,* and *Darby O'Gill and the Little People* netted $42,651,000—a fine pot of gold under the Disney rainbow.

The best and most successful of the year's trio was *Sleeping Beauty,* the classic story of the young princess and her narcoleptic kingdom, the struggle for good and evil, and her eventual winning of the charming Prince Phillip.

This was also the most elaborate (read: expensive) of the Disney animated features to date. Preliminary work on *Sleeping Beauty* began in 1950 and went into full production in 1953, but was delayed with the development and opening of the Disneyland theme park. The film was released in widescreen Technirama-70 at a cost of $6,000,000—nothing to yawn at there. (Only one other Disney animated feature has ever used this process: *The Black Cauldron* in 1985.) Artists found the technique difficult to work with, complaining about working in a "letterbox" format, trying to balance the action in the center of the screen while filling the sides with more supporting characters.

Walt wanted to adapt Tchaikovsky's "Sleeping Beauty Ballet" for the musical score, so the studio's top composer, George Bruns, was dispatched to West Germany, where the music was recorded in six-channel stereo by the Berlin Symphony Orchestra. Additionally, lyrics were added to the main theme—"Once Upon a Dream"—and some new (not very memorable) songs were created.

As in other Disney animated features with human characters, live models were used to aid the artists. For Princess Aurora (the title slumberer), veteran actress Helen Stanley posed, cavorted, waltzed, and snoozed for the artists. In an interview at the time, Ms. Stanley remarked: "We rehearsed the big waltz sequence for three days before we shot it. I had to wear a specially made costume and a cumbersome wig, plus learn all the dialogue." No mention was made of how she survived the sleeping segments.

The voice of Ms. Beauty was supplied by soprano Mary Costa, who went on to a successful operatic career following her vocal appearance in *Sleeping Beauty.* Recently she learned of the huge, uh, royalties earned by the videocassette sales, and has filed suit, claiming her 1952 contract entitles her to a piece of the Disney pie. Yawn.

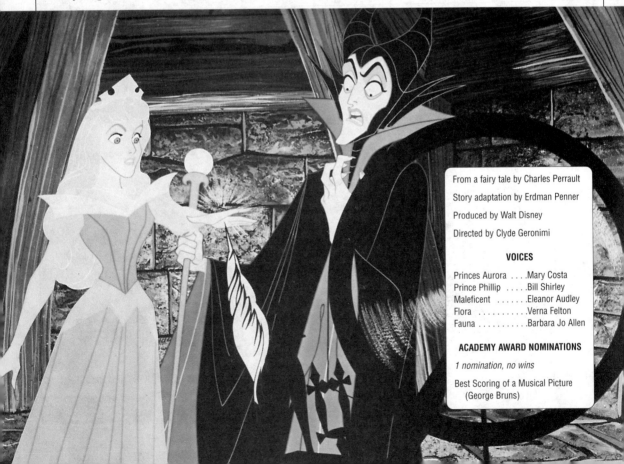

From a fairy tale by Charles Perrault

Story adaptation by Erdman Penner

Produced by Walt Disney

Directed by Clyde Geronimi

VOICES

Princes Aurora . . . .Mary Costa
Prince Phillip . . . . .Bill Shirley
Maleficent . . . . . . .Eleanor Audley
Flora . . . . .Verna Felton
Fauna . . . . .Barbara Jo Allen

ACADEMY AWARD NOMINATIONS

1 nomination, no wins

Best Scoring of a Musical Picture
(George Bruns)

THE SHAGGY DOG

WALT DISNEY PRODUCTIONS
$12,317,000

"In canis corpore transmuto."
—SECRET SPELL

DON'T SAY the above words unless you are seriously interested in spending a good part of your life as a shape-shifter…to wit: a shaggy English sheepdog. While the incantation (translation: "I change into the body of a dog") is likely to produce laughs from the Pope and a few other Latin buffs, it was certainly a successful chant for the folks at Disney, where it translated into "big box office bucks."

Since the '30s, Walt Disney had been planning a film based on the novel *The Hound of Florence* by Felix Salten (author of *Bambi*). The project lapsed during the war, and in 1957 Walt proposed it to ABC as a television series. The network turned it down as being too far-fetched, so Walt went back to his original idea of a feature. He chose to have it shot in black and white rather than color, reasoning that color would add a disturbing note of reality to the supernatural comedics. (Today, however, colorized versions have been made available by Disney Studios.)

Although basically a kid's picture, the film did well with a wide-ranging audience. Part of the reason is the broad appeal of the cast, comprised of child star Kevin "Moochie" Corcoran, some teens, and a few mostly misguided adults. For this slapstick comedy, Disney re-teamed Tommy Kirk and Kevin Corcoran, the brothers in *Old*

Screenplay by Bill Walsh and Lillie Hayward

Suggested by *The Hound of Florence* by Felix Salten

Produced by Walt Disney

Directed by Charles Barton

CAST

Wilson Daniels . . . . . . .Fred MacMurray
Frieda Daniels . . . . . .Jean Hagen
Wilby Daniels . . . . . . .Tommy Kirk
Moochie Daniels . . . . .Kevin Corcoran
Buzz Miller . . . . .Tim Considine
Allison D'Allessio . . . . .Annette Funicello

Yeller, in another dog tale. Fred Mac-Murray was cast as the canine-o-phobic father in the film, and soon found he had a whole new career as a Disney character actor, going on to star in a succession of Disney hits, such as *The Absent-Minded Professor* and *Son of Flubber.* Annette Funicello, fresh out of Mouseketeer ears, made her motion picture debut in this production at the age of 16, and she, too, went on to appear in other Disney films, as well as all those Frankie Avalon beach movies.

But the real star of the show was the dog himself. The three-year-old sheepdog was actually a non-pro belonging to a clerk for the California State Highways. Trainers Bill Koehler and Hal Driscoll spent three months prepping the pooch named Sam (renamed "Shaggy" by the Disney staff) for his first starring role. Although it may appear as if a person

is dressed in a dog suit, the director seldom used a human double, with Sam doing nearly all of his own stunts. One particularly clever bit involved the dog driving a hot-rod convertible. To get the scene, Koehler and Driscoll had mittens put over Sam's feet, and at the command "Feet up," the dog obediently placed his paws on the wheel. Thongs were used to anchor the mittens in the steering position. On the other side of the car, a man crouched to reach a synchronized steering wheel, driving the car while looking through a viewing slot. The effect was realistic, making it appear that the dog was actually driving the car.

The Disney Studios managed to get some mileage out of a couple of sequels—*The Shaggy DA* (1976) and *The Return of the Shaggy Dog* (made-for-TV, 1987). The original, though, is still the best.

OPERATION PETTICOAT

UNIVERSAL-INTERNATIONAL
$9,321,555

IT IS HARD to believe that a comedy about a pink submarine with a cargo of women and toilet paper could be based on fact, but that was the claim made by story writers Paul King and Joseph Stone.

It seems that the United States, for a time, had a bright red sub, the *Sea Dragon,* operating in the Pacific; an explosion near her berth had blistered her surface paint, eventually reducing it to the red priming coat. The USS *Skipjack* got into a bureaucratic hassle with its requisitions for toilet paper. Two pregnant natives of the Solomon Islands gave birth aboard the USS *Geta,* attended by nuns, who'd also been evacuated. Nurses were evacuated onto U.S. ships from islands after the fall of Manila. The USS *Bowfin* accidentally torpedoed a *bus* filled with Japanese sailors. Armed with these historical facts, King and Stone finally convinced producer Robert Arthur to make this unlikely movie.

The teaming of Cary Grant with

Tony Curtis proved to be pure inspiration for Universal-International in this high comedy about the war we didn't find so funny until films like this were made. The story is narrated by Grant, reading to us from the USS *Sea Tiger* captain's journal (a format later used successfully in the television series "Star Trek," which opened each week with excerpts from the Captain's log). But that's about as serious as the film ever gets. Most of this farce deals with Grant's conniving junior officer, played by Tony Curtis, and his attempts to scrounge supplies for the submarine, including a much-needed supply of sexy nurses. Appropriately risqué (for that time) humor abounds, and this early Blake Edwards hit shows the director's skill and promise in directing the type of farcical comedy that has continued to delight audiences through several decades.

Cary Grant garnered the lion's share of critical approval. *Variety* called Grant "a living lesson in getting laughs with-

out lines." *The Hollywood Reporter* also noted this aspect of Grant's performance: "Though he gets many laughs, Cary plays an essentially straight part, and theatrical pros will recognize it as one of the trickiest acting jobs of his long and brilliant career."

Tony Curtis' career was barely underway at the time. Curtis, né Bernard Schwartz, had been signed by Universal as a contract player in 1949 after paying his dues in the Catskills' "Borscht Belt" and on Broadway, but the studio hadn't found the right vehicle to showcase his talents. He was still basically a "pretty-boy" type when signed to do *Operation Petticoat* (although an appearance in *The Defiant Ones* the previous year had already won him a Best Actor nomination). Critics began to sit up and take notice, *Variety* stating that "Tony Curtis is a splendid foil [for Cary Grant], one of the two or three best young comedians around, and his different style of playing meshes easily with Grant's."

Other lesser-known cast members who would go on to greater things included Marion Ross as one of the nurses (she became "Mrs. Cunningham" on TV's "Happy Days"), and Gavin MacLeod as one of the crew (he later became captain of "The Love Boat").

Screenplay by Stanley Shapiro and
  Maurice Richlin

Based on a story by Paul King and
  Joseph Stone

Produced by Robert Arthur

Directed by Blake Edwards

CAST

Comdr. Matt Sherman . . . .Cary Grant
Lieut. Nick Holden . . . . . .Tony Curtis
Dolores Crandall . . . . . . .Joan O'Brien
Barbara Duran . . . . .Dina Merrill
Ernest Hunkle . . . . .Gavin MacLeod
Ruth Colfax . . . . .Marion Ross

ACADEMY AWARD NOMINATIONS

1 nomination, no wins

Best Story and Screenplay Written Directly
  for the Screen

DARBY O'GILL AND THE LITTLE PEOPLE

WALT DISNEY PRODUCTIONS
$8,336,000

"My thanks to King Brian of Knocknasheega and his Leprechauns, whose gracious co-operation made this picture possible. —Walt Disney"
—OPENING CARD

CLEVER, THAT Uncle Walt. In opening his film about the legendary wee folk of Ireland and the human who encounters them, the producer established the "authentic" feeling he wanted to give the picture. True, the credits do list a technical advisor named Michael O'Herlihy, but he was more an expert in Irish lore and a dialogue coach, and not an actual leprechaun himself.

To give this live-acted film (one of Disney's best) even more clout, the special effects were carefully planned and executed by Peter Ellenshaw, whom the studio had used as a matte artist on *20,000 Leagues Under the Sea.*

Under his direction, a huge Throne Room set was designed for *Darby* so that certain scenes could be shot without any special process. Darby and the Little People were all full-size human beings; the apparent difference in their scale was an optical illusion created by their distances relative to the camera. The enormous set required so much light to maintain the depth of field that at one point the production blacked out a portion of Burbank.

The entire picture was filmed on Disney's Burbank lot and on two southern California ranches, with the beautiful scenery of Ireland being filmed by a second unit. This footage was later combined with the matte paintings and live sequences to obtain the overall effect.

Cast in the title role was 73-year-old Irish actor Albert Sharpe, who had retired since his appearance in 1954 in

MGM's *Brigadoon.* Disney's casting people tracked him down in his ivy-covered cottage near Belfast and convinced him to play the feisty old Shanachie (storyteller) who matches wits with the King of the Leprechauns.

The part of the young Irish romantic lead went to a Scotsman, however. Connery—Sean Connery. Two years before he became James Bond, while still virtually unknown in America, the young actor was spotted by Disney's casting people while he was working in Britain on a Paramount film, *Another Time, Another Place.* In *Darby,* not only did Connery get the girl, but he won her heart with his rendition of "Pretty Irish Girl," his first—and last—screen song. Director Robert Stevenson contemplated dubbing him, but the duet with co-star Janet Munro remained on the soundtrack and was later released as a single in Britain.

Written by Lawrence Edward Watkin

Suggested by "Darby O'Gill" stories by H. T. Kavanagh

Produced by Walt Disney

Directed by Robert Stevenson

CAST

Darby O'Gill . . . . .Albert Sharpe
Katie . . . . .Janet Munro
Michael McBride . . . . .Sean Connery
King Brian Connors . . .Jimmy O'Dea
Pony Sugrue . . . . . . .Kieron Moore
Sheelah . . . . .Estelle Winwood

THROUGHOUT the Sixties, Hollywood, still clinging to familiarity, found sustenance in proven success formulas. Musicals were a mainstay, spearheaded by classical Broadway fare like *West Side Story, The Music Man, My Fair Lady, The Sound of Music, Funny Girl,* and *Hello, Dolly!* Biblical epics were history except for *Spartacus* and *The Bible,* and a new genre, the "historical epic," made an entrance. These epics included *Exodus, The Alamo, The Guns of Navarone, El Cid, How the West Was Won, The Longest Day, Lawrence of Arabia, Cleopatra, A Man for All Seasons,* and *The Dirty Dozen.*

The films of the Sixties were becoming more permissive in their content and language. Nudity began appearing not only in bawdy films like *Tom Jones,* but in classics like *Romeo and Juliet.* The 70-millimeter camera now went everywhere, especially into the bedroom.

With Hollywood's new permissiveness came a new rating sys-

1960

tem for movies. Established in 1968 to advise parents in planning film attendance by their offspring, this rating system, in a slightly modified form, is still with us today. The Motion Picture Association of America (MPAA), under the leadership of president Jack Valenti, established the following letter guidelines:

G   Suggested for GENERAL audiences.

M   Suggested for MATURE audiences (parental discretion advised).

R   RESTRICTED—persons under 16 not admitted unless accompanied by parent or adult guardian.

X   Persons under 16 not admitted.

The Hayes Office and its censorship were gone, but so was Hollywood's age of innocence. This new rating system brought with it an implied censorship: if a distributor didn't like a rating a film received, it was up to the studio or producer to make appropriate changes in the film. If not, a whole set of ticket purchasers might be eliminated—box office disaster.

1969

SWISS FAMILY ROBINSON

WALT DISNEY PRODUCTIONS
$20,178,000

OF ALL THE Walt Disney live-acted films, this was certainly one of the most difficult ever undertaken. In searching for the proper remote desert island, the Disney scouts selected Tobago, part of Trinidad in the West Indies. The island was a treasure-trove of all things tropical: sun, sand, colorful water, palm trees—and hurricanes. After spending a fortune constructing sheet-metal soundstages, the crew was hit by Hurricane Edith, one of the biggest storms ever to strike Tobago. It flooded the stage and washed out the treehouse and other sets. They couldn't shoot for weeks, during which time the crew not only reconstructed the sets, but helped the islanders rebuild their homes destroyed by the storm.

The story called for a large tree-house for the Robinson family, and the crew built the most elaborate one imaginable. It was such a hit that Disney decided to have it duplicated for Disneyland. Visitors to that park and to Walt Disney World's Magic Kingdom can climb through the tri-level chalet with its family room and two bedrooms. All the details were reproduced in the 70-foot-high tree-house, including the sailcloth curtains and cracked mirror. A waterfall-operated waterwheel feeds a storage barrel through a system of buckets and bamboo plumbing.

One of the great challenges to the production crew was the large assortment of animals needed, and *Swiss Family Robinson* holds the record for variety. More than 200 birds and animals were used in the six months of

filming. Among the members of the Disney menagerie were ostriches, zebras, anacondas, monitor lizards, iguanas, monkeys, tigers, cheetahs, hyenas, alligators, dogs, goats, a cow, an elephant, and a mule, plus a large variety of tropical birds, fowl, and a couple of dozen vultures.

An excellent cast helped make this film a hit at the box office—again, with an eye to appeal to all age groups. The cast included the third appearance of Kevin Corcoran and Tommy Kirk paired as brothers (by now, *they* even thought they were related); John Mills, renowned British actor, as papa Robinson (although Disney fans couldn't help but think of him as *Hayley's* father); Dorothy McGuire as the mother (she'd been the mother of the young boys in *Old Yeller*); James

MacArthur, Helen Hayes' son, who at the time was starring in "Hawaii Five-O" (playing "Danno," as in "Book him, Danno"); Janet Munro, who had co-starred in the Disney hit *Darby O'Gill and the Little People* the previous year; and Sessue Hayakawa, the heavy from *The Bridge on the River Kwai,* as the Pirate Chief. This basically recycled group always worked well for Disney, with the audience not seeming to mind the same "family" appearing in film after film.

John Mills was one of the most illustrious actors ever to appear in a Disney film. The English-born performer made his professional debut as a chorus boy in a London revue in 1929 at the age of 21. By 1932, he was landing roles in films. His career would see him making nearly a hundred pictures in all, including *The Chalk Garden* (with Hayley, 1963) and *Ryan's Daughter,* for which he won the

Academy Award (1970). His daughter Juliet Mills is also an actress.

While some critics were upset at the license taken by the Disney gang with the 147-year-old tale by Johann Wyss, most gave *Swiss Family Robinson* a nod of approval for its fine production

Screenplay by Lowell S. Hawley

Based on the novel by Johann Wyss

Produced by Bill Anderson

Directed by Ken Annakin

CAST

Father	John Mills
Mother	Dorothy McGuire
Fritz	James MacArthur
Ernst	Tommy Kirk
Roberta	Janet Munro
Francis	Kevin Corcoran
Kuala	Sessue Hayakawa

values and stunning visual imagery. While *Variety* praised the cinematography and the Technicolor views of Tobago, the trade paper lambasted the film for its lack of realism: "Huge boulders and logs dispatched downhill by the Robinsons at their corsair adversaries are so obviously cardboard that the scene just about lapses into sheer slapstick for everyone but tots." When the film opened on December 23, *The New York Times* gave it a terrific notice, writing that "any parent who denies it to the kids deserves to be shipwrecked on a remote island, at least till the new year."

For the Disney organization, *Swiss Family Robinson* was the gift that keeps on giving. Walt Disney Productions had a loss of $1,500,000 during 1960, but the year ended on a happy note, and thanks to re-releases, this movie became one of the studio's most successful films ever.

PSYCHO

PARAMOUNT/UNIVERSAL
$11,200,000

"I aim to provide the public with beneficial shocks. Civilization has become so protective that we're no longer able to get our goose bumps instinctively. The only way to remove the numbness and revive our moral equilibrium is to use artificial means to bring about the shock. The best way to achieve that, it seems to me, is through a movie."

—ALFRED HITCHCOCK, QUOTED IN
THE FILMS OF ALFRED HITCHCOCK

WITHOUT A DOUBT, *Psycho* is one of the scariest pieces of celluloid make-believe to ever run through a projector. Yet Hitch himself saw the picture as a *humorous* film, his idea of the blackest of black comedies. Some joke. After viewing this film, no one would ever feel quite safe in the shower again. And it is not known whether or not the motel business fell off after the film's release, but you can bet that anyone who owned one named "Bates" quickly changed it.

Much of the shock value of this pic-

ture comes from Hitchcock's use of black and white. The director himself selected the monochrome tones because he felt that the bloody shower scene would be *too* realistic for his audience. If anyone should ever decide to colorize this picture (and undoubtedly that day will come), you might be wise to listen to the maestro's warning and turn down the color control, or face the consequences.

Suspense was heightened by the music Hitchcock selected. With the only soundtrack ever to be composed entirely of strings, composer Bernard Herrmann gave the director the "black-and-white music" he sought. The shrieking of the violins coupled with the stabbing in the shower scene make for a moment that virtually every film historian has termed "classic."

Actually, the shower scene was shot with doubles for both stars, Anthony Perkins and Janet Leigh. Perkins was in New York rehearsing for a play when the scene was filmed in Hollywood, and he never actually wielded the knife in this sequence. And

Janet Leigh also used a body double since partial nudity was used, and stars very seldom did their own nude scenes in those days. Most disillusioning of all, no real blood was used. Instead, chocolate sauce was seen flowing out of the body and down the drain! Black and white does have its advantages.

Although the knife never actually makes bodily contact in the shower scene, our minds tell us differently. This sequence set the pace for later violent films of the decade, such as *Bonnie and Clyde.*

Sequels? It took a while, but in 1983 Anthony Perkins reprised his role as Norman Bates in *Psycho II.* It did surprisingly well, so Universal (owner of all Hitchcock properties) did still another sequel, appropriately titled *Psycho III* (1986), with Anthony Perkins not only acting but directing the film. It was a dismal failure, but Universal continues to get mileage out of Norman Bates and his mother—in 1987, NBC aired a two-hour pilot film for a proposed series named "Bates Motel," starring Bud Cort.

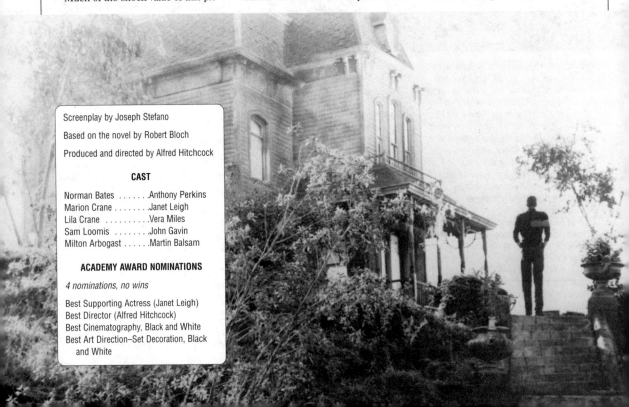

Screenplay by Joseph Stefano

Based on the novel by Robert Bloch

Produced and directed by Alfred Hitchcock

CAST

Norman Bates	Anthony Perkins
Marion Crane	Janet Leigh
Lila Crane	Vera Miles
Sam Loomis	John Gavin
Milton Arbogast	Martin Balsam

ACADEMY AWARD NOMINATIONS

4 nominations, no wins

Best Supporting Actress (Janet Leigh)
Best Director (Alfred Hitchcock)
Best Cinematography, Black and White
Best Art Direction–Set Decoration, Black and White

SPARTACUS

UNIVERSAL INTERNATIONAL
$11,100,000

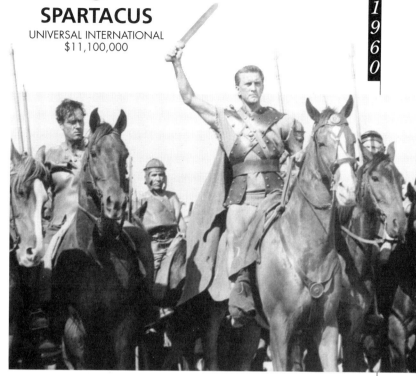

I N SPENDING $12,000,000 on the making of *Spartacus*, Universal/International was banking on the two top box office stars of the year—Tony Curtis (number one) and Kirk Douglas (number two)—to draw people into the theaters for the latest entry in the Biblical-spectacular genre that had been so popular in the '50s. Although far from a flop, the film failed to break even, and it would be a decade more before Universal again had a top-five hit.

Kirk Douglas himself was the film's executive producer, and was particularly drawn to the theme of the film. In *The Films of the Sixties*, Douglas is quoted as saying: "I tended to be attracted to roles of people fighting society. The focus is on a man bucking the system and getting destroyed in the process." Not only was this to be the theme of many a film to come during the decade, but it would be mirrored with the unrest that was to sweep America during the '60s.

For his screenwriter, Douglas selected Dalton Trumbo, one of the so-called "Hollywood Ten," who was sentenced to a year in jail in 1950 for

Screenplay by Dalton Trumbo

Based on the novel by Howard Fast

Produced by Edward Lewis

Directed by Stanley Kubrick

CAST

Spartacus . . . . .Kirk Douglas
Crassus . . . . .Laurence Olivier
Antoninus . . . . .Tony Curtis
Varinia . . . . .Jean Simmons
Gracchus . . . . .Charles Laughton
Batiatus . . . . .Peter Ustinov
Caesar . . . . .John Gavin

ACADEMY AWARD NOMINATIONS

6 nominations, 4 wins*

**Best Supporting Actor (Peter Ustinov)
*Best Cinematography, Color
*Best Art Direction–Set Decoration, Color
Best Scoring of a Dramatic or Comedy
   Picture
Best Film Editing
Best Costume Design, Color

refusing to testify before the House Committee on Un-American Activities. The blacklisted writer had been forced to work under a pseudonym since his release from jail, and the man who had written *30 Seconds Over Tokyo was* reduced to writing a string of "B" movies. In 1957, under the name of Robert Rich, Trumbo won an Oscar for his script of *The Brave One*. And with his work on *Spartacus,* he was able to put the dreaded blacklist behind him.

It was an excellent script, not just because it made use of the wide screen and spectacular visual events in its storytelling, but also because of the fine dialogue, as illustrated by this exchange between Antoninus (Tony Curtis) and Spartacus (Kirk Douglas):

ANTONINUS
Are you afraid to die, Spartacus?

SPARTACUS
No more than I was to be born.

Interesting little bit of philosophy, profound in its simplicity.

There were thousands of extras who made the gladiatorial halftime look like Super Sunday as Roman legions marched before their leaders. And the all-star cast didn't hurt,

either—names like Laurence Olivier, Jean Simmons, Charles Laughton, Peter (can't have a film about Rome without him) Ustinov, John Gavin, and many more known and unknown actors, including a couple of the Canutt boys, Tap and Joe (who also appeared in *Ben-Hur*).

Stanley Kubrick did an excellent job as director, although he was frustrated over his lack of control. Nevertheless, the avant-garde director won praise from the critics. According to *Variety,* "The individual who emerges above all is Director Kubrick. At 31, and with only four other pix behind him…Kubrick has out-DeMilled the old master in spectacle, without ever permitting the story or the people who are the core of the drama to become lost in the shuffle. He demonstrates here a technical talent and comprehension of human values."

Spartacus is frequently shown on independent or cable television stations, its original 196-minute length occasionally shortened by 12 minutes. Its full impact, however, is not diminished, and although its theme is by no means revolutionary today, *Spartacus* still stands as a tribute to the soul's yearning for freedom—written by a man who ought to know.

EXODUS

UNITED ARTISTS
$8,331,582

Leon Uris' novel *Exodus* was a best-seller's best-seller. After 80 weeks on the list and sales upwards of 4,000,000 copies, it arrived on the (wide) screen amidst much well-deserved fanfare. Since filming was done on location in Israel and Cyprus, producer Otto Preminger was able to bring in this 212-minute epic for a cost of only $4,000,000, cheap for a film of this scope. There were the usual thousands of extras—this film claimed to have 45,000 of them—plus a moving script by previously blacklisted "Hollywood Ten" writer Dalton Trumbo. *Spartacus* had not yet been released, and Preminger was actually the first one to give Trumbo a chance to write under his own name once again.

Preminger's casting choices were unusual, since most of the major roles of Jews were played by non-Jews. Paul Newman was selected for the part of Ari Ben Canaan, a hero in the Mosaic tradition, and it is hard to imagine anyone else in the part; Eva Marie Saint is a perfect counterpoint as the WASPish love interest whom he wins over to his cause; Sal Mineo, an Italian-American, was so convincing in his portrayal of the zealous young Jewish terrorist that he won an Academy Award nomination; and even 14-year-old Jill Haworth as Karen was effective as a Nordic Jewish refugee (although she could have used a dialogue coach).

Exodus received generally favorable critical acclaim, although most critics found it overly long. *The New York Times* called the film "a dazzling, eye-filling, nerve-tingling display of a wide variety of individual and mass reaction to awesome challenges and, in some of its sharpest personal details, a free reflection of experience that rips the heart."

Although the production team did its best to try to please both the Arabs and Jews in Israel by constantly rewriting the script during filming, there were still complaints from both groups.

Both Otto Preminger and Paul Newman received threatening letters while on location. Perhaps that is to be expected of any political film. Still, the message of *Exodus* is one that should be heeded by all warring factions. At the end of the picture, Ari Ben Canaan buries two dead patriots—Arab and Jew—in a common grave. In one of the film's most poignant moments, he says: "The dead always share the earth in peace; and that's not enough. It's time for the living to have a turn. The day will come when Arab and Jew will share in a peaceful life this land that they have always shared in death."

More than 35 years have passed since those lines were written. While progress has been made at the bargaining table, with an Arab-Israeli accord being hammered out by the region's leaders, true peace still does not reign. However, the film's prophetic longings seem several steps closer to becoming reality.

Screenplay by Dalton Trumbo

Based on the novel by Leon Uris

Produced and directed by Otto Preminger

CAST

Ari Ben Canaan . . . . . .Paul Newman
Kitty Fremont . . . . . . .Eva Marie Saint
General Sutherland . . .Ralph Richardson
Major Caldwell . . . . . .Peter Lawford
Barak Ben Canaan . . . .Lee J. Cobb
Dov Landau . . . . .Sal Mineo

ACADEMY AWARD NOMINATIONS

3 nominations, 1 win*

Best Supporting Actor (Sal Mineo)
Best Cinematography, Color
*Best Scoring of a Dramatic or Comedy
   Picture (Ernest Gold)

LA DOLCE VITA

ASTOR
$8,000,000

ARMS SPREAD wide as if in benediction, a bigger-than-life statue of Jesus dangles from a helicopter as it makes its way across both ancient and modern Rome. In the opening segment of Federico Fellini's masterpiece *La Dolce Vita* ("The Sweet Life"), the director wastes no time in showing us that this will be an unusual film, and we are quickly swept into the story without beginning or end as another helicopter, bearing leading actor Marcello Mastroianni, swoops into view to record this event. He is a tabloid journalist, and his exploits make up the heart of *La Dolce Vita* as he pursues sordid tales around Rome and encounters characters that make his life more bittersweet than sweet.

This was a landmark film, appearing at the end of the 1950s in Europe and at the beginning of the next decade in America. It broke ground both for its previously taboo treatment of a hedonistic lifestyle of the protagonists, as well as the unique cinematic style of the director. It was one of a very few European films to catch fire at the box office in the United States, and although it is still considered by many an "art film," the cultural influence of

Screenplay by Federico Fellini, Ennio Flaiano, Tullio Pinelli, Brunello Rondi

Produced by Giuseppe Amato, Angelo Rizzoli

Directed by Federico Fellini

CAST

Marcello Rubino	Marcello Mastroianni
Paparazzo	Walter Santesso
Maddalena	Anouk Aimee
Sylvia	Anita Ekberg
Robert	Lex Barker

ACADEMY AWARD NOMINATIONS

4 nominations, 1 win*

Best Director
Best Screenplay (Fellini et al.)
Best Art Direction–Set Decoration, Black and White
*Best Costume Design, Black and White

La Dolce Vita helped it rise above that stereotype. For example, reporter Marcello's ubiquitous photographer, a character named Paparazzo, added a new word to the English language. The term *paparazzi,* meaning photographers who chase after celebrities, is derived from the Italian plural of his name.

La Dolce Vita also made an international star out of Italian unknown Marcello Mastroianni. The handsome ladies' man created a trend based on his character's appearance, and Italian sunglasses, striped shirts and even his fast convertible sports car became objects of emulation for the affluent male audience in Europe as well as the U.S.

Director Fellini had been working as a writer, actor, and director in his native Italy since the 1940s. His first international breakthrough film was *La Strada* (1954), starring his wife, Giulietta Masina. Other minor pictures

followed, but his next successful international film was *La Dolce Vita.* Perhaps the condemnation by both the Catholic Church (for its treatments of suicide and sexuality) and the Italian government (for the film's perceived criticism of Italy) helped make this a box office hit. After that, Fellini's films found success on both sides of the Atlantic. In 1963, he enjoyed moderate success with *8 1/2;* in 1965 with *Juliet of the Spirits* (his first color film), and in 1970 with *Fellini Satyricon.*

Although nominated many times for an Academy Award, the only Oscar Fellini ever received was an honorary one. In 1993, he was awarded a special Oscar for lifetime achievement in filmmaking "in recognition of his cinematic accomplishments that have thrilled and entertained worldwide audiences." His wife of 50 years, Giulietta, was by his side. It was to be his last accolade; he died the following October of a heart attack.

1

101 DALMATIANS
WALT DISNEY PRODUCTIONS
$68,648,000

N O ONE COULD tell a dog story, shaggy or otherwise, like Walt Disney. After successes like *Old Yeller, Lady and the Tramp,* and *The Shaggy Dog,* Walt again turned to the canine kingdom for his next feature-length animated movie. You say you want dogs? Okay, here's *one hundred and one* of them, all adorable and cuddly, with lots of spots, and the ability to make their master a big pile of box office kibble (at $68,648,000 in rentals to date, that's close to $680,000 per puppy).

Based on the book *The Hundred and One Dalmatians* by Dodie Smith, this film represented a significant departure from previous Disney animated fare in several respects. Unlike most of its predecessors, the story was not derived from a classic fairy tale and took place in a contemporary setting instead of a magical or fantasy world. It's a tale of dognapping by one of the meanest villainesses ever creat-

ed, Disney or otherwise. Cruella De Vil is a candidate for animal rights activists' dartboard of the month. With her deathmask-like face and fondness for wearing fur, she plans the demise of the innocent Dalmatian puppies, whose spotted skins she sees as potential coat material ("Poison them, drown them, bash them in the head"). She makes the Wicked Witch in *Snow White* look like a Sunday School teacher.

The fact that audiences identify with the dogs and not the humans in this and other Disney stories is not by accident. The stories are told from the anthropomorphized animals' point of view, emphasized by such comments as "At times she seems almost canine!" (a high compliment) and Pongo's calling his human his "pet."

As with other animated Disney movies about animals, lots of dog models were brought to the studio to be photographed for the artists. As Frank

Thomas, one of the Disney animators, explained in a Disney press release at the time: "The Dalmatians were complicated and tough to draw because of their sleek short-haired bodies. The character design required accurately drawn bones, muscles and structure instead of a more caricatured approach." Another Disney animator, Eric Larson, was responsible for the sequence in which the puppies watch TV. To capture the feeling, according to the same release, he pictured them as a bunch of kids in front of the set. "I just thought of what regular kids would do as they watched TV. . . one of the pups sits directly in front of the set blocking everyone else's view. Another is constantly hungry. It was a lot of fun doing that scene."

At the time of its initial release, *101 Dalmatians* introduced a revolutionary new process—Xerox photography, an electromagnetic technique for transferring animators' drawings directly to cels. It saved an enormous amount of time and money, especially in scenes in which dozens of puppies fill the screen, each of them peppered with spots. The Xerox camera allowed the artists to animate one small group of puppies, then repeat this group across the entire surface, being careful that the scene did not appear too mechanical. Disney statisticians are fond of noting that there are exactly 6,469,952 spots on the backs of the dogs and puppies in 113,760 frames of film ("Pongo" has 72, "Perdita" has 68, and each pup sports 32 spots). Without the Xerox process, we'd probably still be waiting for the first showing of this movie.

Great care went into the selection of the vocal actors for the leading dog and human roles. Rod Taylor is the voice of Pongo. A popular star of science fiction films in the '50s and '60s, the Australian-born actor is best known for his starring roles in *The Birds* and *The Time Machine*.

For Cruella De Vil, the Disney team chose Betty Lou Gerson, who had previously provided the voice-over narra-tion for *Cinderella*. Her impression of the wicked dognapper sounded quite a bit like Tallulah Bankhead, which delighted the producers. She also obliged the animators by modeling for them, slinking around the studio while they photographed and sketched the lean, high-cheekboned actress. As Ms. Gerson said in Disney's press release, "The character you see on the screen is a fairly accurate caricature of me—except for the white streak in Cruella's hair."

Variety called the film "a painstaking creative effort and certainly a valuable and welcome addition to the current theatrical scene," adding that "children are certain to get a big kick out of it." *The New York Times* admitted that "even with a lady Lucifer hell-bent for their hides, those Dalmatians are a friendly lot worth knowing." *Time* described the feature as "one of the nicest things that have happened so far this year to dog's best friend: a full-length animated cartoon that should please just about everybody but cats…the wittiest, most charming, least pretentious cartoon feature Walt Disney has ever made."

In 1996, Walt Disney Productions filmed a live-acted version of *101 Dalmations,* with Glenn Close starring as Cruella. Meanwhile, the animated version of *101 Dalmations* has had several additional theatrical re-releases, and the Disney classic is now available on videocassette for your *dogs'* home viewing. Try not to let them crowd in front of the set.

Story by William Peet

Based on the book by Dodie Smith

Produced by Walt Disney

Directed by Wolfgang Reitherman, Hamilton S. Luske, and Clyde Geronimi

VOICES

Pongo	Rod Taylor
Cruella De Vil	Betty Lou Gerson
Roger	Ben Wright
Anita	Lisa Davis
Horace	Fred Worlock
Jasper	J. Pat O'Malley

2

WEST SIDE STORY

UNITED ARTISTS
$19,645,570

WILLIAM SHAKESPEARE. Leonard Bernstein. Robert Wise. An unlikely trio to produce a Broadway/motion picture hit? Certainly, the Bard would have been delighted to see what had become of his Capulets and Montagues in modern times. And that is just what choreographer-director Jerome Robbins thought when he translated Shakespeare's *Romeo and Juliet* into a Puerto Rican–American gang fight on the mean streets of Manhattan's Upper West Side. When the musical opened in September, 1957, it shattered the mold for Broadway musicals. Three record-breaking years later, it would repeat the magic on the motion picture screen.

The translation to film cost $6,000,000 but more than tripled that amount in profit on a domestic level (and even more when worldwide distribution is considered). At the helm of the expensive production was Robert Wise, a director noted for his sense of artistry and economy of filming. The studio wanted Robbins as co-director, and Wise did his best to work with him. Robbins' only prior film work was the staging for "Small House of Uncle Thomas" in *The King and I*. Wise was distressed when *West Side Story* began running behind schedule due to Robbins' demands for perfection in the choreographed numbers, and after

two-and-a-half months, Wise had Robbins removed. Both directors, however, shared credit, and both received Oscars, the first time the Academy Award went to co-directors.

Leonard Bernstein's score and Stephen Sondheim's lyrics seemed radical when audiences first heard them. The jazzy counterpoint in Bernstein's music at first sounded harsh to ears accustomed to singalong Broadway tunes, but Bernstein offered both, and gradually audiences embraced the music with warmth. Songs like "Maria," "Tonight," and "I Feel Pretty" helped balance the more syncopated numbers like "America" and "Gee, Officer Krupke!" The latter got a lyric-scrubbing for the screen— "My mother is a bastard; my pa's an s.o.b." became "My daddy beats my mommy, my mommy clobbers me." But both film and stage audiences knew that the song's closing line, "Gee, Officer Krupke, krup you!" had a euphemism for the "f" word, making this number quite popular among young people.

The film's executive producers, the Mirisch brothers, had originally wanted Elvis Presley as Tony, with gang members to be played by Frankie Avalon, Fabian, and Paul Anka. Fortunately, Jerome Robbins managed to convince them otherwise. For some actors, starring in the movie *West Side*

Story became a fast rise to the top with nowhere to go from there. Richard Beymer as Tony did little else in what seemed a promising career; ditto George Chakiris, who won an award as Best Supporting Actor. Yet Natalie Wood (whose singing voice was dubbed by the ever-popular Marni Nixon) continued with an acting career that flourished until her tragic death in 1981. Rita Moreno, who also won an Oscar for her portrayal of Chakiris' Puerto Rican girlfriend, has added a Tony and an Emmy to her award collection.

Screenplay by Ernest Lehman

Based on the stage book by Arthur Laurents

From a conception by Jerome Robbins

Lyrics by Stephen Sondheim

Music by Leonard Bernstein

Produced by Robert Wise

Directed by Robert Wise and Jerome Robbins

CAST

Maria	Natalie Wood
Tony	Richard Beymer
Riff	Russ Tamblyn
Anita	Rita Moreno
Bernardo	George Chakiris

ACADEMY AWARD NOMINATIONS

11 nominations, 10 wins*

*Best Picture
*Best Director (Robert Wise and Jerome Robbins)
*Best Supporting Actor (George Chakiris)
*Best Supporting Actress (Rita Moreno)
  Best Screenplay Based on Material from Another Medium
*Best Cinematography, Color
*Best Art Direction–Set Decoration, Color
*Best Sound
*Best Scoring of a Musical Picture
*Best Film Editing
*Best Costume Design, Color

Jerome Robbins was awarded a statuette for "his brilliant achievements in the art of choreography on film."

THE GUNS OF NAVARONE

COLUMBIA
$13,000,000

"The only way to win a war is to be just as nasty as the enemy. One thing that worries me is that we're liable to wake up one morning and find out we're even nastier than they are." —GREGORY PECK

COLUMBIA PICTURES hadn't had a hit since 1957, when *The Bridge on the River Kwai* provided that studio with a box office blockbuster. The war had helped them turn a huge profit, so why not try another war movie? *The Guns of Navarone* proved just the ticket. Written and produced by Carl Foreman (who had been on that infamous blacklist during the '50s but managed to rise above it with the screenplay for *High Noon*), the film was given the full "historical extravaganza" treatment: big budget ($6,000,000), big cast (Gregory Peck, David Niven, Anthony Quinn, and Anthony Quayle), big musical score (Dimitri Tiomkin), and big special effects that were so effective they grabbed the Oscar.

For the location filming in the Aegean Sea, producer Foreman and crew spent a year scouting the Mediterranean and

Screenplay by Carl Foreman

Based on the novel by Alistair MacLean

Produced by Carl Foreman

Directed by J. Lee Thompson

CAST

Mallory	Gregory Peck
Miller	David Niven
Andrea	Anthony Quinn
Franklin	Anthony Quayle
Pappadimos	James Darren
Barnsby	Richard Harris

ACADEMY AWARD NOMINATIONS

7 nominations, 1 win*

Best Picture
Best Director (J. Lee Thompson)
Best Screenplay Based on Material from Another Medium
Best Sound
Best Scoring of a Dramatic or Comedy Picture (Dimitri Tiomkin)
Best Film Editing
*Best Special Effects

Aegean before selecting the 550-square-mile island of Rhodes for principal exterior work. Over a thousand Greek soldiers doubled as Germans invading the island. Access to the area selected to represent the "cliffs of Navarone" was by a two-hour overland donkey trek. The crew rounded up all the local donkeys plus others from 30 miles away, using the beasts to carry the camera and lighting equipment.

The efforts at reality paid off handsomely both at the box office and with the critics. *Time* commented: "*The Guns of Navarone*, a World War II military exercise of the those-poor-devils-haven't-got-a-chance school, is the most enjoyable consignment of baloney in months." *The New York Times* described the film as "one of those muscle-loaded pictures in the thundering tradition of DeMille… J. Lee Thompson has directed it with pace and has seen to it that the actors give the impression of being stout and bold." Audiences agreed, and gave *The Guns of Navarone* their nod of approval at the box office, where the film earned more than double what it cost.

1961

EL CID

ALLIED ARTISTS
$12,000,000

"For God, Alfonso, and for Spain!"
—BATTLE CRY OF EL CID

DON ROBRIGO Diaz de Vivar, Spain's great 11th-century military hero, became the subject of ballads and poems when he routed the Moors from Spanish soil after battling them for 30 years, earning the nickname "al Seid"—Arabic for "the Lord." Producer Samuel Bronston, who had produced *King of Kings* in 1960, figured it was time that modern audiences trembled before El Cid, too, and together with independent production company Allied Artists, produced a 70-millimeter Super Technirama spectacular to rival the original Spanish-Moorish confrontation.

Using the proven formula (Big Budget + Big Cast + Thousands of Extras + Big Screen + Big Score = Big Box Office Bucks), Bronston won over moviegoers and critics alike. His budget was the biggest of any film that year—over $8,000,000, an enormous expenditure, but still yielding its backers a tidy profit. The cast? Big names like Charlton Heston, ranked number three at the box office by American

movie fans, and Sophia Loren, the Italian actress so popular with European audiences and whose presence guaranteed international success for the film.

Reviewers enjoyed the sense of spectacle created by the film, though most noted that the interaction

---

Screenplay by Fredric M. Frank and
 Philip Yordan

Produced by Samuel Bronston

Directed by Anthony Mann

CAST

El Cid . . . . .Charlton Heston
Chimene . . . . .Sophia Loren
Ordonez . . . . .Raf Vallone
Urraca . . . . .Genevieve Page
Alfonso . . . . .John Fraser

ACADEMY AWARD NOMINATIONS

2 nominations, no wins

Best Art Direction–Set Decoration, Color
Best Scoring of a Dramatic or Comedy
 Picture

---

between characters seemed to be its weak point. Wrote *Variety:* " 'El Cid' is a fast-action, color-rich, corpse-strewn battle picture…the one reservation is that the action engages the eye rather than the mind." *The New York Times* agreed, noting that while the film was successful as spectacle, "only the human drama is still and dull in this narrative." Perhaps the unkindest cut of all came from *Newsweek,* which griped that "the dramatics in it explode with all the force of a panful of popcorn…[Anthony] Mann's direction is slow, stately, and confused, while Miss Loren and Heston spend much of the picture simply glaring at each other."

El Cid is occasionally run on independent movie channels, but does not hold the viewer's attention as well as it did in its theatrical release. The above reviews were fairly accurate in that they all made note of the film's main flaw—the lack of meaningful interaction between characters. Oftentimes, a film can get away with this on the big screen, but unfortunately, not on the small one.

THE ABSENT-MINDED PROFESSOR

WALT DISNEY PRODUCTIONS
$11,426,000

FLUBBER—it stood for flying rubber—and its formula brought laughs to the audience and dollars to the ailing Walt Disney Studios. The story line was a simple one: a college professor (Fred MacMurray) invents antigravity. He starts slowly, bouncing a perpetual-motion rubber ball, but quickly graduates to bigger objects—like the college basketball team, the film's villain (played by Keenan Wynn), and a clunky old Model-T automobile known as a flivver. The picture spelled fun for youngsters and their parents as well, which in turn spelled black ink once more for Disney.

Believe it or not, those Disney craftsmen, perfectionists all, hired a bona fide science professor as tech advisor. Among his tasks: create a formula for flubber that didn't sound like gibberish. See what you think of this formula, as described by the "Professor":

"The application of external thermal energy to two previously incompatible metastable compounds brought about fusion at high temperature, combustion, the release of explosive gasses and an accompanying residue—flubber. Never did I hope to find a metastable compound whose mol-ecular configuration is such that the delivery of minute particles of energy to its surface would trigger a change in the configuration. This change in molecular configuration liberates enormous quantities of energy but they act only in a direction opposite of the force which triggered the molecular change. That's why we call it repulsive energy. The total effect is transient, and upon the shutting off of the externally applied energy, the elementary particles return to a state of pseudoequilibrium."

Got that? Good luck.

You might want to try this instead. Here is the recipe that the special-effects guys at Disney used to whip up the stuff that served as the prop for flubber:

To one pound saltwater taffy add one heaping tablespoon polyurethane foam, one cake of crumbled yeast. Mix till smooth, allow to rise. Then pour into saucepan over one cup cracked rice mixed with one cup water. Add topping of molasses. Boil till it lifts lid and says "Quirp."

Proceed at your own risk. Void where prohibited by law and parents!

The movie proved to be a huge hit for Disney. Fred MacMurray had been Tommy Kirk's father in *The Shaggy Dog,* and audiences eagerly welcomed them back with new identities for this Disney picture. And adding to the fun was the casting of three generations of Wynns—Keenan, playing the film's bad guy, his famous father, Ed Wynn, as the fire chief, and son Ned in a small role. It was the first time the trio had acted together.

It was evident that this film truly deserved a sequel, and within two years, *Son of Flubber* (1963) reunited the entire original cast for yet another romp. It did extremely well, narrowly missing the top five. Both movies appear from time to time on television or on Disney cable programming, and can also be rented (though they can be difficult to locate).

Screenplay by Bill Walsh

Based on a story by Samuel W. Taylor

Produced by Walt Disney

Directed by Robert Stevenson

CAST

Prof. Ned Brainard . . . .Fred MacMurray
Betsy Carlisle . . . . .Nancy Olson
Alonzo Hawk . . . . .Keenan Wynn
Bill Hawk . . . . .Tommy Kirk
College President . . . . .Leon Ames
Fire Chief . . . . .Ed Wynn

ACADEMY AWARD NOMINATIONS

3 nominations, no wins

Best Cinematography, Black and White
Best Art Direction–Set Decoration, Black and White
Best Special Effects

HOW THE WEST WAS WON

CINERAMA RELEASING CORPORATION/METRO-GOLDWYN-MAYER
$20,932,883

THE FIRST DRAMATIC Cinerama presentation arrived to trumpets and fanfare, ecstatic reviews, and box office frenzies as people stampeded to get seats. The movie, as sprawling as the great land itself, was the story of the push westward across the American plains in fulfillment of our "manifest destiny."

How the West Was Won was far from a documentary, however. The film was divided into three segments, with three different directors leaving their mark on this wonder: "The Civil War" was directed by John Ford; "The Railroad," by George Marshall; and "The Rivers, the Plains, the Outlaws" was under the command of Henry Hathaway. No less than *four* directors of photography were named in the credits.

Here was a Cinerama picture that, for the first time, was not made just for gawking or as a showcase for effects like roller coaster rides. *How the West Was Won* was a remarkable achievement for a process that required a bank of three simultaneously shooting cameras plus a three-projector system for exhibiting the finished product. Despite the difficulties of getting this epic on film, there were some fine cinematic moments, including lots of POV shots of shooting rapids and trains barreling through tunnels.

As if that weren't enough, there's a real story, narrated by Spencer Tracy. We follow Lilith Prescott (Debbie Reynolds) from youth through old age as our story unfolds across the continent. Along the way we meet nearly every working actor in Hollywood: James Stewart, Henry Fonda, Carroll Baker, Lee J. Cobb, Carolyn Jones, Karl Malden, Gregory Peck, George Peppard, Robert Preston, Eli Wallach, John Wayne, Richard Widmark, Walter Brennan, Andy Devine, Raymond Massey, Agnes Moorehead, Harry Morgan, Thelma Ritter, and Russ Tamblyn.

The film offered incomparable scenery, a star in its own right. Much of the location footage was shot by the Cinerama cameras (with second unit director Yakima Canutt in charge) in national parks and national forests from South Dakota to California.

There were singalong folk songs like "Erie Canal," "Shenandoah," "Poor Wayfaring Stranger," and "When Johnny Comes Marching Home." Some were sung, others were expertly woven into Alfred Newman's Academy Award–nominated score.

The film won the Oscar for Best Original Story and Screenplay, and it's easy to see why. Aside from an enjoyable story, there were cleverly written bits and pieces of history, like the following:

> "Have you seen San Francisco? It's ugly and it's small and it's full of fleas and it burns down about every five minutes, but each time they keep on rebuilding, it gets a little bigger and better than before. It's alive and kicking and nothing can stop it."

And this comment on our early mail service:

> "The Pony Express—the most daring mail route in history. Eighty riders were in the saddle at all times, night and day, in all weather —half of them riding East, half riding West. Five dollars a letter the mail cost, and on thin paper, too."

We learned that "St. Louis [was] the busiest fur trading center in the world" and "California [was] named after a mythical island of pearls and gold in a 15th-century novel." The writing was both philosophical ("[The Civil War] ain't quite what I expected. There ain't much glory to looking at a man with his guts hanging out") and poetic ("After Shiloh, the South never smiled"). Critical acclaim was unbridled. *The Hollywood Reporter* called the film "the best picture ever made in Cinerama" (and it was virtually the last). *Variety* labeled *How the West Was Won* a "blockbuster supreme, a magnificent and exciting spectacle which must inevitably dwarf the earnings of the travelogs in the three-screen process. It will, undoubtedly, run for several years, and will become one of the industry's all-time top grossers…Technically, there's a vast improvement in the process. The print joins are barely noticeable, and the wobble, which beset earlier productions, has been eliminated."

While *How the West Was Won* worked beautifully on the huge Cinerama screen, it suffers terribly when seen on videocassette or TV broadcast, the "seams" plainly visible as the TV editor was forced to pan from side to side trying to center the action for TV's square format, losing two-thirds of the picture in the process.

In 1978, ABC made a television series based on the original movie. It starred James Arness and Bruce Boxleitner and had spectacular settings—location filming was done in Utah, Colorado, Arizona, and California. However, the mixture of Western and soap opera proved too costly, and it ran only five months.

Written by James R. Webb

Produced by Bernard Smith

Directed by John Ford, George Marshall and Henry Hathaway

CAST

Linus Rawlings	James Stewart
Lilith Prescott	Debbie Reynolds
Eve Prescott	Carroll Baker
Zebulon Prescott	Karl Malden
Rebecca Prescott	Agnes Moorehead
Colonel Hawkins	Walter Brennan
Cleve van Valen	Gregory Peck
Roger Morgan	Robert Preston
Abraham Lincoln	Raymond Massey
General Sherman	John Wayne
Jethro Stuart	Henry Fonda

ACADEMY AWARD NOMINATIONS

*8 nominations, 3 wins**

Best Picture
*Best Story and Screenplay Written Directly for the Screen (James R. Webb)
Best Cinematography, Color
Best Art Direction–Set Decoration, Color
*Best Sound
Best Original Score
*Best Film Editing
Best Costume Design, Color

Although released late in 1962, *How the West Was Won* was submitted for Academy Award consideration as a 1963 contender.

LAWRENCE OF ARABIA

COLUMBIA
$20,310,000

To WINSTON Churchill, he was "one of the greatest beings alive in our time." This was T(homas) E(dward) Lawrence, Englishman and honorary Arab sheikh, whose bravery in the desert, perched atop his camel with his burnoose flowing, made him a fit subject for what has become known as *the* classic epic film of our time.

In their first re-teaming since *The Bridge on the River Kwai,* producer Sam Spiegel and director David Lean selected a virtual unknown for the title role. Peter O'Toole, who would long thereafter be identified as Lawrence, had only one other movie credit to his name, a minor Disney production of *Kidnapped.* Lean's choice of the half-Scottish, half-Irish Shakespearean actor proved a fortuitous one, and the director later remarked in a Cable News Network interview, "He was frightfully good in the part." Shortly after the film's release, O'Toole began to have second thoughts. "There we were in the bloody desert doing a bloody drama," he told *Newsweek.* "Only one thing made me stick it out, and that was David Lean. Of all the principals, only he and I were in Jordan for the entire ten months. He

carried the tripod, I the camera. After a horrible day I would see him sitting outside his tent, smoking a cigarette. I thought if he could do it, I could bloody well do it too."

The movie was shot on location in Spain as well as in the desert, and required thousands of extras, camels, and horses working in the 120-degree heat (only one day of interiors was shot on a London soundstage). Over 4,500 separate setups were used, and the total cost of the film ran over $12,000,000. Producer Sam Speigel was nervous before the movie premiered, remarking to *The New York Times:* "Good [pictures] can run for a long time, and over and over. I only hope the public also wants 'Lawrence' to do so."

He needn't have worried. The public and critics alike raved about the film. In 1971, it had its first re-release, but with nearly 20 minutes of Lean's masterpiece cut from its 3-hour 40-minute length. Then, in 1989, *Lawrence of Arabia* was given another re-release, this time with all the missing footage personally restored by the director himself. Not only that, but when the original negative was discovered dam-

aged in parts, Peter O'Toole was called back to redub his lines. Since his voice had changed in the 26 years since he first spoke his lines, state-of-the-art electronic technology was employed to match his voice identically to that of the original recording.

The restored *Lawrence of Arabia* had a black-tie premiere in New York in February, 1989, followed by a limited engagement there, in Los Angeles, and in Washington. The experience of a beautifully restored print with the finest sound system in existence was greeted by thunderous applause with each screening. The *Los Angeles Times* called it "one of the seven wonders of the cinematic world" and *The New York Times* termed it "now more breathtaking than ever…a stirring and spectacularly beautiful epic."

Even with limited engagements, ticket sales for the re-released film brought in excellent returns for the exhibitors and justified the cost of the restoration. For Columbia Pictures, *Lawrence of Arabia* found a gold mine under all that sand.

Screenplay by Robert Bolt

Produced by Sam Spiegel

Directed by David Lean

CAST

Lawrence	Peter O'Toole
Prince Feisal	Alec Guinness
Auda Abu Tayi	Anthony Quinn
Sherif Ali	Omar Sharif
Turkish Bey	Jose Ferrer

ACADEMY AWARD NOMINATIONS

10 nominations, 7 wins*

*Best Picture
 Best Actor (Peter O'Toole)
 Best Supporting Actor (Omar Sharif)
*Best Director (David Lean)
 Best Screenplay Based on Material from
   Another Source
*Best Cinematography, Color
*Best Art Direction–Set Decoration, Color
*Best Sound
*Best Original Score (Maurice Jarre)
*Best Film Editing

THE LONGEST DAY

20TH CENTURY-FOX
$17,600,000

"Sometimes I wonder which side God's on."   —JOHN WAYNE, COMPLAINING ABOUT THE RAIN

"I sometimes wonder whose side God is on."   —GERMAN GENERAL, REALIZING THE GERMANS ARE ABOUT TO LOSE THE WAR

JUNE 6, 1944: D-Day. This was the *Longest Day* of the title, the day of the Allied invasion of Europe, and in re-creating it for this pseudo-documentary film, 20th Century-Fox's new studio boss, Darryl F. Zanuck, stopped just short of the real thing. His cast rivaled the original in its length—the Americans were headed by John Wayne (who else?) and included Robert Mitchum, Henry Fonda, Robert Ryan, Rod Steiger, Robert Wagner, Jeffrey Hunter, Red Buttons, George Segal, and Sal Mineo. Curiously, there was also a large collection of teen-idol recording stars like Paul Anka, Fabian, and Tommy Sands, appearing in their first dramatic roles. Richard Burton topped the list of British players, which also boasted Peter Lawford, Richard Todd, and Sean Connery. The Germans were played by Curt Jurgens, Gert Frobe (he later became "Goldfinger"), and a number of actors who were well-known in their homeland. Furthermore, all the German and the French actors spoke in their native language, subtitled in English. This added to the realism of the film, although it was demanding on

the audience. (Incidentally, this practically all-male cast had only one important female role, played by Irina Demich, Zanuck's girlfriend-du-jour.)

The film boasted 13 military advisors and 10 technical advisors, including an aging Frau Rommel. Many of the advisors were employed in the setup of masterful special effects (which won the Academy Award). For the beach landing at Normandy, for example, 30 second assistant directors were put into uniform, each made a squadron leader in charge of a group of actors playing soldiers. It was up to these ADs to decide which ones would "die" and which would make it onto Omaha Beach. One hundred fifty "explosives" were set to be detonated by the effects personnel, but the smoke from the rigged devices was unpredictable and temporarily blinded some of the actors. Two of them missed their marks and inadvertently ran into some real explosives planted among the dummies; the accident blew them into the air (the footage remained in the movie) and very nearly killed them. Producer Darryl F. Zanuck halted production until the effects team was able to develop a white, non-blinding smoke.

The Longest Day is also one of the longest movies, three hours to the minute. The CinemaScope picture, which *TV Guide* calls "one of the great war films," is frequently run on independent movie stations.

Screenplay by Cornelius Ryan

From the book by Cornelius Ryan

Additional episodes written by Romain Gary, James Jones, David Pursall, and Jack Seddon

Produced by Darryl F. Zanuck

American episodes directed by Andrew Marton

British episodes directed by Ken Annakin

German episodes directed by Bernhard Wicki

CAST

Lt. Col. Benjamin
* Vandervoort . . . . .John Wayne
Brig. Gen. Norman Cota . .Robert Mitchum
Brig. Gen. Theodore
   Roosevelt . . . . .Henry Fonda
Brig. Gen. James M.
   Gavin . . . . .Robert Ryan
Pvt. John Steele . . . . .Red Buttons
Pvt. Flanagan . . . . .Sean Connery

ACADEMY AWARD NOMINATIONS

5 nominations, 2 wins*

 Best Picture
*Best Cinematography, Black and White
 Best Ad Direction–Set Decoration, Black
   and White
 Best Film Editing
*Best Special Effects

4

IN SEARCH OF THE CASTAWAYS

WALT DISNEY PRODUCTIONS
$9,975,000

WALT DISNEY, who had had great success with *20,000 Leagues Under the Sea,* again turned to Jules Verne, this time for a tale that would take them around the world (not in 80 days) on a search for a missing sea captain. Along the way, Hayley Mills, Maurice Chevalier, Wilfrid Hyde-White, and others would encounter earthquakes, floods, fire, landslides (one effect looks like a prototype for a possible Disneyland ride), Andean condors, and crazed New Zealand Maori natives. It was a bit of fluff with great appeal for the younger set, but not too riveting for the adults whose hands they clutched throughout all the mayhem.

The film's meanderings are held firmly together by Hayley Mills, who at 16 was doing her third Disney film in four years. *Pollyana* and *The Parent Trap* had brought her international attention, and Uncle Walt couldn't wait to get her back up on the screen. With so much attention focused on the petite star, Maurice Chevalier almost got lost in the shuffle. His talents are truly wasted, although he does get to sing a half-French/half-English song as they trek through the Andes.

Although *In Search of the Castaways* is by all counts a fantasy, for some reason Disney felt that a note of authenticity would be in order. Forty war-painted Maori dancers did their ancient ceremonial war dance, the Maori Haka, for the cameras at England's Pinewood Studios, where the picture was filmed. The authentic dance culminates with the warriors sticking out their tongues to frighten their enemies. Today these dances are performed mainly for tourists visiting New Zealand.

Critics were mostly favorable to the Disney yarn. *Variety* called it "a splendid piece of spectacular hokum, lavishly colored and packed with incident and special effects." *The New York Times* described the movie as "a whopping fable, more gimmicky than imaginative…it doesn't lack for lively melodrama that is more innocent and wholesome than much of the stuff the children see these days on television."

The movie appears on the Disney Channel from time to time, and is also available for rental. If you have small children, sit them down in front of the tube some rainy day, pop in the videocassette, and watch their faces light up.

Screenplay by Lowell S. Hawley

From a story by Jules Verne

Produced by Walt Disney

Directed by Robert Stevenson

CAST

Professor Paganel	Maurice Chevalier
Mary Grant	Hayley Mills
Thomas Ayerton	George Sanders
Lord Glenarvan	Wilfrid Hyde-White

THE MUSIC MAN

WARNER BROS.
$8,100,000

WHEN WARNER BROS. bought the rights to Meredith Willson's Broadway smash *The Music Man,* they thought they ought to use a "name" to star in the screen version, despite the fact that Tony-winning Robert Preston had appeared in 883 stage performances. Yet the studio still considered top-name actors for the part of the lovable rogue Harold Hill. Among those discussed: Cary Grant. Not a bad choice, considering he actually began his career as a song-and-dance man. Grant, however, would have no part of it. According to *The Guinness Book of Movie Facts and Feats,* he quipped, "Not only won't I play it, but unless Robert Preston plays it, I won't even go to see the picture." End of discussion.

Other members of the cast were of equally high caliber. Shirley Jones had been introduced in *Oklahoma!* back in 1955, and had since done *Carousel, April Love,* and, in a serious role, *Elmer Gantry.* She was a good casting choice, and *The Hollywood Reporter* commented: "Shirley Jones…is happily back in a milieu of her own, musical romance. She is lovely to look at, sings like a flesh-and-blood angel, and carries conviction in every gesture. She is the best singing actress of the screen in her own category, practically the only operetta singer we have."

Buddy Hackett and Hermione Gingold were somewhat bizarrely cast as small-town natives, but no one seemed to mind. Best of all was Ronny Howard as the lisping little Winthrop. Ronny was already a veteran of two years on TV's "The Andy Griffith Show," and he managed to charm critics with the best of them. Wrote *Variety:* "The little boy with the stammer and the bashful ways is a small gem as impersonated by Ronny Howard. He stays safely away from precociousness in all his scenes." And *The Hollywood Reporter* described Ronny, "a pint-sized kid whose talents know no dimension," as "a knockout."

Of course, this is the same talented person who, after appearing in umpteen seasons of Andy's show, starred in his own series, "Happy Days." Still, it wasn't until the '80s that Ron Howard found his true calling as a director, making such hit films as *Splash, Cocoon* and *Apollo 13.*

But the title of the show says it all, and it is *music* that is the star of this movie. As we all know, "Seventy-Six Trombones" led the big parade, with "Marian the Librarian," "Till There Was You," "Trouble," and "Gary, Indiana" right behind.

The soundtrack, surprisingly enough, used only a dozen trombones, electronically amplified and multiplied (uh, 76 divided by 12 equals, hmm… each trombone represents six and one-third trombones?). Don't even think about the 110 cornets.

Screenplay by Marion Hargrove

From the musical comedy by Meredith Willson and Franklin Lacey

Music and lyrics by Meredith Willson

Produced and directed by Morton Da Costa

CAST

"Professor"Harold Hill . .Robert Preston
Marian Paroo . . . . . . .Shirley Jones
Mayor Shinn . . . . .Paul Ford
Eulalie Shinn . . . . .Hermione Gingold
Marcellus Washburn . . .Buddy Hackett
Winthrop Paroo . . . . . .Ronny Howard

ACADEMY AWARD NOMINATIONS

6 nominations, 1 win*

Best Picture
Best Art Direction–Set Decoration, Color
Best Sound
*Best Score—Adaptation or Treatment
  (Ray Heindoff)
Best Film Editing
Best Costume Design, Color

CLEOPATRA

20TH CENTURY-FOX
$26,000,000

THERE WERE romances, battles, clashes in leadership, fortunes spent, and fortunes lost—and that was what went on behind the scenes, not on the screen.

That *Cleopatra* would be a hit was a foregone conclusion. Audiences had been following the soap opera behind the scenes for nearly four years since the film's inception, and before it had even opened, Fox had pre-sold $14,000,000 worth of tickets. Most of the fans weren't history buffs interested in "the glory of Rome" or the fabled Egyptian queen who married her brother (and slept with everyone within earshot). What they came to see was not Cleopatra getting it on with Mark Antony, but Elizabeth Taylor being romanced by Richard Burton, staring passionately into each other's eyes, ignoring the director's pleas to "cut!" Their love affair, which had blossomed while in each other's professional arms, had fueled the hungry public's need for tabloid gossip, and now, wonder of wonders, there they were, and 25 feet high, too!

Yet *Cleopatra* had been termed an "unlucky" film early on by the press. Originally, production was to have taken place in London, but after nine months of shooting at a cost of $5,000,000, the producers had nothing to show for it. The film seemed plagued from the start. There had been a union row over Elizabeth Taylor's hairdresser; the star had had a string of illnesses, including a brush with death caused by double pneumonia requiring an emergency tracheotomy (a freshly healed scar is visible in close-ups); the original director, Rouben Mamoulian, resigned and was replaced by Joseph Mankiewicz; and the wretched English weather finally forced Fox to close down production in Britain and move to Rome for the duration.

The warm, sunny climate of Italy proved just the thing, and the romance between the two leads also began heating up. Although both Taylor and Burton each had a spouse, this seemed a minor problem—to them, at least. (As one anonymous critic put it:

"Elizabeth Taylor is the first Cleopatra to sail down the Nile to Las Vegas.") But the courtship presented problems for the crew. A visit from Burton's wife, Sybil, had thrown Liz into a tizzy, and after staying up all night crying, her eyes were too swollen to shoot the next day. The crew had to film around her scenes (although she voluntarily worked on a Saturday to make up for the lost time). On another occasion, the actress took advantage of the fine weather to sunbathe, tying up her yacht next to the barge set. Whenever she was needed for a shot, she would throw her costume on over her bikini. Lighting directors were driven nuts by her deepening suntan, and much of the footage had to be color-corrected to match her previously filmed interior shots.

The budget eventually ran close to a reported $44,000,000, making it one of

Screenplay by Joseph L. Mankiewicz, Ranald MacDougall, and Sidney Buchman

Based upon histories by Plutarch, Suetonius, and Appian and "The Life and Times of Cleopatra" by C. M. Franzero

Produced by Walter Wanger

Directed by Joseph L. Mankiewicz

CAST

Cleopatra	Elizabeth Taylor
Mark Antony	Richard Burton
Julius Caesar	Rex Harrison
Rufio	Martin Landau
Octavian	Roddy McDowall
Casca	Carroll O'Connor

ACADEMY AWARD NOMINATIONS

9 nominations, 4 wins*

Best Picture
Best Actor (Rex Harrison)
*Best Cinematography, Color
*Best Art Direction–Set Decoration, Color
Best Sound
Best Original Score
Best Film Editing
*Best Costume Design, Color
*Best Special Visual Effects

the most expensive films ever made (with inflation taken into account). Of that, $130,000 was spent on Ms. Taylor's wardrobe of 65 costumes (and another 40 costumes costing $64,800 didn't appear after scenes were cut). The 24-carat gold-covered dress in which she makes her entry into Rome cost $6,500, a lot of moolah in the '60s. Ms. Taylor's salary reportedly also took a big chunk of the budget: the actress received $1,725,000 plus 10 percent of the gross above $7,500,000.

One way in which the studio was able to recoup some of its cash was to charge the highest admission price asked to that date. Audiences didn't seem to mind, and cheerily handed over their money to see the longest commercially made American movie ever released (4 hours 3 minutes), figuring they were getting full value for their dollar. Zanuck, however, came under critics' fire for the length, and took an axe to 22 minutes within the first week. Later it was shortened to

3 hours. The first network television run saw lost footage being restored and the production screened over two nights. Videocassettes are in this longer format. And rumors still abound that there is even more "lost" footage, and that someday a 6-hour version, shown over two successive days, might be edited together. Richard Burton would have been pleased: he always thought his best scenes ended up on the cutting room floor.

2

IT'S A MAD MAD MAD MAD WORLD

UNITED ARTISTS
$20,849,786

I F THERE WAS ONE characteristic of all '60s hits, it seemed to be that "bigger is better," and *It's a Mad Mad Mad Mad World* wrote the textbook. From its redundant title to its lengthy cast (nine stars, two co-stars, 29 also-stars, *and "*Jimmy Durante and a few surprises"), this movie screams "we're bigger!" and never lets up. Not only was it filmed in something called 70-millimeter Ultra Panavision, but it also boasted the new seamless, single-lens Cinerama process. (One wonders why they bothered to call it "Cinerama," since it wasn't the three-camera, three-projector system with which audiences had grown familiar.)

Producer-director Stanley Kramer had a mad, mad time spending $9,400,000 of United Artists' bucks getting the slapstick comedy on film. Virtually every comic available was rounded up and put on the screen: Sid Caesar, Milton Berle, Jonathan Winters, Buddy Hackett, Mickey Rooney, Phil Silvers—it looked like a Friars Club picnic. Also in the cast were Ethel Merman, Dorothy Provine, Edie Adams, Terry-Thomas, Dick Shawn, and, get this, Spencer Tracy!

The list of communities that were disrupted during the location filming runs nearly as long as the cast. The credits noted "Our thanks and apologies to the following California communities—Agoura, Kernville, Long Beach,

Malibu, Oxnard, Palm Desert, Palm Springs, Palos Verdes Estates, San Pedro, Santas Ana, Barbara and Monica, 29 Palms, Universal City and Yucca Valley." All aboard! But don't

---

Original story and screenplay by William and Tania Rose

Produced and directed by Stanley Kramer

CAST

Capt. C. G. Culpepper . . .Spencer Tracy
J. Russell Finch . . . . . .Milton Berle
Melville Crump . . . . . . .Sid Caesar
Benjy Benjamin . . . . . .Buddy Hackett
Mrs. Marcus . . . . .Ethel Merman
Ding Bell . . . . .Mickey Rooney
Sylvester Marcus . . . . . .Dick Shawn
Otto Meyer . . . . .Phil Silvers
J. Algernon
    Hawthorne . . . . . . .Terry-Thomas
Lennie Pike . . . . .Jonathan Winters

ACADEMY AWARD NOMINATIONS

6 nominations, 1 win*

Best Cinematography, Color
Best Sound
Best Song ("It's a Mad Mad Mad Mad World," music and words by Ernest Gold and Mack David)
Best Original Score
Best Film Editing
*Best Sound Effects

---

expect to see much of your hometown if it happens to appear on this list, since most of the film was spent inside cars, in wild chase scenes on the freeways and roads running through these cities.

What did the critics make of all this? *The Hollywood Reporter* termed it a "fun, fun, fun, fun film…it is not the story that matters, it is the development." *Variety* called it "a mad, mad, mad, mad picture, and it's going to make a lot of money…it is a throwback to the wild, wacky and wondrous time of the silent screen comedy, a kind of Keystone Kop Kaper with modern conveniences." But *Newsweek* labeled it "bad, bad, bad, bad," adding: "[It] is redundant, ridiculous, and too insistent…the title writer just didn't know when to stop; neither did the moviemaker Stanley Kramer…at the end of the long, long, long, long film one leaves in about as good a humor as a highway patrolman after a bad day on the freeway."

Yet despite commentary like the above, people still made a mad rush for the box office, and at $4.80 a ticket, they gobbled up the three-and-a-half hour picture like so much popcorn. The plot may have centered around a madcap treasure hunt for $350,000, but the real plot was United Artists' quest for box office gold. With this picture, they struck it rich to the tune of nearly $21,000,000.

BAWDY, LUSTY, scandalous, rollicking, raucous, and veddy, veddy, British— these were the terms used to describe Tony Richardson's innovative film of the 18th-century classic novel by Henry Fielding. That *Tom Jones* should mark a milestone in filmmaking 200 years after the novel appeared is remarkable in itself; but that's just what it did, and audiences couldn't wait to be scandalized by it. Never again would the camera be banished to the hall; with this picture, the bedroom door had been left ajar, and we were all invited in.

Although it wasn't the clinical "this is how you do it" sex of the '80s, the beautiful rustic settings, the fox hunt, and other side stories were all basically foreplay for the movie's sexual raison d'être. Even something as seemingly simple as eating a meal at a tavern became the most memorable scene of the film, each slavering bite, each downing of a morsel of chicken or lobster or oysters becoming an allegory for s-e-x. Audiences would never look at a platter of chicken the same way again!

And the critics, pardon the expression, ate it up. *Newsweek* remarked:

Screenplay by John Osborne

From the novel by Henry Fielding

Produced and directed by
   Tony Richardson

CAST

Tom Jones . . . . .Albert Finney
Sophie Western . . . . . .Susannah York
Squire Western . . . . . .Hugh Griffith
Miss Western . . . . . . .Edith Evans
Lady Bellaston . . . . . .Joan Greenwood

ACADEMY AWARD NOMINATIONS

10 nominations, 4 wins *

**Best Picture
  Best Actor (Albert Finney)
  Best Supporting Actor (Hugh Griffith)
  Best Supporting Actress (Diane Cilento)
  Best Supporting Actress (Edith Evans)
  Best Supporting Actress (Joyce Redman)
*Best Director (Tony Richardson)
*Best Screenplay Based on Material from
    Another Medium (John Osborne)
  Best Art Direction–Set Decoration, Color
Best Original Score (John Addison)

" 'Tom Jones' is a continually delightful, mercurially rhapsodic, and altogether breath-taking film. There is, in fact, no detail, however small, which does not merit unstinting admiration. 'Tom Jones,' an absolute triumph, is the best comedy ever made." *The New York Times'* reviewer admitted: "Perhaps there will be those who will be embarrassed by so much bawdiness on the screen. But I find it too funny to be tasteless, too true to be artistically false."

Tom Jones was re-released late in 1989, and the Academy Award–winning Best Picture of 1963 found a new audience succumbing to the charms of Albert Finney and Susannah York. The print was newly restored and re-edited by director Tony Richardson. The new version had been trimmed by seven minutes, which, Richardson told the *Los Angeles Times,* "I would have done then if I'd been smart enough. It's taken me 25 years to not be so dumb." *Tom Jones* has also been released on videocassette; you might want to rent the tape since, according to the *L.A. Times* reviewer, the film "holds up better than you might expect."

4

IRMA LA DOUCE

UNITED ARTISTS
$11,921,784

THE TEAMING OF director Billy Wilder with actors Jack Lemmon and Shirley MacLaine in 1960 had spelled magic in the highly acclaimed film *The Apartment.* Although it wasn't a box office blockbuster, it still earned a respectable $6,680,000 in North American rentals, placing it in the top 10 films of the year. What's more, it grabbed Oscars for Best Picture and Best Director, along with nominations for Lemmon and MacLaine. With a proven success formula like that, it was only a question of time before the Mirisch brothers, an independent production group, and United Artists, producer-distributor for *The Apartment,* gave it another go.

Irma La Douce had had a successful and lengthy run on the Paris and London stages when it was translated to Broadway in 1960. For the screen version, director Billy Wilder reunited his *Apartment*-mates Jack Lemmon and Shirley MacLaine, but decided to do the film as a comedy sans music. (The songs were eventually adapted as musical score minus the singing, and won an Oscar for composer Andre Previn.)

While the story concerns the life of a Paris streetwalker and her reluctant mentor, it is not raunchy in the sense

---

Screenplay by Billy Wilder and I.A.L. Diamond

Based on the play by Alexandre Breffort

Produced and directed by Billy Wilder

CAST

Nestor . . . . .Jack Lemmon
Irma la Douce . . . . . .Shirley MacLaine
Moustache . . . . .Lou Jacobi
Hippolyte . . . . .Bruce Yarnell
Inspector Lefevre . . . . .Herschel Bernardi
Kiki the Cossack . . . . .Grace Lee Whitney
Concierge . . . . .Howard McNear

ACADEMY AWARD NOMINATIONS

3 nominations, 1 win*

Best Actress (Shirley MacLaine)
Best Cinematography, Color
*Best Score—Adaptation or Treatment (Andre Previn)

---

that *Tom Jones* is; Irma is as matter-of-fact about her career as the average office clerk. Although the subject matter is prostitution, the film is neither social commentary nor a probing psychological study. There are, of course, business-related sexual jokes, like the client who, finding himself short of

---

cash, asks "Do you take traveler's checks?" and Irma's double-entendre remark to another customer, "I'm sorry. I never remember a face."

This was Shirley MacLaine's second important film role, and the critics lauded her. *Time* called her "an adorable golliwog in green lingerie and inky wig; her flamboyant self-assurance is the perfect foil for the bumbling Lemmon [character]." *Variety* took note of Lemmon's performance: "Lemmon plays his juicy role to the hilt, and there are moments when his performance brings to mind some of the great visual comedy of the classic silent film clowns."

Several minor roles in the cast were played by actors who would one day become famous. The desk clerk at the Hotel Casanova was played by Howard McNeer, who won fame as "Floyd" on "The Andy Griffith Show"; Grace Lee Whitney portrayed "Kiki the Cossack" and later went on to become "Yeoman Rand" on "Star Trek"; Bill Bixby, star of various TV shows, including "The Incredible Hulk," had a bit part; and if you look closely, you'll see James Caan in a small walk-on. Caan later co-starred in *The Godfather I* and *II.* But that's another story...

THE SWORD IN THE STONE

WALT DISNEY PRODUCTIONS
$10,475,000

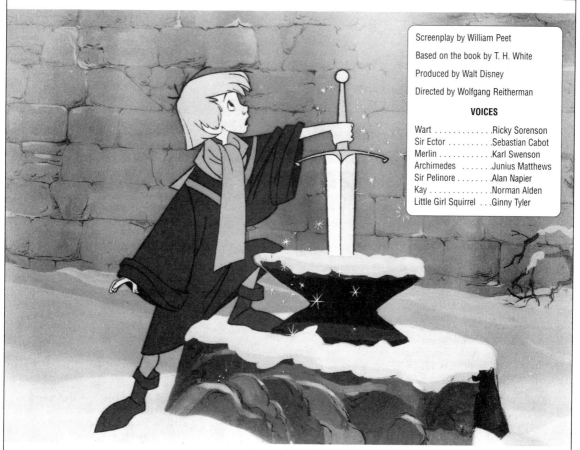

Screenplay by William Peet

Based on the book by T. H. White

Produced by Walt Disney

Directed by Wolfgang Reitherman

VOICES

Wart	Ricky Sorenson
Sir Ector	Sebastian Cabot
Merlin	Karl Swenson
Archimedes	Junius Matthews
Sir Pelinore	Alan Napier
Kay	Norman Alden
Little Girl Squirrel	Ginny Tyler

"Don't take gravity too lightly or it will pull you down." —MERLIN

THEATERGOING audiences in 1960 were treated to *Camelot,* a hugely successful Broadway musical starring Richard Burton and Julie Andrews. It was based in part on English author T. H. White's Arthurian tetralogy, *The Once and Future King,* but because of the magical elements inherent in *The Sword in the Stone,* most of the great storytelling in that book had to be omitted from *Camelot.* Enter Walt Disney.

The story concerns Merlin and his young charge, Wart, the lad who would one day pull the sword from the stone and become the legendary King Arthur. As Wart's tutor, Merlin gives the youngster a variety of transcendental experiences, transmuting him first into a fish, then a bird. (A similar effort at educating a future hero was used when Yoda attempted to train Jedi knight Luke Skywalker in the 1980 film *The Empire Strikes Back* [see page 272].) These moments were perfectly suited to animation, where anything is possible. Disney's first animated feature in two years was another box office success.

In typical Disney fashion, the studio hyped their latest hit with staggering facts, such as: "To paint the characters on celluloid, the backgrounds and all other color effects required 800 gallons of paint weighing nearly five tons, enough in liquid hues to dress the exteriors of 135 average-sized homes."

And: "Some 300 top Disney artists used up exactly 1,325,650 pencils before the three year job was done, enough to keep the New York Stock Exchange in business for a solid year, or redesign all the cities of the world."

For the voices, Disney selected some well-known talent. Veteran English actor Sebastian Cabot read the part of "Sir Ector," Norman Alden portrayed "Kay," and Alan Napier did the characterization of "Sir Pelinore." Napier later went on to co-star in TV's "Batman" series as the butler, "Alfred."

Far from Disney's best, *The Sword in the Stone* is still an enjoyable bit of magic for the younger set. The videocassette is easily available for rental, and the movie can also frequently be found on cable's Disney Channel.

MARY POPPINS

WALT DISNEY PRODUCTIONS
$45,000,000

"Mary Poppins—practically perfect in every way."

S O PROCLAIMS the tape measure that Mary Poppins carries with her, and there's no doubt that she measures up. Not only was she the perfect nanny, but the movie *Mary Poppins* was *perfect* in every way for Walt Disney and company. It was a box office smash, pulling in dollars by the bushel; it was a sensation at the Oscars, grabbing 13 nominations, the most ever for a Disney production and just one short of the record. And it won the hearts of just about everyone—critics, kids, their parents, grandparents. In a word, *Mary Poppins* was supercalifragilisticexpialidocious!

Walt Disney first became aware of P. L. Travers' "Mary Poppins" stories in 1948 when one of his daughters was reading them. But it wasn't until 1960 that he began to plan for a screen version. Much of the success must be attributed to the talented people Walt brought together as the team for this movie. In-house director Robert Stevenson was given the assignment, having successfully directed 17 previous films at Disney Studios.

For the star herself, Walt chose Julie Andrews, whose success on Broadway in *My Fair Lady* and *Camelot* was legendary, but unfortunately not enough to sway the producers of the film version of *Fair Lady* to hire her. Warner Bros. selected Audrey Hepburn, and a bitterly disappointed Julie Andrews accepted what she felt was second prize as the lead in *Mary Poppins.* It proved to be the turning point in her career, and she was awarded the Oscar for Best Actress of 1964. It was an especially sweet victory, since her competition included many film veterans. Also up for Best Actress that year were Anne Bancroft, Sophia Loren, Debbie Reynolds, and Kim Stanley.

Co-starring with Ms. Andrews was Dick Van Dyke, who had just finished both stage and film versions of *Bye Bye Birdie* and was in the third season of his network TV series, "The Dick Van Dyke Show." Dick played the part of Mary's (very platonic) friend Bert, and later doubled as the old bank president.

Rounding out the fine cast were British comedian David Tomlinson as Mr. Banks, Glynis Johns as Mrs. Banks, Hermione Baddeley and Reta Shaw as the maids, Karen Dotrice and Matthew Garber as the Banks children, and special appearances by famed actors Ed Wynn (who appeared in a number of Disney films), Reginald Owen, Elsa Lanchester, and Arthur Treacher (later of Arthur Treacher's Fish and Chips fame).

Two Academy Awards went to the composers of the music for *Mary Poppins.* Richard M. and Robert B. Sherman were brothers who first came to the attention of Walt Disney

---

Screenplay by Bill Walsh and
   Don DaGradi

Music and lyrics by Richard M. Sherman
   and Robert B. Sherman

Based on the books by P. L. Travers

Produced by Walt Disney

Directed by Robert Stevenson

CAST

Mary Poppins	Julie Andrews
Bert	Dick Van Dyke
Mr. Banks	David Tomlinson
Mrs. Banks	Glynis Johns
Uncle Albert	Ed Wynn

ACADEMY AWARD NOMINATIONS

13 nominations, 5 wins *

Best Picture
*Best Actress (Julie Andrews)
Best Director (Robert Stevenson)
Best Screenplay Based on Material from
   Another Medium
Best Cinematography, Color
Best Art Direction–Set Decoration, Color
Best Sound
*Best Song ("Chim Chim Cher-ee," music
   and words by Richard M. Sherman and
   Robert B. Sherman)
*Best Original Music Score (Richard M.
   Sherman and Robert B. Sherman)
Best Score—Adaptation or Treatment
*Best Film Editing
Best Costume Design, Color
*Best Visual Effects

---

when they wrote a 1958 tune called "Tall Paul." Disney wanted to turn blossoming Mouseketeer Annette into a recording star and bought the Shermans' song. They did a couple of other songs for Annette before Disney assigned them their first movie, *The Parent Trap,* with Hayley Mills. Their tune "Let's Get Together" became a hit and won them a cherished position on the Disney staff.

Mary Poppins was their crowning Disney achievement. Their memorable songs included the Award-winning "Chim Chim Cher-ee," "Feed the Birds," "A Spoonful of Sugar," "Jolly Holiday"—a total of 14 all together. But everybody's favorite always seemed to be the tongue-twisting "Supercalifragilisticexpialidocious." According to Richard Sherman, he and his brother first heard a similar word from the kids at their summer camp back in 1937. It was a test of one's verbal agility, something to impress the other kids with, and adults as well. When it came time to write a special song for the film, they recalled the nonsense word of their childhood, and the rest, as they say, is history.

One of the special treats in the movie is the combination of live action and animation. Disney had successfully used the process many times, beginning back in the '20s in something he called *Alice in Cartoonland,* and later in such Disney successes as *The Three Caballeros* and *Song of the South.* Many years after Walt Disney's death, the technique would be put to its most ambitious use in the studio's production of *Who Framed Roger Rabbit* (the producers of that film would even borrow the singing penguin waiters from *Mary Poppins!*).

So many elements were combined by the Disney magicians to make this film that it is impossible to single out one special reason for its success. It was the kind of magic that wouldn't happen again for a long time for that studio. Two years later, the producer of *Mary Poppins* was dead. It was the last feature that Walt Disney would complete, and for us, the perfect ending to a more than "practically perfect" career.

2
MY FAIR LADY
WARNER BROS.
$34,000,000

I T WAS *THE* musical of the 20th century. Many a ticket scalper put his children through college thanks to this Broadway hit. And when Jack L. Warner paid $5,500,000 for the right to bring it to the screen, he thought he'd gotten a bargain. He was wrong, of course. He lost his shirt and a lot more after its production set him back another $17,000,000, and although it ranked as the number-four film for 1964, it failed to break even.

"It," of course, was *My Fair Lady,* the most eagerly awaited cinematic event since *Gone With the Wind.* The success of *My Fair Lady* was truly legendary. The Lerner and Loewe musical adaptation of George Bernard Shaw's *Pygmalion* bowed on Broadway in March, 1956, and its cast took their

final bows six years and 2,717 performances later.

Its stars became legendary, too. Rex Harrison had performed the role in at least a thousand stage performances by the time he was signed to re-create Henry Higgins for the screen (although Jack L. Warner was still pushing for Cary Grant after he failed to get him into *The Music Man* [see page 165]). And everyone who had fallen in love with Eliza Doolittle had come to believe that Julie Andrews would re-create her part as well. But Jack Warner finally did prevail; he was convinced no one would come to see an "unknown" and signed Audrey Hepburn. Although Ms. Hepburn did an admirable acting job, she couldn't sing a note, so Marni Nixon, already an established pro at this type of work, covered for her.

Rex Harrison could barely sing a note either, but he created a style of talking his way through a lyric that is still being emulated today. And what lyrics they were! Alan Jay Lerner managed to write some unbelievably clever rhymes. For example, Henry Higgins'

patter in "You Did It" had "Budapest" rhymed with "a ruder pest." Brilliant lyrics, plus more familiar and singable tunes, helped make *My Fair Lady* the number-three-selling soundtrack album of 1964 (right behind The Beatles' *A Hard Day's Night* and *Mary Poppins*). The disc contained all the Broadway favorites, like "On the Street Where You Live," "Wouldn't It Be Loverly," "Get Me to the Church on Time," "I Could Have Danced All Night," and "The Rain in Spain."

One musical highlight, and certainly one of the most exquisite moments in the film, was "Ascot Gavotte." The entire number is a showcase for the talent of Academy Award–winning costume designer Cecil Beaton, who used gray, black, and white to dress the Edwardian ladies and gentlemen at the racetrack in what is an unforgettable panorama of elegance.

My Fair Lady is one of the real treats of the era when musicals were big box office, and has the rare distinction of becoming more enjoyable with each repeated viewing.

Screenplay by Alan Jay Lerner

Based on the play *Pygmalion* by George Bernard Shaw

Music and lyrics by Alan Jay Lerner and Frederick Loewe

Produced by Jack L. Warner

Directed by George Cukor

CAST

Eliza Doolittle . . . . .Audrey Hepburn
Prof. Henry Higgins . . .Rex Harrison
Alfred Doolittle . . . . . . .Stanley Holloway
Colonel Pickering . . . . .Wilfred Hyde-White
Mrs. Higgins . . . . . . .Gladys Cooper

ACADEMY AWARD NOMINATIONS

12 nominations, 8 wins*

*Best Picture
*Best Actor (Rex Harrison)
Best Supporting Actor (Stanley Holloway)
Best Supporting Actress (Gladys Cooper)
*Best Director (George Cukor)
Best Screenplay Based on Material from Another Medium
*Best Cinematography, Color
*Best Art Direction–Set Decoration, Color
*Best Sound
*Best Score—Adaptation or Treatment (Andre Previn)
Best Film Editing
*Best Costume Design, Color

GOLDFINGER
UNITED ARTISTS
$22,997,706

HIS NAME was Bond, James Bond. He was brought to the attention of the moviegoing audience in 1962 with the first production of Ian Fleming's spy novels, *Dr. No.* It would become the most successful series of films in the history of the cinema: over $2,000,000,000 in worldwide rentals was reached with the 1987 release of *The Living Daylights.* In 1989, the 18th James Bond film, *Licence to Kill,* was released, and no end is in sight. There have been no less than five actors playing the sexy British secret agent,* but for many there can only be one—the original, Sean Connery.

The Scottish-born Connery had appeared seemingly from nowhere (he did have a part in 1959's *Darby O'Gill and the Little People*), and his mischievous grin and puppydog eyes would see a string of ladies—the "Bond Girls," as they later were called—finding their way into his industrial-strength bed.

The plot of *Goldfinger* involves a financier named Auric Goldfinger—played with panache by German actor Gert Frobe—who plans to corner the gold reserves of Britain and the United States.

Goldfinger was actually the third Bond picture released in the United States; *Dr. No* didn't make the top five list, but the second film, *From Russia With Love,* would become the fifth-ranked 1964 movie. With *Goldfinger* in the number-three position, United Artists had a banner year.

Much of the popularity of the Bond series was due to its irreverence toward the sacred cows of cinematic "good taste." It was hard to omit Ian Fleming's frank sexual innuendoes in translating the novels to the screen. To put it bluntly, James got laid a lot, and by women with names like Pussy Galore and Holly Goodhead—there was no doubt what Fleming had in mind.

But audiences also enjoyed watching Bond get out of cliffhanger situations. The man ate danger for breakfast, lunch, and dinner, aided by all sorts of special effects and mechanical gadgetry. *Goldfinger,* for example, had a special smoke-screen-equipped, oil-slick-emitting, passenger-ejecting Aston Martin. Gimmicks, gals, guns—the formula worked.

The 007 "licence to kill" extended to the box office, where British producers Harry Saltzman and Albert "Cubby" Broccoli made a killing of their own. *Goldfinger*'s budget was only $2,500,000. And while the film's villain didn't get to keep all the gold at Fort Knox, the producers certainly came close.

---

*Sean Connery (7), David Niven (1–*Casino Royale*), George Lazenby (1–*On Her Majesty's Secret Service*), Roger Moore (7), Timothy Dalton (2), and Pierce Brosnan (*GoldenEye,* 1995). And that's not counting Woody Allen as nephew Jimmy Bond in *Casino Royale.*

Screenplay by Richard Maibaum and Paul Dehn

Based on the novel by Ian Fleming

Produced by Harry Saltzman and Albert R. Broccoli

Directed by Guy Hamilton

CAST

James Bond . . . . .Sean Connery
Goldfinger . . . . .Gert Frobe
Pussy Galore . . . . .Honor Blackman
Jill Masterson . . . . . . .Shirley Eaton
Tilly Masterson . . . . . .Tania Mallett

ACADEMY AWARD NOMINATIONS

*1 nomination, 1 win**

*Best Sound Effects

THE CARPETBAGGERS

PARAMOUNT
$15,500,000

JONAS (GEORGE PEPPARD):
What would you like to see on your honeymoon?

MONICA (ELIZABETH ASHLEY):
Lots of lovely ceilings.

NOBODY WOULD EVER call *The Carpetbaggers* a film. It was a *movie,* plain and simple, with dialogue like the above, straight out of the sizzling Harold Robbins novel. It didn't win any prizes, unless you can count $15,500,000 at the box office a prize. You can bet Paramount Pictures did. It was their first hit since 1956 and *The Ten Commandments* (a number of which were broken by this movie's characters). The ad copy stated that "it is unlikely that you will experience in a lifetime all that you will see in…*The Carpetbaggers,*" and this was probably true, unless you happened to own an airplane factory *and* a movie studio. Come to think of it, Howard Hughes might have had a bone of contention with the ad copy. Although no mention is ever made of his name, there is an obvious parallel between the life of central character, Jonas Cord, Jr., and that of the late billionaire.

George Peppard plays the ruthless central character who inherits megabucks from his father, then slashes and burns his way to further fortune, taking no prisoners in his greedy quest. He has difficulty in relating to those closest to him, and his wife, Monica (Elizabeth Ashley), and friend/father-figure, Nevada Smith (Alan Ladd), bear the brunt of his misguided psyche.

Many other talented actors appeared in this movie. In addition to the young George Peppard (later to star in many TV series, most recently "The A-Team"), the cast included Bob Cummings, Lew Ayres, Martin Balsam, and Carroll Baker. Ms. Baker had one of the most infamous scenes of the movie—she swings from a chandelier, sending it crashing to the floor.

Outstanding in the cast was Alan Ladd as Nevada Smith. It was his last picture; when a sequel (actually a prequel) was made based on the life of his character, Nevada Smith, Steve McQueen starred in the title role.

Critics were puzzled. Was this to be taken seriously, or was it campy trash? *The Hollywood Reporter* seemed to enjoy the movie, praising its direction and casting. *Time* magazine, however, called *The Carpetbaggers* "a swift, irresistibly vulgar compilation of all the racy stories anyone has ever heard about wicked old Hollywood of the '20s and '30s." And *The New York Times'* critic described it as "a sickly sour distillation of Harold Robbins' big-selling novel…Mr. Dmytryk has gone at this film…with a baseball bat. He has beaten it down to a square flat surface, without cinematic lift or style."

The New York Times predicted that "it will probably be seen by millions." The paper should have also mentioned that it would probably *make* millions—both would have been safe bets, since the public cared not a fig for the reviewers or their opinions. *The Carpetbaggers* bagged a bundle at the box office.

Screenplay by John Michael Hayes

Based on the novel by Harold Robbins

Produced by Joseph E. Levine

Directed by Edward Dmytryk

CAST

Jonas Cord, Jr.	George Peppard
Rina	Carroll Baker
Nevada Smith	Alan Ladd
Dan Pierce	Bob Cummings
Jennie Denton	Martha Hyer
Monica Winthrop	Elizabeth Ashley

FROM RUSSIA WITH LOVE
UNITED ARTISTS
$9,924,279

"My friends call me Tanya."
"Mine call me James Bond."

THIS WAS ONLY the second Bond film,* but already, eager fans of the Fleming novels, along with a whole new audience, had quickly warmed to the sexy British secret agent as portrayed by Sean Connery. *From Russia With Love* had the honor of being the first Bond movie to make it into the top five (later in the year, *Goldfinger* would go all the way to the number-two spot).

In comparison to the later films, this was one of the least gimmicky of the Bond series, which would progressively emphasize more and more action/adventure, eventually entering the realm of science fiction. *From Russia* also boasted one of the classiest of the Bond women—Italian actress Daniela Bianchi as Tatiana Romanova (whose friends, she tells Bond, call her "Tanya"). Her portrayal of the Russian spy-turned-counterspy is warm and realistic, compared with later films in the series, in which the ladies in Bondage are more like male fantasies than real women.

The story line is a complex one, with spies and counterspies abounding. James is sent to Istanbul to liberate a top-secret Russian decoding machine, and tangles with Tatiana—who is really a pawn of the sinister organization called SPECTRE, an international crime syndicate. There is good action in this, and without the complex and clever devices he would later come to depend upon from "Q"

(aside from a trick briefcase), poor James is forced to actually use his fists and his wits to defeat the nasties. There's a great fight sequence with Robert Shaw, a chase by a helicopter, and a motorboat pursuit. Will Double-O-Seven escape? Are you kidding?

Early on, the critics seemed to know that a new phenomenon was afoot and gave the film unanimous praise, something of a phenomenon itself. *The New York Times* wrote: "Secret Agent 007 is very much with us again, and anyone who hasn't yet got to know him is urged to do so right away!" Other critics echoed its praises. *The Hollywood Reporter* called the movie "fast, funny entertainment...[James Bond's] further antics should provide a strong

box office attraction as his movie fame grows and his appeal broadens."

Those who have followed the Bond series since its beginning have often said that the early movies were the best. Whether or not this is true is a matter of opinion, but it's true that *From Russia With Love* sticks closer than any of the others to the Ian Fleming novel. And for purists who prefer their Bond stirred, not shaken, there is no comparison.

---

*The first, *Dr. No* (1962), while not making it into the box office Top Five, turned a respectable profit and established the Bond films throughout the world. (In Japan, they translated the title into *We Don't Want a Doctor!*)

Screenplay by Richard Maibaum

Based on the novel by Ian Fleming

Produced by Harry Saltzman and Albert R. Broccoli

Directed by Terence Young

CAST

James Bond	Sean Connery
Tatiana Romanova	Daniela Bianchi
Kerim Bev	Pedro Armendariz
Rose Klebb	Lotte Lenya
Red Grant	Robert Shaw

1965

THE SOUND OF MUSIC

20TH CENTURY-FOX
$79,975,000

AFTER A YEAR in production (including 10 weeks on location in Austria and Gemany) filming another hit Broadway show, Robert Wise and 20th Century-Fox gave a gift to the American public. *The Sound of Music* had children and dogs, singing nuns and Nazis, and gasp-for-breath scenery. The icing on this wonderful piece of sugar candy was "Mary Poppins" herself—Julie Andrews. She was no longer an unknown, thank you; for the second year in a row, she was the star of the number-one box office hit.

And, to coin a phrase, the box office was alive with the sound of money. The dollars and yen and pounds and deutsche marks and francs came pouring in—you can bet these were a few of Fox's favorite things! And when the take was tallied, *The Sound of Music* had climbed every mountain to reach the top as the industry's all-time highest grossing film to date. Bye-bye, *Gone With the Wind.*

The movie is a three-hour adaptation of Rodgers and Hammerstein's hit musical about the Von Trapp Family Singers. It had all that glorious Salzburg scenery in color by DeLuxe on the wide, wide Todd-AO 70-millimeter screen, with some of the most easily remembered songs of any musical: "Maria," "The Sound of Music,"

"My Favorite Things," "Climb Every Mountain," the beautiful anthem "Edelweiss." Nothing's too musically complex or difficult to hum; even the tone-deaf can follow "Do-Re-Mi."

Julie Andrews herself modestly credits the mood of the movie with contributing to the film's phenomenal success. In an interview with *The New York Times* at the time of its release, she said, "It's very joyous. It's refreshing and not too complicated. A love story, with children and music. That word 'joyous' has an awful lot to do with it." Composer Richard Rodgers, when asked in the same *Times* piece to analyze the reasons for *The Sound of Music*'s success, commented, "It's irresistible if you like people and children."

Originally, William Wyler was set to direct, but delays found him accepting another assignment, and Robert Wise, who had co-directed the hugely suc-

The real Maria von Trapp meets Christopher Plummer as Robert Wise looks on.

Screenplay by Ernest Lehman

Based on the stage musical, book by Howard Lindsay and Russel Crouse

Music and lyrics by Richard Rodgers and Oscar Hammerstein II

Produced and directed by Robert Wise

CAST

Maria . . . . .Julie Andrews
Capt. Von Trapp . . . . . .Christopher Plummer
The Baroness . . . . . . .Eleanor Parker
Max Detweiler . . . . . . .Richard Haydn
Mother Abbess . . . . . .Peggy Wood
Sister Sophia . . . . . . .Marni Nixon

ACADEMY AWARD NOMINATIONS

10 nominations, 5 wins*

*Best Picture
Best Actress (Julie Andrews)
Best Supporting Actress (Peggy Wood)
*Best Director (Robert Wise)
Best Cinematography, Color
Best Art Direction–Set Decoration, Color
*Best Sound
*Best Score—Adaptation or Treatment
*Best Film Editing
Best Costume Design, Color

cessful *West Side Story,* was called in, and won an Oscar for his work. Meanwhile, Fox wanted to cast Doris Day as Maria (the part had been played by Mary Martin on Broadway). Julie was still an unfamiliar face on movie screens, since *Mary Poppins* had yet to be released. The two cinematic roles would typecast her for nearly two decades.

Among the talented children playing the junior Von Trapps was a young actress who was well known to TV audiences. When she was only four, Angela Cartwright had stolen the spotlight from Danny Thomas and company in "Make Room for Daddy." Robert Wise, who had worked with her years earlier in *Somebody Up There Likes Me,* didn't remember her eight years later when he hired the 12-year-old for *The Sound of Music,* but never forgot her after it. "Angela was a real pro," he

recalled to the *Los Angeles Times* recently, "and I cast her for the part because for one so young, she had so much experience on the screen already. She and the other children were easy to work with and they formed a very close-knit community. It has lasted, and they have stayed close throughout their lives."

And don't look now, but there's Marni Nixon as Sister Sophia! This marked the first on-screen appearance of the former ghost-singer. Also doing a walk-on was the real Baroness Maria Von Trapp, a.k.a. Maria, who visited the sets in Salzburg and landed a part as an extra.

When the film premiered at the beginning of March, critics lavished praise on it. *Variety* called it "one of the top musicals to reach the screen," and went on to describe *The Sound of Music* as "a warmly-pulsating, captivat-

ing drama…magnificently mounted and with a brilliant cast." *The Hollywood Reporter* was ecstatic, with a headline proclaiming: " 'SOUND OF MUSIC' RESTORES FAITH IN MOTION PICTURES." What had caused us to lose faith was not made clear. But the trade paper made it perfectly clear that this was not a film to be missed: "Who says you can't buy happiness? As long as Robert Wise's 'The Sound of Music' is playing, you can. And that's going to be for a good long time. Don't, however, wait. Don't deprive yourself of the pleasure a moment longer than necessary. Run, do not walk, to the nearest box office."

Good advice. And if it's been a while since you've seen it (or you've only caught one of the commercially interrupted, abbreviated telecasts), run, do not walk, to your video store and rent a copy.

2
DOCTOR ZHIVAGO
METRO-GOLDWYN-MAYER
$60,964,000

THE SUCCESS OF *Doctor Zhivago* was not an accidental piece of good fortune for MGM: it was a decidedly calculated hit. After acquiring the rights to Boris Pasternak's difficult-to-read Nobel Prize–winning novel, the studio set about securing the services of top industry talent, people like Italian producer Carlo Ponti (once and future spouse of Sophia Loren), and director David Lean, who had proven his mettle with *The Bridge on the River Kwai* and *Lawrence of Arabia.* Cast in important roles were two people already familiar to Lean from these films— Omar Sharif and Alec Guinness. As the film's centerpiece, "Lara," Lean selected a virtual unknown named Julie Christie. It ultimately became *her* picture, Ms. Christie's standout performance catching the attention of all.*

For this artfully conceived piece of movie merchandising, MGM planned a massive campaign, trumpeting the

Screenplay by Robert Bolt

Based on the novel by Boris Pasternak

Executive producer: Arvid L. Griffen

Produced by Carlo Ponti

Directed by David Lean

CAST

Yuri Zhivago . . . . .Omar Sharif
Lara . . . . .Julie Christie
Pasha Antipov . . . . . . .Tom Courtenay
Komarovsky . . . . .Rod Steiger
Tonya Gromeko . . . . . .Geraldine Chaplin
Yevgraf Zhivago . . . . . .Alec Guinness

ACADEMY AWARD NOMINATIONS

10 nominations, 5 wins*

Best Picture
Best Supporting Actor (Tom Courtenay)
Best Director (David Lean)
*Best Screenplay Based on Material from Another Source
*Best Cinematography, Color
*Best Art Direction–Set Decoration, Color
Best Sound
*Best Original Musical Score (Maurice Jarre)
Best Film Editing
*Best Costume Design, Color

$11,000,000 production as the greatest thing since *Gone With the Wind.* Although the *Los Angeles Herald-Examiner* cried yes, indeed it was, most reviews were mixed, and a few critics were downright hostile. *Newsweek* shed tears, not for the film's highly emotional moments, but for what it decried as bad drama: "It is all too bad to be true: that so much has come to so little, that tears must be prompted by dashed hopes instead of enduring drama." Not exactly what the good folks at MGM were longing to hear. However, they probably took comfort in the review by *Hollywood Reporter,* which praised the movie as "a majestic, magnificent picture of war and peace, on a national scale and scaled down to the personal. It has every element that makes a smash, long-run box office hit."

Other reviewers took a stand somewhere between these two positions.

All MGM could do was wait to see whether they had a hit or a costly turkey on their hands.

Fortunately, audience word-of-mouth fulfilled the *Reporter*'s predictions. Moviegoers bought their advance tickets, eager to sit through the 3-hour 17-minute panorama of love and human drama played against the backdrop of the Russian Revolution and World War I. The excellent production values—exquisitely photographed scenery (filmed on location in Spain and Finland), a gripping narrative, striking sets, a moving score (Maurice Jarre's "Lara's Theme" helped push the *Dr. Zhivago* soundtrack album to number three for the year)—and fine performances, all helped to make this one of MGM's biggest moneymaking films ever.

---

*However, she won the Academy Award for a different film that year—*Darling.*

THUNDERBALL

UNITED ARTISTS
$28,621,434

"You don't think I enjoyed what we did this evening, do you? What I did tonight was for Queen and country!" —JAMES BOND, AFTER SEDUCING AN ENEMY AGENT

THE FOURTH in United Artists' by-now-successful James Bond series, *Thunderball* was the first Bond film to receive an Academy Award. It was also the most financially lucrative to date, firmly establishing this action/adventure saga as a genre in its own right.

What was different about this particular Bond film that found an even larger audience than had previous 007 movies? With spy films at their zenith in '65 (*The Ipcress File, The Spy Who Came In from the Cold,* and *Our Man Flint* were just a few), United Artists wanted to take no chances with their hot property. In keeping with the old adage "it takes money to make money," the studio pumped $9,000,000 worth of gimmicks and special effects into *Thunderball* and established James Bond as the king of the gadgetry films. Also present were the traditional "Bond girls," the supervillainous agents from SPECTRE, and some of the most terrific underwater sequences ever filmed

---

Screenplay by Richard Maibaum and John Hopkins

From an original story by Kevin McClory and Jack Whittingham

Based on the novel by Ian Fleming

Produced by Kevin McClory

Directed by Terence Young

CAST

James Bond	Sean Connery
Domino	Claudine Auger
Emilio Largo	Adolfo Cell
Fiona	Luciana Paluzzi
Felix Leiter	Rik Van Nutter

ACADEMY AWARD NOMINATIONS

1 nomination, 1 win*

*Best Special Visual Effects

(location: the Bahamas).

The public was captured by the technology, the very dashing Sean Connery, and the lovely Brazilian co-star Fiona Volpe (the Queen would certainly be proud of her brave agent's success in her name). Even the critics seemed to enjoy watching Bond swing

for old England. Said *Variety:* " 'Thunderball' packs a wallop in its tongue-in-cheek treatment of agent-at-work." And *The Hollywood Reporter* proclaimed: "It's a bird! It's a plane! It's a Super-Bond!...[*Thunderball*] is sure to repeat the stream of gold that 'Goldfinger' unleashed." Indeed it did. With the success of the film came a relatively new phenomenon to the industry, one that is an adjunct to all action/adventure films today—the licensing and merchandising of James Bond products. The likeness of Sean Connery or the "James Bond" copyrighted logo began appearing in department stores worldwide, on items like attaché cases, toys, sweaters, underwear, and dolls. Connery was appalled, complaining to *The New York Times:* "The whole thing has become a Frankenstein's monster. The merchandising, the promotion, the pirating—they're thoroughly distasteful."

In many ways, Connery was right, and there have always been those critical of the exploitation that seems to accompany hit films. But, as with most cult heroes, Connery eventually accepted the merchandising tie-ins in good spirit.

THOSE MAGNIFICENT MEN IN THEIR FLYING MACHINES

20TH CENTURY-FOX
$14,000,000

ACCORDING TO *The Guinness Book of Movie Facts and Feats,* the seventh longest title ever given to a motion picture was *Those Magnificent Men in Their Flying Machines, or: How I Flew From London to Paris in 25 Hours and 11 Minutes.* Just getting the credits on the giant Todd-AO screen was itself a feat, so the producers devised a clever opening sequence that nearly steals the show. The film opens with a striking parallel to *This Is Cinerama*'s format—a pseudo-documentary beginning with historical black-and-white footage. We see classic shots of early attempts at flying—strange egg-beater-like aircraft, flying Venetian blinds with motors attached, and human wing-flappers are just some of the bizarre contraptions. And lest we think this all serious stuff, comedian Red Skelton is intercut throughout, camping it up in his inimitable style. Following this priceless montage, the

actual credits are set forth in a cartoon sequence. It was one of the most cleverly done openings of any film to date.

Basically a slapstick comedy with plenty of sight gags and aerial chases, *Those Magnificent Men* was a British production supervised by American producer Stan Margulies. The only familiar American stars were Red Skelton, who vanished after the opening title sequence, and the Yank played by Stuart Whitman. Aside from the James Bond films and a couple of others, there hadn't been much success at the box office for British fare in the United States. But the comedy was a smash hit on both sides of the Atlantic, thanks to its great photography, straightforward storyline, and natural family appeal. It also boasted a top cast. Among the more familiar Britons in the picture were Sarah Miles, Robert Morley, Benny Hill, and the gap-toothed Terry-Thomas. Gert (*Goldfinger*) Frobe co-

starred as a spiked-helmeted German cavalry officer intent upon bringing glory to the Fatherland, and there were also Italian, French, and Japanese stars to give the movie international appeal.

When the film was made in 1964, there were no airworthy examples of 1910 vintage planes in Britain, so small construction companies were pressed into service, building replicas of the early aircraft, which are the real stars of the film.

In 1969, a re-teaming of writer-director Ken Annakin and actors Terry-Thomas and Gert Frobe resulted in a picture about vintage car racing called *Those Daring Young Men in Their Jaunty Jalopies* (British title: *Monte Carlo or Bust*). It was more like a spin-off than a true sequel, and featured Tony Curtis, Peter Cook, and Dudley Moore. It was cute, but couldn't muster the following of the prototype.

Following *Those Magnificent Men,* comic actor Terry-Thomas appeared in a number of comedy films, but by 1989, he was suffering from declining health due to Parkinson's disease. In April of that year, his show business friends learned that his medical expenses had left him completely penniless; to repay the ailing star for all the years of laughter he had brought them, his colleagues staged a benefit, raising $170,000 to make his last days as comfortable as possible. Terry-Thomas died on January 8, 1990.

Screenplay by Jack Davies and Ken Annakin

Produced by Stan Marguiles

Directed by Ken Annakin

CAST

Orvil Newton . . . . .Stuart Whitman
Patricia Rawnsley . . . . . . .Sarah Miles
Richard Mays . . . . .James Fox
Count Emilio Ponticelli . . .Alberto Sordi
Sir Percy War-Armitage . . .Terry-Thomas

ACADEMY AWARD NOMINATIONS

1 nomination, no wins

Best Writing—Original Story and Screenplay

THAT DARN CAT

WALT DISNEY PRODUCTIONS
$12,628,000

THAT DARN Walt Disney! There he was again with another hit. Animals and kids—it worked every time.

The animal in question was, of course, the title cat, "D.C." (for "Darn Cat"), played admirably by a scene-stealing sealpoint Siamese named Syn, who had also starred in Disney's *The Incredible Journey.* The nine-pound feline did most of his stuntwork, brave thing, using a double only 10 percent of the time; for his performance, he won the animal kingdom's highest honor for four-legged thespians—the "Patsy."

Syn was trained by Bill Koehler (Disney's chief animal trainer for 21 years, who had done likewise for Sam of *Shaggy Dog* fame) and partner Al Niemela. Most people are unaware of how difficult it is to train a cat—ever try to get your house pet to do a trick, like coming to you when called? These professional trainers used a bell signal and reward system to teach all the actions called for in the script to the bright Siamese (the Einstein of domestic cats).

Co-starring with Syn was Disney's favorite contract player, Hayley Mills. She was a veteran of five previous Disney films by now,* and at age 19, this would be her sixth and last for Walt. Two years later, she created a mild scandal by doing a nude scene in

the British film *The Family Way,* thereby shaking forever her Disney image.

The cast also included Dean Jones, who was quickly signed to a contract and became a fixture in the Disney firmament, later appearing in such films as *The Ugly Dachshund, The Love Bug,* and *The Shaggy D.A.* Elsa Lanchester appeared in *That Darn Cat,* her second Disney picture (she played an English nanny in *Mary Poppins*); William Demarest returned to the Disney soundstages following his work in *The Absent-Minded Professor* and *Son of Flubber,* former child star Roddy McDowall made his first Disney appearance in this movie and was later given the title role in the stu-

dio's *Bullwhip Griffin;* and Ed Wynn, whom Walt Disney considered his good luck charm and used in as many comedies as possible, popped up in *That Darn Cat* as a befuddled jeweler.

Walt's director of choice for the film was Britisher Robert Stevenson, who had already helmed ten successful Disney pictures, including *The Absent-Minded Professor, Old Yeller, In Search of the Castaways,* and his Academy Award–nominated *Mary Poppins.*

A classy title song was written by the brothers Sherman, Bob and Dick, and sung by Bobby Darin, whose popularity was at its zenith at that time. The Shermans' music for *Mary Poppins* had brought them two Oscars; "That Darn Cat," however, failed to become a musical hit.

The movie excelled at the box office, continuing in the tradition of Disney's wholesome family fare. In 1995, Walt Disney Productions announced plans for a remake of the 1965 classic, to be a twisted take on the original. Rhett Butler might have been allowed to say "damn" back in 1939, but in the wonderful world of Disney, frankly, my dear, it will always be that "darn" cat.

Screenplay by The Gordons and Bill Walsh

Based on the book *Undercover Cat* by The Gordons

Produced by Bill Walsh and Ron Miller

Directed by Robert Stevenson

CAST

Patti Randall . . . . .Hayley Mills
Zeke Kelso . . . . .Dean Jones
Ingrid Randall . . . . . . .Dorothy Provine
Gregory Benson . . . . . .Roddy McDowall
Dan . . . . .Neville Brand

The Moon-Spinners, Summer Magic, In Search of the Castaways, The Parent Trap, and *Pollyanna.*

HAWAII

UNITED ARTISTS
$15,553,018

NINETEEN SIXTY-SIX was a financially lackluster year at the box office. The combined total of the top five films, $68,000,000, was lower than 1965's number-one *The Sound of Music* alone. Number-one film *Hawaii*'s figure of $15,500,000 was the lowest top amount since 1958, and the lowest for any number-one film since.

James A. Michener's novel *Hawaii* had been a blockbuster, and the same was expected of the film. But although all the elements were there—all-star cast, Panavision screen, lavish sets, costumes, and so on—the episodic Dalton Trumbo–Daniel Taradash script seemed as heavy as the layers of clothing worn in the tropics by the missionaries.

Although the company spent over four months filming in the Islands, there is very little of Hawaii in *Hawaii*. United Airlines does better in their commercials. Only the opening sequence of the ancient Hawaiian creation myth had the breathtaking scenery one might expect of this picture.

The New England village was also shot on location, in Old Sturbridge Village, Massachusetts (a historical replica of an early New England town). Before the missionaries, nicely played by Max Von Sydow and Julie Andrews, set out, we are given a foretaste of things to come for the poor heathen natives they're off to convert. The head of the family intones:

"Almighty God, look down with pity on this miserable company of sinners, conceived in lust, delivered in evil and slaves to every loathsome appetite the flesh is heir to. We have held fast against atheism, Romanism, Unitarianism and a score of lesser evils, and we thank thee that thou has chosen one of us to carry thy holy word and precious light of John Calvin to the wicked and benighted heathen of Hawaii. Amen."

Bye-bye to innocence in Paradise.

The harsh ocean voyage is one of the most dramatic and memorable scenes in the film. To get the right effect, the producers used a two-masted brigantine for the 1820 passenger ship *Thetis,* sailing her from Copenhagen to Honolulu on a 10,000-mile trip across the Atlantic and Pacific Oceans. The Cape Horn footage was actually shot in the Norwegian fjords 140 miles north of the Arctic Circle and doubled as the rugged Straits of Magellan. Even so, the producers didn't find the battering waves mountainous enough, and called upon effects expert Linwood Dunn to optically enhance the stormy seas. Dunn won an Oscar nomination for his efforts.

On arrival in the Hawaiian Islands, the long-suffering missionaries are greeted by the beautiful childlike natives and their Queen, memorably played by Jocelyne La Garde, a 6-foot, 418-pound Tahitian of royal blood who had never acted before. In fact, she'd never even had to work for a living, and took the role of Malama only after she'd been convinced there was no one else available with the huge and regal physique that was required of an Alii Nui. She didn't speak English,

---

Screenplay by Dalton Trumbo and Daniel Taradash

Based on the novel by James Michener

Produced by Walter Mirisch

Directed by George Roy Hill

CAST

Jerusha Bromley	Julie Andrews
Abner Hale	Max Von Sydow
Rafer Hoxworth	Richard Harris
Charles Bromley	Carroll O'Connor
John Whipple	Gene Hackman

ACADEMY AWARD NOMINATIONS

7 nominations, no wins

Best Supporting Actress
   (Jocelyne La Garde)
Best Cinematography, Color
Best Sound
Best Song ("My Wishing Doll," music
   and words by Elmer Bernstein and
   Mack David)
Best Original Music Score
   (Elmer Bernstein)
Best Costume Design, Color
Best Special Visual Effects

---

either, memorizing her lines phonetically. What is most surprising is that the novice actress received the film's only acting nomination, for Best Supporting Actress.

The cast itself was a mini-United Nations. There were the leads, Julie Andrews and Max Von Sydow, an Englishwoman and a Swede, respectively, playing New Englanders (Von Sydow's two boys, ages seven and twelve, played his sons); Englishman Richard Harris; mainland Americans Gene Hackman and Carroll O'Connor; a very young Bette Midler as a passenger aboard the Hawaii-bound ship; plus an assortment of actors of Hawaiian, Tonkinese, Tahitian, and Fijian blood.

One such member of the cast was Manu Tupou, a Tonkinese born in Fiji. Tupou, who plays the role of Keoki, the Hawaiian native whom the missionaries first "civilize," is a graduate of the University of Hawaii, with a master's degree in sociology. Although Tupou made his film debut in *Hawaii,* the 6-foot-4-inch actor admitted to having played a bit in his home island of Fiji in a Dinah Shore TV special called "Christmas Around the World."

The role of Neolani, a young, free-loving Hawaiian, was portrayed by Elizabeth Logue, who was Hawaii's best-known model at the time the movie was made. She was considered a natural for the role, although it was necessary for her to make a slight physical change to win the part—she had to enhance her nose in order to look more like the producers' idea of a native Hawaiian.

Hawaiian location filming took four months, principally at Makua Beach on the Island of Oahu. A village consisting of 107 buildings was constructed and continuously aged during filming to accurately represent the village of Lahaina on Maui as it existed between 1820 and 1848. One of the most difficult scenes to film there was the burning of the missionary church. Tragedy was narrowly averted when Julie Andrew's dress, which was supposed to be scorched, actually caught fire.

The production was plagued by other troubles as well. During the location shooting, which lagged way behind schedule, there was one three-day period during which the film changed directors twice. One Friday afternoon, George Roy Hill was told he was to be removed from the picture, and the Mirisch Corporation announced that Arthur Hiller would be replacing him. No sooner had Hiller flown to Hawaii, however, than a number of Hawaiian bit players and extras announced they would strike, so the producers decided to reinstate Hill, who was back in the director's chair by Monday.

The production company spared no expense in ensuring an authentic look, importing thatch from Japan, since the pili leaves normally used for thatching huts in the story's era are no longer to be found in the Hawaiian Islands. Rooster feathers (for the colorful costumes) had to be imported from the Philippines. Red and gold royal cloaks came from Hong Kong, straw mattings from Mexico, boar's-teeth necklaces and bracelets from India, and silks from Taiwan.

Although *The Hollywood Reporter* predicted that "Mirisch-UA 'Hawaii' looks like box office winner; at least 4 performances are Oscar consideration" (they weren't), most reviewers found *Hawaii* ponderous. *Time* likened the film to a "ten-ton mouse": "Whenever a dull moment threatens, [director George Roy] Hill rummages around in Michener's bottomless bag of epic tricks and comes up with windstorms, conflagrations, eruptions, street fights, breech births, shark attacks, luaus, lava-lavas and assorted shouts and muumuus…The spectator is rather too frequently allowed to feel that he is watching a rather small film on a very large screen…a 3½-hour story that could have been told just as well in two." *The New York Times* had a mixed reaction, enjoying the "eye-popping scenes of storm and seascape, of pomp and pestilence, all laid out in large strokes of brilliant DeLuxe color" while lamenting the fact that *Hawaii* seemed "as big and familiar as Diamond Head, and ultimately almost as heavy."

In 1970, the producers took advantage of the first film's previous location construction to make a sequel film, *The Hawaiians.* It starred Charlton Heston, Geraldine Chaplin, and John Phillip Law. This sequel had Heston returning to a Hawaii undergoing drastic evolutionary changes. The film drew upon the wealth of unused material in Michener's epic tome, involving such dramatic elements as family relationships, conflicts, business ventures, and even the lepers' colony on Molokai. Although cinematically well crafted, the picture proved an enormous box office flop.

2

THE BIBLE
20TH CENTURY-FOX
$15,000,000

O NCE AGAIN, here was a movie based on a book—a best-seller, in fact.

Actually, *The Bible* should really be called *The Book of Genesis,* since that's the only part of the Old Testament covered by the film. It was directed by John Huston, who also assumed the role of Noah (and the Voice of God).

Italian producer Dino De Laurentiis saw himself as a latter-day combination of Cecil B. DeMille and Mike Todd, and the self-appointed heir apparent spent an estimated $18,000,000 shooting in Sardinia, Sicily, North Africa, and at his studio in Rome. It was the most expensive film that year, and worldwide rentals saw it barely breaking even.

The requisite all-star cast was packed with many famous names, like George C. Scott as Abraham, Ava Gardner as Sarah, Michael Parks as Adam, Richard Harris as Cain, Stephen Boyd as Nimrod, and Peter O'Toole as all three Messengers of the Lord. The opening sequences depicting Adam and Eve are well photographed by a very literal, unabashed camera. One blooper, however, was missed by the production staff. Since Adam is supposed to have been created from the elements, rather than born of a woman, he would not have a naval. In an otherwise effective piece of technical crafting, the post-production crew neglected to airbrush

Adam's belly button!

The would-be epic is probably best remembered for the Noah's Ark sequence, since Huston lavished most of his attention on that 45-minute-long segment. We're treated to a regular zoo parade as numerous animals board the giant ark set, two-by-two (although both elephants were female; bull elephants are generally untrainable, since they tend to be rambunctious). It looks very natural on the screen, but Huston once recounted how many months of work it took to train the animals to walk in formation, prey and predator alike, without the use of trick photography.

Huston's original choices for the part of Noah were Charlie Chaplin, who didn't want to work in someone else's film, and Alec Guinness, who had a schedule conflict. An avid animal lover himself, Huston had spent long hours talking to the various beasts, many of them brought from the wild, taming them so they were comfortable around him. In the end, he decided to take the part of Noah only because, as he recalled in his autobiography, *An Open Book,* "I began to realize how important it was that Noah should be on familiar terms with the animals— knowing them was as important as an actor's ability to play the role. So I decided to do the part myself."

Critics again had mixed opinions. *The Hollywood Reporter* proclaimed it a "Box Office Smash," adding: "It looks very much as if Dino De Laurentiis' production is going to be another in 20th-Fox's recent succession of landmark box office smashes. The biblical film has been for so long a standard of Hollywood, and a cliché. It is one of Huston's major achievements that he has found fresh inspiration and vigor." *Time,* on the other hand, had great misgivings: "Unfortunately, it is a long way from The Beginning to the end. The Word is interpreted altogether literally, neither revitalized with the logic of drama nor illuminated by the magic of myth...There is somebody up there, all right, but who? A director, a Deity, or Our Man in Disneyland?" The reviewer summed up by saying, "Better read The Book."

Likewise the critic for *Newsweek,* who wrote that "the film vulgarizes a host of sublime images and metaphors by concretizing them and preserving them in the amber of mediocrity. The Gideons will not be leaving tickets for it in hotel rooms."

But for those who aren't looking for anything more than an entertaining film, *The Bible* is worth seeing, especially when all that went into the filmmaking process is taken into account.

Screenplay by Christopher Fry

Produced by Dino De Laurentiis

Directed by John Huston

CAST

Adam	Michael Parks
Eve	Ulla Bergryd
Cain	Richard Harris
Abel	Franco Nero
Noah	John Huston
Nimrod	Stephen Boyd
Abraham	George C. Scott
Sarah	Ava Gardner
The Three Angels	Peter O'Toole

ACADEMY AWARD NOMINATIONS

1 nomination, no wins

Best Original Music Score (Toshiro Mayuzumi)

WHO'S AFRAID OF VIRGINIA WOOLF?

WARNER BROS.
$14,500,000

WHEN LAST WE MET Richard Burton and Elizabeth Taylor, they were making whoopee while making *Cleopatra*. The world's most watched couple were finally married in March, 1964, and from then on, the twosome made a string of film duets, including *The V.I.P.s* (1963) and *The Sandpiper* (1965). *Who's Afraid of Virginia Woolf?* marked their fourth joint venture.

The movie—if it can be called that, since it is virtually a stage play on film with a few exteriors of campus trees and such thrown in—is a four-person dialogue drama. George and Martha (the Burton-Taylor pairing) are sado-masochists who use words as weapons, aiming their barbs at a young professor and his wife (George Segal and Sandy Dennis) while indulging in an all-night orgy of booze and sexual innuendoes. The unsuspecting visitors gradually undergo a transformation

and an eventual loss of innocence in this profoundly dark, moody, and occasionally depressing film. But the brilliant performances and likewise brilliant directing by first-time filmmaker Mike Nichols has made this a piece of cinematic literature.

As a mainstream film, *Who's Afraid of Virginia Woolf?* broke the old rules of censorship, pushing the Motion Picture Association of America and its production code to the limit. Language was the main barrier; the movie was reported to contain some of the most explicitly frank dialogue ever heard in an American film—by one tally, there were eleven "goddamns," five "son of a bitches," seven "bastards," plus "screw you," "hump the hostess," "up yours," "monkey nipples," and other shocking expletives (but not the still risqué "f" word). Studio boss Jack L. Warner refused to soften on the subject, and the film eventually received an "R" rating, which at that time meant no one under age 18 would be admitted without parent or guardian, so becoming the first film under the new rating system to carry this designation. No doubt this added to the film's mystique and increased box office take.

The avant-garde production received widespread critical acclaim, particularly for its two principals. *Variety* wrote of Taylor: "Miss Taylor, who has proven she can act in response to sensitive direction, earned every penny of her reported million plus. Her characterization is at once sensual, spiteful, cynical, pitiable, loathsome, lustful and tender...the projection of three-dimensional reality requires talent which sustains the interest; the talent is here." And of Burton, the same trade paper wrote: "Burton...delivers a smash portrayal. He evokes sympathy during the public degradations to which his wife subjects him, and his outrage, as well as his deliberate vengeance, are totally believable."

The fact that Richard Burton did not win the Academy Award while Mrs. Burton did was a sore subject for Elizabeth for many years, since she felt (rightfully so) that his-and-hers Oscars were in order. It was Liz Taylor's second Oscar (the first was for *Butterfield 8* in 1960); that year, she aced out some interesting contenders, including Lynn and Vanessa Redgrave, Anouk Aimee, and Ida Kaminski.

Screenplay by Ernest Lehman

Based on the play by Edward Albee

Produced by Ernest Lehman

Directed by Mike Nichols

CAST

Martha	Elizabeth Taylor
George	Richard Burton
Nick	George Segal
Honey	Sandy Dennis

ACADEMY AWARD NOMINATIONS

13 nominations, 5 wins*

Best Picture
Best Actor (Richard Burton)
*Best Actress (Elizabeth Taylor)
Best Supporting Actor (George Segal)
*Best Supporting Actress (Sandy Dennis)
Best Director (Mike Nichols)
Best Screenplay Based on Material from Another Source
*Best Cinematography, Black and White
*Best Art Direction–Set Decoration, Black and White
Best Sound
Best Original Music Score (Alex North)
Best Film Editing
*Best Costume Design, Black and White

A MAN FOR ALL SEASONS

COLUMBIA
$12,750,000

Like other literate filmworks of 1966, *A Man for All Seasons* was a true screen gem for Columbia. The studio hadn't had a hit since 1962's *Lawrence of Arabia,* another historical epic. This time, it turned the clock back three centuries for a historical film that was actually more drama than epic, a serious work in which the production values were an adjunct to the picture and not the main attraction.

The story traces the life of Sir Thomas More as he rises through the ranks of 16th-century England to become one of the most important men in that country's history. The author, politician, humanist, scholar, and lawyer received the honor of being named Henry VIII's Lord Chancellor. Yet he refused to renounce the Pope and accept Henry's Protestant faith (which allowed for divorce, something Henry was very keen on)—with dire consequences.

Many of the English cast members were only recently familiar to American audiences...actors like Robert Shaw as King Henry VIII (he had been seen in *From Russia With Love*), Susannah

Screenplay by Robert Bolt

Based on the play by Robert Bolt

Executive Producer: William N. Graf

Produced and directed by Fred Zinnemann

CAST

Sir Thomas More	Paul Scofield
Alice More	Wendy Hiller
Thomas Cromwell	Leo McKern
King Henry VIII	Robert Shaw
Cardinal Wolsey	Orson Welles

ACADEMY AWARD NOMINATIONS

8 nominations, 6 wins*

* *Best Picture
* *Best Actor (Paul Scofield)
* Best Supporting Actor (Robert Shaw)
* Best Supporting Actress (Wendy Hiller)
* *Best Director (Fred Zinnemann)
* *Best Screenplay Based on Material from Another Medium
* *Best Cinematography, Color
* *Best Costume Design, Color

York in the role of Margaret More (fresh from her part in *Tom Jones*), and, as Anne Boleyn, Vanessa Redgrave, whose sister had just hit the screens in *Georgy Girl.* A minor but important role ("Richard Rich") was played by John Hurt, known to audiences today for many fine performances, including *The Elephant Man,* although he was totally unknown in America back then. Orson Welles as Cardinal Wolsey was perhaps the most instantly recognizable actor in the cast.

But the title role went to the man who had created the part in screenwriter Robert Bolt's stage version. Paul Scofield's name was certainly not a household word in the U.S., yet his performance as the ill-fated More would win him an Oscar, one of only eight Britons (as of 1995) to receive Best Actor awards in 47 years.* Ironically, he would never again equal the success afforded him in this picture.

The critics applauded this motion picture. *The New York Times* wrote that director Zinnemann "has crystallized the essence of this drama in such pictorial terms as to render even its abstractions vibrant...Mr. Scofield is brilliant...'A Man for All Seasons' is a picture that inspires admiration, courage and thought." *The Hollywood Reporter* headlined: "'A Man for All Seasons' is rare film 'for all times.'" Indeed, it is well worth investing a few hours to watch the videocassette version, especially to see all those talented British performers who are somewhat more familiar to us today.

---

*Other winners were Charles Laughton, *The Private Life of Henry VIII*, 1933; Robert Donat, *Goodbye Mr. Chips*, 1939; Laurence Olivier, *Hamlet*, 1948; Ben Kingsley, *Gandhi*, 1982; Daniel Day-Lewis, *My Left Foot*, 1989; Jeremy Irons, *Reversal of Fortune*, 1990; and Anthony Hopkins, *The Silence of the Lambs*, 1991.

LT. ROBIN CRUSOE, USN

WALT DISNEY PRODUCTIONS
$10,164,000

THERE HAVE BEEN no less than 43 film versions (including two porno ones) of Daniel Defoe's shipwreck novel *Robinson Crusoe.* Walt Disney had already made a movie of *Swiss Family Robinson,* which is derivative of Defoe. Yet in 1966, Disney again turned to that classic tale, this time with one of TV's most popular actors—and his own "Bert" from *Mary Poppins*—in the title role.

The credits tell us that the movie was "based on a story by Retlaw Yensid." That's "Walter Disney" backwards— one of the few times Walt actually put his name in the credits. It might have been better if he hadn't. While pleasant enough, *Lt. Robin Crusoe* is one of the weakest of all the Disney films.

For Dick Van Dyke, this role is a tour de force, since he's onscreen virtually all the time. But his talents were wasted, as any Disney fan of *Mary Poppins* can attest; there are no songs,

no dances, and very few other characters with whom he can interact during most of the film. Later on in the picture, he gets his man Friday, or in this case, his girl Wednesday, played by Nancy Kwan, a Eurasian beauty who had made a name for herself in the films *The World of Suzie Wong* (1960) and *Flower Drum Song* (1961). She's fleeing from her overbearing papa, played by the great Russian character actor Akim Tamiroff, and trying to impersonate a superstitious South Seas islander. She's brought along a bunch of giggly beach bunnies, making this seem like a Disney version of the '60s bikini/beach pictures. Worst of all is a very un-Disney-like ending, in which Van Dyke gets rescued and leaves Kwan behind.

Why was this so-so film a hit, then? One big reason was Dick Van Dyke, whose charms were not lost on *The Hollywood Reporter:* "It isn't really the

story that counts…The comic spirit of the picture is provided by Dick Van Dyke, who has the happy faculty of appearing to compose his lines on the spur of the moment, and plays them with an economy of manner and certainty of timing that is always rewarding." Other reviewers weren't so eager to agree. *The New York Times* called *Lt. Robin Crusoe* a "silly, tired business that seems…bedraggled and synthetic…Most of the picture has Mr. Van Dyke mugging and tripping over the lush scenery." And those were the *favorable* comments.

The scenery was indeed lush—aside from shots of the aforementioned bikini-boppers, there was some glorious footage of the Hawaiian island of Kauai, but certainly not enough of it to send ticket-buyers dashing to their nearest box office. The success of this movie can only be attributed to two people: Retlaw Yensid and Ekyd Navkcid.

Screenplay by Bill Walsh and Don DaGradi

Produced by Bill Walsh and Ron Miller

Directed by Bryon Paul

CAST

Lt. Robin Crusoe . . . . .Dick Van Dyke
Wednesday . . . . .Nancy Kwan
Tanamashu . . . . .Akim Tamiroff
Umbrella Man . . . . . . .Arthur Malet
Captain . . . . .Tyler McVey

1

THE JUNGLE BOOK

WALT DISNEY PRODUCTIONS
$60,964,000

THE LAST animated feature to be personally produced by Walt Disney, who died eight months before its initial release, was *The Jungle Book.* The film was based on Rudyard Kipling's stories of a boy raised by wolves, and appeared exactly 30 years after Disney's first animated feature, *Snow White and the Seven Dwarfs.* It was a financial success from the start, right up there with Disney's all-time greatest hits like *Bambi, Pinocchio* and *Fantasia.*

Wolfgang "Woolie" Reitherman, Disney's favorite animation director, was at the helm. He was one of the so-called "nine old men," the original group of animators who had been with Disney since the mid-1930s, when they began work on *Snow White and the Seven Dwarfs.* Reitherman worked with a team of 70 animators and 200 artists, producing approximately 322,000 separate drawings in the course of three years to get the story of the man-cub and his jungle pals on film.

The story chronicles the adventures of Mowgli, a young boy abandoned at birth in the jungles of India and raised by a wolf pack. When the tiger, Shere Khan, stalks Mowgli, Bagheera, a concerned panther, helps the 10-year-old escape and return to human society. Many of these animals were created in response to the personality of the

actor who supplied its voice. Phil Harris played Baloo the Bear, and some of the famous performer's own mannerisms were incorporated by the animators. Sebastian Cabot gave voice to the panther Bagheera. He worked on other Disney films, including *Winnie the Pooh* and *The Sword in the Stone,* but is probably best remembered as "Mr. French" in TV's "Family Affair." Jazz musician Louis Prima spoke the part of King Louie, the swinging ape. Academy Award winner George Sanders (*All About Eve*) provided the voice for the tiger, Shere Khan. Sterling Holloway played Kaa, the lisping hypnotic snake; he was a veteran of many Disney films, appearing as "The Cheshire Cat" in *Alice In Wonderland* and also the voice of "Winnie the Pooh" in many of those cartoons. Woolie Reitherman's son Bruce did the voice of Mowgli the Man-Cub; Clint Howard (Ron's brother and also a child actor at the time) played his baby elephant friend, and a Beatles soundalike—reportedly Chad Stuart, of Chad and Jeremy—played the vulture with the Ringo haircut.

Walt's favorite musical team, the Sherman Brothers, was also called in. They composed five original songs: "I Wanna Be Like You," "Kaa's Song," "My Own Home," and two others. Another song writer, Terry Gilkyson,

contributed the catchy "Bare Necessities" (sung by Phil Harris), which won the film's only Oscar nomination. Gilkyson (along with the Easy Riders) had had a number-four hit in 1957 with the record "Marianne," and had composed mostly pop tunes rather than songs for the movies. At the 40th Academy Awards ceremony held in 1968, life-size recreations of Baloo and King Louis joined Louis Armstrong in a jumping rendition of the nominated song.

It had been four years since the last Disney animated feature (*The Sword in the Stone*), and a new crop of kids and their parents eagerly welcomed this latest offering. Its success at the box office might also be attributed to enthusiasm on the part of the critics. *The New York Times* wrote on December 25: "Merry Christmas right back to the Walt Disney studio! A perfectly dandy cartoon feature, 'The Jungle Book,' scooted into local theatres yesterday just ahead of the big day, and it's ideal for the children…this glowing little picture should be grand fun for all ages…the Disney picture is simple, uncluttered, straight-forward fun." *The Hollywood Reporter* called the movie "Charming," and prophetically hit the nail on the head when it wrote that *The Jungle Book* "should have its strong response at the box office and be another one to put away in the bank for reissue with satisfactory results in years to come."

Just as predicted, there were several re-releases by the Walt Disney Company, the final one in the summer of 1990, adding more box office dollars to the picture's total take, pushing it to the number-one position for movies released in 1967. The movie is available for purchase from time to time on home video, so it can become part of everyone's cherished Disney collection.

Meanwhile, in what must have seemed like a brilliant idea at the time, Disney Studios decided to produce a live-acted version of *The Jungle Book* in 1994. The film starred Jason Scott Lee as Mowgli, plus a cast that included Cary Elwes, Sam Neill, and John Cleese. It did only moderate business at the box office.

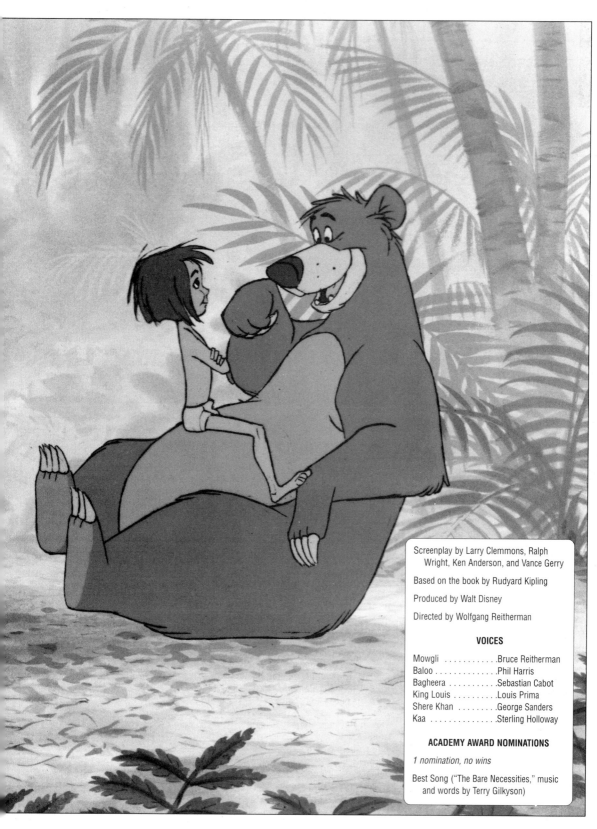

Screenplay by Larry Clemmons, Ralph
    Wright, Ken Anderson, and Vance Gerry

Based on the book by Rudyard Kipling

Produced by Walt Disney

Directed by Wolfgang Reitherman

VOICES

Mowgli . . . . .Bruce Reitherman
Baloo . . . . .Phil Harris
Bagheera . . . . .Sebastian Cabot
King Louis . . . . .Louis Prima
Shere Khan . . . . .George Sanders
Kaa . . . . .Sterling Holloway

ACADEMY AWARD NOMINATIONS

1 nomination, no wins

Best Song ("The Bare Necessities," music
    and words by Terry Gilkyson)

2

THE GRADUATE

AVCO/EMBASSY
$44,090,729

*"Mrs. Robinson, you're trying to
seduce me!"* —DUSTIN HOFFMAN,
TO ANNE BANCROFT

THERE COULDN'T have been a more
fitting title for this film. Not only
was it about Ben Braddock, college
graduate about to enter the School of
Life, but it could be applied to life in
the late '60s in general. Film subject
matter no longer held its earlier sexual
taboos, and in a sense graduated into
maturity. It also marked the graduation
from obscurity to instant fame for director Mike Nichols. This was only his
second film, after 1966's *Who's Afraid
of Virginia Woolf?* (see page 187).
Nichols' career continued well into the
'90s, with such directorial achievements
as *Silkwood* (1983), *Working Girl* (1988),
Postcards from the Edge (1990), *Wolf*
(1994), and *The birdcage* (1996).

The *Graduate* wasn't Hoffman's first
film. The young man who began his
acting career as an automobile-com-
mercial pitchman had made a couple
of low-budget movies that no one ever
heard of—no one, it seems, except
Mike Nichols, who screen-tested
Hoffman after Robert Redford turned
the part down, and paid him $750 a
week to be in the film (Hoffman
earned $20,000 in the role but after-
ward signed up for much-needed
unemployment benefits). The huge
box office success of *The Graduate*
launched Hoffman into instant stardom. This short Jewish kid from L.A.
and New York was not Robert
Redford/drop-dead gorgeous, but he
could *act.* Three decades later, he continued to prove this, making hit after
hit, garnering Oscar after Oscar.

Of his performance in *The
Graduate,* Newsweek wrote: "It is
Dustin Hoffman in his first [sic]
motion-picture performance who turns
Benjamin into an endearing, enduring
hero. He never seems sure of what his
voice, eyes or hands are doing, or
whose orders they are following. He
wears the world like a new pair of

shoes. He nods his head whenever he
doesn't quite know what he means,
which is often. He is wrenchingly simple and vividly intelligent, even with
his self-doubts, and his bumbling
seduction scenes with the wife of his
father's law partner…are as funny as
anything ever committed to film.

One star of the film has to be the
music of Simon & Garfunkel, which,
surprisingly, didn't win any nominations. Their tune "The Sounds of
Silence" had been a number-one hit
for two weeks back in January, 1966,
and was familiar to audiences by the
time it was used as part of the score in
The Graduate. The other popular song
to emerge from the movie was "Mrs.
Robinson," which was a number-one
song for three weeks, beginning June
1, 1968. Rounding out the album
(which was the best-selling soundtrack
of 1967) were "Scarborough Fair/
Canticle" and "April Come She Will."

Screenplay by Calder Willingham and
   Buck Henry

Based on the novel by Charles Webb

Produced by Lawrence Turman

Directed by Mike Nichols

CAST

Mrs. Robinson . . . . . . .Anne Bancroft
Ben Braddock . . . . . . .Dustin Hoffman
Elaine Robinson . . . . . .Katharine Ross
Mr. Braddock . . . . .William Daniels
Mr. Robinson . . . . .Murray Hamilton

ACADEMY AWARD NOMINATIONS

7 nominations, 1 win*

Best Picture
Best Actor (Dustin Hoffman)
Best Actress (Anne Bancroft)
Best Supporting Actress (Katharine Ross)
*Best Director (Mike Nichols)
Best Screenplay Based on Material from
   Another Medium
Best Cinematography

Beginning with 1967, separate "Color"
and "Black and White" divisions were
eliminated for the Best Cinematography
award.

GUESS WHO'S COMING TO DINNER

COLUMBIA
$25,500,000

"You're two wonderful people who happened to fall in love and happen to have a pigmentation problem."
—SPENCER TRACY

THE TIMES, they were a-changing. Sexual taboos in the movies had been overcome for the most part by the late '60s, and it was time to tackle other barriers. The racial intermarriage theme may be dated today, but *Guess Who's Coming to Dinner* was a landmark film in its time. There had been an earlier picture dealing with miscegenation—1959's *Island in the Sun,* which dealt with two interracial romances (John Justin and Dorothy Dandridge, Harry Belafonte and Joan Fontaine). But it took the teaming of Katharine Hepburn and Spencer Tracy to make the theme a box office hit.

Through the years, Hepburn and Tracy had made eight movies together; *Guess Who* was their ninth and last. Ms. Hepburn hadn't made a film in five years, and everyone had assumed she had retired. Not so Stanley Kramer, at whose urging she reunited

with her old partner Spencer Tracy. He hadn't worked in four years, and producer-director Kramer thought it might be therapeutic for him. But Tracy was ill throughout the production, and it proved a challenge to Kramer and the rest of the crew to schedule the shooting around the rapidly weakening actor. Ten days after the last take, Spencer Tracy died.

The story involved a wealthy white couple's daughter bringing home her fiancé, played by charming and handsome Sidney Poitier. So what was all the fuss about? This black man was a parent's dream come true; in the words of *Harper's* reviewer, he was "a world-famous expert on international hygiene problems and in terms of character…a near-perfect mixture of Albert Schweitzer, Louis Pasteur and Ralph Bunche, while looking like Sidney Poitier, who plays the role. Who could resist that?"

Many people, unfortunately, for back in 1967, it was considered a *crime* for people of different races to marry. When Tracy says, "In 16 or 17 states, you'd be breaking the law," he wasn't

exaggerating—at one time, 41 states barred mixed marriages. Back in 1959, for example, a racially mixed couple in Virginia was sentenced to a year in jail. Their name, ironically, was "Loving." The Lovings appealed to the Supreme Court, which overturned their conviction in June, 1967, just six months before the release of *Guess Who's Coming to Dinner.* But people's attitudes weren't so quick to change, and although the laws were struck from the books, the acceptance of racially mixed marriages is far from universal even today.

In March, 1989, 22 years after *Guess Who's Coming to Dinner* premiered, the NBC television network aired its first interracial soap opera, "Generations." In order to compete with other networks' soaps, which were now concerning themselves with once-controversial or taboo subjects like homosexuality, AIDS, child abuse, and alcoholism, NBC gambled that since 20 percent of the daytime audience was black, this drama might boost their ratings. The series ran from 1989 through January, 1991.

Screenplay by William Rose

Produced and directed by Stanley Kramer

CAST

Matt Drayton . . . . .Spencer Tracy
John Prentice . . . . . . .Sidney Poitier
Christina Drayton . . . . .Katharine Hepburn
Joey Drayton . . . . .Katharine Houghton

ACADEMY AWARD NOMINATIONS

10 nominations, 2 wins*

Best Picture
Best Actor (Spencer Tracy)
*Best Actress (Katharine Hepburn)
Best Supporting Actor (Cecil Kellaway)
Best Supporting Actress (Beah Richards)
Best Director (Stanley Kramer)
*Best Story and Screenplay Written Directly for the Screen
Best Art Direction
Best Score—Adaptation or Treatment
Best Film Editing

4

BONNIE AND CLYDE
WARNER BROS.
$22,800,000

"They're young. They're in love. They rob banks."
—ADVERTISING COPY FOR
BONNIE AND CLYDE

WARREN BEATTY, brother of Shirley MacLaine, hadn't had much success with his movie career since he'd acted in two films back in 1961 (*Splendor in the Grass, The Roman Spring of Mrs. Stone*). He figured if he could produce his own vehicle, he could get his career back on track, so he purchased the script for *Bonnie and Clyde* for $75,000. The investment paid off—what began as a film full of little-knowns became the sleeper of the year and Warner Bros.' most financially successful picture of the decade.

Stylish, classy, innovative in its special effects (the overcranked slo-mo footage of their death scene has become a classic), *Bonnie and Clyde* was outwardly a fact-based story of two outlaws of the '30s, a sort of Mr. and Mrs. Jesse James, folk heroes (in this movie, at least) in the Robin Hood

Screenplay by David Newman and
    Robert Benton

Produced by Warren Beatty

Directed by Arthur Penn

CAST

Clyde Barrow . . . . .Warren Beatty
Bonnie Parker . . . . . . .Faye Dunaway
C. W. Moss . . . . .Michael J. Pollard
Buck Barrow . . . . .Gene Hackman
Blanche . . . . .Estelle Parsons
Eugene Grizzard . . . . .Gene Wilder

ACADEMY AWARD NOMINATIONS

10 nominations, 2 wins*

Best Picture
Best Actor (Warren Beatty)
Best Actress (Faye Dunaway)
Best Supporting Actor (Gene Hackman)
Best Supporting Actor (Michael J. Pollard)
*Best Supporting Actress (Estelle Parsons)
Best Director (Arthur Penn)
Best Screenplay Written Directly for the
    Screen
*Best Cinematography
Best Costume Design

tradition—they robbed banks, we are told, because the banks foreclosed on poor people. But in addition to action and graphic violence set to banjo-plunkin' bluegrass music, this movie had a *love* story. Audiences were as drawn to the two central figures as they would have been to any two well-drawn, sympathetically portrayed characters, criminal or otherwise.

Beatty's future was sealed with this picture; after it, he'd never have to beg for financing of his other projects. He not only brought the film in on time, but for a mere $2,500,000—earning back its cost nearly tenfold.

Newcomer Faye Dunaway also established her credibility as an actress after *Bonnie and Clyde*. It was her first major motion picture, and her first Oscar nomination as well. Critics were entranced by her winsome ways. The actress also made the pages of top fashion magazines as the "Bonnie

Parker" look (V-neck sweater, maxiskirt, beret) became an international craze.

Other outstanding performances were turned in by the rest of the cast, as evidenced by their all receiving nominations for Oscars. Gene Hackman and Estelle Parsons made for a memorable couple, and both went on to successful film careers. Michael J. Pollard as C. W. Moss, the goofy moon-faced creature who signs on with the Parker gang, seemed to find equally offbeat roles, playing everything from an alien child in an episode of TV's "Star Trek," to a half-witted psychopath in *Dirty Little Billy* (1972), to a recent role as a sadistic father in *Season for Fear* (1989). In the 1990s, Pollard appeared in two quasi-horror films—*Split Second* (1992), about alien serial killers in the year 2008, and *Skeeter* (1993), a movie about giant killer mosquitos.

THE DIRTY DOZEN

METRO-GOLDWYN-MAYER
$20,403,826

BACK DURING World War II, MGM built its reputation as the studio that made the big musicals, lots of songs and dances with stars like Judy Garland, Fred Astaire, Ginger Rogers. So what was the studio thinking when they turned out a war picture in 1967, at a time when no studio in town was doing war? For one thing, they obviously had a corner on the market. And war wasn't far from our daily thoughts as the Vietnam "living room war" was escalating. Given the right cast and script, the studio knew there was box office money to be made.

The picture was indeed a grim and dirty portrayal of war (yes, it's hell) as we follow a group of convicts on a suicide mission—they're given a choice of death, or death. Crafted almost as a suspense/thriller, the film's well-written script is further enhanced by the chemistry of the dozen assorted types making up the cast.

Lee Marvin stars as the leader of the squad, a no-nonsense guy we're glad is on our side. His hand-picked "dirties" include John Cassavetes as a psychotic hustler, former football star Jim Brown as an anti-white militant, Trini Lopez, a popular singer (he sang the theme song, "The Bramble Bush") as a young Puerto Rican, Telly Savalas as a Bible-quoting sex maniac, and Clint Walker as a psychopath. Other members of the mostly all-male cast included Charles Bronson, Ernest Borgnine, George Kennedy, and Donald Sutherland.

Word-of-mouth was a big plus in selling this picture to a war-weary public, since it received very mixed notices in the press. *Time* put it this way: "*The Dirty Dozen* is the definitive enlisted man's picture. In its view, World War II was a private affair in which officers were hypocritical, stupid or German, and only the dogfaced soldier was gutsy enough to be great. In this film, the lopsided interpretation works largely because of a fine cast and a taut plot that closes the credibility gap...Director Robert Aldrich gets convincingly raw, tough performances in even the smallest roles."

Even *The Hollywood Reporter* had trouble being 100 percent positive about this movie: " 'The Dirty Dozen' ...is the beneficiary of extensive advance publicity and excitement and has a strong, virile cast to deliver both the brutalizing violence and grotesque comedy which will make it one of MGM's big money pictures of the year. It is overlong, uneven and frequently obscure, but will succeed by virtue of its sustained action, even though what it attempts to say, if anything, remains elusive."

The public seemed unaffected by these "good news/bad news" reviews and afforded the picture cult status. A series of TV movies followed: *The Dirty Dozen: The Next Mission* (1985), *The Dirty Dozen: The Deadly Mission* (1987), *The Dirty Dozen: The Fatal Mission* (1988). Some included original cast members like Ernest Borgnine, Telly Savalas, and Lee Marvin. A short-lived TV series ran on the Fox Network from April to July, 1988.

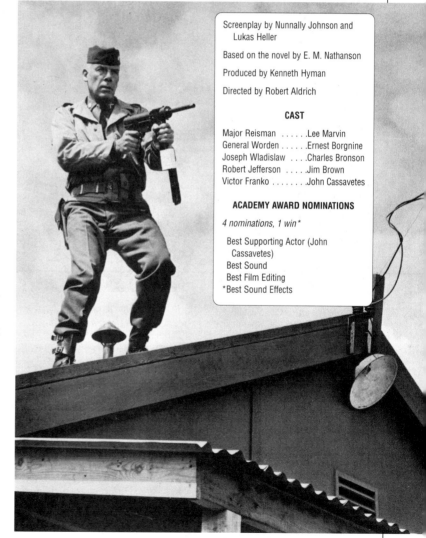

Screenplay by Nunnally Johnson and Lukas Heller

Based on the novel by E. M. Nathanson

Produced by Kenneth Hyman

Directed by Robert Aldrich

CAST

Major Reisman	Lee Marvin
General Worden	Ernest Borgnine
Joseph Wladislaw	Charles Bronson
Robert Jefferson	Jim Brown
Victor Franko	John Cassavetes

ACADEMY AWARD NOMINATIONS

4 nominations, 1 win*

Best Supporting Actor (John Cassavetes)
Best Sound
Best Film Editing
*Best Sound Effects

1

FUNNY GIRL

COLUMBIA
$26,325,000

A S THE '60s drew to a close, the decade of hit Broadway musicals had two more aces left up its sleeve, and both were held by a movie unknown. But after *Funny Girl* and *Hello, Dolly!* the name of Barbra Streisand would become one of the best-known monikers in the industry.

The young Jewish girl from Brooklyn had set her sights on a show business career since childhood, when she would sit in her room singing all the songs on the Broadway original-cast albums she lovingly collected. By her early teens, she was making her own demo records, and later held down jobs as a theater usherette and switchboard operator while she pursued her career. At 19, she was finally signed for a role in the short-lived musical *I Can Get It for You Wholesale*.

The play didn't last, but Barbra did. She was spotted by composer Jule Styne, who had been working on a musical based on the life of comedienne Fanny Brice. Producer Ray Stark had several other screen personalities in mind for his production, like Anne Bancroft, Carol Burnett, Kaye Ballard, Mitzi Gaynor, or possibly Eydie Gorme. But Styne was pre-sold on Streisand, and insisted that Stark consider her, especially as her recording career began to take off. Fortunately, Stark agreed to a contract, and the play opened in March, 1964. It played to packed houses for 1,348 performances before heading for Hollywood

and the movie screen.

Filming began in May, 1967, but with a reluctant Ms. Streisand. She had always been self-conscious about her appearance and now feared that the facial features she considered her worst would be exaggerated by the hugeness of the movie screen. Her main concern was her nose, which many found larger than "standard," whatever that is. Fortunately, she never underwent cosmetic surgery, for it is her slightly flawed nose that reminds us that this woman with the exceptional set of vocal chords is human after all. Nevertheless, she generally prefers to be photographed in left profile, her "better side," as they say in showbiz.

Co-starring with Barbra Streisand was Omar Sharif, perhaps the casting coup of the century. Here was an Egyptian matinee idol, as dashing a male as there could be—an Arab named Omar—cast in the role of Jewish Fanny Brice's Jewish husband, Nick Arnstein. Sharif's credentials were certainly impeccable; he'd actually played an Arab in *Lawrence of Arabia*, and the title Russian in *Doctor Zhivago*. Now he was to kiss a Jewish princess on a 20-foot-high screen. It was only weeks before that the Arab-Israeli Six-Day War had taken place. The Egyptian press denounced him as a traitor, and there was talk of revoking his citizenship. But Sharif had a job to do, and fortunately, he ignored politics.

Others in the cast included Anne Francis as Fanny Brice's friend Georgia, and Walter Pidgeon as Florenz Ziegfeld. The two had appeared together in one other film, back in 1956, as father and daughter in the science fiction movie *Forbidden Planet*.

There are some truly great musical numbers in *Funny Girl*, most notably "People," Streisand's first recording hit and now her theme song; "Don't Rain on My Parade," "Second Hand Rose" (which was added for the movie version), "You Are Woman, I Am Man," and the title song, which was also written for the film and nominated for an Oscar.

Nearly every reviewer had enormous praise for Ms. Streisand. *Newsweek*, for example, described her screen debut as "the most accomplished, original and enjoyable musical-comedy performance that has ever been captured on film." Columbia Pictures charged a six-dollar top for tickets to the New York and Los Angeles engagements, an unheard-of amount in those days. But nobody seemed to mind. The film played at one Times Square theater for over a year and became the highest-grossing film musical since *The Sound of Music*.

In 1975, Columbia produced a sequel called *Funny Lady*, again with Barbra Streisand and Omar Sharif, plus James Caan as her second husband. Ben Vereen and Roddy McDowall co-starred. It pulled in $19,313,000 in North American rentals, not as much as its predecessor, but certainly a respectable amount. It's worth watching once you've seen the first film.

Screenplay by Isobel Lennart

Based on the play and book by Isobel Lennart

Music by Jule Styne

Lyrics by Bob Merrill

Produced by Ray Stark

Directed by William Wyler

CAST

Fanny Brice . . . . .Barbra Streisand
Nick Arnstein . . . . .Omar Sharif
Rose Brice . . . . .Kay Medford
Georgia James . . . . . . .Anne Francis
Florenz Ziegfeld . . . . . .Walter Pidgeon

ACADEMY AWARD NOMINATIONS

8 nominations, 1 win*

Best Picture
*Best Actress (Barbra Streisand)
Best Supporting Actress (Kay Medford)
Best Cinematography
Best Sound
Best Song ("Funny Girl," music by Jule Styne, words by Bob Merrill)
Best Score of a Musical Picture
Best Film Editing

For the first time in the history of the Academy, there was a tie for Best Actress. Co-winner was Katharine Hepburn for *A Lion in Winter*.

2

2001: A SPACE ODYSSEY

METRO-GOLDWYN-MAYER
$25,521,917

TWO THOUSAND and one. The first year of the 21st century. The promise of things to come.

With Stanley Kubrick's masterpiece, filmmaking entered the future, literally leaping galaxies ahead from where it had been. With its sophisticated special effects, the film anticipated the age of high-tech movies such as *Star Wars, Close Encounters of the Third Kind,* and *Alien.* Like the film's black monolith, Kubrick was pointing the way.

To many, especially the younger generation, *2001* was not just a movie—it was the ultimate sensory experience. Humans were just beginning to take their first teetering steps out of cradle Earth; within a year, Neal Armstrong would leave rippled footprints on the moon. Yet here was a movie that zoomed ahead in time and said, "That's ancient history!" And if you sat in the front row of the balcony—theaters had balconies back then—and gazed across the dark void between you and the screen as the orbital space station turned in perfect rhythm to "The Blue Danube" and Pan Am's shuttle prepared to dock…wow! Your heart soared, and you were a space voyager, too.

While much of the film was left open to interpretation by audiences and critics, the movie's strong man vs. machine theme was one aspect of the storyline that was clear to nearly everyone. In the 21st century, it seems, artificial intelligence will be an everyday fact of life. The "protagonist" of *2001* (if there really is one) is the spaceship's on-board computer, HAL 9000,* whose malfunction precipitates a life-or-death struggle for the two hero-astronauts—the major *human* drama in the story.

Although science fiction aficionados eagerly embraced *2001,* mainstream audiences were confused by the story and message. What was the black monolith, anyhow? And what did the ending mean? Were there real chimp babies among the costumed actors? Did our ancestors evolve because of alien intervention, or did the aliens intervene because our ancestors were evolving? How did they shoot the Pan Am hostess walking upside down? (Answer: the same way they shot Fred Astaire's "dancing on the ceiling" scene in *Royal Wedding*—with a turning room and synchronized camera.) And just how *do* you use the zero-G toilet?

2001 was also prophetic in that it shows us to be on speaking terms with our Cold War enemies, actually cooperating with the Russians by the 21st century. Unthinkable back in 1968, but with the dismantling of the Soviet Union, the unthinkable had happened by the 1990s.

But back then, the only people who talked about peace and détente were hippies. This movie was a turn-on for them, and not just because toking up before the "Jupiter and Beyond the Infinite" sequence made it the greatest trip since Dorothy left Kansas and ended up in Oz. *2001* struck a chord in a generation with little hope for a future. It said "Hang on! Humans will survive…and evolve into Future Humans…and in *only 33 years!*"

The film's final moments were among the most controversial of all. Many likened the powerful visual image of the fetal "Star Child" approaching the ancient planet Earth to the images painted on the Sistine Chapel ceiling, in which God reaches out and gives the spark of life to Adam. Perhaps if Michelangelo had been alive in 1968, he would have used the motion picture screen as his medium. And in the tradition of Michelangelo, there is really only one word for the combined genius of Stanley Kubrick, Arthur C. Clarke, and special effects wizard Douglas Trumbull's efforts—masterpiece.

---

*"HAL," fans are delighted to point out, is a parody of "IBM," one letter of the alphabet lower for each initial.

Screenplay by Stanley Kubrick and
  Arthur C. Clarke

Produced and directed by Stanley Kubrick

CAST

Bowman . . . . .Keir Dullea
Poole . . . . .Gary Lockwood
Dr. Heywood Floyd . . . .William Sylvester
Moonwatcher . . . . . . .Dan Richter
HAL 9000 . . . . . .; . . .Douglas Rain

ACADEMY AWARD NOMINATIONS

4 nominations, 1 win*

  Best Director (Stanley Kubrick)
  Best Story and Screenplay Written
    Directly for the Screen
  Best Art Direction–Set Decoration
*Best Special Visual Effects

THE ODD COUPLE

PARAMOUNT
$20,000,000

"I've been sitting here breathing cleaning fluid and ammonia for three hours. Nature didn't intend for poker to be played like that."
—WALTER MATTHAU

BACK IN THE '50s, most of the hit movies were translated to the screen from best-selling novels; yet in the '60s, a goodly number of Broadway shows made their way up onto the screen. 1968 was a perfect example of that trend. Three out of the five top movies were plays: a musical, a comedy, and a Shakespearean tragedy. But despite the possibility of experiencing déjà vu, audiences were more than willing to go with what were already proven successes.

Neil Simon's *The Odd Couple* had been a Broadway hit for more than two years, and it was only a question of time before it became a screen hit as well. Its story line was so basic that nearly everyone in the audience could relate to it (translation: box office success). Quite simply, it's the story of two estranged husbands who are now roomies—Oscar Madison, a happy-as-a-clam slob, and Felix Ungar, your basic compulsive neatnik. Put 'em together and what have you got? In the hands of Neil Simon, nonstop laughs; for Paramount Pictures, non-stop bucks.

Walter Matthau was signed to reprise his Broadway role as the cigar-chomping sportswriter Oscar, a man so messy he should be voted "most likely to be condemned" by the Board of Health. His onstage partner had been Art Carney, but those nervous folks in Hollywood didn't think he would be a big enough draw for the screen version,* so they signed Jack Lemmon for the part of Oscar's neurotic apartment-mate. The team had appeared together in *The Fortune Cookie* (1966), and Lemmon was eager to work with his cohort again.

The movie met with audience approval as well as critical acclaim. *The Hollywood Reporter* predicted a

*Carney had the last laugh, of course, when he walked off with an Academy Award six years later in *Harry and Tonto* (1974).

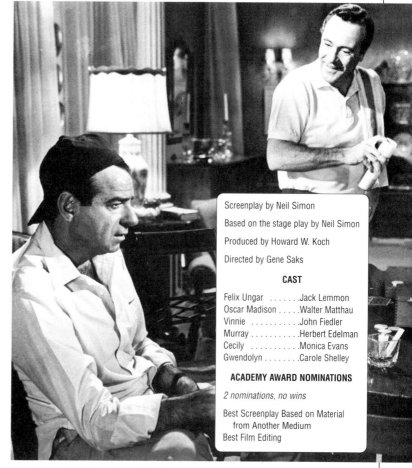

Screenplay by Neil Simon

Based on the stage play by Neil Simon

Produced by Howard W. Koch

Directed by Gene Saks

CAST

Felix Ungar . . . . . . .Jack Lemmon
Oscar Madison . . . . .Walter Matthau
Vinnie . . . . .John Fiedler
Murray . . . . .Herbert Edelman
Cecily . . . . .Monica Evans
Gwendolyn . . . . .Carole Shelley

ACADEMY AWARD NOMINATIONS

2 nominations, no wins

Best Screenplay Based on Material
from Another Medium
Best Film Editing

smash box office hit, writing: "Jack Lemmon as the Saran-wrapped, fanatical argument against toilet training turns in his best performance since 'The Apartment,' and Walter Matthau eclipses his achievement in 'The Fortune Cookie'...Paramount has a hit and laughs will ring to the sound of coin."

The formula of *The Odd Couple*—two mismatched people unwittingly paired for bad or for worse—readily lends itself to derivations. At least four TV shows owe their existence, in whole or in part, to *The Odd Couple*. Paramount launched a situation comedy based on the film, starring Tony Randall and Jack Klugman as Felix

and Oscar; the show had a successful five-year run on ABC. Later, Paramount created a series that was virtually a female *Odd Couple:* "Laverne and Shirley" was spun off the studio's hit, "Happy Days." In 1982–83 they tried it again, this time with two black men as "The New Odd Couple" — Ron Glass played Felix to Demond Wilson's Oscar. Then there's ABC's show "Perfect Strangers"—an American and his Euro-peasant cousin living in Chicago. And Neil Simon himself wrote a female version of his stage play, with Rita Moreno as *Olive Madison* and Sally Struthers as *Florence Ungar.* The combinations and possibilities are endless.

4

BULLITT
WARNER BROS
$19,000,000

"With you, living with violence is a way of life, living with violence and death." —Jacqueline Bisset to Steve McQueen

Escapism ruled at the box office, and *Bullitt* was escapism at its best. A police melodrama with Steve McQueen, an exciting, hot star (fans voted him number two in popularity for the year, right behind Barbra Streisand), this film couldn't miss. The former star of TV's "Wanted—Dead or Alive" as well as films like *The Great Escape* and *The Sand Pebbles* was back for more action as a renegade cop single-handedly taking on corruption in San Francisco. This was no martini-sipping James Bond character either—the aptly named Lieutenant Bullitt (does anyone remember his first name?*) was a down-and-dirty cop who didn't mind mussing his hair.

Yet at first McQueen was dubious about accepting the role that would become one of his most famous.

According to William F. Nolan's *McQueen*, he once said: "I'd never expected to play a cop. As a kid, running the streets, I'd been hassled a lot by the police and I'd always figured that they were on one side of the fence with me on the other. I never felt easy around cops. But here in 'Frisco,' I saw the other side of police work, and it was a real eye-opener." To prepare for the role, McQueen spent weeks driving around in a squad car with actual police detectives. "They really won my respect," the actor said.

But what this picture is best remembered for is the free-wheeling chase scene through the streets of San Francisco. It was this sequence that kept moviegoers coming back to the box office again and again. What *Ben-Hur* had done for the chariot, *Bullitt* did for the car. This roller coaster ride (some people actually got physically sick) ran a full eleven minutes with no music, just the sounds of gears grinding, wheels squealing, sirens blaring. Months had been spent in the planning, rigging the cars for the beating they would take, and the scene required weeks to stage and shoot. An accomplished driver, McQueen insisted on doing his own stunt driving.

Eight cameras were used to record the action—two mounted inside the cars. At one point, one of the cars slammed into a camera platform (similar to what happened in *Ben-Hur*) and blew it up. The footage was left in the picture. The final sequence was edited well enough to impress the Motion Picture Academy members, who nominated the film for an Oscar for Best Film Editing.

Bullitt's main adversary is played by Robert Vaughn in the first of his many "dignified heavy" roles to follow. Until now, fans knew him mostly as "Napoleon Solo," the star of "The Man From U.N.C.L.E.," one of the most popular television series of the '60s. Jacqueline Bissett had a brief but effective role as Bullitt's girlfriend in one of her first screen appearances.

Viewing the movie on your television monitor cannot possibly be as exciting as it was on the big screen. By now, we've all been subjected to car chases as almost nightly fare, so it is important to remember that this was one of the first—and is still one of the best.

---

*Bullitt's first name is Frank.

Screenplay by Alan R. Trustman and Harry Kleiner

Based on the novel *Mute Witness* by Robert L. Pike

Executive Producer: Robert E. Relyea

Produced by Philip D'Antoni

Directed by Peter Yates

CAST

Bullitt	Steve McQueen
Chalmers	Robert Vaughn
Cathy	Jacqueline Bisset
Delgetti	Don Gordon
Weissberg	Robert Duvall

ACADEMY AWARD NOMINATIONS

*2 nominations, 1 win**

Best Sound
*Best Film Editing

ROMEO AND JULIET

PARAMOUNT
$17,473,000

THE STORY of the two star-crossed lovers of Verona is supposedly based on an actual historical occurrence in 1303; the account was first published by Bandello in 1554, translated into French in 1559, and eventually arrived in England in 1562. William Shakespeare's play of *Romeo and Juliet* was first performed in 1597 by the Globe Theatre Company, with the part of Juliet played by a boy, as was the custom, since it was considered inappropriate for women to appear on the stage.

This first of Shakespeare's great tragedies has been filmed 32 times, mostly in silent or ballet renditions. Among the most famous screen versions were a 1935 MGM film starring Norma Shearer and Leslie Howard, directed by George Cukor, and a J. Arthur Rank production from England, with Laurence Harvey and Susan Shentall. And don't forget Robert Wise's production of *West Side Story* (see page 00).

But there were variations that made Franco Zeffirelli's version unique, and subsequently drew audiences to see this highly acclaimed film. For one thing, the casting was historically accurate—both stars were the proper age. Director Zeffirelli is reported to have first offered the role of Romeo to

Screenplay by Franco Brusati and
  Masolino D'Amico

Based on the play by William Shakespeare

Produced by Anthony Havelock-Allan

Directed by Franco Zeffirelli

CAST

Romeo	Leonard Whiting
Juliet	Olivia Hussey
Friar Laurence	Milo O'Shea
Tybalt	Michael York
Mercutio	John McEnery

ACADEMY AWARD NOMINATIONS

4 nominations, 2 wins*

Best Picture
Best Director (Franco Zeffirelli)
*Best Cinematography
*Best Costume Design

Beatle Paul McCartney, who refused because he was afraid of acting in a classic for what would have been his first screen role. The part eventually went to Leonard Whiting, an unknown 17-year-old English teenager without much acting experience. An even younger teen won the role of Juliet— 15-year-old ingenue Olivia Hussey, who went on to become a film and TV star, appearing in such movies as *Death on the Nile* (1978) and a remake of *The Cat and the Canary* (1978). She continued to be active in film and TV in the '90s. Ironically, most people recall her name while forgetting that of Leonard Whiting. He appeared in one other major film, *Royal Hunt of the Sun* (1969), but the much-predicted major acting career failed to materialize.

One of the reasons for the movie's box office success was that it was the right film for the time. Here was a story about young people who bucked the system, idealists who stood up to the Establishment in the era of "turn on, tune in, drop out." It was a time of hippies and flower children, and Romeo and Juliet were their 16th-century equivalents. *Hair* was letting it all hang out on Broadway, and an unoffensive nude scene for the two lovers was almost obligatory. However, so

tastefully done was this scene that most parents weren't offended; even those in charge of bestowing the all-important letter rating gave *Romeo and Juliet* a PG (parental guidance). Exhibitors sighed their relief as most parents happily guided their youngsters straight to the box office.

Purists were disappointed, however, since Zeffirelli took a lot of liberties with the Bard's words; Shakespeare was substantially edited as scenes got shifted around and speeches were given to different characters. But the director must be credited for the outstanding production values he insisted upon for this film. Authentic Italian locations were used; costumes were made from only the finest French velvets and brocades; dialogue coaches, fencing, riding, and dancing lessons were the order of the day for the cast; and cameramen rode horseback to get important handheld shots.

Special mention must also be made of the music by Nino Rota. His soundtrack album was number four for the year, and so impressed Henry Mancini that he did his own arrangement of the theme. Mancini's instrumental recording on RCA of "The Love Theme from Romeo and Juliet" was number one for the week of June 28, 1969.

BUTCH CASSIDY AND THE SUNDANCE KID

20TH CENTURY-FOX
$45,953,000

"The Hole in the Wall Gang led by Butch Cassidy and the Sundance Kid are all dead now. But once they ruled the World! Most of what follows is true."
—OPENING CARD

WITH WARNER BROS.' *Bonnie and Clyde* serving as a successful blueprint, Fox produced its biggest blockbuster since *The Sound of Music*. Based on historical fact, *Butch Cassidy and the Sundance Kid* is a tragicomedy—we laugh ourselves silly right up until the end, when they're sprayed with bullets. But unlike *Bonnie and Clyde,* the final death scene is (mercifully) not revealed to us, since the camera freezes frame and our heroes never die before our eyes.

Fifty years before director George Roy Hill (*Hawaii*) brought us this movie, Harry Longabaugh, a.k.a. The Sundance Kid, teamed up with Robert Leroy Parker, a.k.a. Butch Cassidy, and enjoyed a spree of train holdups and bank robberies. As in the movie, the pair, along with former schoolteacher Etta Place, fled to South America with Pinkerton detectives giving chase. But contrary to the film's ending, there is evidence to support the fact that Sundance may have escaped, returned to the United States, and led the remainder of his life under an assumed identity.

This story fascinated writer William Goldman, who spent more than six years researching Butch's and Sundance's exploits, discovering along the way that they weren't your typical outlaws who shot first, took the money, and ran. His findings showed that they didn't like to shoot or otherwise harm people they were holding up, making the duo likely candidates for a motion picture. Richard Zanuck (son of Darryl F.) at 20th Century-Fox agreed, and paid Goldman a record $400,000 for his script.

Casting for the right twosome proved a chore. Goldman envisioned Paul Newman as Sundance and Jack Lemmon playing Butch. Zanuck disagreed, believing Steve McQueen

would make a better Butch. But Newman and McQueen had an ongoing billing feud dating back to the '50s with *Somebody Up There Likes Me,* and when Newman demanded top billing, McQueen refused to sign on. Enter Robert Redford, whose career was barely getting underway. His fortuitous teaming with Newman provided the chemical magic that moviemakers dream about—heaven couldn't have provided a better match. (They would be re-teamed four years later in *The Sting,* for Universal.)

Goldman kept his script light, and audiences just adored two handsome actors who played so well off each other. One of the most remembered scenes has the two cornered by the law with nowhere to go, except to the river hundreds of feet below:

> BUTCH
> I'll jump first.
>
> SUNDANCE
> No.
>
> BUTCH
> Then you jump first.
>
> SUNDANCE
> No, I said.
>
> BUTCH
> What's the matter with you?
>
> SUNDANCE
> I can't swim!
>
> BUTCH (laughing)
> Why, you're crazy! The fall will probably kill you!

And then, in this most famous bit, the two gather their courage, and with a whoop, leap to the waters below. Even if Butch and Sundance thought they were done for, the audience knew they'd get out of this cliffhanger—there were still several more reels to go.

Another delightful number is the bicycle-riding sequence with Butch and Etta Place (Katharine Ross). Two-wheel bikes were just making their appearance at that time, and there is historical evidence to support the possibility that Butch learned to ride one. In this scene, Newman aptly did his

own stunts, like riding on his stomach, and standing with one foot on the seat and one in the air. Burt Bacharach's accompanying tune, "Raindrops Keep Fallin' on My Head," couldn't have suited the number better. Sung by B. J. Thomas, the song climbed to the top of the charts and remained at number one for four weeks in January, 1970. It produced gold for composers Bacharach and Hal David in the form of an Oscar, as well as a Best Score Oscar.

In 1979, director Richard Lester did a prequel, *Butch and Sundance—The Early Days,* starring Tom Berenger and William Katt. This movie about how Butch and Sundance met and teamed up had mild success, but came nowhere near topping the original *Butch Cassidy and the Sundance Kid,* one of the highest-earning Westerns of all time.

Screenplay by William Goldman

Executive Producer: Paul Monash

Produced by John Foreman

Directed by George Roy Hill

CAST

Butch Cassidy	Paul Newman
The Sundance Kid	Robert Redford
Etta Place	Katharine Ross
Percy Garris	Strother Martin
Bike Salesman	Henry Jones

ACADEMY AWARD NOMINATIONS

7 nominations, 4 wins*

Best Picture
Best Director (George Roy Hill)
*Best Story and Screenplay Based on Material Not Previously Published or Produced (William Goldman)
*Best Cinematography
Best Sound
*Best Song ("Raindrops Keep Fallin' on My Head," music by Burt Bacharach, words by Hal David)
*Best Original Score—Non-Musical (Burt Bacharach)

2

THE LOVE BUG

WALT DISNEY PRODUCTIONS
$23,150,000

WALT WAS GONE, but many of those who were part of his studio roster were determined to carry on the tradition of family entertainment. The first true success to proudly bear the Disney name was a delightful fantasy that would have made the Old Man proud.

The title had a double entendre (a nonsexual one; this is Disney we're talking about). One reference is to the commonly used expression "bitten by the love bug." But the title also describes the film's star car—a Volkswagen Beetle, i.e., "bug." What is really strange, however, is that at no time in the movie (or in any of the Disney press material, for that matter) does anyone ever refer to Herbie as "a Volkswagen" or "a VW." He is *always* "the Little Car." The reasoning behind this is simple: if you're going to personify an automobile, don't call it by a commonplace designation. People should think "little car," not "hunk of metal from Germany."

Bill Walsh was the producer filling Walt's shoes, and he also handled the writing chores on *Love Bug*. Walsh had certainly paid his dues at the Disney factory, having worked there for 22 years on such Disney classics as *The Shaggy Dog, The Absent-Minded Professor, Son of Flubber, Mary Poppins,* and *That Darn Cat*. And Robert Stevenson was back in the director's chair after a successful track record that included such Disney winners as *Mary Poppins, That Darn Cat, The Absent-Minded Professor, In Search of the Castaways,* and many others.

Also returning to the Disney fold

was Dean Jones, appearing as the lead in his sixth film for the studio (other films included *That Darn Cat, Blackbeard's Ghost,* and *The Horse in the Gray Flannel Suit*). His love interest was played by Michele Lee, whose career was just beginning to blossom then. But if there is a scene-stealer (aside from the cutesy car) in the picture, comedian Buddy Hackett fits the bill. Most noted for his appearances on the nightclub circuit, Hackett had also made some top box office hits, including *The Music Man* and *It's a Mad Mad Mad Mad World*. His teaming with Herbie was a bit of inspired casting—there's real chemistry here.

Shot on location in the Bay Area, the film is full of wild street chases through San Francisco—a sort of "Disney Does *Bullitt*," right down to the obligatory run down twisty Lombard Street (also in *Bullitt*). Fisherman's Wharf, Chinatown, the Golden Gate Bridge, the Monterey Peninsula, and even Virginia City, Nevada, all figured prominently in the location shooting. Most of the location work was done by a second unit, with the cast doing the majority of their scenes on a Disney soundstage or at the nearby Paramount Ranch.

Racing sequences dominate a good deal of *The Love Bug,* with over 40 stunt drivers credited. These scenes were filmed at Willow Springs and Riverside Raceway.

Much of the stuntwork involved "Herbie," who had to appear to be doing the driving himself. (It's hard not to think of the car as a "he.") To accomplish this, an assemblage of specially rigged identical VWs were provided by effects expert Eustace Lycett. One was fitted with a Porsche engine for high-speed scenes; another was rigged for blind driving (as in *The Shaggy Dog*); yet another ran on three wheels; one ran on only two; one was cut in half with front and rear sections running on their own; one shook and trembled with fear; and one acted drunk. A number were created for the purpose of totaling them in crash/stunt situations.

Herbie has proved himself a perennial Disney star, and to date, three sequels have been made: *Herbie Rides Again* (1974), *Herbie Goes to Monte Carlo* (1977), and *Herbie Goes Bananas* (1980). In addition, there was a short-run television series on the Disney Channel based on the further adventures of the Little Car.

Screenplay by Bill Walsh and Don DaGradi

Based on a story by Gordon Buford

Produced by Bill Walsh

Directed by Robert Stevenson

CAST

Jim	Dean Jones
Carole	Michele Lee
Thorndyke	David Tomlinson
Tennessee	Buddy Hackett
Haveshaw	Joe Flynn

MIDNIGHT COWBOY

UNITED ARTISTS
$20,499,282

T HE SORDID, depressing tale of a male hustler himself being hustled in New York City and his buddy and part-time pimp "Ratso" Rizzo, *Midnight Cowboy* had the dubious honor of being awarded a Motion Picture Association of America rating of "X." While today's audiences have come to think of the "X" designation mainly in connection with pornography, back in the '60s this film, which contained an explicit (albeit very brief) sex act plus a lot of blue language, could receive nothing less than a scarlet-letter "X." What's more, members of the prestigious Academy of Motion Picture Arts and Sciences—those folks who brought you the Oscar—shocked the world by voting *Midnight Cowboy* the Best Picture of 1969 (as well awarding the film Oscars for Best Director and Best Screenplay), thereby legitimizing the film. A few years later, the MPAA reconsidered (after a few nips and tucks with an editor's scissors) and changed the rating to an "R," thereby increasing the number of potential ticket buyers.

Dustin Hoffman, the naive *Graduate* we had all found so sweet and innocent only two years before, was superb in the about-face role of the gimpy, begrimed Ratso. Hoffman told *The New York Times* in a 1982 interview that early rejections in his acting

---

Screenplay by Waldo Salt

Based on the novel by James Leo Herlihy

Produced by Jerome Hellman

Directed by John Schlesinger

CAST

Ratso Rizzo . . . . .Dustin Hoffman
Joe Buck . . . . .Jon Voight
Cass . . . . .Sylvia Miles
Mr. O'Daniel . . . . .John McGiver
Shirley . . . . .Brenda Vaccaro

ACADEMY AWARD NOMINATIONS

7 nominations, 3 wins*

*Best Picture
 Best Actor (Dustin Hoffman)
 Best Actor (Jon Voight)
 Best Supporting Actress (Sylvia Miles)
*Best Director (John Schlesinger)
*Best Screenplay Based on Material from
   Another Medium
 Best Film Editing

---

career provided him with a powerful resource for acting roles such as this. "Ratso Rizzo was not character acting," said Hoffman. "That was just an autobiography of subjective feelings about oneself." Hoffman's salad days as an actor were over, however; he could say goodbye to the unemployment line

that he'd been on since *The Graduate* (which left him with little cash), since he was paid a cool $250,000 for his work in *Midnight Cowboy.*

Critics applauded his acting abilities but reserved most of the praise for newcomer Jon Voight. A month after the film opened, *Newsweek* wrote: "It was Jon Voight, a sparkling-blue-eyed and moon-faced amalgam of Tab Hunter and early Brandon de Wilde, who captured the imagination of moviegoers. On the strength of his Candide-like portrayal of Midnight Cowboy Joe Buck, the Texas stud turned Times Square hustler, Voight has emerged as one of the industry's new breed of 'instant successes.' "

The Academy agreed, and bestowed an Oscar nomination on the promising actor. Like Dustin Hoffman, Voight had paid his dramatic dues. When he was quite young, he spent six months on Broadway singing "Sixteen Going on Seventeen" in *The Sound of Music,* worked in a few off-Broadway plays, and had one minor movie role before landing *Midnight Cowboy.* Voight then went on to a prosperous career, starring in such films as *Deliverance* (1972), *Runaway Train* (1985), *Chernobyl: The Final Warning* (TV movie, 1991), and *Rainbow Warrior* (1994).

4

EASY RIDER

COLUMBIA
$19,100,000

*"A man went looking for America.
And couldn't find it anywhere."*
—ADVERTISING COPY
FOR *EASY RIDER*

O N THE SURFACE, *Easy Rider* appears to be about two drug dealers who chuck it all and become two for the road. Looking for America? Go East, young men—on Harleys, not horses. Terms like "counterculture" are frequently used when describing the film that was more a statement than a movie.

This labor of love was mounted by Dennis Hopper, who co-wrote, directed, and starred in the picture. He was partnered with another young rebel, Peter Fonda, son of Henry and an actor in his own right. The triumvirate was completed by Jack Nicholson as the Texas lawyer who joins up with the bikers along the way and learns a thing or two about the real world, like how to smoke dope, but more importantly, how to feel really free. While his character is in the film for only a short time, Jack Nicholson created a sensation in the role and garnered an Oscar nomination. He almost didn't get the part; Hopper had signed Rip Torn, but the deal fell through and Nicholson signed on. It proved to be the turning point in a career that still finds him at the top of the box office today.

One other performance is worth mentioning here. Look for Robert

Walker, Jr., as Jack, the Hippie commune leader. He is the spitting image of his father (his mother was Jennifer Jones). Adding to the confusion, he billed himself without the "Jr." designation. ("Star Trek"-kers will remember his performance in an early episode, "Charlie X.")

This Cinderella film was made on the unbelievable budget of $555,000 and grossed over $60,000,000 worldwide, earning more than all of Henry Fonda's films combined (pre–*On Golden Pond*). Shot in only seven weeks, the picture had a limited script, with many of the scenes being enacted by locals who ad-libbed according to Hopper's brief directions. The 127,000 feet of film took Hopper a full year to edit into a completed picture. He premiered it at the Cannes Film Festival in May, 1969, and went on to take the honors as "Best Film by a New Director."

A contemporary rock soundtrack made use of songs by current rock artists and rose to the top of the charts. The best-selling soundtrack album of 1969 featured "Born to Be Wild," the film's theme, recorded by

Steppenwolf, plus songs by The Byrds, The Band, and Jimi Hendrix.

Today *Easy Rider* is sometimes regarded as a cult film, marking the death of the decade of the '60s and the end of an era. Expressions like "groovy," "I'm getting my thing together," and "you do your own thing in your own time" have taken their place as part of our cultural history—a new generation with its own slang expressions has grown up since the premiere of this picture. But there are still some things to be learned from viewing the film, and it's certainly worthwhile watching when it appears on TV, hopefully in an uncut version.

Peter Fonda has continued to act (although not as prolifically as his sister, Jane), and Dennis Hopper has continued to act and direct. But Hopper's dream is to do a sequel to *Easy Rider.* In 1983, he agreed to co-star in a Fonda-produced sequel called *Biker Heaven,* but it failed to materialize. Drug-free and hard at work, he hoped to shoot an *Easy Rider* for the '90s. Meanwhile, his first one has earned the right to be termed "classic."

Screenplay by Peter Fonda, Dennis Hopper, and Terry Southern

Produced by Peter Fonda

Directed by Dennis Hopper

CAST

Wyatt/Capt. America	.Peter Fonda
Billy	.Dennis Hopper
George Hanson	.Jack Nicholson
Rancher	.Warren Finnerty
Karen	.Karen Black

ACADEMY AWARD NOMINATIONS

2 nominations, no wins

Best Supporting Actor (Jack Nicholson)
Best Original Story and Screenplay

HELLO, DOLLY!
20TH CENTURY-FOX
$15,200,000

"**E**XPENSIVE" IS THE best word to describe Fox's lavish production of the Broadway musical success *Hello, Dolly!* Despite the early returns from *Butch Cassidy and the Sundance Kid,* Fox was having a terrible year, and was verging on bankruptcy. The first three quarters of 1969 saw the studio posting a net loss of $21,978,000, yet they continued to pour money into a last-ditch effort at pumping new life into the Big Screen Musical genre. *Hello, Dolly!* cost Fox $26,400,000 and lost them nearly as much. For Fox (and virtually every other studio), Big Screen Musicals were dead, and it would be several years before the studio would be out of the red.

The Broadway version of *Hello, Dolly!* starred Carol Channing as the exuberant matchmaker Dolly Levi, and was an instant hit. (Originally, the producers had wanted Ethel Merman in the part, but she turned it down.*) The title song was a hit as well, landing at the top of the charts in May,

1964, with 63-year-old Louis Armstrong becoming the oldest artist ever to have a number-one song. Five years later, a special role was created for him in the film, and he sang a duet with the film's star, Barbra Streisand.

After viewing *Thoroughly Modern Millie,* producer Ernest Lehman decided he didn't want Carol Charming for the screen version, finding her personality too dominating. He considered Lucille Ball and Elizabeth Taylor, but settled on Streisand, whose *Funny Girl* hadn't yet been released but was certain to be a hit. Walter Matthau was set to co-star, and Gene Kelly, star of many a musical himself, was signed to direct.

All the ingredients were in place—the lavish costumes, fantastic sets (the reconstruction of New York's Fifth Avenue in the 1890s cost $2,000,000 alone), huge cast, great musical numbers, and the memorable title song. So what caused this to be the most lavish flop in musical history?

In conducting the post mortem, it is easy to point to this or that element, but it was a combination of many ele-

ments that rang the death knell for this film as well as the genre. As had been discovered with pictures like *The Graduate* and *Easy Rider,* the moviegoing audience was comprised of mostly under-30s, and young people just weren't impressed with lavish musicals. Also, many felt that Barbra Streisand, at age 27, was miscast as the matronly Dolly. Costs seemed to escalate out of control. Fox took a gamble, and lost.

Watch closely the young man playing Cornelius Hackl. British actor Michael Crawford, seen here in a rare appearance in American films, went on to star in one of the biggest hit musicals of all time, Andrew Lloyd Webber's *The Phantom of the Opera.* The play opened in London in 1986, and Crawford continued playing to SRO crowds with the American touring company through 1991.

---

*In 1970, Ethel Merman finally assumed the role that had been created for her, and several songs that had been dropped for the Channing version were reinstated. Additionally, there had been an all-black cast version (1967) starring Pearl Bailey.

Screenplay by Ernest Lehman

Based on the stage play by Michael Stewart

Adapted from the play *The Matchmaker* by Thorton Wilder

Music & lyrics by Jerry Herman

Produced by Ernest Lehman

Directed by Gene Kelly

CAST

Dolly Levi . . . . .Barbra Streisand
Horace Vandergelder . .Walter Matthau
Cornelius Hackl . . . . . .Michael Crawford
Orchestra Leader . . . . .Louis Armstrong
Irene Molloy . . . . . . .Marianne
                    McAndrew

ACADEMY AWARD NOMINATIONS

7 nominations, 3 wins

Best Picture
Best Cinematography
*Best Art Direction–Set Decoration
*Best Sound
*Best Score of a Musical Picture
Best Film Editing
Best Costume Design

THE SEVENTIES were a mixed movie bag. Gone were most of the extravaganzas, the musicals, and the religious epics. Replacing them was a brand-new genre—the disaster film. People now went to the movies to live out their worst fears—burning to death in a high-rise, drowning in tragic sea disasters, falling from the sky and crashing to earth in airplanes. Even the earth under our feet was suspect and might at any moment open up and swallow us. And if these disasters didn't get us, there was always the Mafia, or giant apes, giant sharks, out-of-control trains, and that old '50s standby, invaders from space.

If our national anxiety was reflected in the types of films we craved, there were also moments of reprieve from all the terror. Comic relief came in the form of pictures like *M*A*S*H, What's Up Doc?* and *Blazing Saddles.*

Perhaps the greatest inspiration for films of the Seventies came from outer space. Toward the end of the decade, the

1970

promises made by the film technology of *2001: A Space Odyssey* were fulfilled with the arrival of *Star Wars* and other features involving special effects. These movies heralded a new age of film, and audiences were the lucky beneficiaries.

The movie ratings system was overhauled in this decade, in keeping with the rapidly growing population of under-30 moviegoers. "G," "M," "R," and "X" were replaced by "G" (all ages admitted), "GP" (general patronage), "R" (now allowing under-17-year-olds to be admitted if accompanied by adults), and "X" (no one under 17 admitted). In 1975, "GP" was changed to "PG" (parental guidance suggested). By the 1990s, "X" was pretty much limited to pornographic movies (usually indicated by "XXX" for clarification as well as hype). In 1990, the MPAA replaced it with "NC-17" (no children under 17) as a new adults-only designation of ratings for mainstream films.

1979

LOVE STORY

PARAMOUNT
$48,700,000

"What can you say about a 25-year-old girl who died? That she was beautiful and brilliant. That she loved Mozart and Bach. And the Beatles. And me."
—OPENING NARRATION

WHAT CAN YOU SAY about a movie that made $48,000,000? That it was the biggest hit Paramount had ever had. That it made stars of its leading players. That it caused whole forests to be felled so tons of Kleenex could be produced.

The novelization alone could have done that. Even as this movie about two lovers from opposite sides of the tracks was being filmed, screenwriter Erich Segal was at work cranking out a novel with virtually the same dialogue, adding a few "he saids" and "she saids," priming the public for the upcoming tearjerker of all time. Until now, movies were made from books that were already on the best-seller list. Beginning with *Love Story,* a whole new genre of fiction was created—the motion picture novelization. Nearly 418,000 hardcover editions and 4,350,000 paperback copies were printed for the first edition—the largest in history. Millions more were sold in later editions. Everyone, it seemed, loved *Love Story.*

Robert Evans loved the script when Segal's agent, William Morris, first showed it to him. Although the project had been turned down by six other studios, Paramount's production chief thought that *Love Story* would be the perfect vehicle for his own romantic interest, Ali MacGraw.

Ali (née Alice) MacGraw was born on April Fool's Day in 1938 in Pound Ridge, New York. The daughter of artists, she graduated from Wellesley College, where she studied art history. Before entering films, she was an editorial assistant on *Harper's Bazaar,* an assistant to a fashion photographer, and a model whose wholesome looks kept her in frequent demand as a cover girl on women's magazines. Ali was catapulted to stardom in her second movie role as an 18-year-old Jewish princess/college girl (she was 30 at the time) in *Goodbye, Columbus* (1968). At the time of *Love Story,* she

was married to Paramount studio boss Robert Evans; they were later divorced, and she subsequently married the late actor Steve McQueen. Since *Love Story,* her film appearances have been sporadic, among them *The Getaway* (1972), and *Just Tell Me What You Want* (1980). During the '80s, MacGraw found new life in television, appearing as a regular on "Dynasty."

Segal's script was loosely based on fact. The associate professor of classics at Yale combined the story of an old girlfriend with a story he had been told by one of his graduate students. Evans had the script rewritten (thirty times), and along the way Jenny was changed from a Brooklyn Jewish girl to an Italian Roman Catholic from Rhode Island.

Several different actors were considered as potential Oliver Barretts. The role of the perennial preppy was turned down by Jon Voight, Michael Sarrazin, Michael York, Beau Bridges, and Michael Douglas. But Ryan O'Neal had just finished a long stint as Rodney Harrington on TV's "Peyton Place" and was anxious to begin a big-screen career. O'Neal, twice married at the

time, with three children (and a prison record), seemed an unlikely candidate for the role of the Ivy Leaguer. But with his looks, charm, and 519 episodes of "Peyton Place" under his belt, Paramount decided to take a chance.

Critics delighted in alternately exalting and slashing this movie soap opera. Wrote *Time:* "Ali MacGraw promises to become the closest thing to a movie star of the '40s…When a Radcliffe girl chooses to die on-screen, the Academy Awards can be heard softly rustling like Kleenexes in the background…Ryan O'Neal gives the character of the neon scion a warmth and vulnerability."

Most people agreed, and lines snaked around the block wherever it played. Soon everyone was quoting the movie's famous slogan, "Love means never having to say you're sorry." For Paramount Pictures, *Love Story* meant never having to say you're sorry, regardless of what the critics might have to say. The studio couldn't have cared less about *Newsweek's* comments: "The ersatz score put together by Francis Lai is so perfectly schmaltzy that one suspects the film was set to music first and then written…'Love Story' is very much [an] exploitation movie, cashing in on crying the way other movies cash in on sex." Critic Roger Ebert, in his *Movie Home Companion's* "Glossary of Movie Terms," defined "Ali MacGraw's Disease" as a "movie illness in which [the] only symptom is that the sufferer grows more beautiful as death approaches." *Variety,* on the other hand, found the film "outstanding," and praised it as "another rare breath of fresh air in the smog of contemporary cinema psychoneurosis."

The huge success of *Love Story* prompted Erich Segal to devise a sequel (how could he resist?), and in 1977 he published *Oliver's Story,* in which the widower discovers that there *is* life after Jenny. In the 1978 film version, Ryan O'Neal reprised his role, with Candice Bergen as his new love interest. But audiences thought him a two-timer, wanting him to mourn his true love the rest of his life. Pass the Kleenex.

Screenplay by Erich Segal

Based on the novel by Erich Segal

Executive Producer: David Golden

Produced by Howard G. Minsky

Directed by Arthur Hiller

CAST

Jenny . . . . .Ali MacGraw
Oliver Barrett IV . . . . .Ryan O'Neal
Phil . . . . .John Marley
Oliver Barrett III . . . . . .Ray Milland
Dean . . . . .Russell Nype

ACADEMY AWARD NOMINATIONS

7 nominations, 1 win*

Best Picture
Best Actor (Ryan O'Neal)
Best Actress (Ali MacGraw)
Best Supporting Actor (John Marley)
Best Director (Arthur Hiller)
Best Original Story and Screenplay
*Best Original Score

2

AIRPORT
UNIVERSAL
$45,220,118

THE "SPECTACULAR" was dead; long live the disaster film. In making Ross Hunter's *Airport,* Universal combined the best of the epic spectaculars from the '50s with this new genre by leaving in the traditional all-star cast, adding the "We're all going to die!" element of terror plus '70s state-of-the-art special effects. The disaster film was based on a formula that guaranteed success throughout the decade.

The basic premise of *Airport* was simple, which is why it was so easily imitated. Create your own scenario: A (plane/building/shark/ship/giant ape) is about to (crash/burn/eat the humans /sink) and everyone will die unless (George Kennedy/Paul Newman/ Steve McQueen/Roy Scheider/Gene Hackman/Jeff Bridges) can figure out a way to save them. See? You, too, can be a movie producer.

Airport, the original disaster movie, had many things going for it, such as a huge cast of really good actors. Among those featured were such names as Burt Lancaster (the airport manager), Dean Martin (the pilot assigned to this unlucky flight), Jacqueline Bisset (a stewardess), Helen Hayes (a shifty old stowaway), and George Kennedy (he

Screenplay by George Seaton

Based on the novel by Arthur Hailey

Produced by Ross Hunter

Directed by George Seaton

CAST

Mel Bakersfeld . . . . . . .Burt Lancaster
Vernon Demerest . . . . .Dean Martin
Tanya Livingston . . . .Jean Seberg
Gwen Meighen . . . . . .Jacqueline Bisset
Patroni . . . . .George Kennedy
Ada Quonsett . . . . . . .Helen Hayes

ACADEMY AWARD NOMINATIONS

10 nominations, 1 win*

Best Picture
*Best Supporting Actress (Helen Hayes)
Best Supporting Actress (Maureen Stapleton)
Best Screenplay Based on Material from Another Medium
Best Cinematography
Best Art Direction–Set Decoration
Best Sound
Best Original Score
Best Film Editing
Best Costume Design

saves the day). Also rounded up for this *Grand Hotel*-ish roll call were Van Heflin, Maureen Stapleton, Barry Nelson, Dana Wynter, Lloyd Nolan, and Barbara Hale.

Critics were cautious in their assessment. *The Hollywood Reporter* wrote: "'Airport' with its superb line-up of talent and already known title should give Universal one of its more popular films of the year…The one place it may find limited appeal will be on transoceanic flights." *Variety* was not quite as optimistic about the film's moneymaking prospects, noting: "This jet age 'Grand Hotel' might do good business for exhibitors, but it's doubtful there will be the kind of stampede necessary to bail out Universal's investment of around $10,000,000."

Wrong. Universal was bailed out many times over by this most successful film they had done to date. Sequelmania also swept the studio, and there were three more *Airport* films, all with the same basic formula: *Airport 1975, Airport '77,* and *Airport '79—The Concorde.* None of these did as well as the original nor, for that matter, as well as the Paramount spoofs *Airplane!* (1980) and *Airplane II: The Sequel* (1982).

M*A*S*H

20TH CENTURY-FOX
$36,720,000

"I now close my military career and just fade away, an old soldier who tried to do his duty as God gave him the light to see that duty."
—GEN. DOUGLAS MACARTHUR,
QUOTED IN OPENING CARD

IT WAS OFFICIALLY called the Korean "Police Action." The State Department never admitted we were in a war, since Congress had never declared war. Yet every day, hundreds of young men gave their blood and their lives in this civil conflict, many of them not even out of their teens yet. It was a nasty little war that propelled World War II hero General Dwight Eisenhower into the presidency in 1952, when he promised to bring an end to it.

The unsung heroes of this, as in any battle, were the doctors and nurses who patched the soldiers together so they could live to fight another day. Ernest Hemingway had written of gruesome front lines and ambulance drivers of World War I with deadly seriousness. Who could ever imagine finding *humor* in such circumstances?

One doctor could, and did. His name was Richard Hooker, and his first-hand experience became the basis

---

Screenplay by Ring Lardner, Jr.

From the novel by Richard Hooker

Produced by Ingo Preminger

Directed by Robert Altman

CAST

Trapper John . . . . .Elliott Gould
Hawkeye . . . . .Donald Sutherland
Duke . . . . .Tom Skerritt
Major Hot Lips . . . . . . .Sally Kellerman
Lt. Dish . . . . .Jo Ann Pflug
Radar O'Reilly . . . . . . .Gary Burghoff

ACADEMY AWARD NOMINATIONS

5 nominations, 1 win*

Best Picture
Best Supporting Actress (Sally Kellerman)
Best Director (Robert Altman)
*Best Screenplay Based on Material from Another Medium (Ring Lardner, Jr.)
Best Film Editing

---

of a novel that had the honor of being rejected by no less than 17 publishers before it became a modest seller. There had never been a blockbuster film about the Korean War, yet Fox saw possibilities in making a film of the *M*A*S*H* novel. With growing unrest and dissatisfaction with the Vietnam "Police Action," this was the right film for the time, and it became a huge success.

The doctors are about as irreverent as they could be without being court-martialed. We never see actual combat, as the doctors in a Mobile Army Surgical Hospital wage their battles with the U.S. military. The film is episodic in style; there are many memorable moments, such as the scene with "Hot Lips" and the hidden mike, the re-enactment of the Last Supper, the Hot-Lips-in-the-shower scene, the trip to Tokyo, and the no-holds-barred football game. Elliot Gould (former husband of Barbra Streisand) co-starred with Canadian actor Donald Sutherland, who rocketed to stardom following this picture. The film also served to introduce John Schuck and Gary Burghoff.*

For Ring Lardner, Jr., it was the high point in what had been a career marked by tragedy. In 1947, he had been subpoenaed by the House Committee on Un-American Activities and convicted of contempt of Congress as one of the "Hollywood Ten." He served 10 months of a one-year sentence in Federal prison and

was blacklisted in the entertainment industry for 15 years. *M*A*S*H* brought him the second of two Academy Awards the gifted writer earned (the other was for *Woman of the Year* in 1942).

The movie itself was a milestone picture, premiering at the Cannes Film Festival and winning the coveted "Palme d'Or" for Best Film of 1970. Most critics agreed with the public that it was unique, so it was bewildering when Fox announced that *M*A*S*H* would become a *television* show for the 1972 fall season. At first, the series seemed like a true flop, as had been so many other attempts at translating hit movies to TV. But the studio and network stuck with it, and gradually the ratings began to climb. Eventually "M*A*S*H" (starring Alan Alda as "Hawkeye," the role Donald Sutherland had created) became number one in TV ratings. And a rare phenomenon occurred: the series actually *surpassed* the movie in popularity. Its longevity was due for the most part to the creative genius of Alda, who later wrote and directed several episodes. After nine years, the program was still on top when Alda convinced Fox to end the show. But high ratings in syndication continue to this day, making "M*A*S*H" one of the truly great properties of all time.

---

*When *M*A*S*H* was translated to TV, Burghoff was the only member of the original cast to make the transition.

4

PATTON

20TH CENTURY-FOX
$28,100,000

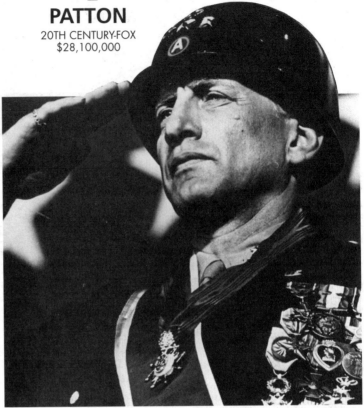

"Compared to war, all other forms of human endeavor shrink to insignificance." —GEORGE S. PATTON, QUOTED IN *PATTON*

BEFORE 20th Century-Fox released *M*A*S*H,* the studio had produced a true war film in the tradition of *The Longest Day.* Desperately in need of a hit after gigantic losses in 1969 with the failure of *Hello, Dolly!,* Fox was not disappointed. While *M*A*S*H* proclaimed war was hell, *Patton*'s title general vowed otherwise.

"Old Blood and Guts," as he became known, was a firm believer in reincarnation; he had distinct feelings of déjà vu on the battlefields of Europe, and used ancient strategies to his advantage. Born into a military family,

Screenplay by Francis Ford Coppola and Edmund H. North

Based on factual material from *Patton: Ordeal and Triumph* by Ladislas Farago and *A Soldier's Story* by Omar N. Bradley

Produced by Frank McCarthy

Directed by Franklin J. Schaffner

CAST

Gen. George
    S. Patton, Jr. . . . . . .George C. Scott
Gen. Omar N. Bradley . .Karl Malden
Field Marshal
    Montgomery . . . . . .Michael Bates
Field Marshal
    Rommel . . . . .Karl Michael Vogler
Gen. Bedell Smith . . . .Edward Binns

ACADEMY AWARD NOMINATIONS

10 nominations, 7 wins*

*Best Picture
*Best Actor (George C. Scott)
*Best Director (Franklin J. Schaffner)
*Best Original Story and Screenplay
    (Francis Ford Coppola and Edmund H.
    North)
Best Cinematography
*Best Art Direction–Set Decoration
*Best Sound
Best Original Score
*Best Film Editing
Best Special Visual Effects

Patton attended West Point and was one of the first American tank commanders in World War I. By the Second World War, he was in charge of the Third Army. He loved war more than life itself, as these words from the film prove: "There's only one proper way for a professional soldier to die. That's from the last bullet of the last battle of the last war."

Patton is portrayed in this movie as a megalomaniac, a human war machine who could be a merciless sadist one minute, a gentle poet the next. He appears as an inadvertent screw-up who makes us believe we won the war in spite of him. When the war ends, a German remarks, "He's an anachronism, a pure warrior. Lack of war will kill him." General Patton never had a chance to find out: he was killed in an auto accident in Germany in 1945.

George C. Scott's portrayal of George S. Patton has become legendary since this film's release. The six-minute-long opening, as he stands at attention addressing the troops in front of what has to be the world's largest American flag, is an image not easily forgotten. All of this takes place before

the opening credits—a departure from the previously standard format—adding to the feeling that we are watching a real event. Later in the film, actual Fox Movietone News footage gives us a further sense of authenticity.

The role of Patton had originally been offered to Lee Marvin; when he refused it, Rod Steiger was sought for the part, but he turned it down on the grounds that it glorified militarism (anti-Vietnam War fever was running high at the time). Scott, whose last big picture had been *The Bible,* accepted the part—but refused the Oscar for Best Actor, becoming the first actor ever to do so. No definitive reason was ever given, but Scott was known to be dissatisfied with the film and especially his performance in it. *Academy Awards Illustrated* quotes him as remarking, "I was much better playing Shylock in a Central Park performance."

In 1986, George C. Scott reprised his Oscar-winning role as Patton in a made-for-television movie called "The Last Days of Patton." It co-starred Eva Marie Saint, Richard Dysart, and Murray Hamilton, and is re-run from time to time on the CBS network.

5

THE ARISTOCATS

WALT DISNEY PRODUCTIONS
$26,462,000

THE DEATH of Walt Disney in 1966 left a void in that famous studio and saw others attempting to duplicate his uncanny talent for spotting potential hit properties. "What would Walt do?" became an oft-asked question. In an effort to hit on a formula for success, his heirs decided on *The Aristocats.* The project had been on the drawing boards at the time of Walt's death, and he had given his blessing on the basis of a few sketches. It proved to have what it takes at the box office, especially in France, where they delighted in the animation of the French settings. Two releases (the initial one in 1970, plus one in 1987) have helped secure a place in the top five for the animated feature.

The plot is hardly original. In many ways it is derivative of *101 Dalmations,* with adorable kittens being kidnapped this time instead of adorable puppies. But it is certainly good entertainment, and children as well as parents can easily sit through the 1-hour 18-minute musical.

Celebrity voices add a great deal to the enjoyment, particularly Phil Harris as Thomas O'Malley, the Alley Cat. Also unforgettable are vocalizations by Eva Gabor as Duchess, Sterling Holloway (remember him as The Cheshire Cat and Winnie the Pooh?) as Roquefort the Mouse, Paul Winchell as the Chinese Cat, Nancy Kulp as Frou-Frou, Pat Buttram (Gene Autry's ex-sidekick) as Napoleon, Hermione Baddeley as Madame, and Monica Evans and Carole Shelley as

the geese, Abigail and Amelia. If these last two voices sound familiar, you may remember them as the "Pigeon Sisters" in *The Odd Couple.*

The Academy Award–winning Sherman Brothers were pressed back into service to write most of the songs for *The Aristocats,* including the title song (sung by Maurice Chevalier), "Scales and Arpeggios," and "She Never Felt Alone." Phil Harris sings "Thomas O'Malley Cat," written by Terry Gilkyson. But the show-stopper is a jazz number headed up by the late Scatman Crothers (as Scat Cat), called "Ev'rybody Wants to Be a Cat," by Floyd Huddleston and Al Rinker. It's truly the best moment in the movie, as Scat Cat leads a group of hippie-cats

on a parade over the rooftops of Paris.

The latest Disney studio Christmas package was well received by *The New York Times,* which wrote: "Bless the Walt Disney organization for 'The Aristocats,' as funny, warm and sweet an animated cartoon package as ever gave a movie marquee a Christmas glow…The real beauty of the picture, which is as amusing, smoothly machined and beautifully colored as any Disney should be, is in the characterizations, sustained within a sprightly but simple format."

In 1996, the Walt Disney Company finally released *The Aristocats* for the home video market, one of the last "classic" animated features to be made available on tape.

Screenplay by Larry Clemmons

Based on a story by Tom McGowan and Tom Rowe

Produced by Wolfgang Reitherman and Winston Hibler

Directed by Wolfgang Reitherman

VOICES

O'Malley . . . . .Phil Harris
Duchess . . . . .Eva Gabor
Roquefort . . . . .Sterling Holloway
Abigail . . . . .Monica Evans
Amelia . . . . .Carole Shelley

1

FIDDLER ON THE ROOF

UNITED ARTISTS
$38,260,954

EVERYONE HAD assumed that musicals were dead, but *Fiddler on the Roof* proved there was life in the genre yet. The successful show (which bowed on Broadway in 1964 and was still running at the time the film version was released) spawned the biggest musical hit movie in many a year, and while still an echo of the '60s screen musicals, *Fiddler* could be counted among the best.

That the story of Tevye the milkman from the Jewish *shtetl* in pogromplagued tsarist Russia could become a popular American hit was something of a miracle itself. Based on the "Tevye" stories of Sholom Aleichem, one of the most popular Yiddish-language writers of all time, *Fiddler on the Roof* was steeped in Jewish culture and tradition, yet also appealed to a broader audience because of its dealings with the universal concepts and emotions of love, joy, sorrow, family, and tradition. The film, set in a Ukrainian village, tells the plight of Tevye, his wife, and the three daughters he's trying to marry off. The violin music of Isaac Stern is featured throughout the soundtrack.

The movie was shot on location at Pinewood Studios, just outside London, where the village of Anatevka was re-created, with exteriors filmed in the countryside of Yugoslavia. It had a budget of $9,000,000, modest by the standards of some musicals, and used a cast of mostly unknowns, at least to the American audience.

Israeli stage performer Topol (born Chaim Topol) had played Tevye in the London stage version of *Fiddler,* performing the part exactly 430 times—he admitted to taking six days off for the Arab-Israeli Six Day War in 1967. (When he was nominated for the Oscar in the film version, he had to secure permission from his Army superiors to attend, since his reservist unit was on active duty at the time.) The Tel Aviv–born actor first began performing with the Israeli Army entertainment unit and later did several films in his native country. In the late '60s, he worked in British films, including *Before Winter Comes* (1969) with David Niven, before landing the part of Tevye.

Another plum role went to actress Molly Picon, as Yente the Matchmaker. Miss Picon was well known to patrons of Yiddish theater, and the late actress was 72 years old when she appeared in the most famous role of her film career. She saw her work as a chance to perform in a document of historical significance. "It's part of a world that's gone," she said in a 1971 interview with *The New York Times.* "There's such a joy and tenderness about this. There's a sadness, too. The world that we're portraying has been destroyed."

Hollywood Reporter wrote: " 'Fiddler on the Roof' is a lavish, carefully made, splendidly designed musical film. It demonstrates once again that ample amounts of time and money, intelligently employed, can indeed buy perfection."

The timeless story of parents watching their flock grow into young adulthood is beautifully captured in the music and lyrics of Jerry Bock and Sheldon M. Harnick. Although the two have collaborated on other projects, *Fiddler* is by far their most successful musical achievement. The songs have just the right feeling of sadness that pervades most Jewish folk music, giving an authentic feeling to the score while still managing to reach a general audience. Songs like "If I Were A Rich Man," "Sunrise, Sunset," "Matchmaker, Matchmaker," and "Tradition," plus Isaac Stern's violin solos (his playing was used to dub the film's opening fiddler), helped make this the number-two-selling soundtrack album of the year.

Screenplay by Joseph Stein

Adapted from stage play by Joseph Stein

Based on the stories of Sholom Aleichem

Music by Jerry Bock

Lyrics by Sheldon Harnick

Produced and directed by Norman Jewison

CAST

Tevye	Topol
Golde	Norma Crane
Motel	Leonard Frey
Yente	Molly Picon
Lazar Wolf	Paul Mann

ACADEMY AWARD NOMINATIONS

8 nominations, 3 wins*

Best Picture
Best Actor (Topol)
Best Supporting Actor (Leonard Frey)
Best Director (Norman Jewison)
*Best Cinematography
Best Art Direction–Set Decoration
*Best Sound
*Best Scoring, Adaptation

Most of the rest of the cast have remained relatively unknown to American audiences in the ensuing years, but one name stands out. Fans of "Starsky and Hutch" will recognize Paul Michael Glaser (now mostly known as a television director), billed as Michael Glaser, in the part of Perchik.

Critical accolades were showered on *Fiddler on the Roof. Variety* said: "Sentimental in a theatrical way, romantic in the old-fashioned way, nostalgic of immigration days, affirmative of human decency, loyalty, bravery and folk humor…'Fiddler on the Roof' is a powerhouse attraction." And *The*

2

BILLY JACK

WARNER BROS.
$32,500,000

"Once in a generation, a hero becomes a legend."

—OPENING STATEMENT

TOM LAUGHLIN'S masterful performance as vigilante for the rights of Native Americans made Billy Jack an unlikely candidate for box office hit status. The producer, director, writer, and star of the film, which was made on a shoestring budget of $800,000, turned it into the sleeper of the decade. It is a simplistic tale of good and evil, youth verses the Establishment, and it reached exactly the audience for which it was intended—the disillusioned young people trying to express their horror over war in general and Vietnam in particular.

The low budget is very apparent in the home-movie-like quality of the film, which is what director Laughlin was seeking. It is part student film, part docudrama, part improvisation. The audience is given the status of out-worlders, privy to sacred Indian tribal rituals like the "Indian Snake Ceremony" and the "Wovoka Friendship Dance." With authentic locations and Native Americans in the cast, Laughlin quickly gains the audience's sympathy for the heretofore overlooked and exploited aboriginal population of our land.

Yet there is something disturbing about *Billy Jack* and its pessimistic attitude. A sample of the dialogue tells why. When one of the characters, tired of being subjected to racist violence and humiliation, says, "We'll go some place else, some place where it doesn't have to be like this," another retorts:

"Oh really? Tell me, where is that place? In what remote corner of this country—no the entire goddamn planet—is there such a place where men really care about one another and really love each other? *Just one place!*"

Laughlin produced the film independently, found he couldn't get the distribution he had been promised by AIP, and struck a deal with Warner Bros. Yet promotion by the distributor was not forthcoming, and *Billy Jack* might have all but disappeared were it not for the persistence of its creator. Laughlin sued Warners for $51,000,000, settled out of court, and eventually won release status for the film in 1974, when it proceeded to double its 1971 grosses. Heavy saturation advertising in a TV blitz campaign turned the trick. Once the enemy of theatrically distributed

movies, television was now harnessed as distributors' most powerful weapon.

Critics failed to predict the success that was forthcoming. *The Hollywood Reporter* said: "Most of the time, the picture seems attenuated and flat, because it's a complicated, tricked-up story that needed a steady pace and strong characterizations to work—neither of which it has…Its box office possibilities look slim."

On that last subject, the trade paper was incorrect. Yet although the film was vastly successful in the early '70s, today the incongruity of an ex-Green beret who preaches nonviolence, then karate-chops his way through half the Southwest makes this picture difficult to watch except as a curiosity piece. Still, the film has remained a cult classic nearly 20 years later.

Screenplay by T. C. Frank and
  Teresa Christina

Produced by Mary Rose Solti

Directed by T. C. Frank

CAST

Billy Jack . . . . .Tom Laughlin
Jean Roberts . . . . .Delores Taylor
Sheriff Cole . . . . .Clark Howat
Posner . . . . .Bert Freed
Barbara . . . . .Julie Webb

THE FRENCH CONNECTION

20TH CENTURY-FOX
$26,315,000

Screenplay by Ernest Tidyman

Based on the novel by Robin Moore

Produced by Philip D'Antoni

Directed by William Friedkin

CAST

Jimmy "Popeye"
  Doyle . . . . .Gene Hackman
Alain Charnier . . . . . . .Fernando Rey
Buddy Russo . . . . .Roy Scheider
Sal Boca . . . . .Tony LoBianco
Pierre Nicoli . . . . .Marcel Bozzuffi

ACADEMY AWARD NOMINATIONS

8 nominations, 5 wins*

*Best Picture
*Best Actor (Gene Hackman)
  Best Supporting Actor (Roy Scheider)
*Best Director (William Friedkin)
*Best Screenplay Based on Material from
  Another Medium (Ernest Tidyman)
  Best Cinematography
  Best Sound
*Best Film Editing

Basically nothing more than a jazzed-up cops-and-robbers movie with a *Bullitt*-derived* car-chase sequence, *The French Connection* somehow won Best Picture over complex productions like *Fiddler on the Roof, Nicholas and Alexandra, A Clockwork Orange,* and *The Last Picture Show*—all nominees for 1971 and all equally worthy of the number-one prize. Seldom had a movie with such a simple premise garnered so much attention and been so well received.

The French Connection, shot almost entirely in and around Manhattan, was based on a novel by Robin Moore, which in turn was based on the true-life exploits of two tough New York cops—Eddie "Popeye" Egan and Sonny Grosso, both of whom appear briefly as other characters in the film. Gene Hackman starred as Jimmy

"Popeye" Doyle, and Grosso, now renamed Buddy Russo, was played by Roy Scheider. The critics and public found their performances so convincing and natural that *Time* seemed certain that the dialogue must have been ad-libbed rather than scripted, commenting that "the actors who play the cops are so well cast that they seem to have grown up next door to the precinct house."

Gene Hackman, who had been nominated as Best Supporting Actor for his roles in *Bonnie and Clyde* (1967) and *I Never Sang For My Father* (1970), was as astonished as anyone when he walked off with the Best Actor award. According to *Academy Awards Illustrated,* Hackman said: "I had no idea…that *Connection* would [be a runaway hit]. I thought it would either be well-received by critics and stand as an example of that kind of film, or that it would be an audience movie. I didn't think it would be both."

There is no doubt that all else paled in the film when compared to that spectacular, superbly edited chase sequence. Plenty of point-of-view shots coupled with expert editing had movie-goers literally on the edge of their seats, and despite an "R" rating—which theoretically should have hurt box office potential—the film was a huge financial success, thanks to repeat business from patrons eager to take additional rides on this Cinerama-like roller coaster.

In 1975, there was the inevitable sequel, which also had a chase sequence (on foot, this time). It failed to live up to both the quality and financial success of the first. There was also a 1986 movie-for-television, *Popeye Doyle.*

In 1989, the original suspect sought as the head of the street-distribution network for the drug ring portrayed in the film was captured in Los Angeles —17 years after he had fled investigators probing his ties to the narcotics underworld.

---

*Highly likely, since Philip D'Antoni was
  producer on both pictures.

4
SUMMER OF '42
WARNER BROS.
$20,500,000

BENJIE (OLIVER CONANT): *My mother and father never did that.*

HERMIE (GARY GRIMES): *Why not?*

BENJIE: *Because it's stupid.*

MANY A YOUNGSTER, especially in the protective era of the '40s, felt as aghast and confused as Benjie and Hermie when they learned the truth about sex and where they came from. Now that films were becoming more sexually permissive, it is easy to see why so many people found *Summer of '42* such a meaningful film, making the "R" rating inconsequential in terms of box office repeat business.

The film was the first of the many modern "coming of age" pictures that would follow. These were especially prevalent in the early '80s when the "how to lose your virginity" genre really came into its own with films like *Little Darlings* (1980) and *Porky's* (1982).

The nostalgic look at the war years was enhanced by the director's attention to the most minute details. Nothing was overlooked, from the totally authentic set decoration, to the price of movie tickets at the box office (adults 25 cents, children 10 cents), to Bette Davis up on the screen uttering her famous ending to *Now Voyager* ("Don't let's ask for the moon—we

have the stars") while the boys played grope-and-tickle with their dates.

It was such a well-crafted film that most critics found little fault in it, except perhaps for some protracted scenes with Hermie, the adolescent protagonist, taking long walks and staring into the sunset. *Newsweek* praised director Mulligan's "knack for drawing natural, charming and, at the same time, complicated performances from young people, and a gentleness and warmth that, when they work, tightrope their way across sentiment to genuinely touch us." Jennifer O'Neill, former model and cover girl, gives a sensitive portrayal as the "older woman," a war widow who initiates Hermie into the art of love while she herself uses the young man for consolation over her grief. Although O'Neill had appeared in minor roles in films since 1968, her performance in *Summer of '42* propelled her to stardom.

One of the film's best and most remembered scenes was Hermie's embarrassing attempt to purchase "rubbers" (condoms). It is important for modern audiences to bear in mind the utter humiliation that young men were made to feel back in those days, when purchasing what was then the common form of birth control was a hush-hush affair. In fact, this classic scene was recently parodied in a British award-winning television commercial that has a young man discreetly trying to purchase condoms while the insensitive druggist blurts out on the loudspeaker, "Stockroom, do we have any condoms left?"

Two years following the success of *Summer of '42,* the studio brought out the sequel, *Class of '44.* It wasn't bad, as sequels go, but it couldn't touch the original's success.

Screenplay by Herman Raucher

Produced by Richard A. Roth

Directed by Robert Mulligan

CAST

Dorothy	Jennifer O'Neill
Hermie	Gary Grimes
Oscy	Jerry Houser
Benjie	Oliver Conant
Aggie	Katherine Allentuck

ACADEMY AWARD NOMINATIONS

4 nominations, 1 win*

Best Original Story and Screenplay
Best Cinematography
*Best Original Dramatic Score
   (Michel Legrand)
Best Film Editing

DIAMONDS ARE FOREVER

UNITED ARTISTS
$19,726,829

"My name is Bond. James Bond."

THOSE WORDS WERE music to the execs at United Artists, who could always count on the superspy to save the day for them at the box office with the same panache with which he saved England.

Diamonds Are Forever was the eighth Bond movie, the seventh to be produced by Albert "Cubby" Broccoli and Harry Saltzman, and the sixth to star Sean Connery. Many thought it the best, although most were just grateful to see Connery back in the harness again, even if he was beginning to gray at the temples. It had been four years since his last Bond picture (*You Only Live Twice,* 1967), and the actor hadn't been able to shake the typecasting. Oh well, why not put the image to good use?

This time, Bond was trying to expose an elaborate diamond smuggling operation, tangling along the way with his old nemesis, Blofeld (played here by Charles Gray). The movie included the usual assortment of Bond girls, such as Jill St. John as Tiffany Case, and Lana Wood (sister of Natalie) as Plenty O'Toole. "M" (Bernard Lee), "Q" (Desmond Llewelyn), Miss Moneypenny (Lois Maxwell), and Felix Leiter (Norman Burton became the fourth actor to

play the part) were by now standard fixtures in any Bond film and favorites with the audience. Willard Whyte, the billionaire kidnapped by Blofeld, is played by Jimmy Dean, the country singer from Texas who gained later fame with his own brand of sausages.

By this time, the Bond films were getting bigger and better budgets, and much of the money went toward authentic locations. *Diamonds* was filmed in England (Pinewood Studios), Germany, Holland, France, and the United States. Direction was by Guy Hamilton (*Goldfinger*) but he brought a much lighter touch to *Diamonds,* emphasizing high camp rather than danger. For example, in the screen's second big chase scene of the year (see *The French Connection,* page 219), Tiffany's Mustang is pitted against the Las Vegas police, with

20 cars totaled in the sequence.

While the audience was obviously happy to have Sean Connery back as James Bond, critics seemed to have mixed feelings. *Time* remarked that "Bond looks better than ever, partly because Sean Connery has returned to play him. During Connery's one-picture absence, some fellow named Lazenby filled the role—the way concrete fills a hole." Yet *Newsweek* wrote: "Connery himself looks a bit long in the tooth to be running around the world scaling buildings, racing cars and generally cutting up."

The actor must have agreed, and loudly proclaimed, "Never again!" But in 1983, the same year Roger Moore played James Bond in *Octopussy,* Sean Connery decided to have another go at male Bonding, with his final (?) venture *Never Say Never Again.*

Screenplay by Richard Maibaum and Tom Mankiewicz

Based on the novel by Ian Fleming

Produced by Harry Saltzman and Albert R. Broccoli

Directed by Guy Hamilton

CAST

James Bond . . . . .Sean Connery
Tiffany Case . . . . .Jill St. John
Blofeld . . . . .Charles Gray
Plenty O'Toole . . . . . . .Lana Wood
Willard Whyte . . . . . . .Jimmy Dean

ACADEMY AWARD NOMINATIONS

1 nomination, no wins

Best Sound

1

THE GODFATHER

PARAMOUNT
$86,275,000

"I'm gonna make him an offer he can't refuse." —MARLON BRANDO

THERE HAD BEEN nothing like it in years. In fact, this was the long-awaited pretender to the box office throne that had been retained by that blockbuster of all time, *Gone With the Wind. The Godfather* handily surpassed the champion to become the reigning king of the box office, netting a phenomenal $86,275,000, nearly double the amount of Paramount's previous biggest hit, *Love Story* (1970).

Back in 1966, Paramount had bought a story from Mario Puzo, paying $7,500 for the 20-page outline. They then made the writer an offer he couldn't refuse—even before the book was published, the studio paid him another $80,000, gave him an office and secretary on the lot, and had him finish the novel. The book went on to become one of the best-sellers of all time: 500,000 copies in hardcover, 10,000,000 paperback copies in print.

Gleefully, Paramount announced plans for filming *The Godfather.* Almost immediately, there was a backlash from the Italian-American Civil Rights League, a group reportedly headed by Joseph Columbo, the reputed don of one of New York City's five Mafia families. The group held an anti-*Godfather*-movie rally in Madison Square Garden, raising $600,000 for their cause. According to reports in *Time,* the offices of Gulf and Western, Paramount's parent company in New York, had to be evacuated twice because of bomb threats. In the end, the League was successful only in getting the producers to substitute all references to "the Mafia" with "the family."

The first order of business was the proper casting of the plum role of Don Vito Corleone, the Godfather himself. Marlon Brando was Coppola's first choice, but many at the studio were skeptical. Actors who were given consideration were George C. Scott, Laurence Olivier, and even Italian producer Carlo Ponti. Melvin Belli, the flamboyant San Francisco attorney and aspiring actor, offered his services. Most of the opposition to Brando centered on the character sketch of the

Don as a man in his sixties, short, stout, graying hair; Brando was in his mid-forties. The decision was finalized one afternoon when Coppola hosted a screening of an actor test for the execs. They nodded approval, then inquired about the vaguely familiar actor. Coppola beamed as he announced it was Brando in full makeup.

Critic Rex Reed commented on Brando's portrayal of the Don, "Most of the time he sounds like he has a mouth full of wet toilet paper," and indeed it was once reported that Brando did stuff his mouth with cotton balls. But it is impossible to imagine anyone else in this role, any more than one can imagine someone other than Clark Gable as Rhett Butler. Brando was simply fated to be Don Corleone.

In a characteristic move, the eccentric Brando refused the Academy's award for Best Actor, sending his proxy to the ceremony in the form of a Native American named Sacheen

---

Screenplay by Mario Puzo and Francis Ford Coppola

Based on the novel by Mario Puzo

Produced by Albert S. Ruddy

Directed by Francis Ford Coppola

CAST

Don Vito Corleone . . . .Marlon Brando
Michael Corleone . . . . .Al Pacino
Sonny Corleone . . . . . .James Caan
Tom Hagen . . . . .Robert Duvall
Kay Adams . . . . .Diane Keaton

ACADEMY AWARD NOMINATIONS

10 nominations, 3 wins*

*Best Picture
*Best Actor (Marlon Brando)
 Best Supporting Actor (James Caan)
 Best Supporting Actor (Robert Duvall)
 Best Supporting Actor (Al Pacino)
 Best Director (Francis Ford Coppola)
*Best Screenplay Based on Material from
 Another Medium (Mario Puzo and
 Francis Ford Coppola)
 Best Sound
 Best Film Editing
 Best Costume Design

Littlefeather, who dolefully walked on stage to refuse the Oscar while bemoaning the treatment of Indians in Hollywood. The Academy didn't seem to mind, and later nominated the twofold winner for his eighth chance at Oscar, for *Last Tango in Paris* (1973).

The others in the film were also well cast. Coppola's sister, Talia Shire, played Vito Corleone's daughter, Connie. She had had limited acting experience but later became a star in her own right (primarily as Mrs. Rocky Balboa in the *Rocky* movies). Al Pacino, a New York stage actor who had won both an Obie and a Tony, landed the pivotal role of Michael even though he had only one previous film credit, *Panic in Needle Park* (1971). He received a nod from the Academy with a nomination for Best Supporting Actor, as did James Caan, who portrayed the explosive Sonny. Recording and nightclub star Al Martino played the part of Johnny Fontane, whom many saw as a parallel to Frank Sinatra (although this was vigorously denied by that singer-actor).

Ninety percent of the movie was shot on the streets of New York City and its suburbs, with the remaining ten percent filmed on a soundstage in the Bronx. Additional footage was shot in Sicily.

Although the violence and language of *The Godfather* mandated an "R" rating, public and critical acclaim made this one of the most successful films of all time, and Paramount immediately began preparing a sequel, *The Godfather, Part II,* which reached the screen in 1974. A special release from Paramount Home Video called *The Godfather Saga* is an edited videocassette version that combines elements of both films but rearranges them into chronological order.

In 1990, Paramount released yet another chapter in *The Godfather* soap opera. *The Godfather, Part III* reunited director Francis Ford Coppola with stars Al Pacino and Diane Keaton while introducing us to many new members of this extended (not to mention dysfunctional) Mafia family. The film, while hardly a blockbuster, pulled in $38,000,000 in rentals, besting the first sequel by $8,000,000.

THE POSEIDON ADVENTURE

20TH CENTURY-FOX
$42,000,000

"At midnight on New Year's Eve, the S.S. Poseidon, enroute from New York to Athens, met with disaster and was lost. There were only a handful of survivors. This is their story." —OPENING CARD

A S WITH THAT other ill-fated ship, the *Titanic,* there was no question in the audience's mind that this was going to be a disaster film and that most of the characters we were about to meet were doomed. Here was the basic premise of all disaster films: the audience, safely noshing in their seats, would calmly bet on who would survive and who would not. If the formula was always the same, so was the predicted box office success.

Screenplay by Stirling Silliphant and Wendell Mayes

Based on the novel by Paul Gallico

Produced by Irwin Allen

Directed by Ronald Neame

CAST

Rev. Frank Scott . . . . .Gene Hackman
Mike Rogo . . . . .Ernest Borgnine
James Madin . . . . . . .Red Buttons
Monnie Parry . . . . . . .Carol Lynley
Acres . . . . .Roddy McDowall
Linda Rogo . . . . .Stella Stevens
Belle Rosen . . . . .Shelley Winters

ACADEMY AWARD NOMINATIONS

8 nominations, 1 win*

Best Supporting Actress (Shelley Winters)
Best Cinematography
Best Art Direction–Set Decoration
Best Sound
*Best Song ("The Morning After," music and words by Al Kasha and Joel Hirschhorn)
Best Original Dramatic Score (John Williams)
Best Film Editing
Best Costume Design

The category of Best Special Visual Effects was dropped for 1972. Instead, *The Poseidon Adventure* was given the Special Achievement Award for visual effects.

What *Airport* had done for the unfriendly skies, *The Poseidon Adventure* did for the high seas. Academy Award winner Gene Hackman (*The French Connection*) played the minister who keeps his cool while all about are losing theirs; others in the star-studded cast were Ernest Borgnine, Red Buttons, Carol Lynley, Roddy McDowall, Stella Stevens, Shelley Winters (probably the most remembered performance—she won an Oscar nomination), Jack Albertson, Pamela Sue Martin (in her pre-"Dallas" days), Arthur O'Connell, Fred Sadoff, Bob Hastings, and Leslie Nielsen as the Captain.

The film was made all the more convincing with the use of visual effects, which won the Academy's Special Achievement Award for effects designers L. B. Abbott and A. D. Flowers. The *Queen Mary,* berthed in Long Beach, was used for exteriors of the ship, while miniatures were set afloat in a tank on the Fox lot in which the storm effects were created. Most ingenious of all was the Grand Salon set, built to tilt 30 degrees with the camera also tilting. To simulate the overturned ship, an upside-down set was also created, with the "ceiling" underfoot and the "floor" carpeted overhead (tables were bolted to it).

The movie's theme song, "The Morning After," won an Oscar as Best Original Song. Maureen McGovern's single of this love theme became a number-one gold record, remaining in that position on the *Billboard* charts for two weeks in August, 1973.

Scoring of "The Morning After" was done by John Williams, earning him an Oscar nomination. Producer Irwin Allen had worked with Williams before—when he was producing a television show called "Lost in Space." Williams wrote the theme to the TV series, billed as "Johnny" Williams in the credits.

There was a sequel, of course. *Beyond the Poseidon Adventure* (1979) found Telly Savalas, Sally Field, Michael Caine, and others attempting a salvage operation on the infamous ship. But the film itself couldn't be salvaged. It was plainly a disaster.

WHAT'S UP DOC?

WARNER BROS.
$28,000,000

"Once upon a time, there was a plaid overnight case."
—OPENING NARRATION

THUS BEGINS Peter Bogdanovich's homage to the screwball comedies so popular in the '30s. Teaming Barbra Streisand and Ryan O'Neal in this irreverent piece of slapstick, Bogdanovich includes every sight gag known to humankind, beginning with the mix-up of four pieces of luggage that opens the film.

If the movie seems derivative of 1938's *Bringing Up Baby,* the Cary Grant–Katharine Hepburn screwball comedy that defined the genre for all time, it is not entirely accidental, since the Howard Hawks–directed classic served as the blueprint for *What's Up Doc?*

During rehearsals, Bogdanovich shot tests of his two stars and showed the footage to Howard Hawks. According to Shaun Considine's *Barbra Streisand,* Hawks told the young director that Streisand had the same problem Hepburn had had. She was trying too hard to be funny. "Tell them to just read the lines. They've got to play off each other and get the laughs from their attitudes," Hawks instructed. He also thought it was wrong for Bogdanovich to admit the plot's source. "You made a mistake telling 'em where you stole it from," Hawks told him. "I never said who I stole it from."

What a breath of fresh air this was for audiences in a year heavy with deadly-serious films like *The Godfather, The Poseidon Adventure,* and *Deliverance.* There were no lessons to

be learned, no social commentary. As the Cole Porter tune says, "Anything Goes" (the film makes heavy use of Porter's songs, including the Streisand-O'Neal duet of "You're the Top" sung over opening credits).

The movie has the second-most-popular California location for its setting, San Francisco, and there was the by-now-obligatory car chase through its hilly streets. Only seven or eight cars get totaled this time, though; after all, this is not *Bullitt.*

Reviews were mixed, with critics uncertain of what to make of this salute to *Bringing Up Baby*—tampering with classics usually doesn't sit well with critics. But *Variety* termed the comedy "terrific" and predicted gold at the box office: "This picture is a total smash. The script and cast are excellent; the direction and comedy staging are outstanding; and there are

literally reels of pure, unadulterated and sustaining laughs…mature audiences haven't seen a new film like this in a generation…The Warner Bros. release has nothing in sight but money, by the carload…Buck Henry, Robert Benton and David Newman have fashioned a great screenplay."

The film's ending pokes fun at *Love Story,* Ryan O'Neal's most famous film to that time:

JUDY
Love means never having to say you're sorry.

HOWARD
That's the dumbest thing I ever heard!

Maybe so, but there was certainly chemistry between the pair—they were reunited in 1979 for another romp in *The Main Event.*

Screenplay by Buck Henry, David Newman, and Robert Benton

From a story by Peter Bogdanovich

Produced and directed by Peter Bogdanovich

CAST

Judy Maxwell . . . . . . .Barbra Streisand
Howard Bannister . . . .Ryan O'Neal
Hugh Simon . . . . . . .Kenneth Mars
Eunice Burns . . . . . . .Madeline Kahn
Frederick Larrabee . . . .Austin Pendleton

DELIVERANCE

WARNER BROS.
$22,600,000

WHEN IT CAME TIME to translate erstwhile poet James Dickey's 1970 best-seller to the screen, Dickey himself was put in charge of writing the screenplay for *Deliverance,* something rarely done in Hollywood. In fact, Dickey managed to get himself cast in a minor part as well, as Sheriff Bullard.

This suspenseful, beautifully photographed film about four Atlanta businessmen off on a weekend of pitting their skills against nature is hardly a joy cruise. Their survivalist, man-against-the-elements whitewater canoeing trip turns to tragedy and death while the river flows angrily, noisily onward. It is almost as if the visitors to this pristine wilderness have themselves raped the virginal forests and landscapes. There is also a profound sense of sadness pervading the latter half of the film, one that lingers even after the lights come up.

The drama is riveting, and audiences obviously related to the gang of four in the film, projecting themselves into each treacherous situation from

the safety of their theater seats. John Boorman's first venture into this all-location film would certainly not be his last, and the style of *Deliverance*—in which the trees and river become characters themselves—is one Boorman would again draw upon for *The Emerald Forest* (1985).

Location shooting used up half of the film's extremely low $2,000,000 budget. Boorman selected a northern Georgia county bisected by the Chattooga River. The location crew filmed there for two months, with most of the budget going to local carpenters, truck drivers, food, and lodging. Boorman filmed in sequence, which is rarely done in filmmaking, and the four stars—Burt Reynolds, Jon Voight, Ned Beatty (in his screen debut), and Ronny Cox (ditto)—did all of their own, sometimes very dangerous, stunts. Following the release and ultimate success of *Deliverance,* Rabun County had a sudden influx of tourists, eager to see the film's location with their own eyes, and three companies

began running guided canoe tours down the river. In order to lure more movie companies and their dollars to avail themselves of the locations, the state of Georgia promptly set up a Film Commission—something virtually every state in the Union has today.

Burt Reynolds may have been one of the main reasons so many people came to see *Deliverance.* Only three months before the film's release, the handsome Floridian had posed in the buff for *Cosmopolitan* magazine, and the publicity hadn't exactly hurt him at the box office. (His other feature of 1972 was Woody Allen's *Everything You Always Wanted to Know About Sex but Were Afraid to Ask*—as far as one can tell, there was no intended correlation between his centerfold and that film's title.)

One of the best-remembered scenes in this movie is the musical interlude of "Dueling Banjos," a lively bluegrass number. Released as a single, the tune became a pop hit, climbing into *Billboard*'s top ten.

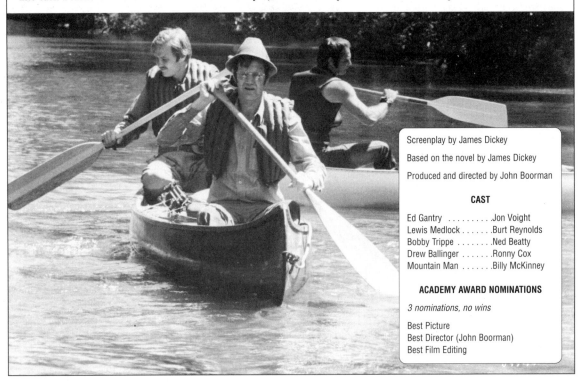

Screenplay by James Dickey

Based on the novel by James Dickey

Produced and directed by John Boorman

CAST

Ed Gantry . . . . .Jon Voight
Lewis Medlock . . . . . .Burt Reynolds
Bobby Trippe . . . . . . .Ned Beatty
Drew Ballinger . . . . . .Ronny Cox
Mountain Man . . . . . .Billy McKinney

ACADEMY AWARD NOMINATIONS

3 nominations, no wins

Best Picture
Best Director (John Boorman)
Best Film Editing

JEREMIAH JOHNSON

WARNER BROS.
$21,900,000

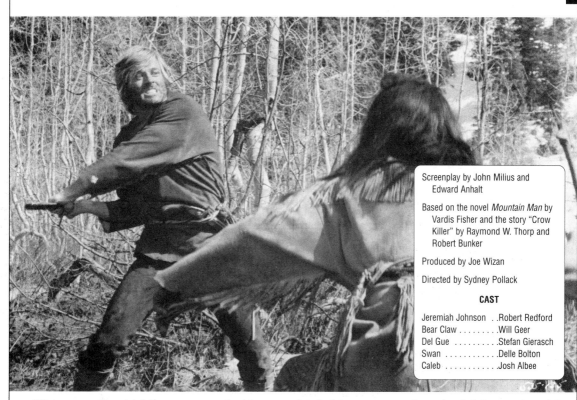

Screenplay by John Milius and Edward Anhalt

Based on the novel *Mountain Man* by Vardis Fisher and the story "Crow Killer" by Raymond W. Thorp and Robert Bunker

Produced by Joe Wizan

Directed by Sydney Pollack

CAST

Jeremiah Johnson	. .Robert Redford
Bear Claw	. . . . .Will Geer
Del Gue	. . . . .Stefan Gierasch
Swan	. . . . .Delle Bolton
Caleb	. . . . .Josh Albee

"His name was Jeremiah Johnson, and he wanted to be a mountain man." —OPENING NARRATION

NINETEEN SEVENTY-TWO was a very good year for Warner Bros. The film studio had three of the top five films for a combined total of $72,500,000 in domestic rentals. Their comedy *What's Up Doc?* was the only one of that genre in the top five. Aside from this exception, we liked our films violent that year, although *Jeremiah Johnson* had less violence than the others. There were some similarities between *Deliverance* and *Jeremiah Johnson:* both featured a return to the wilderness way of life, a remote dream in a country that was in a recession and entangled in a war nobody wanted. "Ride due West as the sun sets; turn left at the Rocky Mountains," he was told, and Jeremiah was off on his back-to-nature trek. Along the way we learned that life was hard back in 1825, and

maybe things weren't so bad for us after all. "I wanted this film to be an antidote to the general feeling in the States today that getting away from civilization is such a terrific thing and is so romantic," Redford told a reporter at the Cannes Film Festival in 1972, where the film had its world premiere. "I wanted to show the kids what it is really like going it on your own in the wilderness and thoroughly deromanticize it for them." Director Sydney Pollack, soon to become a much-sought-after director, agreed, telling *The New York Times:* "You cannot live totally selfishly and be completely independent in the world. You must adjust to the needs of nature or of man." *The Hollywood Reporter* noted: "Sydney Pollack's control of the movie's rich detail is thorough and steady. He knows exactly what he wants and with unusual relaxation and confidence moves from episode to episode with a musical, rhythmic pace which avoids the

sentimental and obvious consistently."

Some saw Robert Redford miscast as the rugged mountaineer who inadvertently marries a Flathead Indian woman, then launches a personal vendetta against the dreaded Crows he despises when they kill his family. According to co-scripter Edward Anhalt, "The real Jeremiah Johnson killed 247 Crow Indians and then ate their livers." Fortunately, Redford doesn't have to eat Crow, or this might not have been the box office hit it was. In fact, it is probably his very miscasting that worked so well for Warners. The public voted him number three at the box office, and climbing rapidly.

The old adage about never working with children and dogs should be appended to include "and Utah" as well, since Redford's only real co-star, aside from by Will Geer ("Grandpa Zeb" in TV's "The Waltons"), is the beautiful scenery of Utah's National Forests and Zion National Park.

THE EXORCIST

WARNER BROS.
$89,000,000

"Have you ever heard of exorcism? It's a stylized ritual in which the rabbi or the priest tries to drive out the so-called invading spirit."
—REGAN'S DOCTOR TO MRS. MACNEIL

WILLIAM PETER BLATTY'S novel *The Exorcist* became one of the hottest sellers of all time, and by the time the film version was released the day after Christmas, 1973, nearly everyone in the country had heard of exorcism. The author claimed to have based his story on fact: when he was a college student at Georgetown University in 1949, the case of a "possessed" 14-year-old boy had hit the newspapers. Catholic priests apparently exorcised the boy's demon, after which the child grew up, married, and led a normal life. The story stayed with the impressionable, Jesuit-trained Blatty, who changed his story's victim to a 12-year-old girl.

The film quickly soared to the top of the box office charts, and all hell broke loose as reports of audience reactions (sympathetic vomiting, fainting, miscarriages, heart attacks, and the like) spread like wildfire, fanned by the gleeful Warner Bros. publicity department. Actually, the book was scarier by far, since the reader's imaginative mind knew no bounds, while the film was limited to special effects, trick photography, and sound effects to tap into people's deepest fears and superstitions. It worked, though, and audiences lined up around the block to be frightened and repulsed by the "R"-rated film.

The rating itself came as something of a shock to many unsuspecting moviegoers, who were suddenly assaulted with every four-letter Anglo-Saxon-derived expression ever conceived, emanating from the mouth of 14-year-old Linda Blair (the expletives were dubbed, however, by the more mature voice of actress Mercedes McCambridge). Despite the "R" rating by the Motion Picture Association of America, many City Fathers decided to restrict the audience to over-17s only. In Los Angeles, the film's young star herself was forbidden to buy a ticket unless accompanied by an adult. As quoted in *Films of the Seventies,*

Jack Valenti, president of the MPAA, defended his organization's position: "Ratings come from what viewers see, not what they imagine they see. In *The Exorcist* there is *no* overt sex. There is *no* excessive violence. There is some strong language, but it is rationally related to the film's theme and is kept to a minimum."

Amazing what could be seen on the screen only four years after *Midnight Cowboy* and not get an "X." If you were under 17, and your parents didn't have a babysitter, they might have taken you to see little Linda spewing forth streams of vomit and obscenities with equal gusto, not to mention masturbating with a crucifix.

The film had expertly crafted special effects and makeup. Oatmeal and pea soup were pumped through a tube concealed in an appliance on Linda's lower lip. (After learning the secret of this trick, many people swore off pea soup for life.) The 360-degree headspin that the possessed child supposedly does was filmed with a full-scale mechanical double of Linda, complete with radio-controlled eyes that blinked. Audiences ate it up.

Critics and film analysts found enough material in this film to keep their columns filled for months. Some saw it as a sign of a depraved society; others attributed its popularity not to a bloodthirsty population, but to the audience's need to see a film in which Good eventually triumphs over Evil (your basic morality play); while still others thought people were simply curious to learn what all the fuss was about.

For Warner Bros., it didn't matter, as they tallied up the receipts of their top film to date, and quickly plotted the sequel. *Exorcist II* arrived in 1977, directed by John Boorman (*Deliverance*), and starred Richard Burton, Louise Fletcher, James Earl Jones, Ned Beatty, and, of course, the Devil's pet possessee, Linda Blair. The movie had a devil of a time at the box office, where even recutting by the director couldn't exorcise the film's problems. The original is still the best, especially when rented intact at the video store, not sanitized and hacked to pieces as it is on local channels.

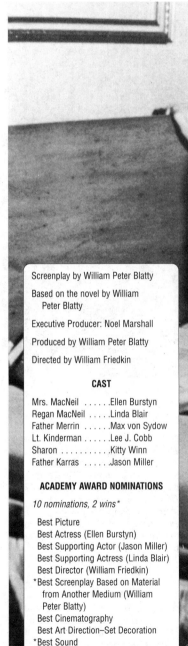

Screenplay by William Peter Blatty

Based on the novel by William Peter Blatty

Executive Producer: Noel Marshall

Produced by William Peter Blatty

Directed by William Friedkin

CAST

Mrs. MacNeil	Ellen Burstyn
Regan MacNeil	Linda Blair
Father Merrin	Max von Sydow
Lt. Kinderman	Lee J. Cobb
Sharon	Kitty Winn
Father Karras	Jason Miller

ACADEMY AWARD NOMINATIONS

10 nominations, 2 wins*

Best Picture
Best Actress (Ellen Burstyn)
Best Supporting Actor (Jason Miller)
Best Supporting Actress (Linda Blair)
Best Director (William Friedkin)
*Best Screenplay Based on Material from Another Medium (William Peter Blatty)
Best Cinematography
Best Art Direction–Set Decoration
*Best Sound
Best Film Editing

2

THE STING

UNIVERSAL
$78,212,000

FROM THE VERY FIRST shot of the old Universal logo, with the single-engine plane putt-putting around the globe, audiences knew they were in for a treat. George Roy Hill, re-teamed here with Paul Newman and Robert Redford—Butch and Sundance—couldn't have selected a more appropriate piece of theme music either: "The Entertainer" aptly describes the director and his picture. *The Sting* is prime entertainment—it doesn't get much better than this.

Hill successfully transports us in a cinematic time machine back to the days of the '30s con artists by never letting any anachronisms slip into this period piece. Each scenic transition is introduced with that '30s technique, "the wipe," as if an invisible hand sweeps across the screen and leads us to the next number. In order to stress this technique, each segment is introduced with a slide telling us what this act will be about. We see:

THE SET-UP
THE HOOK
THE TALE
THE WIRE
THE SHUT-OFF
THE STING

The plot is so well developed and intricately woven that it takes considerable concentration from the audience to follow all its entanglements, one of the reasons for the film's great success, as people returned repeatedly to try to catch what they'd missed the first time. And it didn't hurt that Redford and Newman, the picture's two stars, were also the number-one and number-two box office favorites in the polls.

The movie had opened barely a week before the year's top hit, *The Exorcist,* and part of its popularity had to be due to the comic relief audiences needed after that film's intensity. People were swept along by the whole mystique of *The Sting,* right down to the '30s wardrobe. What Faye Dunaway had done for the beret and maxiskirt in *Bonnie and Clyde,* Redford and Newman did for men's fashions. Lapels broadened and pin-striped gangster suits became the rage. Edith Head also got a lot of

Screenplay by David S. Ward

Produced by Tony Bill, Michael Phillips, and Julia Phillips

Directed by George Roy Hill

CAST

Henry Gondorff . . . . . .Paul Newman
Johnny Hooker . . . . .Robert Redford
Doyle Lonnegan . . . . .Robert Shaw
Lt. Snyder . . . . .Charles Durning
Singleton . . . . .Ray Walston
Billie . . . . .Eileen Brennan

ACADEMY AWARD NOMINATIONS

10 nominations, 7 wins *

*Best Picture
 Best Actor (Robert Redford)
*Best Director (George Roy Hill)
*Best Original Story and Screenplay (David S. Ward)
 Best Cinematography
*Best Ad Direction–Set Decoration
 Best Sound
*Best Scoring: Original Song Score and/ or Adaptation (Marvin Hamlisch)
*Best Film Editing
*Best Costume Design

mileage out of that old standby, the T-shirt. "Whenever I wanted Paul Newman to look mean, I allowed his T-shirt to show," the costume designer said, as quoted in *The Hollywood Reporter* magazine.

The Sting wasn't just a big hit with the fans. The Academy found the picture a winner in the old tradition and showered it with ten Oscar nominations and seven wins (although it seems an inequity that only one of the two leads, Robert Redford, received a Best Actor nod).

Critics were unanimous in their enthusiasm for the movie. Wrote *Variety:* "Paul Newman and Robert Redford are superbly re-teamed… George Roy Hill's outstanding direction of David S. Ward's finely-crafted story of multiple deception and surprise ending will delight both mass and class audiences," *The Hollywood Reporter* called it "a disciplined, delightful film." *Newsweek* said: "Like its heroes, the film succeeds on charm and con. Newman and Redford radiate a charismatic appeal that tilts the movie in their favor." And *The New York Times* described *The Sting* as "a variation on the old Dr. Gillespie–Dr. Kildare relationship, with a bit of Laurel and Hardy thrown in. It is also apparently very good box office."

Indeed it was. Having cost only $5,500,000 to make (with a reported $1,000,000 each for Redford and Newman), the take at Universal proved that the chemistry was still there.

Not so successful, however, was the inevitable sequel, *The Sting II* (1983). Audiences just didn't fall for Jackie Gleason and Mac Davis in the Newman/Redford roles, and it was Universal that got stung this time.

AMERICAN GRAFFITI

UNIVERSAL
$55,128,175

"Where were you in '62?"
—ADVERTISING COPY FOR
AMERICAN GRAFFITI

"Without exception, all players fit perfectly into the concept and execution, and all the young principals and featured players have a bright and lengthy future. And so does Lucas." —VARIETY

INDEED THEY ALL DID. George Lucas had one legitimate film credit to his name—*THX-1138*—and $1,500 in total personal assets in 1973 when he convinced Universal executive Ned Tanen to finance his pet project, a nostalgic look at the early '60s, heavily based on Lucas' own teen years. The young exec reluctantly agreed and gave the 26-year-old Lucas the minuscule budget of $750,000, plus another $500,000 for prints and advertising.* No one could have predicted the kind of phenomenal success *American Graffiti* would become. The film's rental take at the box office returned *50* times the investment. The future director of the legendary *Star Wars* was on his way.

Variety was certainly correct about the future of the young players, too. The cast list read like a "who will be who." Ronny Howard, still only 18, would soon become the lead in a hit

TV series called "Happy Days," which was very much derivative of *American Graffiti;* Mackenzie Phillips, 12-year-old daughter of musician John Phillips, would go on to co-star in TV's "One Day At A Time"; Richard Dreyfuss, who had played only a few walk-ons in some obscure movies, would become one of the major stars of the decade; Cindy Williams, not yet known as half of "Laverne and Shirley," would become the co-star of one of TV's hottest hits; Suzanne Somers, the elusive blonde in the white T-Bird, a former model in her first professional acting job, went on to a TV career also, starring in "Three's Company" and "She's the Sheriff"; and Harrison Ford, who was then supplementing his ailing acting career with part-time carpentry jobs, would eventually star in some of the biggest blockbuster films of all time.

Technically unsophisticated, *American Graffiti* was nevertheless a major hit because of its realistic quality. Lucas shot entirely on location in San Rafael and Petaluma, small Northern California towns. Between the hours of 9:00 P.M., when it was just dark enough, and 5:00 A.M., before the sun would come up, the main streets of these towns were cordoned off for the night shoot. It was grueling work, but there were lighter moments as well. Locals for miles around were encouraged to rent their vintage hot rods for the film at $25 a night, and they really got into the spirit of things, drag racing between takes, having themselves one last fling at the '60s. Over 400 cars were eventually used, among them the yellow dragster driven by Paul Le Mat's character, "John." Look closely at its unusual license plate—THX 138—an obvious inside joke and reference to the Lucas film (but with only three numerals, as permitted by California law).

Further enhancing the nostalgia was the soundtrack, which contained no fewer than 43 rock-and-roll hits from the '50s and '60s. Used basically as "source music" (music emanating from radios or other sources, rather than deliberately orchestrated background), the music was relentless. There was seldom a silent interlude, even during

dialogue, and this seemed to propel the essentially plotless film along.

The movie's climactic drag race was based on Lucas' own high school experiences. Shy, shorter than average, and looking younger than his true age, the teenager found thrills in hot rodding, and nearly killed himself in a serious accident. A lucky break for him, and us, that he didn't. George Lucas has since become one of the most successful producer-directors in motion picture history, reportedly earning over one billion dollars.

In 1979, a sequel, *More American Graffiti,* reunited Clark, Phillips, Williams, and Howard in an episodic film covering the years 1964–67. Lucas did not direct.

---

*Tanen wanted to change the title to *Another Slow Night in Modesto,* afraid audiences would think it was an Italian film or a movie about feet. Producer Francis Coppola suggested *Rock Around the Block.* But Lucas liked his own title, which he felt evoked memories of a bygone civilization, and refused to change it.

Screenplay by George Lucas, Gloria Katz, and Willard Huyck

Produced by Francis Ford Coppola

Directed by George Lucas

CAST

Curt . . . . .Richard Dreyfuss
Steve . . . . .Ronny Howard
John . . . . .Paul Le Mat
Terry . . . . .Charles Martin Smith
Laurie . . . . .Cindy Williams
Bob Falfa . . . . .Harrison Ford

ACADEMY AWARD NOMINATIONS

5 nominations, no wins

Best Picture
Best Supporting Actress (Candy Clark)
Best Director (George Lucas)
Best Original Story and Screenplay
Best Film Editing

4

PAPILLON
ALLIED ARTISTS
$22,500,000

HENRI CHARRIERE was a Frenchman who spent 13 years in captivity for a murder he swore he didn't commit. The court didn't buy it, and sentenced him to life in prison, but he made good his escape time and again. Eventually he was sentenced to Devil's Island off French Guiana in South America, a supposedly "escape-proof" prison. Not for Charriere. Nicknamed "Papillon"— The Butterfly, for a tattoo on his chest, plus his need to soar freely like a butterfly—Charriere became the first man in history to escape from that dreaded penal colony, improvising a raft of dried coconut husks. After many years as a refugee in Venezuela, he went public and did what anyone would do under the circumstances— he wrote his memoirs, and the book became a best-seller.

The property was acquired by independent film company Allied Artists, and the late Franklin J. Schaffner (*Patton*) was signed as director. He chose Steve McQueen for the title role, but felt that the story lacked human interaction. Thus was created the part of Louis Dega, for which he signed the chameleon-like Dustin Hoffman, who was by now becoming an actor's actor. Another "odd couple" was created.

Screenplay by Dalton Trumbo and Lorenzo Semple, Jr.

Based on the book by Henri Charriere

Executive Producer: Ted Richmond

Produced by Robert Dorfmann and Franklin J. Schaffner

Directed by Franklin J. Schaffner

CAST

Papillon . . . . .Steve McQueen
Dega . . . . .Dustin Hoffman
Indian Chief . . . . .Victor Jory
Julot . . . . .Don Gordon
Leper Colony Chief . . .Anthony Zerbe

ACADEMY AWARD NOMINATIONS

1 nomination, no wins

Best Original Dramatic Score

The movie was shot on location in Spain and Jamaica, the latter nearly as punishing as the real Devil's Island for which it doubled, with searing heat, mosquitoes, and crocodiles. Hoffman claims to have lost 20 pounds during the ordeal, and Charriere himself thought the setting so real he kept scanning the horizon for guards who might at any second come and grab him.

The film opened to less than enthusiastic reviews at Christmas time, 1973. Critics complained about its length (150 minutes) and its pessimistic feeling. *Newsweek* wrote: " 'Papillon' offers torture as entertainment but winds up making entertainment a form of torture…the dispiriting, grim tone of the film and its sensational interest in atrocities speak only of the futility of rebellion." *The Hollywood Reporter* called the film "a long, difficult and grim experience which does not do backflips to engage the audience…the screenplay by Trumbo and Semple has awkward expository dialogue, little humor, and except for two major roles, no characterizations." *Variety*'s review seemed

ambiguous: "The atmosphere bores into the brain like it does to its victims, leaving them as well as an audience stunned, disoriented, incredulous and nearly catatonic. It takes literally hours to come out of 'Papillon.' "

Reviews like these piqued moviegoers' curiosity. Surprisingly, the film became a hit, almost doubling its financial outlay of $12,000,000. One reason may be the "PG" rating, which meant more take at the box office from the younger crowd. The rating originally had been an "R," but the distributor argued that the feature was tasteful, discreet, and restrained, thus persuading the Motion Picture Association of America to make the change. Nevertheless, this is an extremely intense film, and certainly isn't for most young teens.

While emphasis is on the McQueen/Hoffman pairing (and their characters' implied homosexual attraction), others in the cast worth noting are Victor Jory as the Indian Chief, Bill Mumy (former child actor on TV's "Lost in Space"), and co-screenwriter Dalton Trumbo as the Commandant.

THE WAY WE WERE

COLUMBIA
$22,457,000

"Can I ask you a question? Do you smile all the time?"
—STREISAND TO REDFORD

O F COURSE he smiled all the time. Wouldn't you if you were the number-one box office star of the year, with two hit movies in a row—*Jeremiah Johnson, The Sting,* and now *The Way We Were*? Make that *three* hit movies.

The pollsters' highest-ranking female star, Barbra Streisand, was cleverly paired opposite Robert Redford—*goy* meets girl, joked some—but it was a chemical combination that ought to have come with a warning label. Hormones stirred in theaters across the land as we watched these two actors, as odd a couple as ever there was, fall in love in this rather improbable story of a golden boy novelist-turned-Hollywood-screenwriter and the idealistic, socialistic, even Communistic object of his affections.

Newsweek cleverly dubbed the couple Miss Left and Mr. Right, then added: "This is one of a vanishing breed of movies in which the stars, by their very presence, alter the

---

Screenplay by Arthur Laurents

Based on the novel by Arthur Laurents

Produced by Ray Stark

Directed by Sydney Pollack

CAST

Katie	Barbra Streisand
Hubbell	Robert Redford
J. J.	Bradford Dillman
Carol Ann	Lois Chiles
George Bissinger	Patrick O'Neal

ACADEMY AWARD NOMINATIONS

6 nominations, 2 wins*

Best Actress (Barbra Streisand)
Best Cinematography
Best Art Direction–Set Decoration
*Best Song ("The Way We Were," music by Marvin Hamlisch, words by Alan and Marilyn Bergman)
*Best Original Dramatic Score
Best Costume Design

---

story. In a way, they *are* the story." This was pretty much the truth, and provoked *Time*'s reviewer to near rage: "This ill-written, wretchedly performed and tediously directed film…does not actually have anything on its mind except to bring together two hot properties in a period setting for which there is currently a lot of nostalgia." Despite less-than-kind reviews like these, word of mouth helped make *The Way We Were* a box office sensation.

Although Streisand doesn't sing in the picture, her recording of the title song became even more popular than the movie. It first appeared on the charts in November, 1973, shortly after the film's release, and by February, "The Way We Were" had steadily climbed to the number-one position, which it held for three weeks. It was also Barbra's first number-one hit. And for composer Marvin Hamlisch, the song brought him one of *three* Academy Awards he took home the night of the 1973 ceremony—one for *The Sting* and two for *The Way We Were*.

THE TOWERING INFERNO

20TH CENTURY-FOX/WARNER BROS.
$48,838,000

"To those who give their lives so that others might live…to the fire fighters of the world…This picture is gratefully dedicated."

—OPENING CARD

THIS IS ONE of those rare films that saw two studios cooperating in a co-production—sort of like Coke and Pepsi collaborating on a new soft drink. Producer Irwin Allen, the man behind 1972's successful *The Poseidon Adventure,* had the blessings of 20th Century-Fox to pursue his forte and do another disaster film. But the property that commanded their attention, a novel called *The Tower,* by Richard Martin Stern, was already owned by Warner Bros. Meanwhile, 20th and Allen obtained the rights to a similar book, *The Glass Inferno,* by Tom Scortia and Frank Robinson. Not wanting any competition from Warners, they approached that studio with the idea of a co-production. Thus was born the child of this unusual mating, *The Towering Inferno.*

It was no secret what the plot concerned; by now audiences were wildly enthusiastic about disaster films and could recite the formula with little difficulty. This time the film's mega-stars weren't on a doomed airliner or in a topsy-turvy steamship, but in a situation much closer to our everyday experiences—trapped inside a burning skyscraper—and the public approbation in the form of box office dollars was the greatest yet. Of course, there were now two leading actors there to save the day: Steve McQueen and Paul Newman. Ever since Newman had starred in *Somebody Up There Likes Me* and received top billing, McQueen had been trying to get one up on him, even turning down the co-starring role in *Butch Cassidy and the Sundance Kid* because his name would come after Newman's. But *The Towering Inferno* appeased his ego once and for all, with *both* men's names appearing simultaneously on the screen, McQueen's positioned higher than Newman's.

For McQueen, the role of the fire captain was a windfall. His share of the gross profits in *The Towering Inferno* came to 7.5 percent. This, coupled with his up-front payment, eventually brought him a whopping $12,000,000. Even by today's standards, this is a staggering amount. Renowned *Los Angeles Times* critic Charles Champlin, however, rushed to McQueen's defense: "McQueen's fire captain in *Towering Inferno* left no doubt why he was worth every penny of the millions he earned. He brought to that role an authority that few other actors could touch."

In August, 1974, three months before *The Towering Inferno*'s release, as part of the advance publicity in connection with the picture, 20th Century-Fox was able to arrange for Steve McQueen to be named an "honorary Los Angeles fire fighter," complete with an official City Hall ceremony.

The rest of the all-star cast (ingredient number two for any disaster-movie recipe) was a true cross section of famous names and faces, some old-timers as well as newcomers, sports figures, and even soap stars. Appearing as those hapless folks whose lives were about to be changed were William Holden, Faye Dunaway, Fred Astaire, Susan Blakely, Richard Chamberlain, Jennifer Jones, O. J. Simpson, Robert Vaughn, Robert Wagner, and Susan Flannery. According to *Inside Oscar,* Paul Newman, still fuming over his credits feud, cracked, "Hell, we all know who the real star of this movie is—that damned fire."

But the film's special effects were probably closer to the real "star"— visuals that made us believe for a harrowing 165 minutes that we were actually watching a burning 138-story skyscraper. Fox built a four-story section of a building for the elevator sequence, with matte paintings and miniatures inserted into the shot for added realism. The exterior of the Hyatt Regency in San Francisco doubled for the skyscraper itself. Dummies were substituted for people being blown out of windows. In all, a team of 25 stuntmen and stuntwomen, under the supervision of coordinator Paul Stader, performed more than 200 individual stunts during the filming.

Paul D. Zimmerman of *Newsweek* loathed the film, yet for some unknown reason, the last paragraph of his review sounds like a course in Film Analysis 101: "The glass tower becomes a combustible symbol of American affluence, built precariously on rotten foundations. 'Towering Inferno' senses that beneath the best of everything lurks the worst of everything. And its torrential climax, when a roomful of enormous top-floor water tanks is blown up, can be read as an apocalyptic ritual cleansing of all that is decayed in our society."

Was this really true? Did anybody really care? Here's what really happened: a big building caught fire, some people died, some lived, audiences loved it, and Fox and Warners made off with a lot of loot—nearly quadruple their $14,000,000 investment. No covert symbolism in that.

Screenplay by Stirling Silliphant

Based on the novels *The Tower* by Richard Martin Stern and *The Glass Inferno* by Thomas N. Scortia and Frank M. Robinson

Produced by Irwin Allen

Directed by John Guillermin

Action scenes directed by Irwin Allen

CAST

Fire Chief O'Hallorhan	Steve McQueen
Doug Roberts	Paul Newman
Jim Duncan	William Holden
Susan	Faye Dunaway
Harlee Claiborne	Fred Astaire
Simmons	Richard Chamberlain
Lisolette	Jennifer Jones

ACADEMY AWARD NOMINATIONS

8 nominations, 3 wins*

Best Picture
Best Supporting Actor (Fred Astaire)
*Best Cinematography
Best Art Direction–Set Decoration
Best Sound
*Best Song ("We May Never Love Like This Again," music and words by Al Kasha and Joel Hirschhorn)
Best Original Dramatic Score (John Williams)
*Best Film Editing

BLAZING SADDLES

WARNER BROS.
$47,800,000

"I must have killed more men than Cecil B. DeMille." —GENE WILDER

MEL BROOKS' humor is a lot like the ads they used to run for Levy's rye bread—you don't have to be Jewish to enjoy it (but it couldn't hurt). The man is simply off-the-wall *meshugge,* and his send-up of the Western genre in *Blazing Saddles* has become a classic in a very short time. The laughs, puns, and surprises come so fast and furious that if you don't already have one, it's worth buying a VCR for this film alone, just so you can reverse-scan for the quickies you're bound to miss on first viewing. There's the sign proclaiming "Howard Johnson's Ice Cream Parlor—1 flavor"; star Cleavon Little's Gucci-emblazoned saddlebags; and Mel Brooks as the Jewish Indian Chief speaking Yiddish to Cleavon's wagon train. Brooks also wrote three songs for the soundtrack—"I'm Tired," "The French Mistake," and "The Ballad of Rock Ridge."

Outstanding comedy casting by Brooks, who directed and co-scripted, enhances the fun: Cleavon Little as the new black sheriff, Harvey Korman as Hedy—oops! that's *Hedley*—Lamarr,

Screenplay by Mel Brooks, Norman Steinberg, Andrew Bergman, Richard Pryor, and Alan Uger

Based on a story by Andrew Bergman

Produced by Michael Hertzberg

Directed by Mel Brooks

CAST

Bart . . . . .Cleavon Little
Jim . . . . .Gene Wilder
Gov. Leoetomane/
 Indian Chief . . . . . . .Mel Brooks
Hedley Lamarr . . . . . . .Harvey Korman
Lili Von Shtupp . . . . .Madeline Kahn

ACADEMY AWARD NOMINATIONS

3 nominations, no wins

Best Supporting Actress (Madeline Kahn)
Best Song ("Blazing Saddles," music by
 John Morris, words by Mel Brooks)
Best Film Editing

and Gene Wilder and Madeline Kahn, a team Brooks would use separately and together in future comedies. Kahn has perhaps the best role in the film, lisping her way through a Marlene Dietrich take-off as Lili von Shtupp (the name is a Yiddish vulgarism, just like it sounds). Only Brooks could get away with having her spout lines like "I'm not a wabbit—I need some west," and her appreciative glee after sizing up Cleavon Little and discovering that he's *not:* "It's twue, it's twue!"

The hilarious comedy was a huge hit at the box office, and with the critics as well. *Newsweek* proclaimed the picture an "insane take-off on the classic Western...triggering laughs that measure a full ten on the Richter scale." *Variety*'s reviewer, although he found the R-rated language "incessant," wrote that "if comedies are measured solely by the number of yocks they generate from audiences, then Mel Brooks' 'Blazing Saddles' must be counted a success...Few viewers will have time between laughs to complain that pic is essentially a raunchy, protracted version of a television comedy skit."

In fact, *Blazing Saddles* generated almost a cultlike following with the college crowd, and continues to find an audience today whenever it is shown on TV. Rent the uncut version on videocassette so you won't miss out on some of the decidedly adult humor.

YOUNG FRANKENSTEIN

20TH CENTURY-FOX
$38,823,000

"Pardon me boy, is this the Transylvania Station?"

"Ya, ya—Track 29. Can I give you a shine?" —DIALOGUE EXCHANGE

THE ABOVE NONSENSE is typical of Mel Brooks' humor: audiences groan with mock disdain but love every second of it. 1974 was definitely the Year of Mel Brooks. After the success of *Blazing Saddles* earlier that year, Brooks' *Young Frankenstein* ("That's Fr*ah*nkenste*en*") fired the second salvo of irreverent humor. Having given us his send-up of the Western genre, Brooks now tackled the classic horror film of the '30s—the original chiller simply titled *Frankenstein*.

The idea of remaking *Frankenstein* was certainly not a new one. The same year would also see a campy 3-D bomb called *Andy Warhol's Frankenstein,* and there have been at least 16 other films about the monster first described by 19th-century novelist Mary Shelley.

Brooks' *Young Frankenstein* is certainly the most financially successful of them all, since he chose to parody the two original (and best) of the lot, *Frankenstein* and *Bride of Frankenstein.* Brooks carefully duplicated the look and feel of the black-and-white classic,

right down to the use of the original Frankenstein laboratory equipment borrowed from Universal Studios, complete with discharging bolts of electricity and skyward-rising platform. Film techniques such as "wipes" and "irising" for scene transitions make this a true parody of the original.

Screenplay by Gene Wilder and Mel Brooks

Based on characters created by
Mary Shelley

Produced by Michael Gruskoff

Directed by Mel Brooks

CAST

Dr. Frankenstein . . . . . .Gene Wilder
Monster . . . . .Peter Boyle
Igor . . . . .Marty Feldman
Elizabeth . . . . .Madeline Kahn
Frau Blucher . . . . .Cloris Leachman
Blind Man . . . . .Gene Hackman

ACADEMY AWARD NOMINATIONS

2 nominations, no wins

Best Screenplay Adapted from Other
    Material
Best Sound

Superb casting heightened the fun of the film. *Newsweek*'s comments summed it up best: "The poodle-haired [Gene] Wilder, in his finest performance to date, is aided by a puckish, addled Igor (Marty Feldman), whose hump keeps shifting shoulders, as well as by the scary Frau Blucher (Cloris Leachman), whose very name makes horses rear. But when [Peter] Boyle takes life, so does the movie, leading to two of the great scenes in screen comedy." The scenes referred to were the musical "Puttin' on the Ritz" number, in which Wilder and his monster, dressed to the nines, break into a tap dance, and the encounter with the blind hermit (Gene Hackman), a klutz who keeps injuring the poor creature.

Another fine performance, often overlooked and underrated, was that of Teri Garr as the German girl, Inga. Known mostly as a television actress prior to this movie (she had guest-starred on a "Star Trek" episode, "Assignment: Earth," when she was only 19, and later became a regular on "The Sonny and Cher Show"), Teri went on to a prosperous career as a character actress for the next several decades, and continued making movies well into the 1990s.

EARTHQUAKE

UNIVERSAL
$35,849,994

"This used to be a helluva town!"
—LLOYD NOLAN

IN THE CONTINUING saga of the disaster film genre, so far there had been tragedy in the skies, on the sea, and in a towering edifice. With *Earthquake,* we were now told that we didn't have to leave home to experience the ultimate in terror—even the very ground under our feet wasn't safe anymore. And this film went them all one better by adding a new dimension of *audience participation,* thanks to a sound system Universal Studios termed "Sensurround." Linked to one of the soundtracks, the low-frequency vibrations made theaters appear to experience "tremors" during the actual earthquake footage; although any stereo buff (and his next-door neighbor) knows you can achieve the same effect at home by turning up the bass on your hi-fi. For this privilege, exhibitors were charged an additional $500 a week by the distributor, while signs in the lobby as well as an on-screen disclaimer warned the squeamish to beware.

It was an added gimmick that more than paid off as moviegoers returned several times for the experience.

Screenplay by George Fox and Mario Puzo

Executive Producer: Jennings Lang

Produced and directed by Mark Robson

CAST

Graft . . . . .Charlton Heston
Remy Graft . . . . .Ava Gardner
Patrolman Slade . . . . .George Kennedy
Royce . . . . .Lorne Greene
Denise . . . . .Genevieve Bujold

ACADEMY AWARD NOMINATIONS

4 nominations, 1 win*

Best Cinematography
Best Art Direction–Set Decoration
*Best Sound
Best Film Editing

This year there were no nominations per se for Best Visual Effects, but the Academy singled out *Earthquake* for a Special Achievement Award for Visual Effects.

(*Midway,* a war movie using the same system, failed to produce the same financial results.) The "star" of the show, the actual quake itself, doesn't appear for quite some time, although there are a few "foreshocks." First, we must meet our all-star cast. Let's see…this time we have Charlton Heston (you just know he's going to make it to the end), Ava Gardner as his bitchy wife, George Kennedy, Lorne Greene, Genevieve Bujold, Richard Roundtree, Marjoe Gortner as The Bad Guy, Barry Sullivan, Lloyd Nolan, Victoria Principal, and Walter Matthau as The Drunk (a cameo billed under his real name, Walter Matuschanskayasky). When the film was recut for TV, 18 minutes of new material was included, which added a character played by Debralee Scott.

The title disaster is supposedly a 9.9 on the Richter scale. All told, we experience 11 actual minutes of shaking, during which time we see the total wasting of Los Angeles (the helluva town mourned by Lloyd Nolan above).

Landslides, crumbling skyscrapers, dam bursts, floods, flames, collapsing bridges, ground fissures opening—you name it, this film's got it. The effects combined mattes, miniatures, and real footage of L.A. very convincingly, although it is obvious when "camera shakes" were used, and one carload of plastic toy cows going over the side of a bridge leaves much to be desired. There was potential danger from all the falling debris and trick shots, providing work for 141 stuntpeople, a Hollywood record.

In the predawn hours of January 17, 1994, Los Angeles residents were awakened to what many thought was the long-awaited "Big One." The 6.8 earthquake did extensive damage and caused loss of life. Universal Studios, reacting with sensitivity, closed the "Earthquake" ride on the studio tour for several weeks. (Author's note: As an L.A. earthquake survivor, I'm fairly confident that the ride would have seemed pretty tame compared to the real thing anyway.)

THE TRIAL OF BILLY JACK

WARNER BROS.
$31,100,000

WHEN LAST WE SAW Billy Jack, he was being hauled off to prison, even though we, the audience, knew he was right. Could a situation like this go unresolved? Not for Tom Laughlin, who had turned that first low-budget "protest" film (see page 218) into a $32,500,000 winner. It was a sleeper of a picture, one that seemed the most unlikely candidate for a sequel, and a successful one at that. Nevertheless, that's exactly what happened.

Tom and his wife, Delores (Taylor), were back, re-creating their previous roles (actually, Laughlin had originated the character of Billy Jack in a 1967 motorcycle gang "B" movie), and not much else is new. Billy's out of jail now, but there are still battles to be fought on behalf of the American Indians and his wife's progressive Freedom School. And again, the message is "nonviolence," meaning that violence should be used only when absolutely necessary, which is about once every five minutes in this film. A Kent State–type massacre by National Guardsmen drives this point home at the picture's climax.

Why were these films so popular? Obviously, there were no big all-star casts. Actors included Laughlin, his wife, his 16-year-old daughter Teresa, director William Wellman's son, Bill Jr., plus an assortment of Native American actors such as Buffalo Horse, Rolling Thunder, Guy Greymountain, Oshannah Fastwolf, and Sacheen Littlefeather (Marlon Brando's proxy at the 1972 Oscar ceremony). There was no Big Name director, either. Tom's son Frank handled those chores. About the biggest name in *The Trial of Billy Jack*'s credits was Elmer Bernstein, the renowned composer, who did the soundtrack.

One theory for the success of this movie was offered by *Variety,* which thought it was due to the "deliberate pitch [it] made to attract youth and 'rebel' audiences." Were there really that many rebels out there? *The New York Times'* reviewer had a different theory: "The average American is a sucker for anything described as homemade. Slap that label on candy, cookies, ice cream, canned soups and…[the American consumer] will buy it, no matter what it tastes like…In at least one respect, 'The Trial of Billy Jack' really is home-made…the only thing the Laughlins aren't doing is making the popcorn being sold in the theaters."

Most reviewers had trouble making sense out of the movie's huge following. This mattered not at all to the Laughlin Family Filmmakers, who followed with yet another sequel, *Billy Jack Goes to Washington* (1977). Like that other man who went to Washington back in 1939,* writer-director-star Tom Laughlin takes on corruption in the Senate in this film. But many thought he had overstepped his bounds this time, and *Billy Jack Goes to Washington* bombed.

---

*Jimmy Stewart in *Mr. Smith Goes to Washington* (see page 19).

Screenplay by Frank and Teresa
  Christina

Produced by Joe Cramer

Directed by Frank Laughlin

CAST

Billy Jack . . . . . . .Tom Laughlin
Jean Roberts . . . .Delores Taylor
Doc . . . . .Victor Izay
Carol . . . . .Teresa Laughlin
National
  Guardsman . . .William Wellman, Jr.

JAWS

UNIVERSAL
$129,549,325

WHAT DO A nude girl, a boy on a raft, a dog, a pier, and a fisherman all have in common? Yes, the answer is: shark food. But not for just any shark. These individuals and objects were all on the menu for *Jaws,* the first megahit for Steven Spielberg. The picture had the honor of being the first film to break the $100,000,000 mark in rentals, becoming the highest grossing film to that date and surpassing previous record-holders *The Godfather, The Sound of Music,* and *Gone With the Wind* (if inflation is not taken into account).

The novel had been a best-seller, so it was only a matter of time before it became a movie. The Peter Benchley novel had five and a half million copies in print at the time the rights were purchased by Richard Zanuck and his partner David Brown for a paltry $175,000. Benchley was signed to write the script as well, but it underwent five drafts before completion, including a final polish by Carl Gottlieb, who received co-credit. (Watch for Benchley as a reporter.)

Steven Spielberg was only 26 when he was assigned director's chores on this $12,000,000 picture. At age 20, the young man had bluffed his way onto

the Universal lot, acting as if he belonged there by setting up shop in an empty office. Pretty soon studio executives began to accept him and, after viewing some of his clever student film efforts, handed him some TV directing assignments, including

---

Screenplay by Peter Benchley and Carl Gottlieb

Based on the novel by Peter Benchley

Produced by Richard D. Zanuck and David Brown

Directed by Steven Spielberg

CAST

Chief Martin Brody	Roy Scheider
Quint	Robert Shaw
Matt Hooper	Richard Dreyfuss
Ellen Brody	Lorraine Gary
Mayor Vaughn	Murray Hamilton

ACADEMY AWARD NOMINATIONS

4 nominations, 3 wins*

 Best Picture
*Best Sound
*Best Original Score (John Williams)
*Best Film Editing

---

episodes of the series "Night Gallery." His early film credits included a thriller called *Duel* (a movie-of-the-week pitting Dennis Weaver against a crazed truck driver) and his only feature, *The Sugarland Express,* a technically difficult picture that convinced the execs at Universal that he was right for *Jaws.*

Spielberg insisted that the film be shot on location rather than in a tank to give it the realism he wanted. "I could have shot the movie in the tank, or even in a protected lake somewhere, but it would not have looked the same," the director told *Time.* Martha's Vineyard was finally selected as the fictional village of Amity, although the residents were less than thrilled at the prospect of having 150 members of a movie crew despoiling their lovely island. Greed won out, however, when they realized the boost this would give local businesses.

Since it's hard to find 20-foot white sharks that can take direction well, the company hired special effects expert Robert A. Mattey to construct a mechanical shark (Mattey had once created the giant squid for Walt Disney's *20,000 Leagues Under the Sea).* Actually, Mattey whipped up three pseudosharks, collectively dubbed "Bruce." Each hydraulically operated plastic creature weighed a ton and a half and cost $150,000. It took 13 scuba-geared technicians to operate the Bruces, which broke down with regularity.

Despite the problems, the film was a huge sensation when it hit the screens just in time for summer. Enormous block-long lines were commonplace wherever it was shown—thanks to word of mouth and the publicity department at Universal, which hyped every shark sighting up and down both the Atlantic and Pacific coasts. Shark hysteria reached an all-time high as the poor, mostly inoffensive creatures were hunted and strung up like Nazi war criminals.

The success of *Jaws* and the baby-faced Spielberg was aided by three human stars as well. Richard Dreyfuss, who had made a couple of moderately successful hits like *American Graffiti* and *The Apprenticeship of Duddy Kravitz,* was certain he was starring in what would turn out to be "the turkey of the year." Fortunately, he was wrong, and the actor, who is the same age as Spielberg, was later given the starring role in one of Spielberg's biggest hits, *Close Encounters of the Third Kind.* Actor Robert Shaw, who had appeared in top hits such as *From Russia With Love* and *The Sting,* was also reluctant to play opposite a shark, terming the story "a piece of shit." Fortunately, his wife disagreed and convinced him to take the part of the crusty old salt who goes after the shark with a vengeance. Rounding out the cast was Roy Scheider (Oscar-nominated in *The French Connection*) as the local sheriff, a role he would repeat in *Jaws*equels.

An unusual star was born from this film, but was never actually seen on camera. Composer John Williams, who had been nominated for an Oscar for his *Towering Inferno* score, won his first Academy Award for his driving music in *Jaws.* The oft-parodied theme brilliantly underscores the anticipatory danger the audience feels well before the shark is ever seen.

Jaws spawned a school of sequels and imitation films plus piles of merchandise all bearing the familiar open-mouthed shark logo, while making piles of money for Universal. A few years later, the studio added a lake to its tour attraction, complete with full-scale town and billboard proclaiming "Amity Island Welcomes You." On cue, Bruce the Shark swam directly toward the tour tram and leaped at the visitors sitting on the right. That is, most of the time; there were those rare occasions when the tour shark was "on a break" (read: break*down*), just like his movie counterpart, Bruce.

ONE FLEW OVER THE CUCKOO'S NEST

UNITED ARTISTS
$59,939,701

IT TOOK 13 years for Ken Kesey's 1962 cult novel about life in a mental ward and a victim of the system to be made into a film. In 1963, the book had been brought to the Broadway stage by Kirk Douglas; after 11 weeks, the play closed (although it did have a successful run off-Broadway starting in March, 1971, with William Devane in the lead role). Douglas attempted to bring it to the screen for years. He eventually turned his option over to son Michael Douglas, then the star of the TV series "The Streets of San Francisco." By "packaging" the property to include Jack Nicholson in the lead, Douglas the younger, now co-producer, was able to raise the $3,000,000 in backing that he needed to make his film. The results proved spectacular, helping to put United Artists (who wisely agreed to release the independent production) on top of the box office in the year following its release.

The icing on the cake came at Oscar

Screenplay by Lawrence Hauben and Bo Goldman

From the novel by Ken Kesey

Produced by Saul Zaentz and Michael Douglas

Directed by Milos Forman

CAST

Randel P. McMurphy . . .Jack Nicholson
Nurse Ratched . . . . . . .Louise Fletcher
Harding . . . . .William Redfield
Orderly Turkle . . . . . . .Scatman Crothers
Martini . . . . .Danny De Vito

ACADEMY AWARD NOMINATIONS

9 nominations, 5 wins *

*Best Picture
*Best Actor (Jack Nicholson)
*Best Actress (Louise Fletcher)
 Best Supporting Actor (Brad Dourif)
*Best Director (Milos Forman)
*Best Screenplay Adapted from Other Material (Lawrence Hauben and Bo Goldman)
 Best Cinematography
 Best Original Score
 Best Film Editing

time, when the Academy blessed *Cuckoo's Nest* with the "Big Five" Awards—Best Picture, Actor, Actress, Director, and Screenplay—the first time this feat had been achieved since 1934's *It Happened One Night.* This shot in the arm saw the take at the box office increase by 70 percent as moviegoers came to see what all the fuss was about.

They weren't disappointed. The counterculture novel adapted well to the screen, with Nicholson giving the performance of his life. *The New York Times* wrote that he "slips into the role of Randel [McMurphy] with such easy grace that it's difficult to remember him in any other film." *Newsweek* went even further, proclaiming that "McMurphy is the ultimate Nicholson performance—the last angry crazy profane wise-guy rebel, blowing himself up in the shrapnel of his own liberating laughter."

Louise Fletcher, in the role of the detestable Nurse Ratched, received

equal acclaim. It was only her second feature; she had concentrated on TV in her early career and later took time out to raise a family. Her performance caught the attention of both the press and her peers in the Academy. When she received her Oscar for Best Actress, she gave an acceptance speech in deaf sign language, the first person ever to do so (both her parents had been deaf from childhood and she was raised "bilingual").

The production was filmed on location at the Oregon State Mental Hospital, with many of the patients playing minor parts and helping the crew. The only mishap occurred when one of the grips (men in charge of setting up equipment) accidentally left a protective screen open on a window after running in cable from the outside, and a patient jumped through the window backwards, falling three floors and fracturing his shoulder. The Salem, Oregon, newspaper headlined: "ONE FLEW *OUT* OF THE CUCKOO'S NEST."

THE ROCKY HORROR PICTURE SHOW

20TH CENTURY-FOX
$40,420,000

> *"I wanna go to the late night double
> feature picture show, by RKO."*
> —LYRIC TO "SCIENCE FICTION/
> DOUBLE FEATURE"

IT WAS BORN in the mind of Richard O'Brien as *They Came From Denton High,* but by the time British producer Michael White (*Sleuth, Oh! Calcutta*) had brought it to the stage, it had been rechristened *The Rocky Horror Show.* The musical spoof of '50s monster movies was spotted by American producer and director Lou Adler, who booked it into his Roxy Theatre on the Sunset Strip in L.A. Even as the play was enjoying a line-around-the-block run, Adler was negotiating the film deal with 20th Century-Fox. What emerged is the biggest cult film of all time.

The Rocky Horror Picture Show opened to very negative reviews by very confused critics. What was this weird thing on the screen about a singing transsexual transvestite from Transylvania in kinky underwear? Both *The Hollywood Reporter* and *Variety* faulted the film for lacking the excitement and sparkle of the stage version; if the critics were to be believed, this was the turkey of all time.

Over at Fox they were about to conduct the post mortem and use the film as a tax write-off when something happened. Like the very monsters the film was sending up, the film seemed to rise from the freshly dug grave and take on a life of its own. Theater owners who

were filling only 50 seats in their 800-seat venues noticed that the *same* 50 people were returning every week, seeing the picture again and again. In the Westwood area of Los Angeles, the theater was selling out every night, not to a new crowd, but to the *same* audience. And the people were singing the songs along with the characters on the screen. The songs were simple enough for a 10-year-old to mimic, admitted the producers. Songs like "Dammit Janet," "Sweet Transvestite," and "Time Warp" had both catchy lyrics and lively rock music. But it wasn't *The Sound of Music,* so why were there so many repeats? Something was happening here.

The film was kept alive by an underground following that refused to let it die. Soon it broke into the midnight circuit in New York City, and in a few weeks word of mouth had produced a flood of exhibitors' requests in Fox's distribution offices begging for a print in Cleveland, Austin, Toronto, Philadelphia…the list goes on and on, and so does the picture. Even in the mid-1990s, midnight showings of the film could still be found in several cities around the U.S.

But this *is* a film of a different color. The key to the phenomenon is audience participation. Fans attend the

Saturday midnight show prepared for an evening of fun. They arrive in costume, dressed as their favorite on-screen character, many wearing Tim Curry drag makeup, she-bitch hose, and garter belts. During the next hour and a half, they will *become* that person. Others come armed with rice to throw in the film's early wedding sequence, squirt guns to shoot during the rainy scene, toast for the "toast," flashlights, Scott toilet paper, and playing cards. Everyone knows and recites every line and song lyric of the film, often talking back to the actors as if fusing with the fantasy. For a "virgin," it is often difficult to know what's going on.

After years of underground videocassettes circulated by die-hard *Rocky Horror* fans, 20th Century-Fox finally released the movie on home video in the early '90s. Rather than trashing movie theaters (always a drawback for theater owners, tired of sweeping up rice and toilet paper streamers every Sunday morning at 2:00 A.M.), fans are now free to throw rice and squirt water guns at their own TV sets. Fox, however, couldn't have been happier with the success of *The Rocky Horror Picture Show,* proving there is occasionally life after premature celluloid death has been pronounced.

Screenplay by Jim Sharman and
   Richard O'Brien

Based on the stage musical by
   Richard O'Brien

Executive Producer: Lou Adler

Produced by Michael White

Directed by Jim Sharman

CAST

Frank N. Furter	Tim Curry
Janet Weiss	Susan Sarandon
Brad Majors	Barry Bostwick
Riff Raff	Richard O'Brien
Dr. Everett Scott	Jonathan Adams

SHAMPOO

COLUMBIA
$23,822,000

"November 4, 1968. Election eve."
—OPENING CARD

DON'T LET the opening card mislead you. This film about a male beauty operator (in the literal sense) had very little to do with the election. If it's about the eve of anything, it's the start of the sexual revolution, and Warren Beatty fires the first shot. What's more, he takes no prisoners in this farcical, triangular romp through the bedrooms of Southern California.

There is certainly nothing new in the story line about a swinging bachelor in the pre-AIDS years of promiscuity. So producer-writer-star Beatty found a way to turn the standard plot into a sure-fire winner at the box office and pick up a few Oscar nominations along the way—he chose beautiful and talented leading ladies with appeal to both sexes. Goldie Hawn had won a Best Supporting Actress Oscar for *Cactus Flower* in 1969; Julie Christie won Best Actress in 1965's *Darling,* as well as another nomination in *McCabe and Mrs. Miller* (1971); and Lee Grant had won an Emmy for her role in TV's "Peyton Place" and one for a TV movie, *The Neon Ceiling* (1971).

Beatty excelled at spotting future star talent, a gift he used successfully in the film. Carrie Fisher, then 17-year-old offspring of Eddie Fisher and Debbie Reynolds, played a minor role in *Shampoo*—her first film appearance. She would be selected by George Lucas a few years later to play Princess Leia, the only female role in his *Star Wars* saga. And it was during the music scoring sessions of this film that Carrie met her future ex-husband, Paul Simon, when Beatty selected that half of the erstwhile Simon & Garfunkel team to do the music.

Another fine performer in a lead role was Jack Warden. He received an Oscar nomination also, and television viewers will probably best remember him as the star of "Crazy Like a Fox," which ran on CBS during the early 1980s.

Watch for a walk-on by Howard Hessman, another future TV star. Hessman co-starred in "WKRP in Cincinnati" and later starred in his own show, "Head of the Class."

When *Shampoo* was released in 1975, it was not well received by the critics, despite its fine cast and script. As *Variety* said, "All the excellent creative components do not add up to a whole," and *The Hollywood Reporter* termed the film "slick, hip entertainment, but also pretty shallow and cynical." *Shampoo* seems dated when you watch it today: the '70s seem very, very long ago, and the '60s time frame makes this film even more like ancient history.

Screenplay by Robert Towne and
  Warren Beatty

Produced by Warren Beatty

Directed by Hal Ashby

CAST

George	.Warren Beatty
Jackie	.Julie Christie
Jill	.Goldie Hawn
Felicia	.Lee Grant
Lester	.Jack Warden
Johnny Pope	.Tony Bill
Lorna	.Carrie Fisher

ACADEMY AWARD NOMINATIONS

4 nominations, 1 win*

  Best Supporting Actor (Jack Warden)
*Best Supporting Actress (Lee Grant)
  Best Original Screenplay
  Best Art Direction–Set Decoration

DOG DAY AFTERNOON

WARNER BROS.
$22,500,000

"I'm a Catholic and I don't want to hurt anybody."—AL PACINO (SONNY)

"How beautiful you were when you were a baby." —JUDITH MALINE (SONNY'S MOTHER)

WERE IT NOT for the fine acting, fine directing, fine scripting, fine… everything, this would be just another police-crime drama about a bank robbery on a hot afternoon in Brooklyn. Although the line is never said, the only cliché that is missing is the familiar "We've got the place surrounded—come out with your hands up."

What makes this different is that we're shown the robbery from the POV of the *robber.* Al Pacino is Sonny, a "nice boy" to his family, a bisexual loved by both his wives, female and male, who keeps digging himself in deeper and deeper, taking us along with him. It is a study in madness, the same kind of madness that once saw Patty Hearst joining her captors. We, the audience, are made to feel the pressures Sonny feels and not the fears of the hostages that are so typical of this sort of film. It might seem

Based on a magazine article by P. F. Kluge and Thomas Moore

Screenplay by Frank Pierson

Produced by Martin Bregman and Martin Elfand

Directed by Sidney Lumet

CAST

Sonny	Al Pacino
Sal	John Cazale
Moretti	Charles Durning
Leon	Chris Sarandon
Jenny	Carol Kane

ACADEMY AWARD NOMINATIONS

6 nominations, 1 win*

Best Picture
Best Actor (Al Pacino)
Best Supporting Actor (Chris Sarandon)
Best Director (Sidney Lumet)
*Best Original Screenplay (Frank Pierson)
Best Film Editing

like fantastic fiction were it not reality-based. At the beginning of the film we are told: "What you are about to see is true—it happened in Brooklyn, New York on August 22, 1972." There ought to be another mention later in the picture, since one tends to forget this could really have taken place. Only at the end are we reminded this was a factual story, when we learn that Sonny was sentenced to 20 years.

Al Pacino gives a powerful performance, so effective it seems almost ad-libbed. His acting technique—the nuances, the gestures, a look here, a nervous tic there—rightfully earned him the Oscar nomination. (He also received nominations for *Godfather I* and his other Lumet-directed film, *Serpico.*) *Godfather I* and *II* made him a star; *Dog Day Afternoon* showcased

him as an actor. The intensity of his performance was not without a price—about halfway through the production, Pacino collapsed from exhaustion and had to be hospitalized for a short time. He swore off movies for a while, returning to his first love, the Broadway stage.

John Cazale gives a memorable performance as Sal, Sonny's partner-in-crime. Cazale had also worked in both *Godfather* pictures, playing Pacino's brother Fredo.

One of the hostages, a young actress named Carol Kane, is worth noting. Ms. Kane received a nomination for Best Actress in 1975 for her starring role in *Hester Street.* She went on to co-star in TV's "Taxi" as well as numerous other films and television series.

ROCKY

UNITED ARTISTS
$56,524,972

HOLLYWOOD LOVES a rags-to-riches tale almost as much as it loves a film about a successful underdog. With *Rocky,* audiences got both and United Artists helped reap the profits. Everyone was a winner.

It almost didn't happen. Thirty-year-old Sylvester Stallone had already written and received rejections on 32 scripts. With a pregnant wife and $106 in his bank account, he sat down to write script number 33. He called it *Rocky,* and within three days the fact-based account of a has-been fighter who stages a comeback and winds up heavyweight boxing champ of the world was completed. It was grabbed by producers Irwin Winkler and Robert Chartoff, who saw it as a star vehicle for the likes of Burt Reynolds or Robert Redford (everyone, it seems, automatically thought of Redford for everything). But Stallone would have no part of a deal that didn't include himself in the lead. He had been a struggling actor even before he was a struggling writer, plus he had the right bod for the role. With a budget just slightly under $1,000,000, the company completed principal photography in 28 days ("the gestation time for a water bug," Stallone pointed out to *The New York Times*), shooting on location in Philadelphia and Los Angeles.

Rocky became the sleeper of the decade and established the formula for the film's Roman-numeraled sequels. Rocky is down and out, but circumstances beyond his control compel him into just one more fight, a fight there's no way in hell he can win. We see him training like an automaton, with lots of sweat and tears (the blood comes later in the ring when he's punished beyond belief). Yes, he wins the bout, but by that time, we've been suckered in and cheered him on like one of our own family, so that when he wins against all the odds, it's practically an orgasmic moment. Audiences almost always cheer wildly, breaking into spontaneous applause, because *Rocky* and the sequels are inspiring, uplifting, stand-up-and-cheer pictures. Rocky Balboa is a hero, a man of the people, and we needed heroes in that decade of Nixon and Watergate. Stallone was quoted by

Academy Awards Illustrated as saying: "It was never a script about boxing. It was always about a man simply fighting for his dignity. People require symbols of humanity and heroism."

Like Rocky himself, this picture came from behind to take the top prize of the Motion Picture Academy—the Oscar for Best Picture. And the contenders were all heavyweights: *All the President's Men, Bound for Glory, Network,* and *Taxi Driver.* Clearly, *Rocky* captured the hearts of Academy members as well as their highest award.

Stallone himself personally made it into the record books as a double Oscar nominee (as actor and screenwriter), a rare feat accomplished at the time by

---

Screenplay by Sylvester Stallone

Executive Producer: Gene Kirkwood

Produced by Irwin Winkler and
Robert Chartoff

Directed by John G. Avildsen

CAST

Rocky Balboa	Sylvester Stallone
Adrian	Talia Shire
Paulie	Burt Young
Apollo Creed	Carl Weathers
Mickey	Burgess Meredith

ACADEMY AWARD NOMINATIONS

*10 nominations, 3 wins ***

*Best Picture
 Best Actor (Sylvester Stallone)
 Best Actress (Talia Shire)
 Best Supporting Actor (Burgess Meredith)
 Best Supporting Actor (Burt Young)
*Best Director (John G. Avildsen)
 Best Screenplay Written Directly for the
   Screen
 Best Sound
 Best Original Song ("Gonna Fly Now,"
   music by Bill Conti, words by Carol
   Connors and Ayn Robbins)
*Best Film Editing

While not winning the Oscar, the single version of "Gonna Fly Now—The Theme from *Rocky*" rose to number one on the *Billboard* charts for the week of July 2, 1977.

---

only two others—Charles Chaplin, for *The Great Dictator* (1940), and Orson Welles, for *Citizen Kane* (1941).

Stallone's co-stars were more like props supporting the centerpiece, but their performances were admirable. Burgess Meredith had become popular back in the late '60s when he played "The Penguin" on TV's "Batman." As Rocky's trainer, Mickey, he found another continuing character he would play in two films to come. The 68-year-old veteran of over 100 films received a Best Supporting Actor nomination, his first recognition by the Academy. He had co-starred in many popular films, including *Advise and Consent* (1962), *The Cardinal* (1963), *Hurry Sundown* (1967), *The Day of the Locust* (1975), and *The Hindenburg* (1975). According to the book *Inside Oscar,* the attention at the Awards ceremony night caused him to comment: "Believe it or not, *Rocky* is my first smash hit out of 120 films. I had many successes artistically, but nothing like *Rocky.*"

Talia Shire played Rocky's lady-love (and later his wife), the only woman's part of any consequence; she's a subservient nonfeminist type, whom audiences met before in the two *Godfather* movies (Shire is Francis Coppola's sister). She appeared in several Roger Corman "B" movies under her maiden name of Talia Coppola before her break in her brother's film. *The New York Times* reserved what little praise it had for Talia Shire: "She's a real actress, genuinely touching and funny as an incipient spinster who comes late to sexual life. She's so good, in fact, that she almost gives weight to Mr. Stallone's performance, which is the large hole in the center of the film." The remainder of the review went on to trash Stallone's performance in no uncertain terms. Did "Sly" (his friends' nickname for him) mind? Not in the least. He had 10 percent of the profits in his contract...for a man who began with $106 in his pocket, that's a lot of money. And he thought of this picture as a one-shot—his next role, he hoped, might be the upcoming movie of *Superman.* But he was never offered that part; it went to another underdog.

2
A STAR IS BORN
WARNER BROS.
$37,100,000

REMAKES are commonplace in the movie industry. The feeling seems to be that if a story is good, it is worth retelling. Even Shakespeare was known to rework a classic story or two. And in Hollywood, a successful remake can often top its predecessor. Such was the case of *The Ten Commandments* (see page 122), *Ben-Hur* (see page 140), and *Cleopatra* (see page 166). All had been successful films of the '20s, yet the remakes surpassed the original in both scope and financial success.

This was the thought of Barbra Streisand and her First Artists production company when they acquired the rights to *A Star Is Born*. But this was not a simple remake of a classic film; it was already a thrice-told tale. The first version, directed by George Cukor, was called *What Price Hollywood* back in 1932, and starred Constance Bennett as the ingenue who rises to the top at the expense of others. It served as the blueprint for the original film titled *A Star Is Born*, the Janet Gaynor–Frederic March 1937 version

that is termed a "classic" today. Then, in 1954, Cukor again directed *A Star Is Born*, starring Judy Garland (in what many believe to her best acting performance) and James Mason.

Screenwriters John Gregory Dunne and Joan Didion had originally conceived of a way for an updated version of the familiar story to find its modern audience by taking their "star" out of Hollywood for her "birth" and placing her in the world of rock music instead of Screenland. Their first choices for the roles were Carly Simon and James Taylor, who passed on the project. Next they considered Liza Minnelli and Elvis Presley, Mick and Bianca Jagger, and even Sonny and Cher. Eventually Jon Peters, Barbra Streisand's hairdresser-turned-producer, obtained the property, and she agreed to star in it. Her co-star choices ranged from Marlon Brando (who had done the musical *Guys and Dolls*) to Elvis Presley. Brando declined, and Presley was already on the way down—the King didn't want this to be the movie he would be remembered

for, even if the two men who had previously played the role had been nominated for Oscars. (Less than a year after the movie's release, Elvis was gone.) Barbra's final choice for co-star was Kris Kristofferson, a singer who could act, an actor who could sing.

Barbra executive-produced this virtual one-woman show as a vehicle for her talents (even her wardrobe was spotlighted—the credit reads: "Ms. Streisand's clothes from her closet"). She obviously has as many fans as the heroine of her story, since the film did incredibly well at the box office, easily surpassing the combined totals of all three previous versions. And while it wasn't the Oscar powerhouse of its forerunners, Streisand managed to pull down an Academy Award for the film's theme song, "Evergreen." The song rose to the top of the *Billboard* charts, where it reached number one in March, 1977, remaining there for three weeks. It also won a Grammy for Song of the Year, while Streisand was voted a Grammy for Best Pop Vocal Performance, Female.

Screenplay by John Gregory Dunne, Joan Didion, and Frank Pierson

Based on a story by William Wellman and Robert Carson

Executive Producer: Barbra Streisand

Produced by Jon Peters

Directed by Frank Pierson

CAST

Esther Hoffman	Barbra Streisand
John Norman Howard . . .	Kris Kristofferson
Brian	Paul Mazursky
Bobby Ritchie	Gary Busey
Gary Danziger	Oliver Clark
Photographer	Sally Kirkland

ACADEMY AWARD NOMINATIONS

4 nominations, 1 win*

Best Cinematography
Best Sound
*Best Song ("Evergreen, Love Theme from
 A Star Is Born," music by Barbra
 Streisand, words by Paul Williams)
Best Original Song Score (Roger
 Kellaway)

KING KONG

PARAMOUNT ·
$36,915,000

"I'm a Libra. What sign are you?"
—JESSICA LANGE TO KING KONG

K ING KONG, that swinging single ape
we all knew and loved in the '30s,
was back, still the perennial bachelor,
size-52 foot(loose) and fancy free. This
time, the studio promised, Kong was
bigger and badder (and meaner than a
junkyard dog).

It was the second remake of the
year (see *A Star Is Born,* page 248),
and like the *Kong* of old, this, too, was
a real crowd pleaser. It was updated, of
course. The original Merian C. Cooper
version had a movie crew stumbling
across the giant anthropoid in the South
Seas; the spectacular $24,000,000 Dino
De Laurentiis remake saw an oil company searching for black gold, the
hottest commodity of the '70s. And for
Kong's demise, the Big Apple's Empire
State Building was deemed too puny for
the Mighty Ape—only the twin towers
of the World Trade Center would do
for his downfall. (Movie posters rather

Screenplay by Lorenzo Semple, Jr.

Based on a story by Edgar Wallace and
Merian C. Cooper

Executive Producers: Federico De
Laurentiis and Christian Ferry

Produced by Dino De Laurentiis

Directed by John Guillermin

CAST

Jack Prescott . . . . .Jeff Bridges
Fred Wilson . . . . .Charles Grodin
Dawn . . . . .Jessica Lange
Capt. Ross . . . . .John Randolph
Bagley . . . . .Rene Auberjonois

ACADEMY AWARD NOMINATIONS

2 nominations, no wins

Best Cinematography
Best Sound

King Kong received a Special Achievement
Award for Visual Effects (Carlo Rambaldi,
Glen Robinson, and Frank Van Der Veer).
Since this was not a contested category,
the Academy also gave the same award to
another film that year, *Logan's Run.*

obscenely depicted the hairy beast
astride the two 110-story buildings.)
Purists were horrified, not by the
creature himself, but at the very
thought of tampering with one of the
classic horror films of all time. The
film took a tongue-in-cheek, campy
attitude one minute, a serious one the
next, making audiences uncertain as
to the film's intent. Was the inane dialogue, like the above parody of '70s
singles-bar ice-breaking chitchat,
meant to be taken seriously? Jessica
Lange, a former fashion model introduced in this film, was saddled with
lines like "You goddamn chauvinist pig
ape!" and "Oh, come on, Kong. Forget
about me. This thing is never gonna
work." Despite this unworthy beginning, Lange persevered in her chosen
career, and eventually won the Best
Actress Oscar for 1994.

Instead of the miniature stop-motion
animation invented by Willis O'Brien,
this new Kong used a combination of
effects to achieve what O'Brien had
done on a tabletop back in the pioneer-
ing days of 1933. First there was
makeup man Rick Baker in a monkey

suit with five different facially expres-
sive masks, depending on Kong's
mood. Then there was a 40-foot-high
mechanical ape weighing six-and-a-half
tons, capable of wiggling his arm, rolling his neck, twitching his ears, rotating his hips, and smiling. There was
also a hydraulically operated arm with
a hand six feet across in which the
gentle giant holds and caresses Ms.
Lange. The genius behind this mechanical miracle was Carlo Rambaldi, who
would go on to become one of the
most sought-after effects men in
Hollywood, later working on *Close
Encounters of the Third Kind* and *E. T.*

While *King Kong* has not replaced
the 1933 version in the hearts and
minds of its enduring fan following
around the world, the remake nevertheless did well at the box office and
more than made back its initial outlay.
In 1986, a sequel was attempted (*King
Kong Lives*), but did poorly.

Perhaps movie makers have now
learned that bigger is not always better. In the case of the remakes of *King
Kong,* to paraphrase an old expression,
"'Twas booty killed the beast."

SILVER STREAK

20TH CENTURY-FOX
$30,018,000

"In ten minutes you're going to have two hundred tons of locomotive smashing its way through Central Station on its way to Marshall Field!" —CHIEF OF POLICE TO AN "AMROAD" OFFICIAL

THE PRODUCERS OF *Silver Streak* (and there were quite of few of them) didn't seem completely certain just what type of genre this film was. More a recipe than a film, it was one part love story, one part action-adventure, one part murder mystery, one part comedy, and one part disaster film (see above dialogue). With something for everyone, one thing was certain— it did well at the box office, although early reviews predicted doom for more than just the runaway train. *Newsweek* called the movie "Train of Fools" and wrote: "It's a sluggish adventure movie about an L.A.-to-Chicago train trip that wastes two considerable talents… when Richard Pryor finally puts in an appearance, well over an hour into the story, his frantic timing and good-natured vulgarity are welcome."

Part of the film's problem for the critics—certainly not with the audience, who returned often enough to push the movie into the year's top five

Screenplay by Colin Higgins

Executive Producers: Frank Yablans and Martin Ransohoff

Produced by Edward K. Milkis and Thomas L. Miller

Directed by Arthur Hiller

CAST

George Caldwell	Gene Wilder
Hilly Burns	Jill Clayburgh
Grover Muldoon	Richard Pryor
Roger Devereau	Patrick McGoohan
Sweet	Ned Beatty

ACADEMY AWARD NOMINATIONS

1 nomination, no wins

Best Sound

—was that Gene Wilder wasn't doing the sort of comedy we'd come to expect from him. After his screen debut as a nervous undertaker in *Bonnie and Clyde,* he had hit his stride playing cuddly, frenetic types in Mel Brooks movies like *Blazing Saddles* and *Young Frankenstein.* With *Silver Streak,* we were asked to believe he was a serious lover one minute, a

comedian the next. Only when Richard Pryor appears on the scene and the two begin to do *schtick* does Wilder's true humor come through.

The critics loved Pryor. Before his role in *Silver Streak,* the black comedian had worked mostly as a nightclub and TV entertainer. He had a small but important role in *Lady Sings the Blues* (1972), but mostly appeared in mediocre films like *The Bingo Long Traveling All-Stars and Motor Kings* (1976) and *Car Wash* (1976). Pryor himself was lukewarm about his participation in *Silver Streak,* describing it to *The New York Times* as "a 'business decision.' "

Others in the cast included Patrick McGoohan as a villain, an interesting departure for the British actor who had a huge following on both sides of the Atlantic for his '60s portrayal of spies in TV's "Secret Agent" and "The Prisoner." Actor Richard Kiel, who would later become known as "Jaws" in the James Bond film series, makes an appearance as Reace/Goldtooth, his character's name derived from the toothy grin that became his trademark.

Happily for fans of the Wilder/Pryor pairing, the two were again teamed in the 1980 film *Stir Crazy.* It, too, became a box office hit (see page 275).

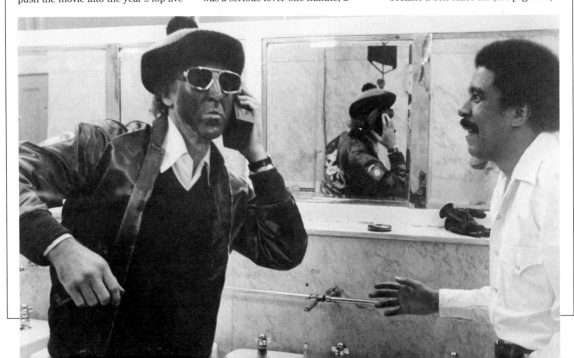

ALL THE PRESIDENT'S MEN

WARNER BROS.
$30,000,000

POLITICAL FILMS usually don't go over well with moviegoers. So when Robert Redford paid $450,000 to option Bob Woodward and Carl Bernstein's best-seller about their exposé of the Watergate cover-up, he had difficulty convincing potential backers that this picture would be a money-maker. Didn't he know how angered television viewers had been during the hearings when their soaps were pre-empted? No one wanted to see more about Watergate, Redford was told, even with him in the lead role. Eventually, he was able to convince Warner Bros. to budget the film at a modest $8,500,000, still a considerable gamble for a political film.

It was not easy bringing such a controversial subject to the screen. Redford, who selected Dustin Hoffman for his co-star, turned to William Goldman for a screenplay adaptation. Goldman had written *Butch Cassidy and the Sundance Kid,* and Redford didn't want to take chances (no problem, as Goldman

Screenplay by William Goldman

Based on a book by Carl Bernstein and Bob Woodward

Produced by Walter Coblenz

Directed by Alan J. Pakula

CAST

Carl Bernstein	Dustin Hoffman
Bob Woodward	Robert Redford
Harry Rosenfeld	Jack Warden
Howard Simons	Martin Balsam
Deep Throat	Hal Holbrook
Ben Bradlee	Jason Robards

ACADEMY AWARD NOMINATIONS

8 nominations, 4 wins*

Best Picture
*Best Supporting Actor (Jason Robards)
Best Supporting Actress (Jane Alexander)
Best Director (Alan J. Pakula)
*Best Screenplay Based on Material from Another Medium (William Goldman)
*Best Art Direction–Set Decoration
*Best Sound
Best Film Editing

proved when he won the Best Screenplay Oscar). "We stuck very close to the book," says Redford on the back of the videocassette version's box. "The story is itself such a thriller that there was no need to resort to literary license or fictionalization."

Shot with the cooperation of the *Washington Post* (Woodward and Bernstein's employing newspaper), the film has a documentary feeling. This is because *All the President's Men* is done as "docudrama," combining elements of both documentary and drama. It begins with actual footage of Richard Nixon about to address Congress, and ends with his taking the Presidential Oath of Office, followed by a montage of headlines leading to his resignation. Intercut throughout the entire film are real news reports, adding to the feeling of authenticity.

The newspaper was also instrumental in aiding the production designers in duplicating the newsroom down to the last detail, including authentic trash. Such attention to minutiae won an Oscar for the art directors and set designers.

There were two Best Supporting Actor/Actress nominations—Jason Robards as *Post* editor Ben Bradlee, and Jane Alexander as a bookkeeper on Nixon's staff who provides key background data. But it is surprising that neither of the principals, Redford

and Hoffman, was nominated for Best Actor, while Sylvester Stallone was nominated for his first major film role that year in *Rocky*. So was an obscure Italian named Giancarlo Giannini, for *Seven Beauties*—another unusual move for the Academy, which rarely nominated foreign actors for the top award.

Others noteworthy in *All the President's Men* were Jack Warden, Martin Balsam, Ned Beatty (he received a nomination from the Academy that year, but for another film, *Network*), and Hal Halbrook as the informant, "Deep Throat." A few future television stars were in other roles: Stephen Collins as Hugh Sloan (he co-starred in the film *Star Trek: The Motion Picture* [1979] and several TV shows); Robert Walden as Donald Segretti (he was in "Lou Grant" and the Showtime series "Brothers"); and a dark-haired Meredith Baxter as Mrs. Sloan (who later added her married name of Birney to her billing when she co-starred as the blonde mom on the TV series "Family Ties").

Critics called it "ingenious" (*Variety*), "spellbinding…the thinking man's 'Jaws'" (*The New York Times*), and "a superb movie" (*Leonard Maltin's TV Movies and Video Guide*). When it's listed in *TV Guide, All the President's Men* is given four stars, a must-see. Good advice; catch it next time it's on.

STAR WARS

20TH CENTURY-FOX
$193,777,000

"A long time ago, in a galaxy far, far away…" —OPENING CRAWL

PART SATURDAY afternoon matinee, part *Wizard of Oz,* part *Star Trek* (even the title was obviously derivative), part Buck Rogers, part Flash Gordon, part Knights of the Round Table—and all George Lucas. That was the magic loosed upon an unsuspecting public in the summer of 1977. The movie that had begun as a germ of an idea in the fertile mind of George Lucas back in 1973 ended up being the sleeper of the century. Movies would never be the same again.

George Lucas had difficulty convincing people to listen to him when, following the success of his first hit, *American Graffiti,* he wrote an outline for what would be his loving tribute to the serials he'd enjoyed so much as a youth, originally entitled *The Star Wars.* No studio in town would give him a tumble. Science fiction films weren't successful, appealing only to a handful of freaks and weirdos, the studios said, and Lucas pounded on several doors before receiving the considerable backing of $9,500,000 he needed when 20th Century-Fox agreed to finance the project.

Actually, it was more fantasy than science fiction. Lucas created an imaginary world of princesses and knights, fighters with movable wings (not necessary in the vacuum of space), and anthropomorphic robots. The plot was as old as fiction itself—the forces of good (Luke Skywalker, all in white) versus the forces of evil (Darth, as in "dark," Vader, all in black). Yet as derivative as it was, *Star Wars* was also the most imaginative use of cinemagic ever, with the finest technical effort ever given any picture, sci-fi or otherwise. Computerized and digitally timed special effects, layer upon layer of stars, ships, backgrounds, animation, humans, and so on made us believe, no matter how shaky the science. Above all, it was *entertainment.* Virtually every second of the picture was filled with excitement, action, or visual interest of some sort. Cliffhangers occurred every ten minutes or so, without the "tune in next week to find out if our heroes

live": the spellbound audience knew immediately.

The critics knew immediately that they were looking not only into the future (or past, as it were), but into the very future of the motion picture industry itself. *The Hollywood Reporter* sized up the situation: " 'Star Wars' will undoubtedly emerge as one of the true classics in the genre of science fiction/fantasy films. In any event, it will be thrilling audiences of all ages for a long time to come." *Newsweek* called the movie "pure sweet fun all the way… [George Lucas] says it's a movie for children—what he means is that he wants to touch the child in all of us… *Star Wars* brims with adventure, charm

Screenplay by George Lucas

Produced by Gary Kurtz

Directed by George Lucas

CAST

Luke Skywalker . . . . .Mark Hamill
Han Solo . . . . .Harrison Ford
Princess Leia . . . . .Carrie Fisher
Grand Moff Tarkin . . . . . .Peter Cushing
Obi-Won (Ben) Kenobi . . .Alec Guinness
C3PO . . . . .Anthony Daniels
R2D2 . . . . .Kenny Baker

ACADEMY AWARD NOMINATIONS

10 nominations, 6 wins

  Best Picture
  Best Supporting Actor (Alec Guinness)
  Best Director (George Lucas)
  Best Screenplay Written Directly for
    the Screen
*Best Art Direction–Set Decoration
*Best Sound
*Best Original Score (John Williams)
*Best Film Editing
*Best Costume Design
*Best Visual Effects

A Special Achievement Award for Sound Effects went to Benjamin Burtt, Jr., for the creation of the alien, creature, and robot voices in *Star Wars.*

A single of the theme and Cantina number by Meco hit the number-one spot on *Billboard* charts in October, 1977, remaining there for two weeks.

and marvels…Lucas makes fun a sparkling pop metaphor for the sheer joy of goodness that could even make friends out of men, mutations and machines."

By now, there's hardly a person alive in *this* galaxy who does not think of characters like C3PO, R2D2, and Chewbacca as close friends. Fans of the film adored the 'droids (short for "androids," of course) and the eight-foot-tall Wookie, Chewbacca. Even Chewie's growling vocalizations were endearing, having been electronically created from mixing the sounds of a bear and a lion.

The public couldn't get enough of *Star Wars* in any form, eagerly embracing the merchandise that poured forth. T-shirts, lunchboxes, bedsheets (one store dubiously advertised, "Now you can have scenes of Luke in action on your mattress!")—the theme song became a number-one hit, and John Williams' music became one of the best-selling soundtracks of all time, with over 3,000,000 copies sold.

The film's ending unintentionally left the story open for sequels. Originally, *Star Wars* was meant as a one-shot, a film complete in itself. But as soon as three-hour-long lines began forming at the box office, Fox executives knew they were on to something. Suddenly, George Lucas and his newly formed company, Lucasfilm, were busy creating a *Star Wars* saga. The film was given a new opening crawl with its next release. Instead of starting with the receding crawl proclaiming simply, "A long time ago, in a galaxy far, far away," the opening slide began with EPISODE IV—A NEW HOPE. (All prints now in release have this beginning title.)

Huh? What about Episodes I, II, and III? Had we slept through them? No, these were (and still are) *prequels,* awaiting the spark of life from their creator, Lucas. Meanwhile, he began prepping Episode V (which is actually only the second in the series), *The Empire Strikes Back,* and Episode VI, *The Return of the Jedi.*

Fans of the series were happy when George Lucas announced in 1995 that he was writing the long-awaited prequel trilogy, with plans for the first film to be in theaters by 1998.

CLOSE ENCOUNTERS OF THE THIRD KIND

COLUMBIA
$82,750,000

Close Encounter of the First Kind: sighting of a UFO

Close Encounter of the Second Kind: physical evidence

Close Encounter of the Third Kind: contact —COLUMBIA PICTURES HANDOUT

THE SIGHTING OF UFOs (unidentified flying objects) was not a new phenomenon. Sightings began appearing with regularity following the Second World War, when people's eyes were focused skyward, looking for enemy aircraft that might at any minute rain down death and destruction. Whether due to mass hysteria or some unexplained mystery, there was definitely *something* being seen, and even the U.S. Air Force began keeping files on reported sightings. During that time, the term "close encounter" was coined to describe the degree to which the sighting was experienced. And although Steven Spielberg originally wanted to call his movie on the subject *Watch the Skies,* he eventually settled on the more technical title of *Close Encounters of the Third Kind.*

There had been a spate of "alien encounter" films during the '50s, when UFO sightings were at their zenith. In many ways, *CE3K* (as the film is frequently abbreviated) was somewhat derivative of those movies: a touch of *The Day the Earth Stood Still,* a little *War of the Worlds,* a tiny bit of *Earth Versus the Flying Saucers, It Came from Outer Space,* and so on. But unlike the latter two "B" movies, *CE3K* was done with a big budget, technical advice, lavish special effects, and a fantastic script written by the director himself, Steven Spielberg.

Like *Star Wars, CE3K* was a technical marvel. Doug Trumbull, the FX genius behind *2001: A Space Odyssey,* worked his spells on this Spielberg production, converting his 13,500-square-foot building into a complete movie studio, with special rooms for developing, optical printing, and editing, "dolly" tracks for camera passes at the models of space ships (expertly crafted by another fine talent, Greg Jein), construction shops, paint shops, and hundreds of thousands of dollars worth of special equipment—much of it designed by Trumbull as the need arose.

The live action was shot in various worldwide locations. The crowd sequences in India took weeks and thousands of extras—DeMille himself couldn't have done better. And the largest indoor set ever used in a film was built in a dirigible hangar in Mobile, Alabama—it was equal to six times the size of the largest soundstage in Hollywood. Here they shot the movie's climax when the chandelier-like Mothership arrives.

Wyoming's Devil's Tower, a unique mountain setting in a desolate area near Huelot, Wyoming, also saw weeks of camera crews trudging through the wilderness. Columbia originally wanted Spielberg to film this on a Burbank soundstage, but the director insisted on authentic location backgrounds.

In 1980, Steven Spielberg did the unheard of—he re-edited his already successful picture, cutting scenes that he felt slowed down the film (e.g., the shots of Richard Dreyfuss obsessively digging up the yard) and adding others, including an all-new ending in which we are actually treated to a look inside the Mothership. The feature was even given a new title: *Close Encounters of the Third Kind: The Special Edition.* Box office earnings again soared. And for Columbia and Spielberg (as well as the audience), it was indeed special.

Screenplay by Steven Spielberg

Produced by Julia and Michael Phillips

Directed by Steven Spielberg

CAST

Roy Neary . . . . .Richard Dreyfuss
Claude Lacombe . . . . .François Truffaut
Ronnie Neary . . . . . . .Teri Garr
Jillian Guiler . . . . .Melinda Dillon
Barry Guiler . . . . .Cary Guffey

ACADEMY AWARD NOMINATIONS

8 nominations, 1 win*

Best Supporting Actress (Melinda Dillon)
Best Director (Steven Spielberg)
*Best Cinematography
Best Art Direction–Set Decoration
Best Sound
Best Original Score
Best Film Editing
Best Visual Effects

Close Encounters of the Third Kind received a Special Achievement Award for Sound Effects Editing (to Frank Warner, sound effects editor).

SATURDAY NIGHT FEVER

PARAMOUNT
$74,100,000

"**T**RIBAL RITES of the New Saturday Night." That was the name of the cover story article by Nik Cohn appearing in *New York Magazine*'s June, 1976, issue. It dealt with kids in Brooklyn, New York, who lived from Saturday to Saturday, "exploding" on the weekends at the local disco. The main character of this fact-based story was "Vincent," a third-generation Italian-American who "owned fourteen floral shirts, five suits, eight pairs of shoes, three overcoats, and had appeared on *American Bandstand*… When Saturday night came round and he walked into 2001 Odyssey, all the other Faces [sic] automatically fell back before him, cleared a space for him to float in, right at the very center of the dance floor."

Producer Robert Stigwood found the story a movie natural and acquired the screen rights for Paramount. Stigwood had a young man under a three-picture-deal contract, and the lead role seemed a natural for him. John Travolta had only been in two movies up until that time, *The Devil's Rain* (1975) and *The Boy in the Plastic Bubble* (made-for-TV, 1976). But audiences were familiar with him from his weekly appearances as "Barbarino" on TV's "Welcome Back, Kotter." And *Fever*'s main character, Tony Manero, was an unintentional clone of Barbarino, making this the ideal vehicle for launching

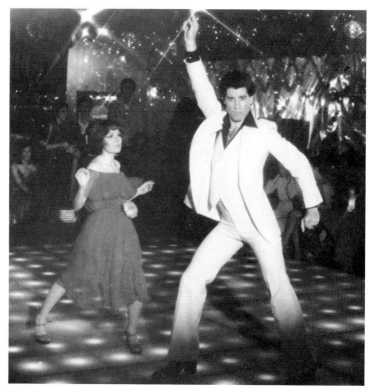

Travolta into mainstream features.

The soundtrack became one of the best-sellers of all time, with over 35,000,000 copies sold worldwide. Bee Gees (for "*Brothers Gibb*") hit songs included "How Deep Is Your Love,"* "Night Fever,"* "Staying Alive,"* "More Than a Woman," "If I Can't Have You"* (performed by Yvonne Elliman), and "You Should Be Dancing."** Amazingly, none of these tunes were nominated for Best Song, nor was the score nominated by the Academy.

The film captured the imagination of young people, who turned disco dancing into a national craze while emulating the fashions worn in the film. By 1978, white three-piece polyester leisure suits with black shirts and Cuban heels were all the rage, along with Travolta look-alike and "Spanish hustle" contests. John Travolta himself emerged as a cult hero, and the charismatic young performer would soon emerge as Paramount/Stigwood's

hottest contract player in decades.

The original 1977 release received an "R" rating, which eliminated much of the young audience, who could not be admitted unless accompanied by an adult. Many potential ticket-buyers wanted to enjoy this musical film with wonderful dance numbers by the multi-talented young star, but there were some sex scenes and a lot of blue language the MPAA rightly termed inappropriate for young teens. So in 1979, Paramount re-edited the feature, deleting seven minutes of offensive footage and, as required by the MPAA, withdrew all copies of the "R"-rated version from circulation. The newly recut edition received a "PG" rating and went on to enjoy a whole new audience.

---

*Became a number-one hit and was written especially for *Saturday Night Fever*.

**Became a number-one hit prior to inclusion in *Saturday Night Fever*.

Screenplay by Norman Wexler

Based on a story by Nik Cohn

Executive Producer: Kevin McCormick

Produced by Robert Stigwood

Directed by John Badham

CAST

Tony Manero . . . . John Travolta
Stephanie . . . . Karen Lynn Gorney
Bobby C . . . . Barry Miller
Joey . . . . Joseph Cali
Annette . . . . Donna Pescow

ACADEMY AWARD NOMINATIONS

1 nomination, no wins

Best Actor (John Travolta)

SMOKEY AND THE BANDIT

UNIVERSAL
$58,949,939

Cᴀʀ ᴄʜᴀsᴇs, when well done, can usually pull any ailing studio out of the doldrums. Toss in a hunky good-ol'-boy type like Burt Reynolds, plus the current fad, whatever it may be, and the lucky studio can count its box office take to the happy tune of plunkin' banjo music from here to Georgia.

For Universal, which hadn't had a top-five hit since 1975's *Jaws, Smokey and the Bandit* saw the studio making out like bandits. Burt Reynolds had proved he could act in *Deliverance* (1972), and polls placed him squarely atop the list of box office favorites in 1977, his fourth year in the top ten. The screenplay about hauling a truckload of bootlegged beer from Texas to Georgia was a textbook on how many different ways to crash a car, with the clichéd Southern redneck potbellied sheriff (played by Jackie Gleason) in hot pursuit. It seems like formula writing at its most generic—except that this is the picture that invented the formula.

The CB craze had peaked while the film was in production in 1976, with the biggest fad since the hula hoop bringing in over $2 billion in sales. So just for good measure, the producers tossed in a heavy dose of CB jive, like "That's a big 10-4, good buddy" (translation: over and out), "What's your handle?" (code name), and "There's a Smokey up the road taking pictures" (a highway patrolman is using radar up ahead).

Along with Burt Reynolds, there was co-star Sally Field, known mostly as the cutesy star of the '60s "Gidget" and "The Flying Nun" TV series. The un-nunlike Ms. Field would go on to co-star as his female sidekick in a number of other Reynolds movies, as well as in real life, when the couple became an "item" for a number of years. She had won an Emmy for her work in the TV movie *Sybil,* and would later shine in films such as *Norma Rae* (1979), for which she received the Oscar, and *Places in the Heart* (1984), another Award-winning role ("You like me! Right now you *like* me!" she crowed on Oscar night in 1984).

Several reviewers crowed as well. *Time* found that *Smokey and the Bandit* "deals in broad comedy and simple emotions…between crashes, Reynolds is given a series of wise- cracks that establish his basic screen character—shrewd, laid-back, a tad reckless and a devil with women…the whole enterprise is fairly tacky, but it is also rather jaunty fun." *The Hollywood Reporter* wrote: "There are a number of amusing sequences which are combined with some exciting road action to provide a mildly entertaining— and totally mindless—film…Reynolds performs with an offhand, easy style and he creates an engaging character."

Reynolds parlayed his success into two less successful sequels, *Smokey and the Bandit II* (1980), again with Field and Gleason, and *Smokey and the Bandit 3** (1983), with Jackie Gleason and Paul Williams, but not Sally Field, who by then had split with Reynolds for good.

---

*There was an unexplained switch from Roman to Arabic numerals in the second sequel.

Screenplay by James Lee Barrett, Charles Shyer, and Alan Mandel

Based on a story by Hal Needham

Executive Producer: Robert L. Levy

Produced by Mort Engelberg

Directed by Hal Needham

CAST

Bandit . . . . .Burt Reynolds
Carrie . . . . .Sally Field
Cledus . . . . .Jerry Reed
Sheriff Justice . . . . . . .Jackie Gleason
Little Enos . . . . .Paul Williams
Big Enos . . . . .Pat McCormick

ACADEMY AWARD NOMINATIONS

1 nomination, no wins

Best Film Editing

Burt Reynolds grabs a look through the camera lens before the next scene is filmed.

*"Oh God, please let me get hit by a
rich man in a Rolls Royce."*
—MARSHA MASON

IN A RARE DEPARTURE from his usual
method, Neil Simon created a play
directly for the screen rather than for
live theater. Writing *The Goodbye Girl*
mainly as a starring vehicle for his
then-wife Marsha Mason, he chose the
medium after careful consideration.
"Any idea ordinarily says to me, 'I'm a
play' or 'I'm a movie,' " the playwright
commented to *The New York Times.*
"But an integral character was a 10-
year-old girl. I didn't want to face the
difficulty of having to get a performance from a child night after night."

The Goodbye Girl is in many ways
reminiscent of Simon's earlier hit film
The Odd Couple. Like Felix and Oscar,
this movie's two protagonists are
thrown together in a New York apartment where their personalities clash
like plaids and stripes. But unlike the
roomies in the first hit, these two are
of *opposite* sexes and inevitably wind
up in love with each other. And the
rest is pure Neil Simon at his best.

Another rare departure was the fact
that this was a co-production of two
studios, Metro-Goldwyn-Mayer and
Warner Bros., with Warner Bros. act-

Screenplay by Neil Simon

Produced by Ray Stark

Directed by Herbert Ross

CAST

Elliot Garfield . . . . . . .Richard Dreyfuss
Paula McFadden . . . . .Marsha Mason
Lucy McFadden . . . . . .Quinn Cummings
Mark . . . . .Paul Benedict
Donna . . . . .Barbara Rhoades

ACADEMY AWARD NOMINATIONS

5 nominations, 1 win*

Best Picture
**Best Actor (Richard Dreyfuss)
Best Actress (Marsha Mason)
Best Supporting Actress (Quinn
Cummings)
Best Screenplay Written Directly for the
Screen

---

ing as the releasing company and handling distribution.

Although the film was intended as a
showcase for Marsha Mason, a.k.a.
Mrs. Simon, most of the accolades
went to Richard Dreyfuss. Although
the actor failed to be nominated for his
hit picture of the year, *Close
Encounters of the Third Kind,* or his
earlier achievement in *Jaws* (1975), he
walked off with the prize for Best
Actor in *The Goodbye Girl.* The role of
Elliot Garfield was as good a role as
any actor dared hope for: an actor
playing an actor. Critics were agog
over Dreyfuss' performance.
According to *Time,* "he gets the girl in
the end, but he gets the audience
first." And *Newsweek,* while noting that
Dreyfuss might appear to be an unlikely romantic lead, praised him as
"charmingly, abrasively funny, perfectly setting the manic rhythm for
Simon's confrontational comedy." The

compliment was echoed by Dreyfuss'
peers at the Motion Picture Academy,
who voted him the Oscar for Best
Actor over the likes of Richard Burton
(*Equus* marked his seventh nomination—and loss), John Travolta (*Saturday Night Fever*), Woody Allen (*Annie
Hall*), and Marcello Mastroianni (*A
Special Day*).

The highlight of the film for many
was the portrayal by Dreyfuss' character of Shakespeare's Richard III as gay.
This outlandish sequence is probably
the scene that clinched the Oscar for
him. Several reviewers likened it to
the "Springtime for Hitler" send-up in
Mel Brooks' *The Producers* (1968).

Young actress Quinn Cummings
surprised many as a Best Supporting
Actress nominee in her first film performance. The child star was quickly
added to the cast of TV's "Family," in
which she co-starred from 1978 until
the show's demise in 1980.

GREASE
PARAMOUNT
$96,300,000

"If you can't be an athlete, be an athletic supporter."
—Eve Arden (Principal McGee)

Nostalgia for the '50s was at an all-time high back in 1972, when off-Broadway first became home to a new musical called *Grease.* The production caught on, in the words of one of its songs, like "Greased Lightning," racking up 3,388 performances before closing in 1980, one of the longest-running productions in Broadway history. Even as Robert Stigwood began shooting his Paramount production back in 1977, the road company was playing an appearance in Los Angeles. But there was never a question about who would play the lead—already under contract in a three-picture deal was the star of Stigwood's *Saturday Night Fever* success of the previous year, John Travolta. Ironically, the star had appeared in *Grease* on Broadway prior to his being signed as "Vinnie Barbarino" in "Welcome Back, Kotter."

Selected as Travolta's co-star was popular Australian recording artist Olivia Newton-John in her American film debut (her Aussie accent is never explained in the movie). There was an unusual chemistry between the virginal character of Sandy, played by Newton-John, and the tough on the outside/soft on the inside, greasy-hood-your-mother-warned-you-about character of Danny, played by Travolta. Musicals may have been essentially dead in this "special effects" decade, but thanks to these two, *Grease* proved there was still a last gasp left in the genre.

Stockard Channing, who would later star in her own TV show and make numerous guest appearances on others, played Rizzo, leader of the girl gang "The Pink Ladies." Jeff Conaway, who eventually co-starred on TV's "Taxi," appeared as Kenickie; Didi Conn, star of the movie *You Light Up My Life,* played Frenchie; and Lorenzo Lamas, later of TV's "Falcon Crest," appeared as Tom Chisum. There were cameo appearances as well by Frankie Avalon, Eve Arden, Edd "Kookie" Byrnes, Joan Blondell, Sid Caesar, Dody Goodman, and a real greaser

rock group, Sha Na Na (they, too, would get their own TV show).

Most of the box office excitement, however, was generated by the animal magnetism of John Travolta. The man knew his way around a dance floor, disco, gymnasium, or even stadium bleachers, as one of the film's big production numbers would have it. This would be his biggest box office hit; although his next film for Paramount, 1980's *Urban Cowboy,* would earn $23,000,000 in domestic rentals, it couldn't touch the success of either *Saturday Night Fever* or *Grease.*

With 17 musical numbers, *Grease* is one of the most ambitious musicals ever to hit the screen. The soundtrack album became the number-two best-seller with 24,000,000 copies, right behind *Saturday Night Fever* and all those Bee Gees tunes. Two of the songs climbed the charts as singles and made it to the number-one spot— "You're the One That I Want," a duet by Travolta and Newton-John, and Frankie Valli's rendition of the title song. Other memorable tunes, each sung in elaborate production numbers, included "Summer Nights," sung by Travolta and Newton-John; "Look at Me, I'm Sandra Dee," performed by Stockard Channing; "Greased

---

Screenplay by Bronte Woodard

Adaptation by Allan Carr

From the Broadway musical by Jim Jacobs and Warren Casey

Produced by Robert Stigwood and Allan Carr

Directed by Randal Kleiser

CAST

Danny . . . . John Travolta
Sandy . . . . Olivia Newton-John
Rizzo . . . . Stockard Channing
Kenickie . . . . Jeff Conaway
Frenchy . . . . Didi Conn

ACADEMY AWARD NOMINATIONS

1 nomination, no wins

Best Song ("Hopelessly Devoted to You," music and words by John Farrar)

Lightning," done by Travolta and Jeff Conaway; "Beauty School Dropout," a fantasy number by Frankie Avalon; and the finale, "We Go Together," again with Travolta and Newton-John.

For the movie, *Grease*'s Broadway score was supplemented by a selection of golden oldies from the '50s, as well as by original songs new to the film. The movie version also differed from the stage version by taking advantage of the possibilities offered by location shooting. Venice High School represented the exteriors of Rydell, with two other local high schools used for the dance contest and the carnival-finale.

"Grease is the word," proclaimed the title song, while reviewers tended toward the word "slick." *Variety* pronounced *Grease* "slick as a ducktail hairdo," commenting: "'Grease' has got it, from the outstanding animated titles of John Wilson all the way through the rousing finale as John Travolta and Olivia Newton-John ride off into pre-Vietnam era teenage happiness. The Robert Stigwood–Allan Carr production values compliment superbly the broad comedy-drama, zesty choreography and very excellent new plus revived music." *The New York Times* saw *Grease* paying homage to '50s films like *Don't Knock the Rock* and *Rock Around the Clock,* in the manner in which *Close Encounters of the Third Kind* acknowledged a debt to the '50s science fiction "B" films. They, too, termed the film "slick." The title didn't translate too well into other languages, though. In Spanish, the word for "grease" is "grasa," which literally means "fat" or "oil," so in Spain the movie was released under the title *Brilliantina/Brilliantine* and in Venezuela as *Vaselina/Vaseline.*

Believe it or not, a non-Travolta sequel was released in 1982. Didi Conn, Eve Arden, Sid Caesar, and Dody Goodman all returned in *Grease 2,* plus new additions Lorna Luft (daughter of Judy Garland and Sid Luft), Connie Stevens, Maxwell Caulfield, Adrian Zmed, and Tab Hunter. The chemistry didn't work, the tunes weren't catchy, and the film bombed, earning only $6,500,000. Ramalama-dingdong.

SUPERMAN

WARNER BROS.
$82,800,000

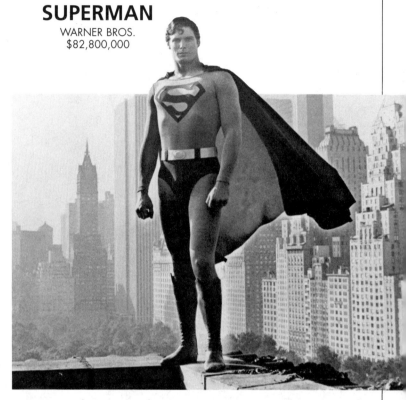

You will believe a man can fly.
—ADVERTISING COPY FOR *SUPERMAN*

BACK DURING the Depression, two teenagers named Jerry Siegel and Joe Shuster created a comic book hero that has survived for generations. "Superman" first flew across the pages of comic books back in 1938, and has been brought to the screen, big and small, many times. There was an early animated cartoon, followed by '40s serials with Kirk Alyn donning cape and tights for Saturday afternoon cliffhangers. In the '50s, an acclaimed television series starred George Reeves and broke ground by filming in color as early as 1954, thus assuring it a place even today in syndicated rerun heaven. But in the '70s, with movie technology soaring even higher than the Man of Steel, the time was right to give *Superman* a big-budget treatment.

First order of business: finding the

Screenplay by Mario Puzo, David Newman, Leslie Newman, and Robert Benton

Story by Mario Puzo

Based on characters created by Jerry Siegel and Joel Shuster

Executive Producer: Ilya Salkind

Produced by Pierre Spengler

Directed by Richard Donner

CAST

Jor-El . . . . .Marlon Brando
Lex Luthor . . . . .Gene Hackman
Superman/Clark Kent . . .Christopher Reeve
Otis . . . . .Ned Beatty
Perry White . . . . .Jackie Cooper
Lois Lane . . . . .Margot Kidder

ACADEMY AWARD NOMINATIONS

3 nominations, no wins

Best Sound
Best Original Score (John Williams)
Best Film Editing

Superman received the Special Achievement Award for Visual Effects (Les Bowie, Colin Chilvers, Denys Coop, Foy Field, Derek Meddings, and Zoran Perisic).

right man for the job. Faster than you can say "speeding bullet," there were muscled hopefuls auditioning at the Warner Bros. lot. Sly Stallone made no secret of the fact he wanted a big "S" on his chest. Another early contender was Bruce Jenner, Olympic decathlon winner. Athlete, yes…actor, no. He kept his day job. Two hundred interviews later, the role was landed by 24-year-old Christopher Reeve (ironically, a name very similar to TV's man from Krypton, although no relation). "We wanted a relative unknown," director Richard Donner told *The New York Times,* "so the public wouldn't think of an established personality pretending he was flying and performing great feats of strength."

The film was budgeted at $25,000,000, but before they finished getting the bugs out (like finding ways to hide the apparatus used in the flying sequences), the cost had escalated to a reported $55,000,000—some claimed even higher.

One reason for the huge success was the characterization. Although certainly a bigger-than-life comic hero, Reeve's Superman was vulnerable, and not just to Kryptonite. When he falls in

love with Lois Lane (played by Margot Kidder), there is something very human about it. Superman becomes Everyman for just a moment, and audiences can identify with that. When she dies, he grieves and disobeys his prime directive by interfering with the laws of nature to bring her back to life. Would we do no less if we could? Men identified strongly with a superhero with human flaws, while women sighed at the looks of Chris Reeve, whose smile could melt hearts faster than his heat vision could melt steel. Kids also adored the PG-rated film, making this the perfect box office draw for families, singles, kids, science fiction and fantasy buffs, and just about everyone else looking for an enjoyable time at the movies.

Three sequels were made to the original film. Actor Christopher Reeve continued to broaden the scope of his acting career with a variety of roles, but his association in the public's eye was always as the Man of Steel. Even in 1995, when Reeve had a tragic accident, suffering paralyzing injuries, when he fell from his horse, fans around the world sent wishes for the speedy recovery of "Superman."

NATIONAL LAMPOON'S ANIMAL HOUSE

UNIVERSAL
$70,826,000

PART RITES of passage, part slapstick comedy, with a touch of "slob humor" tossed in for good measure, *National Lampoon's Animal House* nostalgically harkens back to the year of 1962. This, you may remember, was also the year zeroed in on by George Lucas in *American Graffiti* (1973), but unlike that earlier depiction of tribal rites, *Animal House* pulled very few punches. Food fights, toga parties, sexual hijinks, demolition derbies—this picture had it all. It also had an excellent cast and talented production team, which helped push the movie over the top with the young adult crowd.

Chief party animal was John Belushi, the late actor-comedian who achieved fame on television's popular "Saturday Night Live." Although much of his acting in *Animal House* is limited to grunting or raising eyebrows before letting loose his special brand of humor, it was his name that was the main drawing card. When he crams his mouth with mashed potatoes, then slaps both bulging cheeks and announces "I'm a zit. Get it?" audiences got it, and loved it, and came back for more. Of Belushi's performance, *Newsweek* said: "John Belushi is the movie's heavy slugger. As the oxlike Blutarsky, a fellow given to crunching beer cans on his brutish forehead, Belushi looks as if he'd just taken the first step up the evolutionary ladder…he unleashes his epic appetite on the school's lunch counter, hilariously demonstrating man's genetic link to the industrial vacuum cleaner."

The film's director, John Landis, then only 27 years old, had his finger on the pulse of his equally young audience. He described this kind of comedy to *Newsweek* as "behavioral humor of outrage. It's definitely offensive. It's antagonistic. But it's all in good fun."

As with *American Graffiti,* the cast boasted a long line of future movie and TV stars: Tim Matheson (*1941*), Tom Hulce (*Amadeus*), Karen Allen (*Raiders of the Lost Ark*), Martha Smith ("Scarecrow and Mrs. King"), and Kevin Bacon (*Footloose*). Donald Sutherland as pothead Professor Jennings was the biggest "name" at the time, although he was given last billing. And as in *American Graffiti,* we are given an epilogue of character destinies, in case we care "what ever became of…?" The humor continues right through the credits as we learn that one of the characters, a "Nixon aide, was raped in prison," and that another went on to glory as "a Universal Tour guide—ask for Babs" (the inevitable plug given at the time for the studio's other moneymaker, the Universal Tour).

The movie was co-produced by Ivan Reitman and co-scripted by Harold Ramis. Ramis and Belushi worked together in "Second City," a comedy forerunner to "Saturday Night Live." And six years later, Ramis and Reitman were reunited in *Ghostbusters,* with Reitman directing that picture and Ramis co-starring.

Screenplay by Harold Ramis, Douglas Kenney, and Chris Miller

Produced by Matty Simmons and Ivan Reitman

Directed by John Landis

CAST

John Blutarsky (Bluto)	John Belushi
Eric Stratton (Otter)	Tim Matheson
Dean Wormer	John Vernon
Marion Wormer	Verna Bloom
Katy	Karen Allen
Babs Jensen	Martha Smith
Chip Diller	Kevin Bacon
Prof. Jennings	Donald Sutherland
Larry Kroger (Pinto)	Thomas Hulce

1978

EVERY WHICH WAY BUT LOOSE

WARNER BROS.
$51,900,000

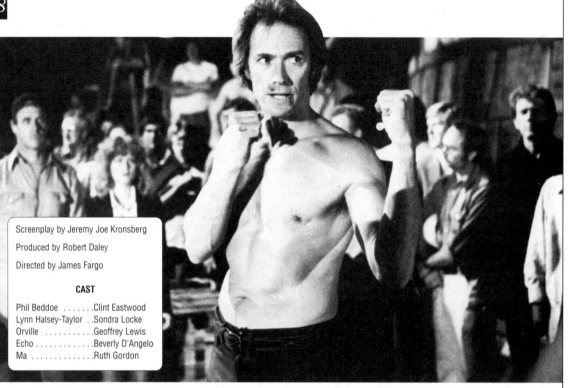

Screenplay by Jeremy Joe Kronsberg

Produced by Robert Daley

Directed by James Fargo

CAST

Phil Beddoe . . . . . . .Clint Eastwood
Lynn Halsey-Taylor . .Sondra Locke
Orville . . . . .Geoffrey Lewis
Echo . . . . .Beverly D'Angelo
Ma . . . . .Ruth Gordon

THERE WAS no doubt about it—we liked our movies light in 1978. There were heavy hitters, to be sure: films like *The Deer Hunter* and *Coming Home* reminded us of the Vietnam War and did well at the Oscars, but not at the box office. What we wanted was *escapism,* and if that meant musicals, fantasy, and "low" humor, so be it.

Every Which Way But Loose, like other popular films of 1978, didn't pick up a single Academy Award nomination. But the statuette wasn't vital to this film's success. What the public wanted was beer, girls, and fist fights, and this movie had all three— with an average of one fight scene every ten minutes. This Warner Bros. release also featured a number of country & western tunes that were fashionable with the latent CB crowd, some of the songs becoming crossover hits on pop or middle-of-the-road radio stations. Charlie Rich's "Behind Closed Doors" and two songs by Mel Tillis set toes tapping in movie theaters across the land. *Every*

Which Way But Loose made money every which way you turned.

There were two main attractions in the feature, one human, one not. Clint Eastwood was the human star, and his pairing with Clyde the Orangutan was the most talked-about human/ape pairing since Ronald Reagan co-starred with a chimp in *Bedtime for Bonzo* (1951). According to *Hollywood Anecdotes,* when Eastwood was elected Mayor of Carmel, California, Reagan exclaimed, "Can you imagine that? What makes him think a middle-aged movie actor who's played with a chimp could have a future in politics?"

The movie soon became a favorite target of critics. *Variety* claimed: "This film is way off the mark. If people line up for this one—and they probably will—they'll line up for any Clint Eastwood picture…for Eastwood fans, the essential elements are there. Lots of people get beat up." *Newsweek*'s review was as subtle as King Kong: "They say that if a million monkeys sat down at typewriters, one of them

would eventually produce 'War and Peace.' Well, one of them—bearing the name of Jeremy Joe Kronsberg— seems to have written *Every Which Way But Loose,* a Clint Eastwood 'comedy' that could not possibly have been created by human hands. The proof is that the only decent part is played by an orangutan…James Fargo directed, every which way but well."

No one else had a fondness for the film either—no one else except the public. Moviegoers enjoyed the chemistry between the bizarre ménage à trois of Clint, Clyde, and Sondra Locke, Clint's love interest in the film and in real life. In 1989, however, that relationship ended, and Sondra Locke brought a palimony suit against Eastwood after the couple had lived together for 13 years. Before separating, however, the pair managed a sequel film, *Any Which Way You Can* (see page 277), and it did surprisingly well, unusual for most sequels. Both pictures are frequently run on television cable channels.

JAWS 2
UNIVERSAL
$50,431,964

*"Just when you thought it was safe
to go back in the water…"*
—ADVERTISING COPY FOR *JAWS 2*

SUMMERTIME and the fish are scarce. What's a hungry shark to do? Why, chow down on Amity, of course, that resort of choice for discriminating great whites. Lots of people too dumb to get out of the water. Mmm, mmm!

You'd think the good folks of Amity would know by now that when Chief Brody (Roy Scheider) blows his whistle, he means business. Unfortunately, not too many people are inclined to listen. And not just people get chomped upon: this shark even takes on boats and helicopters for a second course. Jaws 2, Amity 0.

In the summer of '78, just when you thought it was safe to go back to the theater, *Jaws 2* hit the movie screens. Hoping to take a bite out of the box office dollars, this sequel was a mere minnow compared to the original *Jaws* (page 240), but it still managed a solid fifth place for the year, proving there was life in the old fish yet.

Most of the original human stars were not in the movie, nor did director Steven Spielberg return. But Amity was again saved by Roy Scheider, who admitted to *The New York Times* that he was reluctant to return to the role: "*Jaws* is the best damn movie *ever* made. *Jaws 2* is a contractual commitment that I will fulfill as best I can." Rejoining Scheider were Lorraine Gary as his wife, Murray Hamilton as

the nearsighted mayor ("Shark? What shark?"), and Jeffrey Kramer as the deputy.

Bruce, the mechanical shark-trio from the first film, had gone to that great feeding frenzy in the sky, so designer Bob Mattey had a completely redesigned model built at the cost of about $2,250,000. Bruce II had new skin and two new sets of teeth, plus more valves and hoses to increase his repertoire of movements. Fifteen shark operators were required to put the mechanical marvel through its paces, which included lashing its tail from side to side, opening and closing its jaws, moving its fins, and rolling its eyes.

The critics were not impressed, however. Only *The Hollywood Reporter* genuinely seemed to like the movie: "It's a spin-off, not a rip-off. It promises thrills, and it delivers—in abundance.

It's obviously as meticulously produced as its predecessor, right down to the throbbing John Williams score."

Yet *Time* called the film "the work of a computer that has been programmed by the same drones who used to manufacture Universal Pictures' disaster movies," and *Newsweek* complained that "the new shark has no personality—it's just a set of motorized choppers, a buzz saw with fins."

But if the reviewers weren't happy, the audience certainly was, and so were the brass at Universal. Based on the box office success of *Jaws 2,* there were two additional sequels—*Jaws 3-D* (1983; shown on TV and videocassette as *Jaws III,* in normal 2-D) and *Jaws: The Revenge* (1987), the fourth, and so far, final chapter. Or could it be? Just when you thought you were safe from sequels…

Screenplay by Carl Gottlieb and Howard Sackler

Based on characters created by Peter Benchley

Produced by Richard D. Zanuck and David Brown

Directed by Jeannot Szwarc

CAST

Brody . . . . .Roy Scheider
Ellen Brody . . . . .Lorraine Gary
Mayor Vaughn . . . . . . .Murray Hamilton
Peterson . . . . .Joseph Mascolo
Hendricks . . . . .Jeffrey Kramer

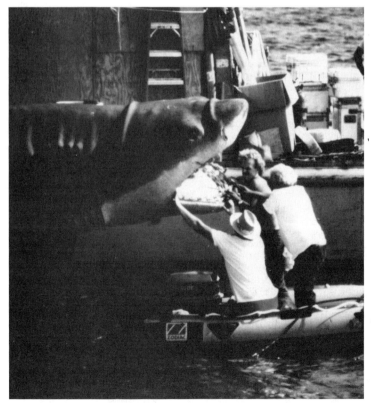

The crew of *Jaws 2* get "Bruce" ready for a shot.

KRAMER VS. KRAMER

COLUMBIA
$59,986,335

*"I'd like to know what law is it that
says that a woman is a better
parent simply by virtue of her sex?"*
—DUSTIN HOFFMAN

DIVORCE was at an all-time high as
the decade of the '70s ended; the
decline of the family unit saw more
and more single-parent situations
become the rule rather than the
exception. With courts across the land
kept busy in deciding child custody
cases, *Kramer vs. Kramer* was the
right film at the right time.

For once, Dustin Hoffman did not
play another unusual character like a
con man, a prisoner, or a super
reporter, but a role that many people
could relate to: an average hard-work-
ing parent trying to make a success of
his career while inadvertently neglect-
ing his family. When his wife leaves
him, even the women in the audience
sided with Ted Kramer and his plight
in trying to raise, then retain custody
of, his young son.

Still, the character portrayed by
Meryl Streep is by no means a loathsome bitch. She's a troubled woman
who belatedly "discovers herself" in
that first full decade of women's libera-
tion. While it's true she leaves her
home and son, she is an accurate portrait of many confident, self-dependent
women. It was the realistic aspects of
Kramer vs. Kramer, plus the fine performances of two of Hollywood's top
actors, that assured this picture a
place at the top of the box office.

The film marked the directorial
debut of 47-year-old Robert Benton.
Benton adapted the screenplay from
Avery Corman's novel, and producer
Stanley Jaffe planned to have François
Truffaut handle the directing chores.
But Benton balked and insisted that
he himself be allowed to direct. Jaffe
relented, but it soon became a free-for-
all, with Hoffman assisting with
rewrites on the script and in the editing, while Streep wrote most of her
own dialogue. In between, there were
feuds on the set as the two personalities jockeyed for scene dominance. Yet
what emerged was an astonishingly
coherent film.

Critics overwhelmingly proclaimed

it a smash. *The Hollywood Reporter*
wrote: "*Kramer vs. Kramer* may not be
what is termed in contemporary usage
an 'event' movie. It has no earthquakes, no towering infernos, no
colossal meteorites on a collision
course with old Manhattan. What this
Stanley R. Jaffe production does have
is wisdom, insight, compassion, and an
extraordinary sensitivity to present-
day problems and pain…*Kramer vs.
Kramer* is not an 'event'—it's an
event." *Variety* also praised the "powerhouse drama" as "a perceptive, touching, intelligent film about one of the
raw sores of contemporary America,
the dissolution of the family
unit…'Kramer' is about people, not
abstract stereotypes."

Both Dustin Hoffman and Meryl
Streep were congratulated by the press
for their outstanding performances,
and both were duly nominated for, and
received, Academy Awards. Ms. Streep
chose to enter the Best Supporting
Actress category, however, raising an
eyebrow or two in Hollywood gossip
columns about her motivation.

Screenplay by Robert Benton

Based on the novel by Avery Corman

Produced by Stanley R. Jaffe

Directed by Robert Benton

CAST

Ted Kramer . . . . .Dustin Hoffman
Joanna Kramer . . . . . .Meryl Streep
Margaret Phelps . . . .Jane Alexander
Billy Kramer . . . . .Justin Henry
John Shaunessy . . . . .Howard Duff

ACADEMY AWARD NOMINATIONS

9 nominations, 5 wins*

*Best Picture
*Best Actor (Dustin Hoffman)
 Best Supporting Actor (Justin Henry)
 Best Supporting Actress (Jane Alexander)
*Best Supporting Actress (Meryl Streep)
*Best Director (Robert Benton)
*Best Screenplay Based on Material from
 Another Medium (Robert Benton)
 Best Cinematography
 Best Film Editing

Many felt she thought she'd have a
better chance against the competition,
including Jane Alexander, another
nominated star from the film. Others
argued that the role of Joanna Kramer
was not a dominant one, with her actual on-screen appearance very limited
(*Variety* called her part "a 'minor' role
she manages to make 'major' ").

There is no doubt, however, that the
Best Picture competition was formida-
ble. *Kramer vs. Kramer* was up against
the likes of *All That Jazz, Apocalypse
Now, Breaking Away,* and *Norma Rae*
(which won the Best Actress award for
Sally Field). The New York Film
Critics earlier had also given the film
their highest award, and proclaimed
Dustin Hoffman their choice for Best
Actor. And the Hollywood Foreign
Press Service, which annually presents the Golden Globe Awards, also
selected Hoffman as their choice for
Best Actor. At that ceremony, the
actor, while noting that he thought
awards made more sense when given
for lifetime achievement to men like
Henry Fonda or Jack Lemmon, nevertheless seemed grateful and quipped,
"I'd like to thank divorce."

The most interesting Academy
Award nomination, however, went to
the youngster who was at the center of
it all. Justin Henry was just six years
old and a novice actor when he was
signed for the part of Billy Kramer. He
was selected from a field of over 200
candidates, with Dustin Hoffman helping to make the final selection for the
right boy to play his son, even screen-
testing with 40 finalists before choosing
Justin. The senior actor spent much
time coaching the boy for their scenes
together. "The first few days his concentration was terrible," said Hoffman,
according to *Inside Oscar.* "He kept
looking at the camera…by the third
week, he was becoming an actor." So
much so that the Academy nominated
him for an Oscar (the youngest person
ever to receive that honor).

As the decade of the '70s drew to a
close, it left us with the legacy of *Kramer vs. Kramer.* This final Best Picture
of the '70s is still timely even today in
the 1990s, a neo-classic worth renting
or catching on cable TV channels.

2

STAR TREK: THE MOTION PICTURE

PARAMOUNT
$56,000,000

"The Human Adventure Is Just Beginning."
—ADVERTISING COPY, FROM A QUOTE BY GENE RODDENBERRY

"Star Trek Lives!"
—RALLYING CRY OF "TREKKERS"

FOR TEN YEARS there had been a void in the world of "Star Trek" fans, commonly called "Trekkies" (although the fans themselves prefer the designation "Trekkers"). The legendary television program, which ran on NBC from 1966 to 1969, had been unceremoniously cancelled by the network back in '69, even after it had been saved for two seasons by an unprecedented letter-writing campaign. Banished to rerun oblivion, its popularity soared to intergalactic heights during the ensuing years, and the clamor for a reunion assaulted the executive offices of the copyright holder, Paramount Pictures, like so many Klingons attacking the Federation.

In 1975, the studio announced a modest film would at last be made, at a budget of $4,000,000. Trekkers were elated. Then Paramount dropped the other spaceboot—a "name" would be sought to sit in Captain Kirk's chair, someone with box office potential, like Robert Redford.

More letters, and intervention from the show's creator, Gene Roddenberry, saved the starship *Enterprise* once again, and the original cast was signed. By now Trekkers knew the roll call: William Shatner (Captain James T. Kirk); Leonard Nimoy (Mr. Spock); DeForest Kelley (Dr. Leonard "Bones" McCoy); James Doohan (Lt. Commander Montgomery "Scotty" Scott); Nichelle Nichols (Lt. Uhura); George Takei (Lt. Sulu); and Walter Koenig (Lt. Chekov).

Work began on a script, but over the next four years, the format shifted with regularity between the big and little screen, as the studio heads tried to find the proper format for what was, after all, *only* a TV series. New series were planned, then abruptly scrapped; films were on drawing boards, only to be abandoned. Eventually, convinced that a science fiction film *could* be successful after witnessing what should have been *Star Trek*'s audience marching to the beat of the *Star Wars* drummer, the studio gave the go-ahead to producer Roddenberry. Robert Wise was signed as director, and the budget was upped to $15,000,000.

Astronomical problems arose during production. There were constant script revisions;* there were special effects promised but not delivered by the originally contracted firm, Robert Abel and Associates, at a loss of $5,000,000 (Doug Trumbull, the wiz behind *2001,* was pressed into last-minute service). With deadlines approaching, editing became a nightmare, some editors even bringing sleeping bags to the studio so round-the-clock shifts could get the film to its exhibitors by the promised delivery date. Costs escalated, with the final price tag reaching $44,000,000, nearly three times the original budget.

For all the *Star Trek: The Motion Picture*–bashing engaged in as new films in the series emerge (last count: seven, including films based on the spin-off TV series), in reality, the first one was the most successful. Only two *Trek* movies to date have made it into the top five: *Star Trek: The Motion Picture* (number two for 1979), and *Star Trek IV: The Voyage Home* (number five for 1986). The latter film made only $820,000 more in domestic rentals than the first movie; with inflation and higher ticket costs taken into account, the most financially successful of the films to date, in terms of rentals at the box office, remains *Star Trek: The Motion Picture.*

The original release ran 132 minutes and omitted some expository footage; subsequent releases and TV runs have added an additional ten minutes, much to the delight of Trekkers.

*The script was the brainchild of Gene Roddenberry, based on his original story "Robot's Return," which in turn became the basis for credited writer Alan Dean Foster's story. The final script, however, was basically a committee effort, and Roddenberry eventually decided to let others take the credit for it.

Screenplay by Harold Livingston

Based on a story by Alan Dean Foster

Produced by Gene Roddenberry

Directed by Robert Wise

CAST

Captain Kirk	William Shatner
Spock	Leonard Nimoy
Dr. McCoy	DeForest Kelley
Scotty	James Doohan
Sulu	George Takei

ACADEMY AWARD NOMINATIONS

3 nominations, no wins

Best Art Direction–Set Decoration
Best Original Score
(Jerry Goldsmith)
Best Visual Effects

THE JERK

UNIVERSAL
$42,989,656

"I was born a poor black child."
—STEVE MARTIN (NAVIN JOHNSON)

STEVE MARTIN was a former TV writer who moved on to a successful career as stand-up comic and television performer. During the '70s, he had garnered a loyal following, and it was his fans' support he was counting on when he co-scripted *The Jerk* with Carl Gottlieb and Michael Elias. His admirers weren't disappointed. Although the film has a lot of vulgar language and was rated "R," it still did surprisingly well, proving that under-17s are a resourceful group who can easily find a way around the MPAA's

rating system.

The character Martin creates in this picture, a white goofus who discovers he's not the natural child of black parents and sets out to seek his fortune, offers a plum role for the talented actor-comedian. He plays the lovable but unlikely moron to the hilt. Sight gags, puns, even tongue twisters—everything is fair game for this Jerry Lewis-like oddball character. He is ably assisted by Bernadette Peters, who plays the perfect straight woman to Martin's character. Typical dialogue:

MARIE
I'm a cosmetologlst.

NAVIN
It must be tough to handle weightlessness.

Naturally, the two become romantically involved, leading to more funny dialogue. For example, after making love, he announces: "I slit the sheet. The sheet I slit. And on the slitted sheet I sit...I've never been relaxed enough around anyone to be able to say that."

Some of the best sequences in this Carl Reiner–directed movie are the spoofs of other hit pictures, among them *2001: A Space Odyssey, The Exorcist,* and *Saturday Night Fever.* Reiner also makes a cameo appearance as a director. Martin himself

makes an appearance in another role—that of "Pig Eye Johnson," the man who juggles cats (don't worry, they're not real, despite the convincing sound effects).

Reviews were mixed, and some papers, like *The Hollywood Reporter,* were downright hostile: "Going the full distance on a feature film is clearly beyond [Steve Martin], and he receives precious little help from Carl Reiner's flat, head-on direction...there are all those Steve Martin fans who turned [his book] *Cruel Shoes* into a best-seller and his record albums into pure Platinum; they may also rally to the support of his movie. But I doubt it. Any picture that calls itself 'The Jerk' deserves what it gets."

What it got was a heaping helping of box office gold, dispelling this critic's gloomy predictions. *Newsweek* was somewhat more favorable, remarking that "if Martin ever finds the proper vehicle, he could become a first-rate screen comedian. 'The Jerk' is a promising warm-up."

Martin and Peters re-teamed in 1981 for *Pennies from Heaven,* and although the movie was not a box office block-buster, each performer has since gone on to enjoy separate, highly successful careers in film, TV, and theater. *The Jerk* had the last laugh after all.

Screenplay by Steve Martin, Carl Gottlieb, and Michael Elias

Based on a story by Steve Martin and Carl Gottlieb

Produced by David V. Picker and William F. McEuen

Directed by Carl Reiner

CAST

Navin Johnson	Steve Martin
Marie	Bernadette Peters
Patty Bernstein	Catlin Adams
Mother	Mabel King
Harry Hartounian	Jackie Mason

"I'm officially retired now."
—ROCKY BALBOA

WANNA BET? Rocky Balboa, that hunk of a punching machine we all cheered to victory in 1976's number-one film and Best Picture, *Rocky* (hereinafter known as *Rocky I*), began this sequel with the above announcement. It didn't take much intelligence or guesswork to realize that there was still an hour and fifty-nine or so minutes of movie to fill, and that *something* was going to happen up there on the screen.

Of course, that something was part of what was now the standard *Rocky* formula: the Champ has sworn off boxing with a "never again" promise; he's coerced into "just this one last fight"; his challenger is a cross between Superman and a 20-megaton bomb; he trains his brains out; he fights an excruciating and nearly deadly fight, and—cue the Oscar-winning "Gonna Fly Now" music—it's a miracle! "This is the greatest day in the history of my life!" exclaims the re-crowned human punching bag as he staggers to his feet and waves his arms in the air, victorious yet again.

Not a film filled with surprises. Yet audiences adored this boxing wonder, created, acted, written, and directed by

Sylvester Stallone. If *Rocky I* had taken Hollywood and the world-at-large by storm, then at first it would seem that *Rocky II* took it by drizzle. No trumpets, no Oscars (not even one nomination) for the previously acclaimed hero, making this even more of an underdog. But audiences *love* an underdog, with both film and hero proving there was plenty of life left in old Rocky yet.

Joining Sly Stallone again were Talia Shire as his devoted wife and Burgess Meredith as his devoted trainer. His devoted opponent, Apollo Creed, was also back for more punishment at the fists of Rocky Balboa. As *The New York Times* commented: "Though the Count de Sade gets no screen credit, it

---

Screenplay by Sylvester Stallone

Produced by Irwin Winkler and Robert Chartoff

Directed by Sylvester Stallone

CAST

Rocky Balboa	Sylvester Stallone
Adrian	Talia Shire
Paulie	Burt Young
Apollo Creed	Carl Weathers
Mickey	Burgess Meredith

---

must have been he who refereed both fights; anybody else would have stopped the first, and there wouldn't have been a sequel."

Stallone attributes the realism to diligent research. "I studied a lot of fight films and borrowed ideas for *Rocky*," he told *The New York Times*. "Real fights, I mean—Marcel Cerdan, Rocky Marciano, Joe Louis, Rocky Graziano…Muhammad Ali." The creator of a legend added, "I like Rocky. [He's] a nice guy. Not smart. I see him with a man's body and the mind of a 15-year-old…he relates to people. I hope audiences still can relate to him."

Time's reviewer had difficulty finding anything to relate to. "There might have been fun in *Rocky II*," he wrote, "but not with Stallone serving as writer and director." The critic added: "The movie's obligatory set piece, a reprise of Rocky's triumphal jog up the steps of the Philadelphia Museum of Art, now looks like a tableau out of Cecil B. DeMille…one almost expects him to wrap himself in the flag; perhaps he is saving that *piece de resistance* for *Rocky III*."

Whether the *Time* reviewer was psychic or Stallone took a cue from this scathing review is not known, but two sequels later, in *Rocky IV* (1985), that's *exactly* what the fighter did.

ALIEN

20TH CENTURY-FOX
$40,300,000

PURPORTEDLY a story about deep space and a group of seven astronauts—five men and two women—working on a battered commercial space-tug, *Alien* was actually a basic "gotcha!" suspense/terror film, more closely aligned to *Psycho* or *Jaws* than to classic science-fiction films like *2001* or *Star Trek*. The first patrons of this release entered the theaters unaware of what to expect; they left in a shaken state, nervously watching every dark shadow, every flutter of a leaf, checking their cars carefully before entering the unknown void of their dark interiors to begin the uncertain drive home.

The film tapped into our deepest nightmares of "something" hiding down the dark, unseen corridors of our minds, lurking there from our childhood. Scary —that was the word most used to describe *Alien*. People screamed, and returned to theaters to scream again. *Variety* sized up the movie's potential instantly, proclaiming: "Another hot summer at the Fox-office."*

Even more interesting than the film's suspenseful plot about an alien "monster" intent on using human bodies as hosts for its next generation was the fact that the film gave birth to the next generation of movie makers, important names we'd be hearing from in the next decade or two.

Although only given second billing, the most successful person aboard the space-tug *Nostromo* would also be the most successful actor in the cast.

Sigourney Weaver (Ripley) had only one other film to her credit (a minor role in 1977's *Annie Hall*) when she was signed to co-star in *Alien*. She has continued her promising career with such '80s hits as *Ghostbusters* (1984); *Aliens* (the 1986 pluralized sequel to *Alien*); *Working Girl* (1988); *Gorillas in the Mist* (1988); *Ghostbusters II* (1989); *Alien 3* (1992); and *Dave* (1993). Along the way, she has picked up several Academy Award nominations, including one for *Aliens* (1986).

The other star to emerge from *Alien* was a man well known to his native British audiences, although only vaguely familiar to Americans—mostly aficionados of Public Television. John Hurt, who plays Kane, the *Nostromo*'s executive officer, has received many accolades, including the British Best TV Actor of the Year Award for his 1975 performance as Quentin Crisp in "The Naked Civil Servant," and critical acclaim for his portrayal of Caligula in

the PBS series "I, Claudius." But his most well-known performance to date has been the lead in the 1980 film *The Elephant Man,* for which Hurt received an Oscar nomination.

The film is also noteworthy for its visual effects, which grabbed the second Oscar for Carlo Rambaldi (his first had been for *King Kong*). Rambaldi had worked on Spielberg's *Close Encounters of the Third Kind,* and his name would soon become a household word with the 1982 hit *E. T. The Extra-Terrestrial.*

So effective were *Alien*'s mechanical and puppet effects that the film's director of photography, Derek Vanlint, became nauseated during "dailies" (viewing of previous day's footage) showing the "birth" sequence, and had to leave the projection room. He spent the rest of the shoot trying to live that moment down.

---

*While the picture cost a mere $11,000,000 to produce, the advertising campaign totaled a whopping $16,000,000—more than the film itself and it took nearly a year for *Alien* to turn a profit.

Screenplay by Dan O'Bannon

Executive Producer: Ronald Shusett

Produced by Gordon Carroll, David Giler, and Walter Hill

Directed by Ridley Scott

CAST

Dallas	Tom Skerritt
Ripley	Sigourney Weaver
Lambert	Veronica Cartwright
Brett	Harry Dean Stanton
Kane	John Hurt

ACADEMY AWARD NOMINATIONS

2 nominations, 1 win*

Best Art Direction–Set Decoration
*Best Visual Effects

T HE EIGHTIES was a decade of escapism. Moviegoers favored larger-than-life heroes, bold and brave personalities who could be counted on to save us or at least themselves from some huge threat. And the decade cracked the nut about sequels not generally doing well, as more and more Roman numerals followed familiar film titles.

More money was made by just *one* number-one film for any given year in the Eighties than by the combined totals of *several* years of top five films of the Forties or Fifties. Certainly, tickets cost more, inflation had occurred, population had increased, and there were more screens in multiplex theaters.

But also motion pictures, as the saying goes, were truly "bigger and better than ever" in the high-tech Eighties. Special effects were convincingly real, thanks to the digital efficiency of the computer age. Wide-screen productions in 70-millimeter were now the norm, and six-channel Dolby-stereo sound systems were installed in thousands of cinemas.

Exhibitors were awash with megamovies from the two biggest (and highest-grossing) names in the business, George Lucas and Steven Spielberg. These producer/directors were the incarnation of Walt Disney for the Eighties, capturing our imaginations and more of our dollars than anyone, including Disney himself, had ever done.

1980

Forget the old "line around the block" cliché—the mere whisper of the name "Spielberg" or "Lucas" was enough to send scores of sleeping-bag-toting fans down to makeshift campsites in front of box offices as early as two days before the picture ever opened.

At the beginning of the decade, a new invention was poised to turn the movie business upside down. Called the videocassette recorder, or VCR for short, it revolutionized the industry by bringing the theater into our homes. But rather than hurt business, the VCR seemed to make no difference whatsoever to exhibitors, whose patrons wanted to see these "events" on the big screen first.

Initially, only a small minority of die-hard movie buffs owned these new gadgets, which frequently cost upwards of $1,000. In 1980, one percent of all households had a VCR, but by 1989, the demand for these wonders pushed prices down to under $200, and the ownership figure had jumped to more than 60 percent. In the long run, this meant huge profits for film studios, whose coffers were further swollen with royalties for videocassette sales. Actors, directors, writers, and other filmmakers threw picket lines around studios demanding their fair share of these profits, and strikes occasionally beset the film industry as this situation sorted itself out. In the end, everyone was happy: filmgoers, cassette buyers, talent, and studio executives. The Eighties were Hollywood's most successful decade to date.

1989

1

THE EMPIRE STRIKES BACK

20TH CENTURY-FOX
$141,672,000

"EPISODE V
THE EMPIRE STRIKES BACK
*It is a dark time for
the Rebellion…*"

THUS BEGINS another chapter in George Lucas' own private Saturday matinee, the one he was kind enough to invite us all to attend with him. "Episode V" was actually only the second look at our friends from *Star Wars* in this first of a promised multitude of sequels from that number-one box office hit. And while it didn't surpass its predecessor financially, many thought it equal to or better than the original in content.

All the Star Warriors were back, of course—Luke Skywalker, his evil nemesis Darth Vader, Princess Leia and Han Solo (whose romance begins to emerge in this film), Chewbacca the Wookie, Droids R2D2 and C3PO, plus some new additions to the gallery of space people. Most innovative was the centuries-old Jedi knight and Luke's reluctant trainer, Yoda. He's sort of a cross between Walter Cronkite and Peter Lorre, with a touch of Burgess Meredith's Mickey to Rocky counterpart Luke, with his "What am I going to do with this kid?" attitude (a formula that would later become the basis of three *Karate Kid* pictures). Urged on by a disembodied Obi-Won Kenobi (Alec Guinness), Yoda (performed by Muppeteer Frank Oz) is the closest thing to a philosopher we'll ever find in a science fiction movie, and he gets the best lines in the film:

LUKE
(observing Yoda levitate his ship)
I don't believe it!

YODA
That is why you fail.

Later he exhorts Luke to "Try not! Do! Or do not. There is no *try.*" Definitely words of wisdom for anyone, not necessarily just a Jedi-in-training. We learn more about the mysterious "Force" that was with us in that first film: "Life creates it and makes it grow," the elfin Yoda explains; "its energy surrounds us and binds us." And Yoda's urging Luke to "feel the flow, feel the Force around you" had mystics and ministers alike busily analyzing the religious overtones inherent in this central philosophy.

Another welcome addition to the cast was the first black character* in what so far had seemed to be an all-white universe. Near the end of the picture, we are introduced to Lando Calrissian (Billy Dee Williams), Cloud City's black ruler (with an unexplained, vaguely Armenian-sounding surname), who sets the movie's denouement into motion.

As in the first film, the action never stops, as our eyes are constantly dazzled with optical magic—walking cameloid tanks (homage to *Lawrence of Arabia,* say some interpretations), hair-raising forays through an asteroid field, plus monsters and creatures of all sizes. Inventive crew members of the executive producer's own company, Industrial Light and Magic, devised optical printers capable of combining layer upon layer of elements to achieve a nearly three-dimensional image in sequences such as the asteroid-dodging scene.

Like its predecessor, *The Empire Strikes Back* was shot at the EMI Elstree Studios outside London. Scenes of the ice planet Hoth were shot on a real glacier at Finse, Norway, where Scott trained for his expedition to the South Pole.

The hugely successful film was not financed by 20th Century-Fox, but only released through that distributor. Although the studio had supplied the $11,000,000 needed to film *Star Wars,* for *Empire* George Lucas put up $18,000,000 of his own money while retaining all worldwide rights to the property for his company, Lucasfilm. This risk caused him to be temporarily overextended, and although he received much criticism from well-meaning friends, the producer eventually made it all back, plus. The Force was certainly with him as, fortunately for us, George Lucas struck back.

*The only other regular black cast member was James Earl Jones, the unseen provider of the voice of Darth Vader (Vader was played by English actor David Prowse).

Screenplay by Leigh Brackett and
Lawrence Kasdan

Based on a story by George Lucas

Executive Producer: George Lucas

Produced by Gary Kurtz

Directed by Irvin Kershner

CAST

Luke Skywalker . . . .Mark Hamill
Han Solo . . . . .Harrison Ford
Princess Leia . . . . .Carrie Fisher
Darth Vader . . . . . .David Prowse
Yoda . . . . .Frank Oz
Lando Calrissian . .Billy Dee Williams
Obi-Won
   (Ben) Kenobi . . . .Alec Guinness

ACADEMY AWARD NOMINATIONS

3 nominations, 1 win*

  Best Art Direction–Set Decoration
*Best Sound
  Best Original Score (John Williams)

With no other nominees in the
category, *The Empire Strikes Back*
was given the Academy's Special
Achievement Award for Visual Effects
(Brian Johnson, Richard Edlund,
Dennis Muren, and Bruce Nicholson)

WOMEN'S LIB had been with us for nearly a decade when *9 to 5* appeared on the scene. It was the perfect film for the '80s, which saw women in every aspect of the work force. Here was a film with three female leads, like that box office hit of the '50s, *How to Marry a Millionaire.* But unlike that earlier movie, *9 to 5* was aimed not at an audience of leering and gawking males but at today's working woman. And women all over the country could certainly relate to this trio and their male chauvinist boss.

The three actresses were especially convincing as secretaries, although Dolly Parton, receiving only third billing, outshone her two co-stars, since she seemed the most natural of the bunch. This was her first movie appearance, and *Newsweek* called her "a sweet and easy comic presence, a natural actress." The country-and-western singer wrote the title song as well, and it climbed the *Billboard* charts to reach number one by February, only two months after the picture's release. The singer also picked up an Oscar nomination for Best Song.

Jane Fonda and Lily Tomlin played the other two secretaries with whom audiences identified. The picture was produced solely by Jane's production company, IPC, but she certainly didn't select the best role for herself. Although she received top billing, she was relegated to playing straightwoman.

Lily Tomlin shines in her part and has the film's best fantasy sequence. Dressed in Snow White costume and wig, surrounded by a Disney gallery of adorable bunnies and bluebirds chirping their hearts out, Tomlin chirps gaily back at the critters in this hilarious send-up of *Snow White, Song of the South,* and *Bambi.*

Cast as their male chauvinist pig of a boss with no redeeming traits whatsoever, Dabney Coleman excels in playing this cardboard-cutout role. During the years that followed, Coleman has played similar characters many

---

Screenplay by Colin Higgins and Patricia Resnick

Based on a story by Patricia Resnick

Produced by Bruce Gilbert

Directed by Colin Higgins

CAST

Judy Bernly	Jane Fonda
Violet Newstead	Lily Tomlin
Doralee Rhodes	Dolly Parton
Franklin Hart, Jr.	Dabney Coleman
Tinsworthy	Sterling Hayden

ACADEMY AWARD NOMINATIONS

1 nomination, no wins

Best Original Song ("9 to 5," music and words by Dolly Parton)

---

times; his own TV show, "Buffalo Bill," had him portraying a sleazy type.

Was the film realistic in its depiction of life at the office? An article that appeared in *The New York Times* two weeks after the film's release noted that "a secretary must be a waitress who serves coffee and snacks to the boss; a personal shopper who buys birthday presents for the wife; a nurse, who administers his eyedrops; a maid, who tends plants and dusts…'We were brought up to do these things,' [an interviewed secretary] said, 'and I guess it seemed a natural extension to do them in the office. But today many more women are demanding to be treated as full-fledged human beings. The movie reflects this.' "

However, the film drew in more than just harassed office workers. No boss could ever be the complete ass depicted by Coleman, so no boss ever recognized himself in that caricature. This gave the picture its wide appeal and gave Fox the number-two box office hit of the year.

In March, 1982, "9 to 5" debuted as an ABC television series. Dolly Parton's sister Rachel Dennison co-starred with Rita Moreno and Valerie Curtin; Jane Fonda co-produced. The show was cancelled by ABC in October, 1983, but was later resurrected for syndication, with James Komack producing and Sally Struthers as one of the stars.

3

STIR CRAZY

COLUMBIA
$58,364,420

"One hundred and twenty five years?! I'll be one hundred and sixty-nine when I get out!"
—RICHARD PRYOR

WILDER WAS BACK, and Pryor got him for the second pairing of this "odd couple." Unlike their earlier duet, *Silver Streak,* there were few other characters to get in their way; the screen was all theirs, as was most of this picture, turned over to the two-some's ad-libs by actor-turned-director Sidney Poitier. What emerged was a semi-funny, semi-serious film that seemed to lose its sense of direction and the love of critics along the way, but never the pair's loyal fans. Wilder and Pryor together were demographically appealing, making for box office dollars and placing the Columbia picture strongly among the year's top five. As *Time* magazine put it: "Recipe for a popular movie: take a series of stock situations, two gifted farceurs, and stir. Crazy!"

The recipe worked. And it didn't hurt that there were some other clichés folded in, like a barroom brawl, a corrupt prison system and warden, the "great" escape, and that favorite gag when all else fails: two grown men in chicken suits. This, more than any of the other gimmicks, did the most to sell the film. Everywhere you looked that Christmas, there were ads and TV promos for *Stir Crazy* with Wilder and Pryor dressed in feathery regalia. For some reason, people found this irresistible and (pardon the pun) flocked to the theaters.

Although audiences enjoyed the tried-but-true formula, *The Hollywood Reporter* found it tough to swallow: "Although Gene Wilder and Richard Pryor again demonstrate that they make excellent foils for each other… it's difficult to avoid the feeling that it's a Bruce Jay Friedman script…should either have been shot straight or not at all…But Pryor, even when working with minimal comic material, manages to give the film liveliness and color."

Pryor seemed to catch the attention of more than one critic. While *Variety* termed the film "saleable," most of the credit also went to Pryor: "His pained look into the camera when he's sentenced to jail, his hopeless reactions to Wilder's eccentricities and his overall stance as the famed fool make a flimsy feature like 'Stir Crazy' worth seeing. To quote an often used line, 'that takes talent.' "

In 1985, a television series was assayed based on the movie, but like many other attempts at translating films into TV shows, it was short-lived.

Wilder and Pryor were reunited again in 1989 for another on-screen romp in the movie *See No Evil, Hear No Evil.* The comedy received rave reviews from "The Today Show" supercritic, Gene Shalit, who exclaimed, "You could die laughing." Not many people did, however, and the film failed to become a block-buster. Like the other Wilder/Pryor pictures, this one is available on video.

Screenplay by Bruce Jay Friedman

Produced by Hannah Weinstein

Directed by Sidney Poitier

CAST

Skip Donahue	Gene Wilder
Harry Monroe	Richard Pryor
Rory Schultebrand	Georg Stanford Brown
Meredith	Jobeth Williams
Deputy Ward Wilson	Craig T. Nelson

4

AIRPLANE!

PARAMOUNT
$40,610,000

AMONG THE films parodied by this zany send-up to end all send-ups were *Airport,* the *Airport* sequels, *Jaws, From Here to Eternity,* and *Saturday Night Fever.* In many ways, *Airplane!* seems like an hour-and-a-half-long "Saturday Night Live" sketch, with the nonstop puns, satire, and looniness never abating.

Back in 1976, Paramount Pictures made their first attempt at satirizing the wave of disaster films popping up all over movie screens in the '70s. The picture was called *The Big Bus,* but it was a big bust instead. It involved a sort of "superbus," but audiences generally preferred their disasters and disaster take-offs to, well, take off.

The film opens with John Williams' driving *Jaws* theme as a plane's tailfin bisects a cloudbank. This is going to be fun, promises Paramount, and the studio keeps its word. Like the disaster-genre films it parodies, *Airplane!* has an all-star cast, including basketball great Kareem Abdul-Jabbar as a co-pilot, Lloyd Bridges as the troubled trouble-shooter, Peter Graves as Captain Oveur, Robert Hays as the former pilot who turns fear of flying into an art form (and of course saves the day), Julie Hagerty as his girlfriend-cum-stewardess, plus a dozen or so television stars like Leslie Nielsen, Robert Stack, Barbara Billingsley ("Leave it to Beaver"), Jimmie Walker ("Good Times"), and Jill Whelan ("The Love Boat").

But that's not all, folks! Ethel

Merman plays a man—a shell-shocked soldier who's deluded into believing he's Ethel Merman. David Leisure (Joe Isuzu and co-star of "Empty Nest") can be seen in an early role as the shaven-head Hare Krishna passenger. And then there's the late Howard Jarvis, author of California's Proposition 13 (a property tax-reform bill), playing a passenger stuck in a taxicab throughout the whole picture! If you watch closely, you'll catch the film's writer-exec producers, Jim Abrahams, David Zucker, and Jerry Zucker, as Religious Zealot #6, Ground Crewman #2, and Ground Crewman #1, respectively.

Airplane! was based on a '50s Paramount drama called *Zero Hour,* in which the pilot and co-pilot of an airlin-er are stricken by food poisoning and one of the passengers, a former fighter pilot who blames himself for the deaths of several of his comrades, assumes command and is "talked" down. Combine this thread of a plot with your basic *Airport* picture, and voilà: a surefire comedy hit.

Two years later, Paramount was back with a sequel, *Airplane II: The Sequel.* It starred William Shatner plus returnees Robert Hays, Julie Hagerty, Peter Graves, and Lloyd Bridges, with cameos by Raymond Burr, Chuck Connors, and Sonny Bono. It wasn't as successful as the original *Airplane!* but is still quite funny. Both movies appear frequently on TV and are also available for rental on videocassette.

Screenplay by Jim Abrahams, David Zucker, and Jerry Zucker

Executive-produced and directed by Jim Abrahams, David Zucker, and Jerry Zucker

CAST

Ted Striker . . . . .Robert Hays
Elaine . . . . .Julie Hagerty
Murdock . . . . . .Kareem Abdul-Jabbar
McCroskey . . . . . . .Lloyd Bridges
Captain Oveur . . . . .Peter Graves
Dr. Rumack . . . . . . .Leslie Nielsen

Cᴸɪɴᴛ Eᴀsᴛᴡᴏᴏᴅ has managed to make a career out of playing three basic characters: the loner cowboy of the *Fistful of Dollars* films, Dirty Harry from the series of films about that self-styled vigilante, and Philo Beddoe, the easy-going westerner who has orang-utan, will travel. His second appearance in the *Every Which Way/Any Which Way* saga saw him reunited with his pal Clyde (*Time* immediately dubbed the film "Philo and Clyde") and significant other Sondra Locke.

Fistfights are one of the main elements fans have come to expect from any Clint Eastwood movie, and fights aplenty arrive like clockwork, averaging about one every 20 minutes. This time, there are a bunch of neo-Nazi bikers who are the baddies, but of course they get their comeuppance.

North Hollywood's Palomino Club (a real-life country-and-western night-club) is again the setting for the musical scenes, with plenty of tunes to help produce a soundtrack album from this urban cowboy watering hole. Fats Domino performs "Whiskey Heaven," and the soundtrack is further enhanced by source music like Glen Campbell doing the title song, "Beers to You" sung by Ray Charles and Clint Eastwood, and "Cow Patti" by Jim Stafford.

There's not much of a guest cast, but the late Ruth Gordon does a memorable job as Clint's crotchety old mother, who feistily takes on the neo-Nazi bikers. There's also a funny parody of the movie *10,* with Ruth's face superimposed over that of Bo Derek.

The original orangutan who played Clyde was not available for this sequel, so an orang named "Buddha" was substituted. According to an article by Jill Donner in the Writers Guild of America West *Journal* for April, 1989, this ape was so mistreated on the set and at its home compound that the instrument designed to hit the poor creature was named a "Buddha club" after him. Donner writes that the club, still in wide use in the movie and TV industry, can be either a metal pipe disguised in a newspaper wrapper or a basic three-and-a-half-foot axe handle.

Clyde/Buddha apparently misbehaved on the set of *Any Which Way* one afternoon, and was "disciplined" on arrival back at his compound. Two weeks after the movie wrapped, Buddha was found dead of a reported cerebral hemorrhage. Whether or not the story of his beating is true, there was much controversy in Hollywood regarding the American Humane Association and its on-set representatives. Conditions have improved since then, with the animals the beneficiaries of this brouhaha.

Screenplay by Stanford Sherman

Based on characters created by Jeremy Joe Kronsberg

Executive Producer: Robert Daley

Produced by Fritz Manes

Directed by Buddy Van Horn

CAST

Philo Beddoe . . . . .Clint Eastwood
Lynne Halsey-Taylor . . .Sondra Locke
Orville . . . . .Geoffrey Lewis
James Beekman . . . . .Harry Guardino
Ma . . . . .Ruth Gordon

1

RAIDERS OF THE LOST ARK

PARAMOUNT
$115,598,000

STEVEN SPIELBERG and George Lucas: their very names above the title guaranteed (a) a good time at the movies and (b) a huge take at the box office. And that was *separately.* Together, the package ought to come with a warning label, the combination was so explosive. Lucky the studio that had such a pairing. Lucky the audience, too.

Paramount Pictures couldn't have been happier. They would get to release the Lucasfilm production, financed by the successful producer of the two (so far) *Star War* epics. The idea for *Raiders* dated back to 1977, when George Lucas was vacationing in Hawaii with Steven Spielberg a week before *Star Wars* opened. "George had gone to Hawaii to get away from what he thought would be a monumental disaster," said Spielberg in a press release at the time. "At dinner one night, when George got the news that the film was a hit the first week, and he was suddenly laughing again, he told me the story of these movies he wanted to make, a series of archeology films…I've always wanted to bring a serial to life that blends Lash LaRue, Spy Smasher, Masked Marvel and Tailspin Tommy with elements from Edgar Rice Burroughs and George's great imagination." Lucas, too, had always wanted to make that kind of serial, but had to put the ideas on the shelf while doing *Star Wars.*

Synchronicity finally happened in 1980, as production on *Raiders* began at EMI Elstree Studios near London, on location in France, Tunisia, and Hawaii. Lucas co-wrote the story with Phil Kaufman (who had once written a draft for *Star Trek: The Motion Picture* and later went on to write and direct *The Right Stuff*). At the same time, he sketched out two additional chapters—*Indiana Jones and the Temple of Doom* (1984) and *Indiana Jones and the Last Crusade* (1989). They set the story in 1936 in order to use some true facts about Adolf Hitler, a student of religious doctrine, artifacts, and the occult. The tale centers around the adventures of a larger-than-life arche-

ology professor who spends his summers hunting for artifacts…in this case, the mythical Ark of the Covenant, which, according to Biblical lore and the film's storyline, contains the broken tablets of the Ten Commandments. It was a film worthy of DeMille himself, with exotic locations, lost cities, power-crazed villains, romantic interludes, and brushes with certain death.

Harrison Ford was selected to portray Indiana Jones, popularly called "Indy" (like the 500 car race of the same name). It was Ford's fourth film for George Lucas—*American Graffiti* and the two *Star Wars* pictures preceded this. He became much more of a sex symbol after playing Indy than he did in the role of Han Solo, and went on to play the dashing archeologist in the film's two sequels. He also moved on to straight dramatic roles, in films

such as *The Mosquito Coast, Witness,* and *The Fugitive.* But in an interview for the Lucasfilm Fan Club newsletter, the actor was quoted as saying, "I think *Raiders of the Lost Ark* was probably the most fun I've had on a film."

Karen Allen played the ballsy Marion Ravenwood, whom he meets and later beds (not on screen, of course; this is "PG"). Her only other major film credit had been in John Landis' *National Lampoon's Animal House* (see page 261).

The other star of the film is the memorable music score by the top motion picture composer of our time, John Williams. The musician has composed scores for more than 50 films, including the *Star Wars* pictures, *Far and Away, Home Alone, Jurassic Park,* and *Schindler's List.*

The critics were blown away by *Raiders of the Lost Ark*; there were no dissenters among all the top reviewers. *The Hollywood Reporter* gushed: "If George Lucas were to say that he could make a terrific entertainment out of Chairman Mao's Little Red Book, at this point I'd be inclined to believe him*—this point being just a few hours after seeing his 'Raiders of the Lost Ark.' And if he wanted to bring along Steven Spielberg to direct, I'd believe him even more." Of all that has been written by critics, Roger Ebert, in his *Movie Home Companion,* seems to have captured the film's feeling the best: "*Raiders of the Lost Ark* is an out-of-body experience, a movie of glorious imagination and breakneck speed that grabs you in the first shot, hurtles you through a series of incredible adventures, and deposits you back in reality two hours later—breathless, dizzy, wrung-out, and with a silly grin on your face."

In 1995, Disneyland added the "Indiana Jones" ride to the theme park's attractions. Not surprisingly, many visitors left breathless, dizzy, wrung out, and with silly grins on their faces.

Screenplay by Lawrence Kasdan

Story by George Lucas and Philip Kaufman

Executive Producers: George Lucas and Howard Kazanjian

Produced by Frank Marshall

Directed by Steven Spielberg

CAST

Indiana Jones . . . . . . .Harrison Ford
Marion . . . . .Karen Allen
Dietrich . . . . .Wolf Kahler
Belloq . . . . .Paul Freeman
Toht . . . . .Ronald Lacey

ACADEMY AWARD NOMINATIONS

8 nominations, 4 wins*

Best Picture
Best Director (Steven Spielberg)
Best Cinematography
*Best Art Direction
*Best Sound
Best Original Score (John Williams)
*Best Film Editing
*Best Visual Effects

A Special Achievement Award for Sound Effects Editing went to Benjamin P. Burtt, Jr., and Richard L. Anderson.

---

*This was, of course, before Lucas' major misstep, *Howard the Duck.*

SUPERMAN II

WARNER BROS.
$65,100,000

HEROES WERE IN. Luke Skywalker, Indiana Jones, even James Bond had captured our hearts and our imaginations. And ever since 1978, fans of the hit movie *Superman* had been patiently awaiting the promised return of their larger-than-life hero. They were not disappointed. When *Superman II* leaped onto the screen this time, the public again sent the movie soaring to box office heights, and like the first opus, it landed squarely in the number-two position, proving that the Man from Krypton still had plenty of bounce left in him.

There were some returnees, of course. Back again were Gene Hackman as Lex Luthor (given top billing over Chris Reeve's title character), Ned Beatty as the bumbling Otis, Jackie Cooper as Perry White, Margot Kidder as Lois Lane, Marc McClure as Jimmy Olsen (a virtual non-role, considering the importance of the character in the comics and TV series), plus a pack of new villains. Most outstanding among these is Sarah Douglas, who seems born to play evil personified. As Ursa, the dominatrix from Krypton with her two greaser cohorts, she creates one of the most charming villainesses since *101 Dalmatians'* Cruella De Vil. (The English actress followed her performance in *Superman II* with a fiendish role in the TV movie *V: The Final Battle* and a recurring part on "Falcon Crest" from 1983 to 1985). When the space trio arrives on Earth hell-bent on stirring up trouble, they land in a small town, and are immediately sized up by the locals: "From the look of them, I'd bet $10 they're from Los Angeles," says one. It's campy, and great fun.

But even better, for the romantics in the audiences, this is the film in which Superman and Lois finally get it on. He first gives up his super powers and becomes—horror of horrors—mortal. Clark Kent shows us unexpected warmth and vulnerability, a tribute to the fine acting of Reeve, whose characterizations must constantly change for his dual role. One of the reasons for the huge success of this sequel is the chance to see our hero in love. Audiences eagerly returned to the theater to see what had never before happened to the Man of Steel.*

Superman II won not only the heart of Lois Lane, but the support of the critics as well. *Newsweek* proclaimed: "*Superman II* is a success, a stirring sequel to the smash of ['78 and] '79. Whether you will prefer it to the original is like choosing between root beer and Fresca. They're both bubbly, but the flavor is different."

The film credits Richard Lester (*A Hard Day's Night, The Three Musketeers*) as director, but it also includes footage shot by Richard Donner when he directed *Superman I* back in 1977. At that time, there were plans to do at least two movies, and the crew immediately segued into *Superman II*. (Some of Lester's shots were likewise included in Donner's picture.) *Superman II* was actually released worldwide in December, 1980, but it was six months before Warner Bros. released it in the United States, earning a pile of money overseas during the winter months in countries like Australia, South Africa, and Brazil before allowing the Man of Steel to migrate for the warm North American summer. The reception at the box office proved warm indeed; we'd be seeing more of Superman in years to come.

---

*In the original '50s "Superman" TV series, there was an episode in which Superman and Lois get married ("The Wedding of Superman"), but alas, it was only Lois' dream. And the '90s series, "Lois and Clark: The New Adventures of Superman," took their relationship to the brink of marriage, then backed off (as of 1996).

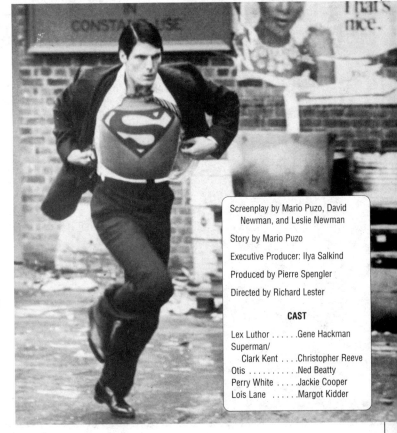

Screenplay by Mario Puzo, David Newman, and Leslie Newman

Story by Mario Puzo

Executive Producer: Ilya Salkind

Produced by Pierre Spengler

Directed by Richard Lester

CAST

Lex Luthor	Gene Hackman
Superman/ Clark Kent	Christopher Reeve
Otis	Ned Beatty
Perry White	Jackie Cooper
Lois Lane	Margot Kidder

ON GOLDEN POND

UNIVERSAL
$61,175,028

presented Hank with Spence's "lucky" hat, which he then wore as part of his *Golden Pond* wardrobe.

"I'm living on borrowed time as it is," gripes Norman Thayer, Henry Fonda's character, all the while Fonda knowing that he himself was doing just that. But he gave it his all, and in the process gave the performance of his life. The film was released in November, 1981, and the following spring's Academy Awards ceremony saw Oscars going to Katharine Hepburn as Best Actress (now she had a record *four* statuettes) and—at last—to Henry Fonda. At ages 76 and 74, respectively, they were the oldest Best Actor and Actress winners in the Academy's history. For Fonda, the Award was long overdue. But sadly, he was too ill to attend the ceremony, so daughter Jane (herself a nominee, although not the winner) accepted for her ailing dad. Five months later, on August 12, 1982, Henry Fonda passed away.

Screenplay by Ernest Thompson

Based on the play by Ernest Thompson

Produced by Bruce Gilbert

Directed by Mark Rydell

CAST

Ethel Thayer . . . . .Katharine Hepburn
Norman Thayer, Jr. . . .Henry Fonda
Chelsea
    Thayer Wayne . . . . .Jane Fonda
Billy Ray . . . . .Doug McKeon
Bill Ray . . . . .Dabney Coleman

ACADEMY AWARD NOMINATIONS

10 nominations, 3 wins *

  Best Picture
*Best Actor (Henry Fonda)
*Best Actress (Katharine Hepburn)
  Best Supporting Actress (Jane Fonda)
  Best Director (Mark Rydell)
*Best Screenplay Based on Material from
    Another Medium (Ernest Thompson)
  Best Cinematography
  Best Sound
  Best Original Score (Dave Grusin)
  Best Film Editing

THERE IS a distinct possibility that today's young generation of filmgoers might have remembered Henry Fonda as "the father of Jane Fonda" had it not been for his final screen performance. The actor had been making movies in Hollywood for 45 years, memorable pictures like *Jesse James, The Grapes of Wrath, Mister Roberts,* and *12 Angry Men.* Yet surprisingly, with over 60 films to his credit, Henry Fonda had never been honored with an Academy Award for Best Actor.*

On the other hand, Katharine Hepburn was one of Hollywood's most honored actresses. In 48 years, she had managed to rack up 12 nominations, more than any other performer, and had already won a record three

Oscars: for *Morning Glory* (1933), *Guess Who's Coming to Dinner* (1967), and *The Lion in Winter* (1968).

Jane Fonda's company had optioned *On Golden Pond,* Ernest Thompson's play about the trauma of facing old age, as a starring vehicle for her father, but also as what would assuredly be her only opportunity to appear together in a film with him. With the Katharine Hepburn/Henry Fonda co-star combination, the company struck pay dirt. Between them, the two venerable performers had a combined 95 years of motion picture acting in 129 films, plus countless stage and television appearances.

On Golden Pond will always be remembered as special for a number of reasons. Surprisingly, Hepburn and Fonda, Sr., had never worked together in all their years in the same industry. She'd made nine films with Spencer Tracy, but had never even met Hank Fonda. The first day on the set, Kate

*In 1980, the Academy presented an Honorary Award to "Henry Fonda, the consummate actor, in recognition of his brilliant accomplishments and enduring contribution to the art of motion pictures."

ARTHUR

WARNER BROS.
$42,000,000

"Isn't this fun? Don't you wish you were me? I know I do."
—DUDLEY MOORE

AT FIVE-FOOT-THREE, puppy-eyed, sheepishly grinning, tousled-haired Dudley Moore was the closest thing to a living teddy bear the screen had ever seen. He could never, for example, play a crazed killer or a truck driver. And he was certainly an unlikely candidate for a romantic lead. Yet this pint-sized cherub from England landed some of the screen's choicest roles opposite babes like Bo Derek in Blake Edwards' movie *10,* which catapulted the composer/pianist/ comedian/British TV personality into international stardom. In 1981, his second major American film, *Arthur,* saw him playing opposite Liza Minnelli, the gifted singer/actress daughter of Judy Garland and Vincente Minnelli, plus Jill Eikenberry, still basically an unknown but soon to become a familiar face after co-starring in TV's "L.A. Law."

In *Arthur,* "Cuddly Dudley," as he was dubbed by nearly every female who saw him, plays what could have been the most repulsive of creatures—a sot, a perpetually plastered drunk.

Dudley manages to make alcoholism almost cute. He is bolstered by his faithful retainer, a latter-day Jeeves to Arthur's Bertie—both P. G. Wodehouse characters of the '30s to whom the film's lead characters bear more than passing resemblance. Jeeves, or in this case Hobson, is the rock on whom Arthur frequently rests his weary but very wealthy head. Sir John Gielgud was 78 when he played the role of Hobson. His career in show business spanned many decades and included recognition by the Motion Picture Academy for his role in *Arthur,* which won him the Oscar for Best Supporting Actor.

Newsweek missed the limousine on this one when its reviewer announced: "*Arthur* is not the best comedy of the season." The fact is that *Arthur* amassed over $42,000,000 in rentals, better than most comedies in several years. There was simple humor, to be sure, like Arthur announcing, "I think I'll take a bath," and Hobson retorting, "I'll alert the media." There was even the old "walk this way" routine, still getting laughs after all these years. Mostly, though, people just came to enjoy the film's star, and to pull for the poor little rich guy of the film's title.

"Arthur's Theme (The Best That You Can Do)" was also a hit, sung by Christopher Cross. It climbed to the top of the *Billboard* charts by October, 1981, remaining there for three weeks. It was the odds-on favorite for an Oscar, the eighth number-one "rock era" song to win the top prize.

In 1988, the sequel, *Arthur 2: On the Rocks,* attempted to recapture the feeling of the first picture. But the more recent audiences had trouble finding the appeal of a character like Arthur, an overgrown man-child whose alcoholism had still not been properly addressed. If he was cute and funny in the first picture, seven years later he was pathetic and obnoxious. Even Dudley's brilliant performance was not enough to sustain interest in the sequel. With more public awareness of the disease of alcoholism, plus ad campaigns like MADD (Mothers Against Drunk Driving), Nancy Reagan's "Just Say No" program, and the valuable services performed by the Betty Ford Center, the public had had enough of "the hilarious drunk" as central character. The sequel was a huge fiasco.

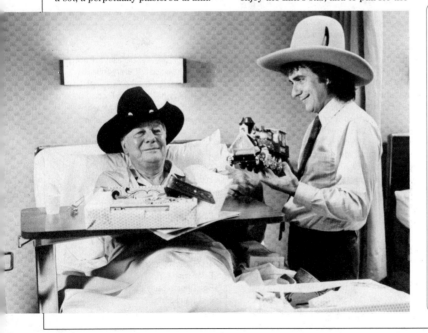

Screenplay by Steve Gordon

Produced by Robert Greenhut

Directed by Steve Gordon

CAST

Arthur Bach	Dudley Moore
Linda Marolla	Liza Minnelli
Hobson	John Gielgud
Martha Bach	Geraldine Fitzgerald
Susan Johnson	Jill Eikenberry

ACADEMY AWARD NOMINATIONS

4 nominations, 2 wins*

Best Actor (Dudley Moore)
*Best Supporting Actor (John Gielgud)
Best Screenplay Written Directly for the Screen
*Best Original Song ("Arthur's Theme [The Best That You Can Do]," music and words by Burt Bacharach, Carole Bayer Sager, Christopher Cross, and Peter Allen)

*"An army without leaders is like a
foot without a big toe."*
—BILL MURRAY

IN 1980, GOLDIE HAWN scored a hit in
Private Benjamin, the story of a
Jewish princess who joins the Army. It
barely missed the top five, but with
$36,000,000 in rentals, the uproarious-
ly funny comedy was a huge success.
A year later, actor-comedian Bill
Murray became the male counterpart
to Hawn's Benjamin with a theme that
had been widely pursued over the
years, beginning with Charlie Chaplin
in *Shoulder Arms* (1918) and continuing through Abbott and Costello in
Buck Privates (1941), Bob Hope in
Caught in the Draft (1941), Danny
Kaye in *Up in Arms* (1944), and Jerry
Lewis in *At War With the Army* (1951).
Completed less than a year after
Goldie's movie, *Stripes* had audiences
laughing even harder, making this film
even more successful at the box office.
Co-produced and directed by Ivan
Reitman, who had showcased Mur-
ray's talents in his previous film, *Meatballs* (1980), *Stripes* was the surprise
comedy hit of the summer of '81. Har-
old Ramis, who had co-written both
Reitman's *National Lampoon's Animal
House* and *Meatballs,* worked on the
script for *Stripes* as well as co-starred
in it. (The trio of Reitman-Murray-

Ramis would be at it again in three
years for *Ghostbusters*; see page 296.)
Ivan Reitman's m.o. was to give
Murray pretty much free rein, since
the actor was at his best when working improvisationally. "Directors might
think, 'Oh, here comes that wild and
wacky guy. I'll just turn on the camera,
and he'll do funny things,' " said Reitman in an interview in *Premiere* magazine. "I start from a premise of his being a gifted actor who's right for a part
that he plays, and I try to help him as
much as I can. I think I have a sense
of his range. And I'm always looking
for him to do his best, to top himself."
Still, Murray was reluctant to do
Stripes—he had also felt the same way

before he agreed to do *Meatballs*—and
Reitman had a hard time convincing
him of the movie's potential. At first it
was "out of the question," but Reitman
enlisted Ramis as a co-star (his first
picture), which turned the trick for
Murray. "The fact that he put Harold
in it was kind of a cheap shot," Murray
admitted to *Premiere.* "If I said no, I
said no to Harold, to his screen debut."
The Hollywood Reporter's Robert
Osborne had mostly pleasant commentary on the movie: "Private
Benjamin, make way for Private
Winger. Columbia, get set for some
tall summer grosses…'Stripes' consistently rolls along with good humor,
solid laughs and a tail-wagging air."
Variety called the picture "The new
Army as frat house & summer camp,"
adding: " 'Stripes' is a cheerful, mildly
outrageous and mostly amiable comedy…there's little in the way of art or
comic subtlety here, but the film really
seems to work."
Watch for appearances by some
actors who would go on to success in
the '80s: John Larroquette, who
became a star of his own TV show;
John Candy, who starred on "SCTV"
and in many movies; actress Sean
Young, who appeared in *Blade Runner,
Dune, No Way Out,* and *Batman*; and
Judge Reinhold, who appeared in
Beverly Hills Cop I and *II.*

Screenplay by Len Blum, Dan Goldberg,
and Harold Ramis

Produced by Ivan Reitman and Dan
Goldberg

Directed by Ivan Reitman

CAST

John	Bill Murray
Russell	Harold Ramis
Sgt. Hulka	Warren Oates
Louise	Sean Young
Ox	John Candy
Capt. Stillman	John Larroquette

E. T. THE EXTRA-TERRESTRIAL

UNIVERSAL
$228,168,939

He is afraid.
He is totally alone.
He is 3,000,000 light years from home.
—ADVERTISING COPY FOR *E. T.*

" 'Jaws,' 'Close Encounters of the Third Kind,' 'Raiders of the Lost Ark.' And now, 'E. T. The Extra-Terrestrial.' Steven Spielberg has done it again. He has created another instant American classic."
—THE HOLLYWOOD REPORTER

IF THERE IS a person alive on this planet who has not yet seen or heard of *E. T. The Extra-Terrestrial,* then they are, in a sense, very lucky. Lucky, because they can still experience seeing *E. T.* for the first time. It's like your first taste of ice cream in the summer, the first time you saw the vast ocean, or the first ray of sunshine after a three-day downpour.

Nineteen eighty-two was the summer we went to the movies and fell in love with a creature from another world: a short, squat, huggable, wrinkly little guy that looked like a shell-less, upright turtle, who touched the innocent child on the screen and the one within our hearts. Just about everyone was caught up in the emotional experience, critic and cynic, child and adult alike. Only those with the hardest of hearts could have refused to adore the wondrous alien.

The film itself seems almost to have been directed by a child, and that is part of the genius of Steven Spielberg. As an adult, he still had one foot in the world of children. That he was gifted when working with children is an understatement: he understood kids even better than that other full-grown child, Walt Disney, understood them, and his ease in directing them was readily apparent. "Their inexperience allows the honesty to come out," he told *Newsweek.* "They *can't* censor. And I *am* a kid."

So at home was Spielberg in the world of children that the story is told entirely from the story's youngsters' point of view, right down to the low angles suggesting the height of a child. When we do meet adults, they are almost invariably antagonistic; even Dee Wallace as the mother, while a sympa-

thetic character, isn't in on the erratic behavior of her kids until the end. In fact, the film was banned in Sweden for children under eleven because the censors felt it showed parents in a poor light.

No problem in America, however, where *E. T.* gave a whole new definition to the term "blockbuster." It wasn't unheard of for people to spend up to two hours waiting patiently in the hot sun for a first (or second or third) chance to catch the on-screen magic. A spate of bumper stickers appeared, urging "E.T. Phone Home!"; Neil Diamond recorded a hit song, "Turn on Your Heart Light" (a reference to the glowing red heart of the creature; the song has since become a hit at Diamond's concerts, where audience members turn on pocket flashlights); people named puppies and kittens "E. T."; and Halloween would never be the same, as thousands of junior E. T.'s waddled door-to-door looking for Reese's Pieces (the merchandising tie-in propelled the candy to an 85 percent increase in revenue).

The creature at the center of all this

Screenplay by Melissa Matheson

Produced by Steven Spielberg and Kathleen Kennedy

Directed by Steven Spielberg

CAST

Mary	Dee Wallace
Elliott	Henry Thomas
Keys	Peter Coyote
Michael	Robert MacNaughton
Gertie	Drew Barrymore

ACADEMY AWARD NOMINATIONS

9 nominations, 3 wins*

Best Picture
Best Director (Steven Spielberg)
Best Screenplay Written Directly for the Screen
Best Cinematography
Best Sound
*Best Original Score (John Williams)
Best Film Editing
*Best Visual Effects
*Best Sound Effects Editing

was a mechanical marvel created by Carlo Rambaldi, the Italian puppet-master behind King Kong and the *CE3K* aliens. In addition to Rambaldi's astonishingly realistic electronic puppet, which had a wide range of facial expressions, there were also live-acted E. T.'s, including one by the shortest adult performer in film. At 2 feet 7 inches, Tamara de Treaux, a little person weighing 40 pounds, was one of three actors playing E. T. Tamara, according to *The Guinness Book of Movie Facts and Feats,* was at that time the shortest adult performer in movies. The San Francisco–born actress and singer did what she called her "Daffy Duck waddle" in the scene when the alien toddles up the ramp into its spacecraft. Other actors were Pat Bilson, 2 feet 10 inches, and a legless schoolboy named Matthew de Merritt, who played the drunk scene while walking on his hands inside an E. T. suit. And the voice of the creature was provided by actress Debra Winger (star of the number-four box office hit of the year, *An Officer and a Gentleman*).

The film was termed "an enchanted fantasy" by *The New York Times* and "an instant American classic" by *The Hollywood Reporter. Variety* proclaimed simply, "*E. T.* equals B. O. [box office]." The latter statement in particular was a prophetic one. Before E. T. was able to phone home and head for his own planet, he managed to haul away enough loot to keep him in Reese's Pieces for the next several millennia. The movie went on to become the number-one box office hit of all time, grossing over $700,000,000 worldwide, with nearly $229,000,000 in domestic rentals (although many are quick to point out that if inflation is taken into account, *Gone With the Wind* is still number one). In 1988, the videocassette was released for home video, and it also quickly rocketed to the top; with 15,000,000 units sold, it was the best-selling videocassette in history at the time, returning another $225,000,000 to MCA (parent company of Universal). Their promotional campaign declared "E. T. Home!" and so at long last he was.

TOOTSIE

COLUMBIA
$94,910,000

EVER SINCE he had won an Oscar for *Kramer vs. Kramer,* Dustin Hoffman had been exploring the idea of what it would be like to be a member of the opposite gender. "The great scripts don't drop out of the sky," the actor told *Time.* "You have to invent them." He kicked the theme of "what is a man/what is a woman?" around for many years, eventually arriving at an early draft of the script to what would be Columbia's biggest hit to that date.

Tootsie began with a script draft by Murray Schisgal, followed by input from seven other writers, including an original script by Don McGuire and rewrites, polishes, and new drafts by Robert Kaufman, Larry Gelbart, Elaine May, Valerie Curtin, Barry Levinson, and Robert Garland. A Writers' Guild arbitration awarded final credit to Larry Gelbart and Murray Schisgal (screenplay) from a story by Don McGuire. But it was pure Dustin Hoffman all the way, with the actor creating the character of Dorothy Michaels from untapped corners of his talented psyche.

Hoffman was the one mainly responsible for the development of Dorothy. Determined to make the character convincing as a woman and not just appear to be another man in drag, Hoffman practiced through a succession of screen tests. In one test Dorothy/Dustin was asked how she

felt about having a baby. "I think it's a little late in the day for that," she said, then suddenly burst into tears. "I felt so terrible I would never have that experience," Hoffman related to *The New York Times.* The father of several children explained, "Nothing like that has ever happened to me. I've been acting for nearly 30 years and I've never had a moment like that before in my life."

It was a great year for films about cross-dressing. While Dustin was proving to audiences that he made a convincing woman, Barbra Streisand portrayed a young man in *Yentl,* while Julie Andrews proved she could do the same in *Victor/Victoria.* But the public's choice was clearly *Tootsie,* at least in terms of box office.

The Academy showered the film with 10 Oscar nominations. Jessica Lange, whose last leading man had been King Kong, welcomed the chance to play opposite Dustin Hoffman, even if he was dressed as a woman for most of their scenes together. The Academy nominated her for two Awards that year—Best Actress, for *Frances,* and Best Supporting Actress, for *Tootsie,* the first time since 1942 that an actress had been nominated in two categories simultaneously. (She won for *Tootsie.*) And Dustin Hoffman was nominated for Best Actor, with his role as Dorothy Michaels rather than the ne'er-do-well

actor Michael Dorsey catching the Academy's, and the public's, eye.

Other noteworthy performances in the movie are Teri Garr as Michael's befuddled girlfriend; Dabney Coleman in his typically lecherous role as the soap opera director; Bill Murray in a rather minor part as Michael's roommate; and Geena Davis as a soap actress, one of her earliest film appearances (both she and Hoffman would be Oscar winners in 1988).

Time knew immediately that *Tootsie* was on a roll, when it noted: "It is not just the best comedy of the year; it is popular art on the way to becoming cultural artifact." And *Newsweek* summed it up quite concisely: "*Tootsie* will make you very happy."

Screenplay by Larry Gelbart and
  Murray Schisgal

From a story by Don McGuire and
  Larry Gelbart

Executive Producer: Charles Evans

Produced by Sydney Pollack and
  Dick Richards

Directed by Sydney Pollack

CAST

Dorothy Michaels . . . .Dustin Hoffman
Julie . . . . .Jessica Lange
Sandy . . . . .Teri Garr
Ron . . . . .Dabney Coleman
Lea . . . . .Charles Durning
Jeff . . . . .Bill Murray

ACADEMY AWARD NOMINATIONS

10 nominations, 1 win*

  Best Picture
  Best Actor (Dustin Hoffman)
*Best Supporting Actress (Jessica Lange)
  Best Supporting Actress (Teri Garr)
  Best Director (Sydney Pollack)
  Best Screenplay Written Directly for the
    Screen
  Best Cinematography
  Best Sound
  Best Song ("It Might Be You," music
    by Dave Grusin, words by Alan and
    Marilyn Bergman)
  Best Film Editing

Director Sydney Pollack (left) appears as Dustin Hoffman's high-powered agent.

ROCKY III

UNITED ARTISTS
$66,262,796

JUST WHEN YOU thought it was safe to go back into the boxing ring, along came *Rocky III,* the third outing for irrepressible prize fighter Rocky Balboa, a.k.a. the Italian Stallion, a.k.a. Sylvester Stallone. This time, the writer-director-star added a few new twists, like a black opponent named Clubber Lang, menacingly played by Mr. T. (né Lawrence Tero), the mohawk-sporting former bodyguard of Leon Spinks. Burgess Meredith returned as his trainer, but only long enough to do a dying scene (and receive a Jewish funeral—surprising audiences, who thought he was supposed to be Irish for two movies). Rocky's former nemesis, Apollo Creed, was now his trainer, guaranteed to turn the champ back into a lean, mean fighting machine.

One of the new additions to the cast was wrestling personality Hulk Hogan, whose career was just beginning to take off in 1982. He is seen here in what is billed as a charity match between Rocky and himself, a must-see for all fans.

Not much is new, however. Stallone slyly stayed with his tried and true formula, the one audiences by now had come to eagerly anticipate. The

Buildup to the Big Fight is the basic plot, yet audiences still delighted in this magic moment, and *Rocky III* made more money than either of its two predecessors (inflation not taken into account). *Newsweek* commented that "just as Sinatra can endlessly reprise 'My Way' and still raise goosebumps, so Stallone can turn out shameless variations on his Believe-in-

---

Screenplay by Sylvester Stallone

Produced by Irwin Winkler and Robert Chartoff

Directed by Sylvester Stallone

CAST

Rocky Balboa . . . . . . .Sylvester Stallone
Adrian . . . . .Talia Shire
Paulie . . . . .Burt Young
Apollo Creed . . . . . . .Carl Weathers
Mickey . . . . .Burgess Meredith
Clubber Lang . . . . . . .Mr. T

ACADEMY AWARD NOMINATIONS

1 nomination, no wins

Best Song ("Eye of the Tiger," music and words by Jim Peterik and Frankie Sullivan III)

Yourself miracle play and still get the old adrenaline pumping." *Time* hailed *Rocky III* as "Winner and Still Champion," describing Stallone's character as a "meat-and-potatoes exemplar of the American dream, a working stiff's contender who battles for his dignity against odds that seem overwhelming."

While *Rocky III* was champion at the box office, the new theme song, "Eye of the Tiger," quickly rose to number one on the *Billboard* charts; the recording by the rock group Survivor (who also did the theme for *Rocky IV*) remained champ for a phenomenal six weeks. The Academy thought "Eye of the Tiger" a good contender for Best Song and nominated the song for an Oscar.

Sylvester Stallone, like the character he portrayed, announced that *Rocky III* was the last chapter in what he had always thought of as a trilogy. Originally, he had planned to set this final episode of his opus in the Roman Colosseum, with Rocky slugging it out with a Russian opponent. Alas, he settled for Mr. T. But there was still plenty of life left in old Rocky B., as audiences were learning with regularity every three years or so.

To be continued…

4

PORKY'S

20TH CENTURY-FOX
$55,559,000

WERE TEENAGERS really sex-crazed in the '50s? The answer supplied by the 20th Century-Fox release *Porky's* seems to be yes, yes, yes. Another in a long line of sexual coming-of-age films, this one caught the public's attention in the spring of '82 (after a pre-release in 1981), a time when young people's fancies seemed likely to turn to thoughts of…pictures like this.

As tasteful as *American Graffiti* had been, its imitators, such as *National Lampoon's Animal House* and *Meatballs,* had become progressively raunchier, culminating in this first of several films consisting mainly of one long dirty joke as storyline. Yet the public adored the "R"-rated picture, and word of mouth, plus an advertising campaign depicting leering youths at a peephole in the girls' locker room, propelled this Canadian-made picture to box office success. The movie seemed to be particularly popular among the members of the under-17 set, the impressionable teens the "R" rating was supposed to be protecting—who somehow managed to produce the requisite "parent or guardian."

Critics sharpened their tongues and let fly their barbs with the same carefree abandonment as the high-schoolers on screen. *Variety* lamented: "[*Porky's*] is undoubtedly one of the grossest [films] ever released by a major studio under an R rating. It also boasts a cast larger than 'The Ten Commandments,' and proceeds to break nearly every one of them. Bob Clark's exposé of teenaged tomfoolery so aggressively wallows in bad taste that it nearly transcends it, and commercial prospects are an open question…hard to say if gross equals grosses." *The Hollywood Reporter* wrote: "In lieu of originality, scripter-director-co-producer Bob Clark unleashes a virtual wall-to-wall avalanche of four-letter words, and all related synonyms, as well as graphic depictions of everything happening in the

---

Screenplay by Bob Clark

Executive Producers: Harold Greenberg and Melvin Simon

Produced by Don Carmody and Bob Clark

Directed by Bob Clark

CAST

Honeywell	.Kim Cattrall
Brian Schwartz	.Scott Colomby
Wendy	.Kaki Hunter
Balbricker	.Nancy Parsons
Cherry Forever	.Susan Clark
Sheriff Wallace	.Alex Karras

---

groin area…everyone at Angel Street [High] is horny, apparently 24 hours a day…under Clark's direction and via his scripting, the kids all come off less like good-spirited hell-raisers and more like mental defectives…the picture was filmed in Florida and should be an embarrassment to all involved."

Two of those involved, who certainly were not embarrassed, were among the only ones receiving critical approval. Susan Clark and her husband, Alex Karras, were later known to TV viewers as the adoptive parents of "Webster," but their roles in this picture were far from parental. Ms. Clark played a backwoods hooker in a short sequence, while her spouse played an exasperated sheriff in another scene. Porky himself was played by Chuck Mitchell, who appeared as the porcine owner of the redneck bawdy house in sequels.

Yes, there were sequels, two at last count. The astonishing success at the box office prompted Fox to follow up with *Porky's II: The Next Day* (1983) and *Porky's Revenge* (1985). About the only thing that had changed was Porky himself, having slimmed down quite a bit. While the teens were as sex-crazed as ever, audiences were not as enthusiastic, and the series had finally run its course.

AN OFFICER AND A GENTLEMAN

PARAMOUNT
$55,223,000

MUCH OF THE SIZZLE of an *Officer and a Gentleman* had to do with the on-screen romance between the two leads, Richard Gere and Debra Winger. This summer movie, which began as a sleeper and emerged as a blockbuster, focuses on sexual attraction, leaving very little to the audience's imagination. While blue-haired ladies gasped at the picture's unabashed eroticism, others in the audience had by now come to accept almost anything as perfectly allowable on screen as long as it enhanced the story—which is what directors had been fighting for lo these many years.

Aside from the hot relationship between Gere and Winger, and the B-story about his Navy buddy, played by David Keith (similarly involved with a local girl), there was a fine performance by Louis Gossett, Jr., as the tough drill instructor whose job it is to turn out officers. *Variety* cited the contribution of one of the screen's finest black actors by noting: " 'Officer' belongs to Louis Gossett, Jr.…[he] takes a near-cliché role of the tough, unrelenting drill instructor and makes him a sympathetic hero without ever softening a whit. Gossett does more with his eyes

and a facial reaction than others can accomplish with pages of dialogue."

The sparks between Gere and Winger flew right off the screen, and the public, which had only recently fallen in love with an extra-terrestrial, immediately took the officer candidate and his ambitious girlfriend into their hearts. Yet it was interesting to watch the critics argue over whether or not this physical attraction worked. *The Hollywood Reporter* proclaimed in no uncertain terms that the picture didn't have what it took: "If Paramount's 'Officer and a Gentleman' fails as a motion picture (and it does, regrettably), one reason is because it painfully lacks the singular ingredient most necessary to successfully orchestrate a romantic motion picture theme: chemistry between its two principals, Richard Gere and Debra Winger."

Could he have seen the same movie as the critic for *Newsweek*? "These days good love stories are almost as hard to

come by on screen as off. One problem is chemical; some of our young actors and actresses…don't know how to strike romantic sparks… Debra Winger and Richard Gere know how in 'An Officer and a Gentleman.' When they're on together the screen exudes a palpable sexuality, a bona fide romantic ache. And it's not just two actors the audience is responding to, but the plight of two well-drawn characters."

Obviously, the audience was more in agreement with the latter critique, if they even bothered to read reviews at all. Most went just because it was good escapist summer fare. The theme song from the film, "Up Where We Belong," sung by Joe Cocker and Jennifer Warnes, climbed the pop charts to land up where it belonged, in the number-one spot, holding that position for three weeks. It also won the Oscar for Best Song, and the music was later used by Continental Airlines as their theme song.

Screenplay by Douglas Day Stewart

Produced by Martin Elfand

Directed by Taylor Hackford

CAST

Zack Mayo . . . . .Richard Gere
Paula Pokrifki . . . . . . .Debra Winger
Sid Worley . . . . .David Keith
Byron Mayo . . . . .Robert Loggia
Sgt. Emil Foley . . . . . .Louis Gossett, Jr.

ACADEMY AWARD NOMINATIONS

6 nominations, 2 wins*

  Best Actress (Debra Winger)
**Best Supporting Actor (Louis Gossett, Jr.)
  Best Screenplay Written Directly for the
  Screen
*Best Song ("Up Where We Belong,"
  music by Jack Nitzsche and Buffy
  Sainte-Marie, words by Will Jennings)
  Best Original Score (Jack Nitzsche)
  Best Film Editing

RETURN OF THE JEDI

20TH CENTURY-FOX
$169,193,000

Je'di (n) 1: an ancient order of Knights of the Empire 2: a member of that order; a Jedi Knight

Re'turn of the Je'di (n) 1: title of the third movie in the *Star Wars* trilogy 2: the amount of money earned at the box office by that film, as in "The return of *The Jedi* was millions and millions of dollars."

ORIGINALLY, IT WAS to be called *The Revenge of the Jedi*. Paramount Pictures, however, had another film in progress at that time with "revenge" in its title, a sequel to *Star Trek I* with the working title of *Star Trek II: The Revenge of Khan*. Lucasfilm's future with Paramount called for a sequel to *Raiders of the Lost Ark,* while *Star Trek* was considered one of the studio's crown jewels. Each creative team desperately tried persuading the other to switch titles. Eventually, *The Revenge of Khan* became *The Vengeance of Khan,* and finally *The Wrath of Khan,* and since Jedi Knights were supposed to be peace-loving types, it was decided that the word "revenge" was unbecoming a knight anyway, and the Lucasfilm project was redubbed *Return of the Jedi*.

But what's in a name? They could easily have used the deliberately misleading "nom de screen" the crew was given for secrecy purposes—*Blue Harvest*—and it would still have made oodles of money. *Star Wars* fans were a loyal lot, and the business generated at the box office for this summer release was enough to propel the film into hyperspace sooner than you could say "Millenium Falcon." In fact, this second sequel did better than the first (*The Empire Strikes Back*), a rarity in the film industry.

It would certainly have helped to have seen one of the film's two predecessors. Anyone going to see *Return of the Jedi* "cold" would probably have felt like Alice falling down the rabbit hole to Wonderland. And one of the reasons for the film's unfaltering success had to be the fan following for the *Star Wars* gang. A cult had quickly formed around the characters, with many fans emulating their favorites at the numerous *Star Wars*/"Star Trek"/science fiction conventions held regularly throughout the United States and in many countries overseas. Princess Leias, Han Solos, Luke Skywalkers, Darth Vaders, and acrylic-clad wookies abounded at these affairs, as did the films' gadgetry, such as light sabers and other role-playing aids. Dealers sold every conceivable tie-in product available, as well as newsletters and "fanzines" (fan-created magazines) for those who craved the printed word on their heroes. Prizes were awarded for the best costume. Many youngsters could not remember a time *without* the *Star Wars* characters. There was a phenomenon afoot, and it instantly propelled this long-awaited sequel to the sequel over the top.

Still, a lot of people were surprised at the picture's success, including a number of critics, who panned the film when it first opened. *The New York Times* wrote: " 'Return of the Jedi'…doesn't really end the trilogy as much as it brings it to a dead stop.

Screenplay by Lawrence Kasdan and George Lucas

Based on a story by George Lucas

Executive Producer: George Lucas

Produced by Howard Kazanjian

Directed by Richard Marquand

CAST

Luke Skywalker . . . . . .Mark Hamill
Han Solo . . . . .Harrison Ford
Princess Leia . . . . . . .Carrie Fisher
Landro Calrissian . . . . .Billy Dee Williams
Yoda . . . . .Frank Oz

ACADEMY AWARD NOMINATIONS

4 nominations, no wins

Best Art Direction–Set Decoration
Best Sound
Best Original Score (John Williams)
Best Sound Effects Editing

Return of the Jedi received a Special Achievement Award for Visual Effects.

The film…is by far the dimmest adventure of the lot. All the members of the old 'Star Wars' gang are back doing what they've done before, but this time with a certain evident boredom." The reviewer for *The Hollywood Reporter* wasn't thrilled either: "Unfortunately, it conveys the sense that the machinery has already begun to wear down, and the inventiveness to wear thin…there's a kind of desperation about it, a feeling that Lucas and co-writer Lawrence Kasdan are simply trying to figure out what they can do next to amuse the kiddies."

Newsweek, on the other hand, seemed to have mixed feelings: "At $32.5 million it is certainly the most expensive of the three. With more special effects per minute than its predecessors, it's definitely the busiest. Also the most battle-ridden, the most cartoony, and let's just spit it right out— the most disappointing…There's no doubt that 'Jedi' gives you your money's worth; it's so packed with wonders you may feel like an oversated child who's just been presented with the entire inventory of F.A.O. Schwarz for his birthday."

This movie was no disappointment act. And the reference to the famous toystore F.A.O. Schwarz was an appropriate one, since the merchandising of cuddly creatures like the Ewoks from Endor, plus the usual assortment of models, laser swords, lunchboxes, bedsheets, and so on, would eventually serve to more than double any profits at the box office. George Lucas' final tribute to the Jedi was profitable for all: Luke was reunited with his father and sister; Han Solo got the girl, and Lucas got the loot.

"I look upon the three *Star Wars* films as chapters in one book," Lucas told *Time* magazine. "Now the book is finished, and I have put it on the shelf."

But not forever. Watch for the return of the *Star Wars* saga in prequel form in 1998.

(Left to right): George Lucas, Harrison Ford, C3PO, Carrie Fisher, Mark Hamill, Chewbacca, R2D2, and director Richard Marquand.

2

TERMS OF ENDEARMENT

PARAMOUNT
$50,250,000

"Have you come to Terms *yet?"*
—ADVERTISING COPY FOR
TERMS OF ENDEARMENT

A LOT OF people did come to *Terms.* This was another "audience picture"—like *Love Story, On Golden Pond,* and even any of the *Rocky* movies, a film that attracts audiences not because of special effects or energetic action, or because of hot-and-cold running bimbos, but simply because there is a story to which audiences can relate.

The picture was virtually a one-man showcase for writer-producer-director James L. Brooks. Brooks began his career as a lowly copy boy at CBS News in New York, later moving to the West Coast, where he formed a profitable partnership with fellow writer Allan Burns. Together, the pair created the beloved "Mary Tyler Moore Show"; Brooks and Burns won four Emmies for their work during the show's seven-year run. While working at Paramount under a development deal, Larry McMurtry's novel *Terms of Endearment* crossed Brooks' path. He was so enthralled by the possibilities that he asked Paramount to option the book for him, reserving the right to direct it himself. "I was overwhelmed by the fact that I was going to take on directing," confessed Brooks in the film's production handbook. "I could absolutely visualize where I'd screw up. But I was secure

about working with actors, and I do have experience as a producer. Everything else I've learned has been by some kind of osmosis."

Brooks was blessed with a winning cast, one of the reasons for the film's huge success. Shirley MacLaine had been in demand constantly since her

---

Screenplay by James L. Brooks

Produced and directed by James L. Brooks

CAST

Emma Horton	Debra Winger
Aurora Greenway	Shirley MacLaine
Garrett Breedlove	Jack Nicholson
Flap Horton	Jeff Daniels
Sam Burns	John Lithgow
Vernon Dahlart	Danny DeVito

ACADEMY AWARD NOMINATIONS

11 nominations, 5 wins*

*Best Picture
*Best Actress (Shirley MacLaine)
 Best Actress (Debra Winger)
 Best Supporting Actor (John Lithgow)
*Best Supporting Actor (Jack Nicholson)
*Best Director (James L. Brooks)
*Best Screenplay Based on Material from
  Another Medium (James L. Brooks)
 Best Art Direction–Set Decoration
 Best Sound
 Best Original Score (Michael Gore)
 Best Film Editing

---

last top-five film at the box office, *Irma La Douce* (see page 170). She had worked in such popular films as *Woman Times Seven, Sweet Charity,* and *Two Mules for Sister Sara.* During much of the '70s, she was politically active, and led the first woman's delegation to China in 1973. She also began a career as a writer of controversial autobiographical books. In 1977, she returned to the screen and received an Oscar nomination for *The Turning Point.* With *Terms of Endearment,* the oft-nominated MacLaine finally received her Award.

Jack Nicholson co-stars as the letch next door, a role he seemed born to. The actor had had six Oscar nominations and one win (*One Flew Over the Cuckoo's Nest;* see page 242) when he accepted the part of former astronaut Garrett Breedlove, Aurora Greenway's (MacLaine's) horny neighbor.

Others in the superlative cast were Debra Winger as Emma Horton, Aurora's daughter; Danny DeVito in an early film role (he had worked with director Brooks on TV's "Taxi"); and John Lithgow, who worked constantly through the ensuing years.

The film, while dealing with a depressing theme, is also comedic, touching, and ultimately uplifting. Stock up on Kleenex when you watch it, but be prepared for smiles, too.

A sequel, *The Evening Star,* was due to open in late 1996.

TRADING PLACES

PARAMOUNT
$40,600,000

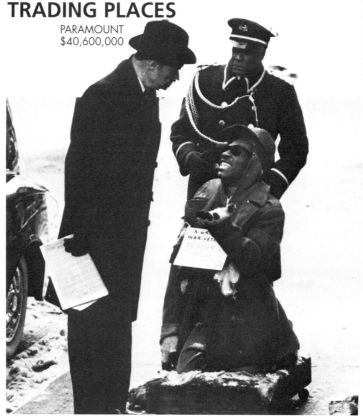

"When I was growing up and we wanted a Jacuzzi, we had to fart in the tub."   —EDDIE MURPHY

EDDIE MURPHY became a household name at the age of 21, when he emerged as a bona fide star from the ranks of TV's "Saturday Night Live" in the early '80s. His first feature, *48 HRS.* (1982), saw the young actor/comedian on the road to further success, and he was signed to a multiple-picture deal with Paramount Pictures. *Trading Places,* a comedy based on a simple premise (remember Mark Twain's *The Prince and the Pauper*?), is up there with the best of Murphy's subsequent films.

Dan Aykroyd and Eddie Murphy play two men whose paths were never meant to cross. Aykroyd is a wealthy investment broker, Murphy a poor but clever survivor of the ghetto. They are thrown together in a scheme devised by the conniving Duke Brothers, played by Ralph Bellamy and Don Ameche (together on the screen for the first time in this film). Suddenly Murphy is given carte blanche at the Dukes' investment firm, while Aykroyd must learn to cope with being a "street person."

The John Landis–directed picture featured some of Murphy's old "Saturday Night Live" buddies in a variety of roles. Murphy actually received second billing in the credits (the last time that would ever happen), with Dan Aykroyd as Louis Winthorpe III listed at the top of the cast. Al Franken,

another "Saturday Night Live" alumnus, played the minor part of "Baggage Handler," while John Belushi's brother Jim was listed as "Harvey." There were a number of well-known names in the cast as well, such as veteran actors Ralph Bellamy (this was his 99th film) and Don Ameche (this was his 49th). When Eddie Murphy found out their combined totals, he quipped, "That means that between the three of us, we've made 150 movies!" Other "names" in the cast included Jamie Lee Curtis as Ophelia the hooker, Frank Oz as the "Corrupt Cop" (you may recall Oz as a Muppeteer and the wizard behind *The Empire Strikes Back*'s Yoda), and rock and roll oldie Bo Diddley as the "Pawnbroker."

While the film loosely addresses racial and cultural prejudices, the emphasis is still on comedy, and the summer release found a wide audience eager for comic relief. Critics also discovered what audiences knew all along—Eddie Murphy was one funny guy. *Newsweek* didn't have much favorable comment for the picture itself, but Murphy captured the

reviewer's complete attention: "John Landis' movie confirms what '48 HRS.' suggested: Murphy is the most dynamic new comic talent around, a quicksilver quick-change artist whose rapport with the audience is instantaneous…Murphy is the movie's hottest—and funniest—commodity." *Time* concurred: "*Trading Places* [is] one of the most emotionally satisfying and morally gratifying comedies of recent times…*Trading Places* also makes Eddie Murphy a force to be reckoned with…[He] demonstrates the powers of invention that signal the arrival of a major comic actor, and possibly a great star. He makes *Trading Places* something more than a good-hearted comedy. He turns it into an event." *The New York Times* predicted: "The film's pleasures are unequivocal, beginning with the lithe, graceful, uproarious performance of Mr. Murphy…A terrific career is in store."

All those predicting a successful career for Eddie Murphy, please raise your hands. In the words of one of Murphy's "Saturday Night Live" characters, "Can you say *very, very rich*?"

Screenplay by Timothy Harris and Herschel Weingrod

Executive Producer: George Folsey, Jr.

Produced by Aaron Russo

Directed by John Landis

CAST

Louis Winthorpe III	Dan Aykroyd
Billy Ray Valentine	Eddie Murphy
Randolph Duke	Ralph Bellamy
Mortimer Duke	Don Ameche
Coleman	Denholm Elliott
Ophelia	Jamie Lee Curtis

4

WARGAMES

METRO-GOLDWYN-MAYER/UNITED ARTISTS
$38,519,833

"Shall we play a game?"
— COMPUTER

"Let's play Global Thermonuclear War." — MATTHEW BRODERICK

VIDEO GAMES and computer technology had reached a fever pitch in the early '80s. The country was in the throes of "Pac-Man" fever, the symptoms of which included young people gluing themselves to joysticks and monitor screens for hours at a time while little creatures gobbled up mazes of small dots. Virtually every red-blooded teenage boy in the country was thus afflicted, along with a goodly number of equally red-blooded young females. (And, lest the games become too sexist, some clever person devised the oxymoronic *Ms.* Pac-Man.")

WarGames targeted this youthful audience and struck home with a 100-megaton hit. It began with a simple "what if…" premise. What if a teenage hacker/gamester were to accidentally launch World War III? Simple, but very scary. The kid thinks he's still playing a game as the countdown to oblivion begins. Eventually it's the youngsters (and the audience, who are in on it from the start) versus the superintelligence of our government.

Screenplay by Lawrence Lasker and Walter F. Parkes

Produced by Harold Schneider

Directed by John Badham

CAST

David . . . . .Matthew Broderick
McKittrick . . . . .Dabney Coleman
Falken . . . . .John Wood
Jennifer . . . . .Ally Sheedy
General Beringer . . . . .Barry Corbin

ACADEMY AWARD NOMINATIONS

3 nominations, no wins

Best Screenplay Written Directly for the Screen
Best Cinematography
Best Sound

Guess who's right all along?

John Badham's tight direction keeps this premise from becoming improbable.* There is suspense aplenty, making the film an "edge of the seat"-er. The director of the 1978 hit *Saturday Night Fever,* Badham also turned out another exciting action-adventure film, *Blue Thunder,* in the summer of '83.

Much of the film's success must go to the young stars. Matthew Broderick and Ally Sheedy were two promising young actors at that time who went on to successful acting careers. *The New York Times* wrote: "Young Mr. Broderick, a Tony nominee for his current Broadway performance in Neil Simon's 'Brighton Beach Memoirs,' is very serious and grave—and thus very appealing—as the unassuming computer wizard…Miss Sheedy…here succeeds in being distinctive in an ordinary role."

Rounding out the cast was Dabney Coleman, again typed as the baddie, in this case a computer defense specialist who thinks David (Broderick) is a Commie spy. Coleman can play "obnoxious" quite well; by now, he'd become the man audiences loved to hate.

WarGames was released domestically in early May, 1983, coinciding with the Cannes Film Festival. It was given the honor of appearing as the final film at that annual world-famous event.

---

*At least we'd all like to *think* it's improbable. Recently, hackers successfully implanted "viruses" in sensitive computer networks.

SUPERMAN III

WARNER BROS.
$37,200,000

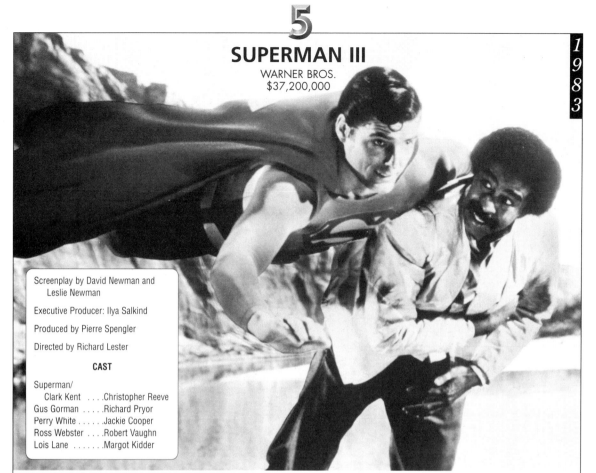

Screenplay by David Newman and
Leslie Newman

Executive Producer: Ilya Salkind

Produced by Pierre Spengler

Directed by Richard Lester

CAST

Superman/
  Clark Kent . . . .Christopher Reeve
Gus Gorman . . . . .Richard Pryor
Perry White . . . . . .Jackie Cooper
Ross Webster . . . .Robert Vaughn
Lois Lane . . . . . . .Margot Kidder

IT'S HARD TO KNOW which came first—Richard Pryor, or the egg laid by *Superman III*. In a severe departure from the format established in the first two *Superman* films, this one plays it for laughs. It may be humorous, and the talented Richard Pryor may have a huge fan following, but somehow this picture isn't on target. Most audiences thought it just didn't *feel* right.

For one thing, there are two leading actors: Chris Reeve, appearing as Superman for the third time, and Pryor, somehow turning the film into "The Richard Pryor Show" whenever he's on screen. It was as if the producers first signed Pryor; then tried to create a movie around him. He certainly was a big box office draw. And Chris Reeve also had a legion of loyal fans who, if need be, would turn up at the box office to watch Superman recite Chaucer for two hours. Still, this film only pulled in half the amount of *Superman II*, and at $37,200,000, it was the lowest-grossing top-five film since 1976.

Pryor plays Gus Gorman, a computer whiz snapped up by the movie's villain, Robert Vaughn, playing a power-hungry bigwig à la *Bullitt* (see page 200), but on a grander scale—he plans to rule the Earth. Along the way, Supe (Pryor actually calls him this!) gets zapped by a strain of Kryptonite, and, in a sequence guaranteed to send Freudians rushing down to the local Bijou, our superhero does battle with himself! Seems this Kryptonite actually splits his superpersonality into "good" and "bad" halves. Under the influence of the "bad" self, he becomes a womanizing, beer-slurping, five-o'clock-shadowed superbum who snuffs out the Olympic flame and straightens up the Leaning Tower of Pisa just for spite.

There also isn't much action with his leading lady of the past two films, Margot Kidder as Lois Lane, although she does put in an appearance. This time, Clark Kent returns to his Smallville High reunion, where he attracts the attention of Lana Lang, his one-time high school crush. In the film's most original development, she actual-ly falls for Clark, not his superalterego.

Critics weren't certain what to write about this film. Most seemed to enjoy Pryor's performance, unaware of any problems Superman purists might have been suffering. *Variety* commented that "virtually none of the film's set action and spectacle pieces...has the scope or the technical imagination of either of the previous pics," and *The New York Times* wrote that "anyone who has been following the 'Superman' saga will find this install-ment enjoyable enough, but some of the magic is missing."

Most true Superman fans agreed, which is why this sequel failed to take off like the others. It was also an embarrassment to Christopher Reeve, who swore off the character. He was eventually persuaded to do one more, *Superman IV: The Quest for Peace* (1987), a return to the style of the first two *Superman* movies. Unfortunately, it fared poorly, earning only $8,000,000 in domestic returns. It seems poor writing, not Kryptonite, kept *Superman IV* from flying at the box office.

GHOSTBUSTERS

COLUMBIA
$132,720,000

"Are you troubled by strange noises in the night? Do you experience feelings of dread in your basement or attic? Have you or your family actually seen a spook, spectre or ghost? If the answer is yes, then don't wait another minute. Just pick up the phone and call the professionals—GHOSTBUSTERS!"
—"COMMERCIAL" IN *GHOSTBUSTERS*

MONTHS BEFORE the public ever heard of *Ghostbusters*, billboards around the country showed a Casper-like apparition popping through the universal symbol for something forbidden—a red circle with a diagonal slash. The message below read "Coming to save the world this summer." It might just as easily have read "Coming to save Columbia Pictures this summer," for that is exactly what it did. The studio had had a big hit back in 1982 with *Tootsie,* but nothing could have prepared Columbia for the huge success that was about to materialize from *Ghostbusters.* Before the year was over, it would become the *fifth* highest-grossing picture of all time.

Some called it a comedy, since the plot involved a Three Musketeers-ish group (Bill Murray, Dan Aykroyd, Harold Ramis) camping it up in New York while in pursuit of some really whimsical supernatural beings (one cute little green ghost's favorite pastime is gorging on hotel food). Others saw this spoof as a fantasy—it does take a bit of imagination to believe that otherworldly creatures live in Sigourney Weaver's fridge, or that she and co-star Rick Moranis can turn into gargoyle-ish red-eyed dogs. Actually, it doesn't matter. It's innovative and entertaining, and audiences ate it up.

The movie was originally conceived as a John Belushi–Dan Aykroyd vehicle called *Ghostsmashers* before Belushi's untimely death from a drug overdose in 1982, and the "eating and drinking ghost" is actually producer-director Ivan Reitman's tribute to that late comedian's character, Bluto, from his previous hit, *National Lampoon's Animal House* (see page 261). With the screenplay by principals Aykroyd and Ramis presenting many opportunities

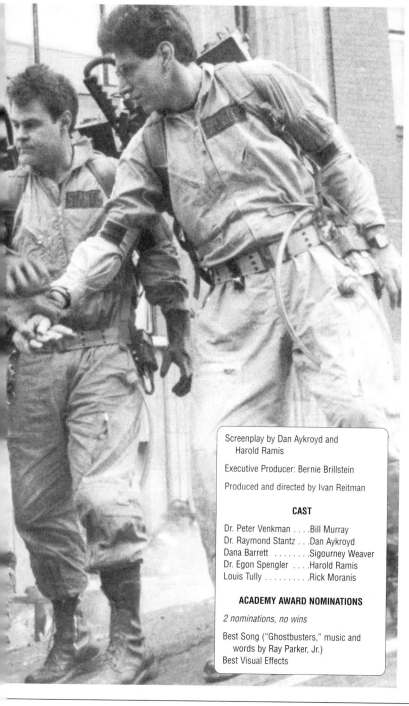

for ad-libbing, director Reitman encouraged improvisation in his actors. And he himself did a cameo as the Mercedes McCambridge-like voice of "possessed" Sigourney Weaver rising on the bed, Linda Blair fashion, as well as providing all the alien voices except that of "Gozer," the Sumerian demigod with designs on planet Earth.

A catchy title song did much to promote the film. "Who you gonna call? GHOSTBUSTERS!" became the sensation of the summer. Ray Parker, Jr., was presented with a dilemma when he was asked by Reitman to compose a title song. Said Parker to *USA Today*: "It's hard to write a song where your main objective is to use the word 'ghost-busters'...I wanted to make a simple, easy song people could sing along with and not have to think about." The song became a number-one hit for three weeks in August, 1984. It was again used as the theme of the 1989 sequel, *Ghostbusters II,* with Run-DMC's version as well as the Ray Parker one appearing in that film.

Time's reviewer really got caught up in the fun: "These spectacular confrontations are well handled by Director Reitman, who always finds the time for the funny aside, the wittily telling detail...But praise is due to everyone connected with *Ghostbusters* for thinking on a grandly comic scale and delivering the goofy goods, neatly timed and perfectly packaged."

The Stay-Puft Marshmallow Man, appearing in one of the film's silliest moments, required a man wearing a suit to stomp through a miniature set of New York City. There were three Fiberglas heads used, each with a different facial expression—smiling, surprised, and grimacing.

Over at Columbia, only smiles were in abundance. The profitable picture ultimately spawned a sequel, *Ghostbusters II,* and although it did well at the box office, its success didn't equal that of its predecessor, earning about half, or $60 million, in rentals.

Screenplay by Dan Aykroyd and Harold Ramis

Executive Producer: Bernie Brillstein

Produced and directed by Ivan Reitman

CAST

Dr. Peter Venkman . . . .Bill Murray
Dr. Raymond Stantz . . .Dan Aykroyd
Dana Barrett . . . . .Sigourney Weaver
Dr. Egon Spengler . . . .Harold Ramis
Louis Tully . . . . .Rick Moranis

ACADEMY AWARD NOMINATIONS

2 nominations, no wins

Best Song ("Ghostbusters," music and words by Ray Parker, Jr.)
Best Visual Effects

INDIANA JONES AND THE TEMPLE OF DOOM

PARAMOUNT
$109,000,000

*"If adventure has a name,
it must be Indiana Jones!"*
—ADVERTISING COPY FOR *INDIANA
JONES AND THE TEMPLE OF DOOM*

THREE YEARS AFTER their highly acclaimed *Raiders of the Lost Ark,* Steven Spielberg and George Lucas brought out the next installment of the adventures of the famous fictional archeologist who matches wits with the forces of evil. Actually a prequel to *Raiders* set three years prior to that movie, *Indiana Jones and the Temple of Doom* has one of the most memorable openings of any film. The Paramountain, the logo seen at the beginning of all Paramount Pictures, suddenly transforms into a gong as the credits are introduced (homage to George Steven's 1939 epic *Gunga Din*). We never actually see the movie's title, which unfolds behind Willie Scott (Kate Capshaw), performer at the Obi Wan Club (get it?), singing "Anything Goes" in Mandarin Chinese, followed by a Busby Berkeley–type production number. All this in the first reel!

A dizzying pace is set in the ensuing sequences, with Spielberg never letting up for a moment. Indy fights for his life in the search for a poison antidote; we meet his newest sidekick, a 10-year-old lad named Short Round (Ke Huy Quan), who drives their getaway car; the threesome wind up in an airplane (a scene that pays homage to the films of the '30s with the old "line across the map" technique of following a plane's progress); followed by a plane crash, a toboggan ride, and an elephant trek through the jungle. And we've still got most of the picture to go!

Despite all this action, many people now believe this to be the weakest of the three *Indiana Jones* movies. Even director Spielberg acknowledged the film's dark and somber feeling. With much of the plot centering on children who have been kidnapped into torturous slavery, plus beatings, devil worship, human sacrifices, and heartsnatching—not fun subjects for youngsters—there was little of the light, uplifting tone of the first picture.

Newsweek called it "pure cinematic energy encumbered with as little soul food as possible," but the reviewer tempered his praise with reservations: "Now I enjoy human sacrifice as much as the next American youth, but at this point the movie loses its stylish integration of violence and humor and becomes a careening juggernaut of beatings, gougings and crunchings… in 'Indiana Jones' Spielberg and Lucas have let their genius for probing deep into us with their mastery of movie rhythms get out of hand."

Audiences didn't pay the least bit of attention to detractors like the above. They paid their money, they took their ride, and came back again for more. *Indiana Jones and the Temple of Doom* took its place as the eighth highest-grossing film of all time to that date, right behind *Raiders of the Lost Ark.*

In 1989, the third Indy film, *Indiana Jones and the Last Crusade,* swept the box office, pulling in $115,500,000 in rentals, better than its predecessor (see page 328). Paramount Pictures also produced a television series during the 1990s based on the films, called "Young Indiana Jones."

Screenplay by Willard Huyck and Gloria Katz

Executive Producers: George Lucas and Frank Marshall

Produced by Robert Watts

Directed by Steven Spielberg

CAST

Indiana Jones	Harrison Ford
Willie Scott	Kate Capshaw
Short Round	Ke Huy Quan
Mola Ram	Amrish Puri
Chattar Lal	Roshan Seth

ACADEMY AWARD NOMINATIONS

2 nominations, 1 win*

Best Original Score (John Williams)
*Best Visual Effects

BEVERLY HILLS COP

PARAMOUNT
$108,000,000

IT WAS A GREAT year for Paramount. In addition to their success with *Indiana Jones and the Temple of Doom,* the studio still had another trump card to play. Eddie Murphy had co-starred in that studio's highly lucrative movie *Trading Places* in 1983. While critics enjoyed the film in general, most of them saved their superlatives for its second-billed star, Eddie Murphy, predicting a phenomenal career for the comedy actor. With *Beverly Hills Cop,* that prediction became a reality.

Murphy stars as Axel Foley, a Detroit policeman tracking the killer of a friend in Beverly Hills. He is certainly more laid back than his California counterparts as he locks horns with the Beverly Hills Police Department. You get the feeling that Murphy could talk his way out of hell itself if called upon to do so, and leave the Devil muttering apologies. He gets excellent support from Judge Reinhold as Detective Billy Rosewood and John Ashton as Sergeant Taggart; these well-scripted characters are perfect foils for Murphy's style and humor. (Believe it or not, the part of Axel Foley was originally written for more of an action picture, with Sylvester

Screenplay by Daniel Petrie, Jr.

Based on a story by Danilo Bach and Daniel Petrie, Jr.

Executive Producer: Mike Moder

Produced by Don Simpson and Jerry Bruckheimer

Directed by Martin Brest

CAST

Axel Foley . . . . .Eddie Murphy
Detective Billy
   Rosewood . . . . . . .Judge Reinhold
Sergeant Taggart . . . . .John Ashton
Jenny Summers . . . . .Lisa Eilbacher
Lieutenant Bogomil . . .Ronny Cox
Serge . . . . .Bronson Pinchot

ACADEMY AWARD NOMINATIONS

1 nomination, no wins

Best Screenplay Written Directly for the Screen

Stallone in mind.) It didn't take long for the critics to heap their praises upon this sure-fire Christmas release. *The Hollywood Reporter* heralded both the film and Murphy's performance: "This lickety-split action comedy is distinguished by the wry, character-conscious direction of Martin Brest, who coaxes a silver-bullet performance from star Eddie Murphy that's practically criminal in its accuracy."

One of the most memorable minor roles in the film went to a then-unknown named Bronson Pinchot. *Newsweek*'s reviewer was quick to spot the actor's potential: "Oddest of all is a salesman in the villain's art gallery who goes by the name of Serge and is of God-knows-what nationality; as played by a singular actor named Bronson Pinchot, Serge is the most unexpectedly and unusually hilarious

bit role within recent memory. The unknown Pinchot may be one of the few people alive who could steal a scene from Eddie Murphy." Pinchot continued that character and accent when he was selected to star in a popular TV series, "Perfect Strangers"; on that show he plays "Balki," the Balkan bumpkin, a character not unlike Serge in *Beverly Hills Cop.*

With the success of *Beverly Hills Cop,* Eddie Murphy's position atop Paramount's roster of talent was assured. The studio eagerly extended his contract and gave him a whole building for his production company, plus practically any perk the superstar might request (his electric golf cart, for example, boasted a Rolls Royce grill).

Sequels? Of course. Three years later, *Beverly Hills Cop II* was back for more fun and bullets (see page 316).

GREMLINS

WARNER BROS.
$79,500,000

"Keep him out of the light…
"Don't get him wet…
"And never, never feed him after
midnight."
—WARNING TO HOYT AXTON
WHEN HE PURCHASES A "MOGWAI"

NATURALLY, all of the above rules about the care and feeding of a "mogwai" are about to be broken, or there'd be no picture. That bit of business having been established before the opening credits, the audience, who had probably seen all kinds of publicity about the film before purchasing their tickets, had only to settle back in their chairs and wait for the fun to unfold.

The movie *Gremlins* is "presented" by Steven Spielberg, a name synonymous with "big box office" (he executive-produced this one), but some began to doubt his sense of humor, wondering if the wunderkind's dark side was beginning to force its way through. The picture begins innocently enough: it's Christmas time in a Frank Capra-esque town (movie send-ups abound); the local theater marquee reads *A Boy's Life* and *Watch the Skies*—early titles of two of Spielberg's biggest hits, *E. T. The Extra-Terrestrial* and *Close Encounters of the Third Kind*. Dad's been out Christmas shopping, and he brings home an unusual gift for son Billy: a mogwai, a cuddly, Disney-eyed creature who sings to himself. What child wouldn't want one for a pet?

But Gizmo, as he's quickly named by Billy's inventor father, isn't just your average mogwai. When he's inadver-

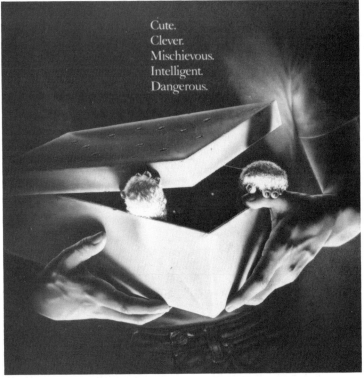

Cute.
Clever.
Mischievous.
Intelligent.
Dangerous.

tently moistened, all hell breaks loose, literally. The Gremlins which eventually materialize as offspring of Gizmo aren't your garden-variety pets at all, and thereby hangs a tale. When these creatures are turned loose on the town, the film goes from cute to grim.

Cute: Gremlins in earmuffs and ski caps, caroling through the town. Gremlins arm-wrestling in the local saloon. Gremlins taking in the local cinema— the film's been changed to Disney's *Snow White*—singing "Heigh-ho" along with the Seven Dwarfs, like kids at a matinee.

Grim: Billy's mom nuking a gremlin in the microwave. Gremlins trashing the town and offing the town grouch.

"Gremlins are not good," admitted director Joe Dante to *Time*. "You can't trust them. You don't want one for a pet. You don't want your daughter to marry one." Steven Spielberg noted that "if they could speak English, they'd probably say, 'Let's party!' It's

how they party that can be hazardous to your health."

Audiences took quite freely to these party animals. In a year filled with fantasies and imaginative action films (*Ghostbusters* and *Indiana Jones and the Temple of Doom* were the top two moneymakers for the year), this picture was in the right place at the right time. The public didn't mind the evil critters, even cheering them on. And since Gizmo remained wide-eyed and innocent throughout the movie, we always knew everything would turn out all right.

In 1990, Warner Bros. and Amblin Entertainment (Spielberg's production company) released a sequel, *Gremlins 2: The New Batch*. The same creative team and stars Zach Calligan and Pheobe Cates returned for more merry mayhem. The movie had only mild box office success, however, earning $20 million in North American rentals.

Screenplay by Chris Columbus

Executive Producers: Steven Spielberg, Frank Marshall, and Kathleen Kennedy

Produced by Michael Finnell

Directed by Joe Dante

CAST

Billy . . . . .Zach Galligan
Kate . . . . .Phoebe Cates
Rand Peltzer . . . . . . .Hoyt Axton
Lynn Peltzer . . . . . . .Frances Lee McCain
Mrs. Deagle . . . . . . .Polly Holliday

THE KARATE KID

COLUMBIA
$43,120,000

SLEEPER: that's what people were calling *The Karate Kid,* 1984's entry into the "feel good" school of movies. The summer release concerned a young 98-pound wimp who gets a dose of Oriental wisdom, along with some practical pointers in the fine art of crunching your aggressor's bones, from a mysterious janitor, superbly played by Pat Morita. Pat was somewhat familiar to audiences as "Arnold," the owner of the drive-in on TV's "Happy Days." Little did audiences suspect that the erstwhile hamburger-slinger was a philosopher. And no one was more surprised by his acting career than Morita himself. "I can't even imagine how I ever got into the entertainment business," the actor told the *San Francisco Chronicle.* "I don't sing, I don't dance, I don't juggle, I don't have an animal act and I can't even do karate, to tell you the truth." Not exactly fighting words from a karate master. "Karate really mystifies me," he continued. "All that stuff about breaking bricks. Why don't they just pick up the brick and hit 'em over the head with it?"

Luckily, none of this attitude came across on the screen. Mr. Miyagi's 17-year-old charge, Daniel, played by

---

Screenplay by Robert Mark Kamen

Executive Producer: R. J. Louis

Produced by Jerry Weintraub

Directed by John G. Avildsen

CAST

Daniel . . . . .Ralph Macchio
Miyagi . . . . .Noriyuki "Pat" Morita
Ali . . . . .Elisabeth Shue
Kreese . . . . .Martin Kove
Lucille . . . . .Randee Heller

ACADEMY AWARD NOMINATIONS

1 nomination, no wins

Best Supporting Actor (Noriyuki "Pat" Morita)

---

then-21-year-old Ralph Macchio, captured the hearts of the underdog-loving public. Sound familiar? Not surprising, since the film's director also made the original *Rocky.* He even referred to this picture jokingly as *The Karocky Kid. The Hollywood Reporter* saw a further parallel: "Put 'Rocky' in 'Alice Doesn't Live Here Anymore,' set it in the Valley and you've got 'The Karate Kid.'…[the film] will have an uphill

battle all the way if it is to be a contender in this summer's heavyweight box office division." The critical bash-fest continued with *Time* noting the picture's similarities to *Flashdance, Rocky,* and even *Star Wars*: "[The film provides Daniel] with a Yoda-like mentor full of gnomic instruction and inspiration in his struggle against evil. In short, *The Karate Kid* presents the smallest imaginable variations on three well-tested formulas for movie success." *The New York Times'* reviewer was one of the few reviewers who saw the potential in *The Karate Kid*: "[The film] has the makings of a genuinely heart-warming two-man drama, with Mr. Morita a charming cut-up and Mr. Macchio gently likable."

The film's popularity in the theaters has been matched only by its popularity in various formats. First, there were the sequels—three of them to date: *The Karate Kid, Part II* (1986; see page 312), *The Karate Kid, Part III* (1989), and *The Next Karate Kid* (1994), this time starring a teenaged girl in the title role. There was also a short-lived animated series on NBC's Saturday morning kiddie schedule, with Pat Morita voicing his original character and dispensing "Miyagi-isms."

BACK TO THE FUTURE

UNIVERSAL
$105,496,267

FIVE WEEKS into the shooting of *Back to the Future,* executive producer Steven Spielberg had the leading actor replaced. He had already spent $4,000,000 and had had to reshoot a number of scenes. But Spielberg was unhappy with Eric Stoltz in the role of Marty McFly, and demanded that he be removed from the cast. His choice for a replacement was a well-known TV actor who had unwittingly turned "Family Ties" into what could easily have been called "The Michael J. Fox Show." The young actor made no bones about the fact that he was "just one of the players" and disliked being the constant center of that show's spotlight. Spielberg had no trouble spotting Fox's talent, though, and nabbed him for his ailing production.

Michael J. Fox* began his TV career in his native Canada at the age of 14 and became an overnight sensation in Paramount's hit TV show "Family Ties," which ran on NBC for seven seasons. Like Ralph Macchio in *The Karate Kid,* Fox was either blessed or cursed, depending on how one looks at it, with appearing much younger than his actual age. In "Family Ties," he played teenager Alex P. Keaton well into his 20s; in *Back to the Future,* he was 24 years old playing 17. Nevertheless, Fox's charisma probably helped turn this cute picture into a real winner.

It wasn't an easy job for Fox, either. He was still working on "Ties," and for six weeks he'd work all day at the Paramount lot, then hop in his black Jeep and head over to the Universal lot for shooting from 6:00 P.M. till midnight, go home for a quick sleep, then do it all again the next day.

The teaming of Fox with another television actor, Christopher Lloyd

("Reverend Jim" from "Taxi") as the kookie mad-professor type, made for beautiful chemistry. Fox plays Marty McFly, a modern teen whose pal Dr. Emmett Brown (Lloyd) sends the lad back to that nostalgic year 1955, just in time for him to meet up with his parents, who were then teens themselves. (Worse, his own future mother develops a crush on him!) There's an old adage in science fiction time-travel stories: If you so much as kill a bug, you may also be destroying the future as we know it. This sort of premise has been a staple of science fiction ever since the genre was invented, and of course, in *Back to the Future,* the chain of events that is set up has exactly the results predicted.

Watch closely for some of the neat touches that director Zemeckis has incorporated into the setting for the film. The little town, for example, shows subtle changes over the decades. A theater marquee in 1955 that had been showing Ronald Reagan in *Cattle Queen of Montana* now exhibits porn films, the Studebaker dealership now sells Toyotas, and the

malt shop has become an aerobics gymnasium. Those visitors to Southern California who take the famed Universal Studios Tour have an opportunity to see this town square as part of the "tram tour."

Robert Zemeckis directed his co-written (with Bob Gale) script, but it was a long struggle getting it made. *Back to the Future* was rejected by all the major studios because, according to Zemeckis, "it wasn't raunchy enough." Spielberg finally gave the 33-year-old Zemeckis a chance; he'd also been the first to recognize Zemeckis' talent when he gave him his first break on *I Wanna Hold Your Hand,* a movie about the Beatles. Zemeckis was also noted for his popular movie *Romancing the Stone* (1984).

A spoof of '50s rock and roll is one of the highlights of the film, right down to Fox's impression of Chuck Berry. One of the musical numbers, "The Power of Love," by Huey Lewis and the News, received an Academy Award nomination, rose to number one on the pop charts for two weeks in August, 1985, and became the fifth best-selling song of the year. (Watch for Huey Lewis in a cameo appearance as a high school teacher.)

In 1989, Universal and Amblin Entertainment produced two long-awaited sequels to *Back to the Future—Back to the Future Part II* (see page 330) and *Part III,* filmed, naturally, back to back. Both films reteamed Michael J. Fox and Chris Lloyd, with Bob Zemeckis again at the helm. One of the reasons for this unusual filming procedure was the availability of both Fox and Zemeckis, popular talents who might not have been available had the films been shot separately. *Future II*'s plot involved sending Fox's character Marty McFly into the 21st century, to the year 2015, where he had to confront his own future and set things aright, while *Future III* sent the time travelers back to the Old West circa 1885.

Meanwhile, the final episode of "Family Ties" was filmed in the spring of 1989, so at least Michael J. Fox was able to get some sleep during these film productions.

---

*When he first joined the Screen Actors Guild, there was already an actor named Michael Fox. Regulations prohibit two actors from belonging to the Guild with the same stage name, so Michael decided to add a middle initial. His own middle initial, "A," would have made him "Michael A. Fox," and he cringed at the prospects of plays upon his name. He finally selected "J," after an actor he admired, Michael J. Pollard.

Screenplay by Robert Zemeckis and Bob Gale

Executive Producers: Steven Spielberg, Kathleen Kennedy, and Frank Marshall

Produced by Bob Gale and Neil Canton

Directed by Robert Zemeckis

CAST

Marty McFly . . . . .Michael J. Fox
Dr. Emmett Brown . . . .Christopher Lloyd
George McFly . . . . . . .Crispin Glover
Lorraine Baines . . . . . .Lea Thompson
Jennifer Parker . . . . . .Claudia Wells

ACADEMY AWARD NOMINATIONS

4 nominations, 1 win

　Best Screenplay Written Directly for the
　　Screen
　Best Sound
　Best Song ("Power of Love," music by
　　Chris Hayes and Johnny Colla, words by
　　Huey Lewis)
　*Best Sound Effects Editing

2

RAMBO: FIRST BLOOD PART II

TRI-STAR
$78,919,250

VIOLENCE LOVERS, unite! Your hero is alive and well and living on the big screen. He's a superman-turned-soldier, a robotic, superbly muscled human who can do one thing well: kill. Already the center of a film called *First Blood*, Sylvester Stallone's character of John Rambo is back and bigger than life once again. This time, there are some MIAs in need of rescuing in Vietnam, and only one man can save them. Machine-gunning, grenading, and sweating his way through the jungles of Southeast Asia, ex-Green Beret John Rambo proves it's brawn, not brains, that counts when you've got right on your side.

Like G.I. Joe of the cartoons, this macho killing machine was a comic-book hero come to life. Fans of Stallone, including President Reagan, all contributed to Rambomania in the summer of '85. In June, following the release of 39 American hostages by Lebanese terrorists, our former President remarked, "Boy, I saw *Rambo* last night. I know what to do the next time this happens!"

"This time do we get to win?" implores the muscled Rambo when given this assignment. Yes, we do, but why did the film have to be so gratuitously violent? According to the National Coalition of Television Violence (which also monitors big-screen features, since they eventually land on the small one), Rambo averaged 161 brutally violent acts per hour. Yet many saw this film as a paean to American patriotism. "People have been waiting for a chance to express their patriotism," said Stallone during the height of the film's popularity. "*Rambo* triggered long-suppressed emotions that had been out of vogue." A few years later, according to *The Cable Guide* magazine, the actor had tired of the "stigma people have put on [Rambo] as a symbol of right-wing aggressiveness…[Rambo's] really Oriental. He thinks more in terms of Muslim or Eastern philosophies. He has no sense of the self. He doesn't stand outside and observe war—he becomes war…Rambo is Zen-like. He's a disenfranchised samurai."

Newsweek, after describing the three *Rocky* films as "bloodbaths," stated that *Rambo*'s violence "makes the 'Rockys' look like 'Winnie-the-Pooh.' It's crunch, slash, ratatat all the way." *The Hollywood Reporter* had similar comments: "Stallone proves his prowess with a knife, a machine gun, a composite bow (complete with explosive heads), a Russian antitank gun and a Russian fighter helicopter…In the orgy of destruction that follows, the audience merely looking for action will have its appetite sated and its prejudices catered to. And these days, for a large segment of the population, that is what is considered entertainment. As a result, look for 'Rambo' to do big business and no doubt 'Rambo 2—First Blood 3' will be on its way soon."

Actually, the sequel was simply called *Rambo III* (1988), and it turned out to be the most expensive film in movie history to that date, costing a reported $63,000,000 to make. *Rambo* and *Rocky* may have made Sly Stallone a wealthy man, but *Rambo III* lost a bundle.

Screenplay by Sylvester Stallone and
    James Cameron

Based on a story by Kevin Jarre

Based on characters created by David
    Morrell

Executive Producers: Mario Kassar and
    Andrew Vajna

Produced by Buzz Feitshans

Directed by George P. Cosmatos

CAST

Rambo	Sylvester Stallone
Trautman	Richard Crenna
Murdock	Charles Napier
Co Bao	Julia Nickson
Podovsky	Steven Berkoff

ACADEMY AWARD NOMINATIONS

1 nomination, no wins

Best Sound Effects Editing

3

ROCKY IV

METRO-GOLDWYN-MAYER/UNITED ARTISTS
$76,023,246

"It's suicide! You can't win!"
—WARNING TO ROCKY BALBOA

ROCKY BALBOA was back for more, in a year that seemed to be dominated by Sly Stallone. His second- and third-place pictures for 1985, *Rambo* and *Rocky IV,* together totalled $155,000,000 in rentals. One might think the public would have had enough by now of this writer-director-actor and his tough-guy characters; not so. In *Rocky IV*, Rocky fulfills the earlier prophecy of one *Rocky II* reviewer by literally wrapping himself in the American flag, after he overcomes the best fighter the Soviet Union has to offer. Following the Big Fight, the triumphant pugilist exclaims: "In here there were two guys killing each other, but I guess that's better than twenty million. I can change, you can change, everybody can change."

Of course, Rocky does more in this film than conjugate the verb "to change." Again the film opens with the has-been Rocky on the brink of nowhere. He's been married to Adrian (Talia Shire) for nine years now—and it feels like it to us, too. Somehow he's persuaded to do just "one more fight"—this time against a Russian from hell. The Big Bad Commie trains; Rocky trains, again with old foe Apollo Creed (Carl Weathers); Rocky runs outdoors; the Russian trains in a high-tech gym. Eventually Rocky climbs a mountain, culminating in the now-

---

Screenplay by Sylvester Stallone

Executive Producers: James D. Brubaker and Arthur Chobanian

Produced by Irwin Winkler and Robert Chartoff

Directed by Sylvester Stallone

CAST

Rocky Balboa	Sylvester Stallone
Drago	Dolph Lundgren
Apollo Creed	Carl Weathers
Adrian	Talia Shire
Paulie	Burt Young
Ludmilla	Brigitte Nielsen

---

familiar fists-over-head gesture from the first *Rocky.*

It's the "fight of his life," of course. The audience is again suckered into thinking maybe Rocky *won't* win this one. But there is good character development, and we've really come to care about Rocky, his wife, and even little Rocky, Jr. Of course, he wins, and even the Russians can't help cheering for our man. (Don't miss the smiling ringside Gorbachev lookalike.)

The most adversarial role went to Brigitte Nielsen as the Russian trainer, Ludmilla. At six feet tall, the Scandinavian beauty walked off with the biggest prize of all—she ended up with Stallone himself, in what proved to be a "rocky" marriage which ended in divorce a few years later.

While *Rocky IV* was a huge success, earning even more money than 1982's *Rocky III,* not so *Rocky V.* The 1990 sequel, which had the familiar formula down pat, barely broke even, earning a mere $20 million in North American rentals. It seemed this time *Rocky* was down for the count.

THE COLOR PURPLE

WARNER BROS.
$49,800,000

"Omission impossible."
—THE NEW YORK POST

"Purple 11, Spielberg 0"
—THE LOS ANGELES
HERALD-EXAMINER

STEVEN SPIELBERG's first attempt at a totally serious film was *The Color Purple.* The man who had won fame as a director of action, fantasy, and supernatural films made a beautiful piece of cinema based on a difficult-to-film book—Alice Walker's diary-style, Pulitzer Prize–winning novel about the metamorphosis of a young black woman. The movie was breathtaking, from the first opening shots, to the well-integrated music, to the splendid tone and texture it established. Spielberg brought Celie, Mister, Shug Avery, and all of Alice Walker's characters to life with a good deal of faithful attention to the novel.

Not surprisingly, *The Color Purple* was showered with Oscar nominations, 11 in all, yet not one was offered to the film's director. Rarely is a film nominated for Best Picture without the director being nominated in his category as well: after all, pictures don't put themselves together. Word of

Spielberg's snubbing generated an audible response throughout the Hollywood film community the day after the Academy Awards were announced. Spielberg could not be reached for comment, but Warner Bros. wasted no time in buying an ad in the trades proclaiming that "the company is shocked and dismayed that the movie's primary creative force—Steven Spielberg—was not recognized." Spielberg did, however, win the Director's Guild Award, viewed by many as a consolation prize. Ironic, too, since it is directors who nominate directors in the Academy. His peers failed to reward him in one organization, while lauding him in another.

The film was noteworthy in another area, too. Both first-time actresses Whoopi Goldberg (née Caryn Johnson) and Oprah Winfrey were nominated for Oscars. Whoopi was best known as a stand-up comic, and many doubted she could handle the role. (She's been disproving such talk ever since.) And Oprah Winfrey was most noted as a talk-show host who had started with a small morning show in Baltimore and had only recently moved on to Chicago. She

would soon hit the big time with a top nationally syndicated TV talk show.

More disappointment followed on Oscar night. With 11 Award nominations, *The Color Purple* received not a single Oscar. Although the NAACP accused the Academy of a deliberate shut-out, this is highly unlikely, due to the strict controls of secret balloting. Financially, the film wasn't a true blockbuster, but at least there was some compensation in its success at the box office.

If you rent the videocassette, try to see this film on a big-screen TV so you can enjoy the breathtaking cinematography.

Screenplay by Menno Meyjes

Based on the novel by Alice Walker

Executive Producers: Jon Peters and Peter Guber

Produced by Steven Spielberg, Kathleen Kennedy, Frank Marshall, and Quincy Jones

Directed by Steven Spielberg

CAST

Albert	Danny Glover
Celie	Whoopi Goldberg
Shug Avery	Margaret Avery
Sofia	Oprah Winfrey
Harpo	Willard Pugh

ACADEMY AWARD NOMINATIONS

11 nominations, no wins

Best Picture
Best Actress (Whoopi Goldberg)
Best Supporting Actress (Margaret Avery)
Best Supporting Actress (Oprah Winfrey)
Best Screenplay Based on Material from Another Medium Best Cinematography
Best Art Direction–Set Decoration
Best Song ("Miss Celie's Blues [Sister]," music by Quincy Jones and Rod Temperton, words by Quincy Jones, Rod Temperton, and Lionel Richie)
Best Original Score (Quincy Jones and 11 others)
Best Costume Design
Best Make-up

OUT OF AFRICA

UNIVERSAL
$43,448,253

"I had a farm in Africa…"
—OPENING TO ISAK DINESEN'S BOOK
OUT OF AFRICA

DANISH WRITER Isak Dinesen emigrated to colonial Africa in the early 20th century. Her real name was Karen Blixen, and she did indeed have a farm. This loosely biographical picture is primarily a tragic love story starring two of the decade's top-drawing names, Meryl Streep and Robert Redford. They make a classy pair, and audiences were moved to fall in love along with them. Set against the splendid scenery of Kenya, the picture follows the young Karen in her loveless marriage to Bror Blixen (Klaus Maria Brandauer) in this episodic film about her affair with Great White Hunter Denys Finch-Hatton.

It's more a tapestry than a movie, with wondrous expanses of the African landscape as seen from Finch-Hatton's airplane, set to soaring music from John Barry (winner of Best Original Score). Other colorful characters from Blixen/Dinesen's books are woven throughout the picture. At 153 minutes, some thought the movie overly long, but not the romantics in the audience, many of whom returned more than once, giving the picture an additional boost at the box office. It was needed, as this was an expensive film to produce, costing a reported $31,000,000.

Screenplay by Kurt Luedtke

Based on the following: *Out of Africa* and other writings by Isak Dinesen

Isak Dinesen: The Life of a Storyteller by Judith Thurman

Silence Will Speak by Errol Trzebinski

Executive Producer: Kim Jorgensen

Produced and directed by Sydney Pollack

CAST

Karen . . . . .Meryl Streep
Denys . . . . .Robert Redford
Bror . . . . .Klaus Maria
Brandauer
Berkeley . . . . .Michael Kitchen
Farah . . . . .Malick Bowens

ACADEMY AWARD NOMINATIONS

11 nominations, 7 wins*

*Best Picture
Best Actress (Meryl Streep)
Best Supporting Actor (Klaus Maria Brandauer)
*Best Director (Sydney Pollack)
*Best Screenplay Based on Material from Another Medium (Kurt Luedtke)
*Best Cinematography
*Best Art Direction–Set Decoration
*Best Sound
*Best Original Score (John Barry)
Best Film Editing
Best Costume Design

Sydney Pollack directed Robert Redford in *Jeremiah Johnson* and again in this movie. He had also directed the popular hit of 1982, *Tootsie* (see page 286). With *Out of Africa,* the director finally received an Academy Award.

The film was made on location during an African drought. Just as the crew was considering a move, the rains finally came. Many of the crew fell victim to malaria. And filming of the animals posed many problems as the crew camped in the bush. Sometimes it was necessary to wait hours for the wild herds to move to the right spot in the shot (it's illegal to touch or maneuver any wild animal). The film featured three dogs, an eagle, and five lions. All these animals had to be imported from California: seems there were no trained lions on their native continent.

Critics praised the picture. *The Hollywood Reporter* called it "a splendid, beautifully composed love story, a resplendent holiday film…Compositionally masterful, 'Out of Africa' moves with carefully modulated visual rhythms …In the leads, Streep and Redford are certain to garner Oscar nominations for their intelligent, gifted portrayals. Brandauer also brings distinction to his role."

Meryl Streep did receive a nomination (her sixth), but oddly enough, Redford did not. And Brandauer, as predicted, was nominated for Best Supporting Actor.

1

TOP GUN
PARAMOUNT
$79,400,000

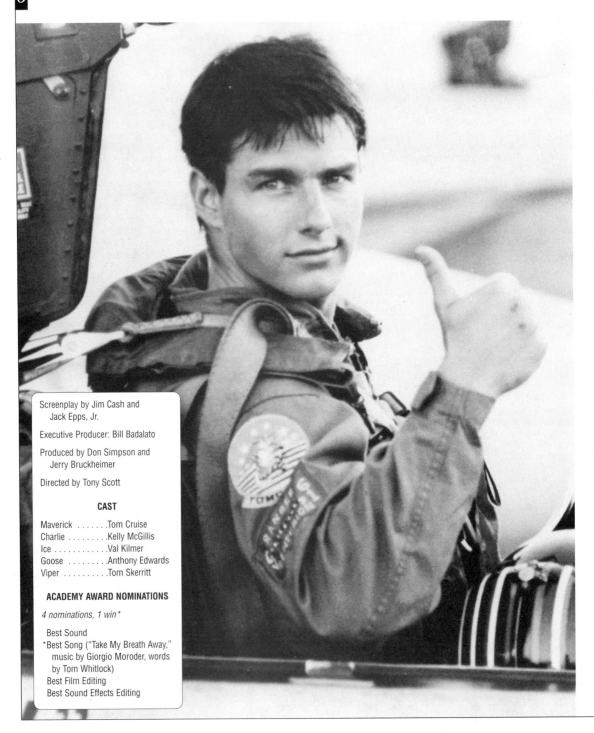

Screenplay by Jim Cash and
    Jack Epps, Jr.

Executive Producer: Bill Badalato

Produced by Don Simpson and
    Jerry Bruckheimer

Directed by Tony Scott

CAST

Maverick . . . . .Tom Cruise
Charlie . . . . .Kelly McGillis
Ice . . . . .Val Kilmer
Goose . . . . .Anthony Edwards
Viper . . . . .Tom Skerritt

ACADEMY AWARD NOMINATIONS

4 nominations, 1 win*

Best Sound
*Best Song ("Take My Breath Away,"
    music by Giorgio Moroder, words
    by Tom Whitlock)
Best Film Editing
Best Sound Effects Editing

"On March 3, 1969, the United States Navy established an elite school for the top one percent of its pilots. Its purpose was to teach the lost art of aerial combat and to insure that the handful of men who graduated were the best fighter pilots in the world. They succeeded. Today, the Navy calls it Fighter Weapons School. The flyers call it: TOP GUN." —OPENING CARDS

THEY COULD HAVE called it *Top Movie.* This number-one hit film had all the ingredients for success: handsome male lead, sexy female to play opposite him, plenty of action for those so inclined, and beautiful machinery—in this case, a fleet of Navy fighter planes. Yet preliminary marketing tests showed that audiences were not completely satisfied. Fearing the worst, producers Don Simpson and Jerry Bruckheimer (the team responsible for *Beverly Hills Cop*) called their principals back for additional photography six months after they had wrapped. Seems the audiences wanted more passion between Maverick (Tom Cruise) and Charlie (Kelly McGillis). That actress, who had appeared as a blonde in the film, had already cropped and darkened her hair for another movie, so in one scene, an encounter in an elevator, she had to wear a military cap.

The story of Maverick and his Radar Intercept Officer, Goose (Anthony Edwards), training to become the elitest of the elite—the best fighter pilots in the world—captured the imagination of the public. There was plenty of action and technical accuracy. The Navy gave its full support to the picture; there is much footage of real Top Gun pilots in evidence. Eight naval F-14 pilots' names are listed in the credits, as well as 16 Top Gun instructors and "MIG" pilots (played by Americans with nicknames like "Horse," "Circus," "Sunshine," "Hollywood," "Tex," "Rat," and "Jaws").

Producers Simpson and Bruckheimer got the idea for the film from a May, 1983 article entitled "Top Guns," which ran in *California* magazine. The creative pair thought there was great potential for a film in the article. "Not only did we like the title and strong aerial photography which accompanied the article," recalled Simpson in the *Top Gun* production handbook, "but we were attracted to this uncommon environment, with its own terminology and its bigger-than-life characters." Bruckheimer added: "The pilots that attend the actual Top Gun school are a combination of Olympic athletes in the sky and rock and roll heroes. We immediately saw a movie."

Part of the thrill for audiences was the true feeling of sitting in the cockpit of an F-14 "pulling G's." It was a Disneyland ride on screen, complete with stomach-wrenching rolls and turns. The film's star, Tom Cruise, spent several months commuting between Los Angeles and the Miramar Naval Air Station north of San Diego, attending Top Gun classes and learning about what it takes to be a pilot. "A Top Gun instructor once told me," said Cruise, quoted in Jolene Anthony's *Tom Cruise,* "that there are only four occupations worthy of a man: actor, rock star, jet fighter pilot, or President of the United States." Cruise's pre-production training was capped by a spectacular ride in the back seat of a TA-4, part of the famous Blue Angels squadron.

Kelly McGillis, Cruise's movie love interest, also did extensive research for her role. "Last year I was studying the Amish people for *Witness,* and the next year, I'm learning about negative Gs and inverted flight tanks for *Top Gun,*" she said during filming, according to the *Top Gun* production handbook.

As part of the location shooting, 35 crew members spent four days at sea aboard the carrier USS *Enterprise.* Tom Cruise brought his own camera to record the events on the flight deck, and found himself being taught by an enlisted man to taxi the airplanes on the flight line. It was any young man's dream come true. Cruise joined the ranks of superstardom with the popularity of *Top Gun,* soaring to the top of the box office polls as the year's number-one performer. His popularity continued to climb throughout the rest of the decade and into the 1990s as he starred in such films as *Rain Man* (1988; see page 320), *A Few Good Men* (1992; see page 351), *The Firm* (1993; see page 356) and *Interview with a Vampire* (1994).

The film's theme song, "Take My Breath Away" (and this picture certainly did just that for a lot of people), became a number-one hit the week of September 13, 1986, and went on to collect Oscars for its composers, Giorgio Moroder and Tom Whitlock. The team wrote two more popular songs for the film, "Danger Zone" and "Lead Me On," plus a number of other soundtrack songs.

Much of *Top Gun*'s aerial action was filmed on a soundstage with rear projection.

2
"CROCODILE" DUNDEE
PARAMOUNT
$70,227,000

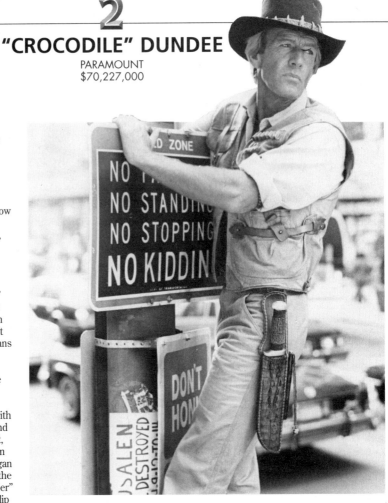

PAUL HOGAN was not exactly a household word in America. The former rigger on the Sydney, Australia, Harbour Bridge, who had gone on to become the Aussie "Johnny Carson," had been seen by only a handful of Yanks who might have caught reruns of his variety show on late-night independent TV channels. So when his Australian hit film, *Crocodile Dundee,* came to America, the releasing studio, Paramount Pictures, decided (after considering 250 alternate titles) to put quotation marks around the word "Crocodile," ⌐t Americans stay away from what th., might suspect was a nature film on the care and feeding of reptiles. It was an unfounded concern. Americans took one look at the charming and sexy Mr. Hogan and couldn't have cared less whether the picture's title had quotes around it or not.

Suddenly Aussie was chic. It was trendy to toss down a few Fosters with your mates (pronounced "mites") and even plan a trip Down Under. In fact, after this picture's release, Australian tourism increased by 40 percent. Hogan himself had been a spokesman for "the land of Wonder, the land Down Under" for years, promising all of us he'd "slip an extra shrimp on the barbie."*

What Paul Hogan did was create a character in the James Bond tradition—

Screenplay by Paul Hogan, Ken Shadie, and John Cornell

Produced by John Cornell

Directed by Peter Faiman

CAST

Mick "Crocodile"
Dundee . . . . .Paul Hogan
Sue Charlton . . . . .Linda Kozlowski
Walter Reilly . . . . .John Meillon
Neville Bell . . . . .David Gulpilil
Con . . . . .Ritchie Singer

ACADEMY AWARD NOMINATIONS

1 nomination, no wins

Best Screenplay Written Directly for the Screen

a hero who could handle himself in any situation—except that this guy was an Aussie babe in the woods. The woods, in this case, was the jungle called New York City, and Hogan as Mick "Crocodile" Dundee proved you can take the Aussie out of the bush, but you can't take the bush out of the Aussie. In the film's story, Dundee is "adopted" by an American reporter, Sue Charlton (Linda Kozlowski), who persuades the croc hunter to journey back to the Big Apple with her so she can finish her story. His childlike reaction to everyday things we take for granted is what gives this story its main appeal.

Some changes in vocabulary had to be made for Americans to understand the Aussie colloquialisms, and several minutes were cut entirely. One scene, however, remained unchanged, although most Americans didn't understand the reference. At the end of the film, Mick is in the New York

subway, fighting his way through the crowd, trying frantically to reach his girlfriend, Sue. In a sequence that parallels the familiar sheepdogs walking across the backs of the sheep in Australia (the world's leading sheep-breeding country), Mick climbs over the backs of subway patrons. Australians roared with laughter at this sight gag, while most Americans didn't catch on.

Paul Hogan's popularity rocketed with this film's surprising success, and Paramount ordered an immediate sequel (see page 324). The actor was inundated with offers, but continued to patriotically promote his native country, as well as its products, including Foster's Lager.

*Chances are your Australian hosts would give you blank stares if you requested one. "Shrimp" are called "prawns" there, and anyway, they usually barbecue steaks and chicken, like the rest of us.

*"Dedicated to the men who fought
and died in the Vietnam War."*
—TITLE CARD

WAR MOVIES have always been box office hits. In the '40s we had *Sergeant York, A Yank in the R.A.F., 30 Seconds Over Tokyo,* and others. In the '50s, there were the "funny" war films, like *Mister Roberts* and *Operation Petticoat,* as well as the dramatic stories of *Battle Cry, From Here to Eternity,* and *The Bridge on the River Kwai.* In the late '80s, with film technology perfected to an art form, war movies reached new heights, culminating in Oliver Stone's masterpiece, *Platoon.*

Never had war been portrayed this realistically. Actor Mickey Rooney was so disturbed by the film that he thought they should have a sign outside theaters banning women, a sexist point of view that may well be merited. *Platoon* is a paean to the insanity that we call war, neither glorifying nor trivializing it. This is humanity at its lowest element, the animal brain stem in con-trol, the cerebrum somehow on hiatus. The film is frightening and depressing and, yes, superb filmmaking. Above all else, viewers must constantly remind themselves that they have not dropped into some jungle during a war, but are still sitting comfortably (by now, uncomfortably) in a theater or living-room chair. It's not the shoot-'em-up-and-let's-hear-a-cheer *Rambo* school of filmmaking violence, but a much more painful, stomach-turning, blood-and-guts movie. Not too many people visited the concession stand during this one.

Oliver Stone had a personal interest in doing this film. He had served for 15 months in Vietnam when, at the age of 21, he dropped out of Yale and joined the infantry. The experiences of his hero, Chris (Charlie Sheen), directly parallel Stone's own wartime hell. Stone spent 10 years trying to get the feature made, meanwhile writing such films as *Midnight Express* (1978) and *Scarface* (1983), and writing and directing *Salvador.* He finally persuaded Orion Productions to make *Platoon,* which he brought in on a budget of only $6,000,000.

It turned out to be the biggest film Orion ever had, returning their investment tenfold. Publicity and word of mouth helped increase the audience for this picture. Besides its harsh realism, there is attention to fine details. Listen for the voice of the real Adrian Cronauer in the background, blaring out "Gooood Morning, Vietnam!" This was not added as an inside joke; that hit film wouldn't even be released for another year.

This picture appears uncut, with all its violence and language intact, on many cable channels. Send the kids to bed early.

Screenplay by Oliver Stone

Executive Producers: John Daly and Derek Gibson

Produced by Arnold Kopelson

Directed by Oliver Stone

CAST

Sergeant Barnes	Tom Berenger
Sergeant Elias	Willem Dafoe
Chris	Charlie Sheen
Big Harold	Forest Whitaker
Rhah	Francesco Quinn

ACADEMY AWARD NOMINATIONS

8 nominations, 4 wins*

*Best Picture
Best Supporting Actor (Tom Berenger)
Best Supporting Actor (Willem Dafoe)
*Best Director (Oliver Stone)
Best Screenplay Written Directly for the Screen
Best Cinematography
*Best Sound
*Best Film Editing

4

THE KARATE KID, PART II

COLUMBIA
$58,310,000

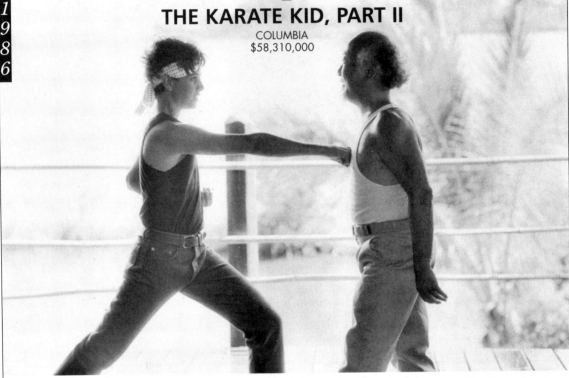

IN DIRECT contrast to violent films like *Platoon, Rambo: First Blood Part II,* and even *Top Gun, The Karate Kid, Part II* was a kinder, gentler type of picture for war-weary audiences. Reprising their original roles were Ralph Macchio as the downtrodden teenaged Daniel (Macchio was now 24 years old) and Pat Morita as his sage advisor/mentor/trainer. Like the first film, this one was a sleeper: no one expected it to do much business. But like its inspiration, *Rocky,* the Roman-numeraled sequel brought in many of the film's original fans, along with many newcomers. This picture actually made more than its predecessor.

Critics immediately took sides. Some thought the movie was merely a rip-off of a rip-off, as if someone at Columbia had perhaps demanded, "Send in the clones!" The Hollywood trade paper *Daily Variety* called the film "a pokey and hokey sequel to the 1984 chop socky kidpic"; yet *The Hollywood Reporter* considered the sequel "a gentle yet exciting film—even rarer, a sequel that's better than the original."

The sequel certainly had more story to it than did its predecessor. Accompanied by his young charge, Miyagi (Morita) returns to his native Okinawa, where his father is dying. Back home, he meets up with an old nemesis and an old girlfriend, while Daniel finds a new nemesis and new girlfriend. Morita has the juicier role here, as noted by *The Hollywood Reporter.* " 'The Karate Kid, Part II' is most certainly Morita's story, and his performance is the film's highlight. It is measured, tender and completely winning. Morita seems a certain bet for Academy consideration as the wise and comical martial arts sage." However, although the actor was nominated for his part in the first *Karate Kid,* the Academy chose to ignore Morita's critically praised performance this time around. The only nomination received was for "Glory of Love" as Best Song. The recording by co-composer Peter Cetera shot to the top of the *Billboard* charts, remaining at number one for two weeks.

In the summer of 1989, yet another installment was released, *The Karate Kid, Part III.* The 27-year-old Macchio was still baby-faced enough to play teenage karate student Daniel LaRusso, but was beginning to fear typecasting. "I guess the thing I want most is to be perceived as a versatile actor who does many things," Macchio told the *Los Angeles Times.* "The challenge is breaking through the mold of being the angelic, identifiable 'Karate Kid' character." *Kid III* completes Macchio's three-picture deal. Says the actor, "My instinct is to move on to other things…I can't feasibly foresee myself just playing this kid getting beat up again and prevailing in the end."

Sylvester Stallone couldn't have put it better.

Screenplay by Robert Mark Kamen

Executive Producer: R. J. Louis

Produced by Jerry Weintraub

Directed by John G. Avildsen

CAST

Daniel . . . . .Ralph Macchio
Miyagi . . . . .Noriyuki "Pat" Morita
Yukie . . . . .Nobu McCarthy
Sato . . . . .Danny Kamekona
Chozen . . . . .Yuji Okumoto

ACADEMY AWARD NOMINATIONS

1 nomination, no wins

Best Song ("Glory of Love," music by Peter Cetera and David Foster, words by Peter Cetera and Diane Nini)

STAR TREK IV: THE VOYAGE HOME

PARAMOUNT
$56,820,071

THERE had been two sequels to the successful *Star Trek: The Motion Picture* (1979; see page 266). In *Star Trek II: The Wrath of Khan,* Ricardo Montalban, as the nefarious Khan, a character created in one of the TV episodes, attacks the *Enterprise* and kills the beloved character of Mr. Spock. Trekkers were furious. Paramount, realizing they may have killed the goose that lays golden eggs for them on a regular basis, found a way to resurrect the popular Vulcan in the third picture in the series, appropriately titled *Star Trek III: The Search for Spock* (they found him, in case you're wondering). For this third movie, Leonard Nimoy, the actor who had fleshed out Gene Roddenberry's creation of the half-Vulcan, half-human Mr. Spock, promised to return only if given directorial chores. The picture did well, and he was given another assignment: *Star Trek IV: The Voyage Home.*

This fourth *Trek* did slightly better financially than *Star Trek I* (but not if inflation is taken into account), since it found a wider audience. The picture has to do with the Enterprise crew trying to return to Earth without their beloved *Enterprise* (they had trashed the starship a picture or two back)— oh, and while they are at it, they have to find a way to save the planet from Destruction by Strange Aliens from Space. The aliens, it seems, are searching for their old pals, the whales from centuries past, but none exist in the 24th century, so Kirk and Company set out to return to an earlier time on Earth when whales hadn't been hunted to extinction. It's a nice thought, if a bit hokey.

Some of the best scenes are not, as one might expect, in space, but on 20th-century Earth—San Francisco, to be exact. There are some delightful numbers with our spacepeople of the future trying to figure out how to use money, operate computers that must be museum pieces to them, take a bus (in a clever bit with Leonard Nimoy's assistant, Kirk Thatcher, as a punker with a boombox), and mix with the population without arousing suspicion about who they really are.

There are shades of *"Crocodile" Dundee* in the "Man from Mars" shtick, but it's all good fun, and main-stream audiences, as well as the hard-core Trekkers and science fiction fans, made this another big hit for Paramount. (The studio, in fact, had three of the top five hits for the year, totalling nearly $200,000,000 in rentals.)

In 1989, Paramount released *Star Trek V: The Final Frontier.* Since Leonard Nimoy had directed *two* of the popular films, it seemed only fair, argued William Shatner, that he be allowed to direct at least one sequel. In fact, his *Star Trek IV* contract already provided for that. In 1988, Shatner co-wrote and directed *Star Trek V: The Final Frontier,* which earned only $27 million in North American rentals. This was followed in 1991 with the final film using the entire original series cast—*Star Trek VI: The Undiscovered Country* ($36 million). In 1994, Paramount released the first film based on the spin-off TV series, "Star Trek: The Next Generation." The movie, *Star Trek: Generations,* earned approximately $37 million in rentals.

Screenplay by Steve Meerson, Peter Krikes, Harve Bennett, and Nicholas Meyer

Executive Producer: Ralph Winter

Produced by Harve Bennett

Directed by Leonard Nimoy

CAST

Kirk . . . . .William Shatner
Spock . . . . .Leonard Nimoy
McCoy . . . . .DeForest Kelley
Scotty . . . . .James Doohan
Sulu . . . . .George Takei

ACADEMY AWARD NOMINATIONS

4 nominations, no wins

Best Cinematography
Best Sound
Best Original Score
Best Sound Effects Editing

THREE MEN AND A BABY

TOUCHSTONE PICTURES (WALT DISNEY PRODUCTIONS)
$81,356,000

*"I think it's your turn to change
her."* —STEVE GUTTENBERG

*"I'll give you a thousand dollars if
you do it."* —TOM SELLECK

I T WAS every leading lady's dream.
Imagine sharing co-credit with Tom
Selleck, Ted Danson, and Steve
Guttenberg, having them fuss over
you, sing to you, share their pent-
house with you. Then imagine you're
their six-month-old baby. That's the
set-up for *Three Men and a Baby*. And
the old warning about never acting
with children and animals goes triple
here…in what borders on armed robbery, the little infant girl steals every
scene she's in.

Screenplay by James Orr and Jim
Cruickshank

Based on the film *Trois Hommes et un
Couffin,* written by Coline Serreau

Executive Producer: Jean Francois Lepetit

Produced by Ted Field and Robert W. Cort

Directed by Leonard Nimoy

CAST

Peter . . . . .Tom Selleck
Michael . . . . .Steve Guttenberg
Jack . . . . .Ted Danson
Sylvia . . . . .Nancy Travis
Rebecca . . . . .Margaret Colin

The Walt Disney Company made
out like bandits at the box office with
this Touchstone release.* Ever since
the creative team from Paramount,
consisting of Michael Eisner, Jeffrey
Katzenberg, and Richard Frank,
defected to Disney, the company,
which had been ailing since Walt's
death, had begun a turnaround that
put Disney Studios once more among
the serious contenders in Hollywood's
film industry.

Three Men and a Baby was a delight
for several reasons. It was based on a
popular French film, *Trois Hommes et
un Couffin* (*Three Men and a Cradle,*
1985). *Trois Hommes* broke box office
records in France and was nominated

in the U.S. for an Academy Award as the Best Foreign Film of 1985. It was also the highest-grossing foreign language film in the U.S. in 1986. Both films have basically the same plot: three bachelors-about-town are suddenly saddled with fatherhood when a baby is abandoned on their doorstep. There's a subplot about drugs and some hoods who mistakenly think our heroes are their contacts, but all that's not really important. Some of the most delightful moments for audiences are whenever the baby (actually twin girls, . Lisa and Michelle Blair) is on screen.

The film was shot in Toronto, Canada, with Leonard Nimoy, fresh from his directing successes on two *Star Trek* films, handling his first non-Trek assignment. Nimoy, a grand-

father, proved that he knew his way around kids as well as around a starship. For the film's huge box office take, Nimoy, in a press release at the time, credited his fine cast: "I think that the relationship between the three actors is palpable on screen. I am particularly sensitive to the importance of this because *Star Trek* was an example of a situation where the chemistry between the performers was crucial to the project's success."

The *Three Men* were popular '80s stars from film and TV. Tom Selleck was best known for his continuing TV series "Magnum, P.I.," which ran for eight seasons on CBS; many hailed him as a modern Clark Gable. During his summer hiatuses from "Magnum," he starred in a number of action-adventure films, including *High Road to China, Runaway,* and *Lassiter.* But his most successful feature was *Three Men and a Baby,* quite a departure for the macho idol.

Steve Guttenberg had an impressively long list of film credits, including the hit fantasy film *Cocoon* (1985), directed by Ron Howard; *Police Academy 1, 2, 3,* and *4* (1984, 1985, 1986, and 1987, respectively); and

Short Circuit (1986). While he had more film credits than his two male co-stars, he admitted his lack of any experience when it came to handling babies. According to *Three Men*'s press release, "this was one time…that not having experience was actually a plus because it made my character all the more believable."

Bachelor number three in the film, Ted Danson, was best known as the perennial bachelor Sam Malone on the hit TV series "Cheers."

To prepare for their roles, Danson, Selleck, and Guttenberg hit the Toronto singles scene. "We went out eating and dancing and had a great time," recalled Danson in the same press release. "Of course, it was all in the name of research and role preparation." (Can you imagine these three guys showing up in a singles bar?)

Both *Three Men and a Cradle,* the original French film, and *Three Men and a Baby* are delightfully funny; the French version is subtitled, rather than dubbed, but if reading subtitles is a chore, these can easily be ignored and you'll still get the picture. A sequel, *Three Men and a Little Lady,* was released in 1990.

*Walt Disney Productions uses the Disney name mostly for the "G"-rated pictures the studio releases; a subsidiary company, Touchstone, is used for the more adult "PG" and "R" releases. Buena Vista (named after the street the studio is on in Burbank) is the name for Disney's distribution arm. For reasons of simplification, Touchstone and Disney productions in this book are all referred to in charts as "Disney" releases.

2

BEVERLY HILLS COP II

PARAMOUNT
$80,857,776

EDDIE MURPHY'S name is so entwined with the comic genre that it's easy to classify *Beverly Hills Cop II* as a comedy. Certainly, there are some hilarious moments in this picture. But there is a serious undertone to this film, as Axel Foley returns to help his Beverly Hills pals, Billy (Judge Reinhold) and Taggart (John Ashton), when their police captain (again played by Ronny Cox) is critically wounded. Dean Stockwell (once a cute child star) plays the heavy, with Brigitte Nielsen (Sly Stallone's former lady) as his hitwoman.

If not for Murphy, this film might just be another Beverly Hills cops-and-robbers picture. For example, there's that old standby, the car chase—this time a demolition derby with a cement truck. Murphy's quick improvisational wit, however, saves the picture from becoming anything close to routine. "I never had aspirations to be in the movie business," admitted Murphy in a Paramount production handbook. "I was always a stand-up comedian, and that's what I am more than anything."

Screenplay by Larry Ferguson and Warren Skaaren

From a story by Eddie Murphy and Robert D. Wachs

Based on characters created by Danilo Bach and Daniel Petrio, Jr.

Executive Producers: Robert D. Wachs and Richard Tienken

Produced by Don Simpson and Jerry Bruckheimer

Directed by Tony Scott

CAST

Axel Foley	Eddie Murphy
Billy Rosewood	Judge Reinhold
Maxwell Dent	Jurgen Prochnow
Andrew Bogomil	Ronny Cox
John Taggart	John Ashton

ACADEMY AWARD NOMINATIONS

1 nomination, no wins

Best Song ("Shakedown," music by Harold Faltermeyer and Keith Forsey, words by Harold Faltermeyer, Keith Forsey, and Bob Seger)

Could be, but the winner of the People's Choice Awards for 1985 could usually be counted on to turn a routine picture into a smash.

Reviews were less than kind for the film. *Variety* complained: " 'Beverly Hills Cop II' is a noisy, numbing, unimaginative, heartless remake of the original film. Everything that was funny and appealing the first time has been attempted again here, but has all gone sour and cold…but none of this will matter at the box office, as Murphy, Simpson, Bruckheimer, et al., will once again laugh all the way to the bank."

Count on it. Eddie Murphy became the highest-paid black film star in history when he banked $7,000,000 for his latest ride down Rodeo Drive. Since then, he has starred in a number of popular films, including *Coming to America* (1988, see page 323), *Another 48 Hrs.* (1990), and a third *Cop* film, *Beverly Hills Cop III*. In 1995, he filmed a remake of the old Jerry Lewis movie *The Nutty Professor.*

The soundtrack for *Beverly Hills Cop* had produced a successful single, "The Heat Is On," which peaked at number two in March, 1985. With the release of *Cop II,* a new song was added to the charts: "Shakedown." The Bob Seger recording climbed the pop charts to number one, where it remained during the first week of August, 1987. It also became a Best Song contender, the movie's only Academy Award nomination.

Eddie Murphy's vocabulary is quite colorful, in addition to the violence and nudity this picture contains. The "R" rating didn't seem to hurt it any at the box office, but it is *not* a family comedy. *Beverly Hills Cop II* can be seen frequently on cable channels, and while not as much fun as the first, it's still an Eddie Murphy showcase, and he doesn't have all those fans for nothing.

FATAL ATTRACTION

PARAMOUNT
$70,000,000

"I WAS ALWAYS interested in lust," said Michael Douglas in *Cable Guide* magazine. "Everybody has someone they've lusted for." If that is true, then this would be the reason behind the huge success of the summer of '87's hit film, *Fatal Attraction.*

In this case, Douglas is the lustee, not the lustor. What starts as a simple little weekend tryst turns into a nightmare for Dan Gallagher (Douglas) when the object of his affections, Alex Forrest (Glenn Close), becomes obsessed, then maniacal, about her one-night-stand lover. Douglas says he is happily married, but Close isn't buying it. When he spurns her attentions, she stalks him like a quarry. Soon we learn this is not a triangular romance picture, but a deadly game of cat and mouse.

Much of this movie's suspense owes a debt to Alfred Hitchcock and the *Psycho* school of filmmaking. It is not a mystery—we know Close is stalking Douglas and terrorizing his family, and she gives new meaning to the words "insanely jealous." The question is, when will she next strike, and how? It is a psychological-suspense thriller/ romance, not for the squeamish, although certainly predictable in outcome.

Newsweek provided something of a warning label for its readers when its reviewer wrote: "Alex is a figure designed to send men rushing off to their shrinks, aquiver with sexual paranoia… What Freddy or Jason is to horny teens, Alex may become to the Yuppie male contemplating an extramarital fling."

Indeed, business was brisk on psychiatric couches across the country, while at the same time declining at singles bars following the film's release. Glenn Close researched her role by taking the script to three psychiatrists, one of whom helped her construct a detailed emotional and psychiatric history for the character. She described Alex to *Newsweek* as "between being a total child and a femme fatale. Her sexuality has been all screwed up, and she has no sense of self-worth. She tries to provoke people to hate her as much as she hates herself."

Most of the audience wasn't interested in psychoanalyzing Douglas' unfortunate choice of a bed partner. According to statistics, a high percentage of the married public are either involved in or contemplating extramarital affairs; many men were reluctantly escorted to this picture by their concerned significant others, who would not believe that the plural of "spouse" is "spice." It became the most talked about film of the summer, and gave Paramount yet another great box office year, with three films in the top five (*Beverly Hills Cop II, Fatal Attraction, The Untouchables*) for a total take of close to $187,000,000 in domestic rentals.

Screenplay by James Dearden

Produced by Stanley R. Jaffe and Sherry Lansing

Directed by Adrian Lyne

CAST

Dan Gallagher . . . . . . .Michael Douglas
Alex Forrest . . . . .Glenn Close
Beth Gallagher . . . . . .Anne Archer
Jimmy . . . . .Stuart Pankin
Hildy . . . . .Ellen Foley
Arthur . . . . .Fred Gwynne

ACADEMY AWARD NOMINATIONS

6 nominations, no wins

Best Picture
Best Actress (Glenn Close)
Best Supporting Actress (Anne Archer)
Best Director (Adrian Lyne)
Best Screenplay Based on Material from Another Medium
Best Film Editing

GOOD MORNING, VIETNAM

TOUCHSTONE PICTURES (WALT DISNEY PRODUCTIONS)
$58,083,108

ROBIN WILLIAMS is always a risk when signed to a picture: a risk in the best sense of the word, since the producer is generally likely to get more than he bargained for. That is precisely what makes Robin Williams so desirable. He is one of the quickest natural wits in the business, a perpetual ad-libber who is virtually always "on," even when relaxing with friends.

As Adrian Cronauer in *Good Morning, Vietnam,* Williams hits his stride. Cronauer was a real Vietnam DJ on the local Armed Forces Radio network. As portrayed by Robin Williams, at least, he was to radio what Hawkeye Pierce was to *M*A*S*H*—a cut-up who refused to take war, or orders, seriously. His instructions were to read propaganda, but Cronauer, as marvelously ad-libbed by Williams, had his own idea about what the soldiers wanted to hear. And of course he was right. Producer Mark Johnson noted in a press release at the time: "Nobody else works with the inventiveness, the quickness and the zaniness of Robin Williams. When he sat down in the control booth to do the scenes involving Cronauer's broadcasts, we just let the cameras roll. He managed to create something new for every single take."

Robin Williams was born in a Chicago suburb in 1952. In Robin's high school years, his father retired to Marin County, California, where

---

Screenplay by Mitch Markowitz

Produced by Mark Johnson and Larry Brezner

Directed by Barry Levinson

CAST

Adrian Cronauer . . . .Robin Williams
Edward Garlick . . . . .Forest Whitaker
Tuan . . . . .Tung Thanh Tran
Trinh . . . . .Chintara Sukapatana
Lt. Steven Hauk . . . .Bruno Kirby

ACADEMY AWARD NOMINATIONS

1 nomination, no wins

Best Actor (Robin Williams)

Williams was voted "Most Humorous" and "Most Likely to Succeed" by his classmates. After briefly studying political science, Williams entered Marin College as a theater major, but soon enrolled at New York's famed Juilliard Academy (Chris Reeve was a classmate), where he spent three years under the tutelage of actor John Houseman, among other notables. After college, he performed on the California nightclub circuit, eventually landing at the Los Angeles Comedy Store. He was spotted by casting agents there, and appeared on TV in what was supposed to be a one-shot performance as "Mork from Ork" on the popular "Happy Days" show. Viewer response encouraged Paramount to spin off his own show, *Mork and Mindy* (1978 premiere), which showcased his outrageous

antics. (Lucky studio audiences got to see an even better show than what was actually written in the script, when Williams ad-libbed nonstop at tapings.) In 1989, Williams starred in the critically acclaimed *Dead Poets Society.* Other credits included *Hook* (1991; see page 344), *Aladdin* (1992; see page 346), *Toys* (1992), and *Mrs. Doubtfire* (1993).

Good Morning, Vietnam was more than a Robin Williams laugh fest; it had a serious side as well. The story marks a departure from many of the recent Vietnam stories like *Platoon* in that its format is a new genre called "dramedy"—drama/comedy. Williams has us clutching our sides in laughter one minute, then director Barry Levinson throws in something from the serious side of war to sober us. It's fine adult entertainment.

5

THE UNTOUCHABLES

PARAMOUNT
$36,866,530

A HIGHLY successful TV show that ran on ABC from 1959 to 1963, "The Untouchables" starred Robert Stack as Eliot Ness, the no-nonsense "Fed" who took a bite out of crime in the days of Prohibition. People who had Stack's portrayal in their minds as they headed for theaters emerged two hours later from the "R"-rated film with a new hero. As Eliot Ness, Kevin Costner created a whole new image for a character that had been mere cardboard for an earlier generation.

"The biggest challenge of Eliot Ness," Costner said during filming, according to the movie's production handbook, "is that he's not a flashy character, and the trick is to try not to make him flashy. He's a really steady character, a homebody with a real sense of what's right and wrong...and he's kind of courageous." Costner found offers pouring in after *The Untouchables,* his first starring role. His 1988 hit, *Bull Durham,* and 1989's *Field of Dreams* landed him on the cover of *Time.* In two short years, his price tag had risen to $5,000,000, and many were calling the handsome, intelligent actor a cross between Jimmy Stewart and Gary Cooper.

Under the direction of Brian De Palma, generally noted for blood-spurting thrillers like *Carrie, Dressed to Kill,* and *Scarface, The Untouchables* focuses on the pursuit of gangster Al Capone (played magnificently by Robert De Niro) by Ness and his cronies, a select team of investigators who couldn't be bought or bribed—hence the designation "untouchables." The team includes George Stone (Andy Garcia), an Italian rookie cop, and Oscar Wallace (Charles Martin Smith), a government accountant sent by Washington to get the goods on Capone. The plum role, though, went to Sean Connery, as Jimmy Malone, a seasoned cop who tests Ness' abilities to take on Capone. Connery proved he had outgrown the James Bond image with his Oscar win for Best Supporting Actor.

Although the picture is violent, as is to be expected with most De Palma films, there are fine production values, and *The Untouchables* received praise from critics. *Daily Variety* called the crime drama "a beautifully crafted portrait of Prohibition-era Chicago" in which "script, directing, characterization, wardrobe, art direction and score jointly evoke the celebrated conflict between gangster bootleggers and Federal agents." The reviewer had special praise for Connery, Costner, and especially De Niro, "a compelling figure who stops just short of caricature. With the addition of 30 pounds and the legendary facial scar, De Niro is quite convincing—perhaps never more so than during one powerful scene in which he wields a baseball bat while philosophizing about business with his lieutenants."

Anyone who has seen this picture will instantly recall this scene, brutal yet wonderfully directed. Like the man said, this is a study in good filmmaking and, incidentally, entertainment on a very adult level.

Kevin Costner (on balcony) awaits the next shot on the set of *The Untouchables.*

Screenplay by David Mamet

Produced by Art Linson

Directed by Brian De Palma

CAST

Eliot Ness	.Kevin Costner
Jim Malone	.Sean Connery
Oscar Wallace	.Charles Martin Smith
George Stone	.Andy Garcia
Al Capone	.Robert De Niro

ACADEMY AWARD NOMINATIONS

4 nominations, 1 win*

*Best Supporting Actor (Sean Connery)
Best Art Direction–Set Decoration
Best Original Score (Ennio Morricone)
Best Costume Design

RAIN MAN

METRO-GOLDWYN-MAYER/UNITED ARTISTS
$86,813,000

A SEEMINGLY unlikely candidate for the top moneymaker of 1988, *Rain Man,* released just in time for the Christmas crowd, immediately began grabbing the public's and critics' attention. The subject matter was autism, a neurological handicap that affects four in 10,000 and is characterized by isolated compulsive behavior, lack of emotional contact with others, and frequently, an extreme sensitivity to sounds and touch. As Raymond Babbitt, Dustin Hoffman portrays a man with this disability who is not only an autistic but also a "savant"—that one percent of autistics who have uncanny abilities to do extraordinary things like multiply huge numbers instantly or memorize half the phone book at one sitting.*

Such is not usually the stuff of box office blockbusters. But Hoffman's remarkable performance, together

---

Screenplay by Ronald Bass and
   Barry Morrow

Based on story by Barry Morrow

Executive Producers: Peter Guber and
   Jon Peters

Produced by Mark Johnson

Directed by Barry Levinson

CAST

Raymond Babbitt . . . . .Dustin Hoffman
Charlie Babbitt . . . . . . .Tom Cruise
Susanna . . . . .Valeria Golino
Dr. Bruner . . . . .Jerry Molen
John Moohey . . . . . .Jack Murdock

ACADEMY AWARD NOMINATIONS

8 nominations, 4 wins *

*Best Picture
*Best Actor (Dustin Hoffman)
*Best Director (Barry Levinson)
*Best Original Screenplay (Ronald Bass,
  Barry Morrow, screenplay; Barry
  Morrow, story)
Best Art Direction–Set Decoration
Best Cinematography
Best Film Editing
Best Original Score (Hans Zimmer)

---

with numerous Oscars and Oscar nominations, saw word of mouth bringing in a brisk business. By mid-'89, the film had passed 1988's box office leader, *Who Framed Roger Rabbit,* in a tortoise-and-hare race across the finish line.

Hoffman's performance is nothing short of brilliant. The actor plays Raymond Babbitt (an early childhood trauma caused him to confuse the sound of his own name with the words "rain man"), who is heir to the family fortune left by a father who had the boy institutionalized. All this comes as a shock to his brother, Charlie (Tom Cruise, proving he can do a serious role), who feels cheated of his inheritance and abducts Raymond for a cross-country trip that will find both men considerably changed by journey's end. It's literally an "Odd Couple" syndrome.

While autism might not sound like a subject befitting comedy, it is the film's light-handed treatment of the disorder that is one of the main reasons for the wide appeal. In one of *Rain Man*'s most humorous sequences, we learn that Raymond is terrified of flying. His brother is frantic to get him on a plane to California, but Raymond throws a tantrum. It seems there is only one airline that doesn't give Raymond nightmares—"Qantas," he says; "Qantas never crashes." Although Australia's national airline doesn't fly from U.S. domestic routes, ticket sales have been rising handsomely ever since this commercial plug.

To prepare for the role of Raymond, Dustin Hoffman intensively studied autism, consulting with experts and autistics and their families. A major source was the UCLA Neuropsychiatric Institute and Hospital. One of their subjects, a young man named Joe Sullivan, was the study of a documentary film. Hoffman viewed the film, then pored over 15 hours of unedited outtakes. "The documentary really moved me," Hoffman told *People* magazine. "Joe's a lovely guy, and if you look closely enough there is a very healthy soul there." Hoffman based

his characterization of Raymond on Joe and another autistic person.

Steven Spielberg turned down an offer of $5,000,000 to direct *Rain Man,* citing other commitments. A deal with Sydney Pollack also fell through, opening the way for Barry Levinson. Levinson had scored a hit with 1987's *Good Morning, Vietnam,* and *Rain Man* was his sixth picture. His first film, *Diner,* was to his career what *American Graffiti* had been to George Lucas: it launched him as a major film director (and coincidentally, launched the acting careers of Steve Guttenberg, Mickey Rourke, and Kevin Bacon, as Lucas' film did for an earlier generation of actors). Although it would be easy to grab credit for *Rain Man*'s success, Levinson was quick in his generosity. "In the best sense of the word," he said in a television interview, "I think it was a terrific collaborative piece. We all knew what we had to ultimately accomplish." In the same interview, co-star Tom Cruise praised his director: "He likes actors, and he allowed Dustin to work, and me to work, and to play around. If you have an idea, he addresses it." To top it all off, Levinson brought the picture in at $2,500,000 *under* budget.

While certainly not made as a public service, the film has nevertheless been widely acclaimed by people working in the field of autism. Brad Tatum, director of the Washington, D.C., chapter of the Autism Association of America, himself the father of an autistic child, told *The Hollywood Reporter*: "The film lets people know that in most cases it is hopeless and that an autistic person stays autistic in the end—there is no cure. But it also shows many of the things autistics can do…the movie gave out the kind of information that we like to give out as an organization…that they are not crazy or dangerous—they just think differently."

---

*In *Rain Man,* Dustin Hoffman's character memorizes a phone book up to the names Marsha and William Gottsegen, Hoffman's real-life in-laws.

WHO FRAMED ROGER RABBIT

TOUCHSTONE PICTURES (WALT DISNEY PRODUCTIONS)
$81,244,000

*"A laugh can be a very powerful
thing. Why, sometimes in life, it's
the only weapon we have."*
　　　　　—ROGER RABBIT

THE WORLD according to Roger
Rabbit can be a very wonderful
thing, as this enormous hit for
Touchstone/Disney proved. It was one
of the cleverest, funniest, happiest
films to come along in many a year, a
picture Walt himself would have been
proud of, to say the least. And no wonder—look who was behind it: none
other than Disney's self-appointed
heir-apparent, Steven Spielberg. For
the first time, Spielberg's Amblin
Entertainment combined forces with
the best talents at the Disney factory
for what is billed as a "Spielberg
Presents" film, directed by *Back to the
Future*'s Robert Zemeckis.

The Disney production notes list 11
pages of names of talent who went into
this picture, all of whom should be
proud to be associated with this

Screenplay by Jeffrey Price and Peter S.
　Seaman

Based on the book *Who Censored Roger
　Rabbit?* by Gary K. Wolf

Executive Producers: Steven Spielberg and
　Kathleen Kennedy

Produced by Robert Watts and Frank
　Marshall

Directed by Robert Zemeckis

CAST

Eddie Valiant . . . . .Bob Hoskins
Judge Doom . . . . .Christopher Lloyd
Dolores . . . . .Joanna Cassidy
Marvin Acme . . . . . . .Stubby Kaye
Voice of Roger Rabbit .Charles Fleischer

ACADEMY AWARD NOMINATIONS

6 nominations, 3 wins*

　Best Art Direction–Set Decoration
　Best Cinematography
　*Best Film Editing
　Best Sound
　*Best Sound Effects Editing
　*Best Visual Effects

---

superb film combining animation with
live action. The concept isn't new, of
course. Walt himself used it in early
"Alice" cartoons, and in *Song of the
South.* But modern computer technology made this state-of-the-art live/
animated movie a wonder to behold.

Credit Bob Hoskins for interactive
believability. As Eddie Valiant, he had
to play to empty space most of the
time, or at best to Charles Fleischer,
the voice of Roger, who often appeared
on the set in a full bunny suit to give
Hoskins something to relate to.

The vocalizations were right on, too.
Fleischer is the perfect rabbit, while
an unbilled Kathleen Turner gives just
the right throatiness to the voice of
sexy Jessica Rabbit.

The story was based on the Gary K.
Wolf book, *Who Censored Roger
Rabbit?,* although it was changed a
great deal. The plot involves the
Toons, stars of cartoons who commute
from Toontown, and their interaction
with human actors in Hollywood.
Roger's honeybunny, Jessica, is photographed with a man who is later
murdered, and Roger becomes the
prime suspect. Chris Lloyd as the villainous Judge Doom plots and
schemes against our heroes. It's up to
detective Eddie Valiant to set things
right for the hapless Roger Rabbit.

There is so much going on here,

though, that the story is almost incidental. Second and third viewings
were not uncommon for moviegoers,
who tried to spot new things and pick
up on missed dialogue with each
return to the theater. There are tributes
and send-ups all over the place. To wit:

• Every item is called "Acme," as in
the old Chuck Jones "Road Runner"
cartoons.
• A "cattle call" at the studio has
preening cartoon cows standing in
line.
• Dumbo flutters by a window, and
the studio boss mutters, "He works for
peanuts."
• When Detective Valiant enters his
office, he hangs his hat on a Maltese
Falcon.

Then there are the "inside" jokes
about Los Angeles:

• "Who needs a car in L.A.?" asks
Eddie. "We've got the best public
transportation system in the world."
• "What's a freeway?" someone asks.
"Eight lanes...smooth, fast...traffic
jams will be a thing of the past."

In 1989, Disney released a new Roger
Rabbit cartoon, *Tummy Trouble* (the
studio's first new cartoon in many
years). Meanwhile, *Who Framed Roger
Rabbit* is now available on videocassette. Go ahead, treat yourself to it.

3

COMING TO AMERICA

PARAMOUNT
$65,000,000

FOR PARAMOUNT Pictures, the two sweetest words in the English language were "Eddie Murphy." At one time, the man could virtually write his own ticket with that studio, and in *Coming to America,* that's just about what he did. As story writer, producer, and star, the triple threat again proved that his name was synonymous with big box office. But it was more than just his name; it was his talent that could turn an ordinary property into a megahit.

Case in point: *Coming to America.* As a royal prince of the mythical African country of Zamunda, Murphy and his devoted friend, played by newcomer Arsenio Hall (Paramount liked Hall's performance so much they gave him his own talk show after this film), set out for America, where the prince hopes to find an old-fashioned girl to be his bride. Naturally, a series of sight gags and *"Crocodile" Dundee*–type mishaps ensues as our rich but naive royal pair stumbles through the Big Apple.

Highlighting the film are the many characters played by Murphy and Hall, who showcase their talents with a number of characterizations—including Murphy as an old Jewish man, complete with thick accent (incredible

make-up actually has him looking like an elderly *white* man). Part of the fun for audiences was trying to spot where Murphy and Hall would pop up next, a gimmick good for repeat business at the box office. In one instance, Murphy plays a cantankerous old New York barber named Clarence, and in yet another he's entertainer Randy Watson. Not to be outdone by Murphy, Arsenio Hall shows his range of comedic abilities in diverse roles. In addition to his first starring role as Semmi, Murphy's American pal, Hall crops up as a fiery preacher and an elderly barber named Morris. Special make-up by two-time Oscar winner Rick Baker, plus some clever optical/photographic work, allowed the two actors to portray six characters within the same scene.

Baker had previously collaborated with director John Landis on *An American Werewolf in London* and *Michael Jackson's Thriller.* His work for *Coming to America* required him to create "life masks" of Murphy's and Hall's faces, from which he could sculpt the necessary appliances. In one of his best jobs ever, Baker made

up Murphy as the aforementioned elderly Jewish man, then had one of the film's producers introduce Murphy to the Paramount brass who had known him for years. No one recognized him.

Reviews bordered on scathing. *The Hollywood Reporter* lamented: "Eddie Murphy's latest 'Coming' is likely to leave the wreath-bearers, the frantic faithful, the crowd herders, and the legions of line-waiters in numbed disbelieving disappointment…Distressingly, the film flops into the blandest of sitcom formats…except for the effervescent Murphy, this very common comedy doesn't have much more to strut than your average network re-run. Box office will undoubtedly be gargantuan at first, but Paramount's gold mine has been short-shafted by *Coming to America*'s dull-witted screenplay."

Did Murphy's fans notice? Did they even read *The Hollywood Reporter*? *Variety,* too, called the film a "true test for loyal [Murphy] fans."

Eddie Murphy must have had millions of them, since they made this the number-three film of the year.

Screenplay by David Sheffield and
    Barry W. Blaustein

Based on a story by Eddie Murphy

Executive Producers: Mark Lipsky and
    Leslie Belzberg

Produced by George Folsey, Jr. and
    Robert D. Wachs

Directed by John Landis

CAST

Prince Akeem . . . . . . .Eddie Murphy
Semmi . . . . .Arsenio Hall
Cleo McDowell . . . . . . .John Amos
King Jaffe Joffer . . . . .James Earl Jones
Lisa McDowell . . . . . . .Shari Headley

ACADEMY AWARD NOMINATIONS

2 nominations, no wins

Best Costume Design
Best Make-up

TWINS

UNIVERSAL
$57,715,127

1988

"Actually, I hate violence."
—ARNOLD SCHWARZENEGGER

"But you're so good at it!"
—DANNY DEVITO

IVAN REITMAN directed this outrageous comedy, which hit movie screens during the Christmas rush and was, amazingly, still running in a few theaters by late summer of 1989, even after the picture had been released on home video. It was definitely a last-minute entry into the top five race for 1988, pulling away from a pack that included big hits like *Big, Beetlejuice, A Fish Called Wanda,* and *The Naked Gun,* any of which might have ended up in the top film list of the year. But there was something enduring and endearing about this story of *Twins,* separated from birth and reunited again at age 35. Something…familiar.

For one thing, there were similarities to the number-one film of the year, *Rain Man.* Obviously, since these were simultaneous releases, the parallels were not intentional. But the stories of both films involve brothers, separated in childhood, reunited later in adult life. And, as in the case of *Rain Man,* one brother is bent on exploitation of the other. There are still further analogies in that they travel cross-country together on a quest. In both instances, we have the familiar "Odd Couple" syndrome.

But there are differences, since this is an Ivan Reitman (*National Lampoon's Animal House, Ghostbusters*) comedy. An odder couple you couldn't find. Schwarzenegger plays Julius Benedict, a genetic experiment gone right. When he learns that he has an unknown twin brother, also part of that long-ago experiment, his superbly conditioned heart leaps as he leaves his lifelong island habitat in search of his long-lost sibling in the Big Orange (L.A.). Lots of crowd-pleasing "Man from Mars" shtick à la *"Crocodile" Dundee* when Arnold discovers the other half of that experiment, a genetic boo-boo played by Danny DeVito. "It's like looking in a mirror!" wisecracks DeVito (Vincent) when confronted by the brother whose kneecaps he barely clears.

It's played strictly for laughs, and as such, critics found very little to criticize. *Variety* described the pairing of Schwarzenegger and DeVito as inspired, praising the film's "near-perfect execution in Reitman's hands" and its "lively mix of sight gags and fresh, topical jokes."

One of the best sight gags finds Schwarzenegger stopping in front of a *Rambo* poster to compare musculature. And on that subject, check out the physique of Hugh O'Brian, who at the age of 65 never looked better. O'Brian rose to popularity in the '50s as the star of TV's "The Life and Legend of Wyatt Earp"; he appeared in *Twins* as one of the guys' fathers.

TWINS

Only their mother can tell them apart.

AN IVAN REITMAN FILM

Screenplay by William Davies,
    William Osborne, Timothy Harris, and
    Herschel Weingrod

Executive Producers: Joe Medjuck and
    Michael C. Gross

Produced and directed by Ivan Reitman

CAST

Julius Benedict . . . . . .Arnold
                            Schwarzenegger
Vincent Benedict . . . . .Danny DeVito
Marnie Mason . . . . . . .Kelly Preston
Linda Mason . . . . . . .Chloe Webb
Mary Ann Benedict . . .Bonnie Bartlett

"CROCODILE" DUNDEE II

PARAMOUNT
$57,300,000

THE SUCCESS of Paul Hogan's first film, the Australian-made *"Crocodile" Dundee,* saw Paramount Pictures eagerly signing the actor to a contract for a sequel. This time, he wouldn't have to put up his own money for the movie, then try to market it in America. This time, Paramount gave him carte blanche. And with both Eddie Murphy and Paul Hogan in its fold, Paramount had a very good year.

Hogan wrote his own screenplay with assistance from his son, Brett, for whom it was a first experience. Hogan pére commented in a Paramount production handbook: "Brett's enthusiasm and contributions made the movie happen sooner that it would have oth-erwise. He brought a fresh outlook, imaginative dialogue and some great gags to the film."

This story of Michael J. "Crocodile" Dundee (call him "Mick") picks up where the first one left off, with our Aussie living with girlfriend Sue in New York City. A series of adventures eventually lands the characters back Down Under, where the famous crocodile hunter is really in his element. Aborigines, crocs, and a water buffalo all cross paths with our hero, who must do battle with…Latino drug dealers? Oh well. Hogan is an old-fashioned man's man, and his popularity is as legendary as his screen counterpart's croc-fighting escapades.

The studio was banking on that (lit-erally) when they opened the picture on an unprecedented number of screens—2,837 North American venues—on May 25, 1988. Lines immediately formed, and *The Hollywood Reporter* predicted: "Paramount should be able to stride right past the Labor Day weekend with sizable print offerings of this engaging, likable sequel. While star Paul Hogan's enjoying a long cool one with his real-life mates, the studio will be savoring a long hot one at the ticket windows; when the summer glut clears, 'Croc II' will likely have put all its box office competition down under."

Although big box office was taken for granted, it wasn't helped any by many of the less than favorable reviews of the film. *Variety* called it "a disappointing follow-up to the disarmingly charming first feature…too slow to constitute an adventure and has too few laughs to be a comedy…initial box office probably will be good until word of mouth gets out."

Or until people read that review. Which, it would appear, they did not. The picture did about three-fourths the business of the first, which is excellent for a sequel and made for happy executives at Paramount.

Following the release of *Croc II,* Paul Hogan swore off ever playing crocodile hunter Mick Dundee again, claiming burnout. Since then he has made only a few films, including *Almost an Angel* (1990) and *Lightning Jack* (1994), which he also scripted and produced. Hogan eventually married his *Crocodile* co-star, Linda Kozlowski.

Screenplay by Paul Hogan and Brett Hogan

Executive Producer: Paul Hogan

Produced by John Cornell and Jane Scott

Directed by John Cornell

CAST

Mick "Crocodile" Dundee	Paul Hogan
Sue Charlton	Linda Kozlowski
LeRoy Brown	Charles Dutton
Rico	Hechter Ubarry
Miguel	Juan Fernandez

BATMAN

WARNER BROS.
$150,500,000

BATMAN was an old idea whose time had come—again. Back in 1939, 18-year-old artist Bob Kane had created this comic book hero, and generations of fans were well aware of the exploits of millionaire playboy Bruce Wayne, "who unbeknownst to the good people of crime-ridden Gotham, leads a secret life as the dark avenger of the night," the Caped Crusader. The original Batman was assisted by Robin, the Boy Wonder, and his faithful retainer, Alfred, as they took on a host of archvillains who peopled Gotham City. There had been Saturday matinees for the kids back in the '40s and a couple of "Batman" episodes on the "Superman" radio series of those days. In the 1960s, the American public came down with a full-blown case of Batmania when a camp-defining television series landed twice a week in living rooms with a zap! pow! wham!

Warner Bros. decided the time was ripe to dust off the mask and cape and give "Batman" the big-screen treatment. Plans were under way as early as 1979 to produce the film, but it took another decade to iron out all the licensing details. Jon Peters, who had hated the original '60s TV series, was assigned to produce. He decided to take his *Batman* 360 degrees from the television version. "All those pinks," he told *Newsweek* magazine in an interview coinciding with the film's June, 1989, release, referring to the hit TV

series. "I didn't like it. I wanted the guy to be New York, to be street."

In fact, he virtually turned off all the lights. The Gotham of the "updated" *Batman* was a darkened, gloomy city of perpetual night, a film noir landscape where only a bat-themed superhero could thrive and triumph over evil. And *Batman,* as always, was about the age-old central theme of

good vs. evil. The good, in this case, was portrayed in a rather toned-down performance by Michael Keaton, most noted until this film for his comic and light dramatic performances. Keaton had charmed audiences in 1983's *Mr. Mom* and had worked with *Batman*'s director Tim Burton in the lighthearted film *Beetlejuice* (1988) just prior to donning cape, mask, and tights. When comic book fans learned of this unusual casting, they were furious at first. Not to worry—Keaton's characterization of Bruce Wayne/Batman was anything but comedic. (One attempt at comedy does come off quite well: When Bruce Wayne plans to reveal his secret identity to love interest Vicki Vale, he begins to practice nervously before she enters the room, mouthing "I'm Batman" over and over. Unfortunately, when she arrives, he never has the chance.)

Actually, the plum role went to the picture's main "heavy"—Jack Nicholson as "The Joker." While critics weren't overly kind with their praise of *Batman,* most of them reserved their kudos for Nicholson. "It comes as no surprise that Jack Nicholson steals every scene in a sizable role as the hideously disfigured Joker," wrote *Variety.* "It's a masterpiece of sinister comic acting. But his Joker is disturbing enough to cause small kids to run up the aisles screaming." And with a "PG-13" rating, there were a number of children in attendance at all showings of *Batman*; however, all but the youngest seemed to have a good enough time to provide the much-desired repeat business which determines box office success or failure. In the case of *Batman,* this proved to be one of the most financially successful pictures of all time, soaring to the top of the list of major money-making films and knocking off all the competition for the entire season and then some.

A sequel seemed inevitable. Tim Burton directed *Batman Returns,* released in 1992 (see page 349). The box-office returns were nearly as good as for the original—$100,100,000 in North American rentals. This second film again starred Michael Keaton, with Danny DeVito as his latest neme-

Screenplay by Sam Hamm and Warren Skaaren

Produced by Jon Peters and Peter Guber

Directed by Tim Burton

CAST

Batman/Bruce Wayne	. . .Michael Keaton
Joker/Jack Napier	. . . . .Jack Nicholson
Vicki Vale	. . . . .Kim Basinger
Commissioner Gordon	. .Pat Hingle
Harvey Dent	. . . . .Billy Dee Williams
Grissom	. . . . .Jack Palance

ACADEMY AWARD NOMINATIONS

1 nomination, 1 win*

*Best Art Direction–Set Decoration

sis, "The Penguin." But most agreed it was Michelle Pfeiffer who stole this show as "Catwoman."

In the summer of 1995, the third installment in the series, *Batman Forever,* premiered (see page 364). Val Kilmer was now the big, black bat inside the cape and cowl, while Joel Schumacher took over the director's reins from Burton. The emphasis this time was once again on the villains, with a lighter touch being provided by rubber-faced comedian Jim Carrey as "The Riddler," and far-from-lovable Tommy Lee Jones as "Two-Face." The film's noir-ishness was still in evidence, however. As director Schumacher put it (as told to *Daily Variety*): "There's always a dark edge to Batman; it's never going to be 'The Care Bears.'"

INDIANA JONES AND THE LAST CRUSADE

PARAMÓUNT
$115,500,000

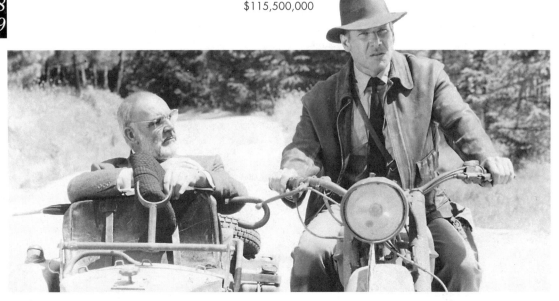

I T HAD BEEN almost eight years since Paramount Pictures first introduced the character of Indiana Jones, mild-mannered archeology professor who spends his summer vacations facing down various forces of evil while earning big bucks at the box office. Indy's first film—*Raiders of the Lost Ark*—had won its place atop the 1981 list of high rollers, with $115,598,000 (see page 278), while a second, much darker sequel—*Indiana Jones and the Temple of Doom*—had netted a bit less in 1984—just(!) $109 million (see page 298). Meanwhile, the studio had begun planning the third installment even as the coffers were bulging at the seams from the first two adventures.

Aware of the criticism surrounding the depressing first sequel, the new film—*Indiana Jones and the Last Crusade*—was given a much lighter touch. The picture reunited most of the original cast and crew, including Harrison Ford, now fitting comfortably into Indy's well-worn outfit, complete with trademark hat and whip. (And in *Last Crusade*, the audience even learns how he acquired these.) Steven Spielberg was back to direct this latest on-screen theme park ride,* with his old pal George Lucas returning as one of the three executive producers, as well as co-storywriter.

For the first time, audiences got to see young Indiana Jones, as portrayed

by the late actor River Phoenix. Paramount liked the idea of this youthful version of the character so much that, during the early 1990s, they recast the role and aired a critically acclaimed television series, "Young Indiana Jones," about the exploits of the hero as a lad.

Best of all, however, was the addition of a father figure for Indy, played by an aging but not aged 59-year-old Sean Connery—dubbed "the sexiest man alive" not long afterward by *People* magazine. Connery's role as Indy's reunited dad created the central

---

Screenplay by Jeffrey Boam

Produced by Robert Watts

Directed by Steven Spielberg

CAST

Indiana Jones . . . . .Harrison Ford
Prof. Henry Jones . . . . .Sean Connery
Marcus Brody . . . . . . .Denholm Elliott
Elsa . . . . .Alison Doody
Sallah . . . . .John Rhys-Davies
Young Indy . . . . .River Phoenix

ACADEMY AWARD NOMINATIONS

3 nominations, 1 win *

Best Original Score (John Williams)
Best Sound
*Best Sound Effects Editing

---

core for this buddy picture in which the two pursue deeds of derring-do in a plot not too dissimilar from that of *Raiders*—the search for a religious artifact, the Holy Grail, complete with supernatural mumbo-jumbo about curses upon the unworthy. And those pesky Nazis are back again, as in the first movie, allowing Indy to utter that immortal line, "Nazis—I hate these guys." So much for heavy dialogue.

Unlike the previous sequel, this picture was able to capture a Holy Grail-full of box office dollars, earning virtually the same amount as the first film while at the same time clinching rave reviews. *People* urged audiences to "Take a good look at this movie. In fact, go back four or five times and take four or five good looks. In this imperfect world, you're not likely to see many manmade objects come this close to perfection." *Newsweek* declared that "Spielberg still does it best. Only a determined grouch could deny that *The Last Crusade* is a lot of fun." Fans, however, aren't much for reading what critics have to say. The film was able to pull in audiences simply by word of mouth, and the word was "go."

---

*Someone at Disneyland caught on to the "thrill ride" potential in the Indiana Jones movies. In 1995, the new "Indiana Jones Adventure" quickly became Disneyland's most popular attraction.

LETHAL WEAPON 2
WARNER BROS.
$79,500,000

NINETEEN EIGHTY-NINE was a summer of sequels. Three out of the top five films were further installments of previous adventures: *Indiana Jones and the Last Crusade* could have been called *Indiana Jones III; Back to the Future Part II* chose the fancier Roman numeral designation, while the less pretentious *Lethal Weapon 2* did not. (The other two top films, *Batman* and *Honey, I Shrunk the Kids* would have offspring of their own within a few years.)

Lethal Weapon 2 did not behave like a proper sequel, however. This second in the series actually did better at the box office than its progenitor (and the third edition, *Lethal Weapon 3,* released in 1992, would do better still; see page 350). Perhaps it was because the audience was now familiar with the two lead characters, a happy pairing of heroic hunk Mel Gibson and his affable pal, Danny Glover. Or perhaps it was the madcap, comic-book, pulp-fictional atmosphere that pervaded the film. Or the car chases, explosions, rivers of bullets, buckets of blood, helicopters, and just the right mixture of violence and comedy that held the

Screenplay by Jeffrey Boam

Produced by Richard Donner and Joel Silver

Directed by Richard Donner

CAST

Martin Riggs . . . . .Mel Gibson
Roger Murtaugh . . . . .Danny Glover
Leo Getz . . . . .Joe Pesci
Arjen Rudd . . . . .Joss Ackland
Rika van den Haas . . . .Patsy Kensit

ACADEMY AWARD NOMINATIONS

1 nomination, no wins

Best Sound Effects Editing

attention span of a generation of MTViewers and channel surfers.

Lethal Weapon 2 was, above all, a generic buddy film, rooted in the obvious chemistry between the two leads—mad-to-the-max Mel Gibson as Riggs and sensible charmer Danny Glover as Murtaugh. There was a plot stringing their antics together, a bit about some racist South African drug lords and the evils of apartheid, and an endangered money-launderer, played most effectively by Joe Pesci, whose career was just taking off.

The film was directed by Richard Donner, who had been responsible for the first *Lethal Weapon* two years earlier, in 1987. That picture had earned only $29,500,000, not even placing in the top five for the year. Donner had directed the popular films *The Omen* (1976) and *Superman* (1978), and would go on to direct the third *Lethal Weapon* in 1992, as well as the moderately successful 1994 film *Maverick*.

Mel Gibson's varied career had seen him play comedy, action, and high drama equally well, appearing in such films as the *Mad Max* series, *The River* (1984), *Bird on a Wire* (1990), *Hamlet* (1990), *Forever Young* (1992), *The Man Without a Face* (1993; he also directed), *Maverick* (1994), and 1995's Best Picture, *Braveheart,* which he also directed.

Danny Glover appeared in all three *Lethal Weapon* pictures as Gibson's buddy. He is best remembered for his role as Whoopi Goldberg's abusive husband in *The Color Purple* (1985; see page 306).

BACK TO THE FUTURE PART II

UNIVERSAL
$72,319,000

PICKING UP with a replay of the final scene from the original *Back to the Future,* this first of two sequels to 1985's most popular film at the box office heads off to the 21st century at a frenetic pace that never lets up. The filmgoers were mere passengers in this ride through time, courtesy of Doc Brown's DeLorean time machine.

First, it's full speed ahead to century 21, circa 2015, where Michael J. Fox as Marty McFly must deal with his future children. Here Marty learns that his son is a wimp and he himself has become a loser. Fox plays the role of Marty as well as his children—including his future *daughter*—a gimmick that tickled Fox's many adoring fans. And while Marty's future seems in jeopardy, for many Americans, the 21st century is bright indeed, especially for fans of the Chicago Cubs, who finally win the World Series. The legal system in the U.S. will also show improvement in this future where lawyers have at last been eliminated from the criminal justice system.

But all is not well in 2015. Marty's nemesis has managed to change history for his own benefit, naturally ruining the lives of our hero and his family and forcing Marty's return from the future back to 1955 to set things right.

Screenplay by Bob Gale

Produced by Bob Gale and Neil Canton

Directed by Robert Zemeckis

CAST

Marty McFly/
   Marty McFly Jr./
   Marlene McFly . . . . .Michael J. Fox
Dr. Emmett
   "Doc" Brown . . . . .Christopher Lloyd
Lorraine . . . . .Lea Thompson
Biff Tannen/Griff . . . . . .Thomas F. Wilson
Jennifer . . . . .Elizabeth Shue

ACADEMY AWARD NOMINATIONS

1 nomination, no wins

Best Achievement in Visual Effects

All this time traveling can become a bit hard to follow, especially since director Robert Zemeckis and screenwriter/producer Bob Gale plotted this sequel as if everyone was familiar with the original. Without some prior knowledge of the characters, it could easily have left a number of viewers bewildered. Fortunately, the roller coaster pacing was a great draw to young audiences, whose repeat box

office business kept the bucks pouring in. Although it did only about half the business of the first film, the take was healthy enough to place *Back to the Future Part II* in fourth place for 1989.

The ending of the original film might have made it appear that a sequel had been planned all along, but surprisingly, the tag, which had Doc returning from the 21st century to warn Marty and his girlfriend Jennifer (Elizabeth Shue) about their kids' trouble, was intended just as a joke. According to the production notes, the first hint actor Michael J. Fox had of sequel possibilities came from watching a video of the first film, to which a "To Be Continued" had been added. He was still starring in his NBC hit series "Family Ties," but managed to work the sequel into his busy schedule. Or rather, two sequels, since *Back to the Future Part II* and *Back to the Future Part III* were shot back-to-back over a period of 10 months, then released only six months apart. And although *Part III* was the conclusion to the trilogy, the roller-coaster ride was far from over. Visitors to Universal Studios Southern California or Florida tours could sit in a DeLorean and travel through time in the popular "Back to the Future" ride.

HONEY, I SHRUNK THE KIDS

WALT DISNEY PRODUCTIONS
$72,007,000

THERE WAS a time when the name Walt Disney evoked not only animated features like *Snow White and the Seven Dwarfs* and *Bambi,* but clever, live-acted films like *The Absent-Minded Professor, Darby O'Gill and the Little People,* and *Mary Poppins.* But it had been many years since the Mouse Factory had given the public an acceptable *family* film with human beings (no matter how transformed) instead of talking critters. (*Who Framed Roger Rabbit* in 1988 was a mixture of animated plus live-acted, and it was not for the real young 'uns.) All that changed in 1989 with *Honey, I Shrunk the Kids.* For the first time since 1969's *The Love Bug,* the studio had a hit fantasy film that didn't involve cartoons.

The full-sentence title said it all. Rick Moranis starred as an heir to the throne of absent-minded professor; when his experiment in the attic goes haywire, he unknowingly shrinks not only his kids, but the neighbors' children too. With that premise in place early in the film, the wonderful special effects can begin. For this was, above all, a special effects smorgasbord, in the tradition of *The Incredible Shrinking Man/Woman.* For children, already small in a world made primarily for adults, it wasn't too much of a stretch to imagine being towered over by giant blades of grass, or sitting atop an ant for transportation, or being chased down by a killer lawn mower, or even being swallowed for breakfast along with inner-tube-sized Cheerios.

Getting all this on film proved surprisingly inexpensive, thanks to a wise decision by the production company to film at Churubusco Studios in Mexico City. With the peso affording more for each dollar spent, other productions had long ago discovered the advantages of filming in this Mexican studio. *The Treasure of the Sierra Madre* had been made there in back in 1948, and the James Bond film *Licence to Kill* was filmed at Churubusco the same year as *Honey, I Shrunk the Kids.*

To create these illusions took all the skill the effects wizards could muster. The 35-foot-high blades of grass were constructed out of urethane foam. The giant Cheerios were created from nine-foot-diameter inner tubes, while a tank was filled with 16,000 gallons of artificial "milk." Often the adults and children didn't work together—it just appeared that way. One such sequence, in the attic where the children are swept up by a giant broom and dust pan, was deemed the most difficult. Two sets had to be built—a normal-sized room for the adult actors, and an oversized attic with the "shrunken" kids—identical in every way except the scale. Actor Rick Moranis, quoted in *The New York Times,* recalled: "In the scenes where I'm trying to search for the shrunken kids, I had to imagine the other half of the scenes, because they were filmed separately."

The success of this film prompted Disney Studios to commission a sequel —*Honey, I Blew Up the Kid* (1992)— the converse of the original concept, with a giant baby running amok through scaled-down sets. A third film in 1996, *Honey, We Shrunk Ourselves,* was set to go straight to video.

Screenplay by Ed Naha and Tom Schulman

Produced by Penney Finkelman Cox

Directed by Joe Johnston

CAST

Wayne Szalinski . . . . . .Rick Moranis
Big Russ Thompson . .Matt Frewer
Diane Szalinski . . . . . .Marcia Strassman
Mae Thompson . . . . . .Kristine Sutherland

THE FINAL DECADE of the 20th century brought few surprises to the world of movies. People are, after all, mere humans who enjoy a hearty laugh, a good cry, a few thrills, and a box of overpriced popcorn at the cineplex. Comedies, love stories, and action packed 'em in; it was business as usual.

Sequels were popular. Nothing succeeds at the box office like success, and picture after picture tacked on Arabic numerals after a familiar name (Roman numerals were, for the moment, out of vogue): *Terminator 2, Lethal Weapon 2* and *3,* and so on. Other sequels were simply cleverly named, like *Batman Returns,* and some combined two names for even more box office clout, like *Home Alone 2: Lost in New York.* Movies based on the classics also proved this adage: *Hook, Beauty and the Beast,* and *Robin Hood: Prince of Thieves* were just a few.

Another trend was the television series brought to the big screen. The first TV show to do this successfully was *Star Trek: The Motion Picture,* back in 1979. By the 1990s,

1990

it seemed that every TV series sooner or later was destined to become the focal point of a movie. A few, like *Dragnet, The Untouchables, The Fugitive* and *The Flintstones,* actually made it into the top five. Others proving mildly popular included *The Addams Family* (1991) and its PC-titled sequel, *Addams Family Values* (1993), *Maverick* (1994), *Wyatt Earp* (1994), *The Beverly Hillbillies* (1994), and *The Brady Bunch Movie* (1995). With the limitless supply of TV series to choose from, it seems only a matter of time before we see the likes of *Married…with Children, The Movie* or *Roseanne: The Motion Picture.*

The remainder of the decade will probably be a mixture of all of the above. Several classics are already on the boards, slated for remakes, and several sequels for box office successes have been green-lighted. Many more will have direct-to-video sequels, now that approximately 90 percent of homes have VCRs (as of 1995). But one thing is clear: Whatever form the films of future decades take, the real winners will always be us—the movie audience.

1995

HOME ALONE
20TH CENTURY-FOX
$140,099,000

THAT OLD ADAGE "Be careful what you wish for—you might get it" became the theme for the most successful comedy film to date, Fox's money machine called *Home Alone,* a Christmas present to children of all ages. Eight-year-old Macaulay Culkin became a household name after he starred as Kevin McCallister, a normal kid who seems to be alone in his home even when surrounded by his huge, extended family as they prepare to leave on a Christmas flight to Paris. Sent to the attic as punishment for some childish transgression, Kevin awakes the next morning to find that his folks, brothers, sisters, and assorted relatives have departed without him. By the time mama McCallister realizes her precious Kevin isn't on the plane, they're halfway across the Atlantic. But before Mom and Dad can return, let the adventure begin...or in the words of Kevin, "Yesss!"

John Hughes, who wrote and produced *Home Alone,* had made a career of capturing the heart of youth and adolescence, with such films as *The Breakfast Club* (1985), *Pretty in Pink* (1986), and *Uncle Buck* (1989). It was in the latter that he "discovered" Macaulay, or "Mack," as he was nicknamed—he played John Candy's nephew in that picture. As with many of his films, Hughes got the idea for *Home Alone* from his personal life, in this case while he was making preparations for a Christmas trip with his own family. "I was going away on vacation and making a list of everything I didn't want to forget," he told *Time* magazine. "I thought, 'Well, I'd better not forget my kids.' Then I thought, 'What if I left my 10-year-old son at home? What would he do?' " It was these simple musings of Hughes that became the basis for the blockbuster film, one of the largest-grossing pictures of all time.

Twentieth Century-Fox was amazed to find they had a hit on their hands. The movie had been planned for a Thanksgiving opening, but they feared the competition from *Three Men and a Little Lady,* the sequel to the highly popular *Three Men and a Baby.* So the film was moved up to November 16, opposite the opening of Sylvester

Stallone in *Rocky V.* It soared past the proven *Rocky* franchise, to the delight of Fox, which almost hadn't gotten the property. *Home Alone* had been on the boards at Warner Bros. But at the last minute, just prior to the beginning of principal photography, that studio bowed out due to a disagreement over production costs. Three weeks before shooting was to begin, Hughes was list of upcoming films for the holiday, not even in the longshot dark-horse column," Hughes recalled in the same interview. "But I felt that the concept, the idea of a kid taking care of himself, was the most important thing."

And oh, how this kid could take care of himself! This was the essential fun of the picture—a child who gets to fulfill every kid's fantasies—eating all the ice cream he wants, staying up late to watch TV, reading *Playboy* ("No clothes on anybody. Sickening"), thwarting burglars, and splashing on Dad's aftershave. It was the latter, which prompts Kevin to slap his peach-fuzzy cheeks with both hands, that became the film's (and Mack's) trademark. It was soon the gesture of the year (although no one seemed to realize it wasn't original to the film but rather a parody of the famous Edvard Munch painting *The Scream*).

Mack Culkin's price went up considerably after this film. His reported earnings for *Home Alone* were in the low six-figure range; from then onward, he commanded millions for his youthful services. A sequel, *Home Alone 2: Lost in New York* (1992; see page 348) was his next successful project, but after that, his cuteness factor began to wane, and his career—guided by what many in Hollywood saw as an overly difficult father—took a nose dive.

Screenplay by John Hughes

Produced by John Hughes

Directed by Chris Columbus

CAST

Kevin McCallister . . . . .Macaulay Culkin
Harry . . . . .Joe Pesci
Marv . . . . .Daniel Stern
Peter . . . . .John Heard
Gus Polinski . . . . . . .John Candy

ACADEMY AWARD NOMINATIONS

2 nominations, no wins

Best Original Song ("Somewhere in My Memory," music by John Williams, words by Leslie Bricusse)
Best Original Score

---

able to persuade Fox to take on the project. "I knew I had to go somewhere where I could get it made right away," Hughes recalled in a *New York Times* interview. "I had a cast and

crew that were waiting and didn't know what was going on."

Even after the film was made, Fox didn't realize the huge potential in what they had. "We weren't on anybody's

2

GHOST
PARAMOUNT
$98,200,000

THE HOTTEST summer picture of 1990 starred a dead dude. Well, actually *Ghost* starred Patrick Swayze, who played the murdered hero, Sam Wheat, in this fantasy/romantic comedy/sometimes drama. Demi Moore co-starred as Sam's bereft significant other, now stalked by the same no-good murdering business associate who "done in" Sam. She cries a lot, and the audience cries with her. Meanwhile, this *is* a Hollywood story, after all, where heaven can wait while all good guys are given one last chance to set things right on earth. Sam is no exception; he stays earth-bound, unseen by everyone but the audience and heard only by a charlatan psychic named Oda Mae. In the end, the criminal gets his comeuppance, or rather his come-downance. Sometimes it seems that Hollywood's images of an afterlife are lifted directly from Christian fundamentalist concepts. Such a theory was proffered by *People* magazine, which went on to say: "When a villain dies, he is dragged off screaming—dragged *down*, into the floor—by animated black shapes who look like refugees from *Fantasia*. When a nice guy buys it, he is led in his ascent by a squadron

> Screenplay by Bruce Joel Rubin
>
> Produced by Lisa Weinstein
>
> Directed by Jerry Zucker
>
> ### CAST
>
> Sam Wheat . . . . .Patrick Swayze
> Molly Jensen . . . . .Demi Moore
> Oda Mae Brown . . . . .Whoopi Goldberg
> Carl Bruner . . . . .Tony Goldwyn
> Subway Ghost . . . . . .Vincent Schiavelli
>
> ### ACADEMY AWARD NOMINATIONS
>
> *5 nominations, 2 wins*
>
> Best Picture
> *Best Supporting Actress (Whoopi Goldberg)
> *Best Original Screenplay (Bruce Joel Rubin)
> Best Original Score
> Best Film Editing

of luminous Ping-Pong balls, who are clearly leading him to Heaven."

Not all the black guys (or gals) in *Ghost* were bad. Whoopi Goldberg found her niche as Oda Mae. It was a part she knew was hers long before the studio realized it. "They didn't give it to me for six months," she told *Jet*

magazine. "But I knew there wasn't anybody else out there to do this role but me…When they said they were looking for an unknown, I said, 'great, if you change your mind let me know.' And six months later, they did." A wise choice. Goldberg played the medium well enough to receive an Oscar for her performance.

Goldberg's comic relief, coupled with the romantic elements (complete with haunting—pun intentional—soundtrack by Maurice Jarre, making nice use of the Righteous Brothers' hit "Unchained Melody") helped the film achieve its hit status. There was an Oscar in the Tarot cards for the film's writer, too. Bruce Joel Rubin, whose most noted prior screen credit was for Natalie Wood's last film, *Brainstorm* (another film about what lies "beyond"), won the statuette for Best Screenplay Written Directly for the Screen. According to the writer (in an interview with *People*), his script, which underwent more than 25 drafts with input from director Jerry Zucker, "not only acknowledged the spiritual life but affirmed it." Rubin claimed he drew on his own experiences, including his journey to Tibet and India and daily meditation sessions.

3

PRETTY WOMAN

TOUCHSTONE PICTURES (WALT DISNEY PRODUCTIONS)
$81,905,530

"We both screw people for money."
—VIVIAN, TO EDWARD

IT WAS ORIGINALLY going to be called *$3000.* Screenwriter J. F. Lawton's title referred to the amount his heroine, Vivian, charges for a week's worth of her time as an "escort" for the film's lead character, Edward. There were also going to be a lot of drugs and sex, with an unhappy ending. But once the script was in the hands of filmmakers at the Disney studios, things began to change rapidly.

Rewrites turned Lawton's story into a *Pygmalion/My Fair Lady* with a touch of *Cinderella* and *The Owl and the Pussycat.* Garry Marshall, best known at that time for *Beaches* (1988) and a lot of TV, including sister Penny Marshall's series, "Laverne and Shirley," was brought on board to direct. *3000* was retitled *Pretty Woman* and softened into a romantic comedy, perfect summer movie fare. Suddenly Lawton's hard-edged script was a family picture. Or at least the writer felt it was: "[My script has] become the *Turner & Hooch* of the '90s," he lamented in *Entertainment Weekly.* In reality, though, this was still an "R"-rated picture, the outer limits for a Disney film.

A majority of critics panned this tale of the money-grubbing executive, played by Richard Gere, and the heart-of-gold hooker he transforms (Julia

Roberts). The critic-ignoring public stayed true to form as people flocked to theaters to catch a glimpse of a movie star in the making. Ms. Roberts, fresh from her Academy Award nomination and Golden Globe win as Best Supporting Actress in *Steel Magnolias* (1989), was awarded her first starring role. The Smyrna, Georgia, native had graduated from high school only four years earlier and now, at age 22, had Hollywood sitting up and taking notice. So were moviegoers, who took to her slight drawl, "four-headlight smile" (as one critic put it), and definite screen presence.

Roberts, grateful to be working at all, insisted on researching her character on Hollywood Boulevard. "These are girls, not unlike me, who look like your average girl, talk like your average girl," she told *The New York Times.* "They have aspirations just like

any girl does, except they're in this situation, and they don't really acknowledge it that much." Apparently the research of their "situation" paid off, and Roberts' performance earned her another Academy Award nomination.

Other performances were noteworthy. Watch for Jason Alexander as an unscrupulous (is there any other kind in movies?) lawyer. Alexander became well known during the '90s for his television role as the whiney George Costanza on "Seinfeld." *Pretty Woman* also marked the end of a long acting career for Ralph Bellamy, who appeared in the film as a business owner. Bellamy died a year after the picture was released, in 1991, at the age of 87.

In 1995, Walt Disney Productions announced plans for a sequel, *Pretty Woman II,* to begin filming in the fall. It was hoped that Richard Gere and Julia Roberts would return.

Screenplay by J. F. Lawton

Produced by Arnon Milchan and Steven Reuther

Directed by Garry Marshall

CAST

Edward Lewis . . . . . .Richard Gere
Vivian Ward . . . . . . .Julia Roberts
James Morse . . . . . .Ralph Bellamy
Philip Stuckey . . . . .Jason Alexander
Kit De Luca . . . . . . .Laura San Giacomo
Hotel Manager . . . . .Hector Elizondo
Briget . . . . .Elinor Donahue

ACADEMY AWARD NOMINATIONS

1 nomination, no wins

Best Actress (Julia Roberts)

DANCES WITH WOLVES

ORION
$81,537,971

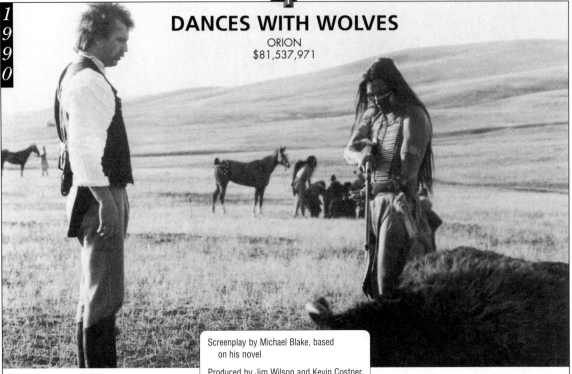

Screenplay by Michael Blake, based on his novel

Produced by Jim Wilson and Kevin Costner

Directed by Kevin Costner

CAST

Lt. John Dunbar . . . . . . Kevin Costner
Stands with a Fist . . . . Mary McDonnell
Kicking Bird . . . . Graham Greene
Wind in his Hair . . . . . Rodney A. Grant
Ten Bears . . . . Floyd Red Crow
                                    Westerman
Timmons . . . . Robert Pastorelli

ACADEMY AWARD NOMINATIONS

12 nominations, 7 wins*

* *Best Picture
  Best Actor (Kevin Costner)
  Best Supporting Actor (Graham Greene)
  Best Supporting Actress (Mary McDonnell)
* *Best Director (Kevin Costner)
* *Best Screenplay Based on Material from Another Medium (Michael Blake)
* *Best Cinematography
  Best Art Direction–Set Decoration
* *Best Sound
* *Best Original Score (John Barry)
* *Best Film Editing
  Best Costume Design

I F EVER there was a motion picture that was a labor of love, Kevin Costner's *Dances with Wolves* was it. Yes, *Kevin Costner's Dances with Wolves.* For although the co-producer/director/star of this film would never have had the chutzpah to put his name above the title, by all rights it might easily have been so. This is a classic tour-de-force film, Costner's dream fulfilled on celluloid.

Costner first met Jim Wilson, his future co-producer, and Michael Blake, the writer of the film and the novel on which it is based, back in 1981 when the three were filming Costner's first starring role, in *Stacy's Knights.* Five years later, Blake published a novel drawn from his love of the American frontier. It was called *Dances with Wolves,* but Costner and Wilson, who had encouraged Blake to write the book, saw it more as a first draft of a screenplay for the film they hoped to produce as a starring vehicle for Costner.

Dances with Wolves may be the most politically correct Western ever made. In a complete role reversal, the good guys are the Indians—in this case, the Sioux—while the white men of the American Cavalry are all depicted as brutish louts with no proper respect for the Native Americans. All, that is, except Lt. John Dunbar, a Civil War veteran who heads west and ends up being adopted by the local natives (who name him "Dances with Wolves," referring to his taming and frolicking with a wild wolf of the plains).

In an unprecedented move, approximately one-third of the three-hour film's dialogue is spoken in the Sioux's native Lakota tongue, with English subtitles. A teacher from the local college on the Rosebud Reservation was hired to translate the screenplay into Lakota and to act as technical advisor. The Sioux nation couldn't have been more pleased. Just prior to the film's benefit premiere (for the Smithsonian's new Museum of the American Indian), Kevin Costner, Jim Wilson, and co-star Mary McDonnell were adopted as full tribal members.

Great care was taken not to harm any of the animals, including the 3,500 stampeding buffalo in one of the film's highlights. The scenes were shot near the Triple U Ranch in South Dakota, with trained "stunt" buffalo used for the tricky shots and "articulated" (dummy) beasts portraying the falling and trampled animals.

The Academy at last had the kind of sweeping epic movie on which it loves to bestow multiple Oscar nominations. When the dust had cleared from the buffalo, the 300 horses, and the 42 period wagons, the first-time director was rewarded with seven Academy Awards, including Best Picture and Best Director.

Cowabunga! The hottest summer treat for the kids was a film starring four anthropomorphic reptiles, better known as the Teenage Mutant Ninja Turtles. Part superheroes, part pizza-craving teens with a vocabulary steeped in surfer dude Valley-speak, these "heroes on the half-shell" attained cult status faster than you can say "Turtle power!," the foursome's rallying cry. Not since the Beatles or the Monkees had there been a fab four this, um, totally awesome.

The Turtles—named Leonardo, Donatello, Michelangelo, and Raphael, after those Renaissance dudes—had their beginnings back in 1983, when two struggling young Massachusetts comic book artists, Peter Laird and Kevin Eastman, created their first "Teenage Mutant Ninja Turtles" comic book. After landing in a mess of radioactive ooze when dropped into the New York City sewer system as baby turtles, the four reptiles grew to become teens who had metamorphosed into a sort of turtle-human hybrid. For five years, they were found only in comic books, until Mark Freedman, president of Surge Licensing, Inc., recognized the marketability of the creatures and signed up Laird and Eastman. Under Freedman's guidance, the Turtles were soon on network television as a Saturday morning cartoon, produced by Group W. From there, it was only a short while until Turtlemania caught on.

The next logical step was a movie for the quartet, but no Hollywood studio seemed interested. Then Raymond Chow, president of Hong Kong–based Golden Harvest International Co. Ltd., and the man who had discovered Bruce Lee, decided to back the $13,000,000 production. When he couldn't find a major Hollywood studio to release the film, he turned to a small independent, New Line Cinema.

The Turtles took the country—and eventually the world—by storm. Critics tried hard to find things to dislike about the film, prepared to dissect it based on the inherent violence of anything with the word "Ninja" in the title. But by and large, most raved about it and urged attendance by anyone under 14. Parents and children obliged, and the movie soon became one of the top films of the summer and the number-five picture for the year.

The inevitable onslaught of Turtle merchandise overflowed the shelves.

There were Turtle cookies, cereal, clothing, sheets, shampoo, key chains, T-shirts, lunchboxes, toys, action figures and even cans of "radioactive" ooze just like the kind the Turtles fell into. Actually, much of this stuff was already in place long before the movie first appeared, based on the phenomenon created by the TV series. That series was still running on the CBS Saturday morning lineup in 1996.

There were two sequels, *Teenage Mutant Ninja Turtles II* (1991) and *Teenage Mutant Ninja Turtles III* (1993), earning $41,900,000 and $19,868,000 respectively. About the time the interest in Turtles seemed to be waning, the "Power Rangers" were just powering up, and the interest in these new superheroes may have been responsible for the flagging Turtlemania. Still, in 1996 there were ongoing discussions for at least two new future *TMNT* movies.

Screenplay by Todd W. Langen and Bobby Herbeck

Based upon characters created by Kevin Eastman and Peter Laird

Produced by Kim Dawson, Simon Fields, and David Chan

Directed by Steve Barron

CAST

Raphael . . . . .Joch Pais
Michelangelo . . . . . . .Michelan Sisti
Donatello . . . . .Leif Tilden
Leonardo . . . . .David Forman

1

TERMINATOR 2: JUDGMENT DAY

TRI-STAR
$112,500,000

"I'll be back."
—ARNOLD SCHWARZENEGGER,
THE TERMINATOR (1984)

H E KEPT his word. It took seven years and a $94,000,000 budget (including $12,000,000 to Arnie, in the form of a Gulfstream III jet), but sure enough, Arnold Schwarzenegger, a.k.a. The Terminator, returned. And this time, the box office returns were over the top. While the first picture had earned a meager $16,000,000 in North American rentals, *Terminator 2: Judgment Day*—or *T-2,* as it quickly was dubbed—soared past the century mark, pulling in $112,500,000.

Schwarzenegger was still a relatively minor actor when the first film appeared. He did an outstanding job as the cyborg sent from the future to kill the mother of a yet-unborn future leader, and helped establish the action genre, one of the most popular forms of cinema in the '80s and '90s. The former Mr. World, Mr. Universe, and Mr. Olympia made a name for himself after his first breakthrough movie, *Conan the Barbarian* (1982). In 1984, he appeared in *The Terminator,* as well as a *Conan* sequel, *Conan the Destroyer.* In 1987, he starred in *Predator* and *The Running Man.* His appearance in 1988's *Twins* (see page 324) proved his versatility with humor, making him the perfect actor for 1990's *Kindergarten Cop,* a combined genre picture. This was immediately followed by *Total Recall,* one of his heaviest-demanding roles as an actor, i.e., he had more dialogue than writers generally trusted the heavily accented Austrian with. Actually, most fans agreed that his accent was part of his charm, although even that couldn't save his 1993 film, *Last Action Hero,* one of his few flops.

As a cyborg in *T-2,* the Schwarzenegger charm shines through. This time, at least, he's not the "bad" cyborg he had been in the first *Terminator* picture. His murderous intent now subdued, his goal is to be a protector, to stop another cyborg, the mighty morphin' T-1000, from doing harm to the future leader.

The star of this film, though, was neither a human nor a cyborg. It was the special effects. This was the first picture to feature the new technique of "morphing" (a term derived from "met*amorph*osing"), which makes it appear that one creature or object "morphs," or shape-shifts, seamlessly into another. Morphing had previously been used to a lesser extent in other films, including *Willow* (1988), in which it first appeared, and the 1989 Oscar winner for special effects, *The Abyss,* directed by James Cameron, who also directed *T-2.* The process, perfected by George Lucas' special effects house, Industrial Light & Magic (ILM), resulted from the perfect marriage of camera and computer-generated imagery. It uses "digital compositing" to break down a film image into a complex numerical code that can be manipulated by a computer. Footage of the beginning and ending appearance of the "morphees" are coded and fed into the computer, which then blends the two together seamlessly. Morphing has become the darling of the '90s and can be seen in hundreds of films, TV shows such as "Star Trek: Deep Space Nine" and "The X-Files," and even shaving cream commercials.

Linda Hamilton reprised her role as Sarah Connor, the mother of the future leader now under The Terminator's protection. Hamilton's muscles ripple almost as much as Arnie's, her *machisma* image in direct contrast to her familiar television persona at the time. She had co-starred in TV's "Beauty and the Beast" (hint: she wasn't the Beast) from 1987 to 1989, until her character was killed off. *Newsweek* called her "a fanatical matriarchal warrior...a wonderfully gaga heroine, as ferocious as a lioness protecting her cub, and twice as butch as Sigourney Weaver in *Aliens*" (1986; also directed by James Cameron).

But it was Schwarzenegger who received the lion's share of attention, a "kinder, gentler Terminator," as he referred to himself. With the blockbuster success of *T-2,* it seemed only a matter of time until there would be a *T-3,* although the only hint of future sequels might be found in Arnold's trademark line from this picture: *"Hasta la vista,* baby!"

Screenplay by James Cameron
and William Wisher

Produced and directed by
James Cameron

CAST

The Terminator . . .Arnold
Schwarzenegger
Sarah Connor . . . .Linda Hamilton
T-1000 . . . . .Robert Patrick
John Connor . . . . .Edward Furlong

ACADEMY AWARD NOMINATIONS

6 nominations, 4 wins*

Best Cinematography
*Best Sound
Best Film Editing
*Best Makeup
*Best Visual Effects
*Best Sound Effects Editing

ROBIN HOOD: PRINCE OF THIEVES

WARNER BROS.
$86,000,000

AN AMERICAN-ACCENTED Robin Hood, living in Sherwood Forest with his Merry Persons and a feminist Marian (no *Maid* for this liberated woman)? And what's this—a black sidekick? Could this be a 1991 updated and PC *Robin Hood: Prince of Thieves*? Absolutely. Quicker than you can say "Warner Bros. box office hit," this modernized retelling of the ancient story played summer theaters in 1991 and began hauling in the loot faster than Robin and his hip gang ever dreamed of.

The story of loyal Richardian monarchist Robin of Locksley is an oft-told one, with a long cinematic tradition dating back to the silent era and Douglas Fairbanks, Sr., as the most gymnastic Robin ever to buckle a swash. Since then, there have been no less than a dozen retellings—everything from romantic versions (*Robin and Marian,* 1976) to campy comedy and satire (*Robin and the Seven Hoods,* 1964; *Robin Hood: Men in Tights,* 1993) to westerns *Robin Hood of the Pecos,* 1941; *Robin Hood of Texas,* 1947) to the Walt Disney animated (with animals) version, called simply *Robin Hood* (1973). So it seemed likely that a serious modern movie of the original legend, complete with the Sheriff of Nottingham, Guy of

Screenplay by Pen Densham and John Watson

Produced by Richard B. Lewis, Pen Densham, and John Watson

Directed by Kevin Reynolds

CAST

Robin of Locksley . . . .Kevin Costner
Azeem . . . . .Morgan Freeman
Marian . . . . .Mary Elizabeth
 Mastrantonio
Will Scarlett . . . . .Christian Slater
Sheriff of Nottingham   .Alan Rickman
King Richard . . . . . . .Sean Connery

ACADEMY AWARD NOMINATIONS

1 nomination, no wins

Best Song ("[Everything I Do] I Do It For You," music by Michael Kamen; words by Bryan Adams and Robert John Lange)

Gisborne, and the usual suspects, not to mention merry men Will Scarlett, Little John, Friar Tuck, and the rest of the gang (along with a few merry *women*), was bound to happen.

For the first time in cinematic history, however, a Robin Hood film was able to take full advantage of modern movie-making methods, such as state-of-the-art special effects and authentic locations, modern cinematography and sound techniques. Add to the mix one of the decade's true actors of star quality—Kevin Costner—and this was a picture that couldn't miss.

Costner arrived on the set in England to film *Robin Hood: Prince of Thieves* just days after completing his work on his own magnum opus, *Dances with Wolves* (see page 338). Director Kevin Reynolds was already behind schedule, so Costner wasn't afforded the luxury of rehearsals. He had hoped to work with a dialogue coach to sound more British, but there was no time, so Robin of Locksley now sounded more like Robin of Los Angeles. Audiences seemed willing to overlook this, given the success at the box office.

Reynolds and Costner, longtime pals, would find their friendship tested during the ordeal of getting this version of *Robin Hood* on film. But it would be nothing compared to their next project together. While shooting the megabucks-over-budget film *Waterworld* (1995), director Reynolds' and Costner's "creative differences" saw Reynolds walking out of the project and dumping it into Costner's lap. It reportedly cost Costner and Reynolds their 10-year friendship.

BEAUTY AND THE BEAST

WALT DISNEY PRODUCTIONS
$69,415,000

BEAUTY *and the Beast* marked the 30th animated film from Walt Disney Studios since *Snow White and the Seven Dwarfs* debuted back in 1937. Constant throughout the ensuing years were female "leads" of the old school. Snow White, Cinderella, Sleeping Beauty, even the Little Mermaid—all were high-born young ladies without much gray matter between their pretty ears. And then along came Belle. The leading, very animated female of *Beauty and the Beast* (she was the first half of the title) actually liked to *read books.* What's more, she was low-born, not the daughter of a king or queen, nor did she have ambitions, à la Cinderella, to become royalty. Just a nice simple country girl, right in tune with the politically correct '90s.

But not for long. While retaining her literary predilection, she was destined to fall for a beastly male who just happened to be an enchanted prince. The formulaic Disney royalty fixation was still intact. (In fact, it was still there well into the '90s, two blockbusters later, with Aladdin getting involved

with an Arabian princess, and Pocahontas herself being an Indian princess.)

It was a "tale as old as time," the telling and retelling of *Beauty and the Beast. King Kong* (1933 and 1976) and *The Hunchback of Notre Dame* (1939) had been earlier versions of the classic fairy tale. Perhaps the best rendering yet to be found on celluloid is French director Jean Cocteau's 1946 masterpiece in its original, lyrical French (with English subtitles), available on video. Disney's 1991 animated film owes a great deal to this live-acted predecessor. It, too, was a fantasy, complete with talking spellbound household objects—candelabra held by disembodied hands, talking doors, and wall statuary that follow Belle with their eyes. The movie is noted for its dazzling costumes, sets, and makeup, as well as its poignant performances.

Disney's version of the classic successfully captures the heart of the Cocteau classic. There are singing and dancing table settings, talking clocks and teapots, all equally charming. In fact, the whole film has the feel of a

Broadway production, thanks to the glorious score by Alan Menken and the late Howard Ashman. Fortunately, this was just what the composers had in mind; they were trying to capture that feeling for the big screen, and it worked. Not only did they receive an Oscar (for the title song), but two years later, the live-acted stage version of *Beauty and the Beast* landed on the boards in New York and, in 1995, Los Angeles. It was Disney's first venture into the world of the "theatuh," and most critics predicted (or longed for) failure. Instead, the Tony-nominated legit version, with six original and seven new songs (penned by Menken with lyricist Tim Rice) broke records on both coasts.

Disney's movie edition of *Beauty and the Beast* itself set several records. It was the highest-grossing animated film to that date; it was the first animated film ever to be nominated for an Academy Award for Best Picture (for a total of six nominations), a salute from those usually sedate Academy members to the film's excellence, and it was also the first film to receive three (out of five) Best Song nominations.

Screenplay by Linda Woolverton

Based on the fairy tale by Mme. Leprince de Beaumont

Produced by Don Hahn

Directed by Gary Trousdale and Kirk Wise

VOICES

Belle . . . . .Paige O'Hara
Beast . . . . .Robby Benson
Lumiere . . . . .Jerry Orbach
Mrs. Potts . . . . .Angela Lansbury
Gaston . . . . .Richard White
Cogsworth/Narrator . . .David Ogden Stiers

ACADEMY AWARD NOMINATIONS

6 nominations, 2 wins*

Best Picture
Best Sound
*Best Original Song ("Beauty and the Beast," winner; "Belle" and "Be Our Guest," nominated; all music by Alan Menken, words by Howard Ashman)
*Best Original Score (Alan Menken)

4
HOOK
TRI-STAR
$65,000,000

WHAT IF Peter Pan grew up? That was the premise—and an advertising copy line—of *Hook,* a 1991 Christmas movie that promised toys for adults in its revisit to Neverland. Some critics said it delivered; others, er, panned it. But audiences found enough magic in the $60,000,000 production to make it a fairly lucrative venture for Tri-Star.

The premise was actually the brainchild of a child—screenwriter Jim Hart's son Jake. The family regularly played rounds of "What if…?" at the dinner table, and one night 12-year-old Jake threw out the line about Peter Pan. It became his dad's "hook," so to speak.

Steven Spielberg, often called an adult Peter Pan himself, was signed to direct. The award-winning director counted the film among one of his milestones. "I was finally able to break through my 20-year fear of working with movie stars," Spielberg told *People* magazine. "My God, it was so easy!" The director even generously

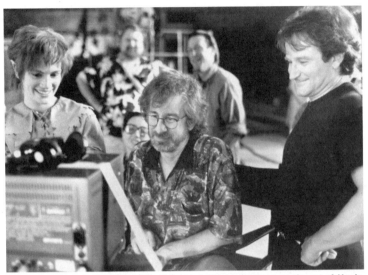

Steven Spielberg (center) with Julia Roberts and Robin Williams on the set of *Hook.*

allowed star Dustin Hoffman, in the title role, to offer pointers behind the camera, something most directors won't tolerate. But Spielberg graciously welcomed Hoffman's input, calling *Hook* "the most collaborative movie" he'd ever made.

Dustin Hoffman played Peter Pan's nemesis, Captain Hook, with gusto. The actor admitted he took the role, which he did with a William F. Buckley vocal impression, because he had always wanted to play an archvillain. "I was dying to do the Joker in *Batman,*" he told *People.*

Robin Williams played Peter Banning, a.k.a. Peter Pan, a virtual casting to type, since Williams had always been thought of as a sort of man-child. In this revisionist tale, the workaholic Banning, addicted to his cell phone, has lost his memories of his childhood, in which he was Peter Pan. His kids are kidnapped, and he must fly off to Neverland to rescue them from the evil clutches of Hook. It's a gimmicky excuse to get him (and the audience) off to this magical island.

Julia Roberts as Tinkerbell completed the all-star cast. There was talk of strife on the set because of her breakup with fiancé Keifer Sutherland, but Steven Spielberg stood by her

throughout. Roberts had a particularly difficult role, having to play Tink suspended on wires for hours at a time against a bluescreen, rather than interacting with her fellow performers. To boost her spirits, Williams and Hoffman would stand off-camera and read lines with her.

As the reputation of the $8,000,000 Neverland set quickly spread throughout Hollywood, celebrities began elbowing each other for a chance to visit the Sony soundstage where filming took place. It was not unusual to find Tom Cruise, Whoopi Goldberg, Demi Moore, or even Jordan's Queen Noor ogling the Lost Boys' treehouse or the huge 70-foot pirate ship.

Casting for the pirates was simple. The crew merely offered the roles to a number of local bikers, again casting to type. The biker/pirates, however, were not treated like celebrities on the set. They were given a list of 35 "Do's and Don'ts" such as Don't talk to the actors, Don't ask for autographs, and Do not eat or drink the crew's food (they were instead given pretzels and saltines). Two pirates were the exception: Glenn Close, in an uncredited cameo, cross-dressed as a disloyal pirate, and singer-actor Phil Collins also appeared in a bit part.

Screenplay by Jim V. Hart and Malia Scotch Marmo

From the story by Hart and Nick Castle

Adapted from the original stage play and books by Sir James M. Barrie

Produced by Kathleen Kennedy, Frank Marshall, and Gerald R. Molen

Directed by Steven Spielberg

CAST

Captain Hook	Dustin Hoffman
Peter Banning/Peter Pan	Robin Williams
Tinkerbell	Julia Roberts
Smee	Bob Hoskins
Granny Wendy	Maggie Smith

ACADEMY AWARD NOMINATIONS

5 nominations, no wins

Best Art Direction–Set Decoration
Best Original Song ("When You're Alone," music by John Williams, words by Leslie Bricusse)
Best Costume Design
Best Makeup
Best Visual Effects

CITY SLICKERS

COLUMBIA
$60,750,000

"You look like one of the Village People." —BILLY CRYSTAL TO FELLOW "DUDE"

BILLY CRYSTAL wasn't happy. He wasn't getting the kinds of scripts he'd hoped for after his appearance in the successful Rob Reiner–directed *When Harry Met Sally* (1989). So he decided to develop his own. As executive producer, he was able to give input on the kind of script he wanted: something funny, naturally; perhaps about a midlife crisis of some city folk; a lot of male bonding; and maybe a western setting.

Welcome to "thirtysomething" meets *Red River.* When the trail dust had cleared, it was evident that Crystal's wildly popular summer comedy, *City Slickers,* owed a debt to both. The story involved three New York City dudes (in the original sense of the word) who set out to spend a few weeks roundin' up cattle and getting in touch with their feelings. Sensitivity training on horseback, with that sarcastic Crystal humor.

Hiring just the right team was important. For screenwriters, Crystal chose Lowell Ganz and Babaloo Mandel, who had written the popular movie *Parenthood* (1989) (and later *A*

Screenplay by Lowell Ganz and Babaloo Mandel

Produced by Irby Smith

Executive Producer: Billy Crystal

Directed by Ron Underwood

CAST

Mitch Robbins . . . . . . .Billy Crystal
Phil Berquist . . . . .Daniel Stern
Ed Furillo . . . . .Bruno Kirby
Barbara Robbins . . . . .Patricia Wettig
Curly . . . . .Jack Palance

ACADEMY AWARD NOMINATIONS

1 nomination, 1 win*

*Best Supporting Actor (Jack Palance)

League of Their Own, 1992). Oscar-winning cinematographer Dean Semler, who had won the Academy Award for his sweeping vistas in *Dances with Wolves* (1990) was brought on board. And Marc Shaiman, himself a future Oscar nominee (for "A Wink and a Smile," from 1993's *Sleepless in Seattle*), was selected to do the rich western pastiche score.

But basically, this was a comedy. Cowboy wannabes with horse-phones, discussing how to program their VCRs and humming the theme to "Bonanza," had audiences roaring with laughter and returning for more.

Then there was Jack Palance, in an Oscar-winning role as the stereotypical trail boss, Curly. Says Mitch (Crystal): "Did you see how leathery he was? He was like a saddlebag with eyes." The real Palance proved to be a softy, though. According to Crystal, in the scene where his character, Mitch, delivers a calf, Palance started to cry. The graphic dogie-delivery sequence was actually a bit of Hollywood trickery. A synthetic uterus was developed, and a week-old calf was actually "delivered," complete with slimy chicken innards for effect. "It was like bathing in liver," Crystal told *Macleans.*

The film did so well that a sequel was immediately planned. *City Slickers II: The Legend of Curly's Gold* (1994) was a modest success, doing only about a third as much business ($20,000,000) as the original.

1

ALADDIN

WALT DISNEY PRODUCTIONS
$111,740,683

THE FIRST animated feature to become number one at the box office since *The Jungle Book* back in 1967, *Aladdin* was also the highest-grossing animated film of all time to its date, as well as the highest-grossing Walt Disney production to date (surpassed in 1994 by *The Lion King*). The reasons were many.

The 31st animated film from Disney, *Aladdin* was one of the studio's first real cross-over animated pictures, appealing to both children and adults. Children took to the fantasy aspects—once again, a royal princess raised by a single parent, her father the sultan. There was magic and mayhem in old

Bagdad, along with a cohesive story, a rich musical score, and great state-of-the-art animation. Adults, on the other hand, were treated not only to all of the above, but to a Robin Williams laugh fest.

Williams was cast in the role of the magic Genie, the one who lives in the lamp and presents "Al" with his three wishes. But when our hero rubs this lamp, the movie becomes more like "Robin Williams Unplugged." The renowned star of television, screen, and stand-up night clubs, Williams practically stole the picture, at least for the adult audience. Yet although the animation team had Williams in mind

from the beginning, the actor almost didn't sign to appear. It wasn't until they presented him with a mock-up of the Genie doing Robin's stand-up routines and comedy records that he was convinced. In fact, he liked it so much that he worked for scale—$485 per day, Screen Actors Guild minimum. According to *TV Guide*'s sources, the studio was so pleased they sent him a token of their gratitude—an original Picasso!

In *Aladdin*, Robin as the Genie gives a whole new meaning to the term "free spirit" as he ad-libs about 60 different impressions, including Ed Sullivan, Arnold Schwarzenegger,

Arsenio Hall, Robert De Niro, and William F. Buckley (apparently a popular figure in fantasy films; see *Hook,* page 344). This use of contemporary figures was a real departure for Disney, locking an animated feature in time with references to American pop culture, including game shows, recent movie hits, TV commercials, and politics. But it worked, and word of mouth about Williams' antics helped make the film an even bigger hit.

So did the memorable score by Academy Award winners Alan Menken and Howard Ashman. When Ashman died of AIDS in 1991 before completing the lyrics to all the film's songs, a devastated Menken continued the work with Tim Rice (Andrew Lloyd Webber's former writing partner). The complete soundtrack became one of the hottest albums of the year, and the composers received two out of the five Oscar nominations, winning Best Song with "A Whole New World." The songs also won five

Screenplay by Ron Clements, John Musker, Ted Elliott, and Terry Rossio

Produced and directed by John Musker and Ron Clements

VOICES

Aladdin	. . . . .Scott Weinger, Brad Kane (singing)
Genie	. . . . .Robin Williams
Jasmine	. . . . .Linda Larkin, Lea Salonga (singing)
Jafar	. . . . .Jonathan Freeman

ACADEMY AWARD NOMINATIONS

5 nominations, 2 wins*

*Best Song ("A Whole New World," winner, music by Alan Menken, words by Tim Rice; "Friend Like Me," nominated, music by Alan Menken, words by Howard Ashman)
*Best Score (Alan Menken)
Best Sound
Best Sound Effects Editing

Grammys, including song of the year. The album was also voted best instrumental for a motion picture or television, as well as best children's recording. "A Whole New World" won for best song written specifically for a film and for best pop performance by a duo or group (sung by Peabo Bryson and Regina Belle).

The popularity of *Aladdin* continued long after the film's release. There was the usual merchandise, of course—the lunchboxes, clothing, and toys. The videocassette sold the most units ever for a video to that date. That was followed by an unusual video release of an animated film based on the original movie. *The Return of Jafar* (1994) went straight to video, rather than having a theatrical release. It, too, proved a top seller, even sans Robin Williams as the Genie (he's replaced by Dan Castellaneta, the voice of Homer on "The Simpsons"). And there was a TV cartoon of *Aladdin,* running on CBS as well as the Disney channel and in syndication.

HOME ALONE 2: LOST IN NEW YORK

20TH CENTURY-FOX
$103,377,614

LIKE ITS predecessor, *Home Alone, Home Alone 2: Lost in New York* was one long series of slapstick tricks to outwit the bad guys, perpetrated by a now-11-year-old Kevin McCallister (Macaulay Culkin). When "Mack" made the first *Home* film for director Chris Columbus, he was paid the whopping sum of $100,000. Not bad for a child actor. But that picture went on to become the third-highest grossing movie to that date (behind *E. T.: The Extra-Terrestrial,* 1982, and *Star Wars,* 1977) and the highest-ranked comedy to that date as well. Suddenly Mack Culkin was hot. Following his sensational success in the first *Home Alone,* the film offers flooded in. But a series of mistakes on the part of the young star's handlers had caused him to appear in one box office flop after another. Still, what did the youngster earn for the sequel to *Home Alone*? A reported $4,500,000 plus 5 percent of the grosses, or about 50 times his earnings for the first *Home.*

With all the hype surrounding the sequel, the second coming of *Home Alone* should have been one special sequel. It wasn't. It was basically a rerun of the first movie, but audiences were so loyal to Culkin and his movie persona that they didn't care. The film, while not setting any records, did a brisk business at the box office, not to mention in merchandising, with dozens of "Kevin" products licensed with Mack Culkin's smile that could thaw glaciers. Perhaps this retread was successful because, despite the plot, there's something about a little boy all alone at Christmastime that appeals to the humanistic, mothering/fathering instincts in most adults. Not that this kid needed any adult assistance. In the basic plot, Kevin is once again abandoned by his family on their annual Christmas trip. This time, they board the plane for Miami while Kevin accidentally heads for New York. Once in the Big Apple, he naturally checks into the Plaza (on his father's credit card) and begins a sequence of implausible but entertaining events.

One encounter has him befriending a "Pigeon Lady," à la the "Feed the Birds" number from *Mary Poppins* (see page 172). To get the scene, Columbus had 350 pigeons trained for 12 weeks to land just right on Brenda Fricker, playing the Pigeon Lady.

Other events aren't so benevolent. In the best "Road Runner" cartoon tradition, Kevin manages to outwit the same two burglars he encountered in the first movie. The notorious "Wet Bandits" (played again by Joe Pesci and Daniel Stern) manage to get hit with bricks, stapled, electrocuted, burned, smashed, and bonked umpteen times and still live to tell their woeful tale. Did this encourage kids to try these pranks? Not according to Columbus, who told *People* magazine: "We throw out gags if we feel kids could duplicate them. I have to laugh when people question the so-called violence—the same people, myself included, who grew up watching cartoons where Bugs Bunny would blow off Daffy Duck's head with a shotgun, his beak would fall off and he'd put it back on." Still, the films ought to come with a warning: Kids, don't try this at home alone.

Screenplay by John Hughes

Produced by John Hughes

Directed by Chris Columbus

CAST

Kevin McCallister	Macaulay Culkin
Harry	Joe Pesci
Marv	Daniel Stern
Kate	Catherine O'Hara
Pigeon Lady	Brenda Fricker
Concierge	Tim Curry

BATMAN RETURNS

WARNER BROS.
$100,100,000

ONE OF THE FEW sequels to actually have its own title (rather than a numeral and colon followed by a subtitle), *Batman Returns* was the second in a planned series by Warner Bros., the proud franchise licensee. And, as was hoped, the box office returns for *Batman Returns* were many and happy.

This picture had two new nemeses for the Caped Crusader—"The Penguin" and "Catwoman." New, that is, to the film series. Both had antecedents in the "Batman" comics and TV series. In *Batman Returns,* The Penguin was given life by Danny DeVito, bringing a sort of warped Dickensian characterization to this creature. It was quite unlike the TV version created by Burgess Meredith, camping it up, complete with FDR-esque cigarette holder and monocle. Tim Burton, back once again in the director's chair, envisioned a quite different Penguin from the TV character. "We didn't want Danny DeVito in a top

hat and tuxedo quacking. We decided to take the word 'penguin' and let the images conjure themselves for that," he told *The Hollywood Reporter.* DeVito also bristled at the thought, telling *Time, "*I didn't see myself playing a weird Nick Charles [from *The Thin Man*] with a martini glass and a tuxedo. It just didn't tickle my fancy."

Casting of the sexy Catwoman, the film's other "villain" (although in a sense, she's just a slightly demented Everywoman, not a true villain), nearly created a catfight as numerous Hollywood female performers vied for the role. Annette Bening was initially signed for the part, but then became pregnant and had to bow out before filming began. When word quickly spread that the part was up for grabs, Julie Newmar, one of the original TV Catwomen (others were Lee Ann Meriwether and Eartha Kitt), lobbied for the part. Actress Sean Young also fought hard to win the role, marching onto the Warners lot dressed in a cat

suit and scaring Tim Burton, Michael Keaton (reprising his role as Batman), and a production executive who panicked at the sight of her walkie-talkie, mistaking it for a gun. Sean didn't get the part. Instead, it went to Michelle Pfeiffer, whose portrayal received applause from most critics, despite often lukewarm words for others in the cast. "Catwoman was a childhood heroine of mine," Pfeiffer told *The Hollywood Reporter. "*I used to watch the TV series and wait for her to come on." To *Time,* she added: "She's good, bad, evil, dangerous, vulnerable and sexual. She is allowed to be all of those things, and we are still allowed to care about her."

Audiences cared a great deal about all these animal-humans, the cat and the bat and the penguin, plunking down bucks to the tune of slightly more than $100,000,000 (in North American rental figures) to see Michael Keaton's second (and last) performance as Batman.

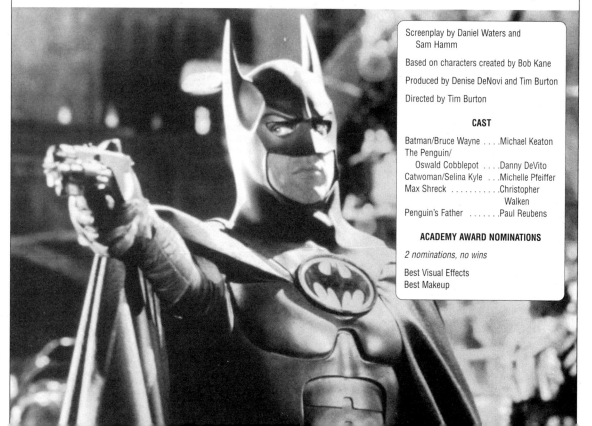

Screenplay by Daniel Waters and
   Sam Hamm

Based on characters created by Bob Kane

Produced by Denise DeNovi and Tim Burton

Directed by Tim Burton

CAST

Batman/Bruce Wayne . . . .Michael Keaton
The Penguin/
   Oswald Cobblepot . . . .Danny DeVito
Catwoman/Selina Kyle . . .Michelle Pfeiffer
Max Shreck . . . . .Christopher
                                 Walken
Penguin's Father . . . . . . .Paul Reubens

ACADEMY AWARD NOMINATIONS

2 nominations, no wins

Best Visual Effects
Best Makeup

LETHAL WEAPON 3

WARNER BROS.
$80,000,000

"Close is a lingerie shop without a front window."
—RENE RUSSO TO MEL GIBSON

DON'T PONDER the meaning of the above line from *Lethal Weapon 3* too heavily. It has none. This third entry into the *Lethal Weapon* blood-and-explosions derbies introduced audiences to a new partner and a love interest for Det. Martin Riggs (Mel Gibson), the trilogy's loose cannon. The meaningless dialogue was at the behest of director Richard Donner, who requested a non-sequitur, something completely off-the-wall, from screenwriter Jeffrey Boam. Boam in turn thought up dozens of strange suggestions, beginning with "Close is...," while the crew had fun thinking up others. The actual line, though, was invented by actress Rene Russo herself.

Originally, Russo's character was to have been another man, but Donner's wife, producer Lauren Shuler-Donner (appearing in this film in a cameo as a nurse), thought the picture was too man-heavy and suggested making the character a female. "I knew instantly she was right," Donner told *The New*

Screenplay by Jeffrey Boam and
  Robert Kamen

Produced by Richard Donner and
  Joel Silver

Directed by Richard Donner

CAST

Martin Riggs . . . . .Mel Gibson
Roger Murtaugh . . . . .Danny Glover
Leo Getz . . . . .Joe Pesci
Lorna Cole . . . . .Rene Russo

York Times. "We didn't need another guy. We needed a 'Lethal Weaponette.' "

The addition did nothing to soften the film's tenor, however. From the opening shot of a car bomb exploding and taking out an entire building (eerily and unintentionally foreshadowing the Oklahoma City bombing tragedy of April, 1995) to the various car wrecks (5), killings (16), and other explosions (3 more), there was little to differentiate this *Weapon* from the previous ones. Instead of the plot having to do with nasty white South Africans in the previous sequel, it was brought a little closer to home this time—the

mean streets of South Central L.A.'s gangs.

That opening building explosion was not, as some might have speculated, done with miniatures or magic Hollywood special effects. The producers searched for actual buildings slated for demolition. As it just so happened, Orlando, Florida, was about to raze its old city hall. For a mere $110,000, the city fathers allowed the *Lethal Weapon 3* crew the privilege of blowing it up. Other cities got wind of this transaction and began petitioning the producers to use their defunct properties. However, the film crew only utilized the services of one other community, Lancaster, California, where the local savings and loan had gone belly up, leaving a number of half-finished houses. This time it cost the crew only $100,000 to trash and burn the houses—a scene that was deliberately worked into the script. The money was peanuts to this production; *Lethal Weapon 3* made even more than the first sequel back in 1989, and at $80,000,000 in rentals, nearly triple the amount taken in by the original 1987 release.

A FEW GOOD MEN

COLUMBIA
$71,000,000

WHEN DIRECTOR Rob Reiner needed a few good men to star in his Castle Rock production company's *A Few Good Men,* he and his partners got out their checkbook—a very large checkbook. This military courtroom drama about the murder of a young private by two Marines on the Guantanamo naval base in Cuba had no special effects, no big car chases or crashes, no pyrotechnics, and no heavy sex scenes (in fact, no sex at all, not even a kiss) to entice an MTV-paced audience. So what did Reiner & Co. get for their bucks? A few good men, and a woman. But it cost them a quite a few good dollars, starting with Tom Cruise in the lead—price tag: $12,000,000. Jack Nicholson, who appeared in only three major scenes and worked for 10 shooting days, took home a paycheck totaling $5,000,000. The director awarded himself a cool $4,000,000. And the film's only female star, Demi Moore, was paid $2,000,000. The other two male leads made even less; Kevin Bacon took home $650,000, while Keifer Sutherland's check came to $250,000. Total cost: $40,000,000, not counting promotion.

Screenplay by Aaron Sorkin, based on his play

Produced by David Brown, Rob Reiner, and Andrew Scheinman

Directed by Rob Reiner

CAST

Lieutenant j.g.
  Daniel Kaffee . . . . . . .Tom Cruise
Colonel Nathan Jessep . .Jack Nicholson
Lieutenant Commander
  Jo Anne Galloway . . .Demi Moore
Captain Jack Ross . . . . .Kevin Bacon
Lieutenant Jonathan
  Kendrick . . . . .Keifer Sutherland

ACADEMY AWARD NOMINATIONS

4 nominations, no wins

Best Picture
Best Supporting Actor (Jack Nicholson)
Best Editing
Best Sound

Was it worth it? Moviegoers seemed to think so, even without special effects or rapid pacing. The film brought in $71,000,000 in domestic rentals, more if the international market is factored in, which helped replenish Castle Rocks' and co-producer/distributor Columbia Pictures') coffers. What's more, this character-driven drama received four Academy Award nominations; nothing is sweeter than recognition by one's own peers.

The film originated as a play that ran on Broadway for slightly more than a year, beginning in 1989. Translating it to the screen wasn't the easy task it might seem for playwright Aaron Sorkin. Reiner didn't care for the ending of the stage version, but Sorkin had difficulties "fixing" it. "I worked on the play for three years," he told the director in a story meeting (as quoted in *Premiere* magazine), "and if I haven't solved it by now, it's not solvable." Reiner disagreed. "We CAN fix it. I'll do it. I'll make YOU do it!" he told Sorkin. Sorkin (along with help from uncredited script doctor William Goldman) eventually yielded to the director's pleas. "What really

turned me around," Sorkin told *Premiere,* "was the discovery that…it's getting better. This guy is helping me make it better, and once that happens, you're in love." The rewrite took five months, but Sorkin liked the changes so much he rewrote the play, which is now based on the screenplay, based on his original play.

Tom Cruise was always the first choice for the lead. He first learned about *A Few Good Men* when his wife, Nicole Kidman, caught the play and urged her husband to go, thinking there might be a great role for him. He never saw a performance until Reiner called him to offer him the lead part of the young attorney for the defense. Then Cruise saw the play and immediately enlisted.

Finding the female lead proved more of a challenge. The part demanded a strong woman in the role, since the character was Cruise's superior officer. Many actresses read for the part, including Linda Hamilton, Helen Hunt, Elizabeth Perkins, and Julie Warner. Eventually the part went to Demi Moore, who landed it despite being eight months pregnant when she read for the director.

1

JURASSIC PARK

UNIVERSAL
$208,000,000

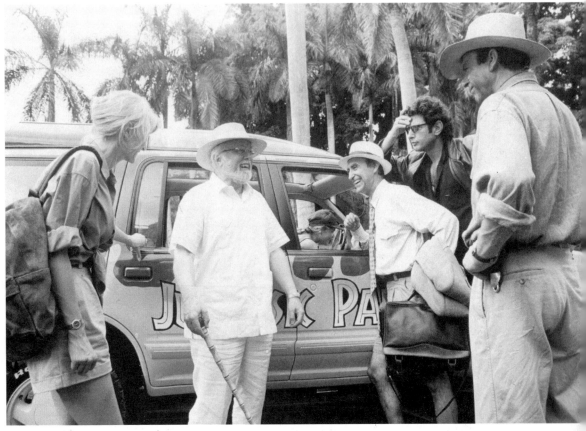

"I can't get Jurassic Park back on line."
—SAMUEL L. JACKSON

*J*AWS with dinosaurs. That's how some might describe this megahit from director Steven Spielberg, who was responsible for the 1975 blockbuster chew-'em-up and the 1993 monster movie *Jurassic Park.* The renowned director was once again back in his element, even if it was 100,000,000 years ago.

The film was based on the best-selling novel by Michael Crichton, himself a director who knew how to lay out the chapters of the book like so many scene changes in a film. All that was left for Spielberg to do was make it convincing, something the director had been doing for years. When John Hammond (Richard Attenborough)

bids his guests (and the audience), "Welcome to Jurassic Park!" it's time for audiences to grab a fistful of popcorn, hold on tight, and let the ride begin.

The concept for *Jurassic Park* was a fairly simple, almost plausible one. Given the present-day facility scientists have at the molecular level with DNA, the blueprint for life itself, what if (all good stories begin thusly)…what if some dinosaur DNA could be used to re-create a wildlife theme park, populated not with lions and tigers and bears, but, oh my, living, breathing dinos? Once you suspend disbelief—scientists admit they're good, but not that good, yet—presto! Keep your hands inside and please don't pet the *T. Rex.*

Years earlier, Michael Crichton had

written and directed a spooky thriller called *Westworld,* about an amusement park populated by run-amok robots—a *Jurassic Park* with cowboys. This latest plot was not unique—naturally, things go wrong. Dinosaurs on the loose. Dilophosaurs spit venom; tyrannosaurs chomp people, while velociraptors try to eat the kids. In the 1950s, this would have been silly stuff for Saturday matinees. With the Spielbergian take on this ancient movie plot (*The Lost World,** 1925, and *King Kong,* 1933, immediately come to mind), it became real. No little animated miniatures on a tabletop for this special effects wonder. Life-sized models, including a full-scale, 40-foot-long

---

*Coincidentally the title of Crichton's 1995 sequel novel and planned sequel film.

T. Rex, as well as byte-sized (computer-enhanced) reptiles lifted this sort of filmmaking from the stop-motion animation dinosaur age into the high-tech present.

Sam Winston, the special effects wizard who created the models in his shop, spoke lovingly of his creations in an interview with the *Los Angeles Times* (June 6, 1993): "This isn't a movie where you're going to be impressed by special effects—they're characters. We did what Hammond wanted to do. We've brought them back to life."

While the original Jurassic Park had a Central American island location, Spielberg brought his crew to Hawaii to film on the lush tropical island of Kauai. Filming had just about finished when a rare Pacific hurricane named Iniki struck the island. To Spielberg, it was just another adventure, and the director took to the airwaves to broadcast live, blow-by-blow descriptions to news channels on the mainland. Once the hurricane ended, he finished the

Screenplay by David Koepp, Michael Crichton and Malia Scotch Marmo

Based upon the novel by Michael Crichton

Produced by Kathleen Kennedy, Gerald R. Molen

Directed by Steven Spielberg

CAST

Dr. Alan Grant . . . . . . .Sam Neill
Dr. Ellie Sattler . . . . . .Laura Dern
Ian Malcolm . . . . . . .Jeff Goldblum
Dr. John Hammond . . .Richard Attenborough
Arnold . . . . .Samuel L. Jackson
Jurrasic Park
 Tour Voice . . . . . . .Richard Kiley

ACADEMY AWARD NOMINATIONS

3 nominations, 3 wins*

*Best Sound
*Best Sound Effects Editing
*Best Visual Effects

picture with little time to spare, and headed off to Poland to work on his next project, the acclaimed *Schindler's List,* leaving much of the post-production work on *Jurassic* to his old pal George Lucas.

When the final bill was in, *Jurassic Park* was remarkably inexpensive, given what was needed in the way of effects. The picture cost roughly $65,000,000. Compared to the $40,000,000 for the previous year's number five film (*A Few Good Men,* 1992), there was certainly more bang for Universal's buck. This was partly because the cast consisted of less well-known actors who didn't demand huge salaries. *Jurassic Park* managed to make the executives and shareholders of MCA-Universal extremely happy; it pulled in $208,000,000 in domestic rentals alone, making it the number-two-grossing picture of all time to that date, right behind another Universal gem, *E. T. The Extra-Terrestrial,* also directed by Spielberg.

2

MRS. DOUBTFIRE

20TH CENTURY-FOX
$109,761,240

A ND NOW FOR something completely different. For Robin Williams, that is. In his last box office hit, *Hook* (1991), two years earlier, he was a modern-day Peter Pan. In *Mrs. Doubtfire*, he took on the role of a British nanny, the first popular cross-dressing-themed movie since *Tootsie* (1982).

The plot that thrust Williams into this highly acclaimed role was not very complex. He plays a divorced father who hits upon a unique way to be around his beloved children—by becoming the family's Scottish housekeeper. In undoubtedly one of the funniest, if a bit clichéd, scenes in the movie, he turns to his makeup artist gay brother (Harvey Fierstein) for assistance in his makeover. The highlight of this montage is not Williams' transformation into Mrs. D., but the choices from which he must select, giving him ample opportunity to mug before the camera, including one hilarious bit as every drag queen's dream, Barbra Streisand, belting out "Don't Rain on My Parade." (The makeup was so successful that the real

artists—Greg Cannom, Ve Neill, and Yolanda Toussieng—won Oscars for their efforts.)

The daily on-set transformation for Williams took up to four hours as makeup artists and costumers suited him up in a thick body suit, latex mask, graying wig, Fair Isle cardigan, sensible Oxfords, and other middle-aged feminine attire. Williams endured it all with his usual good nature, although he drew the line at shaving his legs, adding humor to a scene in which a flirtatious male bus driver remarks, "I like that Mediterranean look in women."

Once the metamorphosis takes place, the rest of the film is a Robin-in-drag fun fest, for the audience as well as for Williams. The actor/comedian seems to be having the time of his life in his gender-bender role, doing what he does best—pulling out all the stops as he transforms into a one-man (or one-woman) dervish, ad-libbing whenever director Chris Columbus (*Home Alone I* and *II*) would let him get away with it.

Others in the cast were merely along for the ride. Academy Award–winning actress Sally Field's talents are wasted as his ex-wife. Future James Bond hunk Pierce Brosnan phones in his appearance as her new suitor. Polly Holliday, once the star of her own TV series, "Flo," is curiously fifth-billed in the opening credits, playing the role of the next-door neighbor, Gloria. (Her only two lines are uttered before the opening titles are completed!) Among the supporting cast, only Fierstein's role was a highlight.

Critics were not overwhelmingly enthusiastic; many thought Robin Williams was becoming a parody of himself. But director Columbus disagreed, telling *The New Yorker*: "Robin gives two hundred and fifty percent. I've never met an actor so giving. He's concerned about every aspect of the performance. He's not at all a guy who rests on his laurels." Equally appreciative audiences gave the picture enthusiastic "thumbs up," once again boosting Fox into the year's top five.

Screenplay by Randi Mayem Singer and Leslie Dixon

Based upon the novel *Alias Madame Doubtfire*, by Anne Fine

Produced by Marsha Garces Williams, Robin Williams, and Mark Radcliffe

Directed by Chris Columbus

CAST

Daniel Hillard/
  Mrs. Doubtfire . . . . . Robin Williams
Miranda Hillard . . . . . . Sally Field
Stu . . . . Pierce Brosnan
Frank . . . . Harvey Fierstein
Gloria . . . . Polly Holliday

ACADEMY AWARD NOMINATIONS

1 nomination, 1 win*

*Best Makeup

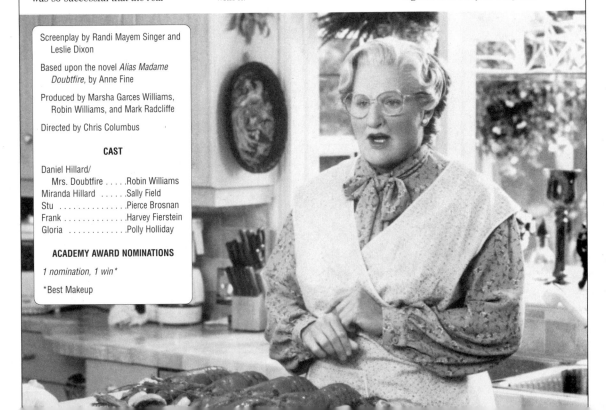

THE FUGITIVE
WARNER BROS.
$92,600,000

NINETEENTH-CENTURY writer Victor Hugo probably never envisioned the longevity his work would have when he penned his classic novel *Les Misérables*. His story of Frenchman Jean Valjean, accused of stealing a loaf of bread, then escaping, and Inspector Javert, the police chief who doggedly pursues his quarry, became the blueprint, one century later, for a popular television show that ran from 1963 to 1967. Ran, literally, since that is exactly what the hero, a latter-day Valjean, did each week for four years. Dr. Richard Kimble (David Janssen), wrongly accused of murdering his wife, hit the high (and sometimes low) road, trying to keep one step ahead of Lieutenant Gerard (Barry Morse) while trying to find the one-armed man actually guilty of the crime. It was one of those rare TV series that actually had a happy ending, when the one-armed man was caught in the highly watched final episode.

Cut to 1993, thirty years after the TV show's premiere. Warner Bros. decided to build this concept into a feature-length motion picture. Surprisingly, it worked quite well, even though the original episodes were still rerunning occasionally, and everyone knew the presumed climax of the film. There were many reasons for the movie's success at the box office, including brilliant casting, a fine director, and one very memorable special effects sequence.

The movie starred Harrison Ford (in the David Janssen role), one of the most bankable action stars of the century. Of the top 20 films of all time as of 1993, Ford had appeared in seven, including three *Star Wars* pictures and three *Indiana Jones* movies. Co-starring as the cat to Ford's mouse was Tommy Lee Jones—a sort of "Everyheavy" for the '90s—as the by-the-book Gerard. And Andrew Davis, a former cinematographer who had directed the previous year's Steven Seagal hit, *Under Siege* (1992), which also co-starred Tommy Lee Jones, brought new energy to the time-honored plot.

Credit Davis' cinematic skills with the film's set-piece, the great train

Screenplay by Jeb Stuart and David Twohy

Based on characters created by Roy Huggins

Executive Producer: Roy Huggins

Produced by Arnold Kopelson

Directed by Andrew Davis

CAST

Dr. Richard Kimble . . .Harrison Ford
Samuel Gerard . . . . .Tommy Lee Jones
Helen Kimble . . . . . .Sela Ward
Dr. Anne Eastman . . .Julianne Moore
Cosmo Renfro . . . . .Joe Pantoliano

ACADEMY AWARD NOMINATIONS

7 nominations, 1 win*

Best Picture
**Best Supporting Actor (Tommy Lee Jones)
Best Cinematography
Best Editing
Best Original Score
Best Sound
Best Sound Effects Editing

wreck. This most-talked-about scene in the whole movie was as much an asset as its stars or director. In this sequence, the bus on which prisoner Kimble (Ford) is traveling accidentally ends up on train tracks, in the path of an oncoming locomotive. He makes good his escape, but not before being chased by the out-of-control train after it strikes the bus. The scene was filmed using a full-scale bus and train, rather than the usual miniatures. To capture the action on film, 13 remote-controlled, specially shielded cameras actually developed for use in combat were strategically placed in front of the runaway locomotive. It was a one-take-or-nothing shot, filmed on location in the Great Smoky Mountains of North Carolina. Harrison Ford, suffering from an injured knee and only days away from surgery, insisted on doing his own stunts for the scene, which involved him actually escaping through the bus window and running like hell. After the shot was completed, the cameras had to be dug out of the dirt, their motors still eerily whirring away. And the demolished bus was sold to the railway company for one dollar, to become a tourist attraction.

THE FIRM

PARAMOUNT
$77,047,044

JOHN GRISHAM was a southern defense attorney who dreamed of becoming a writer on the side. He plugged away at his hobby, eventually selling his first novel, *A Time to Kill.* It had modest sales, but most Americans still had never heard of him. Then came *The Firm,* his breakthrough novel, published in 1991. Suddenly, that shuffling sound heard above the drone of jet engines was the turning of thousands of pages, all written by Grisham. Paperback racks everywhere were loaded with this legal thriller, and people couldn't get enough of *The Firm.* Or Grisham's next four books, as of 1995—*The Pelican Brief, The Client, The Chamber,* and *The Rainmaker*—best-sellers all.* And motion pictures all, filmed or about to be, even his least known and the one many still consider his best writing, *A Time to Kill.*

The first book to be filmed, *The Firm,* had a ready-made audience. So it was natural that it would do well at the box office. The story was not kept intact, however, and many moviegoers were surprised (and some disappointed) to find the ending changed from the one in the book. But huge crowds still turned out over the Christmas, 1993, holiday season to watch Tom Cruise flee from the mob. The basic plot was unchanged: top-of-his-class Harvard grad accepts cushy job from prestigious Memphis law firm after numerous perks—money, car, house, trips—are dangled before his besotted eyes. The only catch to winning this lottery is that he's now married to the mob. The dream firm is a money-laundering front for the Mafia. Once he stumbles onto their dirty little secret, it's "run for your life" time, a typical theme in most Grisham novels.

Although critics bemoaned the film's deviations from the book, audiences enjoyed the thrilling run-and-jump action, as well as the impressive cast. Gene Hackman played Cruise's mentor; Jeanne Tripplehorn (future co-star of Kevin Costner's *Waterworld,* 1995) played Cruise's savvy wife; Hal Holbrook played a not-to-type corrupt partner in the firm, while Holly Hunter

put on her best southern accent to play his secretary/ally in his stand against corruption. Hunter's performance caught the attention of the Academy, who nominated her for Best Supporting Actress.

Most of the film was shot on location in Memphis, a typical Grisham setting, with local members of the legal profession providing some of the nonspeaking talent. There were no law firms, however, with the opulence required by the script, so John Willett, the film's art director, created his own in the old International Harvester plant, strewing his sets with rich mahogany furniture and moldings, antique oriental carpets, and lots of marble. To further add to the look of success, 40,000 books, filling three tractor-trailers, were trucked down to Memphis. It took two full days for ten people just to set up the books on the shelves. Many of these tomes, rented from the West Publishing Company, were seasoned movie veterans, having appeared in such recent law-related films as *The Verdict, Presumed Innocent,* and *Other People's Money.*

---

*With the publication of his 1995 novel, *The Rainmaker,* the author could claim over 50,000,000 copies of his books in print.

Screenplay by David Rabe, Robert Towne, and David Rayfiel

Based upon the novel by John Grisham

Produced by Scott Rudin, John A. Davis, Michael Hausman, and Sydney Pollack

Directed by Sydney Pollack

CAST

Mitch McDeere	Tom Cruise
Abby McDeere	Jeanne Tripplehorn
Avery Tolar	Gene Hackman
Oliver Lambert	Hal Holbrook
Tammy Hemphill	Holly Hunter

ACADEMY AWARD NOMINATIONS

2 nominations, no wins

Best Supporting Actress (Holly Hunter)
Best Original Score

SLEEPLESS IN SEATTLE

TRI-STAR
$64,930,137

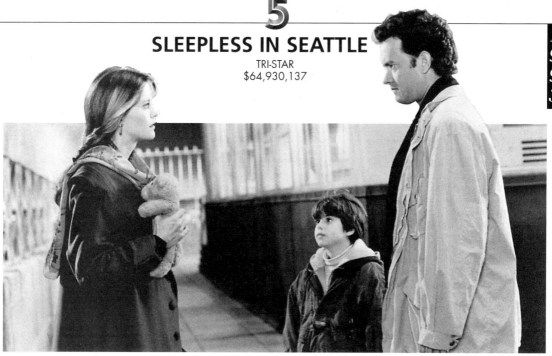

Sleepless in Seattle was easily 1993's summer sleeper. The reaction to *Sleepless* was amazing for a movie that was not an action film, the kind usually needed to pull in summer crowds. Although it was burdened with that sometimes-fatal label of "date movie" or "chick flick," word of mouth keep *Sleepless* awake at the box office long enough to become a must-see picture, right along with the summer's other hits, *Jurassic Park* and *The Fugitive*.

Sleepless was a love story, but there was no sex, and the romance was implied; the two lovers never meet until the last scene of the last reel. Yet this was a true romantic comedy. The story concerns recent widow Sam Baldwin, played by Tom Hanks, and his young son, Jonah (Ross Malinger), who wants a new mom, which means finding the right wife for dad. The boy phones a nationwide radio talk show, and eventually Sam is drawn into the conversation. Women all across America begin to fantasize about romance with Sam, dubbed "Sleepless in Seattle," after the city where he and Jonah have relocated from Chicago. One woman especially is drawn to him—Annie (Meg Ryan) of Baltimore. The plot twists and turns, with Jonah doing his young Machiavellian best to bring these two together. It finally happens, in a not-so-subtle salute to the 1957 Cary Grant–Deborah Kerr film *An Affair to Remember,* when the two

get together for the first time, at the top of the Empire State Building. Pass the Kleenex.

Nora Ephron, who directed *Sleepless in Seattle,* came from a family of writers; her parents, Henry and Phoebe Ephron, were screenwriters, so Nora was raised in the Hollywood community. She remembered seeing the original *An Affair to Remember* at its premiere in L.A., when she nearly lost it after being introduced by her folks to Cary Grant. After that, she always had a soft spot for the movie. She even

managed to work a clip of it into *Sleepless.* In fact, after *Sleepless* took on hit status, video stores were jammed with requests for *An Affair to Remember,* making the tape nearly impossible to rent for a while.

Another attribute of *Sleepless* was its memorable soundtrack. Ephron wanted the songs selected to be timeless. She didn't want anything in the movie—clothes, furniture, and especially music—to be dated. So the director and music composer Marc Shaiman selected some classics, then used the songs to identify the various moods and characters, giving each person his or her own little theme. For example, there's a comment about how Sam's deceased wife used to sing "Bye Bye Blackbird" to Jonah when he was a baby, so this tune, performed by Joe Cocker, becomes Jonah's theme. Other classic songs used included "As Time Goes By," performed by Jimmy Durante; "A Kiss to Build a Dream On," by Louis Armstrong; "Stardust," by Nat King Cole; "In the Wee Small Hours of the Morning," performed by Carly Simon; and "A Wink and a Smile," performed by Harry Connick, Jr. This latter song, written by Marc Shaiman and Ramsey McLean, received an Academy Award nomination. The soundtrack itself proved as much a sensation as the picture, reaching number one on *Billboard*'s album chart in August, 1993.

Screenplay by Nora Ephron, David S. Ward, and Jeffrey Arch

Executive producers: Pat Crowley and Lynda Obst

Directed by Nora Ephron

CAST

Sam Baldwin	Tom Hanks
Annie Reed	Meg Ryan
Jonah Baldwin	Ross Malinger
Becky	Rosie O'Donnell
Jay	Rob Reiner

ACADEMY AWARD NOMINATIONS

2 nominations, no wins

Best Original Screenplay
Best Original Song ("A Wink and a Smile," music and words by Marc Shaiman and Ramsey McLean)

1

THE LION KING

WALT DISNEY PRODUCTIONS
$173,057,366

THE LIGHTS dim, darkening the theater. A voice cries out in song, starting slowly, mysteriously, as on the screen a panorama of African life spreads before the audience. The animals gather in groups of their kind, each bowing to an unseen master as the "Circle of Life" anthem swells and finally crescendos, climaxing with the presentation of the new cub, the future king of the beasts. Then, with a gasp, the moment abruptly ends and the audience, tears welling from emotion, bursts into applause. And the opening credits haven't even rolled yet.

Thus begins the highest-grossing animated film as of 1996, Walt Disney's *The Lion King.* This was no *Bambi,* no *Snow White* with her furry friends, no panoply of cutesy, pop-eyed critters out for a stroll in the enchanted forest. *The Lion King* was a beautifully illustrated fable of life on the African veldt, backed by an all-star cast and terrific Elton John–Tim Rice songs. But it was tough on kids. (Disney has always been tough on kids, killing off Bambi's mother and Old Yeller, for starters.) Adults could take it, but many young children had a hard time dealing with the stampede scene and the death of lion cub Simba's father. (Disney has always loved stories about orphans, too.) Yet despite the rough ride for some, *The Lion King* was acclaimed a masterpiece by critics and audiences alike. "A certain blockbuster and a future classic…a scrumptiously delightful moviegoing experience," proclaimed *The Hollywood Reporter.*

Many compared the story to either *Hamlet* or *I, Claudius.* In this coming-of-age tale, the young lion heir to the throne is deceived by his evil Uncle Scar (malevolently voiced by Jeremy Irons), who has kingly designs of his own. He's assisted by a trio of equally villainous hyena henchmen, voiced by Whoopi Goldberg, Cheech Marin, and Jim Cummings. Indeed, perhaps more than in any other Disney film, the talents lending their voices to the lead roles in *The Lion King* were well-known actors: Matthew Broderick as the adult Simba; James Earl Jones as Mufasa, his father; and Jonathan Taylor Thomas of TV's "Home Improvement" as the young Simba.

The record-breaking soundtrack included three Oscar-nominated tunes, tying with another Disney animated feature, *Beauty and the Beast* (1991), for the most songs ever nominated from one film. The nominees were the "no worries" tune "Hakuna Matata," "Circle of Life," and the movie's love theme that won the Oscar, "Can You Feel the Love Tonight?" The music also captured four out of its six Grammy nominations.

When the videocassette was released in March, 1995, it too broke records, surpassing the previous record-holder, *Aladdin,* to become the best-selling tape of all time— 26,000,000 units in the first two weeks alone. As with *Aladdin,* a direct-to-video sequel, rather than theatrical release, was planned. And an animated weekly children's series, "Timon & Pumbaa," based on the comic-relief characters from *The Lion King,* debuted in the fall of 1995. For the Walt Disney studios, it was "hakuna matata" all the way.

Screenplay by Irene Mecchi, Jonathan Roberts, Linda Woolverton

Produced by Don Hahn

Directed by Roger Allers, Rob Minkoff

VOICES

Young Simba . . . .Jonathan Taylor Thomas
Adult Simba . . . .Matthew Broderick
Mufasa . . . . .James Earl Jones
Scar . . . . .Jeremy Irons
Pumbaa . . . . . . .Ernie Sabella
Timon . . . . .Nathan Lane
Rafiki . . . . .Robert Guillaume
Shenzi . . . . .Whoopi Goldberg

ACADEMY AWARD NOMINATIONS

4 nominations, 2 wins*

*Best Original Score (Hans Zimmer)
Best Original Song ("Can You Feel the Love Tonight?," "Circle of Life," "Hakuna Matata," music by Elton John, words by Tim Rice)

FORREST GUMP

PARAMOUNT
$156,000,000

> *"Mama always said, 'Life is like a box of chocolates; you never know what you're gonna get.' "*
> —FORREST GUMP

GUMP happened. It happened a lot. Moviegoers fell in love with the simple-minded Forrest Gump, who blunders his way through life, succeeding without trying, peppering his narration of his own life story with "Gumpisms." These little homilies, like the one his mother told him about life and the chocolates, or "Stupid is as stupid does," and so on, became the most quoted expressions of the year.

In this uniquely American slice of apple-pie innocence, *Forrest* had gumption and huge appeal—but mainly on the national level. Not surprisingly, the film did not do as well overseas—they just didn't get it. The story centers on an American icon, a young, handicapped lad, both physically as a child and mentally throughout all his life, who doesn't know the meaning of the word "can't." He becomes a running hero, then a military one, then a successful businessman, and finally finds romance and parenthood. The American dream realized by a simpleton, giving hope and inspiration to millions in this feel-good summer film.

In that old advertising cliché, Tom Hanks *is* Forrest Gump, at least in this movie. The versatile actor, fresh from his Academy Award for 1993 in *Philadelphia,* proved that he was definitely *the* actor of our time. Hanks got his start in television, doing bit parts in such series as "Taxi" and "The Love Boat." From 1980 to 1982, he co-starred in his own TV comedy series, "Bosom Buddies," in which he worked in drag throughout that show, playing a man living at an all-girls hotel. Successes in films soon followed, mostly in comedies like *Splash* (1984), *The Money Pit* (1986), *Dragnet* (1987), *Big* (1988), *A League of Their Own* (1992), and the 1993 sleeper, *Sleepless in Seattle* (see page 357). That year he proved his great dramatic acting ability, taking home the Oscar for the part of a dying gay lawyer in *Philadelphia.* (In 1995, he would again add to his repertoire, playing an astronaut in the summer's box office hit *Apollo 13*). And it came as no surprise when Hanks was named 1995's NATO/Showest Star of the Year, an entertainment industry honor heaped upon Hanks' other honors.

At Oscar time, *Forrest Gump,* like its lead character, was running well ahead of the pack. The film earned 13 nominations, the most a film had received since *Who's Afraid of Virginia Woolf?* also garnered 13 back in 1966.* Oscar night was like a box of chocolates for *Forrest;* you never knew how many statuettes you were going to get. By evening's end, *Forrest* had captured six awards, including Best Picture. And Hanks took home his second Best Actor award in two years, the fifth actor to win back-to-back Oscars. Others in this exclusive club were Luise Rainer (1936–37), Spencer Tracy (1937–38), Katharine Hepburn (1967–68) and Jason Robards (for supporting actor, 1976–77). The movie also won Golden Globe awards for Best Picture, Best Actor in a Drama, and Best Director (Robert Zemeckis). Additionally, Zemeckis received the top honor from the Directors Guild of America, as well as being named NATO/Showest Director of the Year.

The incredible special effects were another award-winning aspect of this film, although they were certainly not the "star" of the movie the way they were in so many action or science fiction films. Thanks to the advent of computer digital technology, Gump is seen hobnobbing with JFK, LBJ, and RMN (Nixon), and his buddy, played by Gary Sinise, has his legs lopped off via computer in a very convincing piece of cinema.

With a property with this much appeal, is it any wonder that Paramount Pictures optioned author Groom's 1995 sequel for $4,000,000? *Gump & Company* opens with a Gumpism, "Everybody makes mistakes, which is why they put a rubber mat around spittoons," and is about the further adventures of Forrest and his son in the '80s. At the time it was published, Tom Hanks declined to reprise his role. *Gump* had been good to him the first time around, but now he swore off chocolates. With all those honors, no wonder his sweet tooth seemed to be sated.

---

*The record is 14 nominations, for *All About Eve,* in 1950.

Screenplay by Eric Roth

Based upon the novel by Winston Groom

Produced by Wendy Finerman, Steve Tisch, and Steve Starkey

Directed by Robert Zemeckis

CAST

Forrest Gump	Tom Hanks
Lieut. Dan Taylor	Gary Sinise
Jenny Curran	Robin Wright
Mrs. Gump	Sally Field
Benjamin Buford Blue ("Bubba")	Mykelti Williamson

ACADEMY AWARD NOMINATIONS

*13 nominations, 6 wins**

*Best Picture
*Best Actor (Tom Hanks)
 Best Supporting Actor (Gary Sinise)
*Best Director (Robert Zemeckis)
*Best Screenplay Adaption (Eric Roth)
 Best Cinematography
*Best Film Editing
 Best Original Score
 Best Art Direction
 Best Makeup
 Best Sound
 Best Sound Effects Editing
*Best Visual Effects

TRUE LIES
20TH CENTURY-FOX
$80,000,000

WHAT WOULD the summer be without an Arnold Schwarzenegger action picture? Not much, according to whatever studio was lucky enough to have the services of the actor who turned bullets and explosions into box office cash. In the "how high is up" derby, Fox touted *True Lies*—its Schwarzenegger vs. the terrorists shoot-'em-up—as one of the most expensive movies ever made. Although rumored to have cost $120,000,000, it didn't deliver much bang per buck, at least in domestic rental figures; the movie would have to depend on the foreign take to reach the break-even point.

The high-concept story line was actually a remake of a French comedy called *La Totale!* (1991). Yes, comedy. The farcical French version only managed to kill 10 people, while *True Lies* left a body count of 100 in its wake. The stories of both involved a milquetoasty computer sales rep who is really a government agent straight out of the James Bond school for spies. His wife, of course, doesn't know this. Her rude awakening comes when she's thrust right into his latest caper, trying to stop Arab terrorists from wreaking havoc with nuclear bombs all across

Screenplay by James Cameron

Produced by James Cameron, Stephanie Austin

Directed by James Cameron

CAST

Harry Tasker . . . . .Arnold Schwarzenegger
Helen Tasker . . . . .Jamie Lee Curtis
Simon . . . . .Bill Paxon
Gib . . . . .Tom Arnold
Juno Skinner . . . .Tia Carrere
Spencer Trilby . . . .Charlton Heston

ACADEMY AWARD NOMINATIONS

1 nomination, no wins

Best Visual Effects

the United States. It's typical action fare, good guys vs. bad guys, one-dimensional characters all. The only exception is Jamie Lee Curtis as Arnie's mousy wife, inadvertently caught up in the action. She evolves from disbelieving hausfrau to assistant spy, just like that. And along the Mata Hari trail, she does a sexy dance in her lingerie and learns to play hardball with the big guys. In the film's truly spectacular end sequence, featuring an

out-of-control car racing down the Florida Keys' Overseas Highway, she shows her stuff with gusto. And the helicopter rescue is one for the record books too, one of the most exciting moments ever put on celluloid.

One drawback was the constant Arab-bashing. The apparent heirs to the cinema bad-guy crown once worn by Native Americans in westerns, Arabs have become racially stereotyped as terrorists—witness the first accusations that flew following the Oklahoma City bombing of April, 1995. In the first few weeks following the release of *True Lies,* several Islamic groups around the U.S. filed the now-routine complaints.

Movie fans, however, continued to invade theaters, eager to see the movie that reunited director James Cameron and actor Arnold Schwarzenegger. The two had made box office music previously in the hit *Terminator* movies. Thanks to the smooth workings of this team, plus the efforts of the special effects whizzes, film editors, and skilled cinematographer Russell Carpenter, not to mention all that money from Fox, *True Lies* tells the truth about what a riveting action film is all about.

THE SANTA CLAUSE

WALT DISNEY PRODUCTIONS
$72,348,689

"If something should happen to me, put on my suit. The reindeer will know what to do."
—CARD FOUND ON SANTA AFTER HE FALLS OFF TIM ALLEN'S ROOF

SUMMERTIME, and its polar opposite, Christmastime, are opportunities for motion picture studios to play to the largest audiences, mainly because people are on vacation during both periods. Generally, the most popular films of the year bow at these times. Summertime usually brings roller-coaster-ride action films, while Christmas can offer warm-and-fuzzy family movies full of mirth and jollity. Just like that jolly old man himself. Who better, then, to create a starring vehicle for, than that Man for All (Christmas) Seasons, Santa Claus.

The Santa Clause—note the play on words—used a clever premise. Santa is not Santa, at least not the same Santa year after year. (Please suspend disbelief if you're not a child; think of this as science fiction/fantasy.) There has been a long line of Santas, each replacing the previously obsolete one. Suddenly, Santa falls off the roof of yuppie Tim Allen, who's pressed into service after signing the Santa *clause*—hence, the title.

Allen, star of "Home Improvement," one of TV's most popular shows of the

'90s, was drawn to the script from the moment he first saw it. "I was attracted to this screenplay," he said in a Walt Disney Studios press handout, "because it's the story of a man caught between his dedication to his career and to his family. In the beginning he's really not a good parent to his son. Then this amazing situation happens and motivates a change in his behavior and life."

Sounds like serious stuff. It wasn't. The Yuletide comedy had the typical Tim Allen touch. As he strives to be a better dad, Allen cracks wise throughout. Typical repartee:

SON:
Dad, you're flying!

DAD:
It's okay, I'm used to it. I lived through the '60s.

Another time there is a reference to the awaiting reindeer on the roof being a gift from the cable company because "We're getting the Disney Channel now!" (a not-so-subtle reference to the movie's production company).

The North Pole sets were clever, too. Great detail went into the research for the look of the North Pole (yes, it's marked by a barber pole), a kind of Santaland—the poten-

tial for a new Disney theme ride is unlimited. The production designer utilized mythological influences not just from the Norse countries, but from Turkish, Gothic, Egyptian, and Celtic lands as well. An unusual casting ploy had a multi-ethnic cast of 125 children ranging in age from 2 to 13 years playing the part of elves supposedly hundreds of years old.

The film had all the earmarks of a Christmas classic. With its appeal to both kids and adults, this holiday-themed movie will likely become a perennial, right up there with *It's a Wonderful Life*.

Screenplay by Leo Benvenuti and Steve Rudnick

Produced by Brian Reilly, Jeffrey Silver, and Robert Newmyer

Directed by John Pasquin

CAST

Scott Calvin	Tim Allen
Dr. Neal Miller	Judge Reinhold
Laura Calvin	Wendy Crewson
Charlie Calvin	Eric Lloyd
Bernard	David Krumholtz
Mr. Whittle	Peter Boyle
Det. Nunzio	Larry Brandenburg
Ms. Daniels	Mary Gross

THE FLINTSTONES

UNIVERSAL
$70,753,383

"Yabba-Dabba-Doo!"
—FRED FLINTSTONE

IF YOU LIKE puns about rocks, this is the movie for you. Based on the original animated TV series made popular in the '60s, *The Flintstones* was a live-acted cartoon for the big screen. The familiarity with this "modern stone-age family" should have made it easy to translate to film. It wasn't. Aside from the clever casting—John Goodman *looked* the part of Fred Flintstone, and the clever makeup and costumes did wonders to make the rest of the gang (including Elizabeth Taylor as Wilma Flintstone's mother) resemble their cartoon counterparts—the difficulty lay in trying to nail down a script that would attract a wide (read: adult) audience.

The final tally claimed 14 screenwriters and 18 TV gag writers who slugged it out for screen credit. Most of their work consisted of those bad puns on rocks and stones, starting with "Steven Spielrock Presents"* in the opening credits, and including a newspaper headline that reads "Rock Market falls—it's an avalanche." Most

surnames end in -stone—or *are* Stone, with no apologies to Sharon. (The role of Fred's new secretary, Sharon Stone, was actually offered to that actress. She couldn't do it, but allowed her name to be used.) No stone, it seems, was left unturned.

Bad science also thrived in Bedrock. Dinosaurs ruled the earth along with these rock-happy humans (although the real dinos had been gone for 61,000,000 years before the first proto-humans evolved). A clever line in the closing credits reads: "No dinosaurs were harmed in the making of this motion picture."

An incredible amount of detail went into the set design of beautiful downtown Bedrock ("Welcome to Bedrock—First with Fire" reads the town's slogan). The shopping mall has a "Toy-S-AURUS" store, there's a "RocDonald's (over 19 dozen sold)" and so on.

Was there a story? Probably, but most moviegoers were too busy observing the landscape and catching the bad puns to care. Mostly, the movie had great appeal to kids, thus generating a lot of return business in a

movie market that doesn't produce that much fare suitable for youngsters.

Critics lobbed stones of their own at the film. There were those who liked it: "Yabba-dabba-do! for rock-solid family values" (*Boston Herald*); "Yabba-dabba-do see this film" (*Middlesex* [Mass.] *News*). And there were those who didn't: "Yabba-dabba-don't," "Yabba-dabba-doo-doo," "Yabba-dabba-dull," "Yabba-dabba-dumb," and on and on. The best, however, may have been from *The Hollywood Reporter,* which hit the rock, er, nail on the head with their headline "Yabba-dabba-dough" when, a week after opening, *The Flintstones* had box office hit written all over it.

---

*Steven Spielberg's production company, Amblin Entertainment, co-produced with Hanna-Barbera.

Screenplay by Tom S. Parker, Jim Jennewein, and Steven E. de Souza

Based on the animated series by Hanna-Barbera

Produced by Bruce Cohen

Executive producers: William Hanna, Joseph Barbera, Kathleen Kennedy, David Kirschner, and Gerald R. Molen

Directed by Brian Levant

CAST

Fred Flintstone . . . . . . .John Goodman
Wilma Flintstone . . . . .Elizabeth Perkins
Barney Rubble . . . . . . .Rick Moranis
Betty Rubble . . . . .Rosie O'Donnell
Pearl Slaghoople . . . . .Elizabeth Taylor
Cliff Vandercave . . . . . .Kyle MacLachlan
Sharon Stone . . . . . . .Halle Berry

1

BATMAN FOREVER
WARNER BROS.
$105,100,000

For the 1995 entry into the continuing saga of a man called Bat, original star Michael Keaton was replaced by Val Kilmer; director Tim Burton was ousted by Joel Schumacher, while previous villains made way for "The Riddler" (Jim Carrey) and "Two-Face" (Tommy Lee Jones). But our hero, as we were reminded in the non-numbered title, would always be *Batman Forever.*

There were major similarities, as well as the above innovations, in this latest incarnation of the successful Warner Bros. franchise. Most obvious was the ability of this *Batman,* like its predecessors, to fly at the box office. In fact, the film surpassed the second batmovie in box office rentals.

The replacement of Keaton with Kilmer, best known for his portrayal of Jim Morrison in the Oliver Stone film *The Doors* (1991), as well as Tom Cruise's rival in *Top Gun* (1986), didn't create any problems winning the audience's acceptance of the latest Caped Crusader. There were reports that Kilmer won the role after Keaton's salary requests soared higher than the batsignal over Gotham City—a whopping $15,000,000. Kilmer accepted far less and seemingly jumped at the chance to wear the 40-pound latex batsuit (so confining, he dropped five pounds during one day's stunt shooting); the actor told *Entertainment Weekly* he never requested a copy of the script before signing. "How many different variations [of *Batman*] can there be?…I knew I wasn't going to read anything that would make me gravely concerned about playing the part."

The stellar supporting cast was almost as weighty as the costume. Heavy-hitters Tommy Lee Jones and Jim Carrey, plus Chris O'Donnell as sidekick Robin, made this screen comic book roundly entertaining. Jones, playing a schizophrenic character aptly named Two-Face (with appropriate bifurcated makeup), never seemed to be taking his part too seriously—just the right touch for this fantasy. Carrey, on the other hand, one of the emerging megastars of the '90s (his follow-up film contract for *The Cable Guy* paid him $20,000,000), played his Riddler almost as an over-the-top parody of himself playing an over-the-top character. He should have been charged with the crime of stealing the film, for whenever he was on the screen, even Batman had to compete for audience attention.

The plot is basic—the bad guys are out to get Batman and Robin. More intriguing is the subplot, which revolves around identity crises—everyone in this film seems to be having one. Batman's concerned over the feelings of his latest lady love, sexy psychiatrist Dr. Chase Meridien (Nicole Kidman). Does she prefer him or alter ego Bruce Wayne? Two-Face's dilemma is an obvious one, and director Schumacher has riotous fun with the character, especially in a scene where Two-Face romances two totally opposite women at once. The Riddler also is an alter ego, although it isn't much of a stretch for his nerdy, deranged other half, Edward Nygma (E. Nygma—get it?) to devise his evil persona.

Also appearing in a *Batman* film for the first time, and fitting right in with the angst-ridden crowd by reluctantly donning superhero garb, is the Robin character, a staple of "Batman" comic books. And true to that pulp tradition, Robin's family is killed in a high-wire "accident," and Robin, a.k.a. Dick Grayson, vows revenge. At age 24, though, it takes a certain amount of suspension of disbelief to embrace actor Chris O'Donnell as Batman's ward and the "Boy Wonder." But his characterization does lend itself to the '90s, complete with rock music and a fondness for motor biking.

Batman Forever's rock soundtrack is estimated to have cost more than $1,000,000 to produce, but generated several hit singles. The most important hit was "Hold Me, Thrill Me, Kiss Me, Kill Me," by U2 (with lyrics by Bono). The song received a Golden Globe nomination for Best Original Song from a Motion Picture. Other offerings on the Atlantic Records soundtrack were from Seal ("Kiss from a Rose"), Brandy, The Offspring, PJ Harvey, Method Man, Nick Cave, and Mazzy Star.

With the success this film had at the box office, is it any wonder that theater owners are eagerly crying, "Batman Forever!" as they await with certainty the next installment. In 1996, plans were under way for a fourth film, *Batman and Robin,* with George Clooney set as the newest Batman.

Screenplay by Lee Batchler, Janet Scott Batchler, and Akiva Goldsman

Produced by Tim Burton and Peter Macgregor-Scott

Directed by Joel Schumacher

CAST

Batman/Bruce Wayne . . .Val Kilmer
Two-Face . . . . .Tommy Lee Jones
The Riddler/
   Edward Nygma . . . . .Jim Carrey
Dr. Chase Meridien . . . .Nicole Kidman
Dick Grayson/Robin . . .Chris O'Donnell
Sugar . . . . .Drew Barrymore
Spice . . . . .Debi Mazar

ACADEMY AWARD NOMINATIONS

3 nominations, no wins

Best Cinematography
Best Sound
Best Sound Effects Editing

TOY STORY

WALT DISNEY PRODUCTIONS
$92,217,831*

TOY STORY is based on a truth known to every child who ever had a toy box in his or her room: When you aren't looking, your toys are alive. What child hasn't believed that toys have a secret life, talking among themselves when you're not playing with them? And thanks to the computer animation techniques pioneered by a company called Pixar, in collaboration with Walt Disney Productions, audiences were now able to enter that clandestine realm.

Most of the initial attraction of this box office smash was generated around the much-ballyhooed computer animation, which gave a unique three-dimensional look to the characters. But a gimmick alone, even one as clever as this, cannot sustain any picture, and *Toy Story* proved that it had what it needed to take it "to infinity and beyond."

The film can be viewed on many levels. There is the simple story of boy meets toy, boy loses toy, boy gets toy. This is also a "buddy" film inspired by *48 HRS., Midnight Run,* and *The Defiant Ones,* in which the two dominant toy characters, Woody, a "pull-my-string" talking cowboy doll, and Buzz Lightyear, the new boytoy in town, develop a rivalry for owner Andy's affections. Eventually they become pals who must overcome obstacles in an Indiana Jones-like, classic Saturday matinee cliffhanger drama.

In fact, there are multiple examples of homage paid to movie classics. Most of the children in the audience would not catch on, but savvy adults find their attention captured by tributes to such films as *The Wizard of Oz,* with the actual line "There's no place like home"; *E. T. The Extra-Terrestrial,* in the tea party scene in which the young girl dresses Buzz in girl's apron and hat; and even *The Exorcist,* when Woody's head whips around 360 degrees.

There are also not-so-subtle salutes to "Star Trek." The astronaut toy, Buzz

Lightyear (his first name is from number-two moon-walker, astronaut Buzz Aldrin), is constantly recording Captain Kirk-type logs, right down to the stardate. At one point in the film, he bids his fellow toys "Farewell" with the Vulcan hand salute used by Mr. Spock in "Star Trek." He uses "lasers on stun," and other quasi-trekian lingo.

Several allusions seem to trip over each other in competing for the audience's attention. There is a signage reference to the fictitious Binford Tools, the "sponsor" of "Tool Time," the equally fictitious TV show that stars Tim Allen (the voice of Buzz Lightyear) in his Disney-produced hit TV series, "Home Improvement."

When Andy's family is out in the car, the radio can be heard playing "Hakuna Matata," the Academy Award–nominated song from Disney's 1994 box office hit, *The Lion King.* And most subtle of all, there is a book on the shelf in Andy's room called *Tin Toy,* a reference to the first Pixar short by the same title, winner of a 1989 Academy Award.

Toy Story also benefited from the voices of talented actors. Multiple Academy Award winner Tom Hanks as the voice of Woody, Tim Allen as Buzz Lightyear, Don Rickles as Mr. Potato Head, John Ratzenberger (Cliff, of "Cheers" fame), and Annie Potts as Bo Peep may be recognizable at first to adults, but they quickly mesh with and seem perfectly suited to their toy characters. Despite this all-star lineup, none of the talent were paid their usual big bucks. The money went into the animation, not the stars' pockets—they received slightly more than union scale for voice-overs.

Screenplay by Joss Whedon, Andrew Stanton, Joel Cohen, and Alec Sokolow

Story by John Lasseter, Pete Docter, Andrew Stanton, Joe Ranft

Produced by Ralph Guggenheim and Bonnie Arnold

Directed by John Lasseter

VOICES

Woody	Tom Hanks
Buzz Lightyear	Tim Allen
Mr. Potato Head	Don Rickles
Slinky Dog	Jim Varney
Hamm	John Ratzenberger
Bo Peep	Annie Potts

ACADEMY AWARD NOMINATIONS

3 nominations, no wins

Best Screenplay Written Directly for the Screen
Best Original Musical or Comedy Score
Best Song ("You've Got a Friend," by Randy Newman)

A Special Achievement Award was given to director John Lasseter.

---

*Rental figure is approximate and is based on projected figure from the film's 1995–96 grosses.

APOLLO 13

UNIVERSAL
$84,309,770

"Houston, we have a problem."

IN 1970, LESS than a year after Neil Armstrong took his first small step on the surface of the moon, the 13th mission in the Apollo space program was launched. It was to be just an average trek through space, a sequel to the earlier historic event that no one on the ground seemed to care about, when Commander Jim Lovell unexpectedly uttered the above phrase. Perhaps someone at NASA should have suffered from triskaidekaphobia —even elevators don't launch to a 13th floor, since most modern skyscrapers succumb to a bit of superstition.

Apollo 13 lived up to that irrational fear. A series of unbelievable mishaps occurred in what was to be a routine space flight whose biggest problem was public indifference. Fifty-five hours into the voyage, one of the craft's two oxygen tanks exploded, preventing the moon landing and placing the lives of the three astronauts aboard in mortal danger. Electrical power failed, vital oxygen bled into space, and the crew had to cram into their tiny lunar module to conserve power. Freezing temperatures and the danger of carbon dioxide poisoning, plus the likelihood of burning up on re-entry, all combined to make this a very real drama in space. Only now did they grab the attention of the previously apathetic populace of planet Earth.

Director Ron Howard's *Apollo 13* film version capitalizes on this true-life space opera, and although the eventual safe outcome of the mission is historical fact, the edge-of-your-seat tension he brings to the screen had audiences vicariously experiencing every crisis along with Jim Lovell (Tom Hanks), Fred Haise (Bill Paxton), and Jack Swigert (Kevin Bacon). Add to that a big budget of $51,000,000, plus the technical advice of Apollo 15's commander, Dave Scott, and the services of NASA available to train the crew and assist in filming, and this movie had no choice but to become a box office hit.

The cast trained at the U.S. Space Camp in Huntsville, Alabama, where they flew simulated shuttle missions.

Multiple Oscar winner Tom Hanks joyfully discovered his inner astronaut, proclaiming (in *People* magazine), "If they said, 'You can go on the shuttle, but you'll have to give away two years to train, study and prepare,' I'd gladly do it. You bet."

To capture the actual look and feel of weightlessness, Howard refused to rely on special effects. Instead, he filmed his actors and crew aboard a NASA KC-135 jet—basically a stripped-down, padded 707 actually used to train astronauts, which climbs to 36,000 feet, arcs parabolically, then dives toward the ground creating 23 seconds of pure weightlessness at the peak of the parabola. NASA veterans call it the "Vomit Comet," a plane that frequently lives up to its name. Howard and his people made 600 such trips in this plane as he captured the weightless scenes needed, second by precious second.

Howard also insisted on authenticity for the sequences filmed on the soundstage. He ordered the temperature lowered to 34 degrees Fahrenheit in order to film the actors' frozen breath and give the appearance of the frigid conditions the real astronauts endured for three days in space.

Screenplay by William Broyles, Jr., and Al Reinert

Based on the book *Lost Moon,* by Jim Lovell and Jeffrey Kluger

Produced by Brian Grazer

Directed by Ron Howard

CAST

Jim Lovell . . . . .Tom Hanks
Jack Swigert . . . . .Kevin Bacon
Fred Haise . . . . .Bill Paxton
Ken Mattingly . . . . . . .Gary Sinise
Gene Kranz . . . . .Ed Harris

ACADEMY AWARD NOMINATIONS

9 nominations, 2 wins

Best Picture
Best Supporting Actor (Ed Harris)
Best Supporting Actress (Kathleen Quinlan)
Best Screenplay Based on Material Previously Produced or Published
Best Art Direction
*Best Sound
Best Original Dramatic Score
*Best Film Editing
Best Visual Effects

POCAHONTAS
WALT DISNEY PRODUCTIONS
$67,848,010

"Can you paint with all the colors of the wind?"

THE ABOVE LINE from the breakout song from Walt Disney's *Pocahontas* would seem an apt description of the film itself. When "Colors of the Wind" asked the musical question, the production company clearly answered with a resounding "Yes!" This 33rd full-length animated feature from the Mouse Factory created yet another hit film while painting, if not with all the wind's colors, then certainly a potful of paint from Hollywood's lionized king of animation.

Pocahontas had its debut before the largest, wettest audience ever assembled. Over 100,000 eager celebrants gathered at the opening event, billed as "The Premiere in the Park," on the Great (but soggy from drizzle) Lawn of New York's Central Park. There were parades, musicians, concession stands selling Poca-goodies (T-shirts, picnic blankets, and yes, Poca-ponchos for the rain). The crowd, however, gave the film, which was shown on four eight-story-tall screens, a warm New York welcome and quickly spread the word: go see this film. Audiences around the country obliged, propelling it into hit status (although far from the megahits of the two top-grossing Disney films to date, 1992's *Aladdin* and 1994's *The Lion King*.)

Pocahontas marked the first time a Disney animated picture was based on the life of a real person, and perhaps no other film from that studio was ever prepared with such attention to political correctness. Set in Virginia in 1607, the story of the young Indian woman who pleads with her father, Chief Powhatan, to spare the life of the English settler John Smith is one familiar to nearly every school child. But it is more myth than truth, and the

---

Screenplay by Carl Binder, Susannah Grant, Philip LaZebnik

Produced by James Pentecost

Directed by Mike Gabriel and Eric Goldberg

VOICES

Pocahontas . . . . .Irene Bedard,
                    Judy Kuhn (singing)
John Smith . . . . .Mel Gibson
Governor Ratcliffe . . . .David Ogden Stiers
Meeko . . . . .John Kassir
Powhatan . . . . .Russell Means
Grandmother Willow . .Linda Hunt

ACADEMY AWARD NOMINATIONS

2 nominations, 2 wins

*Best Original Musical or Comedy Score
  (Alan Menken and Stephen Schwartz)
*Best Original Song ("Colors of the Wind,"
  by Alan Menken and Stephen Schwartz)

---

producers at Disney were quick to admit they had taken dramatic liberties with history. Whereas the real Pocahontas was probably around 10 or 11 years old when John Smith's ship reached her shores, she is portrayed as much older in the movie. The historical Pocahontas married another Englishman, John Rolfe, underwent baptism (probably forced), had her name changed to Rebecca (again, probably against her will), and was paraded at the royal palace in England. She was stricken with either smallpox or TB in that country, and died in 1617, at the age of 21, survived by the couple's two-year-old son.

The Disney production team worked with many Native Americans to attain as much authenticity as a semi-fictional entertainment piece might achieve. Whenever possible, they sought the advice and participation of people like Jim "Great Elk" Waters, a Native American tribal leader and an artist, musician, and poet. He and his ensemble provided authentic Algonquin music and speech for the film. Indian choreographers and storytellers were consulted to ensure authenticity in portraying the Powhatan tribal customs. The technical advisor for the film was Shirley "Little Dove" Custalow McGowan of the Mattaponi Indians. The colorful songs by Disney veteran composer Alan Menken and lyricist partner Stephen Schwartz were also apropos the film's historical period. Menken drew on Baroque influences for songs associated with the British, and for the Native American melodies he paid homage to the music of the Eastern Indian tribes and the Algonquins. The movie boasted eight original songs, including "Colors of the Wind," "Just Around the Riverbend," and "If I Never Knew You." And yes, that was superstar Mel Gibson, the voice of John Smith, singing his own songs.

"Colors of the Wind" was the first song Menken and Schwartz wrote for the film. Vanessa Williams released a hit single of the tune. "Colors of the Wind" received the Golden Globe award from Best Song, and was also the winner of the 1995 Best Song Oscar.

ACE VENTURA: WHEN NATURE CALLS

WARNER BROS.
$54,122,769*

Fʀᴏᴍ ɪᴛꜱ latrine-evoking imagery in the title, to its anally fixated humor (including a "birth" scene through the tail end of a rhino), *Ace Ventura: When Nature Calls* was strictly lowbrow fare. Yet there was something appealing about the film. In a word, Jim Carrey, the movie's tour-de-*farce* star.

When Nature Calls proved to be a more-popular-than-the-original sequel to the lucrative *Ace Ventura: Pet Detective* (1994), also a starring vehicle for its Carrey-ismatic lead. It seemed the actor could do no wrong, having starred in a string of mid-'90s box office hits, from the three 1994 hits—the first *Ace Ventura* movie, *Dumb and Dumber*, and *The Mask*—to his 1995 success in *Batman Forever* and Thanksgiving release *When Nature Calls*.

Written and directed by Steve Oedekerk, who worked with Jim Carrey writing sketches for him when he was an ensemble player on TV's "In Living Color," the unpretentious sequel saw the rubber-faced star Carrey-ing on in the role of the Miami pet detective, now an innocent abroad. Throughout

the movie, the hyperkinetic star, who has been likened variously to Jerry Lewis, Steve Martin, and even Laurel *and* Hardy, continues his frantic antics, adding '90s buzzwords to America's lexicon, like "All righty, then" and "Spank you very much." In the opening sequence, which pays homage to Sylvester Stallone's *Cliffhanger,* Ace attempts to rescue a raccoon. After he fails, he heads for a Tibetan monastery (a tribute to *Rambo III*). From there, he's summoned to Africa to search for a rare white bat, and the picture becomes a salute to several African jungle-movie stereotypes.

The use of so many critters proved a challenge to animal maven Cathy Morrison of Birds and Animals Unlimited. Her company supplied and trained spike, Ace's white-throated monkey companion, Boba the elephant, and the animals Boba leads in Ace's rescue at the end of the film—everything from giraffes, zebras, lions, and water buffalo to three varieties of antelopes, ostriches, chimps, and birds.

Sides were quickly drawn by critics. *The Hollywood Reporter* called the movie "remarkably layered with some nifty noir-complexity. Luckily, the narrative does not muck up the real entertaining stuff: elephants, guano, horny apes, snitty Englishmen, farting and a mechanical rhino." Critic Roger Ebert wrote of the comic (in an on-line review for CompuServe), "Carrey himself is so manic he makes Jerry Lewis look like a narcolepsy victim." Still, Ebert found little to recommend the film, claiming "there aren't enough laughs." Richard Corliss of *Time* took the movie to task, saying "*When Nature Calls* in this awful sequel, don't answer…[the film] would be a career ender for Carrey—except that a zillion people have seen it. Stop this, folks. It'll only encourage him."

Apparently the public did encourage him. Carrey carved a niche for himself as Hollywood's resident nut, with a price tag to match. His next two pictures reportedly paid him $20,000,000 each, as he continued to get rich and richer. CBS began airing "Ace Ventura: Pet Detective" as a Saturday morning cartoon, while further live-acted sequels were on the Warner Bros. drawing boards. The franchise seemed destined to continue, lowbrow or not. Or, in the words of Ace Ventura, "All righty, then!" Better make that, "Spank you very much!"

*Rental figure is approximate and is based on projected figure from the film's 1995–96 grosses.

Screenplay by Steve Oedekerk

Produced by James G. Robinson

Directed by Steve Oedekerk

CAST

Ace Ventura	Jim Carrey
Fulton Greenwall	Ian McNeice
Vincent Cadby	Simon Callow
Ouda	Maynard Eziashi
Burton Quinn	Bob Gunton
The Princess	Sophie Okonedo
The Tiny Warrior	Tommy Davidson

APPENDIXES

FILMS BY YEAR

GONE WITH THE WIND	1939	MGM	$79,375,080
THE WIZARD OF OZ	1939	MGM	4,759,890
MR. SMITH GOES TO WASHINGTON	1939	Columbia	3,500,000
THE HUNCHBACK OF NOTRE DAME	1939	RKO	1,500,000
JESSE JAMES	1939	Fox	1,500,000
FANTASIA	1940	Disney	41,660,000
PINOCCHIO	1940	Disney	40,442,000
BOOM TOWN	1940	MGM	4,586,415
THE GREAT DICTATOR	1940	United Artists	3,500,000
REBECCA	1940	Selznick	3,000,000
SERGEANT YORK	1941	Warner Bros.	6,135,707
DUMBO	1941	Disney	3,000,000
DIVE BOMBER	1941	Warner Bros.	1,500,000*
HONKY TONK	1941	MGM	1,500,000*
THE PHILADELPHIA STORY	1941	MGM	1,500,000*
BAMBI	1942	Disney	47,265,000
MRS. MINIVER	1942	MGM	5,390,009
CASABLANCA	1942	Warner Bros.	4,750,000
YANKEE DOODLE DANDY	1942	Warner Bros.	4,719,681
RANDOM HARVEST	1942	MGM	4,665,501
THIS IS THE ARMY	1943	Warner Bros.	8,500,000
FOR WHOM THE BELL TOLLS	1943	Paramount	7,100,000
THE OUTLAW	1943	RKO	5,075,000
THE SONG OF BERNADETTE	1943	Fox	4,701,000
STAGE DOOR CANTEEN	1943	United Artists	4,339,532
GOING MY WAY	1944	Paramount	6,500,000
MEET ME IN ST. LOUIS	1944	MGM	5,132,202
SINCE YOU WENT AWAY	1944	United Artists	4,924,756
30 SECONDS OVER TOKYO	1944	MGM	4,471,080
HOLLYWOOD CANTEEN	1944	Warner Bros.	4,200,000
THE BELLS OF ST. MARY'S	1945	RKO	8,000,000
LEAVE HER TO HEAVEN	1945	Fox	5,505,000
SPELLBOUND	1945	United Artists	4,970,583
ANCHORS AWEIGH	1945	MGM	4,778,679
THE VALLEY OF DECISION	1945	MGM	4,566,755
SONG OF THE SOUTH	1946	Disney	29,228,717
THE BEST YEARS OF OUR LIVES	1946	RKO	11,300,000
DUEL IN THE SUN	1946	Selznick	11,300,000
THE JOLSON STORY	1946	Columbia	7,600,000
BLUE SKIES	1946	Paramount	5,700,000

WELCOME STRANGER	1947	Paramount	6,100,000
THE BACHELOR AND THE BOBBY-SOXER	1947	RKO	5,500,000
THE EGG AND I	1947	Universal	5,500,000
UNCONQUERED	1947	Paramount	5,250,000
LIFE WITH FATHER	1947	Warner Bros.	5,057,000
THE RED SHOES	1948	Archers/Eagle-Lion	5,000,000
RED RIVER	1948	United Artists	4,506,825
THE PALEFACE	1948	Paramount	4,500,000
THE THREE MUSKETEERS	1948	MGM	4,306,876
EASTER PARADE	1948	MGM	4,189,997
SAMSON AND DELILAH	1949	Paramount	11,500,000
BATTLEGROUND	1949	MGM	5,051,143
JOLSON SINGS AGAIN	1949	Columbia	5,000,000
THE SANDS OF IWO JIMA	1949	Republic	5,000,000
I WAS A MALE WAR BRIDE	1949	Fox	4,100,000
CINDERELLA	1950	Disney	41,087,000
KING SOLOMON'S MINES	1950	MGM	5,586,000
ANNIE GET YOUR GUN	1950	MGM	4,919,394
CHEAPER BY THE DOZEN	1950	Fox	4,425,000
BORN YESTERDAY	1950	Columbia	4,115,000
QUO VADIS?	1951	MGM	11,901,662
ALICE IN WONDERLAND	1951	Disney	7,196,000
SHOW BOAT	1951	MGM	5,533,000
A STREETCAR NAMED DESIRE	1951	Warner Bros.	4,800,000
DAVID AND BATHSHEBA	1951	Fox	4,720,000
THIS IS CINERAMA	1952	CRC	15,400,000
THE GREATEST SHOW ON EARTH	1952	Paramount	14,000,000
THE SNOWS OF KILIMANJARO	1952	Fox	6,500,000
IVANHOE	1952	MGM	6,258,000
HANS CHRISTIAN ANDERSEN	1952	RKO	6,000,000
PETER PAN	1953	Disney	37,584,000
THE ROBE	1953	Fox	17,500,000
FROM HERE TO ETERNITY	1953	Columbia	12,200,000
HOUSE OF WAX	1953	Warner Bros.	9,500,000
SHANE	1953	Paramount	9,000,000
WHITE CHRISTMAS	1954	Paramount	12,000,000
20,000 LEAGUES UNDER THE SEA	1954	Disney	11,267,000
REAR WINDOW	1954	Paramount	9,812,271
THE CAINE MUTINY	1954	Columbia	8,700,000
THE GLENN MILLER STORY	1954	Universal	7,590,994

LADY AND THE TRAMP	1955	Disney	40,249,000
CINERAMA HOLIDAY	1955	CRC	12,000,000
MISTER ROBERTS	1955	Warner Bros.	8,500,000
BATTLE CRY	1955	Warner Bros.	8,100,000
OKLAHOMA!	1955	Magna	7,100,000
THE TEN COMMANDMENTS	1956	Paramount	43,000,000
AROUND THE WORLD IN 80 DAYS	1956	United Artists/WB	23,120,000
GIANT	1956	Warner Bros.	14,000,000
SEVEN WONDERS OF THE WORLD	1956	CRC	12,500,000
THE KING AND I	1956	Fox	8,500,000
THE BRIDGE ON THE RIVER KWAI	1957	Columbia	17,195,000
PEYTON PLACE	1957	Fox	11,500,000
SAYONARA	1957	Warner Bros.	10,500,000
OLD YELLER	1957	Disney	10,050,000
POOR WHITE TRASH (BAYOU)	1957	United Artists	6,000,000
SOUTH PACIFIC	1958	Fox	17,500,000
AUNTIE MAME	1958	Warner Bros.	9,300,000
CAT ON A HOT TIN ROOF	1958	MGM	8,785,162
NO TIME FOR SERGEANTS	1958	Warner Bros.	7,500,000
GIGI	1958	MGM	7,321,423
BEN-HUR	1959	MGM	36,992,088
SLEEPING BEAUTY	1959	Disney	21,998,000
THE SHAGGY DOG	1959	Disney	12,317,000
OPERATION PETTICOAT	1959	Universal	9,321,555
DARBY O'GILL AND THE LITTLE PEOPLE	1959	Disney	8,336,000
SWISS FAMILY ROBINSON	1960	Disney	20,178,000
PSYCHO	1960	Paramount/Universal	11,200,000
SPARTACUS	1960	Universal	11,100,000
EXODUS	1960	United Artists	8,331,582
LA DOLCE VITA	1960	Astor	8,000,000
101 DALMATIANS	1961	Disney	68,648,000
WEST SIDE STORY	1961	United Artists	19,645,570
THE GUNS OF NAVARONE	1961	Columbia	13,000,000
EL CID	1961	Allied Artists	12,000,000
THE ABSENT-MINDED PROFESSOR	1961	Disney	11,426,000
HOW THE WEST WAS WON	1962	CRC/MGM	20,932,883
LAWRENCE OF ARABIA	1962	Columbia	20,310,000
THE LONGEST DAY	1962	Fox	17,600,000
IN SEARCH OF THE CASTAWAYS	1962	Disney	9,975,000
THE MUSIC MAN	1962	Warner Bros.	8,100,000

CLEOPATRA	1963	Fox	26,000,000
IT'S A MAD MAD MAD MAD WORLD	1963	United Artists	20,849,786
TOM JONES	1963	United Artists	17,070,000
IRMA LA DOUCE	1963	United Artists	11,921,784
THE SWORD IN THE STONE	1963	Disney	10,475,000
MARY POPPINS	1964	Disney	45,000,000
MY FAIR LADY	1964	Warner Bros.	34,000,000
GOLDFINGER	1964	United Artists	22,997,706
THE CARPETBAGGERS	1964	Paramount	15,500,000
FROM RUSSIA WITH LOVE	1964	United Artists	9,924,279
THE SOUND OF MUSIC	1965	Fox	79,975,000
DOCTOR ZHIVAGO	1965	MGM	60,964,000
THUNDERBALL	1965	United Artists	28,621,434
THOSE MAGNIFICENT MEN IN THEIR FLYING MACHINES	1965	Fox	14,000,000
THAT DARN CAT	1965	Disney	12,628,000
HAWAII	1966	United Artists	15,553,018
THE BIBLE	1966	Fox	15,000,000
WHO'S AFRAID OF VIRGINIA WOOLF?	1966	Warner Bros.	14,500,000
A MAN FOR ALL SEASONS	1966	Columbia	12,750,000
LT. ROBIN CRUSOE, USN	1966	Disney	10,164,000
THE JUNGLE BOOK	1967	Disney	60,964,000
THE GRADUATE	1967	Avco/Embassy	44,090,729
GUESS WHO'S COMING TO DINNER	1967	Columbia	25,500,000
BONNIE AND CLYDE	1967	Warner Bros.	22,800,000
THE DIRTY DOZEN	1967	MGM	20,403,826
FUNNY GIRL	1968	Columbia	26,325,000
2001: A SPACE ODYSSEY	1968	MGM	25,521,917
THE ODD COUPLE	1968	Paramount	20,000,000
BULLITT	1968	Warner Bros.	19,000,000
ROMEO AND JULIET	1968	Paramount	17,473,000
BUTCH CASSIDY AND THE SUNDANCE KID	1969	Fox	45,953,000
THE LOVE BUG	1969	Disney	23,150,000
MIDNIGHT COWBOY	1969	United Artists	20,499,282
EASY RIDER	1969	Columbia	19,100,000
HELLO, DOLLY!	1969	Fox	15,200,000
LOVE STORY	1970	Paramount	48,700,000
AIRPORT	1970	Universal	45,220,118
M*A*S*H	1970	Fox	36,720,000
PATTON	1970	Fox	28,100,000
THE ARISTOCATS	1970	Disney	26,462,000

FIDDLER ON THE ROOF	1971	United Artists	38,260,954
BILLY JACK	1971	Warner Bros.	32,500,000
THE FRENCH CONNECTION	1971	Fox	26,315,000
SUMMER OF '42	1971	Warner Bros.	20,500,000
DIAMONDS ARE FOREVER	1971	United Artists	19,726,829
THE GODFATHER	1972	Paramount	86,275,000
THE POSEIDON ADVENTURE	1972	Fox	42,000,000
WHAT'S UP DOC?	1972	Warner Bros.	28,000,000
DELIVERANCE	1972	Warner Bros.	22,600,000
JEREMIAH JOHNSON	1972	Warner Bros.	21,900,000
THE EXORCIST	1973	Warner Bros.	89,000,000
THE STING	1973	Universal	78,212,000
AMERICAN GRAFFITI	1973	Universal	55,128,175
PAPILLON	1973	Allied Artists	22,500,000
THE WAY WE WERE	1973	Columbia	22,457,000
THE TOWERING INFERNO	1974	Fox/WB	48,838,000
BLAZING SADDLES	1974	Warner Bros.	47,800,000
YOUNG FRANKENSTEIN	1974	Fox	38,823,000
EARTHQUAKE	1974	Universal	35,849,994
THE TRIAL OF BILLY JACK	1974	Warner Bros.	31,100,000
JAWS	1975	Universal	129,549,325
ONE FLEW OVER THE CUCKOO'S NEST	1975	United Artists	59,939,701
THE ROCKY HORROR PICTURE SHOW	1975	Fox	40,420,000
SHAMPOO	1975	Columbia	23,822,000
DOG DAY AFTERNOON	1975	Warner Bros.	22,500,000
ROCKY	1976	United Artists	56,524,972
A STAR IS BORN	1976	Warner Bros.	37,100,000
KING KONG	1976	Paramount	36,915,000
SILVER STREAK	1976	Fox	30,018,000
ALL THE PRESIDENT'S MEN	1976	Warner Bros.	30,000,000
STAR WARS	1977	Fox	193,777,000
CLOSE ENCOUNTERS OF THE THIRD KIND	1977	Columbia	82,750,000
SATURDAY NIGHT FEVER	1977	Paramount	74,100,000
SMOKEY AND THE BANDIT	1977	Universal	58,949,939
THE GOODBYE GIRL	1977	MGM/WB	41,839,170
GREASE	1978	Paramount	96,300,000
SUPERMAN	1978	Warner Bros.	82,800,000
NATIONAL LAMPOON'S ANIMAL HOUSE	1978	Universal	70,826,000
EVERY WHICH WAY BUT LOOSE	1978	Warner Bros.	51,900,000
JAWS 2	1978	Universal	50,431,964

KRAMER VS. KRAMER	1979	Columbia	59,986,335
STAR TREK: THE MOTION PICTURE	1979	Paramount	56,000,000
THE JERK	1979	Universal	42,989,656
ROCKY II	1979	United Artists	42,169,387
ALIEN	1979	Fox	40,300,000
THE EMPIRE STRIKES BACK	1980	Fox	141,672,000
9 TO 5	1980	Fox	59,068,000
STIR CRAZY	1980	Columbia	58,364,420
AIRPLANE!	1980	Paramount	40,610,000
ANY WHICH WAY YOU CAN	1980	Warner Bros.	40,500,000
RAIDERS OF THE LOST ARK	1981	Paramount	115,598,000
SUPERMAN II	1981	Warner Bros.	65,100,000
ON GOLDEN POND	1981	Universal	61,175,028
ARTHUR	1981	Warner Bros.	42,000,000
STRIPES	1981	Columbia	40,886,589
E. T. THE EXTRA-TERRESTRIAL	1982	Universal	228,168,939
TOOTSIE	1982	Columbia	94,910,000
ROCKY III	1982	MGM/UA	66,262,796
PORKY'S	1982	Fox	55,559,000
AN OFFICER AND A GENTLEMAN	1982	Paramount	55,223,000
RETURN OF THE JEDI	1983	Fox	169,193,000
TERMS OF ENDEARMENT	1983	Paramount	50,250,000
TRADING PLACES	1983	Paramount	40,600,000
WARGAMES	1983	MGM/UA	38,519,833
SUPERMAN III	1983	Warner Bros.	37,200,000
GHOSTBUSTERS	1984	Columbia	132,720,000
INDIANA JONES AND THE TEMPLE OF DOOM	1984	Paramount	109,000,000
BEVERLY HILLS COP	1984	Paramount	108,000,000
GREMLINS	1984	Warner Bros.	79,500,000
THE KARATE KID	1984	Columbia	43,120,000
BACK TO THE FUTURE	1985	Universal	105,496,267
RAMBO: FIRST BLOOD PART II	1985	TriStar	78,919,250
ROCKY IV	1985	MGM/UA	76,023,246
THE COLOR PURPLE	1985	Warner Bros.	49,800,000
OUT OF AFRICA	1985	Universal	43,448,253
TOP GUN	1986	Paramount	79,400,000
"CROCODILE" DUNDEE	1986	Paramount	70,227,000
PLATOON	1986	Orion	69,937,092
THE KARATE KID PT. II	1986	Columbia	58,310,000
STAR TREK IV: THE VOYAGE HOME	1986	Paramount	56,820,071

THREE MEN AND A BABY	1987	Disney	81,356,000
BEVERLY HILLS COP II	1987	Paramount	80,857,776
FATAL ATTRACTION	1987	Paramount	70,000,000
GOOD MORNING, VIETNAM	1987	Disney	58,083,108
THE UNTOUCHABLES	1987	Paramount	36,866,530
RAIN MAN	1988	MGM/UA	86,813,000
WHO FRAMED ROGER RABBIT	1988	Disney	81,244,000
COMING TO AMERICA	1988	Paramount	65,000,000
TWINS	1988	Universal	57,715,127
"CROCODILE" DUNDEE II	1988	Paramount	57,300,000
BATMAN	1989	Warner Bros.	150,500,000
INDIANA JONES AND THE LAST CRUSADE	1989	Paramount	115,500,000*
LETHAL WEAPON 2	1989	Warner Bros.	79,500,000
BACK TO THE FUTURE, PT. II	1989	Universal	72,319,630
HONEY, I SHRUNK THE KIDS	1989	Disney	72,007,000*
HOME ALONE	1990	Fox	140,099,000
GHOST	1990	Paramount	98,200,000
PRETTY WOMAN	1990	Disney	81,905,530
DANCES WITH WOLVES	1990	Orion	81,537,971
TEENAGE MUTANT NINJA TURTLES	1990	New Line Cinema	67,650,000
TERMINATOR 2: JUDGMENT DAY	1991	TriStar	112,500,000
ROBIN HOOD: PRINCE OF THIEVES	1991	Warner Bros.	86,000,000
BEAUTY AND THE BEAST	1991	Disney	69,415,000
HOOK	1991	TriStar	65,000,000
CITY SLICKERS	1991	Columbia	60,750,000
ALADDIN	1992	Disney	111,740,683
HOME ALONE 2: LOST IN NEW YORK	1992	Fox	103,377,614
BATMAN RETURNS	1992	Warner Bros.	100,100,000
LETHAL WEAPON 3	1992	Warner Bros.	80,000,000
A FEW GOOD MEN	1992	Columbia	71,000,000
JURASSIC PARK	1993	Universal	208,000,000
MRS. DOUBTFIRE	1993	Fox	109,761,240
THE FUGITIVE	1993	Warner Bros	92,600,000
THE FIRM	1993	Paramount	77,047,044
SLEEPLESS IN SEATTLE	1993	TriStar	64,930,137
THE LION KING	1994	Disney	173,057,366
FORREST GUMP	1994	Paramount	156,000,000
TRUE LIES	1994	Fox	80,000,000
THE SANTA CLAUSE	1994	Disney	72,348,689
THE FLINTSTONES	1994	Universal	70,753,383

BATMAN FOREVER	1995	Warner Bros.	105,100,000
TOY STORY	1995	Disney	92,217,831
APOLLO 13	1995	Universal	84,309,770
POCAHONTAS	1995	Disney	67,848,010
ACE VENTURA: WHEN NATURE CALLS	1995	Warner Bros.	54,122,769

*Figures are informed estimates

FILMS BY TITLE

ABSENT-MINDED PROFESSOR, THE	1961	Disney	11,426,000
ACE VENTURA: WHEN NATURE CALLS	1995	Warner Bros.	54,122,769*
AIRPLANE!	1980	Paramount	40,610,000
AIRPORT	1970	Universal	45,220,118
ALADDIN	1992	Disney	111,740,683
ALICE IN WONDERLAND	1951	Disney	7,196,000
ALIEN	1979	Fox	40,300,000
ALL THE PRESIDENT'S MEN	1976	Warner Bros.	30,000,000
AMERICAN GRAFFITI	1973	Universal	55,128,175
ANCHORS AWEIGH	1945	MGM	4,778,679
ANNIE GET YOUR GUN	1950	MGM	4,919,394
ANY WHICH WAY YOU CAN	1980	Warner Bros.	40,500,000
APOLLO 13	1995	Universal	84,309,770
ARISTOCATS, THE	1970	Disney	26,462,000
AROUND THE WORLD IN 80 DAYS	1956	United Artists/WB	23,120,000
ARTHUR	1981	Warner Bros.	42,000,000
AUNTIE MAME	1958	Warner Bros.	9,300,000
BACHELOR AND THE BOBBY-SOXER, THE	1947	RKO	5,500,000
BACK TO THE FUTURE	1985	Universal	105,496,267
BACK TO THE FUTURE, PART II	1989	Universal	72,319,630
BAMBI	1942	Disney	47,265,000
BATMAN	1989	Warner Bros.	150,500,000
BATMAN FOREVER	1995	Warner Bros.	105,100,000
BATMAN RETURNS	1992	Warner Bros.	100,100,000
BATTLE CRY	1955	Warner Bros.	8,100,000
BATTLEGROUND	1949	MGM	5,051,143
BEAUTY AND THE BEAST	1991	Disney	69,415,000
BELLS OF ST. MARY'S, THE	1945	RKO	8,000,000
BEN-HUR	1959	MGM	36,992,088
BEST YEARS OF OUR LIVES, THE	1946	RKO	11,300,000
BEVERLY HILLS COP	1984	Paramount	108,000,000
BEVERLY HILLS COP II	1987	Paramount	80,857,776
BIBLE, THE	1966	Fox	15,000,000
BILLY JACK	1971	Warner Bros.	32,500,000
BLAZING SADDLES	1974	Warner Bros.	47,800,000
BLUE SKIES	1946	Paramount	5,700,000
BONNIE AND CLYDE	1967	Warner Bros.	22,800,000
BOOM TOWN	1940	MGM	4,586,415
BORN YESTERDAY	1950	Columbia	4,115,000
BRIDGE ON THE RIVER KWAI, THE	1957	Columbia	17,195,000
BULLITT	1968	Warner Bros.	19,000,000
BUTCH CASSIDY AND THE SUNDANCE KID	1969	Fox	45,953,000
CAINE MUTINY, THE	1954	Columbia	8,700,000
CARPETBAGGERS, THE	1964	Paramount	15,500,000
CASABLANCA	1942	Warner Bros.	4,750,000

CAT ON A HOT TIN ROOF	1958	MGM	8,785,162
CHEAPER BY THE DOZEN	1950	Fox	4,425,000
CINDERELLA	1950	Disney	41,087,000
CINERAMA HOLIDAY	1955	CRC	12,000,000
CITY SLICKERS	1991	Columbia	60,750,000
CLEOPATRA	1963	Fox	26,000,000
CLOSE ENCOUNTERS OF THE THIRD KIND	1977	Columbia	82,750,000
COLOR PURPLE, THE	1985	Warner Bros.	49,800,000
COMING TO AMERICA	1988	Paramount	65,000,000
"CROCODILE" DUNDEE	1986	Paramount	70,227,000
"CROCODILE" DUNDEE II	1988	Paramount	57,300,000
DANCES WITH WOLVES	1990	Orion	81,537,971
DARBY O'GILL AND THE LITTLE PEOPLE	1959	Disney	8,336,000
DAVID AND BATHSHEBA	1951	Fox	4,720,000
DELIVERANCE	1972	Warner Bros.	22,600,000
DIAMONDS ARE FOREVER	1971	United Artists	19,726,829
DIRTY DOZEN, THE	1967	MGM	20,403,826
DIVE BOMBER	1941	Warner Bros.	1,500,000*
DOCTOR ZHIVAGO	1965	MGM	60,964,000
DOG DAY AFTERNOON	1975	Warner Bros.	22,500,000
DUEL IN THE SUN	1946	Selznick	11,300,000
DUMBO	1941	Disney	3,000,000
EARTHQUAKE	1974	Universal	35,849,994
EASTER PARADE	1948	MGM	4,189,997
EASY RIDER	1969	Columbia	19,100,000
EGG AND I, THE	1947	Universal	5,500,000
EL CID	1961	Allied Artists	12,000,000
EMPIRE STRIKES BACK, THE	1980	Fox	141,672,000
E.T. THE EXTRA-TERRESTRIAL	1982	Universal	228,168,939
EVERY WHICH WAY BUT LOOSE	1978	Warner Bros.	51,900,000
EXODUS	1960	United Artists	8,331,582
EXORCIST, THE	1973	Warner Bros.	89,000,000
FANTASIA	1940	Disney	41,660,000
FATAL ATTRACTION	1987	Paramount	70,000,000
FEW GOOD MEN, A	1992	Columbia	71,000,000
FIDDLER ON THE ROOF	1971	United Artists	38,260,954
FIRM, THE	1993	Paramount	77,047,044
FLINTSTONES, THE	1994	Universal	70,753,383
FORREST GUMP	1994	Paramount	156,000,000
FOR WHOM THE BELL TOLLS	1943	Paramount	7,100,000
FRENCH CONNECTION, THE	1971	Fox	26,315,000
FROM HERE TO ETERNITY	1953	Columbia	12,200,000
FROM RUSSIA WITH LOVE	1964	United Artists	9,924,279
FUGITIVE, THE	1993	Warner Bros.	92,600,000

FUNNY GIRL	1968	Columbia	26,325,000
GHOST	1990	Paramount	98,200,000
GHOSTBUSTERS	1984	Columbia	132,720,000
GIANT	1956	Warner Bros.	14,000,000
GIGI	1958	MGM	7,321,423
GLENN MILLER STORY, THE	1954	Universal	7,590,994
GODFATHER, THE	1972	Paramount	86,275,000
GOING MY WAY	1944	Paramount	6,500,000
GOLDFINGER	1964	United Artists	22,997,706
GONE WITH THE WIND	1939	MGM	79,375,080
GOODBYE GIRL, THE	1977	MGM/Warner Bros.	41,839,170
GOOD MORNING, VIETNAM	1987	Disney	58,083,108
GRADUATE, THE	1967	Avco Embassy	44,090,729
GREASE	1978	Paramount	96,300,000
GREAT DICTATOR, THE	1940	United Artists	3,500,000
GREATEST SHOW ON EARTH, THE	1952	Paramount	14,000,000
GREMLINS	1984	Warner Bros.	79,500,000
GUESS WHO'S COMING TO DINNER	1967	Columbia	25,500,000
GUNS OF NAVARONE	1961	Columbia	13,000,000
HANS CHRISTIAN ANDERSEN	1952	RKO	6,000,000
HAWAII	1966	United Artists	15,553,018
HELLO, DOLLY!	1969	Fox	15,200,000
HOLLYWOOD CANTEEN	1944	Warner Bros.	4,200,000
HOME ALONE	1990	Fox	140,099,000
HOME ALONE 2: LOST IN NEW YORK	1992	Fox	103,377,614
HONEY, I SHRUNK THE KIDS	1989	Disney	72,007,000
HONKY TONK	1941	MGM	1,500,000*
HOOK	1991	TriStar	65,000,000
HOUSE OF WAX	1953	Warner Bros.	9,500,000
HOW THE WEST WAS WON	1962	CRC/MGM	20,932,883
HUNCHBACK OF NOTRE DAME, THE	1939	RKO	1,500,000
INDIANA JONES AND THE LAST CRUSADE	1989	Paramount	115,500,000
INDIANA JONES AND THE TEMPLE OF DOOM	1984	Paramount	109,000,000
IN SEARCH OF THE CASTAWAYS	1962	Disney	9,975,000
IRMA LA DOUCE	1963	United Artists	11,921,784
IT'S A MAD MAD MAD MAD WORLD	1963	United Artists	20,849,786
IVANHOE	1952	MGM	6,258,000
I WAS A MALE WAR BRIDE	1949	Fox	4,100,000
JAWS	1975	Universal	129,549,325
JAWS 2	1978	Universal	50,431,964
JEREMIAH JOHNSON	1972	Warner Bros.	21,900,000
JERK, THE	1979	Universal	42,989,656
JESSE JAMES	1939	Fox	1,500,000

JOLSON SINGS AGAIN	1949	Columbia	5,000,000
JOLSON STORY, THE	1946	Columbia	7,600,000
JUNGLE BOOK, THE	1967	Disney	60,964,000
JURASSIC PARK	1993	Universal	208,000,000
KARATE KID, THE	1984	Columbia	43,120,000
KARATE KID, PART II, THE	1986	Columbia	58,310,000
KING AND I, THE	1956	Fox	8,500,000
KING KONG	1976	Paramount	36,915,000
KING SOLOMON'S MINES	1950	MGM	5,586,000
KRAMER VS. KRAMER	1979	Columbia	59,986,335
LA DOLCE VITA	1960	Astor	8,000,000
LADY AND THE TRAMP	1955	Disney	40,249,000
LAWRENCE OF ARABIA	1962	Columbia	20,310,000
LEAVE HER TO HEAVEN	1945	Fox	5,505,000
LETHAL WEAPON 2	1989	Warner Bros.	79,500,000
LETHAL WEAPON 3	1992	Warner Bros.	80,000,000
LIFE WITH FATHER	1947	Warner Bros.	5,057,000
LION KING, THE	1994	Disney	173,057,366
LONGEST DAY, THE	1962	Fox	17,600,000
LOVE BUG, THE	1969	Disney	23,150,000
LOVE STORY	1970	Paramount	48,700,000
LT. ROBIN CRUSOE, USN	1966	Disney	10,164,000
MAN FOR ALL SEASONS, A	1966	Columbia	12,750,000
MARY POPPINS	1964	Disney	45,000,000
M*A*S*H	1970	Fox	36,720,000
MEET ME IN ST. LOUIS	1944	MGM	5,132,202
MIDNIGHT COWBOY	1969	United Artists	20,499,282
MISTER ROBERTS	1955	Warner Bros.	8,500,000
MRS. DOUBTFIRE	1993	Fox	109,761,240
MRS. MINIVER	1942	MGM	5,390,009
MR. SMITH GOES TO WASHINGTON	1939	Columbia	3,500,000
MUSIC MAN, THE	1962	Warner Bros.	8,100,000
MY FAIR LADY	1964	Warner Bros.	34,000,000
NATIONAL LAMPOON'S ANIMAL HOUSE	1978	Universal	70,826,000
9 TO 5	1980	Fox	59,068,000
NO TIME FOR SERGEANTS	1958	Warner Bros.	7,500,000
ODD COUPLE, THE	1968	Paramount	20,000,000
OFFICER AND A GENTLEMAN, AN	1982	Paramount	55,223,000
OKLAHOMA	1955	Magna	7,100,000
OLD YELLER	1957	Disney	10,050,000
ON GOLDEN POND	1981	Universal	61,175,028
ONE FLEW OVER THE CUCKOO'S NEST	1975	United Artists	59,939,701

101 DALMATIANS	1961	Disney	68,648,000
OPERATION PETTICOAT	1959	Universal	9,321,555
OUTLAW, THE	1943	RKO	5,075,000
OUT OF AFRICA	1985	Universal	43,448,253
PALEFACE, THE	1948	Paramount	4,500,000
PAPILLON	1973	Allied Artists	22,500,000
PATTON	1970	Fox	28,100,000
PETER PAN	1953	Disney	37,584,000
PEYTON PLACE	1957	Fox	11,500,000
PHILADELPHIA STORY, THE	1941	MGM	1,500,000*
PINOCCHIO	1940	Disney	40,442,000
PLATOON	1986	Orion	69,937,092
POCAHONTAS	1995	Disney	67,848,010
POOR WHITE TRASH (BAYOU)	1957	United Artists	6,000,000
PORKY'S	1982	Fox	55,559,000
POSEIDON ADVENTURE, THE	1972	Fox	42,000,000
PRETTY WOMAN	1990	Disney	81,905,530
PSYCHO	1960	Paramount/Universal	11,200,000
QUO VADIS?	1951	MGM	11,901,662
RAIDERS OF THE LOST ARK	1981	Paramount	115,598,000
RAIN MAN	1988	MGM/United Artists	86,813,000
RAMBO: FIRST BLOOD PART II	1985	TriStar	78,919,250
RANDOM HARVEST	1942	MGM	4,665,501
REAR WINDOW	1954	Paramount	9,812,271
REBECCA	1940	Selznick	3,000,000
RED RIVER	1948	United Artists	4,506,825
RED SHOES, THE	1948	Archers/Eagle-Lion	5,000,000
RETURN OF THE JEDI	1983	Fox	169,193,000
ROBE, THE	1953	Fox	17,500,000
ROBIN HOOD: PRINCE OF THIEVES	1991	Warner Bros.	86,000,000
ROCKY	1976	United Artists	56,524,972
ROCKY II	1979	United Artists	42,169,387
ROCKY III	1982	MGM/United Artists	66,262,796
ROCKY IV	1985	MGM/United Artists	76,023,246
ROCKY HORROR PICTURE SHOW, THE	1975	Fox	40,420,000
ROMEO AND JULIET	1968	Paramount	17,473,000
SAMSON AND DELILAH	1949	Paramount	11,500,000
SANDS OF IWO JIMA, THE	1949	Republic	5,000,000
SANTA CLAUSE, THE	1994	Disney	72,348,689
SATURDAY NIGHT FEVER	1977	Paramount	74,100,000
SAYONARA	1957	Warner Bros.	10,500,000
SERGEANT YORK	1941	Warner Bros.	6,135,707
SEVEN WONDERS OF THE WORLD	1956	CRC	12,500,000

SHAGGY DOG, THE	1959	Disney	12,317,000
SHAMPOO	1975	Columbia	23,822,000
SHANE	1953	Paramount	9,000,000
SHOW BOAT	1951	MGM	5,533,000
SILVER STREAK	1976	Fox	30,018,000
SINCE YOU WENT AWAY	1944	United Artists	4,924,756
SLEEPING BEAUTY	1959	Disney	21,998,000
SLEEPLESS IN SEATTLE	1993	TriStar	64,930,137
SMOKEY AND THE BANDIT	1977	Universal	58,949,939
SNOWS OF KILIMANJARO, THE	1952	Fox	6,500,000
SONG OF BERNADETTE, THE	1943	Fox	4,701,000
SONG OF THE SOUTH	1946	Disney	29,228,717
SOUND OF MUSIC, THE	1965	Fox	79,975,000
SOUTH PACIFIC	1958	Fox	17,500,000
SPARTACUS	1960	Universal	11,100,000
SPELLBOUND	1945	United Artists	4,970,583
STAGE DOOR CANTEEN	1943	United Artists	4,339,532
STAR IS BORN, A	1976	Warner Bros.	37,100,000
STAR TREK: THE MOTION PICTURE	1979	Paramount	56,000,000
STAR TREK IV: THE VOYAGE HOME	1986	Paramount	56,820,071
STAR WARS	1977	Fox	193,777,000
STING, THE	1973	Universal	78,212,000
STIR CRAZY	1980	Columbia	58,364,420
STREETCAR NAMED DESIRE, A	1951	Warner Bros.	4,800,000
STRIPES	1981	Columbia	40,886,589
SUMMER OF '42	1971	Warner Bros.	20,500,000
SUPERMAN	1978	Warner Bros.	82,800,000
SUPERMAN II	1981	Warner Bros.	65,100,000
SUPERMAN III	1983	Warner Bros.	37,200,000
SWISS FAMILY ROBINSON	1960	Disney	20,178,000
SWORD IN THE STONE, THE	1963	Disney	10,475,000
TEENAGE MUTANT NINJA TURTLES	1990	New Line Cinema	67,650,000
TEN COMMANDMENTS, THE	1956	Paramount	43,000,000
TERMINATOR 2: JUDGMENT DAY	1991	TriStar	112,500,000
TERMS OF ENDEARMENT	1983	Paramount	50,250,000
THAT DARN CAT	1965	Disney	12,628,000
30 SECONDS OVER TOKYO	1944	MGM	4,471,080
THIS IS CINERAMA	1952	CRC	15,400,000
THIS IS THE ARMY	1943	Warner Bros.	8,500,000
THOSE MAGNIFICENT MEN IN THEIR FLYING MACHINES	1965	Fox	14,000,000
THREE MEN AND A BABY	1987	Disney	81,356,000
THREE MUSKETEERS, THE	1948	MGM	4,306,876
THUNDERBALL	1965	United Artists	28,621,434
TOM JONES	1963	United Artists	17,070,000
TOOTSIE	1982	Columbia	94,910,000
TOP GUN	1986	Paramount	79,400,000

TOWERING INFERNO, THE	1974	Fox/Warner Bros.	48,838,000
TOY STORY	1995	Disney	92,217,831 *
TRADING PLACES	1983	Paramount	40,600,000
TRIAL OF BILLY JACK, THE	1974	Warner Bros.	31,100,000
TRUE LIES	1994	Fox	80,000,000
20,000 LEAGUES UNDER THE SEA	1954	Disney	11,267,000
TWINS	1988	Universal	57,715,127
2001: A SPACE ODYSSEY	1968	MGM	25,521,917
UNCONQUERED	1947	Paramount	5,250,000
UNTOUCHABLES, THE	1987	Paramount	36,866,530
VALLEY OF DECISION, THE	1945	MGM	4,566,755
WARGAMES	1983	MGM/United Artists	38,519,833
WAY WE WERE, THE	1973	Columbia	22,457,000
WELCOME STRANGER	1947	Paramount	6,100,000
WEST SIDE STORY	1961	United Artists	19,645,570
WHAT'S UP DOC?	1972	Warner Bros.	28,000,000
WHITE CHRISTMAS	1954	Paramount	12,000,000
WHO FRAMED ROGER RABBIT	1988	Disney	81,244,000
WHO'S AFRAID OF VIRGINIA WOOLF?	1966	Warner Bros.	14,500,000
WIZARD OF OZ, THE	1939	MGM	4,759,890
YANKEE DOODLE DANDY	1942	Warner Bros.	4,719,681
YOUNG FRANKENSTEIN	1974	Fox	38,823,000

*Figures are informed estimates

FILMS BY STUDIO/DISTRIBUTOR

EL CID	1961	Allied Artists	$12,000,000
PAPILLON	1973	Allied Artists	22,500,000
THE RED SHOES	1948	Archers/Eagle-Lion	5,000,000
LA DOLCE VITA	1960	Astor	8,000,000
THE GRADUATE	1967	Avco Embassy	44,090,729
BORN YESTERDAY	1950	Columbia	4,115,000
THE BRIDGE ON THE RIVER KWAI	1957	Columbia	17,195,000
THE CAINE MUTINY	1954	Columbia	8,700,000
CITY SLICKERS	1991	Columbia	60,750,000
CLOSE ENCOUNTERS OF THE THIRD KIND	1977	Columbia	82,750,000
EASY RIDER	1969	Columbia	19,100,000
A FEW GOOD MEN	1992	Columbia	71,000,000
FROM HERE TO ETERNITY	1953	Columbia	12,200,000
FUNNY GIRL	1968	Columbia	26,325,000
GHOSTBUSTERS	1984	Columbia	132,720,000
GUESS WHO'S COMING TO DINNER	1967	Columbia	25,500,000
GUNS OF NAVARONE	1961	Columbia	13,000,000
JOLSON SINGS AGAIN	1949	Columbia	5,000,000
THE JOLSON STORY	1946	Columbia	7,600,000
THE KARATE KID	1984	Columbia	43,120,000
THE KARATE KID, PART II	1986	Columbia	58,310,000
KRAMER VS. KRAMER	1979	Columbia	59,986,335
LAWRENCE OF ARABIA	1962	Columbia	20,310,000
A MAN FOR ALL SEASONS	1966	Columbia	12,750,000
MR. SMITH GOES TO WASHINGTON	1939	Columbia	3,500,000
SHAMPOO	1975	Columbia	23,822,000
STIR CRAZY	1980	Columbia	58,364,420
STRIPES	1981	Columbia	40,886,589
TOOTSIE	1982	Columbia	94,910,000
THE WAY WE WERE	1973	Columbia	22,457,000
CINERAMA HOLIDAY	1955	CRC	12,000,000
SEVEN WONDERS OF THE WORLD	1956	CRC	12,500,000
THIS IS CINERAMA	1952	CRC	15,400,000
HOW THE WEST WAS WON	1962	CRC/MGM	20,932,883
THE ABSENT-MINDED PROFESSOR	1961	Disney	11,426,000
ALADDIN	1992	Disney	111,740,683
ALICE IN WONDERLAND	1951	Disney	7,196,000
THE ARISTOCATS	1970	Disney	26,462,000
BAMBI	1942	Disney	47,265,000
BEAUTY AND THE BEAST	1991	Disney	69,415,000
CINDERELLA	1950	Disney	41,087,000

DARBY O'GILL AND THE LITTLE PEOPLE	1959	Disney	8,336,000
DUMBO	1941	Disney	3,000,000
FANTASIA	1940	Disney	41,660,000
GOOD MORNING, VIETNAM	1987	Disney	58,083,108
HONEY, I SHRUNK THE KIDS	1989	Disney	72,007,000
IN SEARCH OF THE CASTAWAYS	1962	Disney	9,975,000
THE JUNGLE BOOK	1967	Disney	60,964,000
LADY AND THE TRAMP	1955	Disney	40,249,000
THE LION KING	1994	Disney	173,057,366
THE LOVE BUG	1969	Disney	23,150,000
LT. ROBIN CRUSOE, USN	1966	Disney	10,164,000
MARY POPPINS	1964	Disney	45,000,000
OLD YELLER	1957	Disney	10,050,000
101 DALMATIONS	1961	Disney	68,648,000
PETER PAN	1953	Disney	37,584,000
PINOCCHIO	1940	Disney	40,442,000
POCAHONTAS	1995	Disney	67,848,010
PRETTY WOMAN	1990	Disney	81,905,530
THE SANTA CLAUSE	1994	Disney	72,348,689
THE SHAGGY DOG	1959	Disney	12,317,000
SLEEPING BEAUTY	1959	Disney	21,998,000
SONG OF THE SOUTH	1946	Disney	29,228,717
SWISS FAMILY ROBINSON	1960	Disney	20,178,000
THE SWORD IN THE STONE	1963	Disney	10,475,000
THAT DARN CAT	1965	Disney	12,628,000
THREE MEN AND A BABY	1987	Disney	81,356,000
TOY STORY	1995	Disney	92,217,831*
20,000 LEAGUES UNDER THE SEA	1954	Disney	11,267,000
WHO FRAMED ROGER RABBIT	1988	Disney	81,244,000
ALIEN	1979	Fox	40,300,000
THE BIBLE	1966	Fox	15,000,000
BUTCH CASSIDY AND THE SUNDANCE KID	1969	Fox	45,953,000
CHEAPER BY THE DOZEN	1950	Fox	4,425,000
CLEOPATRA	1963	Fox	26,000,000
DAVID AND BATHSHEBA	1951	Fox	4,720,000
THE EMPIRE STRIKES BACK	1980	Fox	141,672,000
THE FRENCH CONNECTION	1971	Fox	26,315,000
HELLO, DOLLY!	1969	Fox	15,200,000
HOME ALONE	1990	Fox	140,099,000
HOME ALONE 2: LOST IN NEW YORK	1992	Fox	103,377,614
I WAS A MALE WAR BRIDE	1949	Fox	4,100,000
JESSE JAMES	1939	Fox	1,500,000
THE KING AND I	1956	Fox	8,500,000
LEAVE HER TO HEAVEN	1945	Fox	5,505,000
THE LONGEST DAY	1962	Fox	17,600,000
M*A*S*H	1970	Fox	36,720,000

MRS. DOUBTFIRE	1993	Fox	109,761,240
9 TO 5	1980	Fox	59,068,000
PATTON	1970	Fox	28,100,000
PEYTON PLACE	1957	Fox	11,500,000
PORKY'S	1982	Fox	55,559,000
THE POSEIDON ADVENTURE	1972	Fox	42,000,000
RETURN OF THE JEDI	1983	Fox	169,193,000
THE ROBE	1953	Fox	17,500,000
THE ROCKY HORROR PICTURE SHOW	1975	Fox	40,420,000
SILVER STREAK	1976	Fox	30,018,000
THE SNOWS OF KILIMANJARO	1952	Fox	6,500,000
THE SONG OF BERNADETTE	1943	Fox	4,701,000
THE SOUND OF MUSIC	1965	Fox	79,975,000
SOUTH PACIFIC	1958	Fox	17,500,000
STAR WARS	1977	Fox	193,777,000
THOSE MAGNIFICENT MEN IN THEIR FLYING MACHINES	1965	Fox	14,000,000
TRUE LIES	1994	Fox	80,000,000
YOUNG FRANKENSTEIN	1974	Fox	38,823,000
THE TOWERING INFERNO	1974	Fox/Warner Bros.	48,838,000
OKLAHOMA!	1955	Magna	7,100,000
ANCHORS AWEIGH	1945	MGM	4,778,679
ANNIE GET YOUR GUN	1950	MGM	4,919,394
BATTLEGROUND	1949	MGM	5,051,143
BEN-HUR	1959	MGM	36,992,088
BOOM TOWN	1940	MGM	4,586,415
CAT ON A HOT TIN ROOF	1958	MGM	8,785,162
THE DIRTY DOZEN	1967	MGM	20,403,826
DOCTOR ZHIVAGO	1965	MGM	60,964,000
EASTER PARADE	1948	MGM	4,189,997
GIGI	1958	MGM	7,321,423
GONE WITH THE WIND	1939	MGM	79,375,080
HONKY TONK	1941	MGM	1,500,000*
IVANHOE	1952	MGM	6,258,000
KING SOLOMON'S MINES	1950	MGM	5,586,000
MEET ME IN ST. LOUIS	1944	MGM	5,132,202
MRS. MINIVER	1942	MGM	5,390,009
THE PHILADELPHIA STORY	1941	MGM	1,500,000*
QUO VADIS?	1951	MGM	11,901,662
RANDOM HARVEST	1942	MGM	4,665,501
SHOWBOAT	1951	MGM	5,533,000
30 SECONDS OVER TOKYO	1944	MGM	4,471,080
THE THREE MUSKETEERS	1948	MGM	4,306,876
2001: A SPACE ODYSSEY	1968	MGM	25,521,917
THE VALLEY OF DECISION	1945	MGM	4,566,755
THE WIZARD OF OZ	1939	MGM	4,759,890

RAIN MAN	1988	MGM/UA	86,813,000
ROCKY III	1982	MGM/UA	66,262,796
ROCKY IV	1985	MGM/UA	76,023,246
WARGAMES	1983	MGM/UA	38,519,833
THE GOODBYE GIRL	1977	MGM/Warner Bros.	41,839,170
TEENAGE MUTANT NINJA TURTLES	1990	New Line Cinema	67,650,000
DANCES WITH WOLVES	1990	Orion	81,537,971
PLATOON	1986	Orion	69,937,092
AIRPLANE!	1980	Paramount	40,610,000
BEVERLY HILLS COP	1984	Paramount	108,000,000
BEVERLY HILLS COP II	1987	Paramount	80,857,776
BLUE SKIES	1946	Paramount	5,700,000
THE CARPETBAGGERS	1964	Paramount	15,500,000
COMING TO AMERICA	1988	Paramount	65,000,000
"CROCODILE" DUNDEE	1986	Paramount	70,227,000
"CROCODILE" DUNDEE II	1988	Paramount	57,300,000
FATAL ATTRACTION	1987	Paramount	70,000,000
THE FIRM	1992	Paramount	77,047,044
FORREST GUMP	1994	Paramount	156,000,000
FOR WHOM THE BELL TOLLS	1943	Paramount	7,100,000
GHOST	1990	Paramount	98,200,000
THE GODFATHER	1972	Paramount	86,275,000
GOING MY WAY	1944	Paramount	6,500,000
GREASE	1978	Paramount	96,300,000
THE GREATEST SHOW ON EARTH	1952	Paramount	14,000,000
INDIANA JONES AND THE LAST CRUSADE	1989	Paramount	115,500,000
INDIANA JONES AND THE TEMPLE OF DOOM	1984	Paramount	109,000,000
KING KONG	1976	Paramount	36,915,000
LOVE STORY	1970	Paramount	48,700,000
THE ODD COUPLE	1968	Paramount	20,000,000
AN OFFICER AND A GENTLEMAN	1982	Paramount	55,223,000
THE PALEFACE	1948	Paramount	4,500,000
RAIDERS OF THE LOST ARK	1981	Paramount	115,598,000
REAR WINDOW	1954	Paramount	9,812,271
ROMEO AND JULIET	1968	Paramount	17,473,000
SAMSOM AND DELILAH	1949	Paramount	11,500,000
SATURDAY NIGHT FEVER	1977	Paramount	74,100,000
SHANE	1953	Paramount	9,000,000
STAR TREK: THE MOTION PICTURE	1979	Paramount	56,000,000
STAR TREK IV: THE VOYAGE HOME	1986	Paramount	56,820,071
THE TEN COMMANDMENTS	1956	Paramount	43,000,000
TERMS OF ENDEARMENT	1983	Paramount	50,250,000
TOP GUN	1986	Paramount	79,400,000
TRADING PLACES	1983	Paramount	40,600,000

UNCOUNQUERED	1947	Paramount	5,250,000
THE UNTOUCHABLES	1987	Paramount	36,866,530
WELCOME STRANGER	1947	Paramount	6,100,000
WHITE CHRISTMAS	1954	Paramount	12,000,000
PSYCHO	1960	Paramount/Universal	11,200,000
THE SANDS OF IWO JIMA	1949	Republic	5,000,000
THE BACHELOR AND THE BOBBY-SOXER	1947	RKO	5,500,000
THE BELLS OF ST. MARY'S	1945	RKO	8,000,000
THE BEST YEARS OF OUR LIVES	1946	RKO	11,300,000
HANS CHRISTIAN ANDERSEN	1952	RKO	6,000,000
THE HUNCHBACK OF NOTRE DAME	1939	RKO	1,500,000
THE OUTLAW	1943	RKO	5,075,000
DUEL IN THE SUN	1946	Selznick	11,300,000
REBECCA	1940	Selznick	1,500,000
HOOK	1991	TriStar	65,000,000
RAMBO: FIRST BLOOD PART II	1985	TriStar	78,919,250
SLEEPLESS IN SEATTLE	1993	TriStar	64,930,137
TERMINATOR 2: JUDGMENT DAY	1991	TriStar	112,500,000
DIAMONDS ARE FOREVER	1971	United Artists	19,726,829
EXODUS	1960	United Artists	8,331,582
FIDDLER ON THE ROOF	1971	United Artists	38,260,954
FROM RUSSIA WITH LOVE	1964	United Artists	9,924,279
GOLDFINGER	1964	United Artists	22,997,706
THE GREAT DICTATOR	1940	United Artists	3,500,000
HAWAII	1966	United Artists	15,553,018
IRMA LA DOUCE	1963	United Artists	11,921,784
IT'S A MAD MAD MAD MAD WORLD	1963	United Artists	20,849,786
MIDNIGHT COWBOY	1969	United Artists	20,499,282
ONE FLEW OVER THE CUCKOO'S NEST	1975	United Artists	59,939,701
POOR WHITE TRASH (BAYOU)	1957	United Artists	6,000,000
RED RIVER	1948	United Artists	4,506,825
ROCKY	1976	United Artists	56,524,972
ROCKY II	1979	United Artists	42,169,387
SINCE YOU WENT AWAY	1944	United Artists	4,924,756
SPELLBOUND	1945	United Artists	4,970,583
STAGE DOOR CANTEEN	1943	United Artists	4,339,532
THUNDERBALL	1965	United Artists	28,621,434
TOM JONES	1963	United Artists	17,070,000
WEST SIDE STORY	1961	United Artists	19,645,570
AROUND THE WORLD IN 80 DAYS	1956	United Artists/WB	23,120,000
AIRPORT	1970	Universal	45,220,118

AMERICAN GRAFFITI	1973	Universal	55,128,175
APOLLO 13	1995	Universal	84,309,770
BACK TO THE FUTURE	1985	Universal	105,496,267
BACK TO THE FUTURE, PART II	1989	Universal	72,319,630
E.T. THE EXTRA-TERRESTRIAL	1982	Universal	228,168,939
EARTHQUAKE	1974	Universal	35,849,994
THE EGG AND I	1947	Universal	5,500,000
THE FLINTSTONES	1994	Universal	70,753,383
THE GLENN MILLER STORY	1954	Universal	7,590,994
JAWS	1975	Universal	129,549,325
JAWS 2	1978	Universal	50,431,964
THE JERK	1979	Universal	42,989,656
JURASSIC PARK	1993	Universal	208,000,000
NATIONAL LAMPOON'S ANIMAL HOUSE	1978	Universal	70,826,000
ON GOLDEN POND	1981	Universal	61,175,028
OPERATION PETTICOAT	1959	Universal	9,321,555
OUT OF AFRICA	1985	Universal	43,448,253*
SMOKEY AND THE BANDIT	1977	Universal	58,949,939
SPARTACUS	1960	Universal	11,100,000
THE STING	1973	Universal	78,212,000
TWINS	1988	Universal	57,715,127
ACE VENTURA: WHEN NATURE CALLS	1995	Warner Bros.	54,122,769
ALL THE PRESIDENT'S MEN	1976	Warner Bros.	30,000,000
ANY WHICH WAY YOU CAN	1980	Warner Bros.	40,500,000
ARTHUR	1981	Warner Bros.	42,000,000
AUNTIE MAME	1958	Warner Bros.	9,300,000
BATMAN	1989	Warner Bros.	150,500,000
BATMAN FOREVER	1995	Warner Bros.	105,100,000
BATMAN RETURNS	1992	Warner Bros.	100,100,000
BATTLE CRY	1955	Warner Bros.	8,100,000
BILLY JACK	1971	Warner Bros.	32,500,000
BLAZING SADDLES	1974	Warner Bros.	47,800,000*
BONNIE AND CLYDE	1967	Warner Bros.	22,800,000
BULLITT	1968	Warner Bros.	19,000,000
CASABLANCA	1942	Warner Bros.	4,750,000
THE COLOR PURPLE	1985	Warner Bros.	49,800,000
DELIVERANCE	1972	Warner Bros.	22,600,000
DIVE BOMBER	1941	Warner Bros.	1,500,000
DOG DAY AFTERNOON	1975	Warner Bros.	22,500,000
EVERY WHICH WAY BUT LOOSE	1978	Warner Bros.	51,900,000
THE EXORCIST	1973	Warner Bros.	89,000,000
THE FUGITIVE	1993	Warner Bros.	92,600,000
GIANT	1956	Warner Bros.	14,000,000
GREMLINS	1984	Warner Bros.	79,500,000
HOLLYWOOD CANTEEN	1944	Warner Bros.	4,200,000
HOUSE OF WAX	1953	Warner Bros.	9,500,000

JEREMIAH JOHNSON	1972	Warner Bros.	21,900,000
LETHAL WEAPON 2	1989	Warner Bros.	79,500,000
LETHAL WEAPON 3	1992	Warner Bros.	80,000,000
LIFE WITH FATHER	1947	Warner Bros.	5,057,000
MISTER ROBERTS	1955	Warner Bros.	8,500,000
THE MUSIC MAN	1962	Warner Bros.	8,100,000
MY FAIR LADY	1964	Warner Bros.	34,000,000
NO TIME FOR SERGEANTS	1958	Warner Bros.	7,500,000
ROBIN HOOD: PRINCE OF THIEVES	1991	Warner Bros.	86,000,000
SAYONARA	1957	Warner Bros.	10,500,000
SERGEANT YORK	1941	Warner Bros.	6,135,707
A STAR IS BORN	1976	Warner Bros.	37,100,000
A STREETCAR NAMED DESIRE	1951	Warner Bros.	4,800,000
SUMMER OF '42	1971	Warner Bros.	20,500,000
SUPERMAN	1978	Warner Bros.	82,800,000
SUPERMAN II	1981	Warner Bros.	65,100,000
SUPERMAN III	1983	Warner Bros.	37,200,000
THIS IS THE ARMY	1943	Warner Bros.	8,500,000
THE TRIAL OF BILLY JACK	1974	Warner Bros.	31,100,000
WHAT'S UP DOC?	1972	Warner Bros.	28,000,000
WHO'S AFRAID OF VIRGINIA WOOLF?	1966	Warner Bros.	14,500,000
YANKEE DOODLE DANDY	1942	Warner Bros.	4,719,681

*Figures are informed estimates.

BUT WHAT ABOUT . . . ?

A number of important films fail to appear on the list of the top five hits of each year. Many will be surprised that these aren't number-ones or at least runners-up. While generally box office success is a measure of quality, this is not always the case. The following motion pictures are generally remembered by audiences as successful, if not financially, then in emotional impact and/or quality of production (these are alphabetically listed and not ranked according to gross or rental dollars):

1939

DARK VICTORY
DESTRY RIDES AGAIN
ELIZABETH AND ESSEX
GOODBYE, MR. CHIPS
NINOTCHKA
STAGECOACH

1940

THE GRAPES OF WRATH
NORTHWEST MOUNTED POLICE
NORTHWEST PASSAGE
OUR TOWN
THE ROAD TO SINGAPORE
SANTA FE TRAIL
STRIKE UP THE BAND
A YANK IN THE RAF

1941

CITIZEN KANE
DR. JEKYLL & MR. HYDE
HOW GREEN WAS MY VALLEY
THE MALTESE FALCON

1942

HOLIDAY INN
NOW, VOYAGER
THE PRIDE OF THE YANKEES
THE ROAD TO MOROCCO

1943

CABIN IN THE SKY
A GUY NAMED JOE
LASSIE COME HOME
THE PHANTOM OF THE OPERA

1944

ARSENIC AND OLD LACE
THE CANTERVILLE GHOST
GASLIGHT
NATIONAL VELVET
TO HAVE AND HAVE NOT
WHITE CLIFFS OF DOVER

1945

THE CORN IS GREEN
THE LOST WEEKEND
MILDRED PIERCE
SARATOGA TRUNK
A TREE GROWS IN BROOKLYN

1946

THE BIG SLEEP
GILDA
GREAT EXPECTATIONS
IT'S A WONDERFUL LIFE
NOTORIOUS
THE POSTMAN ALWAYS RINGS TWICE
THE RAZOR'S EDGE
THE YEARLING

1947

THE FARMER'S DAUGHTER
FOREVER AMBER
GENTLEMAN'S AGREEMENT
THE GHOST AND MRS. MUIR
MIRACLE ON 34TH STREET
THE ROAD TO RIO

1948

HAMLET
JOHNNY BELINDA
KEY LARGO
THE SNAKE PIT
TREASURE OF SIERRA MADRE

1949

ADAM'S RIB
ALL THE KING'S MEN
LITTLE WOMEN
THE THIRD MAN
TWELVE O'CLOCK HIGH

1950

ALL ABOUT EVE
THE ASPHALT JUNGLE
FATHER OF THE BRIDE
HARVEY
SUNSET BOULEVARD

1951

THE AFRICAN QUEEN
AN AMERICAN IN PARIS
THE DAY THE EARTH STOOD STILL
DEATH OF A SALESMAN
THE GREAT CARUSO
A PLACE IN THE SUN

1952

COME BACK, LITTLE SHEBA
HIGH NOON
THE MEMBER OF THE WEDDING
MOULIN ROUGE
THE QUIET MAN
SINGING IN THE RAIN

1953

CALL ME MADAM
GENTLEMEN PREFER BLONDES
HOW TO MARRY A MILLIONAIRE
MOGAMBO
ROMAN HOLIDAY
STALAG 17
WAR OF THE WORLDS

1954

THE COUNTRY GIRL
THE HIGH AND THE MIGHTY
ON THE WATERFRONT
SEVEN BRIDES FOR SEVEN BROTHERS
A STAR IS BORN
THREE COINS IN THE FOUNTAIN

1955

EAST OF EDEN
LOVE IS A MANY-SPLENDORED THING
MARTY
PICNIC
REBEL WITHOUT A CAUSE
TO CATCH A THIEF

1956

BUS STOP
CAROUSEL
FRIENDLY PERSUASION
HIGH SOCIETY
SOMEBODY UP THERE LIKES ME

1957

A FAREWELL TO ARMS
FUNNY FACE
RAINTREE COUNTY
SILK STOCKINGS
12 ANGRY MEN
THE THREE FACES OF EVE
WITNESS FOR THE PROSECUTION

1958

THE BROTHERS KARAMAZOV
DAMN YANKEES
THE DEFIANT ONES
THE OLD MAN AND THE SEA
VERTIGO

1959

ANATOMY OF A MURDER
THE DIARY OF ANNE FRANK
THE FIVE PENNIES
NORTH BY NORTHWEST
THE NUN'S STORY
PILLOW TALK
PORGY AND BESS
SOME LIKE IT HOT

1960

THE ALAMO
THE APARTMENT
BUTTERFIELD 8
ELMER GANTRY
THE MAGNIFICENT SEVEN
NEVER ON SUNDAY

1961

BREAKFAST AT TIFFANY'S
FANNY
FLOWER DRUM SONG
JUDGEMENT AT NUREMBERG
LOVER COME BACK
THE PARENT TRAP

1962

THE DAYS OF WINE AND ROSES
DR. NO
GYPSY
THE MIRACLE WORKER
MUTINY ON THE BOUNTY
TO KILL A MOCKINGBIRD
WHAT EVER HAPPENED TO BABY JANE?

1963

THE BIRDS
BYE BYE BIRDIE
THE GREAT ESCAPE
HUD
LILIES OF THE FIELD
SON OF FLUBBER

1964

BECKET
DR. STRANGELOVE
A HARD DAY'S NIGHT
THE PINK PANTHER
A SHOT IN THE DARK
THE UNSINKABLE MOLLY BROWN
ZORBA THE GREEK

1965

THE AGONY AND THE ECSTASY
CAT BALLOU
DARLING
THE GREATEST STORY EVER TOLD
HELP!
THE SANDPIPER
SHIP OF FOOLS
A THOUSAND CLOWNS

1966

ALFIE
GEORGY GIRL
A MAN AND A WOMAN
THE RUSSIANS ARE COMING, THE RUSSIANS ARE COMING
THE SAND PEBBLES

1967

CAMELOT
DOCTOR DOLITTLE
IN THE HEAT OF THE NIGHT
THOROUGHLY MODERN MILLIE
VALLEY OF THE DOLLS
YOU ONLY LIVE TWICE

1968

THE LION IN WINTER
OLIVER!
PLANET OF THE APES
ROSEMARY'S BABY
STAR!
YELLOW SUBMARINE

1969

ANNE OF THE THOUSAND DAYS
BOB & CAROL & TED & ALICE
CACTUS FLOWER
GOODBYE, COLUMBUS
ON HER MAJESTY'S SECRET SERVICE
PAINT YOUR WAGON
THEY SHOOT HORSES, DON'T THEY?
TRUE GRIT

1970

CATCH-22
FIVE EASY PIECES
LITTLE BIG MAN

1971

CARNAL KNOWLEDGE
A CLOCKWORK ORANGE
DIRTY HARRY
THE LAST PICTURE SHOW
NICHOLAS AND ALEXANDRA

1972

CABARET
DEEP THROAT
LADY SINGS THE BLUES
SOUNDER

1973

DAY FOR NIGHT
LAST TANGO IN PARIS
LIVE AND LET DIE
MAGNUM FORCE
PAPER MOON
ROBIN HOOD
SERPICO
A TOUCH OF CLASS

1974

AIRPORT 1975
CHINATOWN
THE GODFATHER PART TWO
HARRY AND TONTO
THE LONGEST YARD
THE THREE MUSKETEERS

1975

FUNNY LADY
THE MAN WHO WOULD BE KING
NASHVILLE
THE SUNSHINE BOYS
THREE DAYS OF THE CONDOR

1976

BOUND FOR GLORY
CARRIE
NETWORK
THE OMEN
SILENT MOVIE
TAXI DRIVER

1977

ANNIE HALL
THE DEEP
JULIA
OH GOD!
THE SPY WHO LOVED ME
THE TURNING POINT

1978

THE BUDDY HOLLY STORY
COMING HOME
THE DEER HUNTER
HEAVEN CAN WAIT
UP IN SMOKE

1979

ALL THAT JAZZ
THE AMITYVILLE HORROR
. . . AND JUSTICE FOR ALL
APOCALYPSE NOW
THE CHINA SYNDROME
MANHATTAN
MOONRAKER
NORMA RAE

1980

COAL MINER'S DAUGHTER
THE ELEPHANT MAN
ORDINARY PEOPLE
PRIVATE BENJAMIN
URBAN COWBOY

1981

ABSENCE OF MALICE
THE CANNONBALL RUN
CHARIOTS OF FIRE
THE FOX AND THE HOUND
THE GODS MUST BE CRAZY
MOMMIE DEAREST
REDS

1982

ANNIE
GANDHI
POLTERGEIST
SOPHIE'S CHOICE
STAR TREK II: THE WRATH OF KHAN
THE VERDICT

1983

THE BIG CHILL
FANNY AND ALEXANDER
FLASHDANCE
THE RIGHT STUFF
RISKY BUSINESS
SILKWOOD
YENTL
ZELIG

1984

AMADEUS
FOOTLOOSE
THE KILLING FIELDS
A PASSAGE TO INDIA
PLACES IN THE HEART
POLICE ACADEMY
ROMANCING THE STONE
A SOLDIER'S STORY
SPLASH
STAR TREK III: THE SEARCH FOR SPOCK
2010

1985

AGNES OF GOD
COCOON
THE JEWEL OF THE NILE
KISS OF THE SPIDER WOMAN
PRIZZI'S HONOR
RUNAWAY TRAIN
WITNESS

1986

ALIENS
CHILDREN OF A LESSER GOD
DOWN AND OUT IN BEVERLY HILLS
FERRIS BUELLER'S DAY OFF
THE FLY
HANNAH AND HER SISTERS
THE MISSION
STAND BY ME

1987

BROADCAST NEWS
CRY FREEDOM
DIRTY DANCING
HOPE AND GLORY
THE LAST EMPEROR
LETHAL WEAPON
MOONSTRUCK
WALL STREET
THE WITCHES OF EASTWICK

1988

THE ACCIDENTAL TOURIST
BEETLEJUICE
BIG
COCKTAIL
DANGEROUS LIAISONS
A FISH CALLED WANDA
GORILLAS IN THE MIST
MISSISSIPPI BURNING
THE NAKED GUN
OLIVER AND COMPANY
SCROOGED
WILLOW
WORKING GIRL

1989

DEAD POETS SOCIETY
DRIVING MISS DAISY
GHOSTBUSTERS II
THE LITTLE MERMAID
LOOK WHO'S TALKING
PARENTHOOD
STEEL MAGNOLIAS
THE WAR OF THE ROSES
WHEN HARRY MET SALLY

1990

DICK TRACY
DIE HARD 2
EDWARD SCISSORHANDS
THE HUNT FOR RED OCTOBER
KINDERGARTEN COP
PRESUMED INNOCENT
TOTAL RECALL

1991

THE ADDAMS FAMILY
BACKDRAFT
JFK
THE NAKED GUN: 2 1/2
THE SILENCE OF THE LAMBS
SLEEPING WITH THE ENEMY
THE PRINCE OF TIDES
TEENAGE MUTANT NINJA TURTLES II
THELMA AND LOUISE

1992

BASIC INSTINCT
THE BODYGUARD
BRAM STOKER'S DRACULA
A LEAGUE OF THEIR OWN
SISTER ACT
UNFORGIVEN
WAYNE'S WORLD

1993

CLIFFHANGER
THE CRYING GAME
FREE WILLY
INDECENT PROPOSAL
IN THE LINE OF FIRE
THE PELICAN BRIEF
PHILADELPHIA
SCHINDLER'S LIST

1994

CLEAR AND PRESENT DANGER
FOUR WEDDINGS AND A FUNERAL
INTERVIEW WITH THE VAMPIRE
THE MASK
MAVERICK
PULP FICTION
SPEED
STARGATE
WOLF
WYATT EARP

1995

BRAVEHEART
CASPER
CRIMSON TIDE
DIE HARD WITH A VENGEANCE
GOLDENEYE
JUMANJI
SEVEN

BIBLIOGRAPHY

Adler, Bill. *Fred Astaire: A Wonderful Life.* New York: Carroll & Graf Publishers, Inc., 1987.

Anthony, Jolene M. *Tom Cruise.* New York: St. Martin's Press, 1988.

Balaban, Bob. *Close Encounters of the Third Kind Diary.* A Paradise Press Book, 1978.

Beckerman, Bernard, and Howard Siegman. *On Stage: Selected Theater Reviews from The New York Times, 1920–1970.* New York: Arno Press/Quadrangle/The New York Times Book Co., 1970.

Benson, Raymond. *The James Bond Bedside Companion.* New York: Dodd, Mead & Co., 1984.

Bergan, Ronald, Graham Fuller, and David Malcolm. *Academy Award Winners.* New York: Crescent Books, 1986.

Bergreen, Laurence. *As Thousands Cheer: The Life of Irving Berlin.* New York: Viking, 1990.

Boller, Paul F., Jr., and Ronald L. Davis. *Hollywood Anecdotes.* New York: Ballantine Books, 1987.

Bookbinder, Robert. *The Films of the Seventies.* Secaucus, N.J.: Citadel Press, 1980.

Brode, Douglas. *The Films of the Fifties.* Secaucus, N.J.: Citadel Press, 1976.

Brode, Douglas. *The Films of the Sixties.* Secaucus, N.J.: Citadel Press, 1980.

Brodsky, Jack, and Nathan Weiss. *The Cleopatra Papers.* New York: Simon & Schuster, 1963.

Bronson, Fred. *The Billboard Book of Number One Hits.* New York: Billboard Books, 1988.

Brooks, Tim. *The Complete Directory to Prime Time TV Stars, 1946–Present.* New York: Ballantine Books, 1987.

Brooks, Tim, and Earle Marsh. *The Complete Directory to Prime Time Network TV Shows, 1946–Present.* Fifth Edition. New York: Ballantine Books, 1992.

Cagin, Seth, and Philip Dray. *Hollywood Films of the Seventies.* New York: Harper & Row, 1984.

Callan, Michael Feeney. *Sean Connery.* New York: Stein & Day, 1983.

Chaplin, Charles. *My Autobiography.* New York: Simon & Schuster, 1964.

Connors, Martin, and Julia Furtaw, Editors. *VideoHound's Golden Movie Retriever.* Detroit: Visible Ink Press, a division of Gale Research Inc., 1995.

Considine, Shaun. *Barbra Streisand.* New York: Delacorte Press, 1985.

Culhane, John. *Special Effects in the Movies.* New York: Ballantine Books, 1981.

Deschner, Donald. *The Films of Cary Grant.* Secaucus: Citadel Press, 1973.

Dewey, Donald. *Marcello Mastroianni: His Life and Art.* New York: Carol Publishing Group, 1993.

Eames, John Douglas. *The MGM Story.* New York: Crown Publishers, 1977.

Ebert, Roger. *Roger Ebert's Movie Home Companion, 1989 Edition.* Kansas City: Andrews & McMeel, 1988.

Edwards, Anne. *Early Reagan.* New York: William Morrow & Co., 1987.

Ewen, David. *The New Complete Book of the American Musical Theater.* New York: Holt, Rinehart and Winston, 1970.

Finch, Christopher. *The Art of Walt Disney.* New York: Harry N. Abrams, 1975.

Finler, Joel. *All-Time Box-Office Hits.* New York: Gallery Books, 1985.

Finler, Joel W. *The Hollywood Story.* New York: Crown Publishers, 1988.

Fitzgerald, Michael G. *Universal Pictures.* New York: Arlington House, 1977.

Freedland, Michael. *Irving Berlin.* New York: Stein and Day, 1974.

Friedrich, Otto. *City of Nets.* New York: Harper & Row, 1986.

Gifford, Denis. *Chaplin.* Garden City: Doubleday & Co., Inc., 1974.

Gifford, Denis. *A Pictorial History of Horror Movies.* London: Hamlyn, 1973.

Grossman, Gary. *Superman, Serial to Cereal.* New York: Popular Library, 1977.

Guiles, Fred Lawrence. *Jane Fonda.* New York: Doubleday & Co., 1982.

Halliwell, Leslie. *The Filmgoer's Companion, Sixth Edition.* New York: Hill & Wang, 1977.

Harmetz, Aljean. *The Making of The Wizard of Oz.* New York: Limelight Editions, 1984.

Henkin, Bill. *The Rocky Horror Picture Show Book.* Hawthorn Books, 1979.

Higham, Charles. *Brando: The Unauthorized Biography.* New York: New American Library, 1987.

Huston, John. *An Open Book.* New York: Alfred A. Knopf, 1980.

Kanin, Garson. *Hollywood: Stars and Starlets, Tycoons and Flesh-Peddlers, Moviemakers and Moneymakers, Frauds and Geniuses, Hopefuls and Has-Beens, Great Lovers and Sex Symbols.* New York: The Viking Press, 1967.

Kaplan, Mike. *Variety Who's Who in Show Business.* New York: Garland Publishing, 1983.

Katz, Ephraim. *The Film Encyclopedia.* New York: HarperCollins, 1994.

Klain, Jane; British Ed., William Pay; Canadian Ed., Patricia Thompson. *International Motion Picture Almanac, 60th Edition.* New York: Quigley Publishing Company, 1989.

Kobal, John. *John Kobal Presents the Top 100 Movies.* New York: New American Library, 1988.

Koehler, William R. *The Wonderful World of Disney Animals.* New York: Howell Book House, 1979.

Koszarski, Richard. *Hollywood Directors.* Oxford: Oxford University Press, 1977.

Lasky, Michael S., and Robert A. Harris. *The Films of Alfred Hitchcock.* Secaucus, N.J.: Citadel Press, 1976.

Lenburg, Jeff. *Dustin Hoffman.* New York: St. Martin's Press, 1983.

Lloyd, Ann, and Graham Fuller. *The Illustrated Who's Who of the Cinema.* New York: Portland House, 1987.

Lyon, Richard Sean. *The 1989 Investor's Guide to Films.* West Los Angeles: LyonHeart Publishers, 1989.

Maltin, Leonard. *The Disney Films, New Updated Edition.* New York: Crown Publishers, 1984.

Maltin, Leonard. *Leonard Maltin's Movie and Video Guide, 1995 Edition.* New York: Signet, The Penguin Group, 1994.

Martin, Mick, and Marsha Porter. *Video Movie Guide.* New York: Ballantine Books, 1987.

McNeil, Alex. *Total Television.* New York: Penguin Books, 1991.

Minelli, Vincent, with Hector Arce. *I Remember It Well.* Garden City: Doubleday & Company, Inc., 1974.

Morella, Joe, Edward Z. Epstein, and John Griggs. *The Films of World War II.* Secaucus, N.J.: Citadel Press, 1980.

Nolan, William E. *McQueen.* New York: Congdon & Weed, 1984.

Osborne, Robert. *Academy Awards Illustrated.* La Habra, Cal.: ESE California, 1977.

Parish, James Robert. *The Fox Girls.* New York: Arlington House, 1971.

Parish, James Robert, and William T. Leonard with Gregory W. Mank and Charles Hoyt. *The Funsters.* New Rochelle: Arlington House, 1979.

Parish, James Robert, and Steven Whitney. *Vincent Price Unmasked.* New York: Drake Publishers Inc., 1974.

Preminger, Otto. *Preminger.* New York: Doubleday & Co., 1977.

Robbins, Jhan. *Yul Brynner.* New York: Dodd, Mead & Co., 1987.

Robertson, Patrick. *The Guinness Book of Movie Facts and Feats.* Great Britain: Guinness Books, 1988.

Sackett, Susan. *Hollywood Sings!* New York: Billboard Books, 1995.

Sackett, Susan, and Gene Roddenberry. *The Making of Star Trek: The Motion Picture.* New York: Pocket Books, 1980.

Scheuer, Steven H. *Movies on TV and VideoCassette.* New York: Bantam Books, 1989.

Sennett, Ted. *Great Movie Directors.* New York: Harry N. Abrams, 1986.

Sharif, Omar, with Marie-Therese Guinchard. *The Eternal Male.* New York: Doubleday & Co., 1977.

Solmi, Angelo. *Fellini.* New York: Humanities Press, 1967.

Spoto, Donald. *Stanley Kramer, Film Maker.* New York: G. P. Putnam's Sons, 1978.

Taylor, Elizabeth. *Elizabeth Takes Off.* New York: G. P. Putnam's Sons, 1987.

Terrace, Vincent. *The Complete Encyclopedia of Television Programs, Vols. 1 & 2.* New Jersey: A. S. Barnes & Co., 1976.

Thomas, Bob. *Astaire: The Man, The Dancer.* New York: St. Martin's Press, 1984.

Thomas, Bob. *Walt Disney.* New York: Pocket Books, 1976.

Thomas, Tony. *The Films of the Forties.* Secaucus, N.J.: Citadel Press, 1975.

Thomson, David. *A Biographical Dictionary of Film.* Third Edition. New York: Alfred A. Knopf, 1994.

Wiley, Mason, and Damien Bona. *Inside Oscar.* New York: Ballantine Books, 1993.

Wilkerson, Tichi, and Marcia Borie. *Hollywood Legends.* Los Angeles: Tale Weaver Publishing, 1988.

Windeler, Robert. *The Films of Shirley Temple.* Secaucus: Citadel Press, 1978.

CD-ROMS

Microsoft CINEMANIA '95.

The Motion Picture Guide. New York: CineBooks, 1995.

PHOTO CREDITS

THE ABSENT MINDED PROFESSOR © The Walt Disney Company.

ACE VENTURA: WHEN NATURE CALLS © Warner Bros. Inc. All Rights Reserved.

AIRPLANE! Copyright © 1980 by Paramount Pictures Corporation. All Rights Reserved.

AIRPORT Copyright © by Universal Pictures, A Division of Universal City Studios, Inc. Courtesy of MCA Publishing Rights, A Division of MCA Inc.

ALADDIN © The Walt Disney Company. All Rights Reserved.

ALICE IN WONDERLAND © The Walt Disney Company.

ALIEN © 1979 Twentieth Century-Fox Film Corporation. All Rights Reserved.

ALL THE PRESIDENT'S MEN © 1976 Warner Bros. Inc. and Wildwood Enterprises, Inc. All Rights Reserved.

AMERICAN GRAFFITI Copyright © by Universal Pictures, a Division of Universal City Studios, Inc. Courtesy of MCA Publishing Rights, A Division of MCA Inc.

ANCHORS AWEIGH © 1945 Loew's Inc. Ren. 1972 Metro-Goldwyn-Mayer Inc.

ANNIE GET YOUR GUN © 1950 Loew's Inc. Ren. 1977 Metro-Goldwyn-Mayer Inc. Courtesy of Marvin Paige's Motion Picture & TV Research Service.

ANY WHICH WAY YOU CAN © 1980 Warner Bros. Inc. All Rights Reserved.

APOLLO 13 © Universal City Studios. All Rights Reserved.

THE ARISTOCATS © The Walt Disney Company.

AROUND THE WORLD IN 80 DAYS © 1956 Michael Todd Co., Inc. Renewed 1984 Warner Bros. Inc. All Rights Reserved.

ARTHUR © 1981 Orion Pictures Company. All Rights Reserved.

AUNTIE MAME © 1958 Warner Bros. Pictures, Inc. Renewed 1986 Warner Bros. Inc. All Rights Reserved. Courtesy of Marvin Paige's Motion Picture & TV Research Service.

THE BACHELOR AND THE BOBBY-SOXER © 1947 RKO.

BACK TO THE FUTURE Copyright © by Universal Pictures, a Division of Universal City Studios, Inc. Courtesy of MCA Publishing Rights, A Division of MCA Inc.

BACK TO THE FUTURE PART II © by Universal Pictures, a Division of Universal City Studios, Inc. Courtesy of MCA Publishing Rights, A Division of MCA Inc.

BAMBI © The Walt Disney Company.

BATMAN © DC Comics Inc. All Rights Reserved.

BATMAN FOREVER © DC Comics Inc. All Rights Reserved.

BATMAN RETURNS © 1992 DC Comics Inc. All Rights Reserved.

BATTLE CRY © 1954 Warner Bros. Pictures, Inc. Renewed 1982 Warner Bros. Inc. All Rights Reserved.

BATTLEGROUND © 1949 Loew's Inc. Ren. 1976 Metro-Goldwyn-Mayer Inc.

BEAUTY AND THE BEAST © The Walt Disney Company. All Rights Reserved.

THE BELLS OF ST. MARY'S Courtesy of the Academy of Motion Picture Arts and Sciences.

BEN-HUR © 1959 Loew's Inc. Ren. 1987 Turner Entertainment Co.

THE BEST YEARS OF OUR LIVES Courtesy of Marvin Paige's Motion Picture & TV Research Service.

BEVERLY HILLS COP Copyright © 1984 by Paramount Pictures Corporation. All Rights Reserved.

BEVERLY HILLS COP II Copyright © 1986 by Paramount Pictures Corporation. All Rights Reserved.

THE BIBLE © 1966 Dino De Laurentiis Cinematografica, S.A.

BILLY JACK © 1971 National Student Film Corp. All Rights Reserved.

BLAZING SADDLES © 1974 Warner Bros. Inc. All Rights Reserved.

BLUE SKIES Copyright © by Universal Pictures, a Division of Universal City Studios, Inc. Courtesy of MCA Publishing Rights, A Division of MCA Inc.

BONNIE & CLYDE © 1967 Warner Bros.–Seven Arts and Tatira-Hiller Productions. All Rights Reserved.

BOOM TOWN © 1940 Loew's Inc. Ren. 1967 Metro-Goldwyn-Mayer Inc.

BORN YESTERDAY © 1951 Columbia Pictures Industries, Inc. All Rights Reserved.

THE BRIDGE ON THE RIVER KWAI © 1957 Columbia Pictures Industries, Inc. All Rights Reserved. Page 128: Courtesy of the Academy of Motion Picture Arts and Sciences.

BULLITT © 1968 Warner Bros.–Seven Arts and Solar Productions, Inc. All Rights Reserved.

BUTCH CASSIDY AND THE SUNDANCE KID © 1969 Campanile Productions, Inc. and Twentieth Century-Fox Film Corporation. All Rights Reserved.

THE CAINE MUTINY © 1954 Columbia Pictures Industries, Inc. All Rights Reserved.

THE CARPETBAGGERS Copyright © 1963 by Paramount Pictures Corporation and Embassy Pictures Corporation. All Rights Reserved.

CASABLANCA © 1943 Warner Bros. Pictures, Inc. Ren. 1970 United Artists Television, Inc.

CAT ON A HOT TIN ROOF © 1958 Loew's Inc. and Avon Productions Inc. Ren. 1986 MGM/UA Entertainment Co., Weingarten Dec. 12, 1967 Trust, and Pandro C. Berman and Kathryn Berman.

CHEAPER BY THE DOZEN © 1950, renewed 1977 Twentieth Century-Fox Film Corporation. All rights reserved.

GIANT © 1956 Giant Productions. Renewed 1984 Warner Bros. Inc., George Stevens, Jr. and Jess S. Morgan. All Rights Reserved.

GIGI © 1958 Loew's Inc. and Arthur Freed Productions, Inc. Ren. 1986 MGM/UA Entertainment Co. and Arthur Freed Productions, Inc. Courtesy of Marvin Paige's Motion Picture & TV Research Service.

THE GLENN MILLER STORY Copyright © by Universal Pictures, a Division of Universal City Studios, Inc. Courtesy of MCA Publishing Rights, A Division of MCA Inc. Courtesy of Marvin Paige's Motion Picture & TV Research Service.

THE GODFATHER Copyright © 1972 by Paramount Pictures Corporation. All Rights Reserved.

GOING MY WAY Copyright © by Universal Pictures, a Division of Universal City Studios, Inc. Courtesy of MCA Publishing Rights, a Division of MCA Inc.

GOLDFINGER © 1964 Danjaq S.A. All Rights Reserved.

GONE WITH THE WIND © 1939 Selznick International Pictures, Inc. Ren. 1967 Metro-Goldwyn-Mayer Inc.

GOOD MORNING, VIETNAM © Touchstone Pictures.

THE GOODBYE GIRL © 1977 Metro-Goldwyn-Mayer Inc. and Warner Bros. Inc.. All Rights Reserved.

GREASE Copyright © 1977 by Paramount Pictures Corporation. All Rights Reserved.

THE GREAT DICTATOR © 1940 United Artists. All Rights Reserved.

THE GREATEST SHOW ON EARTH Copyright © 1952 by Paramount Pictures Corporation. All Rights Reserved.

GREMLINS © 1984 Warner Bros. Inc. All Rights Reserved.

GUESS WHO'S COMING TO DINNER © 1967 Columbia Pictures Industries, Inc. All Rights Reserved.

THE GUNS OF NAVARONE © Columbia Pictures Industries, Inc. All Rights Reserved.

HAWAII © 1966 The Mirisch Corporation. Assigned © 1985 United Artist Corporation. All Rights Reserved.

HELLO, DOLLY! © 1969 Chenault Productions, Inc. and Twentieth Century-Fox Film Corporation. All Rights Reserved.

HOLLYWOOD CANTEEN © 1944 Warner Bros. Inc. All Rights Reserved.

HOME ALONE 2: LOST IN NEW YORK © 1992 Twentieth Century-Fox. All Rights Reserved.

HONEY, I SHRUNK THE KIDS © The Walt Disney Company. All Rights Reserved.

HONKY TONK © 1941 Loew's Inc. Ren. 1968 Metro-Goldwyn-Mayer Inc.

HOOK © 1991 TriStar Pictures, Inc. All Rights Reserved.

HOUSE OF WAX © 1953 Warner Bros., Inc. All Rights Reserved.

HOW THE WEST WAS WON © 1962 Metro-Goldwyn-Mayer Inc., and Cinerama, Inc.

THE HUNCHBACK OF NOTRE DAME © 1939 RKO Radio Picture, Inc. Ren. 1967 RKO General, Inc. Courtesy of the Academy of Motion Picture Arts and Sciences.

INDIANA JONES AND THE LAST CRUSADE © 1989 Lucasfilm Ltd. All Rights Reserved.

INDIANA JONES AND THE TEMPLE OF DOOM © Lucasfilm Ltd. 1983. All Rights Reserved.

IN SEARCH OF THE CASTAWAYS © The Walt Disney Company.

I WAS A MALE WAR BRIDE © 1949, renewed 1977 Twentieth Century-Fox Corporation. All Rights Reserved.

IRMA LA DOUCE © 1963 The Mirisch Company, Inc. Assigned © 1985 United Artists Corporation. All Rights Reserved.

IT'S A MAD MAD MAD MAD WORLD © 1963 Casey Productions, Inc. All Rights Reserved.

IVANHOE © 1952 Loew's Inc. Ren. 1980 Metro-Goldwyn-Mayer Inc.

JAWS Copyright © by Universal Pictures, a Division of Universal City Studios, Inc. Courtesy of MCA Publishing Rights, a Division of MCA Inc.

JAWS 2 Copyright © by Universal Pictures, a Division of Universal City Studios, Inc. Courtesy of MCA Publishing Rights, A Division of MCA Inc.

JEREMIAH JOHNSON © 1972 Warner Bros. Inc. and Sanford Productions, Inc.

THE JERK Copyright © by Universal Pictures, a Division of Universal Studios, Inc. Courtesy of MCA Publishing Rights, A Division of MCA Inc.

JESSE JAMES © 1939, renewed 1968 Twentieth Century-Fox Film Corporation. All Rights Reserved. Courtesy of Marvin Paige's Motion Picture & TV Research Service.

JOLSON SINGS AGAIN © 1949 Columbia Pictures Industries, Inc. All Rights Reserved.

THE JOLSON STORY © 1946 Columbia Pictures Industries, Inc. All Rights Reserved. Courtesy of Marvin Paige's Motion Picture & TV Research Service.

THE JUNGLE BOOK © The Walt Disney Company.

JURASSIC PARK © 1993 Universal City Studios Inc. and Amblin Entertainment Inc. All Rights Reserved.

THE KARATE KID © 1984 Columbia Pictures Industries, Inc. All Rights Reserved.

THE POSEIDON ADVENTURE ©
1972 Twentieth Century-Fox Film
Corporation. All Rights Reserved.

PRETTY WOMAN © Touchstone
Pictures. All Rights Reserved.

PSYCHO Copyright © by Universal
Pictures, a Division of Universal
City Studios, Inc. Courtesy of MCA
Publishing Rights, A Division of
MCA Inc.

QUO VADIS? © 1951 Loew's Inc. Ren.
1979 Metro-Goldwyn-Mayer Inc.
Courtesy of the Academy of
Motion Picture Arts and Sciences.

RAIDERS OF THE LOST ARK ©
Lucasfilm Ltd. 1981. All Rights
Reserved.

RAIN MAN © 1988 United Artists
Pictures, Inc. All Rights Reserved.

RAINTREE COUNTY © 1957 Loew's
Inc. Ren. 1985 MGM/UA
Entertainment Co.

RANDOM HARVEST © 1942 Loew's
Inc. Ren. 1969 Metro-Goldwyn-
Mayer Inc.

REAR WINDOW Copyright © by
Universal Pictures, a Division of
Universal City Studios, Inc.
Courtesy of MCA Publishing
Rights, A Division of MCA Inc.

RED RIVER © 1948 Monterey
Productions. Renewal © 1975
United Artists Corporation. All
Rights Reserved.

THE RED SHOES Courtesy of the
Academy of Motion Picture Arts
and Sciences.

RETURN OF THE JEDI © Lucasfilm
Ltd. 1983. All Rights Reserved.

THE ROBE © 1953, renewed © 1981
Twentieth Century-Fox Film
Corporation. All Rights Reserved.

ROBIN HOOD: PRINCE OF
THIEVES © 1991 Warner Bros.
Inc. All Rights Reserved.

ROCKY © 1976 United Artists
Corporation. All Rights Reserved.
Courtesy of Marvin Paige's Motion
Picture & TV Research Service.

ROCKY II © 1979 United Artists
Corporation. All Rights Reserved.

ROCKY III © 1982 United Artists
Corporation. All Rights Reserved.

ROCKY IV © 1985 United Artists
Corporation. All Rights Reserved.

THE ROCKY HORROR PICTURE
SHOW © 1975 Houtsnede
Maatschappi N.V.

ROMEO AND JULIET Copyright ©
1968 by Paramount Pictures, Inc.
All Rights Reserved.

SAMSON AND DELILAH Copyright
© 1949 by Paramount Pictures,
Inc. All Rights Reserved.

THE SANTA CLAUSE © The Walt
Disney Company. All Rights
Reserved.

SATURDAY NIGHT FEVER
Copyright © 1977 by Paramount
Pictures Corporation. All Rights
Reserved.

SERGEANT YORK © 1941 Warner
Bros. Pictures, Inc. Ren. 1969
United Artists Television, Inc.
Courtesy of the Academy of
Motion Picture Arts and Sciences.

THE SHAGGY DOG © The Walt
Disney Company.

SHAMPOO © 1975 Columbia Pictures
Industries, Inc. All Rights
Reserved.

SHANE Copyright © 1952 by
Paramount Pictures Corporation.
All Rights Reserved.

SHOW BOAT © 1951 Loew's Inc. Ren.
1979 Metro-Goldwyn-Mayer Inc.

SILVER STREAK © 1976 Twentieth
Century-Fox Film Corporation. All
Rights Reserved.

SLEEPING BEAUTY © The Walt
Disney Company.

SLEEPLESS IN SEATTLE © 1993
TriStar Pictures Inc. All Rights
Reserved.

SMOKEY AND THE BANDIT
Copyright © by Universal Pictures,
a Division of Universal City
Studios, Inc. Courtesy of MCA
Publishing Rights, A Division of
MCA Inc.

THE SONG OF BERNADETTE ©
1943, renewed 1971 Twentieth
Century-Fox Film Corporation. All
Rights Reserved.

SONG OF THE SOUTH © The Walt
Disney Company.

THE SOUND OF MUSIC Page 178:
Courtesy of the Academy of
Motion Picture Arts and Sciences.

SOUTH PACIFIC Courtesy of the
Academy of Motion Picture Arts
and Sciences.

SPARTACUS Copyright © by
Universal Pictures, a Division of
Universal City Studios, Inc.
Courtesy of MCA Publishing
Rights, A Division of MCA Inc.

A STAR IS BORN © 1976 Barwood
Films Ltd., The First Artist
Production Company Ltd. and
Warner Bros. Inc. All Rights
Reserved.

STAR TREK: THE MOTION
PICTURE Copyright © 1979 by
Century Associates. All Rights
Reserved.

STAR TREK IV: THE VOYAGE
HOME Copyright © 1986 by
Paramount Pictures Corporation.
All Rights Reserved.

STAR WARS © 1977 Twentieth
Century-Fox Film Corporation. All
rights reserved.

THE STING Copyright © by Universal
Pictures, a Division of Universal
City Studios, Inc. Courtesy of MCA
Publishing Rights, A Division of
MCA Inc.

STIR CRAZY © 1980 Columbia
Pictures Industries, Inc. All Rights
Reserved.

A STREETCAR NAMED DESIRE ©
1951 Warner Bros. Inc. All Rights
Reserved.

STRIPES © 1981 Columbia Pictures
Industries, Inc. All Rights
Reserved.

SUMMER OF '42 © 1971 Warner
Bros. Inc. and Mulligan-Roth
Productions. All Rights Reserved.

INDEX

ABOUT THE AUTHOR

Susan Sackett grew up in Connecticut and Florida, receiving both her Bachelor's and Master's degrees from the University of Florida in Gainesville. After teaching elementary school in Miami and Los Angeles, she quit to pursue her lifelong dream of working in Hollywood. She spent the next four years with NBC as a publicity assistant and commercial coordinator.

In 1974 Susan began an association with Gene Roddenberry, creator of the television legend *Star Trek*, serving as his personal executive assistant for over 17 years until his death in 1991. She also functioned as Roddenberry's production assistant on the first *Star Trek* film and worked closely with him on the five subsequent *Star Trek* movies. In addition, she served as Production Associate during the first five seasons of the television series *Star Trek: The Next Generation*, and with fellow Billboard author Fred Bronson contributed several stories and a teleplay to the series.

Since 1977 Susan has authored or co-authored nine books on film and television, including three for Billboard. Her publications have included *Letters to "Star Trek," "Star Trek" Speaks!, The Making of "Star Trek: The Motion Picture," "Star Trek": 'Where No One Has Gone Before': A History in Pictures*, You *can be a Game Show Contestant and Win!, Say Goodnight, Gracie!— The Story of Burns and Allen*, and for Billboard Books, *The Hollywood Reporter Book of Box Office Hits, Prime Time Hits*, and *Hollywood Sings!*